**PROFESSIONAL
SECRETARIES
INTERNATIONAL®**
THE ASSOCIATION FOR
OFFICE PROFESSIONALS™

COMPLETE

OFFICE

HANDBOOK

Second Edition

The Definitive Reference for Today's Electronic Office

Susan Jaderstrom, Leonard Kruk, and Joanne Miller
GENERAL EDITOR: *Susan W. Fenner*

RANDOM HOUSE   NEW YORK

Complete Office Handbook: The Definitive Reference for Today's Electronic Office

Copyright © 1997 by Professional Secretaries International®

All inquiries should be addressed to Reference & Information Publishing, Random House, Inc., 201 East 50th Street, New York, NY 10022.

Published in the United States by Reference & Information Publishing, Random House, Inc., New York, and simultaneously in Canada by Random House of Canada, Limited.

"Random House" and colophon are trademarks of Random House, Inc.

This a revised and completely retypeset edition of the *Professional Secretaries International® Complete Office Handbook* originally published in 1992 by Random House, Inc.

Library of Congress Cataloging-in-publication data

Jaderstrom, Susan.
    Professional Secretaries International complete office handbook :
  the definitive reference for today's electronic office / Susan
  Jaderstrom, Leonard Kruk, and Joanne Miller : general editor, Susan
  W. Fenner. — 2nd ed.
      p.   cm.
    Includes index.
    ISBN 0-679-44962-0 (hc). — ISBN 0-679-77038-0 (pb)
    1. Office practice—Automation. I. Kruk, Leonard B. II. Miller,
 Joanne. III. Fenner, Susan W. IV. Professional Secretaries
 International. V. Title.
    HF5548.J34   1997
    651.8—dc20   96-38330
                                       CIP

Typeset and printed in the United States of America.

Cover design: Laura Shaw

Interior book design: Nancy Etheredge, REM Studio

Page Composition: ComCom, Inc.

Second Edition

0 9 8 7 6 5 4 3 2 1

ISBN 0-679-44962-0 (Hardcover Edition)

ISBN 0-679-77038-0 (Paperback Edition)

New York Toronto London Sydney Auckland

CONTENTS

93500

LIST OF ILLUSTRATIONS

FIGURE   **PAGE**

PART I

PROFESSIONAL

DEVELOPMENT

AND

HUMAN

RELATIONS

Career options for office professionals at all levels are rapidly expanding as a result of automation of office tasks. Technology has created an information age that has changed the way offices operate and the way information is handled, affording new opportunities for professional growth.

Computer and telecommunication technologies will continue as engines of change, constantly redefining the role of the office professional. As requirements become increasingly complex, office professionals will need to have strong technical and interpersonal skills and function as integral parts of the management team. In addition, office-support positions will require the lifelong education and retraining of workers just so they can keep pace with changing office technology and be responsive to marketplace demands.

CHAPTER 1

GROWING

PROFESSIONALLY

CHANGING ROLES: FROM SECRETARY TO EXECUTIVE ASSISTANT

The position of secretary has its earliest recorded mention in the sixteenth century. Then a secretary was usually a man with the ability to read, write, and calculate; he wrote all manuscripts, letters, and records by hand.

Not until the late nineteenth and early twentieth centuries did the mechanized office come into being. The invention of the typewriter, telephone, duplicating equipment, and calculating machine helped to speed up information processing within business. As a result, the male secretary's support role evolved into management as he became an understudy for the executive and the executive's successor in managing the business. With that change, more and more women were hired and trained to perform clerical support tasks for this male-dominated management.

The office today, however, is very different from the one that existed earlier in the twentieth century. Several important factors have contributed to this change.

One factor is technology. The computer has replaced the typewriter. The ease of having facts and figures available and able to be manipulated by electronic tools makes computer literacy essential for everyone in business.

Business is also increasing in size and complexity. The economic need to reduce office costs through greater productivity has made the secretarial role emerge as a major responsible position within the office.

No longer is the secretary necessarily a woman, nor is the secretary viewed as a lowly clerk. Both men and women are opting for administrative support careers. These office positions are recognized as a significant factor in the efficient operation of an organization, especially given the rising costs of information processing. The position of office professional has thus become a management apprenticeship with nearly unlimited opportunities.

The recent evolution of the secretary to administrative or executive assistant is significant. Although expert keyboarding and language skills are still critical, the role is evolving to one of a paraprofessional who supports management in the processing and organizing of information.

Professional Secretaries International® (PSI®) defines today's secretary as "an executive assistant who possesses a mastery of office skills, who demonstrates the ability to assume responsibility without direct supervision, who exercises initiative and judgment and who makes decisions within the scope of assigned authority."

Job titles and responsibilities vary dramatically from organization to organization. The title "secretary" is rapidly being replaced by other terms, such as "office professional," to reflect the changing office environment and responsibilities of today's office support staff.

In addition, some of the other titles used for the secretarial position include "executive secretary," "executive assistant," "administrative assistant," "administrative secretary," "office manager," and "senior secretary."

Revolutionary changes in today's offices are providing a window of opportunity for office professionals. Everyone from top management to the stock clerk is faced with change arising from continual advances in computer and communications technologies, changing organizational behavior, and new work routines.

The greatest challenge, however, will be to accept change, adapt, be willing to learn new equipment and software, and to share this information with others. A "change enabler" is one who facilities the acceptance, implementation, and evolution of change. Become a change enabler by following these steps:

1. Determine the types of changes that are having the greatest impact on the group that you support. Embrace these changes and help others who may be having difficulties.

2. Create a short- and long-term plan for yourself. This may include enrolling in seminars or courses, or a degree program at a local college. It is also a good idea to keep up to date by reading appropriate trade magazines. Photocopy interesting articles and distribute them to your group.

3. Recommend the formation of a change-enablers team. Ask if you can be the chairperson. This interdisciplinary group should meet at least quarterly, preferably monthly, to discuss your company's changing organizational behavior and work routines. Each team member should become an avid reader in at least one area, for example, personal computers, word processing software, groupware, desktop

videoconferencing, ergonomics, and teaming. Communicate the minutes of the team meetings to all employees via the company newsletter or some other means.

4. Become an active member of your local Professional Secretaries International® chapter. This association for office professionals will help you to develop professionally, give you a local support network of colleagues, and help you to stay up to date. (See page 576 for information on contacting PSI.)

ENTRY-LEVEL OPPORTUNITIES

As more positions are evolving, the term "secretary" is now increasingly applied to entry-level or clerical positions. There is no standardization within this field, nor is there a single, clear definition for different job titles. However, a number of entry-level opportunities exist for office professionals to begin their careers in the office-support field.

It is relatively easy to enter this profession. At least a high school education with an emphasis on keyboarding, effective written and oral communication, and information management is necessary. Knowledge of office procedures and familiarity with word processing and computer equipment and software packages are additional assets.

Professional Secretaries International® recently conducted an entry-level competency study and found that beginning office workers should know how to manage records; handle telephone calls, mail, and appointments; keyboard; prepare correspondence; and use language skills. In addition, the ability to use word processing and financial software packages is important, as is projecting a professional image and self-direction in learning.

A number of entry-level positions exist. Persons in entry-level positions must be prepared to perform a variety of office functions, with broad emphasis on professional attitudes, behaviors, and skills rather than on particular job titles or stereotyped roles. Since each organization is different, job titles may vary.

Administrative support (AS): generally includes most of the nonclerical functions previously performed by the traditional secretary. Skills and characteristics needed within the area of administrative support include ability to work as part of a team, good communication and organization skills, and initiative.

Beginning positions include the following:

Switchboard operator: Handles incoming calls and processes outgoing calls, has a good telephone voice, takes messages, answers inquiries, and handles fax transmissions.

Receptionist: Welcomes, orients, and directs visitors, handles phone system or switchboard, does some filing and correspondence, handles fax transmissions, controls petty cash, uses office equipment, distributes mail, and controls courier and messenger dispatch.

Secretary: Handles routine functions in the office, such as processing the mail and answering telephones.

Customer services representative: Interfaces with customers by phone and/or in person regarding the company's product(s) and customers' accounts.

Telemarketing representative: Calls prospective customers to determine their interest in purchasing a company's product(s).

With new technology being used in business almost as quickly as it is introduced, nearly all medium- to large-sized businesses use integrated office systems, that is, office equipment, including computers, connected via a communications network. These systems require specially-trained personnel with traditional basic skills as well as new skills to manage and operate the office.

Skills and characteristics needed for those interested in a secretarial career include the ability to work independently, a technical orientation, computer skills, a knowledge of computer software, a team consciousness, accuracy, language arts and grammatical skills, audio acuity for transcription, and the ability to proofread, edit, and prioritize tasks.

Records management has become a technically-specialized field, but it offers entry-level opportunities in three major areas: filing and micrographics, archiving, and destruction of records. Micrographics is the process of recording information in a reduced form through microfilming, microfishe, or scanning.

Entry-level job opportunities in records management include:

Records clerk/trainee: Performs simple sorting and retrieving of information.

Junior file clerk: Processes material already classified by a senior clerk.

Micrographics technician: Operates technology in the preparation of microforms under supervision.

Skills and characteristics needed for this field include having a team consciousness and being detail-minded, logical, systematic, and security conscious.

Several other entry-level opportunities exist in office services. Among them is:

Travel services clerk: Delivers tickets, car keys, and communications related to travel; uses data processing and telecommunications to provide travel services.

ADVANCED-LEVEL OPPORTUNITIES

Advancement from an entry-level position within an organization largely depends on the perseverance and hard work of the entry-level professional. Each organization varies in how far it will advance its office-support personnel. Titles such as administrative assistant, executive assistant, and executive secretary are often used interchangeably to describe secretaries performing higher-level office tasks or working for higher-level executives.

Entry-level professionals often advance into administrative support, which generally involves the following:

- Providing support services to executives
- Performing general office duties in addition to buying
- Carrying out administrative assistance tasks

Other important skills and abilities for office administrators to have include:

- English skills
- Human relations skills
- Problem-solving abilities
- Analytical and decision-making abilities
- Computer literacy
- Supervisory and managerial techniques
- Communication skills, including speaking, listening, and writing
- Research skills

These skills may also qualify office professionals for other positions.

Administrative support supervisor: Hires, evaluates, and trains new personnel; delegates and assigns work; coordinates work schedules; keeps attendance and payroll records; tracks new office technology; develops, writes, and implements office procedures; establishes and maintains work production standards; supervises and motivates personnel.

Information manager: Manages records, paper and electronic files, and databases; organizes and retrieves information and may also draft specifications for new computer programs.

Communications manager: Manages communications technologies, such as modems, fax machines, photocopiers, multifunction image processors, and local area networks (LANs); may be the LAN administrator or the supervisor of the new scanning technology.

Records manager: Manages the records center and personnel documents; assumes responsibility for records' protection and security; coordinates work flow; determines priorities; manages the budget; manages the conversion of paper to electronic documents.

Meetings or travel manager: Schedules meetings; plans agendas; orders or requisitions multimedia presentation technologies; makes business travel arrangements.

Employee relations manager: Works in a human resources department, interviews and makes recommendations on hiring new employees; assists with employee benefits, work schedules, and personal concerns of employees; in a small firm, a secretary may also function as the employee relations manager.

Other advanced-level duties that you may be asked to perform include:

- Managing data and follow-up reports in a computerized accounting system
- Monitoring reports generated by electronic data interchange
- Disseminating press releases and other types of internal and external communications
- Assisting in research and gathering information for special projects

- Training personnel and others on computer hardware and software, as well as office procedures
- Facilitating electronic meetings using groupware and other technologies

SPECIALIZED OFFICE CAREER OPPORTUNITIES

Just as in any career, office professionals have an opportunity to specialize in many fields. In the fields of law, medicine, education, government, and technology, numerous career opportunities exist for the office professional.

Although the basic duties within each specialized field may be similar and the use of office technology the same, terminology, applications, and procedures vary greatly from field to field. A quick look at each field will help to clarify some of the differences.

The Legal Office Professional

Accuracy and speed are important requirements for a career in the legal field. Whether in a one-lawyer office or a large firm, the work of a law office is detailed and exacting. Terminology is precise; timing, organization, and confidentiality are essential in this field.

Duties include keying and transcription. A knowledge of legal documents and legal terminology as well as good oral and written skills are important. The work is highly varied, ranging from managing the office to preparing legal documents and court papers; it also includes extensive contact with clients.

Many kinds of positions are available within the legal profession. They include opportunities in single-attorney offices; in partnerships; in large law firms; in the legal departments of major corporations; and in the local, state, and federal court systems. Legal firms' practices vary from general law to specialization in such areas as real estate, corporate law, tax law, criminal law, estate planning, marital law, or labor law.

The Medical Office Professional

The medical office professional's special duties include managing the office, scheduling patients, quoting and collecting fees, preparing and processing insurance claim forms, ordering and maintaining supplies and equipment, transcribing dictation, maintaining patients' records, assisting and supporting patients, and performing clinical duties if trained to do so by attending physicians. Confidentiality of patient records must always be maintained.

Opportunities within the medical profession exist in physicians' offices, medical clinics, public health facilities, hospitals, health maintenance organizations, nursing homes, research centers, medical centers, foundations, laboratories, insurance agencies, private agencies, medical departments of large companies, educational institutions, companies that manufacture medical supplies and equipment, and medical transcription service companies.

The Educational Office Professional

A career in the educational field can be multifaceted regardless of the educational level. This office professional must have excellent communication skills and the ability to work under established policies and practices as well as to plan and organize work schedules. Computer skills and dictation transcription are important, as is familiarity with other office equipment. The educational office professional must serve as liaison between students, teachers, administrators, coworkers, parents, and the local community, so interpersonal skills are essential.

The duties of educational office professionals vary from institution to institution. Opportunities for such personnel exist from the preschool to the graduate level and can be in public, private, or church-affiliated schools, large or small. Specialized schools for special need students, vocational schools, and correctional schools also need office professionals. Many not-for-profit organizations, such as the National Education Association and the American Association of School Administrators offer job opportunities.

The Government Office Professional

The largest employer in the United States is the federal government, which offers numerous opportunities both here and abroad for office professionals. To become eligible for most government positions, you must take a written civil service examination. Promotions are usually made from within based on the availability, demonstrated skills, and seniority of those applying.

Other positions are available in state, county, and municipal governments as well as in quasi-governmental agencies. Contact the Office of Personnel Management in the region in which you desire employment; it is the best source for checking available jobs in the public sector.

The Technical Office Professional

Aerospace, agriculture, engineering, environmental protection, chemistry, life sciences, mathematics, and the physical sciences are just some of the career fields available to the technical office professional.

Knowledge of electronic office equipment is essential for the technical office professional. Technical documents such as scientific reports and abstracts, require proper formatting. Technical office professionals must have the ability to key technical data accurately and to proofread text that includes mathematical equations, symbols, and technical data. A strong background in mathematics or science and a knowledge of technical terminology are definite assets. Confidentiality is also a critical element for this field.

The growth of research and technology, within both government and private companies, has created many opportunities for office professionals who have the ability to deal with technical terms and symbols. Because these offices deal with technology, most such offices use modern electronic equipment that can provide additional experience.

PART-TIME, TEMPORARY, AND HOME OFFICE CAREERS

Changes in the demographics of the work force, labor shortages, and the advancement of technology have made the options for office professionals more flexible. While most are employed on a full-time basis in a particular office, today's office professional also works part-time, as a temporary, or even from home.

Some businesses prefer hiring on a part-time rather than a full-time basis. An individual or firm may require only a few hours of work each day or a few days of work per week in order to fulfill necessary work requirements. For some companies, dividing a full-time job between two part-time employees has proven to be a plus and has added to job flexibility. Part-time work enables individuals to maintain important career skiffs while at the same time allowing them to pursue other responsibilities and interests.

Temporary Career Options

More than a million temporary workers (temps) are used by businesses every day, according to the National Association of Temporary Services (NATS), a trade group based in Alexandria, Virginia. Businesses use outsourcing for a variety of reasons. Many firms outsource in order to handle seasonal peak workloads better. Some companies use outsourcing or temporary agencies to avoid the problems of recruiting and training permanent workers or as a way to maintain lean permanent staffs. For various reasons, the temp career is a viable option for today's office professional

Two economic trends are also contributing to the use of temps. The first is a shortage of qualified workers. According to *The Occupational Outlook Handbook,* an annual publication from the U.S. Department of Labor, the demand for skilled clerical and technical help is forecasted to grow significantly faster than the demand for the work force as a whole.

The second trend is the changing lifestyles of the work force itself. Factors such as down-sizing, the women's movement, the aging of the work force, and increased labor-force mobility have created a labor shortage.

As a result of these trends, a temporary office career fits with many workers' career goals. Temps come in all ages and both genders and are highly trained. To keep pace with the growing demand for computer-literate office workers, outsourcing services provide training to sharpen computer skills and to provide knowledge of current hardware and software. This not only helps the employer, but can also provide temps with skills that might otherwise never be learned or upgraded.

The Home Office Career and Telecommuting

For at least 34 million Americans, modern technology has allowed the world of work to shift from offices to homes, part-time or full-time. The trend toward working at home is driven by the personal computer, which can be connected to a phone line in order for the worker to "telecommute" to the office. Increasingly, clerical workers use this option to do tasks formerly performed in offices, as do home-based entrepreneurs who provide services to numerous organizations. A home office career allows professionals to maintain skills and pursue a career. They can contribute to the organization while following other interests or while managing the household, all without having to leave home.

Here are some guidelines to follow when working at home:

- Establish a work schedule, specific hours when you plan to do your tasks, with "to do" and "follow-up" lists as if you were in the office. (Good home office workers or telecommuters are generally people who are able to manage their own time and workload well, solve many of their own problems, and find satisfaction in completing tasks with minimal supervision.)

- Establish with your manager(s) the hours when you will be available by phone or else call in at specified times. Consider a personal pager for crises.

- Organize your work schedule so that most of the individual work is reserved for telecommuting days and collaborative work for times when everyone is in the office. But even when you are working at home, telecommunication tools—such as phones, e-mail, groupware, and faxes—can be used to connect to your manager(s).

- Work out with your manager such issues as security and which files you may take home. Be sure to log all files that you take out of the office. Electronic records management systems that can be accessed from remote locations with proper security codes are the best solution for home office workers who need access to information.

- Be sure you have appropriate technology and home office furniture. For example, a mobile telecommuter who will be working in many locations should have a laptop computer with a docking station in the office rather than a desktop computer. A person who spends a lot of time in a home office inputting data into a computer should have a desktop computer and correct ergonomic furniture, including an ergonomic chair and keyboard support, to minimize potential injuries. (See Chapter 10—the same guidelines given there apply to setting up a home office workstation.) ISDN phone lines or, at a minimum, a 28.8-baud computer modem is essential if you will be spending considerable time on the Internet or up- or downloading files. Also, fax equipment is essential for most telecommuting employees. Many employers will provide the technology for the employee, and some will help defray the cost of the home office furniture.

- Consult your organization's policies regarding an employee's personal use of company-owned computer and fax equipment, as well as maintaining the integrity of information (i.e., formatted, filed, categorized) stored on paper and in electronic form.

- Sign an agreement that summarizes your organization's expectations. This agreement should include the days and hours you will be working at home, work assignments, reimbursement policy for phone calls and supplies, management contact expectations, company equipment and furniture to be provided, telecommunications hookup, equipment maintenance, and any additional conditions you feel pertinent.

- Know that there is no "right" number of days for telecommuting. On the average, one to three days a week seems to be the practice. More time away can give you the feeling of being "out of the loop" and create morale problems, as well as make it hard for managers to schedule departmental or group meetings.

- Remember that telecommuting is not a perk, an entitlement, or a benefit. It is an alternative way to work that is not for everyone. Not all jobs or personalities are suited for this type of work.

- Keep in mind that working at a distance is, in some respects, similar to working in the office. Good employees set expectations, give feedback to their managers, and do all the other required tasks no matter where they work.

- You can contact the Telecommuting Advisory Council (TAC) (204 E Street N.E., Washington, D.C. 20002, 202-547-6157 voice, 202-546-3289 fax, http://www. telecommute.org) for more information about telecommuting programs. TAC comprises individuals, corporations, educators, consultants, and vendors involved in telecommuting in both the private and public sectors.

PREPARATION FOR OTHER CAREERS

Unlike many other professions, the office professional field offers many career options. Neither extensive preparation nor a degree in business administration or a technical or scientific field is necessary.

For example, a secretary who is interested in a career in the communications industry might take a position at a television station or public relations firm to gain firsthand experience. With that experience, an office worker could advance to being an account executive or a salesperson. A secretary interested in law might train as a legal secretary, obtain a position in a law firm, and then advance to a paralegal position.

With the increased knowledge needed to use office technology, office professionals have found positions as equipment salespersons and as marketing support representatives. They have also become customer service representatives, who provide training and backup services for customers.

Traditional furniture vendors are expanding and diversifying their marketing horizons to include office furniture that is especially designed to meet the needs of the electronic office. Managers of such vendors often seek marketing representatives who are knowledgeable about the furniture required by the integrated office, its effects on personnel, and the expectations of users.

Other advanced office career options in the computer field include training directors, who train personnel in various software applications such as word processing, spreadsheet, or desktop publishing; programmers, who write the software that tells computers what operations to perform; systems analysts, who develop appropriate programs, systems, and applications for users; and equipment technicians, who repair and service computer hardware and accessories. Another option is to become an independent contractor, who works at home for firms that have no computer equipment or that need additional support during peak periods.

The likelihood for an entry-level secretary in today's office to advance to an operational or managerial job is great, thanks to automation. Automation has freed the office professional to make more decisions and receive more recognition. Within this profession, you can guide your career in a direction that will be in harmony with your own talents. Growing numbers of office professionals find their careers following a path into computers, finance, desktop publishing, administration, personnel, and management.

PROFESSIONAL DEVELOPMENT AND GROWTH

To advance in your career, it is important to continue education in your field. Reading is the best and easiest way to grow professionally. Current news magazines, business-oriented publications, and trade publications can help keep you informed about events, trends, policies, and procedures.

If you can, enroll in a local college or in continuing education courses. Colleges offer evening and weekend courses; many give credit for life experiences. Take advantage of company-sponsored workshops and seminars. In addition, many professional organizations offer seminars to help office professionals understand and perform better in their jobs.

Another good step is to join professional organizations, such as the Professional Secretaries International® (PSI®); the National Association of Legal Secretaries (NALS); the American Association for Medical Assistants (AAMA); the American Association for Medical Transcription (AAMT); and many others. These groups provide a wealth of information on word and information processing and office automation. Most offer newsletters, magazines, seminars, workshops, and equipment exhibits.

Other groups, such as consultants, retailers, and manufacturers, offer seminars and information on such topics as how to integrate word and data processing and how to increase office productivity as well as training in time management, office organization, and filing techniques.

See About Professional Secretaries International: The Association for Office Professionals® on page 560.

PROFESSIONAL DEVELOPMENT THROUGH CERTIFICATION

Professional Secretaries International® administers two business-oriented certification programs in the office professional field. Receiving these certifications is indicative of meeting the highest professional standards. The registered service mark for the rating that measures secretarial proficiency is the Certified Professional Secretary® (CPS®) rating. The rating is obtained by (1) completing and verifying educational and secretarial employment experience requirements and (2) passing a three-part, one-day examination administered each May and November by the Institute for Certification (IC), a department of PSI.

Working secretaries, students, and business educators are eligible to take the CPS examination. Many colleges and universities grant academic credit hours to those with the CPS rating who are enrolled in a degree program.

The examination is divided into three parts:

1. *Finance and Business Law:* 30% economics, 35% accounting, 35% business law (120 questions; 2 hours and 30 minutes).
2. *Office Systems and Administration:* 50% office technology; 25% office administration, 25% business communications (150 questions; 2 hours).
3. *Management:* 36% behavioral science in business, 19% human resources management, 45% organizations and management (150 questions; 2 hours).

The Office Proficiency Assessment & Certification® (OPAC®) System is a computerized office skills testing system that is a tremendous timesaver for administrators due to completely automated, self-scoring tests. Hard-copy results are generated on completion of testing. The OPAC System offers a battery of different tests, measuring skills in language arts, keyboarding, 10-key data entry, filing, basic arithmetic, word processing, spreadsheets, and databases. It is IBM-compatible and interacts with live versions of leading software applications. The OPAC System was developed and validated by Professional Secretaries International®. OPAC certification indicates entry-level office skills, as determined by PSI. For more information, contact PSI at the number listed below.

Certification is also possible in certain specialized fields. A legal secretary may become a Professional Legal Secretary (PLS). This is the only certification program for legal secretaries; it provides a standard measurement of legal secretarial knowledge and skills. Additional information can be obtained by contacting the National Association of Legal Secretaries.

Medical assistants are eligible to join the American Association of Medical Assistants (AAMA). The AAMA offers a certifying examination that upon successful passing leads to certification as a Certified Medical Assistant (CMA). This can be achieved through continuing education or through reexamination. For more information contact the American Association of Medical Assistants.

Certification as a medical transcriptionist can be obtained through the American Association for Medical Transcription (AAMT). Their examination leads to certification as a Certified Medical Transcriptionist (CMT). Additional information can be obtained by contacting the American Association for Medical Transcription.

Office personnel in the educational field can obtain certification through the National Association of Educational Office Personnel (NAEOP). Their Professional Standards Program leads to the distinction of a Certified Educational Office Employee. This is awarded to those who meet established criteria.

Organizations for office professionals include:

General
Professional Secretaries International®—The Association for
Office Professionals™

10502 NW Ambassador Drive
P.O. Box 20404
Kansas City, MO 64195-0404
(816) 891-6600
Fax number: (816) 891-9118
E-mail: service@psi.org
Homepage: http://www.gvi.net/psi

Legal
National Association of Legal Secretaries
2250 East 73 Street, Suite 550
Tulsa, OK 74136
(918) 493-3540

Educational
National Association of Educational Office Personnel
7223 Lee Highway, Suite 301
Falls Church, VA 22046
(703) 533-0810

Medical
American Association of Medical Assistants
20 North Wacker, Suite 1575
Chicago, IL 60606
(312) 899-1500
(800) 228-2262

American Association for Medical Transcription
P.O. Box 6187
Modesto, CA 95355
(800) 982-2182

SEMINARS, WORKSHOPS, AND TRAINING

In addition to certification, office professionals today must rely on seminars, workshops, and other training programs to achieve ongoing career development and to keep up with changing technology in the automated office. Many professional associations sponsor seminars on professional development. Other organizations train businesspeople through workshops and seminars.

Many companies provide in-house training programs to their employees as a means of keeping their work-force's skills at optimum levels. Some programs are taught by instructors from within the organization. Others are hired from outside the company for their expertise in particular topics.

Other training programs are self-taught. They may use manuals, which may be combined with a computer software program; tutorials; audiotapes; videotapes; or interactive video instruction. Interactive video instruction allows the trainee to become actively involved with the computer screen and keyboard. The trainee in effect directs the lesson by "dialoguing" with the computer.

SETTING PERSONAL GOALS

The growth in jobs for office professionals represents 50 percent of the total growth in jobs for white-collar workers. The office and all its related support areas offer some of the greatest growth potential ever known. As an office professional you have a better chance to achieve your personal goals if you know your own goals as well as the goals of your organization.

In order to set personal goals, you must know what you want out of life and how hard you are willing to work for it. Goals define where you want to go and how you want to get there. They are benchmarks by which you can measure your progress. By setting goals, high achievers are able to seize opportunities to make those goals realities.

Every job you hold is a critical step in the development of your career. A career requires long-term planning and commitment to help you reach your professional potential. A master career plan should consist of long-range goals and short-range, more immediate objectives. An inventory of the skills you have—the things you do well and enjoy—is the very core of a plan for your career.

To build a successful career, you also must know the basic skills and components of your career. For example, if your goal is to become a computer trainer, you must know software, the equipment used, and the procedures involved in order to be an effective teacher. Such knowledge is usually gained through work experience.

The development of job and career objectives is a continuous process. Each day, month, and year you know more about yourself. At the same time, you deepen and broaden your knowledge of the world of work and continue to work toward meeting your goals—whatever they may be.

When planning goals for your career, you need to decide what role you want to pursue in the offices of both today and tomorrow. You must be open-minded in order to maintain the flexibility needed to work within this ever-changing environment.

CAREER PATHS AND CAREER LADDERS

The average American today will work for 10 different employers, keep each job only 3.6 years, and change entire careers three times before retirement. These statistics may sound somewhat astonishing, but they show that career paths and career ladders are important elements in this process. A **career path** is a course of action in a career and the various steps taken to achieve an end result. A **career ladder** is a list of the promotions achieved during one's career.

A career path addresses goals that have been established. For instance, suppose an office professional determined that their desired career is to be a lawyer specializing in the medical field. Initially, they took a job as a secretary at a medical office. Then time was spent getting a law degree at night from a local university. Their career path showed the steps to take to achieve her career goal.

Climbing the career ladder, on the other hand, begins when one has determined one's career path and is advancing up the "rungs" through promotion. In any career, several career ladders exist. Within an office, a career ladder for word processing may exist as well as one for administrative services. Only you can determine which ladder you want to climb and only you can create opportunities in order to climb the ladder.

FUTUREVISIONEERING™ YOUR CAREER

Technology is creating a new information age that will forever change the way offices operate and the way information is handled. High technology is proliferating in the office environment. FutureVisioneering™ your career path by identifying emerging computer and communications technologies that can significantly impact how you work can lead to expanded job opportunities as we enter a new century.

Emerging information technology of one kind or another will produce revolutionary changes in organizations. Secretaries will be even more dependent than today on technologies such as desktop videoconferencing, artificial intelligence (AI), and voice recognition. Networking technology, both local area networks (LANs) and wide area networks (WANs), has made transmission of voice, data, and images faster, less expensive, and more widespread. Interactive three-dimensional video, very-high-bandwidth communication channels, virtual reality as a communications medium, and shape-recognition cameras may be part of an office assistant's future.

New technologies will also revolutionize how workers share information. More secretaries will individually manage information, making group sharing of knowledge increasingly important, either face-to-face or by electronic means. Portable laptop computers, video/audio teleconferencing equipment, liquid crystal display (LCD) and video projectors, visualizers, fax machines, optical scanners, smart electronic information display boards that connect to computers, and input tablets that process handwriting are examples of standard equipment for the modern business meeting. In addition, new electronic communication feedback systems and video WEBbing technology will be integrated into some of the more sophisticated meeting and training rooms.

One thing is certain—machines are not replacing the secretary in the office. If anything, they are enhancing and expanding the position to one of greater importance than ever. The future will be dominated by a new discipline, termed "knowledge management." As the office environment becomes electronic, the key to the office professional's career success lies in his or her ability to connect—to connect phone calls, messages, schedules, information, reports, and data—and to put information together for a particular use. Administrative support personnel are the gatekeepers of the electronic channels. As these channels become more prevalent and better developed, the role of controlling and making sense of all this electronic traffic will become even more important.

Staying up to date with the latest technologies and incorporating them into one's work routines is necessary for both job security and job enhancement. Executive-search firms are reporting an increased demand for people with strong computer and telecommunications skills. They also report that because of technology, new supervisory jobs, such as Help Desk Manager, are arising in most organizations, especially growing companies. Continue to keep up to date by attending seminars, reading computer and communications magazines, and learning the latest versions of software applications. Become the office expert on software and in finding valuable business-related information on the Internet. Keeping everyone in your department up to date and serving as an end-user technology resource person ensures that you will be of great value to your departmental group.

Actively reengineering your job description must be an ongoing activity. Secretaries can no longer continue to accept the status quo but must create future career opportunities. Perhaps it is time to become a FutureVisioneer™ by looking ahead, seeing the future, and creating the pathway to it.

Career advancement can be a job promotion or new job within your present company or a new position with another firm. In order to prepare for career opportunities, you must be able to:

- Prepare a resume
- Write a cover letter
- Fill out an employment application
- Interview successfully
- Follow up on the interview
- Complete employment tests
- Determine when to use employment agencies or other support networks

THE RESUME

A resume is a written summary of abilities, accomplishments, and work history. The purpose of the resume is to get an interview, not a job. Employers do not hire on the basis of a resume alone, but the resume should motivate an employer to meet you. Successful job seekers should prepare at least two versions of their resume. One version is read by people in 6 to 8 seconds. The other version is designed to be electronically examined and analyzed by a computer. Both resumes should have the following qualities:

- Resumes should be well organized. The preferred length is one or two pages of 8½-by-11-inch paper, no matter how many previous jobs or how much experience and education a candidate has.
- Resumes should emphasize strengths and accomplishments and show that the candidate is qualified for the available job. It should demonstrate excellent writing skills, with perfect grammar, spelling, and punctuation. A well-written resume is tailored to the available job, showing a knowledge of the necessary skills, talents, and background. A resume is not a life history, lengthy job description, or detailed listing of irrelevant earlier jobs.

All resumes should also have the following components:

- Heading
- Job objective

CHAPTER 2

CAREER

ADVANCEMENT

- Work experience
- Education

Resumes Screened by an Individual: Resumes screened by an individual (as opposed to being scanned by a computer) should be attractive to the eye. Word-processed resumes may be easily and quickly customized, changed, or corrected. The following are suggestions for this style of resume:

- Use no more than two or three different typefaces and type sizes.
- Do not overuse type styles such as bold, italic, and uppercase.
- Use wide margins, proportional spacing, and indentions.
- Select off-white, beige, or gray 16- to 20-pound bond paper.
- Print on a laser printer.

Optically-Scannable Resumes: At most large companies and many medium-sized ones, resumes are scanned by computers. A software program searches for keywords, which are words or phrases that define the requisites of a job. Because computer-read resumes are designed to be scanned and not read by an individual, use the following guidelines:

- Left-justify the entire document with 1½-inch left and right margins.
- Use a plain, standard sans serif font such as Helvetica or, if only a serif font is available, Times or Courier in 10- to 14-point type size.
- Avoid tabs, which can cause an error for the optical scanning equipment.
- Avoid italic text, script, underlining, columns, graphics or pictures, and shading. Bold, however, can be scanned but that too tends to cause more errors.
- Avoid horizontal and vertical lines as well as parentheses and brackets.
- Use a paper clip, not a staple, to hold more than one page together. Be sure to include name, telephone number, and date at the top of each page. Also, label pages out of total number of pages sent (e.g., page 1 of 2, page 2 of 2, etc.).
- Use 20-pound white paper with black ink printed on a laser printer. Copies and faxed resumes will not work.
- Send the resume unfolded and flat in a large envelope.

Heading

The heading includes your name, address (including ZIP code), and home and/or work telephone numbers (including area codes). If a home telephone answering machine is used, the recording should be professional and to the point. If your present employer is aware of your job search, then include your work number. If it is impossible to talk with a prospective employer at a work phone, then omit it.

Some suggested styles for resume headings are shown in the sample resumes. (See Figures 2-1, 2-2, and 2-3 for examples.)

The following are suggestions for an optically scanned heading:

- Use a middle initial if you have one.
- Do not abbreviate the state, the word *street* or *avenue,* or any other part of the address.
- Avoid parentheses and the dash when entering your home/work phone number. They can cause an error for the optical scanning equipment.

See Figure 2-4 for an example of an optically scannable resume.

Job Objective

Start with a clear job objective. The job objective lets the employer know that you have gone through a thorough self-analysis and know what you want in your career.

The job objective immediately follows the heading and states a job title or specific occupational field. Unless the job objective is general, it should be restated to reflect each different position you apply for.

Here are some possible job objectives:

- Administrative assistant to the director of sales
- Legal secretary for a law firm specializing in litigation
- Office support in the insurance industry
- Medical transcriptionist in a metropolitan hospital
- Records management specialist for a manufacturing firm

The job objective for an optically-scanned resume should stand alone in bold type and match the job title advertised. If possible, the objective should match the wording of the advertisement.

Highlights of Qualifications

Immediately after the objective comes a "profile" that states, in five or six lines, why you are the ideal person for this particular position. This section can also be called "Summary of Skills" or "Qualifications and Skills."

This section can include skills, years of experience, character traits, schools attended, hardware and software you are proficient in, or anything else the employer might find important. Below is a list of suggestions for qualifications, which will work well in either a traditional or scanned resume.

Marcia Hernandez
                38 South Hawthorne Way • Washington, DC 20009
                202-555-7236

Job Objective   Administrative assistant with sales firm

QUALIFICATIONS AND SKILLS

- Sixteen years of office support experience, including customer relations
- Excellent time-management and organizational skills
- Self-motivated, dependable, and goal-oriented employee
- Skilled in written and verbal communications
- Professional appearance and high professional standards

PROFESSIONAL EXPERIENCE

1990–present   SENIOR SALES ASSISTANT
                Bigelow Publishing Co., Washington, D.C.

                Primary focus of this position is marketing and technical support for six sales representatives in Florida, West Virginia, Virginia, North Carolina, South Carolina, and Pennsylvania.

- Develop specialized education materials.
- Coordinate regional sales exhibits and conferences.
- Serve as liaison among central office, editorial staff, customers, and sales representatives.
- Research and compose correspondence for representatives.
- Coordinate city and county textbook adoptions, and develop and maintain production information.
- Access computerized inventory and customer database.

1985–1990   DISPATCHER
                3M Business Products Sales, Inc., Reston, Virginia

                Routed and dispatched 20 service representatives for copy machines in the greater Washington, D.C., area.

1980–1985   ORDER CLERK
                3M Business Products Sales, Inc., Reston, Virginia

                Received orders for 300 businesses over the telephone for office and school supplies in the greater Washington, D.C., area.

Figure 2-1 A reverse chronological resume for a person who is looking for work in the same field and who has no education beyond a high school diploma.

Joanne Jacobson
3948 Grove Street • Kansas City, Missouri 64112
816-555-4930

Objective: Position as an executive secretary involving information services
with a high degree of public contact.

HIGHLIGHTS OF QUALIFICATIONS

- Ten years of experience as an administrative assistant.
- Familiar with Windows 3x, Windows 95, and Macintosh plus a variety of
  word processing, database, and spreadsheet software.
- Learn new computer systems quickly.
- Consistently earned outstanding performance evaluations.
- Achieved the Certified Professional Secretary (CPS) rating, 1992.

PROFESSIONAL EXPERIENCE

Organizational and Planning Skills

- Conducted in-house systems training on the computer network for
  200 employees.
- Developed office procedures, including office manuals.
- Planned and supervised yearly national sales meetings for 200 employees,
  including choosing the meeting site, confirming speakers, and arranging for
  support services.
- Prepared all reports for the Board of Directors' monthly meetings.

Interpersonal/Communication Skills

- Served as a liaison with computer systems manager and outside consulting
  firm to coordinate the network.
- Coordinated payroll preparation with outside processing firm.
- Wrote press releases.
- Prepared correspondence.

Computer Skills

- Researched, proposed, and supervised the installation of a $55,000 purchase
  of telecommunications and computer equipment.
- Prepared income and expense spreadsheets using Excel on the PC.
- Designed company newsletter on the Macintosh using Word and PageMaker
  software.

—Continued—

Figure 2-2 A resume highlighting job duties for a person with similar work experience in a variety of firms.

JOANNE JACOBSON
Page 2 of 2

EMPLOYMENT HISTORY

1994–present	Administrative Assistant	First Interstate Bank Kansas City, Missouri
1991–1994	Administrative Assistant	Valley Bank Overland Park, Kansas
1988–1991	Secretary	Kellogg and Sons Blue Springs, Kansas
1986–1988	Secretary	Borden Foods Company East Point, Georgia

EDUCATION AND PROFESSIONAL AFFILIATIONS

Enrolled in Administrative Management program at Mission College, Kansas City, Misouri.

Member of Professional Secretaries International—The Association for Office Professionals

Figure 2-2 (continued).

KATHLEEN GLENN
102 Rancho Coati Drive
White Plains, New York 10604
914-555-9999

Objective   Office Assistant

QUALIFICATIONS

- Five years' experience in office environment; familiar with office procedures.
- Two years experience on the Macintosh using word processing, spreadsheet, and desktop publishing software.
- Proficient in usingIBM-compatible computers.
- Developed and implemented alphabetic and numeric filing systems.
- Excellent telephone communication skills; patient, personable, and loyal.
- Demonstrated ability to work independently and as a cooperative team member.

EXPERIENCE

1991–present   GABLER SALES COMPANY, White Plains, New York

Secretary: Duties include communicating with customers by telephone and scheduling appointments, creating and maintaining a database of customers, organizing an accurate alphabetic filing system, keyboarding correspondence and generating price lists and brochures, processing mail and shipping, preparing bank deposits, and maintaining records for taxes.

VOLUNTEER EXPERIENCE

1990–1991   THE PRACTICAL PRESS, White Plains, New York

Office assistant: Duties included answering marketing questions for telephone customers. Handled mail order of books, processed invoices, implemented bookkeeping procedures.

EDUCATION

Currently attending White Plains Community College, White Plains, New York

Working toward Administrative Assistant Certificate. To be completed May 19—.

Figure 2-3 A resume highlighting qualifications and accomplishments for a person with recent work experience.

Kimberly Gilstrap, CPS
4489 Horseshoe Bay Court
Sebastopol, California 94143
Telephone: 707.337.3992

Administrative Assistant
Responsible position as an assistant to upper management in an insurance firm

Summary of Skills
....formal education....proficient using Microsoft Word for Windows, WordPerfect 6.1, Excel, Lotus 1-2-3, Quicken....10 key by touch....customer relations and service....staff supervision and training....filing....excellent communication skills....enjoys challenges....works well with all levels of management and personnel....self-motivated...

Professional Highlights
Redford Insurance Company 1997– present
Petaluma, California

Administrative Assistant

Position responsibilities include:
• Keyboarding insurance policies, including homeowner's, automobile, and life.
• Proofreading and editing premium notices.
• Preparing correspondence for three individuals by keyboarding memorandums, letters, medical reports, and legal documents.
• Managing the reception desk, answering phones for an office of 20 people.
• Maintaining alphabetic and numeric files.

United Leasing Corporation 1991–1997
San Francisco, California

Operations Manager

Position responsibilities included:
• Managed a staff of five, including supervisor and lease processors.
• Developed strong professional relationships with vendors.
• Administered lease processing and documentation control.
• Handled scheduled input and backlog management.
• Managed credit analysis and approval.
• Maintained budget and profitability levels.

Education
AA Degree in Administrative Support, 1995,
Santa Rosa Junior College, Petaluma, California. GPA 3.5.

Figure 2-4 An optically scannable resume.

- Ability to work well under pressure
- Ability to work well with all levels of management and personnel
- Able to learn new tasks quickly
- Bilingual; fluent in English and Spanish
- Innovative in developing work-flow systems
- Proficient in use of Microsoft Office software

Professional Highlights

This is the core of the resume. Experience is listed in reverse chronological order or according to job functions. Reverse chronological order is preferable if you are staying in the same field, especially if your job history shows growth and development and no gaps in work history. Reverse chronological resumes list the most recent job first. (See Figures 2-1 and 2-3.) If there are many jobs to list, select the last four or five.

Listing experience by job functions is useful if you are changing careers, entering the job market for the first time, reentering the job market after an absence, have an irregular work history, or need to highlight volunteer experience. This type of resume describes your responsibilities over the years, starting with the most important work-related tasks. Your employers are listed separately.

Any major accomplishment can be included under the job function without stating the name of the employer. (See Figure 2-2.) Separating the job functions from employer names is particularly useful when changing from one type of business to another (for example, applying for a job in a nonprofit association after working for a manufacturer).

Whether the resume lists jobs reverse chronologically or by job functions, all descriptions should be clear. Phrases such as "worked as acting administrative assistant" or "worked as accountant" are too vague and will not give employers an idea of the work performed. Even the phrase "responsible for" does not give a good idea of job duties.

Employers want to know what you accomplished on the job, not just what your job description was. If you are writing a resume to be read by a person, you should use action verbs, which are verbs that help create a well-defined image of contributions and accomplishments. Listed below are some action verbs you could use to describe your accomplishments:

Analyze	Evaluate	Present
Assist	Examine	Process
Calculate	Generate	Produce
Collect	Implement	Purchase
Compose	Instruct	Recommend
Conduct	Interpret	Represent
Consult	Maintain	Research
Coordinate	Manage	Review
Create	Order	Save
Design	Organize	Schedule
Develop	Perform	Supervise

Diagnose	Plan	Train
Direct	Prepare	Write

If you are writing a scannable resume, keywords are important. Keywords are more of the noun or noun-phrase type, such as total quality management, customer support, cash-flow management, payroll, computerized systems, or documentation of patient charts.

Numbers and figures should be included whenever possible. Money-saving techniques should be stated. "Managed yearly operating budget of $170,000" is more impressive than "managed budget." Supervisory experience should be emphasized, stating how many people were hired, trained, and supervised.

The following are additional suggestions for writing about your experience:

- Avoid long sentences. A description of a job or job duty should be ten lines long or less and list the accomplishments most relevant to the position you would like to fill. Omit accomplishments that have nothing to do with the target job.
- Avoid using "I," for example, "I was responsible for supervising five employees. In this position I did…" Instead, use action verbs without a pronoun: "Managed and maintained local area network of 15 office computers. Recommended selection and purchase of new database software."
- Use years instead of months and days: 1992–present or 1990–1997.
- Write "continued" on the bottom of the first page of a two-page resume and your full name and "page two" on the second page. (See Figure 2-2.)
- Omit jobs that go back 10 or 15 years if space is limited. It is not necessary to list every position ever held. Jobs can be summarized with a statement such as "1980–1990. A variety of office support positions."
- Describe duties in detail only once if several jobs involved similar responsibilities. Avoid giving several examples of work performed when one is adequate.
- Omit company addresses; the name and location of the company are adequate.
- Include home-based and volunteer work if job experience is limited. (See Figure 2-3 for an example of how to include volunteer work on a resume.) Volunteer work and part-time jobs should not be included if work experience is extensive.

Education

If your education occurred within the last five years and is related to the job, it can be emphasized by placing the information about it (including the years) immediately after the job objective. If you have been out of school for some time or your education is not related to the job, you may decide to deemphasize it by placing this information at the bottom of the resume and omitting the years. However, most scanning software are not programmed to read education if the dates are omitted.

Providing graduation years will give an employer an idea of your age, which could be used to eliminate qualified candidates. Omit reference to high school if you attended college or hold post-high school degrees. List each associate, bachelor's, or master's degree separately unless they were earned from the same institution. The date should be included if a degree was earned recently.

If an associate, bachelor's, or master's degree has been earned, list the degrees as follows:

▲ Santa Rosa Junior College, Santa Rosa, CA
  Associate Degree in Business Office Technology

▲ Dana College, Blair, NE
  Bachelor's Degree in Business Administration

▲ University of Wyoming, Laramie, WY
  Master of Business Administration

If you have taken classes beyond high school but have not earned a degree, list the institution and courses relevant to the prospective job. Include seminars or other job training. It is also appropriate to list professional certifications such as the Certified Professional Secretary® (CPS®) rating. The following are examples:

▲ College of Marin, Kentfield, CA
  Completed courses include: Computerized Accounting, Word for Windows, and Excel.

▲ Findlay University, Findlay, OH
  Will receive a Bachelor of Science degree in Accounting, August 19—.
  Achieved a 3.8 grade point (out of a possible 4.0).

▲ San Francisco State University, San Francisco, CA
  Completed 10 hours graduate work in Business Administration.

▲ Achieved the Certified Professional Secretary® (CPS®) rating, 19—.

▲ Attended Certified Professional Secretary® (CPS®) Seminar, June 19—, Savannah, GA
  Received 2.1 CEU for the Local Area Network courses.

If you have completed no education beyond high school, high school can be either included or omitted. The year of graduation is not necessary unless it was recent. The following is an example:

▲ Graduated from Petaluma High School, Petaluma, CA

Here are some other resume preparation techniques:

- Include academic awards and grade point average if they are impressive.
- Include major awards if they are relevant to your profession. For example, "Won a national award for designing a computerized loan amortization program."
- Include leadership roles, such as holding an office in a professional association or an important club. This information is stated under a "Professional Associations" heading. For example, "President of the Dallas chapter, Professional Secretaries International, 1994–1996."
- Omit hobbies unless they are relevant to the job.
- Do not include references. They can be given when the employer is serious about a candidate. It is not necessary to say "References provided upon request."
- Avoid buzzwords and abbreviations unless they are related to the industry to which you are applying. If the employer uses jargon and detailed technical terms to describe required qualifications, it is acceptable to use such words.
- Omit salary requirements; they will be discussed during the interview.
- Do not give reasons for leaving previous jobs. This information will come up either on the employment application or during the interview.
- Never include personal information such as height, age, weight, sex, health, and status. It is illegal for a job interviewer to ask you about such matters.

CHECKLIST FOR RESUMES

▲ Is it no more than one or two pages?

▲ Is it printed on good-quality bond paper?

▲ Is the layout (organization) attractive?

▲ Is it easy to scan?

▲ Are there any spelling, grammar, or punctuation errors?

▲ Are the following items in the heading?

    Name

    Address (including ZIP code)

    Phone numbers (including area code)

▲ Is the job objective clearly stated (if included)?

▲ Is your experience presented effectively?

    Included necessary information?

    Omitted days and months?

    Omitted employer addresses?

    Used action words?

       Limited descriptions to fewer than ten lines?

       Avoided use of "I"?

       Listed previous jobs relevant to the position?

▲ Is your education presented effectively?

       Included necessary information?

       Placed at the top of the page if recent?

       Provided dates if recent?

▲ Included special courses, certificates, and leadership roles that apply to the job?

Faxing a Resume

If an employer has asked for a faxed resume, include a cover sheet indicating the name of the person requesting the resume and a brief message stating why the resume is being faxed. If you have the address, mail the original resume immediately with a cover letter explaining that the resume has been faxed. If you are called for an interview, take a copy of your resume with you to the appointment.

THE COVER LETTER

A cover letter is sent to a prospective employer with the resume. A personalized cover letter gives applicants an additional opportunity to sell themselves. It usually describes how the qualifications and skills listed on the resume correspond with those required for the job. A three-paragraph letter will be sufficient in most cases. Your cover letter should cover the following points:

- It should be readable, to the point, and refer to the specific job. Some job openings attract hundreds of responses, so the cover letter should be so well-written as to place it in the category of applicants the firm "definitely will interview."
- It should be keyed, no longer than one page (8½ by 11 inches), and printed on paper that matches the paper used for the resume. Perfect spelling, grammar, and punctuation are necessary, because they show the care you put into your work.
- It should be addressed to a specific individual. If an individual's name is not listed in an advertisement or job announcement, phone the company to find out the name of the person making the hiring decision, the correct spelling of the name, and the person's title. If there is no company name or phone number listed in an advertisement, address your letter "Dear Manager" or "Dear Selection Committee."
- Do not use an envelope from your current company to mail in your letter. You are using office supplies for personal use. Also, always weigh and affix the correct postage.

First Paragraph

The first paragraph is the introduction and answers the following questions:

- Why are you writing?
- Where or how did you learn about the job?
- What is your most important qualification for the job?

Avoid starting out in an unconventional or annoying way. A direct statement is more positive and professional than a question, such as "Are you looking for a dynamic and talented administrative assistant?" The following is an example of an opening for a job advertised in a newspaper. It is not necessary to repeat the exact words of an advertisement.

▲ I am applying for the bookkeeping position advertised in the May 10 edition of the *San Francisco Chronicle*.

If an instructor, friend, or employee of the firm told you of a job opening, state that fact also.

▲ Carol Starnes, instructor at Glendale College, suggested I contact you about the office support position available at XYZ Company.

▲ Richard Kerry of Interstate Bank told me a new branch bank was opening in Fremont.

The second part of the first paragraph indicates your main qualifications for the job. Select one fact that justifies suitability for the job.

▲ I have ten years' experience as an office manager for the national headquarters of an insurance agency.

▲ I have been an administrative assistant to the president for the last five years.

▲ I am a recent graduate of San Jose State University, with a degree in Accounting.

Second Paragraph

The second paragraph emphasizes education and work background and creates interest in you as an applicant. It may be six or seven sentences long and it must relate your education and experience d1irectly to the available job. It should describe exactly how schoolwork and job experience qualify you to function in the job advertised. Your goal is to create interest in you as an applicant. State your knowledge about the company in the opening sentence to show your interest in a job with that firm. The following is an example of an opening statement about the company:

▲ Because Company X is well known for its technical expertise, you are looking for employees who are experienced in handling technical information.

The work experience description indicates how your experience will be valuable to an employer and does not describe your desire for a job. (See Figures 2-5 and 2-6.) For example, avoid this kind of sentence when replying to an advertisement for a position requiring word processing skills: "I have worked with WordPerfect software before, and this experience will give me the edge in operating it. I can adjust quickly to any working environment." The following sentence is more meaningful to an employer, because it describes what you can do for him or her:

▲ I am a highly motivated self-starter with three years' experience using Microsoft Office software on a PC. My work experience includes writing and editing customer reply letters, keying and formatting the company newsletter, developing promotional brochures and flyers, and producing the company's annual report.

Third Paragraph

The third paragraph asks for an interview and indicates your availability for one. This paragraph is usually only two or three sentences long. The following is an example:

▲ I would like to schedule an interview to further discuss the possibilities of our working together. I can be reached at 415-555-3994 after 4 p.m. during the week.

Some people recommend stating that you will call in a week to ten days to set up a meeting. This tactic may or may not work. Depending on the size of the company and the number of applications received, employers might not accept calls from a prospective employee. Employers who travel may not be available at the time the call is made.

CHECKLIST FOR COVER LETTERS

▲ Is it no more than one page?

▲ Is it printed on good-quality bond paper?

▲ Is the layout attractive?

▲ Are spelling, grammar, and punctuation correct?

▲ Is it addressed to an individual?

394 East Forest Avenue
Sonoma, California 95476
May 7, 19—

Mr. Richard Herndon, Director
Valley of the Moon Hospital
384 Oak Leaf Lane
Sonoma, California 95476

Dear Mr. Herndon:

I am applying for the administrative assistant position advertised on May 7 in the *Press Democrat*. I am skilled on the PC, detail-oriented, and able to work under pressure.

With five years of experience as an administrative assistant in the advertising department of a Fortune 500 firm, I know the importance of meeting deadlines and following through on details. I am exceptionally well organized and have a wide range of experience, including supervising and training a staff of twenty. My computer skills include expertise in Excel, Microsoft Word, PowerPoint, PageMaker, and Access software.

I feel I have much to offer Valley of the Moon Hospital, and I would enjoy discussing my qualifications and your needs in person. Please contact me at 707-555-4883 after 3:00 p.m. to schedule an appointment.

Sincerely,

Maralee Shadle

Figure 2-5 Cover letter showing work experience correlating closely with the job opening.

4390 Olive Street
Pasadena, California 91104
June 23, 19—

Ms. Christine Rummler
Personnel Manager
Lifetime, Inc.
Department 2093, Box 24
Pasadena, California 91109-7237

Dear Ms. Rummler:

I am applying for the administrative position advertised on June 22 in the *Los Angeles Times*. I have extensive experience in office procedures and support functions and have been trained in word processing and spreadsheet software on the PC.

My last five years have been spent as an administrative assistant to an executive vice president. Some of my accomplishments have included complete organization and management of office procedures for our division of fifty support staff. I have designed brochures and flyers with Microsoft Word. Although the enclosed resume states some of my skills, it does not take into consideration my willingness to take on new tasks, ability to learn quickly, and desire to succeed.

I welcome the opportunity to talk with you about the position and my interest in working for Lifetime. I can be reached at 818-555-9938 after 5:00 p.m.

Sincerely,

Peggy Giradi

Figure 2-6 Cover letter showing a willingness to take on new responsibilities.

▲ Does the first paragraph:

    state why you are writing?

    tell where you heard about the job?

    mention your major qualification for the job?

    italicize or underline the newspaper name?

▲ Does the second paragraph:

    show that you know something about the company?

    relate educational accomplishments to the job?

    relate experience to the job?

    match your qualifications with the needs of the company?

▲ Does the third paragraph:

    ask for an interview?

    include a phone number where you can be reached?

    indicate the best times to call?

▲ Does it make an employer want to meet you?

THE EMPLOYMENT APPLICATION

Many employers ask a prospective employee to complete an employment application. It is important that the employment application be filled out neatly and accurately. If the application can be completed out at home, where there are fewer distractions, there will be less possibility of error. Make a copy of the application and fill out as practice before completing the actual application. Answer all questions truthfully and as accurately as possible.

Read the directions carefully. If it says to print or type all responses, a keyboarded copy will make the most favorable impression, assuming corrections can easily be made. If a typewriter is not available, use a pen with dark ink that will not smear. Do not use a pencil.

Fill in all blanks. If an item does not apply, write "N/A," which means "not applicable," or use a dash (—). Usually an application requires more information than is on a resume. There may be questions about salary, your reason for leaving your last job, and references.

Personal Information

Your name, address (including ZIP code), and home phone number will always be requested. Other items may include work telephone number, Social Security number, and driver's license number.

Unless height and weight directly relate to a job requirement (police officer, for example), these questions are illegal. Nor should an employer ask about marital status, number and ages of children, or date of birth. Asking for proof of age after hiring is acceptable. (For other illegal questions that should not be asked on an application form, see the section Illegal Questions later in this chapter.)

Candidates for civic appointments or government positions may be asked to waive the privilege of confidentiality of information on file at federal, state, or city agencies. To know ahead of time what is in those records, contact the Federal Information Center in the nearest city.

Education

Most applications have a section for education. Unless the application states otherwise, list the most recent education first and work backwards. Information requested often includes the name of the educational institution, dates attended, grade-point average, credits completed, and the full address.

Job Experience

This will ask for the names and addresses (including ZIP Codes) of current and previous employers and dates employed. Usually the current job is listed first. The application may ask the name of your supervisor, their phone number, and job title.

If a job description is asked for, use action verbs. There will probably only be room for a few words, so use the ones most relevant to the job. If you prefer that the interviewer not contact your present employee without your permission, a note to that effect can be placed in the margin.

You may be asked your reason for leaving past jobs. If the reason is that you received a promotion, make certain the next job listed actually is a promotion. Try to avoid using the term "fired"; reword to "looking for a more responsible position" or "prefer to discuss in interview." "To raise a family" and "to return to school" are also possible responses.

If the application has a blank for "salary requested," you can either list a salary range or write "negotiable" or "open." It is also appropriate to leave this item blank if you wish. If you fill in an amount, however, be sure it is accurate.

References

The best references are former employers or teachers who can relate positive information about you. Friends and relatives are not appropriate. All references should be contacted ahead of time so they are not surprised by phone calls. Their names, addresses, phone numbers, and occupations will probably be requested.

CHECKLIST FOR EMPLOYMENT APPLICATIONS

▲ Is every blank completed with information or N/A?

▲ Is the application typewritten or printed in dark ink?

▲ Is it neat and legible?

▲ Is it free of spelling, grammar, and punctuation errors?

▲ Is all personal information given as requested?

▲ Is all education information complete?

▲ Is all work experience information complete?

▲ Are appropriate references listed?

▲ Is the application signed and dated?

THE JOB INTERVIEW

A job interview is an opportunity for you to learn more about a company and a job and for the employer to see if you will match the needs of the company. Some positions may require two or three interviews. The higher the job level and the more bureaucratic the organization, the more interviews there will be.

A successful job interview calls for a candidate to do the following:

- Dress conservatively and appropriately.
- Arrive on time.
- Maintain eye contact.
- Greet interviewer with a firm handshake.
- Demonstrate enthusiasm and initiative.
- Use good speech and grammar and the same kind of action verbs used in the resume.
- Indicate specific job goals.
- Bring extra resumes, samples of work, educational transcripts, or performance reviews.
- Listen carefully to questions.
- Think before you answer.
- Act naturally.
- Be informed about the company.
- Have questions to ask about the position.
- Be realistic about salary.

Appearance and Behavior

Research shows that most interviewers decide whether to hire someone in the first 10 to 30 seconds of the interview. The goal of a prospective employee is to make that first impression positive.

One of the ways to make a good first impression is to be well-groomed and appropriately dressed. Your clothes must be clean, pressed, and in good condition. When interviewing, you should wear the kinds of clothes that would be worn in the office. When in doubt, dress conservatively and avoid both overdressing and dressing too casually.

Good manners require eye contact and a firm handshake. Eye contact is absolutely essential, and a lack of it may cost you the job. A firm handshake is also important. If you get nervous, hold a cotton handkerchief in your hands to absorb any moisture before shaking hands.

It is best to act self-confident, rather than shy. Most employers are looking for someone who is assertive, self-assured, and competent. Even if you desperately need or want the job, you should not convey this during the interview.

Researching the Company

If you learn as much as possible about the company, its products, and the interviewer prior to the interview, you will show the interviewer how interested you are in the job. The reference librarian at a public library is a good source of information. Newspaper articles and Internet searches also provide information about the company.

Before going to the job interview, you should:

- Secure a copy of the company's annual report, if possible, through the company, the public library, or the Chamber of Commerce.
- Know the company's major products and services.
- Be aware of the company's competition.
- Find out about the company's reputation.
- Ask others about the organization and the interviewer. Try to find someone who works for the company and talk with them. Try to find someone who has been interviewed by the person who will be interviewing you.
- Know the supervisory role of the person doing the interviewing.

Interview Questions

An effective interviewer evaluates skills, abilities, and experience. At the same time, the interviewer makes judgments about a candidate's motivation, enthusiasm, and ability to fit into the organization. Keep your answers on a professional, not a personal, level. Some possible interview questions may include:

Q: Tell me something about yourself.

HINT: *Outline several strong work-related points and accomplishments; make a summary statement and then stop talking.*

Q: Tell me about your professional experience. What are your most important achievements?

HINT: *Mention the most impressive achievement first; prepare success stories ahead of time.*

Q: What are your goals?

HINT: *Be general and mention that you see yourself gaining increased responsibility, if the firm has opportunities for advancement.*

Q: What are your major strengths?

HINT: *Highlight qualities that will help you succeed in the job available (for example, you work hard, learn quickly, and are conscientious).*

Q: What are your major weaknesses? What areas do you need to improve?

HINT: *Disguise weaknesses as strengths (for example, "I like to stick with a problem until I solve it"; "Sometimes I have ignored my family to finish a project"); select a problem you encountered early in your career and describe how you overcame it.*

Q: Why are you looking for a new position? Why did you leave Company X?

HINT: *Indicate a desire for greater responsibility and challenge or an opportunity to use talents not used in the present position; avoid mentioning money, personality conflicts, or anything that is not a major component of the job. Never deride a former employer.*

Q: Why do you want to work for this company?

HINT: *Show familiarity with the company; draw on the research you did. By asking open-ended questions such as these, the employer can learn about a prospective employee's communication skills and thought processes.*

The following are some suggestions for answering open-ended questions:

- Listen to the question and answer all parts of it.
- Show that the question has been anticipated by answering questions directly.
- Describe education and work experience in a clear, concise way.
- Describe the most important results and accomplishments of your career or experiences.
- Ask the interviewer to clarify the question if you are in doubt about its meaning.

- Let the interviewer set the pace of the discussion. An interviewer should be in control.
- Avoid giving either lengthy answers or simple "yes" or "no" answers. Keep your answers to the point.
- Discuss problem areas briefly and honestly.
- Do not criticize former employers. Avoid displaying bitterness and a negative attitude.

Illegal Questions

When applying for a job, a person cannot be discriminated against because of race, color, national origin, religion, sex, age, or, in many cases, physical or mental handicaps. The following questions are illegal:

- Are you married (single, divorced)?
- Do you have children? How old are they? What are your childcare arrangements?
- Are you planning a family?
- How old are you?
- Do you have any handicaps?
- Have you ever received psychiatric or psychological treatment?
- What race are you?
- Where were you born? Where were your parents (spouse) born?
- Of what country are you a citizen?
- Have you ever been arrested?
- What is your credit rating?
- What is your religion?
- You went to St. Michael's College. Is that a religiously affiliated school?
- Do you belong to any unions?

If an illegal question is asked, there are several options available:

- If the job is interesting and the answer will help rather than hurt your chances, answer the question. After you are hired, bring the illegal question to the attention of the interviewer.
- Do not answer immediately. After a long pause, quietly ask, "Why did you ask that question?"
- Ask politely what the question has to do with job performance. Explain that the question does not pertain to your ability to do the job.

- State that you would like to discuss the job to see whether you are interested and that after that discussion, you would be willing to talk about other things.

Advice and assistance on job discrimination issues are available from state labor and rights agencies or from an office of the Equal Employment Opportunity Commission.

Panel Interviews

This type of interview is becoming common and is used frequently by government employers, schools, banks, and consulting firms. Usually each interviewer will have a specialty or concern that he or she feels is important and will ask more technical questions. Because several people are involved, you may feel more pressure.

The following are techniques for dealing with a panel interview:

- Rephrase the question to give yourself more time to think of an answer.
- If you do not know the answer to a question, say so.
- Make eye contact with all members of the panel, not just the one who has asked you the question. Do not ignore anyone in the group.
- Include the information you want the group to know. Do not merely respond; treat the group interview as if it were a regular interview.
- Avoid the tendency to feel overconfident if you know one or two members of the panel. Approach each question as if the members of the panel know nothing about your work experience and background.

Computer Interview

Some companies are conducting screening interviews by computer. Applicants answer carefully-selected questions on the computer. The human interviewer reviews the report generated by the computer, which includes contradictory responses and highlights any potential problem areas. The report also generates a list of structured interview questions to ask if the applicant is invited back for a face-to-face interview.

Research has shown that applicants respond more honestly to computer-generated questions and are less likely to provide socially acceptable responses. Be careful to be consistent and not to divulge too much information during a computer interview.

Video Interview

Some companies are recognizing the cost benefits of screening or interviewing an out-of-state candidate using video technology. The candidate visits a branch office or public video-conference facility. The technology allows for two-way viewing and listening. One or more corporate interviewers participates. Except for the fact that the candidate is not physically in the same room as the interviewer, the process is about the same as a face-to-face interview.

Voice Mail Interview

Some employers use voice mail systems to screen applicants. Typically an applicant is asked a series of questions, such as "What can you tell us about yourself?" or "Identify four characteristics that others use in describing you."

The best way to handle a voice mail interview is to hang up after you hear the questions, think about what you want to say, and call back. Have your resume, cover letter, and an outline of answers to the questions in front of you as you complete the voice mail interview.

Problem Areas

Several problem areas may come up in the interview. However, they can be neutralized with the right strategy. Major problem areas are discussed below.

Being fired, although problematic, is not the worst thing that can happen. The reason for being fired is important. If you were fired because you were unqualified for a job, you have a serious problem to overcome. A response might be: "I realized after I took the job it was wrong for me. I tried to stay with it, but they asked me to leave. Now I have a better idea of the kind of job that would be best for me."

If the firing resulted from a personality conflict, indicate that to the interviewer. Give the employer names of people who can describe the work you did and the circumstances of the dismissal. Do not go into lengthy details but do offer an honest perspective.

If you were dismissed as part of a major change in the company, explain that. Mergers and acquisitions have made layoffs common.

Emotional problems can be another area of concern. You need to use your own judgment before discussing emotional, alcohol, or drug problems. Some companies may understand, but others may hold these problems against job candidates. Unless such a problem became an issue in a previous job, it may be better to refrain from discussing it.

Health problems can also raise questions. An employer may ask whether applicants have any health problems or handicaps that may affect work performance. If you do have physical limitations (such as the inability to lift more than 20 pounds) that will affect your ability to do the job, mention this during the interview. If your limitation does not affect your work performance, do not discuss it during the interview.

Past criminal activity can present difficulties. Some employers will ask whether you have been convicted of a crime other than a minor traffic violation. The key word is "conviction." If you were arrested but not convicted, then the arrest requires no further discussion.

It is illegal for an employer to check a person's arrest, court, or conviction record if it does not substantially relate to the responsibilities of the prospective job. Any lawful questions about past encounters with the law should be answered truthfully. If a record has been sealed, a conviction has been reversed, or you have been pardoned, it is legal to answer any questions about the conviction in the negative.

Gaps in work history may raise a few eyebrows. Do not be defensive. Explain that the job market was tight or that you took time off to go back to school, travel, take care of your children, or define career objectives.

Job hopping, too, can be an issue. Explain that it was necessary to change jobs frequently because of factors beyond your control, such as company layoffs or company moves. Mention your eagerness to make a long-term commitment to the next employer.

Questions to Ask the Interviewer

An important goal of the job interview is to discover whether you are interested in the job. Here are some questions to ask the prospective employer:

- Why is this job open?
- Would you describe a typical day?
- Why did the person who previously held this job leave?
- What are your expectations for this job?
- To whom would I be reporting?
- What are the promotional and career opportunities in the organization?
- With what kind of team will I work?
- Does the company promote or sponsor advanced education for its employees?
- Are my background and experience a good match for this job?
- When do you expect to make a decision on this position?
- When can I expect to hear from you?
- Please show me where my work area will be. (This gives you an idea of whether the work space is comfortable and attractive and a chance to see what the other workers are like.)

Salary Negotiation

You should know the salary range for the open position or for similar jobs before going to the interview. Researching the company and the job often reveals this type of information. If your research shows that the salary is significantly below what you are willing to accept, it is best to decline the interview.

Here are some ways to negotiate salary:

- Let the interviewer introduce the subject of money.
- Avoid disclosing your present salary until it looks like the company is serious about hiring you.
- Turn a direct question to you about salary into a question to the interviewer, such as, "What kind of range does this position pay?"
- Be prepared to answer any questions about salary. Be honest about previous salaries.
- Start negotiating as high in the range as possible, preferably toward the top of the range.

- Never react with anger or surprise. Pause to think.
- Take 24 hours to think about every job offer.
- If the salary is lower than you are willing to accept, look for other areas for negotiation, such as vacation time, shorter working hours, or tuition for additional school or training. It may also be possible to negotiate a performance review and salary increase in three months.

THE FOLLOW-UP LETTER

Follow up on every job interview. A follow-up letter is usually more effective than a telephone call because the employer can review the letter during the decision-making process. The letter can also bring up any additional information you may have omitted during the interview, although there is no need to restate information already on the resume or in the cover letter. In the follow-up letter, you can express interest in the job or indicate otherwise. (See Figure 2-7.)

Here are some tips for the follow-up letter:

- Print it on good-quality bond paper. The envelope should not be handwritten.
- Send it within 24 hours of the interview.
- Keep it short and to the point.
- Proofread it carefully so there are no errors in grammar, spelling, or punctuation. Spell the interviewer's name and company name correctly and use the exact title of the interviewer. Call the company to get this information if necessary.
- Thank the interviewer for taking the time to interview you and to explain the job.
- Express interest in the position (or explain why you are no longer interested).
- Reemphasize why your skills match the job.
- Give a phone number where you can be reached.

EMPLOYMENT TESTING

Some companies use employment tests to screen applicants further. If the applicant wants a job, taking the tests is necessary. When the interview is arranged, ask whether any tests will be given. Tests may analyze personality, determine skill level, assess knowledge about a subject, or test for illegal drug use or health conditions; some companies may also perform credit checks, honesty testing, and handwriting analyses.

Personality Tests

Some employers test personality in order to determine whether the applicant's personal and behavioral preferences match the job. Some companies use standardized tests such as the Minnesota Multiphasic Personality Inventory (MMPI) and others use ones they have developed themselves. Sometimes companies administer personality tests to current employees as one factor in making promotion decisions.

There is no way to prepare for this kind of test. It may be possible to guess what an employer is looking for, but then you might have to act that way on the job. When taking a personality test, it is best to be honest and mark the first reaction to the question. A possible question on a personality test might be, "What would you prefer? (a) stay home and read a book; (b) go to a party; (c) don't know."

Skill Tests

The purpose of skill testing is to determine whether the applicant has the skill level needed to perform the job. Skill tests may include the following:

- Knowledge of computer software, including word processing, spreadsheet, and desktop publishing applications.
- Proofreading.
- Spelling, Grammar, and Punctuation.
- Using the 10-key machine or calculator.
- Keyboarding speed and accuracy.
- Record keeping and Filing.
- Transcription of dictated material.
- Composition and transcription of correspondence.
- General math, including fractions, percentages, and decimals.

If the skill being tested is something used every day on your present job, little review is necessary. If, however, you feel insecure about any skill area, it is best to postpone the test for a few days and spend time preparing for it.

To review, go to a library or bookstore and find a current book on the subject. General reference books review the rules of grammar, spelling, punctuation, and letter styles. Computer software is available that tests and analyzes keyboarding skill. College and other bookstores have workbooks with math problems and explanations on how to solve them. Self-help books are available at bookstores and computer stores.

Professional Secretaries International®—The Association for Office Professionals™ developed and validated the Office Proficiency Assessment & Certification (OPAC) System. The OPAC System, a test used by employment agencies, offers a battery of tests measuring skills in keyboarding, word processing, language arts, filing, basic arithmetic, financial recordkeeping, spreadsheets, and databases. The OPAC System is completely automated and self-scoring and interacts with live versions of leading software applications. Any person who passes one or all of the OPAC tests within the standards set by PSI may apply for OPAC Certification.

In order to feel confident about taking a skill test, you need to know details of the testing procedure. Some questions to ask before the interview are:

638 Sixth Street
Petaluma, California 94952
June 1, 19—

Ms. Mona Garza
Personnel Director
Transamerica Insurance
384 Sutter Street
San Francisco, California 94132

Dear Ms. Garza:

Thank you for the opportunity to discuss the administrative assistant position with Transamerica. It seems to be a very challenging position requiring flexibility, initiative, and imagination. I am very interested in the position and would welcome the opportunity to discuss my qualifications further with you.

After talking with you, I feel my skills and abilities would help you meet the goals you are trying to accomplish in your department. When you mentioned the purchase of a new network system, I started thinking of all the preparations that could be done ahead of time to make the transition smooth, including the development of manuals and procedures.

Again, thank you for your time. I look forward to hearing from you soon.

Sincerely,

Marilyn Meyer
707-555-5523

Figure 2-7 A follow-up letter should be sent after every interview.

- What kind of test is it—multiple choice? true/false? problem-solving? fill in the blank?
- How much time does each test take?
- Will there be an opportunity to repeat any test?
- Will the testing be on a typewriter, electronic typewriter, or computer? What is the brand name of the equipment?
- For computers and software: Is the computer a Mac or PC? Is it a hard disk or floppy disk system? What is the operating system? What is the software? What version is the software? Is spell-checker software allowed? Can the software reference manual be used during the testing?
- Are dictionaries or reference manuals allowed?

Subject-Matter Tests

Some professional positions require either oral or written tests or a combination of both. The purpose of the tests is to find out how much you know about a subject or how well you can analyze and solve hypothetical cases in a subject area, such as management, sales, personnel, or training.

Try to get as many details as possible about the test from the interviewer or others who have taken the test. Often it is difficult to review or prepare ahead of time, but it builds confidence to know what to anticipate. If the questions are written ones about a specific subject, practice writing out answers. Review important aspects of the particular field. Find out how long the test takes to complete.

Drug Tests

Some employers test prospective employees for the use of illegal drugs. Civil libertarians have expressed concern about drug testing because, among other issues, the tests may not be accurate. Unless you are willing to go to court, you will probably have to submit to drug testing in order to get a job at a company that has a policy of testing new employees. Also, be aware that some prescriptions and over-the-counter medications may cause a false-positive test result.

LOCATING JOB OPPORTUNITIES THROUGH
EMPLOYMENT AGENCIES AND OTHER MEANS

Employment agencies, or placement firms, as they are also called, work as intermediaries between employers and prospective employees. Their job is to match the talents and interests of the prospective employee with the company and the job. Most placement firms prefer to work with candidates who have solid job experience or training.

Agencies may deal with permanent or temporary positions, or both, and usually specialize in specific fields, such as accounting, marketing, secretarial, engineering, chemical, heavy industry, or technology. If an agency does not specialize in one particular field, it may employ counselors who do.

Placement Firms

A placement firm is useful when you have a good idea of the career area you are interested in, although some agencies provide career information and counseling. As a part of their service, agencies usually provide help with interviewing techniques, resumes, and salary negotiations. They also conduct appropriate skill testing.

Placement firms depend on the premise that they can get you a better job than you can get on your own. Often the jobs are listed only with the firm. A fee is charged for this service. In most cases, the company doing the hiring pays the fee. In some cases, however, the new employee and the company split the fee or the employee pays the entire fee. The fee varies and may be a percentage of salary. Sometimes the employee may pay the fee on an installment basis.

The placement firm arranges all interviews. A prospective employee may interview at several companies before accepting a job. To increase job opportunities, some people use more than one placement firm. Even if you use a placement firm, you should still watch the want ads and network with your coworkers and friends.

The following questions may assist you in deciding whether to use placement firms:

- In what areas does the firm specialize?
- Does the office look well organized?
- Is the placement firm well known? Does it have a good reputation? Do you know of anyone who has used its service?

HINT: *Phone the personnel departments of major employers and ask with which agencies they work and which ones have a good reputation. Check with the Better Business Bureau to see whether there have been any complaints against them.*

- How many people work for the firm? How long have they worked there?

HINT: *If a counselor has no business cards, assume he or she is new. Ask the agency manager to switch you to another counselor.*

- Does the counselor seem really interested in your background and career goals? Is the counselor familiar with the job market?
- Does the firm do career counseling and testing? Does it help with resumes? Does it help with interviewing skills?
- Is there a fee involved? If so, who pays? If you pay, could you get the job on your own? If you quit the job after a short period, will any part of the fee be refunded?

HINT: *Never pay a fee unless an employer has offered you a job and you have accepted.*
Get all promises in writing.

Other types of firms also provide services to job-hunters. Headhunters, executive search firms, and consultants are paid to find people to fill positions that may or may not be open. They usually deal with high-level executive secretaries and executives. Headhunters typically contact job candidates themselves, although people looking for jobs also contact headhunters.

Resume services help write and print resumes. For an additional fee, they will send out resumes to a list of companies they have compiled.

Career counselors charge a fee to provide testing and career counseling. They also give advice on a job search. They do not make job placements, and they charge a fee whether a job is secured or not. Career counselors can be located in the Yellow Pages under "Career and Vocational Counseling." Free career counseling may be offered through college and business schools to students and graduates. Some schools have a lifetime commitment to counsel and/or place graduates.

Temporary Employment Agencies

Temporary employment agencies quickly find jobs for people on a temporary basis. These jobs may range in length from one day to several months or even years. The temporary agency serves as your employer. It interviews and evaluates the skills and preferences of temporary employees, tests employees' skills, trains employees on software packages, and finds prospective employers. A company uses temporary employees for peak work periods, temporary replacements, one-time projects, specialized work, or vacation replacements.

The skills, capabilities, and requirements requested by the company determine the level of pay. Temporary employees submit timecards each week and receive paychecks from the temporary agency. The agency bills the company for salary and fees. There are no fees or deductions from wages other than legally required payroll taxes that all employees must pay. After a period of time, paid vacation or sick leave may become available. Many temporary agencies make health benefits and 401(k) plans available to their workers.

Temping is recommended for the following situations:

- You have little or no experience in your targeted position.
- The company you want to work for is not hiring at the present time.
- You are changing careers or reentering the labor market, or you are a student or a recent graduate.

Temping lets you get inside a company so that you can sell yourself in person rather than on paper. Numerous networking opportunities are available through temping, especially if you make people aware of your qualifications and ambitions.

A growing number of secretaries are choosing temporary work as a career. Advantages include pay increases without extensive performance reviews, vacations when desired, and opportunities to experience a wide variety of people and companies. Career temps typically avoid assignments of indefinite length so that they do not feel the same obligation as a permanent employee. Pay raises, negotiated through the agency by the temp, can occur after a temp has been requested back by customers on a few assignments. The highest rates are paid for the most current skills.

Many temps register with a number of agencies, try them out, then narrow them down to their favorite two or three. This method is ethical and expected by most temp agencies.

Ask the following questions when deciding whether to choose temporary work:

- In what areas does the temporary agency specialize?
- Is it well known? Does it have a good reputation? Do you know of anyone who has been a temporary for this firm?
- How often will you be called for work?
- Do you have enough financial security to go without work if you are not called?
- Are there enough jobs available that you can work as much as you want?
- How often can you turn down jobs if they do not interest you?
- What is the pay period? Can the check be mailed? How promptly will you receive it? Can your salary be directly-deposited into your bank account?
- Are insurance benefits available? If not, where can you get insurance and what will it cost?
- Can you accept a full-time position if one is offered?
- Is workers' compensation available if you are injured on the job?
- Are there any bonus incentives, such as holiday pay, for working for a temporary agency for a long period of time?

Networking

Networking is a way to use friends and colleagues in the job search. It is estimated that up to 90 percent of jobs are filled by word of mouth. The aim of networking is to expand your list of contacts until you reach the ones who are hiring.

Start by talking with friends and close business associates; then contact people you have met at associations and professional organizations, people in different departments at your present company, and people in other companies or organizations. The goal is to get names of other people you can contact. It is important to remember that you are asking for information, not a job.

Evening classes at local colleges can connect you with other employees. Often the instructor works professionally in the field in which he or she teaches and can direct you to people and companies. Another technique is to find out where employees of a company you are interested in go for lunch and after work. Often a relaxed atmosphere is a good context in which to meet people from a company and get a feeling about a company or industry. If you are unemployed, working as a temporary is a quick way to acquire contacts in and knowledge of a company before interviews or applications take place; in addition, many openings are posted on internal bulletin boards or e-mail systems before they are publicly advertised.

Online Resumes and Positions

The Internet and commercial online services are the fastest-growing employment marketplace in the world. Thousands of employment recruiters and companies recruit exclusively online because it is faster, less expensive, and global. The cost of going online varies widely, as do fees for specific databases or areas.

Computerized job databases let a job seeker access up-to-date information on employment opportunities throughout the world. These computerized job openings are like electronic classified ads.

Software programs are available to help develop a resume for use in keyword searches. Multimedia resumes can be developed with sound, video, text, and graphics. Resumes may either be scanned to databases by a service company or uploaded through a modem.

Online resumes can be searched by anyone who has access to the database. Resume databases have been developed by associations, groups, and companies. Often the resumes are searched by another computer, which is looking for particular keywords. The computer finds a "hit" when resumes match the keyword criteria.

Preparing for Advancement

Developing a personal portfolio is an excellent tool for preparing for advancement or a career change. A portfolio is organized according to what you consider important for advancing your career. The following are suggestions for inclusion in the portfolio:

- Forms or templates you designed
- Printouts of software macros you created
- Style sheets and memo or letter formats you use
- Time- and money-saving ideas the company adopted; include appreciation letters and awards, which prove that others value your work
- Copies of certificates, academic degrees; a list of courses and seminars attended
- Documentation of self-directed computer training
- Management tasks and responsibilities you handle on a regular basis
- Documentation on helping others with specialized computer features and software and hardware troubleshooting
- Examples of situations that demonstrate you are a team player

Organize the portfolio with dividers so your accomplishments are easy to review. If you are preparing the portfolio for an in-house evaluation, organize the dividers according to the categories that are used in your performance evaluation.

CAREER ADVICE AFTER A LAYOFF

Layoffs are a frequent reason to look for a new position. The following are steps to take immediately after finding out about a layoff:

- Apply for unemployment compensation. It typically takes between three and five weeks to get the first unemployment check, which will amount to only a fraction of your normal salary.
- Consider health insurance options. The COBRA law requires that companies allow ex-employees to stay on their health plan for up to 18 months, provided the worker pays the insurance premiums.
- Examine retirement account savings. See if you can borrow from your 401(k) or pension. These loans are not considered distributions, so they usually do not incur a tax liability on the amount borrowed.
- Suggest "consulting" for your former employer. Your work still may need to be done, and you are the most qualified person to do it. Your former employer may have more flexibility in hiring consultants, and consultants cost the company less money than a full-time employee.
- Consider doing temporary work, part-time work, or contract work—the biggest growth industry for the recently unemployed. The benefits of temporary or contract work include autonomy, flexibility, and variety. Such work also brings in money, builds self-esteem, and develops contacts. The major disadvantage is the uncertain cash flow.
- If your former employer has not offered the services of an outplacement firm, request it or seek out nonprofit organizations that offer career counseling, interviewing, resume-writing, and networking workshops for a nominal fee. Community colleges also offer career testing, placement services, and computer classes at reasonable fees.

CHAPTER 3

TIME

MANAGEMENT

AND

PROBLEM

SOLVING

Businesses view time as an extremely valuable resource. Applying effective time management principles to office tasks is crucial for office professionals because many businesses are downsizing their operations and implementing new technologies to remain competitive.

Effective time management requires that important tasks and projects be identified and completed in the time available and that they be done well. Ineffective use of time results in unnecessary confusion and last-minute upheavals, personnel misunderstandings, disgruntled customers, and stress. To avoid these pitfalls, office professionals must *analyze, plan, schedule,* and *control* the use of their time.

ANALYZING CURRENT USE OF WORK TIME

Analyzing your current use of work time allows you to adopt more realistic approaches to planning time use and to find alternative ways to do certain tasks.

Daily Time Log

To begin, prepare a chart that lists the typical tasks you do each day. Divide the day into 15-minute blocks and record the amount of time you spend on each task. You may wish to indicate the priority status (Rush [R], Same Day [SD], Next Day [ND], Later [L]) of these tasks. You will also find it helpful to record the interruptions (I) that occur. It is important to keep a log for each day. (A sample log appears in Figure 3-1.)

Maintain this log for one week and repeat the process quarterly. Review the answers to the following questions. Your responses may provide you with valuable insights about the current use of your time.

- What time period or time periods during the day were the most productive? the least productive? Why?
- During what hours of the day did the most interruptions occur? Who caused the interruptions? Supervisors, coworkers, or outside visitors?
- How much time was spent on crises that materialized during the day?
- How much of the day was spent handling your personal concerns? your supervisor's?

TIME	Entering Information on Computer	Proofreading/Editing Copy	Copying Documents	Transcribing Dictated Material	Filing Records	Greeting Clients/Making Appointments	Handling Incoming/Outgoing Mail	Attending Meetings	Composing Communications	Answering the Phone	Placing Outgoing Calls	Conferring with Supervisor	Conferring with Coworkers	Arranging Meetings/Travel	Supervising Personnel	Handling Personnel Requirements	Other
A.M. 7:45–8:00																	
8:00–8:15																	
8:15–8:30																	
8:30-8:45																	
8:45–9:00																	
9:00–9:15																	
9:15–9:30																	
9:30–9:45																	
9:45–10:00																	
10:00–10:15																	
10:15–10:30																	
10:30–10:45																	
10:45–11:00																	
11:00–11:15																	
11:15–11:30																	
11:30–11:45																	
11:45–12:00																	
P.M. 12:00–12:15																	
12:15–12:30																	
12:30–12:45																	
12:45–1:00																	
1:00–1:15																	
1:15–1:30																	
1:30–1:45																	
1:45–2:00																	
2:00–2:15																	
2:15–2:30																	
2:30–2:45																	
2:45–3:00																	
3:00–3:15																	
3:15–3:30																	
3:30–3:45																	
3:45–4:00																	
4:00–4:15																	
4:15–4:30																	
4:30–4:45																	
4:45–5:00																	
5:00–5:15																	
5:15–5:30																	
5:30–5:45																	
5:45–6:00																	

EVALUATION

Tasks to simplify _____

Tasks to modify _____

Tasks to group _____

Interruptions/with whom _____

Tasks to delegate _____

Figure 3-1. Sample daily log.

- Were there any daily routines or tasks that could have been streamlined, combined with other tasks, or delegated?
- Were the tasks requiring 15 minutes (or less) "Rush" tasks or were these tasks to fill time? When are you most productive?
- Could the "Rush" tasks have been started sooner? Could large tasks have been broken down into smaller daily segments?
- Were there times in the day when the pace was slow? Were there specific times when the stress level was particularly high? Were there specific times when you needed extra assistance?

Special Considerations for Analyzing Time

It is important to analyze, evaluate, and make comments about your use of time on *each* day's log. Record tasks as you work on them; don't wait until the end of the day to record them. The task of improving time management will become overwhelming if you try to solve too many problems immediately. Attempt to solve only one problem at a time, but set a realistic deadline for solving it.

Your supervisors may be able to recommend suggestions for more effective use of your time. Share the time log you have completed with them. In addition to asking for their input, present a tentative list of suggestions for improvement. If other workers are part of the problem, make them part of the solution.

The time logs may indicate there are slow- and fast-paced time periods. Determine if these periods are predictable. Use the analyses to request extra assistance, overtime or outsourcing services during peak periods. Include the request as a part of the normal budgetary process so you are not caught unprepared during a peak period.

TAKING TIME TO PLAN

A written plan can assist you in directing your efforts to reach predetermined goals. Doing random tasks without a plan can be expensive and inefficient. On the other hand, adhering to a plan so rigidly that it does not allow for interruptions or special requests can also be self-defeating.

A simple planning technique that most time management experts recommend involves a master list and a "to do" list. Tasks that need to be accomplished that week and tasks that should be done daily are listed on these forms.

Master Lists

A weekly master list allows you to record projects or tasks as you think of them or as your supervisor requests them. Do not set priorities for these activities; just record them as they occur. Estimate the amount of time you will require to complete each activity and indicate the due date.

If a task is large, break it down into smaller segments. Before leaving work each day, select several of the tasks or subtasks and place them on the next day's "to do" list. Use the following headings on your master list:

- Week of _____
- Activity description
- Starting date
- Due date
- Estimated time to complete

It is easy to enter your master list on your computer.

"To Do" Lists

From the master list, calendar, and the tasks that come up during the day, prepare the daily "to do" list. Although there is no one right way to prepare "to do" lists, several suggestions include:

- Organize the next day's "to do" list at the end of each day if possible; if not, do the day's list first thing each morning. Preparing the list before you leave for the day shows what you accomplished, and the next day's priorities may be clearer.
- Prioritize each task; label each task A (must do), B (should do), or C (nice to do). Category A tasks are important and must be done without delay; category B tasks should be completed as soon as possible, preferably the same day; and category C tasks may be completed the same day, if there is time, or later. All items listed on a "to do" list are not of equal value; therefore, treat each task individually.
- Highlight the top three A items on the "to do" list to signify that these tasks should take precedence over the other A tasks. This is especially useful when there are numerous A tasks on the "to do" list. Using a combination letter and number system is another method that identifies precedence (A-1, A-2).
- Keep the list visible. If you tape it to a reading stand or place it in a desktop planner holder, it will not get lost on your desk. Cross out tasks that are completed; add tasks to the list when necessary. Indicate those tasks that you delegate or that are in progress.
- Rewrite the list at the end of the day by carrying forward those tasks that were not completed to the next day's "to do" list. Reorder the priorities of the tasks. Limit the number of daily tasks to 10 or 12 depending on their complexity. Do not place too many tasks in category A; overscheduling A tasks can cause stress and fatigue.
- Include names of people to contact and their telephone numbers. Use a "to do" list format that allows a place to record telephone calls you must make. If you highlight the names of the people who cannot be reached, you will be reminded to try them again at a later time. Indicate "VM" if you left a voice mail message.

- Use a calendar to record monthly and yearly events; e.g., dates for payroll reports, staff meetings, sales conferences, and budget deadlines. These reminders can then be worked into the planning of the master lists and "to do" lists.

- Divide a major project, such as planning a conference, into many subparts. Prioritize these subparts; keep a project notebook with a page for each subpart; list all contacts, phone numbers, and sources of information associated with that subpart; establish feasible deadlines for each subpart; check the notebook regularly and include the appropriate subtasks on the daily "to do" list.

Special Considerations for Planning Time

Interruptions happen, so be flexible when listing tasks and their priorities. You can achieve this flexibility by adding 10 to 20 percent to your estimated time. Adopt a realistic attitude toward planning. Do not list *all* the long-range projects in need of completion. The result will be too overwhelming, and you will only get frustrated. Listing the subtasks involved with a long-range project will help you *get started* on complicated or lengthy tasks.

When you do not complete all the tasks on the list, there is no need for you to criticize yourself. If the tasks are identified realistically, the process will work. However, if a task appears on a "to do" list three or four times, try to determine why. If you are avoiding the task because it is too difficult or uninteresting, handle it immediately or at least begin it rather than take the time to transfer it to the next day's list. Sometimes it is better to just do the task and eliminate writing it on a list. If too much time is spent in listing minor items, the tasks may never get done.

Planning *how* to do a project requires time. When reviewing your master list, identify alternative methods for completing tasks in case the original plan goes awry. Be sure to include sufficient time for organizing the materials and collecting the resources you will need. Allow at least half an hour of planning time for new projects. Consult with the people involved to see what they need and when you can expect information from them. If you don't receive the information on time, begin the project anyway. Do a draft and fill in the blank information when it arrives.

MAKING A REALISTIC SCHEDULE

A plan requires action in order for it to be useful. If you schedule tasks realistically, you can expect to accomplish the *important* things within the time available. Before determining your schedule, you need to consider several questions:

- Who is requesting the work? The more important or senior the person, the higher the priority of the task.

- When must each task be completed?

- What types of materials must be available before starting each task? Do you need someone's approval?

- Where does the work go after it is completed? If it goes to another department, how much time must be allowed for completion there?

- What tasks require service outside the company; e.g., typesetting?

- What tasks can best be accomplished by others?

- Which of the tasks will take the longest to complete? Are there subtasks that can be identified and started immediately?

- Are there similar activities in any of the tasks that may be subgrouped and done at the same time?

Scheduling Time to Spend on Each Task

Here are some ways to schedule the time you need to spend on each task:

- Estimate the time it takes to complete a task; then compare the estimated time to the actual time. Revise your estimate in the future to better reflect the actual time. If you are a perfectionist, ask yourself whether the job has to be done perfectly or whether something less than perfect will be acceptable in order to finish the task on schedule. Perfectionists need to watch their priorities and make adjustments.

- Set more specific, self-imposed deadlines. Instead of deciding to finish a task "today," set a deadline of late morning or early afternoon.

- Determine the best time of your day to do creative work or work that requires concentration. Use "your best" time for thinking and planning or for tackling your most difficult task.

- Complete routine tasks such as handling mail at the same time each day. Schedule blocks of time for completing similar tasks. For example, it is more efficient to return and place calls during a single block of time than to make them periodically throughout the day.

- Play games with unpleasant or routine tasks. For example, set aside 15 minutes before a break or before lunch to file, so you will get a "reward" at the end. Try to complete routine tasks five minutes before the self-imposed deadline.

- Place work with the highest priority in a brightly colored folder in the center of your desk before you leave the office.

- Collect ideas of things to do to keep busy during slow days or hours. Examples of such tasks include purging files from the hard disk, ordering supplies, or reviewing infrequently used computer procedures.

- Schedule time for self-improvement. Review career goals to determine if you are making progress in reaching these goals. Inquire about company-paid tuition plans, or check the possibility of getting time off from work to take additional coursework.

Special Considerations for Scheduling Time

It is more efficient to start a long, complex project than to concentrate on tasks that are simple and quick to complete. Also, it is important to perform high-priority tasks—those in category A on your "to do" list—first.

Without a schedule, it is easy to get sidetracked. Concentrate on one task at a time. Finish a task rather than place it aside, thinking it will just take 15 minutes to finish and so can be done later. Unfinished tasks can create chaos on days that suddenly become filled with crises. If you prefer having several projects underway at one time, be sure you schedule your time so you meet each project's deadline. Completing a subtask early in the day often gives you the psychological motivation you need.

There is no one right way to get started. Some people begin a project by doing the most difficult parts first. Others begin with the easiest parts and work into the project. Waiting for "free time" to do a lengthy project is not wise. It is more efficient to start the project today.

CONTROLLING WORK TIME

There are two important steps to take to make your work time efficient and productive: organize your work and minimize interruptions.

Procedures for Organizing Work

The following suggestions are a few ways to organize work in order to make the best use of your time. Additional suggestions may be found in each of the chapters covering specific topics.

- Arrange your working environment so it is more efficient. Keep frequently-used supplies within close reach. Clear the working area of distractions and clutter. Arrange equipment, such as the computer and printer, so that each piece can be comfortably reached.

- Handle each piece of paper as few times as possible. When handling a piece of paper, try to take at least one step in moving it to its appropriate destination. Sort materials into action folders such as "Urgent," "To Read," "To Sign," and "To Check Later."

- Prepare form letters, form paragraphs, frequently-used phrases, and formats for computer storage. Create macros to minimize keystrokes. Note the date each form letter was used and the person to whom the letter was sent so the same items are not used in the next mailing. Prepare checklists that outline the steps required for procedures you do frequently; e.g., travel details or conference planning.

- Keep samples of previously completed forms as references. Attach a description of how the data were obtained, what sources were used, and who should receive copies.
- Prepare a list of facts for future reference. The facts may be accessed by computer or recorded in a notebook.

  ▲ Temporary agencies—contact persons; fee schedules; and, if applicable, the names of individuals who have done excellent work on previous assignments.

  ▲ Bank names—account numbers, hours, and names of people to contact.

  ▲ Organizations—dues, current contact person, and meeting dates, times, and locations.

  ▲ Supervisor's credit card names and numbers, expiration dates, and telephone numbers to call in case the cards are lost or stolen.

  ▲ Supervisor's preferences for rental cars, hotels, restaurants, airline carriers, airline seating, and flight times. Include telephone numbers and addresses where appropriate.

  ▲ Conference or meeting room availability, contact person, and room capacity.

  ▲ Computer network hotline sources—numbers to call and hours of operation.

  ▲ Equipment repair contacts—numbers to call, hours, warranties, notes on repairs already made, and signatures required to authorize repairs.

- Know your organization. Identify sources of assistance; express your appreciation to those who have helped you. Most people will willingly assist someone in a crisis who has taken the time to recognize another's previous efforts.
- Organize a tickler file to avoid missing deadlines. Label 12 folders with the months of the year, 31 folders for the days of the month, and one folder for the next year. Decide on what day a document should be handled and place the item in that day's tickler folder. If a document needs to be handled in a future month, place it in that month's folder; then at the end of the current month, remove the items and place them in the appropriate daily tickler folders. Check the files daily and place tasks that need to be completed on your "to do" list. It is helpful to place some tasks in a tickler file labeled a day or two before the deadline to be sure they are handled on time. To avoid placing material in tickler files with weekend or holiday dates, use colored adhesive circles to identify those dates. Assign these to appropriate work days each month.
- Plan outgoing calls carefully. Have the information needed for each call and a checklist of questions available. For the people you call frequently, make a list of the things you want to ask or tell them. When the list is a few items long, make the call. If you do not reach a person, leave a detailed message so a return call is not needed. If you do need to talk to the person, indicate a precise time frame (e.g., 1:30 to 2:30 p.m.) that you will be available for the call.

Minimizing Interruptions

An analysis of your time log (see section on analyzing time in this chapter) can be helpful in determining whether interruptions are interfering with your getting the necessary work completed. Interruptions are a part of a normal day; however, the effects of interruptions may be minimized by taking some of the following steps:

- Block a period of "quiet time" when you ask a coworker to cover your telephone and greet clients. Reciprocate by doing the same for your coworker. Schedule activities that require concentration for this uninterrupted time.

- Listen attentively to telephone calls and take complete notes so additional time will not be wasted making another call.

- Keep a telephone message pad, pencil, and notebook within reach at all times for telephone messages, directions, or notes. If your supervisor is not available to speak with a caller, ask the caller the best time for your supervisor to return the call. Record the time of day when you can most easily reach those people with whom you have frequent contact.

- Discourage lengthy telephone conversations and excessive socializing with coworkers, personal friends, and clients. Suggest that the discussions be continued during break or lunch periods, or indicate it is necessary to complete your present task within the hour to meet a deadline.

- Use your own discretion in handling interruptions. Is it something that requires immediate attention or is it a matter that you or your supervisor can handle later?

Special Considerations for Controlling Time

It is more impressive to do a task right the first time than to use overtime to redo it. Listen attentively to instructions and think through the strategies for completing tasks. Ask questions when instructions are not clear or discrepancies exist in the materials. Take enough time to understand the assignment. Being too hasty often results in more serious problems later.

Refrain from interrupting others. Do not just "drop in" for a chat with your colleagues.

If you cannot complete work by the time requested, communicate this to the person making the request. It is more prudent to say "no" and suggest an alternative solution than to accept an impossible deadline.

SCHEDULING A SUPERVISOR'S TIME

Office professionals not only have their own time to manage, they often must schedule the time of their supervisors. Here are some ways to schedule the time of your supervisor.

Suggestions for Scheduling a Supervisor's Time

- Understand thoroughly the goals of your organization and your supervisor. Find out how you and the office staff can assist in meeting those goals.

- Determine how your supervisor prefers you to schedule appointments, handle interruptions, and take messages. Ask about these matters the first week you are in a new position.

- Organize a system for telephone messages. Place all messages in a special message box on your desk; arrange the messages in the order of their importance or by the time of the call.

- Schedule a time to discuss goals, priorities, and changes with your supervisor for 5 to 10 minutes each day. Ask for instructions so you will not have to interrupt your supervisor all the time. Throughout each day write your questions, ideas, and suggestions in a notebook so you can refer to them the next time you meet.

- Use an electronic organizer or personal information manager (PIM) software to remind your supervisor of things to do, meetings, and appointments. If software is not available or appropriate, prepare an appointment reminder form that highlights important events scheduled for the next day and give it to your supervisor before you leave the office. Schedule time daily to compare calendars.

- If you and your supervisor agree to do so, underline, circle, highlight, or summarize information in documents that may be of interest to your supervisor. If the material is to be read at a later time, identify it by topic and prepare a file for each.

- Keep track of where your supervisor is throughout the day in case you need to contact him or her on an urgent matter. Be persistent in reminding your supervisor of meetings or deadlines. Also, inform your supervisor when you leave your desk area. Forward your telephone calls to an appropriate location if you will be away from your desk for 15 minutes or longer.

Special Concerns About Scheduling a Supervisor's Time

Your assumptions about what items have high priority may be incorrect, so check with your supervisor to determine the relative importance of your projects.

Several warning signs may indicate impending time crises—a supervisor's procrastination, equipment malfunctions, or missed intermediate deadlines by people to whom work has been delegated. When you notice such warning signs, stay ahead of your own schedule so these last-minute crises can be handled with a minimum of frustration.

Request assistance before a rush period occurs. Monitor work schedules and check for assignments to other departments so you can estimate more accurately the amount of assistance and the amount of time you will need.

Keep abreast of sources of help or costs of outsourcing. If you need assistance for rush jobs, you will have the information available and save your own and your supervisor's time.

Keep your supervisor apprised of your workload. If you see overscheduling about to occur, request a review of priorities. One approach is to say "I'm willing to try to finish it by the deadline, but I have several other projects that also require immediate attention. What would you suggest I do first?"

WORKING FOR MORE THAN ONE MANAGER

Reengineering and downsizing will continue to create changes for office professionals. You may find you are now handling work for more than one manager or for an entire department or work group. A work group may not be permanent since it may change with the project.

Suggestions for Handling Work Flow

To avoid chaos and conflicts, here are some suggestions for working for more than one manager.

- Use different-colored folders containing completed work or messages for each supervisor. Place these folders in a stand on the corner of your desk so that managers can take them without interrupting your work on other tasks. Stacked individual out-boxes may also work, but they become unwieldy if you have five or more people in your work group.

- Maintain a checkout board so you know if people are in or out of the area. Keep reminding people to use the board. If necessary, explain how this helps you respond to customer/client needs and, in turn, improves the image of the firm.

- Prepare a master calendar showing everyone's days away from the office, such as those involving vacations, travel, conference attendance, and work-at-home time. With appropriate software, you can get a daily update on when people in your work group will be away from the office. This information is vital for planning your work schedule and deadlines.

- Schedule five minutes each day with individual managers or leaders of work groups to go over the day's priorities or discuss an impending crisis or deadline.

- Create a work priority form for each manager to use when requesting work. Information to include on the form consists of current date, project deadline date and time, notes from the originator, and the account or accounts to charge. These completed forms are helpful in preparing your master lists and "to do" lists.

- Become familiar with the working habits of individual managers. By recognizing the perfectionistic, procrastinating, detail-oriented, disorganized type of worker, you will be in a position to accommodate your own work schedule more effectively. Discover how to get information when you need it.

Special Concerns When Working for More Than One Manager

Working for more than one manager requires multiple skills. If you do not understand a set of instructions, ask for help. Do not say, "I don't understand this." Instead say, "I know what to do with the first section, but I'm not clear about the section on recording your expenses. This is what I understood you to say, but I want to be sure I have all the details."

Meeting a deadline may not always be feasible. When you discover that you cannot complete a task by the due date, inform the manager soon enough so other arrangements can be made. Try to suggest an alternative plan. For example, "I have these tasks [indicate your master list] to complete by this Friday, but I'll be able to complete this project by next Wednesday." Do not wait until the last minute and give an excuse or produce incomplete or poor work.

Working for more than one manager also may cause problems with prioritizing work. Do work from the manager with the most seniority or authority first. In many work groups, managers are on an equal basis. Then use the first-in, first-out method. If two managers have equal authority and have a rush job at the same time, ask the managers involved to make the decision. Refrain from mediating such disputes.

SCHEDULING TIME OF SUPERVISEES

Office professionals often find they must schedule and supervise the work of others, such as other office professionals, temporary workers, independent contractors, interns, or work–study students. In addition, office professionals may schedule training or actually do the training as well as schedule and monitor work that is outsourced. The following suggestions may help you in scheduling the time and work of your supervisees:

- Review your strengths and weaknesses. Are there tasks others can do or become trained to do? A review of your daily "to do" list can help you answer that question. Obtain your supervisor's approval before you delegate the work to another office professional or to an outside firm.

- Select carefully the people to whom you delegate tasks. Do not always delegate the work you do not like to do or delegate to the same person each time. Those you supervise must also have the opportunity to progress professionally. Let them know they are capable.

- Provide sufficient information about doing the job and be very specific about what you need and when you need it. Do not assume everyone knows what is expected.

- Follow up on the progress of the delegated tasks periodically.

- Introduce new skills slowly. Break a complicated task into subtasks. You will save time if the trainee practices the skill soon after you give instructions. Be there when the trainee does the task the first time.

- Create a form to keep track of work that you delegate. Include space for such items as name of the worker, date delegated, description of work delegated, date due, follow-up, and problem areas.
- Provide feedback to the worker or source of service. Keep notes on the tasks so you can refer to them the next time a similar situation arises.
- Follow precisely the IRS guidelines for hiring independent contractors.
- Keep notes on temporary workers. Ask temporary agencies how they test, screen, and guarantee satisfaction. Request a temp who has done satisfactory work for you previously. If you are not satisfied with a temporary worker, intern, or student worker, inform the recruiter or appropriate placement coordinator.

Special Considerations for Scheduling the Time of Others

You may think that no one does the task as well as you do. However, your supervisees may become defensive and eventually fail to cooperate if you cannot curb your need for perfection. But under no circumstances should you allow slovenly work. You are still accountable for the final results.

Interns and work–study students require time and space. Weigh the pros and cons of their presence carefully. Are you able to schedule the time needed to supervise them? If you can demonstrate to your supervisees that you can schedule work so as to limit major crises and that you can maintain an even workflow, your rush periods will become a cooperative effort.

Some of the work that you believed to be "yours" to do may be outsourced to an outside business service. You may be the liaison between your office and this service. Maintain a schedule of work that leaves the office. Work out completion schedules with the service center that allow for breakdowns or other unforeseen incidents.

The Human Resources Department in your company may offer training sessions for office professionals to become trainers. Take advantage of these opportunities. The sessions will not only help you schedule improved training sessions for your supervisees but may also provide an opportunity for you to train others in the firm.

MANAGING TIME IN A HOME OFFICE

Telecommuting—working for a company away from the office in a mobile office, home office, or outlying work area—is increasing in popularity. The right technology combined with the right people working away from the office can result in increased productivity. Workers save time because they are not commuting, and they don't have to deal with interruptions or office politics.

Becoming the sole proprietor of a home-based business is a goal for many office professionals. For some, a home-based business is a second-income generator or the result of company downsizing; for others, it is a chance to test their expertise and gain financial security. Although home-based businesses are not new, they have become more popular because of technology and the expertise office professionals have in using this technology.

Telecommuters and home-based business owners require time management skills. Here are some suggestions:

- Plan how to set up your home office in advance. Once you begin working with clients, your focus will be on providing service. Read the trade journals. If you are connected to any of the online services or have access to the Internet, check the "home office" information sections. Talk with others who have set up businesses to find out about their successes and failures.

- Analyze your strengths and weaknesses. Invest the time to brush up on skills that need improvement; for example, small business bookkeeping practices. Invest the time *before* you begin your business. Even though seeking good legal and accounting advice may be advised, you need to understand every part of your company's own business.

- Prepare a detailed list of equipment specifications so you buy equipment that fits in your home office space and that is compatible with your company's equipment or your clients' needs.

- Keep sufficient supplies on hand. Running out of toner cartridge at 10 p.m. with a project due at 9 a.m. the next day is stressful and wastes time.

- Install a separate telephone line with voice mail or an answering machine. Do not allow family members to answer the office telephone.

- Develop self-discipline by keeping regular work hours in your office at home. Keep family interruptions to a minimum. Having a separate area (preferably a room that is separated by walls from the other areas of the house) is more conducive to making efficient use of your time. If you are telecommuting, let your supervisor know that you will be available during certain hours.

- Move about the room or do stretching exercises every hour or so if you work at the computer for long time periods. It is easy to become so involved with a project that you forget to take scheduled breaks. When you're tired and your muscles ache, you begin to make mistakes and waste time.

- Use e-mail, since you can read it or send it at any time. If you are a telecommuter and already have an e-mail address at your company, maintain that address. Home-based businesses can obtain access to e-mail through a local Internet access provider or an online service such as America Online or CompuServe. Inexpensive or free e-mail software is also available.

- Remain in touch with the people in your office. The lack of social contact is a major disadvantage of a home office. If you are a member of a team, set your goals for the week and communicate these to the other team members. Take time to report on each day's progress. Schedule a regular weekly meeting at the office. By maintaining communication with your supervisor, you are less likely to feel that those who are physically present in the office are more likely to be promoted or given more interesting tasks. If you are a home-based business owner, continue your networking efforts.

- Evaluate your goals and services every six months. If your business is not generating a profit after two years, it is time to review your procedures. You may be spending too much time on tasks that generate limited revenue or you may need to find another niche for service. It is, however, normal to have slow months. Have enough money set aside to see you through the difficult times.

USING TECHNOLOGY TO MANAGE TIME

Software and other tools are helpful in such areas as scheduling, making appointments, prioritizing tasks, and managing projects. The software varies in capabilities, complexity, and power.

Personal Information Managers (PIMS)

Personal information manager (PIM) software is multifunctional. It manages business-related details such as calendars, addresses, "to do" lists, appointment books, file drawers, fax machines, telephone calls, and notepads. In addition, PIM software is capable of linking and presenting these details so they are all easy to access.

The three basic modules found in PIM software are contact management, scheduling, and task management. **Contact management software** allows you to list names and multiple addresses and telephone numbers. It can remind you to call and give you information on why you are calling; e.g., follow-up referrals. You can search the directory in several ways; e.g., by company, city, or product. Notes can be added to any contact. **Scheduling software** allows you to record meeting times and the people with whom you are meeting. The program automatically checks for conflicts, records regularly scheduled meetings, includes reminders of meeting times, and prints your schedule in a daily, weekly, or monthly format. **Task management software** allows you to list tasks, make notes, prioritize the tasks, and sort by due date, priority, or person to whom assigned. It may also identify any task that is off schedule. Other available functions, many of them quite sophisticated, depend on the software. The modules may be stand-alone packages, or the functions may be integrated into one program.

SELECTING PIM SOFTWARE

Large companies have an information systems department that selects software. You learn the program and use it. In smaller companies, you often have input in the selection process. Answers to the following questions will assist your selection analysis:

- Which tasks need the most help in your office? Is your biggest bottleneck managing your supervisor's calendars and your own, keeping an up-to-date client address list, or completing tasks on time? Do you need a stand-alone program for the bottleneck, or do you want to integrate the functions?

- Where does your information come from now? How do you access it? What type of fingertip information do you need to access daily? How do you link your data?

- Do you keep detailed notes on your clients or contacts? How large a field do you need for a notepad?

- In what format do you want your information? For example, do you want a weekly calendar only, or do you want a weekly, monthly, and yearly format? Do you prefer a program format that looks like your "to do" list, or do you prefer an outline, free-form format? Do you have the graphics capability to produce calendars?

- Can the software print labels and Rolodex cards? Is it capable of rescheduling a task if it does not get done that day? Is there a scheduling option to handle rooms and equipment? Is there sufficient space for multiple addresses and telephone numbers, such as home, work, e-mail, and fax?

- What reports do you need to prepare from the data collected?

- Do you need a program with network capabilities? Do you want access to external word processors or printers? Will the software be used for work-group functions?

- Are you away from your computer a great amount of time during working hours? Do you need software for a laptop computer?

- Are you operating under a DOS or under a Windows system?

SPECIAL CONSIDERATIONS FOR USING PIM SOFTWARE

Personal information managers are not magic. You must be self-motivated to enter the data and maintain the information regularly. Software packages vary in features and price. Some allow more freedom to customize fields and on-screen views than others. For example, if you do not want 15-minute intervals for calendaring, you have the flexibility to customize your own program. The notepad field, which allows you to attach notes to any contact, schedule, or task component, varies in size. Be sure the field will accommodate your type of notes.

Individual personalities and working styles should determine the software you and your supervisor eventually use. If you use a program that does not "work" like you prefer working, you will be frustrated. Before selecting PIM software, ask for a demonstration of each function and see how the modules work together. Request a demonstration disk or check with other office professionals to see what works best for them. Check product reviews in current trade magazines. The complexity of PIM software determines the learning time.

Access to your PIM software is not always going to be convenient. You may be at your desk most of the day; your supervisor may not. It is important to set aside time to coordinate schedules and tasks.

If addresses, master lists, and other personal data are now in a text file that originated in a word processor, you may have to reenter the data into your PIM program. Check the link to your word processor and the way that your import function operates. Field order and length become important when importing or exporting information.

Electronic Organizers

Two other types of hand-held organizers for people away from their desks a great deal are pen-based digital assistants and voice-activated organizers. Pen-based digital assistants are the size of a paperback book and can track appointments and project due dates. They also have the capability of storing telephone numbers and messages, creating multiple lists, and recording notes. These organizers can recognize precise printed letters, punctuation marks, and numbers and can produce an acceptable transcript. The organizers have such features as dictionaries, built-in calculators, world clocks, and currency conversions.

The voice-activated organizer is operated by your voice. You need some training with the organizer so the equipment will understand you. You enter your information, such as a name and phone number, by speaking. Most electronic organizers can be linked to microcomputers, which allows notes and calculations to be easily transferred, updated, and printed.

Office Application Suites and Integrated Packages

An office application suite combines the full features and processing power of the individual programs. These linked programs include word processing, spreadsheet, database, presentation graphics, and PIM software. Using a suite eliminates the time you waste when you want to switch from one program to another. It also makes it easy to view and move data between applications. If you need service or assistance, often one call will provide help. These suites, however, require a considerable amount of disk space.

Office application integrated packages are not as powerful and do not have the extensive features that suites have. However, they do link basic word processing, spreadsheet, and database functions. They are easy to use and less expensive than stand-alone programs or suites.

PROJECT MANAGEMENT

Project management requires organization and time management skills. Project managers require information about the completion time for a project and the chances that it will be finished in that time. They must break down the project and identify specific tasks, estimate starting and ending times for each task, request the people and materials needed, and operate within a budget. If delays occur, project managers need to know what effects these delays can cause for a company. Gantt charts, PERT (Program Evaluation and Review Technique) programs, and project management software provide project managers with assistance in these tasks.

Gantt Chart: A Gantt chart is a scheduling tool that project managers use to monitor small projects. The project manager needs a breakdown of the work and starting and ending times for each step. To obtain realistic subtask deadlines, begin with the due date and work backward. The bar chart shows scheduled and actual progress for each task; managers can use this information to see if scheduled tasks are on schedule or if problems need to be solved. The chart does not give project managers data about interrelationships among the tasks.

You can also use a simple paper form to keep track of your projects. Keep information on each project in a separate folder. Some items you will need to record are: name of project, start date, due date, project description, subtasks, individuals responsible for each subtask, action to be taken on each subtask, date due for each subtask, and date completed for each subtask.

PERT: The PERT chart helps project managers find the best way to complete a project. It requires managers from all departments involved with the project to plan together. Managers use the technique not only to determine how long it will take to complete a project but also to indicate problem tasks that may affect the date of completion. PERT allows plans to be updated as the project moves along. The chart includes (1) project activities or tasks (represented by arrows) and (2) events or completions of activities (represented by circles). The path is a line that connects the activities; the longest path is the critical path. If an activity on the critical path falls behind schedule, it causes a delay in the project.

Project Management Software

Project management software also creates a graphic timeline for a project and can display information for keeping track of deadlines in Gantt chart formats. Your first step is to arrange your tasks and subtasks in order of importance. The software allows you to change personal deadline dates or budget items easily. You can review selected portions of a schedule, such as time period or one person's schedule. Doing project management electronically enables you to keep everyone informed and on schedule and assists you in identifying problem areas before they are out of control.

A PROCESS FOR SOLVING PROBLEMS

Problems can result in an office from uncertainty, disagreement, and unanswered questions. Ignoring problems usually creates greater chaos. Problems require solutions that will bring about change. Bringing about change requires special skills, and office professionals with effective problem-solving skills are valuable employees.

Whether office professionals are working alone or in a work group, one systematic process for solving problems involves the following steps:

1. Define and analyze the problem.
2. Consider possible solutions.
3. Select the best solution and defend it.
4. Evaluate the results.

Define and Analyze the Problem

To define and analyze a problem may be the most difficult step in solving it. The symptoms of a problem are often more evident than its causes. Everyone may have a different perception of the problem. To define the underlying problem accurately, answers to several questions may be helpful.

- From your perspective, is there really a problem?
- Has this problem occurred before? If so, were the conditions similar? How was the problem solved before? Did that solution work or is a new approach needed?
- How can you learn more about the problem?
- With whom can the problem be discussed? Are there other viewpoints?
- What are the specific circumstances surrounding this problem?
- What company policies and procedures are involved? What are the legal implications? Are there budget limitations?
- What is the desired outcome?

Consider Possible Solutions

The second step is to explore numerous possible approaches to solving the problem. Brainstorming is one effective technique for seeking creative solutions to problems. It is a technique that does not restrict or judge any suggestions so that as many ideas as possible are generated. Include the people who are involved in the solution-generating process. Use suggestions others have used or modify them to work for you. Speak with someone who has been in the company for some time. Several questions that will assist you in generating alternative solutions include:

- What is the first solution that you considered?
- What would be the easiest solution? What would you *like* to occur?
- What are the conventional approaches to solving the problem?

- What other ideas (workable or not) can be used as alternative solutions?
- How did another supervisor solve the problem?

Select the Best Solution and Defend It

After identifying all the possible solutions, the next step is to list the likely consequences of each solution, select the best solution, and prepare to defend it. In most situations, some factors will have an impact on those decisions, such as time, money, convenience, and impact on personnel. Although each solution will have strengths and weaknesses, the best solution should be selected on the basis of all the factors that you have identified and ranked. Here are some questions to help select the best solution:

- What individual department or company limitations must be considered? What solutions are eliminated because of these restraints?
- What are the weaknesses and strengths of each solution?
- What factors are used to judge all solutions? Rank the factors by importance.
- What justification can be made for a decision? How will it solve the problem? What will be the outcome if applied?

Evaluate the Results

After you have identified the best solution, try out the solution and evaluate the results. Establish some timelines and follow up on the outcome. If successful, the solution will be helpful in solving similar problems and eliminating a recurrence of the same problem. The answers to the following questions may be helpful in evaluating the problem-solving process:

- What step-by-step tasks were involved in trying out the solution? Were all the subtasks identified and approved?
- Was the solution successful? Was it necessary to put a second solution into effect? What were the positive and negative consequences? What improvements were needed?
- What experiences with this process could be applied to other problems? What changes would be recommended if these solution procedures were used again?

Special Concerns About Problem Solving

Frustration with a problem may cause it to be blown out of proportion. After you go through the steps in solving a problem, focus your attention on the solution selected; do not waste time imagining every horrible consequence that may result.

Personnel need frequent updates. Don't forget to keep those employees with vested interests informed of your decisions.

It often helps to write a sentence or two describing the desired goal. The focus of your problem definition should not be on who or what gets the blame. How you present the problem will remain in people's memories a long time. Always communicate with respect for others in the group.

When the problem involves a group, you need each member to at least accept the solution and the process. This can be a lengthy, tedious task, so don't give up and handle it yourself.

If a solution doesn't work, review the mistakes. Obtain more feedback or use another approach.

Some problems are difficult to solve and may need input from your supervisor. Ask for assistance if the authority to solve a problem rests with another department or a colleague. Do whatever is necessary to handle a problem, but if it becomes too complex, consult with your supervisor before the situation becomes unmanageable.

USING TECHNOLOGY TO SOLVE PROBLEMS

There is a wide range of software to aid management in solving problems. The array of products increases as companies reorganize and struggle to maintain their competitive edge. Office professionals will find it helpful to understand some of the technology.

Decision-Making Software (Groupware)

Groupware is software that requires a multiuser environment. In that type of environment, the software allows work groups to manage and share information, solve problems, and develop collaborative applications with a minimum of paperwork exchange. In addition to e-mail and other messaging services, groupware can support such functions as bulletin boards, group calendaring and scheduling, task management, project management, workflow routing, electronic document exchange and tracking, forms routing, desktop videoconferencing, and access to a database. Groupware can also support remote users. Desktop videoconferencing adds another dimension to groupware. This growth technology has implications for work groups who need face-to-face feedback.

Groupware is not suitable for every office since it requires a heavy investment of money and training time and raises a security issue. Groupware solutions change the working environment; sometimes users are uncomfortable with the new procedures. Pilot testing with a selected work group usually alleviates the stress and indicates appropriate ways to implement the groupware concept.

Desktop Asset Management

Managing the various hardware and software assets in a firm of any real size creates problems because in large companies there are so many pieces of equipment and software packages in use. The location of the equipment changes because of its mobility. Remote offices and home offices cause additional concerns. Companies are not only concerned about the type and location of equipment and software; they also want to know these details: internal configurations, purchase and warranty agreements, depreciation, cost basis, maintenance, software licensing agreements, and replacement schedules. Managing this type of inventory is costly in both time and money; it becomes obsolete quickly. Desktop asset management software concentrates on personal computers and other easily transportable items such as audiovisual aids. Software features vary in power and sophistication. Companies, however, often decide to use an outsource firm to handle the growing volume of desktop assets that require management.

Artificial Intelligence (AI)

Artificial intelligence (AI) is a broad scientific field that involves making machines more intelligent and therefore more useful. In making machines smarter, AI researchers also try to study and understand the human intellect.

An intelligent computer is more than a storage area for facts or programmed instructions. AI researchers want to find ways that allow the computer to reason, link facts, and solve problems. As computer power increases, perhaps new applications for computers that think like humans will emerge.

Expert Systems

Developing expert systems is a branch of artificial intelligence. An expert system is a powerful business tool. It is software that is based on the knowledge of experts and is used in supporting decisions and in problem solving rather than in developing applications.

Expert-system engineers ask experts what they know and how they use that expertise to solve problems relevant to a specific task. The amount of knowledge gained from these experts must be large, and the questioning technique requires skill and quick comprehension of the experts' reasoning processes. After the questioning period, the developers of the expert system include the acquired knowledge in a computer program. Businesses can use that software to assist them in their problem solving.

CHAPTER 4

ORGANIZATIONAL

STRUCTURES

AND

OFFICE

RELATIONSHIPS

Organizational structures vary widely from company to company, even in the same industry. Within any given company, especially a large one, the relationships between functions and subfunctions undergo continual change, reflecting external changes in market demands, corporate objectives, and employee needs. Organizations usually develop a chart indicating what positions exist and how these positions are related to each other. The authority and responsibilities of personnel are also shown. Understanding the office professional's place, authority, and responsibilities in an organization can contribute to your overall effectiveness in the company.

ORGANIZATIONAL PRINCIPLES

All organizations are built on a number of principles. Among them are:

1. *Lines of authority:* An organization plan makes one person responsible for each worker and/or group of workers in an organization.
2. *Responsibility and authority:* Each position must be clearly defined through job descriptions.
3. *Equating responsibility and authority:* Responsibility is coupled with corresponding authority.
4. *Delegation:* Authority needs to be delegated as far down as possible. However, the delegator remains fully responsible and accountable for what has been delegated.
5. *Simple structure:* An organizational structure should be kept as simple as possible, with minimal levels of authority.

ORGANIZATIONAL STRUCTURES

Based on these principles, businesses develop an organizational structure and an organization chart in order to depict the organization graphically. In an organization with a **line structure,** management has direct authority over, and is responsible for, the performance of all workers reporting to them. This is the most common structure. A line organization chart usually takes the form of a pyramid, with the president or CEO at the apex. (See Figure 4-1.)

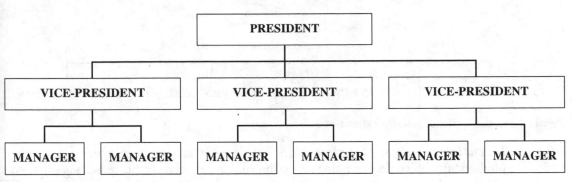

Figure 4-1 Line organization.

In a **line and staff** organization, assistants are assigned to executives. These assistants handle specific advisory responsibilities, such as research, planning, accounting, distribution, public relations, and industrial relations. Staff personnel have advisory or support positions with no direct authority over workers down the line. Staff positions are usually designated by a dotted line on the organization chart. (See Figure 4-2.)

Charting Activities Within an Organization

Office professionals are occasionally called upon to chart an organization's structure. There are four general ways to chart the activities of an organization:

1. *By function, activity, or process:* An organization chart arranged by function breaks the enterprise into groups involved in a single class of activity, such as finance or sales. (See Figure 4-3.) Such a chart can use either broad categories, such as sales, or a specific activity, such as sales promotion.

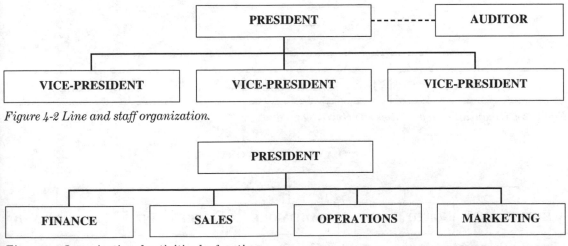

Figure 4-2 Line and staff organization.

Figure 4-3 Organizational activities by function.

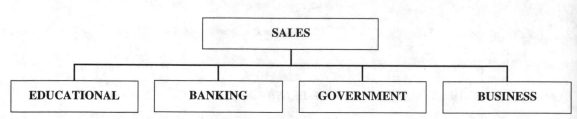

Figure 4-4 Organizational activities structured by customer.

2. ***By customer or type of customer:*** In this kind of chart, workers can be listed alphabetically by customer name or by the customer's type of business, e.g., insurance, banking, transportation, or government. (See Figure 4-4.) Such an organization fits products more closely with customer needs.

3. ***By product:*** A chart in which activities are grouped by product is useful for an organization that focuses on a specialized product and has experts about that product. (See Figure 4-5.)

4. ***By geography:*** A chart structured by geographical location permits special attention to local conditions and requirements. It is particularly important in sales and marketing, where local traditions and habits have great influence on success. However, such an organization may duplicate common activities, such as accounting and marketing. (See Figure 4-6.)

The Matrix Structure

An alternative to these four structures is the matrix structure. In a matrix structure, each person reports to two executives: the person in charge of the particular project or product on which the employee is working, and the person in charge of the particular area in which the employee works. For example, in a high-tech company, a software design spe-

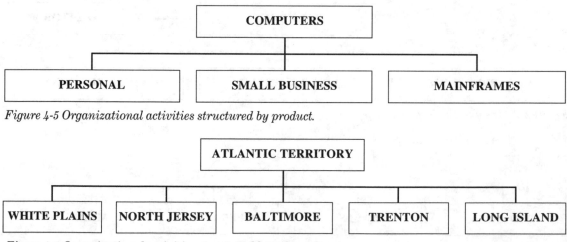

Figure 4-5 Organizational activities structured by product.

Figure 4-6 Organizational activities structured by geography.

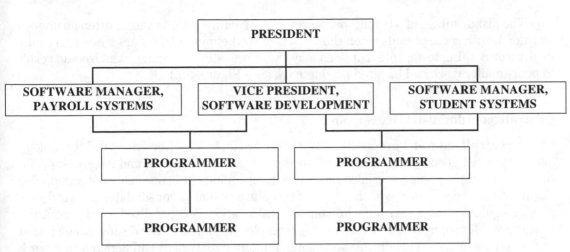

Figure 4-7 Organizational activities as a matrix structure.

cialist may report to both the manager of the product on which the specialist is working and the manager of software for the organization. (See Figure 4-7.)

This structure is complex. It often works best when employees and management are well educated and professionally oriented, and the company is small and entrepreneurial. Many companies use a matrix structure as a transition between being functionally organized and being organized by product or market.

THE MODERN OFFICE STRUCTURE

Because each organization is different, there is no ideal way to place administrative support personnel in the organizational structure. In fact, many businesses are restructuring to better suit their needs and to maximize productivity. Business costs have also increased, partly because white-collar workers now comprise more than 60 percent of the total work force. As a result, the office is now viewed as a professional environment where skilled people perform functions vital to the smooth operation of an organization. Businesses are placing more emphasis on the management of office support, and in the process they are creating new career opportunities.

Traditional Office Support

Traditionally, offices have been organized so that upper-level managers have private or personal secretaries or executive assistants. Moving down in the organization, middle- and lower-level managers have often shared secretaries. Within the traditional structure, executives have immediate access to secretarial support. There is more flexibility in scheduling and prioritizing managerial work. The executive assistant works with his or her boss on a one-to-one basis and does a variety of tasks.

The disadvantage of a traditional secretarial structure is that there is often an uneven workload, with some periods when the work is overwhelming and others when there may be little or nothing to do. Interruptions may cause priorities to change, which could result in poor-quality work and lowered productivity. (See Figure 4-8.)

Centralized Administrative Support

A **centralized word processing (WP) center** can be an effective use of technology and people. All document preparation—memos, reports, proposals, and letters—is completed by word processing specialists on text-editing equipment in one central location. (See Figure 4-9.) The advantage of this type of structure is that it consolidates all word processing equipment and personnel into one central location. A centralized word processing center provides sophisticated equipment for complex documents. The disadvantage is that there may be delays in producing documents if many departments all demand that work be done at the same time.

In some organizations, administrative support specialists are also located in a centralized location. These specialists perform all tasks other than producing documents, such as scheduling meetings, customer relations, making travel arrangements, and re-

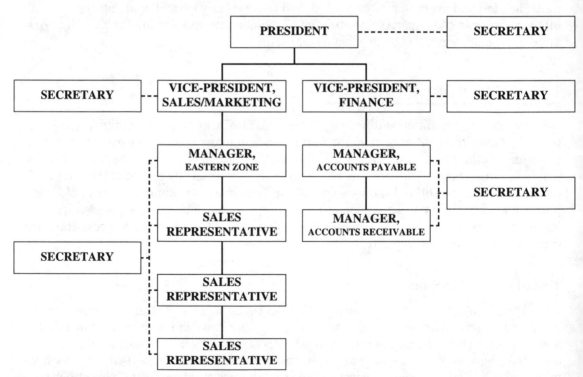

Figure 4-8 Traditional office secretarial support organization structure.

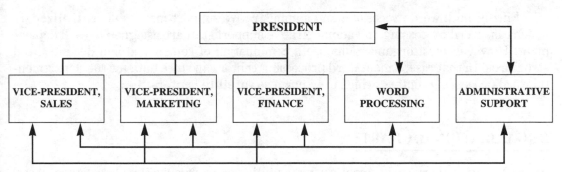

Figure 4-9 Centralized word processing and administrative support organization.

search. Work in an organization with this structure comes to the administrative group from each department as well as from the word processing center.

Decentralized Administrative Support

In other organizations, the word processing center may be centralized, but the administrative support staff is **decentralized.** Staff may be located in several locations near users. For example, departments such as sales, marketing, or personnel may each have an administrative secretary. The word processing center, however, remains centralized for all departments to use for document-producing tasks. The advantage of this structure is that there is a cost-effective word processing center, but managers have easier access to administrative support personnel. The disadvantage is that the work flow may be inconsistent. (See Figure 4-10.)

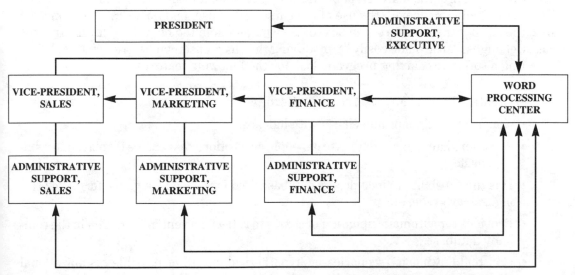

Figure 4-10 Centralized word processing with decentralized administartive support organization.

Finally, both word processing and administrative support may be **decentralized,** in which case word processing and administrative support staff are assigned to each department. However, most organizations use a combination of centralized and decentralized structures. In that case, a main word processing center can store data for the departmental word processing centers, which are known as **satellite centers.**

ORGANIZATIONAL CHARTS

An organization chart is a schematic representation of an organizational structure, showing lines of authority and the relationships among employees. A properly constructed chart:

- Provides a view of the general structure of the company's work by showing relationships and areas of responsibilities.
- Serves as a historical record of organizational changes.
- Serves as information for orienting new employees.
- Can be a work plan for expanding a business and an information piece for the general public or special groups.

The design of an organization chart can range from a simple line chart of job titles to a more detailed chart that includes titles, job responsibilities, and photos of the top company executives.

Computer programs are available for use in creating organization charts. Lines can be automatically drawn with the use of the cursor or mouse, and boxes can be formatted with the use of a menu. Charts can be created with an unlimited number of levels. In most cases, changes can be made easily by modifying the chart onscreen before printing. When selecting a software charting program, look for the following features:

- Creates charts in any size, shape, style, or color.
- Generates wall maps and charts with indexes.
- Accommodates a large database of people or positions that can be displayed in a single chart.
- Has the capability to include any database field in the chart, e.g., performance rating, salary grade, etc.
- Provides for automatic updating of charts to reflect current information in the company database.
- Can build "what-if" scenarios or hypothetical charts of possible organizational changes.

- Has a batch printing feature allowing integration of any number of charts into one master chart with a consolidated index; any number of people or positions can be included.
- Has relationship paths that allow for cross-referencing information about candidates, supervisors, next planned positions, etc., with incumbent data in the same box.

After creating an organization chart, whether it is done via a software program or manually, the following questions should be answered:

- Are titles correct and up to date?
- Are names spelled correctly?
- Is the reporting structure correct?
- Is the organization chart dated to show latest revision?
- Has management reviewed the chart and approved its distribution?
- Has the organization chart been revised according to an established schedule, e.g., semiannually or annually?

OFFICE RELATIONSHIPS AND TEAMS

As today's companies merge, downsize, and invest in technology to meet the changing demands of business, team management is emphasized more than ever before. The team approach allows management to share responsibility for implementation of corporate goals. The team approach also helps office professionals to build a framework for professional and greater efficiency.

Teams of people may work together in common facilities or may be physically separated from one another. For example, key team members may be located in different offices in different parts of the country or world and be connected by means of a telecommunications network. A team may be composed of members from the same department or may be interdisciplinary, with members from various departments. Teams are generally assigned to work on a specific goal or project. The team's assignment may run for as little as one month or as much as a year and a half. A project room is often made available to facilitate the work. The most common type of team is a **linear team,** which is generally organized by function and is process-oriented. An example is a health and safety team organized to review office workstation ergonomics. Team members have fixed roles, such as chairperson, secretary, etc. A team focusing on solving a problem, such as developing a new customer service software program in the next year, is referred to as a **parallel team.** This type of team will have members with specialized skills that contribute toward a directed goal. Another type of team is called a **circular team.** Such a team usually consists of highly creative individuals who function democratically and even set their own goals. A new product development team is an example.

A team has the following characteristics:

Results: A team's purpose is to accomplish something.

Goals: A team must have a common purpose that is understood and pursued by the whole group.

Energy: An extra dimension of energy is created as a team works together to achieve an end result.

Structure: An organization should be orderly and members should respond to workflow in a uniform way. However, the structure should be flexible as the team tries to accomplish its goals.

Spirit: Team spirit reflects the quality of the team's work.

Identity: Having a sense of belonging is important.

Collective learning: Because teams learn together as they answer difficult questions and solve hard problems, their collective knowledge will become part of the team as well as part of each individual member.

The relationship between manager and administrative assistant is the most common team within the office. This unit is motivated by the goal of making the workplace more efficient. Managers and administrative assistants must address face-to-face such issues as trust, joint problem solving, giving and receiving feedback, time management, and behavioral styles. Team building commands the presence of all the players.

Everyone in an office works together in a team effort, whether formally or informally, at some level. Acting as a team member:

- Maximizes work distribution for the organization.
- Allows an interchange of office professionals when one person is out ill or on vacation.
- Provides a career path and opportunities for career development for the office professional.
- Maximizes productivity through fall utilization of human resources and technology.

To be an effective team member, you must:

- Understand the group's objective. What is the group expected to achieve? Is the purpose of a particular meeting to exchange information or to solve a conflict? Ask questions to help clarify the purpose, but do so in a nonthreatening way. For example, you might ask, "Am I correct in my understanding of our goal? As I see it we are..." "As I see it" is a useful phrase because it implies that you are receptive to other viewpoints.
- Focus on the objective. Keep to the subject and try not to deviate.
- Be economical with words. Do not ramble. Try to use strong nouns and active verbs.

- Listen carefully. Concentrate on ideas, not just facts. Watch for nonverbal cues from the speaker. Reserve judgment until the speaker has finished. Be open-minded.
- Interact informally. Important information exchanges are often made in informal settings. Informal interactions offer opportunities to express opinions, influence others, compare information, and learn about decisions that have not yet been made.

To work effectively in a team-managed organization and enhance your opportunities for career advancement, you should:

1. Assess the needs of each member of the team for computer skills, education, experience, and certification. Such an assessment will pinpoint the technical, administrative, and interpersonal skills needed by members of the team.
2. Focus on developing and improving communication skills such as writing, speaking, and listening.
3. Understand and keep informed about the organization's goals, products, and competition. Be aware of changes within the company and industry.
4. Develop self-initiative.
5. Learn to delegate. (See Figure 4-11.)
6. Be organized and manage your time well, not only for yourself but for others in the team.

COMMUNICATION IN THE OFFICE

Effective communication helps create a desirable work climate in which individuals can cooperate to accomplish personal, group, and organizational goals. In organizations, communication occurs between overlapping and interdependent groups as well as individuals. Organizations rely on communication in order to work effectively. For that reason, they develop communication networks to facilitate the flow of messages. An administrative assistant is often the controller of the communication network and therefore must have good communication skills.

Finally, keep in mind that office professionals also communicate and interact with clients, customers, stockholders, financial institutions, and civic and community groups. How an office professional responds to people outside the organization reflects on the organization's image.

PERSONAL NETWORKING

Developing personal contacts in a company can be very helpful in getting information for your managers as well as for your personal advancement. Since it isn't possible to network with everyone, apply your efforts to the people who can help you the most, that is, those

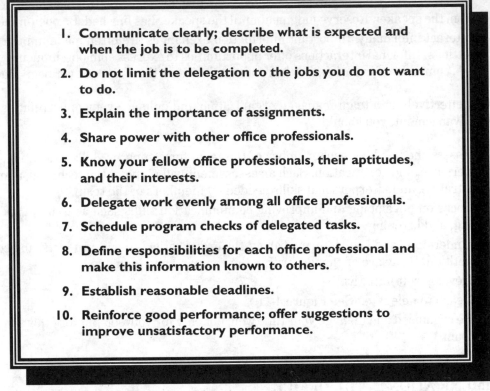

1. Communicate clearly; describe what is expected and when the job is to be completed.

2. Do not limit the delegation to the jobs you do not want to do.

3. Explain the importance of assignments.

4. Share power with other office professionals.

5. Know your fellow office professionals, their aptitudes, and their interests.

6. Delegate work evenly among all office professionals.

7. Schedule program checks of delegated tasks.

8. Define responsibilities for each office professional and make this information known to others.

9. Establish reasonable deadlines.

10. Reinforce good performance; offer suggestions to improve unsatisfactory performance.

Figure 4-11 Ten rules for effective delegation.

who have information you or your manager may need in the decision process. Remember that it takes time to build relationships with people whom you can count on and trust to provide you with reliable information. Ask yourself these questions:

- Which people in the organization have information my executive or I may need from time to time?
- How can I help others in the organization by providing useful information to them?
- What is the best method of contacting others: telephone, e-mail, or personal visit?
- Can I build relationships with people outside the organization via the Internet? (Although this can be an excellent way to network, be careful you do not become involved in a conflict-of-interest situation whereby you provide confidential and critical information to someone unauthorized to receive it.)

As a supervisor, overseeing, assisting, and monitoring the work of those reporting to you is only one aspect of your job. Other responsibilities include interviewing and hiring, training new and temporary employees, conducting performance appraisals, and administering discipline.

THE HIRING PROCESS

Hiring good people can be a long and difficult process or a short and simple one. There are many steps involved, from writing the job description to interviewing potential candidates to checking references. As today's office professionals advance to supervisory positions, they are increasingly involved in hiring others to work for them.

Writing a Job Description

Organizations require division of responsibilities. As more and more people are added to the organization, this division becomes greater. Job descriptions have several important advantages. They help the manager analyze and improve organization structure and determine whether all company responsibilities are fully covered. They can also help in the reallocation of responsibilities to achieve a better balance, if necessary. An effective job description does more than simply list specific duties and responsibilities. It also indicates the relative importance of each duty and responsibility.

(See Chapter 11, Office Manuals and Publications.)

Writing a Job Advertisement

Once the decision has been made to create a new job, a job advertisement may have to be written for the newspaper or for posting within the company. The human resources department (if one exists in the organization) is the best source of assistance in writing the ad. (See Figure 5-1.) However, if it is left to you or your supervisor, the following considerations should be noted:

- An advertisement should explain as succinctly as possible what the job is.
- Job requirements or prerequisites should be stated to screen out unsuitable applicants.

CHAPTER 5

SUPERVISION

AND

TRAINING

Blind ad (no listing of company's name, only post office box number):

Educational organization needs organized, outgoing person with strong word processing and interpersonal skills to coordinate production and planning of public presentations and management seminars. Desktop publishing and graphic arts a plus. Send resume to this newspaper, P.O. Box 1011.

Open company ad:

Detail-oriented individual needed with minimum 2 yrs. exp. to handle work analysis. Write job descriptions, conduct surveys, and assist in personnel screening. Send resume to the XYZ Corp., 91 Victor St., Scotch Plains, NJ 07091.

Figure 5-1 Sample job advertisements.

- The advertisement should reflect the legal issues in hiring, such as stating that your organization is an equal employment opportunity employer.
- Being creative in the advertisement can help attract a higher quality of applicant.
- The advertisement should not misrepresent the job but rather explain it, indicating the most important points of the job. Beware of the ad that promises too much.
- Use a post office box if the company wants to protect its identity, or avoid a possible flood of applicants.
- The ad can be placed in trade magazines and newsletters as well as in the classified section of local newspapers (usually placed on Sunday and running for three to five days), business newspapers, and professional association publications.

Interviewing

Conducting a successful interview involves a number of steps. First, screen the written applications. The basic screening device is the application form or resume. Once you have done this, talking to candidates by phone is also a good way to narrow the field further. Try to turn such conversations into mini-interviews.

Before each interview, familiarize yourself with the candidate's application form or resume. Jot down some questions that you want to ask to make sure you control the conversation. The eight most common questions asked during an interview are:

1. What are your major strengths?
2. What are your major weaknesses?

3. How is your previous experience applicable to the work we do here?
4. Why are you changing jobs?
5. Is there someone we can contact who is familiar with your work activities?
6. Where do you see yourself in this company five, ten years from now?
7. What kind of work are you looking for?
8. What kind of compensation do you expect?

During the initial interview, which should last about 30 minutes, you should acquaint the applicant with the company and position(s) available and try to learn as much as possible about his or her background. A good rule of thumb is for the interviewer to talk about 20 percent of the time and the applicant 80 percent.

Write down your impressions during and after the interview. This can help you begin further to narrow down the list of applicants. An initial interview helps in gathering factual information about the applicant's background, attitudes, reasoning process, motives, and personal goals.

Certain questions that are illegal to ask during the interview are shown in Table 5-1. Here are some additional interviewing techniques:

- Create a proper interview environment by holding the interview in a place free from interruptions.
- Put the candidate at ease. This helps to generate a useful flow of information; it also indicates to the candidate this could be a good place to work.
- Perfect your questioning techniques. Vary your use of questions from those that require a simple "yes" or "no" and to those that require more explanation so that the end result is a conversation, not a grilling session.
- Give the applicants feedback to their responses; this encourages more in-depth answers.
- Keep your reactions to yourself; stay in control and maintain a professional rapport.
- Be honest. Conclude the interview by letting the candidates know whether they are being considered for the position and will be called for additional interviews.

If you know after the interview that this is not the candidate for the job, write to the applicant indicating your decision to hire someone else and thank him or her for applying. If the applicant calls, this information should be conveyed orally.

Finally, when choosing one candidate over another ask yourself the following questions:

1. Does this candidate fit in with the people already here? Does this person have compatible perspectives, integrity, and a desire to work as part of the team?
2. Does this candidate show enthusiasm for this particular job?
3. Does this candidate project a good image?

Table 5-1
ACCEPTABLE AND UNACCEPTABLE QUESTIONS TO ASK IN AN INTERVIEW

CATEGORY	UNACCEPTABLE	ACCEPTABLE
Name	The fact of a change of name or the original name of an applicant whose name has been legally changed	Maiden name of a married woman
Birthplace	Birthplace of applicant Birthplace of applicant's parents Requirement that applicant submit birth certificate or naturalization and/or baptismal record	Applicant's place of residence Length of applicant's residence there
Religion	Applicant's religious affiliation Church, parish, or religious holidays observed	
Race/color	Applicant's race Color of applicant's skin, eyes, hair, etc.	
Age	Date of birth, except when information is needed for: 1. Apprenticeship requirements based on a reasonable minimum age 2. Satisfying the provisions of either state or federal minimum age statutes 3. Verifying that applicant is above the minimum legal age 4. Avoiding interference with the operation of the terms and conditions and administration of any bona fide retirement, pension, or employee benefit program	
Citizenship	Any inquiries concerning citizenship	Can applicant produce documentation of eligibility to work in this country
National origin/ancestry	Applicant's lineage, ancestry, etc. Nationality of applicant's parents or spouse	
Language	Applicant's primary language Language used at home How the ability to read, write, or speak a foreign language was acquired	Language(s) the applicant speaks fluently

(continued)

Table 5-1 *(cont.)*

CATEGORY	UNACCEPTABLE	ACCEPTABLE
Relatives	Name and address of any relative	Names of relatives employed by company Person to be notified in case of emergency Whether the applicant has ever worked for the employer under a different name
Military experience	Applicant's military experience, other than 1. U.S. National Guard or Reserve 2. Draft classification 3. Dates and conditions of discharge	Military experience in U.S. Whether applicant has received any notice to report for duty
Organizations	Membership in any club, social fraternity, society, or lodge	Membership in any union or professional, trade, or service organization
References	Name of pastor or religious leader	Names of persons willing to provide professional and/or character references
Sex and marital status	Sex of applicant Marital status Dependents	Maiden name
Arrest	Number and kinds of arrests	
Height	Only if it is a bona fide occupational requirement	

4. Would this candidate go the extra distance to get the work done?
5. Does this candidate have a genuine enthusiasm for this organization and its goals?

Following the initial screening and interview process, the top candidates can be invited back for further interviews with other members of the staff. If the position requires certain skills, such as keyboarding or dictation proficiency, tests may be given.

Hiring Temporary Help

Temporary help is used to fill in for unplanned absences (such as illness), planned leaves, vacations, and seasonal or short-term workloads. Before you can effectively use temporaries, however, you must:

- Identify what positions can be filled by temporaries and specific duties the temporaries will be performing.
- Summarize skills needed for each position, being as specific as possible.
- Compile a short outline of company-specific procedures, based on job descriptions. Give copies to the agency for its reference and be sure they are available to temporaries when they arrive for work.

In selecting a temporary agency, make appointments for interviews with several firms. Evaluate according to:

Prompt and accurate response: The agency should confirm requests quickly and provide the names of other qualified agencies should it not be able to accommodate your request.

Feedback and quality control: The agency should monitor the temporary the first day to ensure that the temporary has the proper skills and should be ready to respond if problems occur.

Adequate insurance coverage: The agency should provide insurance in several areas to protect both the employee and your employer. Bonded personnel should be available if required.

Solid references: An agency should provide references from other clients and employees.

The key to working with temporary agencies is to develop a long-term relationship.

Checking the Resume and References

In the process of selecting a candidate, you should thoroughly review the resume and check the candidate's references. According to national personnel surveys, 33 percent of the resumes submitted contain false information. Employment dates, salary levels, job responsibilities and titles, and reasons for termination are the most frequent areas where the truth gets stretched.

A starting point for detecting dishonest resumes is to question such things as emissions, abbreviations, peculiar wording, and ambiguous information. Copies of transcripts, W-2 forms, and letters of reference in conjunction with thorough interviews are also common means to counter resume fraud. However, heavy workloads compounded by understaffing may not give you enough time to check resumes. The best alternative, to make sure you hire the right person for the job, is to use a professional resume checking service. A good background checking service has the expertise to spot areas that should be questioned and the resources to check them out.

Giving References

As a supervisor or as a colleague, you may be called on to give potential employers references on people you have worked with or trained. In today's litigious society, this is not always as easy as it seems.

Because of the threat of lawsuits, many companies refuse to give references unless they are positive ones. Often employers will have employees sign a waiver granting the company permission to give references. Despite these seemingly careful measures, companies that refuse to give references or give them with employees' permission may still end up being sued.

The best way to approach references is to assume your information will be heard in court and be prepared to defend what you say as fact. Consult your company's legal representative to determine the best policy in providing references.

Some guidelines to follow in giving references:

If you give a telephone reference, maintain a written record of who called you, when they called, and what you said. If you provide a letter of reference, keep a copy for your files.

Check your company policy to find out what information you may provide. This policy should be stated in writing as part of any waiver that employees sign granting the company permission to give information to potential new employers.

Provide only information regarding verified and documented job performance. References are not the place to advertise a personal grudge against a past employee.

If you do make a personal statement, it should begin with the phrase "in my opinion" or "I believe" to make it clear it is your personal opinion and not an objective fact. Trying to prove objectively that a person lacks motivation or has a difficult personality is extremely hard.

Provide only the information asked of you. If you give information beyond that requested by the caller, make it clear that this information should be treated as confidential. One way to convey that the information you are providing is not intended to damage an employee's reputation is to qualify it. Use phrases such as, "This information is for professional use only."

SEXUAL HARASSMENT

Sexual harassment in the workplace is difficult to define and it is not confined to males harassing females. The reverse is also a possibility. The Equal Employment Opportunity Commission (EEOC) provides the following guideline:

> Unwelcome sexual advances, requests for sexual favors, and other verbal or physical conduct of a sexual nature constitutes sexual harassment when 1. Submission to such conduct is made either explicitly or implicitly a term or condition of an individual's employment; 2. Submission to or rejection of such conduct by an individual is used as the basis for employment decisions affecting such individual; or 3. Such conduct has the purpose or effect of substantially interfering with an individual's work performance or creating an intimidating, hostile, or offensive working environment (Federal Register, 1980:25025).

A recent study by the Professional Secretaries International®—The Association for Office Professionals™ and Nan DeMars CPS (1995) reported that office workers considered behaviors related to sex in the workplace—including certain physical contact, verbal discussion of sex, and the display of pornographic material—to be a basis for a formal complaint or a lawsuit. Based on this study and good management sense, follow these guidelines:

- Document all complaints and give each of the parties involved an opportunity to clearly state the case.
- Stop inappropriate behaviors before they become pervasive. Doing so can help improve an employee's performance as well as minimize the threat of lawsuits.
- Become familiar with your company's sexual harassment policy.

TRAINING EMPLOYEES

Because today's office professional has become the main interface between management and computer-based office systems, a sound knowledge of office automation is imperative. The office professional is expected to be able to access a database, manipulate financial models, output to graphic displays, and integrate the applications into a comprehensive word processing document. A professional is also expected to apply conceptual and human relations skills within this fast-paced environment. Effective training fills gaps in an individual's skills and knowledge.

Professional Secretaries International recently introduced the Office Proficiency Assessment and Certification® program (OPAC®), a three-and-a-half-hour computerized assessment tool to help entry-level students, business teachers, job applicants, and employers determine proficiency in five areas: word and information processing, keyboarding, administrative support skills, records management, and language skills. Data can be used to verify skills or identify areas needing skill development.

Training can be handled through several methods:

- Classroom training
- Self-study manuals, audiotapes, and videotapes
- Seminars, workshops, or structured on-the-job training
- Videodisk training packages
- Computer-assisted instruction (CAI)

Training can be done by the organization's in-house personnel or conducted by outside vendors either on-site or at off-site locations.

Classroom Training

Despite a new focus on self-paced training, instructor-led training is still the most popular form. Instructor-led training has the following advantages:

- Trainees receive immediate feedback from an acknowledged leader.
- It is scheduled training with a specific time set aside.
- It is less expensive than one-on-one tutoring.

On-site training is more convergent and eliminates the cost of travel. Off-site training is more concentrated and eliminates office interruptions and having equipment tied up for training purposes. Electronic materials are also available to supplement classroom instruction.

Audiotapes

Through the use of a cassette, a voice prompts the learner through a series of programmed segments. An accompanying diskette controlled from the computer keyboard works along with the tape, displaying additional course materials on the screen and illustrating particular points.

Videotapes

Trainees can also watch a training videotape on a TV screen and may also perform exercises on a microcomputer.

Interactive Video Instruction

Considered the state-of the-art in self-paced instruction, interactive video instruction (IVI) allows the user to control the pace and concept of a video. It takes advantage of the educational precept that people retain only about 25 percent of what they hear, 45 percent of what they see and hear, and 70 percent of what they see, hear, and do. IVI lets the user see, hear, and do.

Computer-Aided Instruction

Computer-aided instruction (CAI) uses a program encoded onto a diskette along with courseware that introduces features of the program frame by frame. The learner turns on the computer, inserts the disk, and hits the proper start-up keys; the system then takes over, showing and telling the student what to do next.

Training Temporary Help

If a position needs to be filled by temporary help, you must effectively organize the temp's time. Here are some pointers for using temporary help:

- Arrange the work to be done in sequence. Prioritize.
- Set aside a specific place for the temp to work.

- Provide all equipment and supplies needed.
- Prepare instructions and write them out.
- Furnish samples of company brochures, letters, forms, etc.
- Assign a full-time person to assist the temp. Let that person monitor the temp's performance.
- Keep your expectations reasonable.
- Introduce the temp to other office personnel. Make the temp welcome as a team member.
- Keep a list of temps who work out well, and ask the agency to send one of these temps the next time you need one.

SUPERVISING EMPLOYEES

How effectively work is accomplished depends a great deal on the supervision people receive. Good supervision encompasses motivation, performance review, the ability to make decisions and communicate expectations and disappointments, and ordinary common sense.

Managing for Change

A manager's greatest challenge will be motivating a high level of employee morale while maintaining a high level of productivity. People will be the major challenge as offices enter the twenty-first century. Downsizing, erosion of loyalty, virtual officing, and obsolescence, as well as the need to upgrade hardware/software skills are among the many factors contributing to increased worker stress.

Change often creates uncertainty and fear of the unknown, especially in the initial stages of reorganization or introduction of something new. Some workers may challenge a software upgrade as unnecessary because the old version worked just fine. Managers will have to guard against employees believing they are overworked, unimportant, and unappreciated.

Educating and informing are two of the most effective tools in dispelling misunderstanding and overcoming resistance. Once people are properly informed and are shown how the new system works, resistance will generally decrease, especially as they begin to experience benefits from the change.

A needs assessment is the first step in educating your staff. This will help you to pinpoint the technical, administrative, and interpersonal skills in need of improvement. Assessments may reveal needs in such areas as software applications, self-esteem, career development, stress and time management, and dealing with change. Next, implement an improvement program by providing classroom training, self-study manuals or audio/video tapes, seminars, or structured on-the-job training. Use your own personnel to provide the training or hire a specialist from the outside.

A failure to communicate is often the real problem in dealing with acceptance of change. Employees are expected to accept or at least try the proposed change. Simply telling people is only part of an effective communications program. Feedback is critical, and supervisors need to analyze the situation and consider the following:

- What is the level of the employees' technical knowledge and expertise?
- What are the individuals' specific needs and aspirations?
- What is the overall business and social climate?
- What are the ages and other demographics of the group?
- What other changes have occurred recently?
- Will the change cause anyone to lose their job or be demoted?
- How supportive is management of the change?

When a change is proposed, people will react to the message according to their experiences and understanding. If they are uninformed and inexperienced, they will not receive the message the way that you intended.

Motivating Employees

Motivation comes from the Latin word meaning "to move." Thus motivation is the internal process that moves or energizes you to fulfill various goals. Motivation techniques are important to your job of supervising others. Such techniques include the following:

Set objectives: Help employees establish challenging, measurable objectives that will motivate them. Supervisors with little experience frequently fail to motivate workers because they are afraid to demand too much. Once you have helped set the objectives, you must follow through to see that the objectives are achieved.

Give recognition: Recognition should be given through verbal praise, a thank-you letter, the company newsletter, etc.

Enrich the job: Give employees a greater variety of duties to perform, especially if the employee wants them and has the time to do them. By making the job more challenging, you help prepare the employee for advancement. Job enrichment can also be achieved through additional education. Seminars, workshops, or classes can provide a greater understanding of the jobs and duties of office professionals. Additional responsibility has been shown to increase the employee's sense of satisfaction. It also contributes to promotional possibilities, since new skills will be acquired by performing additional duties.

Develop a team: Productivity can increase when each person in the group contributes to the effectiveness of the team. Motivation starts when you give your undivided attention to the people you supervise

Compensate the job appropriately: Yearly or semiannual performance reviews that reward good work can help motivate individuals. A pay increase should be the result of a good review. It not only motivates; it helps to develop loyalty and dedication to the organization.

Delegate: Delegation is the process of entrusting the performance of a specific job to another person. Delegation is one of the keys to effective supervision, but it is also one of the hardest things for most supervisors to do. Some supervisors may not understand their role and therefore cannot delegate what they do not understand. Some believe that the work will not be done properly unless they do it themselves. Some fear competition or loss of credit and recognition. Delegation is important, however, to distribute work fairly and to motivate employees and give them an opportunity to grow.

Conducting a Needs Assessment

Having up-to-date computer hardware and software and providing related training are not all that is required to improve an office worker's productivity. Nor is sufficient motivation. Productivity can often suffer because of procedural and reporting issues. An effective tool for analyzing "productivity bottlenecks" is to conduct a needs assessment. This tool can also be helpful when assessing computer hardware and software requirements for end-users, since the data gathered can help answer many questions and provide necessary information on which to base decisions. The following points will guide you:

- A positive commitment by management is vital to a successful study. Get the support of both the senior and middle managers in the department to be studied. Solicit specific issues they want to have included or outcomes they would like to see result from the study.
- Define the exact scope of the study. For example, "to determine the cost/benefits of an alternative administrative support structure" is a clearly defined, measurable objective. All departments and personnel to be included should be listed, along with the project leaders (if any) for each department.
- Communicate the scope and objectives of the study effectively to the administrative support staff. Gain their support by explaining fully and patiently the reasons for the study and its possible benefits for them and the departmental managers. Let each person know at the outset that the results of the study will not necessarily be used to eliminate jobs; rather, the results will be used to improve the current administrative support system. A good technique is to conduct orientation sessions in which you discuss the purpose of the study, timetables, who will be included in the study, and what is to be expected from each participant.
- Establish a needs assessment team of at least three people to help you design the study instruments, conduct the study, and analyze the findings. Since data may be comprised of many items, it must be reduced to a meaningful, manageable form. Several approaches to gathering the data may be taken. These include interviews, questionnaires, work measurement, and identification of all tasks. A combination of an interview and a questionnaire is usually successful.

- For the managers, use open-ended questions that get at the issues that could increase or decrease administrative support productivity. For example, ask the managers questions about what they like best and least about the current system and the reporting relationships; have them identify tasks they currently delegate and other tasks they might want to delegate; ask how they would reorganize the administrative support to be more effective. Most importantly, help them feel that they are participating in the solution. Be sure to keep the manager's interview to a maximum of 30 minutes.

- Use both open- and closed-ended questions for the administrative support group. The open-ended questions could be similar to those used for the managers. The closed-ended questions should be task-related and elicit the information about telephone activity, time spent at the photocopy and fax machines, messenger/errand services, maintenance of manuals and data libraries, research activities (online and in the corporate library), audiovisual services, mail procedures, filing (both paper and electronic), time spent in meetings with managers or others in the organization, nature of computer activities, time spent performing various software applications, and any other activities pertinent to administrative support in the organization. Time survey sheets and work samplings are also effective approaches to augment and validate the information gathered through interviews and closed-ended questionnaires. And, just as with the managers, help the staff to feel as if they also are participating in coming up with appropriate solutions.

- Activities to perform during an interview include introducing yourself and the other team members, reiterating the objective of the study, reviewing the topics you will discuss, and taking notes. But also listen (ask if it is all right to use a tape recorder), assure them that their input will be kept confidential within the survey team, keep the interview focused, summarize at the end, and thank the interviewees for their time.

- Immediately after the interview, organize your notes with a team member and summarize the findings. Identify points that are still unclear and may require you to ask for a second interview. Evaluate your own performance!

- The analysis of the study should be presented in a final report to the department's senior manager, although others may also be involved when the report is presented. Keep the statistics to a minimum, using them only as needed, such as to clarify the findings in a graph format. Just as in any other type of report, one picture or graph is "worth a thousand words." If needed, statistical analysis software with graphic output for inclusion in reports exists. Support each of your recommendations with data from the study. Should your recommendations impact on "nuts and bolts" issues, such as adding administrative personnel, reorganizing the office layout, or purchasing more equipment, provide the required budget.

- Urge management to announce the results of the administrative study. Open lines of communication among all of the departmental members is a basic requisite for productivity improvement.

Conducting Job Evaluations

A job evaluation or performance **review** is a private meeting between an employee and an immediate supervisor to discuss the employee's past, present, and future performance. Through a systematic rating procedure, management should maintain a record of the performance of its personnel and make decisions regarding employment, placement, transfers, promotions, dismissals, and individual salary rewards.

Evaluations answer the basic question, "How am I doing?" A formal evaluation is scheduled at least once a year. Informal evaluations occur on a continuous basis.

Here are a number of suggestions for conducting formal and informal evaluations:

1. Prepare the employee: Do not evaluate without letting the employee know why the appraisal is required.
2. Evaluate on the basis of current behavior and performance.
3. Assess all the facts objectively. Be fair.
4. Be consistent. Do not say one thing in the evaluation and write something else on the evaluation form.
5. Appraisal information should be given only to those who need it. Such information should be kept confidential.
6. Be clear, concise, and accurate in writing the evaluation report.
7. Allow adequate time for the evaluation.
8. Listen to what the employee says in the meeting.
9. Establish attainable objectives. Set down in writing a plan of action for improvement, with dates for achieving each objective.
10. Support these objectives by providing opportunities for professional development such as internal training programs, outside seminars, or classes to build skills and promote career advancement.

The evaluation should be constructive. The main objective of such a process is to improve performance. Keep in mind that you should evaluate an employee as if you were the person being evaluated.

A performance appraisal should include the following elements:

- Quality of work.
- Quantity of work, or productivity under normal daily requirements.
- Performance under stress.
- Knowledge of work, e.g., utilization of training and experience and understanding of the job in the organization.
- Initiative.
- Adaptability and flexibility.

- Judgment.
- Resourcefulness.
- Cooperation or teamwork.
- Job presence, e.g., lateness, absenteeism.
- Administrative ability.
- Professional appearance and behavior.

For those personnel involved in word processing, the performance appraisal would also encompass such skills as typing, dictation, and telephone manners.

Giving and Receiving Criticism

Learning to give and take criticism is an important skill for supervisors. Since no one is perfect, criticism should be expected. The way in which you deliver criticism, however, determines whether its effect will be productive or disastrous. Whether you are receiving or giving criticism, some important points should be remembered and practiced.

If you must criticize, keep the following points in mind:

- Stay calm. Anger creates a physical reaction that can make you tense and unreasonable. Walk away. Sit at your desk or some quiet place and relax. Uncross your legs and arms and close your eyes and think of a peaceful scene. Holding your body in this fashion helps to relieve the anger.
- The best times to criticize someone are early in the morning and at midday. This gives you a chance to speak to your coworker again during the day in a casual manner, reassuring the person that you have found fault with the behavior, not the person.
- Listen to what the other person has to say. Create an open environment for discussion. Use body language and a tone of voice to let the person being criticized know that you are on his or her side. Criticize the person's actions or behavior only.
- Criticize in private but compliment in public. Criticizing in public alienates the person you are criticizing and may lower the opinion of you held by people overhearing your remarks.
- Be specific. Say exactly what the person is doing wrong, such as, "This is what I don't like and here's why."
- Be supportive. Give the sense that the criticism is meant to help the person do better.
- Help solve the problem. Suggest a solution or offer to help find a way to improve things.
- Be timely. Give the message soon after the problem occurs.

These destructive ways to give criticism should be avoided:

- Being vague by offering no specifics, merely making a blanket statement, such as "That was a lousy job."
- Blaming the person by attributing the problem to personality or some other unchangeable trait.
- Being threatening, and making the person feel attacked, by saying things such as, "Next time, you're fired."
- Being pessimistic by offering no hope for change or suggestions for doing better.

If you are being criticized:

- Listen without becoming defensive.
- Remain calm. Remind yourself that you can learn from criticism.
- Take notes and repeat the main points to make sure you understand correctly. Doing so allows you time to calm down and shows the other person that you are considering his or her statements.
- Thank the other person if it is a justified and helpful criticism. But if you feel it is unjustified, present your side.
- Tell the person you would like to consider the criticism and discuss it later.
- Outline your responses to the criticism. Explain why you think the criticism is unjustified (if that is the case) and try to end the discussion on a firm and friendly note.

Not all criticism is negative, however. Criticism can also suggest a better method of doing an assignment or a different approach to handling a situation. Such criticism should be viewed as a growth and learning experience.

Supervising Home-Based Office Employees

Telecommuting, or allowing some employees to work part- or full-time at a site other than their primary location, is increasing greatly in many business organizations. This trend is significantly impacting the day-to-day supervisory role of the manager.

Neither all employees nor all jobs are suitable for telecommuting. Good telecommuters are generally people with a demonstrated ability to manage their own time and workload well, solve many of their own problems, and find satisfaction in completing tasks with minimal supervision. Jobs most appropriate for telecommuting are those that are information-based and require a minimum amount of face-to-face contact. Also suitable are jobs that are mobile or can be performed largely via a phone line and computer, such as sales, auditing, consulting, and customer service.

Here are some guidelines to help you effectively supervise your telecommuters:

- Provide training regarding telecommuting for both supervisors and telecommuters.
- Set the hours that telecommuters are to be available by phone or require them to call in at specified times. Rely on phones and personal pagers for crises.
- Organize the team's work so that most of the individual work is reserved for telecommuting days and collaborative work for a time when everyone is in the office.
- Handle issues such as security and access to files by using logs and electronic records management systems that can be accessed from remote locations with proper security codes.
- Provide telecommuters with appropriate technology and home office furniture. For example, a mobile telecommuter who will be working in many locations should have a laptop computer with a docking station in the office rather than a desktop computer. A person who spends a lot of time in a home office inputting data into a computer should have correct ergonomic furniture to minimize workers' compensation liabilities. ISDN phone lines or, at a minimum, a 28.8 baud computer modem is essential for employees who will spend considerable time on the Internet or up- or downloading files. Also, fax equipment is essential for most telecommuting employees. It is important to establish a policy regarding the employee's personal use of the company-owned computer and fax equipment, as well as to maintain the integrity of information stored on both paper and other media.
- Realize that there is no "right" number of days for telecommuting. On the average, one to three days a week seems to be the practice. More time away can give employees the feeling of being "out of the loop" and create morale problems, as well as make it hard for supervisors to schedule group meetings.
- Experiment with telecommuting and have a few volunteers or selected personnel try working at home for one month. This gives you the option of expanding or contracting the program. When doing so, make it clear that telecommuting is not a perk, an entitlement, or a benefit but an alternative way to work and that it will not be suitable for everyone.
- Have each telecommuting employee sign an agreement that summarizes your organization's expectations. This agreement should address such topics as days and hours, work assignments, reimbursement policy for phone calls and supplies, management contact expectations, company equipment and furniture, telecommunications hookup, and any additional conditions you feel pertinent.
- You can contact the Telecommuting Advisory Council (TAC) (204 E Street N.E., Washington, D.C. 20002, 202-547-6157 voice, 202-546-3289 fax, http://www.telecommute.org) for more information about telecommuting programs.

EMPLOYEE DISCIPLINE

Experts indicate that over the course of a management or supervisory career, there is a 90 percent chance of being confronted with a problem employee. Problem employees can be, among other things, chronic complainers, constant talkers, rumormongers, incompetents, habitual latecomers, persistent arguers, or practical jokers.

Dealing with such employees requires a systematic, legal-awareness approach, particularly with today's lawsuits for discrimination and unfair treatment.

Several elements are involved in determining how to discipline an employee:

Facts: The supervisor must seek to discover the facts—the who, what, when, where, why, and how of the incident.

Reason: The supervisor must act as a counselor and listen directly to the employee's account of the incident. This may mean allowing the employee to give the reasons for his or her absence, explain poor performance, or deny an accusation of theft. If an employer fails to give an opportunity for the employee to give his or her side of the story, an arbitrator can reverse the disciplinary action.

Audit: A review of the employee's personnel file must be made as a means of gathering data. The audit should review past performance evaluations and any disciplinary actions that may have been taken. Not all infractions are documented, however, which can make it difficult to support an allegation. By documenting the infraction, support for the disciplinary action can be upheld later in court, if necessary.

Consequences: The supervisor must analyze the impact of the infraction. An employee's behavior can result, for example, in loss of productivity or delay in getting work done.

Type of infraction: The supervisor must define which policy or procedure has been violated. Some offenses are more serious, resulting in more severe discipline or termination.

Improving the Problem Employee's Performance

The first thing to do when you are having problems with an employee is to find out the cause of the problem. Personal problems as well as work-related ones often result in poor performance. Personal problems that affect work performance range from car trouble to divorce, mortgage problems to the death of a close friend or family member. Work-related problems range from poor lighting to insufficient training, from smoke in the office to a poor relationship with the manager.

Personal problems often manifest themselves at work through mood swings or attendance problems. A supervisor's involvement in personal problems should be kept at a minimum. It is not your role to act as a therapist; rather, you should counsel the employee on job performance and help resolve the problem, using your authority and leverage to encourage and persuade people to do things they might not be interested in doing on their own.

In dealing with work-related problems, several steps need to be taken:

1. Analyze the employee's performance, taking positive and negative behaviors into account.
2. Develop specific goals for improvement.
3. Meet with the employee for a performance improvement interview. Find out from the employee how things are going on the job, if there are any problems, and what you can do to help.
4. Ask the employee to do a self-analysis in order to identify concrete examples of effective performance and areas needing improvement.
5. Present your own analysis to the employee and negotiate a performance agreement that assigns both of you specific tasks designed to improve the employee's work performance within a three- to six-week period.
6. Follow up with a formal interview within a month to evaluate progress.

Firing is only one of several options at the time of the follow-up. The employee's behavior may have worsened, remained the same, or changed only minimally. Before considering firing, a supervisor should explore the possibility of restructuring the employee's job to take advantage of strengths or transfer the employee to another, more suitable position in the organization. Firing may be the only alternative if these options are not feasible, as well as in cases of dishonesty, excessive absenteeism, substance abuse, insubordination, or general lack of productivity. However, thorough documentation of the entire performance improvement process should be made to avoid legal difficulties, and other types of disciplinary action can be taken.

Types of Disciplinary Action

When all else fails with problem employees, disciplinary action generally is taken. Based on the infraction and a review of the steps outlined, the following types of discipline can be administered:

Oral warning: This is used for minor infractions and as a first step in progressive discipline. Documentation of a verbal warning is usually not placed in the employee's personnel file, but the supervisor should keep a record of the discussion.

Written warning: A written warning is given by the employee's supervisor as documentation of an infraction. It clearly states future expectations for the employee and indicates what future action will take place if further infractions occur.

Suspension: Suspension is used when the seriousness of either the present infraction alone or a combination of the employee's past and present behavior warrants a more severe form of discipline. Loss of pay highlights the seriousness and the fact the employee is in jeopardy of losing his or her job.

Sending an employee home: If an infraction is dangerous to the employee or to others, the best course of action is to have the employee leave work for the day. The employee should be told that he or she is to report to work the next day and that management will then inform him or her of the discipline that will be administered.

Discharge: Discharge, or firing, should happen only when it is no longer possible to correct the employee's behavior. The rationale for discharging is that the employee's actions gave management no other alternative.

BUSINESS ETHICS

The most successful people and companies are those who behave ethically. The leaders of a corporation set the tone for ethical behavior, and this determines how employees, customers, and competitors are treated. Ethical problems in business are not just a matter of knowing right from wrong but involve looking at business questions from a reasonable, responsible, and consistent point of view.

Legality Versus Morality

The legality of an action is determined by law. The morality of an action is determined by ethical rules of right and wrong. Ethical behavior requires following the spirit as well as the letter of the law. An ethical business follows rules and trusts that other businesses and their employees will do the same, despite the fact that some unscrupulous businesspeople take advantage of this trust.

Employees may behave unethically because they do what they are told to do without considering the consequences. They may be afraid of losing their jobs, or they may not understand management expectations. The corporate climate often determines employee behavior. For example, when there are slack internal controls, employees may feel free to take home office supplies or to make an excessive number of personal telephone calls. Employees may be asked to tell "white lies" to protect their supervisors. On the other hand, when management treats employees as trustworthy adults, employees are more likely to act responsibly.

Corporate Image

The reputation of a company is judged by its image in the public eye. One factor of a corporation's image is the care and upkeep of its building, grounds, and offices. Its logo and letterhead also communicate a message about the company. One of the most important factors in a company's image is the way its employees treat its customers and clients as well as the general public. Finally, the way a company treats its own employees is another important factor in corporate image.

A positive corporate image creates respect and confidence in the company and its product or service. Every employee can contribute to a positive image by wearing

CHAPTER 6

BUSINESS ETHICS AND ETIQUETTE

appropriate business attire, by being courteous in telephone calls and written correspondence, by treating visitors well, and by participating in community activities.

More and more people determine where they want to work and with whom they wish to do business based on corporate ethics. Here are some questions to ask in determining whether or not to work for or do business with a company:

- Does the company make quality products or offer superior service?
- Is the company trusted by customers and employees?
- Is the company comfortable and personal for employees, no matter what the size?
- Does the company sacrifice quality for profit?
- Do employees feel that unethical behavior "goes on all the time"?
- Does the company have a code of ethics?
- Has the company been involved in any sexual harassment or civil rights lawsuits, or in any coverups?
- Does the company contribute to the community through public service, charity, youth activities, or the like?

Handling Ethical Problems

As an employee, you may be faced with a situation that is unethical or illegal or both. You will have to decide how best to handle the problem. PSI/Nan DeMars' CPS 1995 office ethics survey asked 2,000 readers of *The Secretary*® magazine questions on ethical dilemmas at work and office conduct. The issues office personnel deal with range from "telling a little white lie" (which approximately 85 percent said they regularly did) to being asked or forced to perform illegal, immoral, and/or unethical tasks on the job. In addition, respondents reported that they are often in a position to observe unethical activities done by others. Such situations call for a choice of action. All choices have consequences. When making a choice, you must define the problem and weigh the potential consequences. You need to assess the risks of stepping forward and of keeping silent, and to calculate your chances of being fired, reprimanded, demoted, or of having a promotion withheld. You must also live with the possible stress the situation causes.

In order to help you best solve such borderline ethical problems, it is helpful to answer the following questions:

- What is the problem?
- Is there a law against it? Is there a company policy against it?

HINT: *If the action is against company policy, repeat the request back: "Do I understand you want me to falsify this expense report?"*

- Who is affected by your decision? How are they affected?
- What are the alternatives? What are the consequences of the alternatives?

HINT: *Try to come up with two or three possible solutions.*

• Who can be consulted for help?

HINT: *Discuss the problem with several of your peers.*

• How will your decision make you feel? How does it relate to your personal values? Does it reflect the kind of person you are or want to be and the kind of company you want to work for?

Loyalty is not to be confused with blind allegiance that compromises integrity. Office professionals are responsible and accountable for their own actions. Most managers encourage office staff to bring ethical issues to their attention. Since the majority of office workers will have to face ethical decisions, prepare yourself ahead of time by analyzing your own principles and ethics. If your personal ethics and those of your manager or company do not match, you will not be comfortable in the position. It may be best to find a new position that matches your personal ethics.

Copying Printed Materials and Software

An important issue of legality in today's office involves copyright law. Copyright law defines the rights of copyright owners to authorize others to use their work. Copyright protection applies to published material, software, musical works, pictures, sound recordings, and motion pictures. Reproducing, displaying, or performing copyrighted work without permission is a copyright infringement.

The courts permit "fair use" in copying protected works. Therefore, copying printed documents for purposes such as criticism, comment, news reporting, teaching, or research usually does not violate copyright laws. For example, an article in a newspaper or magazine can be legally copied and distributed to employees. However, copying an article and using it in a seminar where enrollment fees are charged is illegal.

It is illegal to copy software if it is copyrighted. Although licenses vary, software should be treated as if it were a single item, like a book, and should not be used by more than one individual at a time. Software can be moved from computer to computer, but installing copies of the same program on more than one computer is illegal. The copyright law applies to both copy-protected and non-copy-protected software. (See Chapter 8, Office Computer Software, for a discussion of other sorts of programs, such as shareware.)

In order to help firms with many users, most software producers have reasonable pricing for multiple copies. Advantages to purchasing rather than copying software include free customer support, usually via a toll-free number, and notification of price breaks on software upgrades.

Many businesses have scanners (optical computer input devices for graphics and text), but it is not legal to copy and scan all graphics. For example, most cartoons are copyrighted and should not be scanned without getting prior permission in writing from the publisher or copyright holder. Clip art is the term for graphics that can be purchased and legally scanned.

Business Versus Personal Phone Calls

Each company sets its own policy, either formally in writing or informally by example, regarding personal phone calls at work. Charging personal long-distance calls to the company and tying up company phones with personal calls are commonly unacceptable practices. Some companies scrutinize phone bills more closely than others and confront employees about questionable calls.

It is best to ask about the company policy when you are hired to avoid embarrassment or questions about your personal integrity. Just because "everybody else is doing it" does not make it right.

Business Versus Personal Office Supplies

Is it permissible to take home paper, pens, and staplers? These questions should be asked at the time of hiring. Employees who travel or do company business at home may have permission to take supplies out of the office. Employees who take company supplies for their personal use, however, may be accused of stealing. Some businesses have tighter controls than others over the supply area and are able to monitor how many supplies are taken and by whom. If the company uses an honor system for supplies, it is a violation of trust to use supplies for personal use.

Sharing Confidential Information

A key role of office support personnel is safeguarding information, both written and oral. PSI/Nan DeMars' CPS 1995 office ethics survey discovered that while approximately 27 percent of the office support staff had personally shared confidential information, over 50 percent were aware of others sharing information about hiring, firing, and layoffs. The issue of confidentiality is an ethical issue secretaries encounter regularly in the workplace.

If you are uncertain whether a topic should be treated confidentially, err on the safe side. If you decide to share confidential information, understand that your actions constitute grounds for dismissal with no recourse if it is discovered.

The following are suggestions for safeguarding confidential information:

- Say, "I can't discuss that since it is confidential."
- Avoid leaving information on the computer screen, on a desk, or in a fax machine.
- Use a password (available on software packages) to keep others from accessing computer files. Transfer confidential information to a floppy disk that can be locked in a drawer instead of leaving it on the hard drive or network.
- Create special locked files either in a desk drawer or in a separate file cabinet.

Covering Up a Manager's Absence

In PSI/Nan DeMars' CPS 1995 office ethics survey, over 50 percent of the respondents had been asked to lie about their supervisor's absence. Avoid saying the manager is in a meeting or out of the office if this information is not true. Saying "Ms. Manager is unavailable" is the truth.

If a manager specifically asks you to lie about his or her whereabouts, do not go into a lengthy explanation as to why you feel this is unethical. Simply state, "'I am sorry. I do not feel comfortable in saying that. If you like, I can say…" Most managers do not expect support staff to carry out unethical requests. Even if a manager disagrees with your assessment of a situation, you probably will not be asked to perform the task again.

Additional Ethical Mistakes to Avoid

In a work setting, it is important to consider the needs of others, not just your own. Listed below are ethical mistakes to avoid:

- Blaming "the company" or manager for your own mistakes or those of other employees.
- Taking credit for another employee's ideas or suggestions.
- Protecting poor performers from corrective discipline or termination.
- Suppressing information about on-the-job accidents or failing to report health and safety hazards.

On-the-Job Harassment

Many companies have a harassment policy, which protects employees from harassment because of race, color, ancestry, national origin, religion, sex, marital status, age, or medical condition or disability. Workplace harassment takes many forms, including the following:

- Verbal conduct such as swearing, derogatory comments, slurs, or inappropriate sexual suggestions.
- Visual conduct such as derogatory posters, cartoons, drawings, or gestures.
- Physical conduct such as assault, blocking normal movement, touching, or unwanted sexual advances.
- Demands to submit to sexual requests in order to keep a job or avoid some other loss as well as offers of job benefits in return for sexual favors.
- Retaliation for having reported harassment.

The victim of harassment has a responsibility to complain. The employer has a responsibility to establish a procedure to handle such complaints.

Corporations are held responsible for sexual harassment by their employees (even if top management was not aware of the problem) and could be forced to pay damages. An employer is legally responsible for preventing sexual harassment and providing a harassment-free environment.

The PSI/Nan DeMars' CPS 1995 office ethics survey discovered that nearly one-third of the 2,000 respondents had personally experienced sexual harassment and approximately 38 percent knew others who had been harassed. Sexual harassment is not just men harassing females. Men may be harassed by women, and sometimes a person is harassed by someone of the same sex. There are no objective criteria for determining what is or is not sexual harassment. Some situations are more obvious than others (e.g., "If you don't have sex with me, you don't get the promotion or get to keep your job.").

To determine whether you are being harassed, ask the following questions:

- Is the action unwelcome?
- Does the behavior continue on a regular basis?
- Is your job at stake if you do not go along with sexual propositions or if you speak up about the verbal or emotional harassment?
- Does it affect your ability to function at work?

If you feel that your answers indicate you are being harassed, here is a series of steps to take:

1. Tell the harasser that the behavior is offensive and that you want it to stop. Be specific about the behavior. Say "No" as soon as something happens to make you uncomfortable.
2. Keep a record of the behavior with dates, times, and detailed circumstances, including names of witnesses. Store your journal in a safe place.
3. Write a letter to the harasser specifying what is objectionable and why. Keep a copy.
4. Keep copies of positive work evaluations and memos or letters of praise. These records can refute allegations by the harasser that your work was poor.
5. Try to get witnesses. Ask them to keep a written record of what is happening to you.
6. Follow the company's complaint procedure, which usually means reporting the problem to your supervisor. If the person is your supervisor, go to the harasser's supervisor.
7. If these steps fail, file a formal complaint with the state's department of labor or human resources, the local human rights commission, or the local EEOC office. It is illegal for the harasser to retaliate by firing or demoting you for these actions.
8. Consider conciliation, such as a transfer to another department. If you have a solid case, you may deserve financial compensation.

9. If conciliation fails, decide whether it is worth suing. The court case may take years to settle though, so this should be only a final step.

BUSINESS ETIQUETTE

Proper business etiquette is essential for good human relations in the office. Good etiquette sets a high standard for handling daily encounters and situations. Treating others with respect and courtesy increases cooperation and enhances working relationships. Most business etiquette is based on common sense and sensitivity.

Introductions

When introducing yourself, extend your hand and give your name. In social settings, the woman is traditionally introduced first. In business, however, decisions on who is introduced to whom depend on the ranks of the individuals, not their gender. The higher-ranking person should be named first (e.g., "Ms. Higher Rank, I would like you to meet Ms. Lower Rank").

When making introductions, always use both names in a sentence (e.g., "Ms. Jones, I'd like you to meet Ms. Smith"). It is not necessary to repeat the introduction in reverse (e.g., "Ms. Smith, I'd like you to meet Mr. Jones; Mr. Jones, this is Ms. Smith").

When being introduced, always stand if you are sitting and extend your hand. It is appropriate for both men and women to shake hands. When someone is introduced to you, stand up, maintain eye contact, and shake hands firmly. The handshake should communicate sincere enthusiasm.

An older man introduced to a woman may not extend his hand unless the woman extends hers. If the other party does not extend a hand, withdraw yours and do not worry about it. Having arthritis or other health problems may make shaking hands uncomfortable. If someone is handicapped, take the lead from them on their preferred manner of greeting.

In foreign countries, a handshake is not always the accepted means of greeting. In Japan, the preferred form of greeting is a bow from the waist. Most Japanese business-people visiting the United States will bow slightly from the waist, and then shake hands. In India and South Asia, one form of greeting is placing the palms together at chest level or higher and giving a slight bow. Indian customs discourage a man from touching a woman or talking with her alone in public. In Europe, a handshake is used, but it is not as firm as the American handshake. In Northern Africa and Central Europe, greetings may be an embrace and a kiss on one or both checks.

The following are general guidelines for introductions:

- The person making the introduction should give a little information about each person to make small talk easier. This information might include titles and areas of responsibility.

- Whether or not to use first names depends on the location and size of the company. Some cities and companies are more formal than others. Generally a lower-ranking person should not use the first name of a higher-ranking person unless asked or given permission to do so.
- After being introduced, repeat the other person's name and say something like, "I am pleased to meet you, Ms. Senior Executive."
- When introducing a company employee to a client, always name the client first: "Mr. Client, I would like you to meet Bob Green, assistant to the president. Mr. Client is with Jones, Inc."
- Introduce a person individually to each member of a group and leave time to shake hands before going on to the next person in the group. Always name the new person first unless the people in the group outrank the new person: "Jim, I would like to introduce my colleagues—June Cortez, John Baker, and Doris Hing. This is Jim Hernandez, manager of information services."
- When introducing people of equal rank, titles (Mr., Ms., Dr.) are not necessary.
- If you forget a name, introduce the person to those whose names you remember. This should be a cue to the omitted person to give his or her name. If this does not happen, admit lapse of memory and say something like, "I'm sorry I've forgotten your name," or "Your name is—?"
- Present a spouse to someone who outranks you. Always name the higher-ranking person first: "Ms. Senior Executive, I'd like you to meet my husband, Mark."

Responding to Invitations

Any invitation, whether to a cocktail party introducing a new product line or from a client celebrating a tenth anniversary, should be responded to promptly, to the person named on the invitation. If an invitation was accepted and at the last minute something prevents attendance, it is important to notify the host immediately. If someone other than the person who received the invitation will attend, the host should be notified of this substitution.

Interrupting a Conference

Occasionally an important client or manager asks to talk with another manager who is in a meeting or conference. It is the role of the administrative assistant to determine whether or not to interrupt the conference.

If the decision is made to interrupt the meeting, the most unobtrusive method is to wait for a break in the meeting to speak with the manager. If the administrative assistant does not know when the next break will occur, a folded note can be given to the manager. The administrative assistant waits for a response, typically a nod of the head, before leaving the room.

Business Cards

Business cards have become an important part of every business occasion, and all office professionals should have them. The purpose of the business card is to identify you and give the recipient information about you and your company. The business card can be attached when sending someone a magazine article or the company annual report and even used when sending someone a present or flowers.

The typical business card is 3½ inches long and 2 inches high. Most businesses have designed their business cards to match their corporate image, including the company logo and the placement of information on the card.

The following information should appear on the business card:

- Company logo
- Company name, exactly as the official name is written (e.g., if the word "company" is abbreviated it must be abbreviated on the card)
- Company business address, including city, state, and ZIP Code (including all nine digits)

HINT: *If a company uses a post office box number and a street address, both are included. The U.S. Postal Service prefers that the street address be listed before the post office box number.*

- Company business phone number and car phone, including area code and extension

HINT: *Some businesspeople also list their home phone number on their cards.*

- Incoming toll-free number or Telex number
- E-mail address
- Fax number
- Name in full

HINT: *Omit the middle name if it is not used (the initial could be included). Any nicknames should be in parentheses after the first name or in quotation marks (e.g., Margaret "Peggy" Martin). Avoid Mr. or Ms. unless the name could be mistaken for either sex (e.g., Chris or Marion). Titles such as Ph.D. are placed after the name (e.g., Jennifer E. Ubarra, Ph.D., Susan Smith CPS).*

- Job Title

HINT: *Put the title in smaller type under the name.*

- Department (if appropriate)
- Office hours (if unusual, such as evening or weekend hours)

HINT: *Office hours are helpful for the medical profession.*

Suggestions for printing the business card:

Paper: Thicker paper gives a higher quality look and feel. The card should be strong enough to withstand a certain amount of wear and still look attractive.

Printing: Engraved cards, where the letters can be felt, are usually reserved for senior management. Offset or letterpress printing is less expensive than engraving, but can produce an effective card with the proper choice of paper and design.

Type style: The style of type should be legible, and it should be the same style as that used in the logo.

Color: The color should match company stationery.

When enclosing your business card with a business gift, write a message on the back and sign your first name. When using the business card for forwarding material, clip the card on the upper left side of the material. When exchanging cards, let senior management make the first move.

It generally is not appropriate to give a business card out socially. Business cards should not be wrinkled or soiled, nor should they include handwritten information (such as a new phone number or address). If business is done internationally, the cards should be in English on one side and in the other country's language on the other.

Usually it is the responsibility of the office professional to order business cards. It is extremely important to proofread any business card order carefully before it is given to the printer and to proofread it again after it has been printed. It may take several weeks to receive an order.

The Business Lunch

A popular way of entertaining employees or clients is the business lunch, which gives people an opportunity to relax and get to know one another away from the office. When a guest is invited to lunch, careful planning and a caring attitude are important.

Here are some tips on inviting guests to lunch:

- Let guests choose the best time.
- Ask for culinary preferences (Italian, Chinese, vegetarian, etc.).
- Decide on the restaurant. Ask coworkers for suggestions, check on the price range, and make certain the location is convenient for the guest.
- Make a reservation, even though one may not be required. Avoid tables near the kitchen, waiters' station, or door. If the location is unacceptable, request another table before sitting down.
- Check for credit card or cash before leaving for the restaurant. If using a credit card, make certain the restaurant accepts that card.
- Make arrangements with the maitre d' and/or waiter to pay for the guest's parking and coat check if necessary.

- Arrive earlier than the guest (you may be seated or wait just inside the restaurant door).

Here are some suggestions for dining with a business associate:

- Sit opposite each other for best eye contact. Guests should have the best seat.
- Decide what beverage is appropriate. If the other person has ordered an alcoholic beverage, it is acceptable (but not necessary) also to drink alcohol.
- Avoid eating anything that will distract you from the conversation.
- Wait at least ten minutes before discussing business. Do not expect anyone to do a great deal of reading or note taking during the meal.
- Start with the utensil farthest from the plate and work inward.
- Ask the guest whether there is time for dessert and coffee before ordering them.

Here are some suggestions for handling the check:

- Notify the waiter during the meal that you are picking up the check. Pick it up quickly and do not make a scene. If the check is presented to your guest, let the guest know the company is paying and ask for the check back.
- Leave a 15 percent tip before tax at a moderate restaurant, 20 percent if the restaurant is expensive. Tip even if the service was not good; bring the problem to the attention of the restaurant's management later.

Smoking and Fragrances

Smokers should always be aware of federal, state, and local laws regarding smoking in public places. Many businesses regulate smoking in the office. If smoking is allowed only in designated areas, it is important to abide by all rules, including not smoking in rest rooms. When dining with a group and no one is smoking at the table, assume that you may not. If smoking is permissible, do not light up until everyone has finished eating. When visiting someone's office or conference room where there are no ashtrays, assume smoking is not permitted. Fragrances are inappropriate in the workplace because of possible allergic reaction of coworkers to perfume or cologne. In addition, fragrances have a social implication not suitable in a business setting.

The Diverse Workplace

In today's workplace it is important to be able to communicate with an increasingly diverse group of people. A diversity of ethnic groups and cultures exist in nearly every workplace. Diversity includes:

- Gender
- Age

- Ethnicity
- Physical abilities
- Religious affiliation
- Sexual orientation

Conflicts may occur in a work setting because colleagues have different cultural expectations regarding work standards, punctuality, relationships, status, or verbal and nonverbal behaviors. To become an effective communicator, you must be flexible, nonjudgmental, and have respect for others. Complete knowledge about numerous cultures is not possible, but the following strategies will increase your effectiveness in the diverse office environment:

- Learn about values, etiquette, and attitudes of diverse colleagues. Spend time with people of different backgrounds.

- Ask questions of individuals in private to help understand and demonstrate your interest in the other person. Explain why you are asking the questions.

- Read about diversity and attend diversity training workshops. Avoid misinterpreting the information and forming conclusions.

- Do not generalize from one person to the other. See each person as an individual. Identify stereotypes you currently hold and remind yourself that they have little validity as accurate indicators of an individual's character, skills, or personality.

- Use nonprejudicial language and/or humor.

- Find shared interests, goals, and values.

- Avoid using the term *minority* to describe ethnic groups. In California, for example, the minority groups and majority groups are changing.

- Ask what someone wishes to be called. For example, "Do you prefer the term *black* or *African-American?*"

- Work on ways to become more verbal when you are aware of inappropriate behavior by others. Trying to play it safe by remaining silent is often perceived as acceptance.

Bias-Free Language

An office professional cannot afford the risk of communicating an insensitive message that may alienate other employees and customers. Using bias-free language focuses on the message. Below are some suggestions for communicating in a diverse workplace.

- Avoid using the masculine pronouns *he* or *him* when the gender could be either male or female. Use the plural *they* or use *he or she.*

- Do not use male and female pronouns in a way that stereotypes roles and occupations; for example, "The office support person should remember to call security when *she* leaves."
- Substitute gender-free words for gender-biased words:

Gender-Biased	Gender-Free
▲ businessman	manager, supervisor, executive, business-person
▲ chairman	chair, chairperson, group leader, department head
▲ stewardess or steward	flight attendant
▲ waiter or waitress	server, waitperson
▲ authoress	author
▲ fireman	firefighter
▲ workman	worker
▲ salesman	salesperson, sales representative

- Omit unnecessary references to ethnicity. For example, avoid "Our new manager is black and from Detroit." Say instead, "Our new manager is from Detroit."
- Avoid religious references to holidays. For example, say "Our office will be closed for the holidays" instead of "Our office will be closed for Christmas."
- Avoid referring to those with disabilities in a negative way. For example, avoid "The ramp is for the handicapped only; normal people should use the steps." Instead say, "The ramp is provided as an alternative to the stairs." The term "disabled" is acceptable, but do not use terms like *victim* or *afflicted*.

The Changing Roles of Men and Women in the Office

Traditional social etiquette suggested that a man should always let women leave elevators first, stand up when a woman enters a room, open doors for women, and walk next to the curb. These rules are considerate, but they no longer apply in today's office.

Office etiquette is now based on rank in the company. Never automatically assume that one person (usually a man) ranks higher than another. The following etiquette is appropriate:

- The person closest to an elevator door should exit first.
- The first person to a door should open it and hold it open until all have passed through. If the door is heavy or if a person is carrying something, it is courteous to

help regardless of gender. A visitor to an office should be treated like a guest and be allowed to go through a door first.

- Men and women should help each other with coats.

- A person of either gender can hail a taxi.

- When riding with several people in a car (especially if the car belongs to a person of higher rank), it is best to ask where to sit.

- All staff should rise when a visitor of either sex comes into the office from the outside. Staff should also rise for a higher-ranking executive unless that executive is frequently in the office, in which case the lower-ranking person should stop work and acknowledge the presence of the senior person. It is not necessary to stand when a colleague (man or woman) enters or leaves a room.

Office Politics

In any job it is important to know who has the power, who will be inheriting the power, and how to assimilate into the organization. Balance is important in office politics. Being overly political and not concentrating on your work will cause people to notice, and not being politically savvy may mean you get overlooked for promotions. Managers in every organization periodically change; the key to surviving office politics is being respectful to everyone.

Be careful of office gossip. People gossip out of boredom or jealousy. Office gossip can give early warnings about corporate reorganizations, the effect of a competitor's product on corporate sales, or the loss of a major client. However, gossiping about personal or work problems of coworkers is counterproductive and dangerous and should be avoided.

Here are some suggestions for dealing with office politics:

- Avoid sharing confidential information unless you are prepared to have the rest of the office know.

- Treat all coworkers with respect and interest. Give everyone a chance to express his or her opinion. If you avoid negative remarks, coworkers are more likely to treat you with the same respect.

- Avoid criticizing a subordinate in front of others.

- Counteract untruths by mentioning the truth when the subject comes up in a conversation. Avoid arguing or losing your temper.

- Ignore harmless gossip and do not pass it on.

It is important for administrative assistants to be discreet and not to talk about company business inside or outside the business. An executive must feel secure that all information will be confidential, including any knowledge about financial matters or private life.

Domestic Partners

Domestic partners is a term to describe live-in lovers of the same or opposite gender. Some companies are offering benefits to domestic partners and including them in company activities. The following suggestions avoid discrimination against domestic partners.

- Use *guest* instead of *spouse* when issuing invitations to company activities.
- Avoid asking personal questions about relationships or activities outside the workplace. Do not gossip.
- Treat domestic partners the same way you would treat spouses.

Holiday and Birthday Gifts

Many companies have a standard gift or a set amount of money to give to employees during the holidays, a standard gift for customers or clients, and inexpensive promotional items to give away. Companies vary widely in their holiday gift giving, ranging from none at all to giving a turkey or to having or sponsoring a company party.

Employees are usually not expected to give gifts to their employers during the holidays unless the relationship is longstanding and close. Follow the lead of other employees or rely on tradition.

Many businesses send out holiday greeting cards to clients or customers with an imprinted company name. Use a card with "Season's Greetings" to avoid the problem of sending religious cards. Each card should be personalized with a signature and a short message.

Some businesspeople send holiday greetings to employees and their families at their home address. This is a nice gesture but not expected or necessary. Office professionals may wish to remember those who have done them favors throughout the year, such as maintenance or security employees.

It is often the responsibility of the administrative assistant to keep an up-to-date holiday mailing list each year. This mailing list is best kept on a computerized database program for easy updating and printing of address labels, and to avoid duplication of gifts from one year to the next.

Holiday cards should be ordered at least two months in advance, particularly if cards are sent abroad. If company gifts are given to clients and customers, they should also be ordered in advance. In many cultures, gift giving is a sign of trust, and the more elaborate gift, the better. When giving a gift to someone from another country, make certain it cannot be interpreted as a bribe under the definition of the 1977 Foreign Corrupt Practices Act. If uncertain about the proper gift to give someone from another country, ask a colleague who is familiar with that country or call that country's embassy. In Argentina, for example, giving a set of knives is interpreted as a desire to cut off the business relationship. In China a clock is a symbol of death. Sometimes the best gift is something inexpensive but hard to find in another country. Know the important gift-giving times of the year.

Many businesses keep a list of employee birthdays and celebrate by bringing in a cake and having employees sign a card. Donations for a gift may be requested from coworkers, but it is perfectly acceptable to politely say "no" when asked to contribute.

Procedures for an Employee Illness or Death

If an employee or client has been injured, is seriously ill, or is in the hospital, a card is usually sent. Depending on office policy, flowers may also be sent. Some offices have a special fund for purchasing cards and flowers, or donations may be solicited as needed. Other offices have written procedures describing when cards or flowers are to be sent.

In the case of death, a letter of sympathy should be sent to the family. Flowers may also be sent, if appropriate. Some families prefer that donations be made to charities or other organizations. The family should be consulted to determine their wishes.

If a manager dies, the administrative assistant may be asked to notify other employees, clients, and associates. Depending on the family circumstances, a company employee may be responsible for helping make the funeral arrangements as well as acknowledging all flowers and memorials. Writing an obituary notice for the newspaper may also be necessary. The obituary notice should include the following information:

- Name.
- Address.
- Age.
- Education, including degrees and honorary degrees.
- Current title and important past career information, including any major awards received.
- Date, place, and cause of death.
- Names and relationships of survivors (spouse, children, parents, brothers, sisters).
- Details about the funeral.

The administrative assistant may also be asked to gather all personal effects for the family. Someone in the company should be designated to receive and place all calls about the death.

PART II

EQUIPMENT

AND

SUPPLIES

The last half of the twentieth century has seen vast changes in office tasks. In the 1960s, data processing significantly changed the way information was handled in the office; in the 1970s, word processing, or automated text editing, was introduced as a substitute for repetitive typing; in the 1980s, information processing, the integration of data and text, became a reality through the widespread use of the personal computer; and in the 1990s, networks linking computers increased the ability of groups to work together electronically. As a result, the role of the administrative assistant has changed dramatically.

Personal computers (PCs), desktop videoconferencing, voice input, multifunction image processors, multimedia, and other products will continue to impact the processing of information at a faster rate than ever before. Office workers of the new century will be at the center of this information explosion, using technologies that will connect them worldwide. This chapter provides an overview of current and emerging office equipment.

CHAPTER 7

OFFICE EQUIPMENT

THE COMPUTER

A computer is an electromechanical, programmable machine that accepts, processes, interrelates, and displays data. All digital computers have the following components:

- A *central processing unit (CPU),* the device that contains the central control and arithmetic units used for controlling the system.
- *Memory* for temporary storage of programs and data.
- *Mass storage* for permanent storage of programs and files.
- A *visual display monitor,* usually a cathode-ray tube (CRT), for viewing text, graphics, and numerical data
- An *input device* for entering data.
- *Software* to give instructions to the computer. (See Chapter 8, Office Computer Software.)
- An *output device,* usually a printer. See below under the heading *Printers* for more information.

Central Processing Unit (CPU)

This is the "brain" of a computer. The CPU accepts data, manipulates it according to programmed instructions, and then can direct storage and output of the data. The CPU consists of a control unit and arithmetic logic unit. The control unit is like a telephone switchboard, controlling and coordinating the parts of the computer system as directed by a set of instructions called a **program.** The arithmetic logic unit does the actual calculating or data processing. The speed of a computer system's CPU clock is rated in megahertz (MHz) (a measure of frequency in millions of cycles per second). For example, a 100 MHz CPU requires memory rated at 10 nanoseconds, whereas a 50 MHz CPU requires memory rated at 20 nanoseconds.

Memory

Memory enables a computer to store program instructions, data to be processed, and the intermediate results of the mathematical and logical operations it has performed. The size of a computer's memory is given in bytes. A **byte** is roughly the size of one character (single letter, number, or graphics symbol) and is equal to eight bits. A **bit** is the smallest electrical unit of data and is represented as either 1 or 0 in the electronic circuits making up the computer. Three other frequently used terms are **kilobyte (KB),** which is 1,024 bytes of information; **megabyte (MB),** which is 1,084,576 bytes; and **gigabyte (GB),** which is 1,000 MB.

A computer has two types of memory, **read-only memory (ROM)** and **random-access memory (RAM).** Measurements of a computer's memory normally refer to RAM.

READ-ONLY MEMORY (ROM)

ROM is the permanent internal memory of a computer. It contains the computer's instructions for starting up (or "booting") the system and for reading the **operating system** instructions. An operating system controls the input, processing, storage, and output of the computer's operations, by managing the interaction between the computer and its peripheral devices, such as the keyboard, printer, and disk drives. (See the section on Systems Software in Chapter 8.)

ROM instructions are generally nonprogrammable, that is, their contents cannot be altered by the user. The CPU can only access instructions in ROM; it cannot write instructions to ROM.

RANDOM-ACCESS MEMORY (RAM)

RAM is the computer's temporary memory; its contents are erased when the power is turned off. It is used to store programs and information only while the computer is operating. The size of the program and amount of data you are working with are limited by the amount of RAM memory installed in your computer. For example, if your computer has 4 MB of RAM and the operating system you want to use requires 8 or more MB of RAM, you will have to purchase additional RAM memory chips which are installed and expand memory. Some software programs, such as high-end graphics, desktop publishing, and large database programs, may require 16 MB or more of RAM.

Mass Storage

A variety of magnetically coated materials are used for data and program storage. The main types include:

Floppy disk (or diskette): This is a magnetically coated disk that comes in two basic sizes: 5¼-inch disks (minifloppies) are found primarily on older computers. They are flexible and come enclosed in a protective envelope. They commonly store either 360K (double-density disks) or 1.2 MB (high-density disks) of information; 3½-inch disks (microfloppies) are encased in rigid plastic and commonly store 720K (double-density disks) or 1.44 MB (high-density disks) of information. An extra-high-density 3½-inch disk holds 2.88 MB of data. A disk drive with a higher capacity can read from and write to a lower-capacity disk. However, the reverse is not possible. For example, if your system has a 1.2 MB minifloppy drive, you can read and write to a 360K disk in that drive. You cannot read a 1.2 MB disk in a 360K drive.

Hard disk: This is a rigid, random-access, high-capacity magnetic storage medium. Disks may be removable, providing off-line archival storage, or nonremovable. Capacities of hard drives can exceed 1 GB of memory. The major advantages of a hard disk over a floppy disk are speed, capacity, and permanent storage. You can retrieve and store information almost 100 times faster with a hard disk system. Also, you do not have to continually insert floppy disks when using a hard drive.

Cartridge: This is a magnetic tape loaded into a cartridge (such as a single reel or reel-to-reel) that holds multiple pages of text.

Cassette: This is a magnetic tape loaded into reel-to-reel cassette with a capacity of approximately 30 text pages.

Other storage options include:

Magneto (rewritable) optical disk: This uses a laser beam to store and read data on a magneto-optical substrate over a layer of aluminum. These disks are erasable and perform similarly to hard disks, but they are removable and support as much as 230 MB of storage on 3½-inch disks.

WORM disk: This stands for "write once, read many" times. A WORM disk is generally used to store items that are going to be retrieved many times but do not need to be updated. It is available in several sizes—5¼, 8, 12, and 14 inches in diameter. It is used primarily to store correspondence, invoices, and other business documents. It can be read thousands of times without degradation, and the information cannot be changed. Since they are slow, in comparison to magnetic hard disks, WORM disks are primarily used for data archival purposes.

CD-ROM: This stands for "compact disk read-only memory." CD-ROMs are similar to music CDs. They are 4.71 inches in diameter, capable of storing digitized text, data, images, and sound. Capacity generally is up to 650 MB per disk. CD-ROM disks have data stored on them when a user receives them and cannot be changed. Typical applications include large databases of information, such as encyclopedias, catalogs, or other reference information.

DVD-ROM: This storage medium offers eight times the storage capacity and two times the data transfer rate of CD-ROM technology. A DVD (digital video disk) can hold up to 4 GB of information and is backwards-compatible with CD-ROMs.

Display Monitors

A monitor is an output device that provides a temporary image of information on a video screen. When combined with a keyboard it is called a **video display terminal (VDT).** A display screen can be like a television or can be a flat panel. Monitors vary in size, type, and quality of resolution.

The television-like display screen is called a **cathode-ray tube (CRT)** and typically comes in sizes ranging from 12 to 30 inches. They can be monochrome (one background color and one foreground color) or multicolor. Monochrome screens are available in green or amber on black and in black on white.

The larger CRTs, 17 inches or more, are suitable for such applications as **presentation graphics,** which generate, display, and print line drawings, organization charts, bar graphs, and pie charts; **computer-aided design (CAD),** which generates, displays, and prints standard engineering drawings to assist engineers and designers; and **desktop publishing,** which creates a document of typeset quality using personal computers and appropriate software.

The following are among the common display standards:

Color Graphics Adapter (CGA): This offers a resolution of 320 by 200 pixels (picture elements) in 4 colors selected from a palette of 16 colors. (A pixel is one or more dots treated as a unit. The pixel can represent as little as one dot for monochrome screens or three dots—red, green, blue—for color screens.)

Enhanced Graphics Adapter (EGA): This offers a resolution of 640 by 360 pixels, with 16 colors that can be selected from a palette of 64 colors.

Video Graphics Array (VGA): This offers greater resolution than EGA—up to 720 by 400 pixels in text mode and, in graphics mode, up to 640 by 480 pixels, in 16 colors that can be selected from a palette of 256.

Super VGA (SVGA): Compatible with the older VGA standard, SVGA also offers even greater resolution, usually 800 by 600 pixels but, in some instances, as high as 1024 by 768 pixels. Although SVGA has no clearcut standards for colors, the graphics cards that support it offer a much wider choice than VGA does, with 256 available colors not uncommon.

A video card's **refresh or vertical scan rate**—that is, the number of complete screens the monitor draws per second—is measured in hertz (Hz). Screen flicker is often caused by a slow vertical refresh rate. A video card should meet the refresh standards of the Video

Electronics Standards Association (VESA), which are 72 Hz at 640 × 480 and 800 × 600, and 70 Hz at 1,024 × 768. **Noninterlaced monitors** (which draw all the lines on the screen one by one during each pass versus **interlaced monitors,** which draw every other line, half during one pass and the other half during the next) are available with a refresh rate of 70Hz to 75Hz.

The amount of **video memory** required varies with the type of application. Most business users need just 4-bit for 16 or 8-bit for 256 colors. However, if typical applications might include desktop publishing, presentation graphics, or computer-aided design (CAD), then 16-bit for 65,000 colors or 32-bit for 16.7 million colors is recommended. Graphics cards are also available for very high resolutions at 64-bit, 128-bit and 192-bit. The more expensive and faster boards use video memory (VRAM) or Window RAM (WRAM).

To play digital video clips on screen, your computer must be equipped with hardware or software that allows for the rapid compression and decompression of graphics and sound data. QuickTime software, developed primarily for the Macintosh, is one way to generate sound synchronized with moving pictures or animations. Other common standards for audio and moving pictures are provided by **MPEG** (Moving Picture Experts Group). The **MPEG-1** standard, for example, calls for a resolution only slightly less than that provided by a VCR and for a minimum rate of 30 frames per second to produce the effect of full-motion video. Although software decompression is less expensive, hardware **MPEG** provides pictures of a higher quality.

Flat panel displays are usually 5 inches to 12 inches in diameter and are classified as follows:

Liquid crystal display (LCD): An LCD forms characters by subjecting a liquid crystal solution to an electrical charge. The readout is either dark characters on a dull white background or the reverse. A backlight option can enhance the quality of the image.

Gas plasma display (GASP): A GASP is characterized by an exceptionally clear, flicker-free image. It has a sharper image than the LCD and does not depend on any external light source.

Input Devices

An input device is a means through which a user can enter data and instructions into the computer. The most common device is a **keyboard.** Computer keyboards are similar to standard typewriter keyboards with the addition of function keys. When a key is pressed down, an electrical pulse is emitted that translates the symbol represented by that key into a digital code that the computer can interpret. The code most often used is **ASCII** (American Standard Code for Information Interchange). This code enables one computer to communicate with other computers.

Most keyboards are arranged in a QWERTY layout, which is the same as for the typewriter and is named after the left portion of the top row of alphabetic keys. An alternative to the QWERTY keyboard is the Dvorak keyboard, named after its designer, August Dvorak. The layout is based on the frequency of use of the letters of the alphabet. Both keyboards are available from many manufacturers.

In addition to alphabetic and numeric characters, keyboards have other special purpose keys:

Function keys are programmable, changeable keys, switches, or buttons that initiate predetermined instructions when depressed, such as storage, insertion, or deletion of characters.

Cursor control keys are used to position the **cursor,** the marker that shows the exact location on the screen where one is working. These keys are usually labeled with arrows, one each pointing up, down, left, and right.

Designated-purpose keys include ctrl, alt, caps-lock, and shift keys and special software program command keys. Some keyboards also have a separate numeric keypad similar to an adding machine.

Other input devices or techniques include:

Touchscreen: A video terminal input device using a clear panel overlaid on the CRT screen. The user simply touches the screen with a finger to select available options.

Mouse: A handheld input device that when rolled across a flat surface moves the cursor to a corresponding location on the display.

Voice input: A means of recognizing spoken words and converting them into digital signals that are then changed into characters. With voice-input or voice-recognition software you can work with your PC entirely by voice or by combining voice with a keyboard and a mouse. You can dictate text or numbers, move around a document, format paragraphs, and even move a mouse with your voice.

Light pen: A pen-shaped light-sensitive device that when touched to the display screen can create or change images on the display.

Digitizer or *scanner:* A device used to transform a graphic image into signals that can be accepted for processing by the computer.

Optical character reader (OCR): A device that can read printed or typed characters and then digitally convert them into text and/or numeric data.

Pen-based computer: Characters are written by hand on an LCD display and converted into text or saved as images.

Types of Computers

There are three types of computers: the mainframe, the minicomputer, and the personal computer (PC) also known as the microcomputer.

MAINFRAME COMPUTERS

The earliest computers were **mainframes,** developed in the late 1940s. Mainframe computers have CPUs that can process millions of bytes of information at extremely fast speeds. These systems can support hundreds of input terminals tied directly into the com-

Figure 7-1 Personal computer. (Photo reprinted with permission from Micron Electronics, Inc.)

puter. Mainframes are used to manipulate large databases and for payroll, inventory, and other large-volume applications in business and science.

MINICOMPUTERS

The **minicomputer** was developed in the 1960s. It uses the integrated circuit, in which hundreds of electronic components are formed chemically on a piece of semiconductor material, or "chip." Minicomputers are midsized computers, smaller than a mainframe and usually with much more memory than a microcomputer. They are sometimes referred to as small business computers. Minicomputers are frequently used at the department level to perform functions such as accounting or word processing. They can share peripheral devices and can support multiple users.

PERSONAL COMPUTERS

Personal computers (PCs) are also known as microcomputers. Developed in the mid-1970s, they are reprogrammable electronic devices that process information. A microcomputer uses a microprocessor, a single chip containing all the elements of a computer's CPU. These computers are meant for a single user and generally have a smaller CPU than the minicomputer. They usually fit on the top of a desk. More and more offices are networking microcomputers together to provide capabilities similar to those of minicomputers.

Stripped-down, low-cost personal computers with no CPU are called **InterPersonal Computers (IPCs).** These devices are similar to **dumb terminals** and are attached to an internal or public network for accessing storage, memory, and processing power. Applications include e-mail, word processing, Internet and database access, and videoconferencing.

Personal computers are available in portable versions. These units use the same basic components as their desktop counterparts and are called **laptops.** They weigh from 4 to 14 pounds and can be powered by electricity or by batteries. The smaller, lighter laptops are called "notebooks."

Portables provide a wide range of computing power, although they do not always have the memory capacity of a desktop. They may include a flat panel display using LCD or GASP. Most can be used with the monitor and printer of a compatible PC.

Personal Digital Assistants (PDAs), or **hand-held computers,** are lightweight and mobile. PDAs use internal RAM storage and removable PCMCIA memory cards for software applications, such as a notepad, "to do" list, datebook, telephone log, personal finance

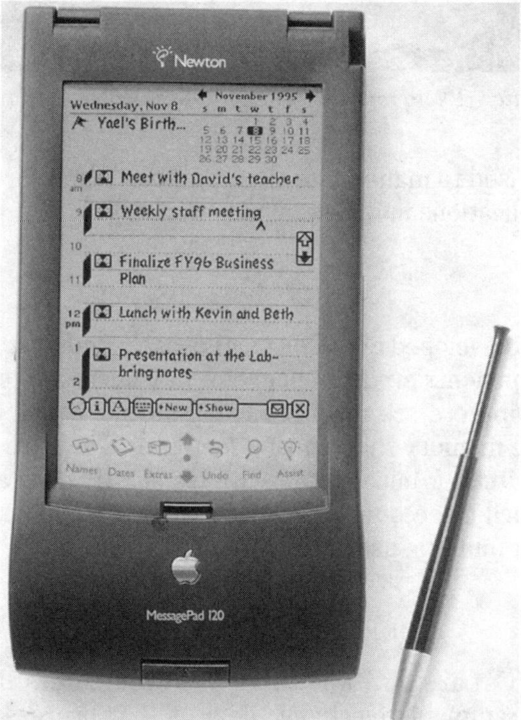

Figure 7-2 A Personal Digital Assistant (PDA).
(Courtesy of Apple Computer, Inc.)

organizer, or spreadsheet. Specialized software applications for such areas as sales, inventory, bar-coding, and medical data collection are available as well. You can also receive wireless messages and alphanumeric pages, as well as send and receive faxes and e-mail or connect with the Internet. Information is entered directly on the screen via a pen or with an onscreen or attachable keyboard. Handwriting recognition software transforms handwriting into typed text. (See Figure 7-2.)

Miniaturization and wireless communications are the basis for **wearable computers,** consisting of a small PC and a battery pack. This type of unit is worn on a belt and includes a head-mounted display consisting of a 0.7-inch diagonal LCD. These systems are used primarily in industrial and field applications for storing documentation, entering inventory data, and similar procedures.

DICTATION EQUIPMENT

Dictation equipment records spoken dictation so that the office professional may key the material later while listening to the playback. Dictating systems use either an endless loop or discrete media. An endless loop system uses a loop of tape that records the dictation and erases it after it has been transcribed, allowing new dictation to be recorded. It resembles a reel-to-reel tape recorder. The tape fits within a case called a "tank." A discrete media dictation system is one in which the recording medium can be removed. It uses cassettes (mini, micro, or standard), magnetic disks, or magnetic belts.

These tapes, disks, and belts are reusable and semipermanent. They may be stored for some time but will eventually deteriorate. Therefore, it is important to have critical information filed on paper or stored on a computer disk.

Dictating systems use analog recording, the same as magnetic audiotapes, or digital recording, which translates the spoken word into the 1s and 0s of binary machine language to interface with a computer. Users of analog systems, the older of the two technologies, can retrieve a document only by fast-forwarding through previous documents on the tape. A cue tone or electronic signal is used to mark the beginning of a document or to alert the transcriber to editing instructions.

Digital systems can store more information in less space, and they offer random access to documents. They also include more efficient editing functions as well as computer compatibility. Insert and delete functions allow the user to dictate changes within the document itself so that the transcriber can work with one continuous document.

Central Dictation System

A central dictation system provides a telephone-like handset for dictation from each executive's office; it can also be accessed from elsewhere by a touch-tone telephone. A central system permits more than one person to record simultaneously.

The following features are found in most central dictation systems:

▲ Digital or analog recording.

▲ Immediate access to transcription.

▲ Automatic job identification.

▲ Display status of job.

▲ Priority coding: Allows the user to designate to the word processing center or transcriber which recording has priority.

▲ Productivity tracking: Provides a printed summary of activity and data to analyze the performance and productivity of the word processing department.

▲ Editing capabilities: Allows corrections to be put on a separate track on the tape from the body of the dictation. Where insertions are indicated, the tape automatically switches to the correction track as it is played back and returns to the right spot on the main track at the end of the insertions.

▲ Programmability to suit the specific needs of a business.

▲ Random access.

▲ Built-in telephone recording.

▲ Voice mail.

▲ Intercom.

▲ Multiple simultaneous inputs and outputs.

▲ Computerized work routing.

▲ Redundant voice storage.

▲ Compatibility with various computer operating systems.

▲ Identification entry.

Desktop Dictation System

A desktop dictation system is about the size of a desktop telephone and may include a conventional handheld microphone or a telephone-like handset. Desktop systems store and record on tape inside the desktop unit. When the document is ready for transcription, the author must remove the tape from the machine and deliver it to the transcriber. The transcriber unit is usually controlled by a foot pedal so the transcriber's hands need not leave the keyboard while typing.

HINT: *A desktop system is useful for offices where two to four people each dictate several hours daily.*

The following features are found in most desktop dictation systems:

▲ Analog recording.

▲ Voice-activated recording: Begins recording when the user begins to speak into the microphone without turning on the machine.

▲ Cue tones: Allows an author to alert the transcriber to the end of a document, beginning of a new document, or special instruction.

▲ Conference recording: Records conversations of two or more people without losing the voices farthest from the microphone.

▲ Pitch and speed control: Automatically corrects for variations in speed and keeps the recorder's voice intelligible at any speed.

▲ Instant review: Allows the user to listen to what has been recorded without rewinding.

▲ Push-button control.

▲ Dual speed recording: Allows user to run the tape at two speeds, with the lower speed doubling the capacity of storage.

▲ Audible fast-forward: Allows user to locate a specific portion on a tape.

▲ Tape counter or liquid crystal display (LCD).

▲ Clocks, alarms, and appointment reminders.

▲ Record meter: Alerts user when voice becomes too soft or too loud for quality recording.

▲ Electrical pause control.

▲ Fail-safe warning: Alerts user to cassette malfunction or approach of end of tape.

▲ Intercom.

▲ Ability to double as answering machine.

Portable Dictation Machines

A portable dictation machine is battery operated and fits in the palm of one's hand. It is about the size of a midsized calculator and has a built-in microphone. The transcriber unit is often controlled by a foot pedal so the transcriber's hands need not leave the keyboard while typing.

The following features are found in most portable dictation machines:

▲ Portability.

▲ Analog recording.

▲ Voice-activated recording.

▲ Cue tones.

- ▲ Push-button control.
- ▲ Dual speed recording.
- ▲ Audible fast-forward.
- ▲ Tape counter or liquid crystal display (LCD).
- ▲ Clocks, alarms, and appointment reminders.
- ▲ Record meter.
- ▲ Electrical pause control.
- ▲ Fail-safe warning.

REPROGRAPHICS

Reprographics is the reproduction of documents by any process that uses light or photography. A wide variety of reprographics equipment is available. The choice of which process to use depends on the quality and quantity of copies needed, cost, and the time factor involved.

Photocopiers

Photocopiers are the most commonly used office machines for reproducing documents. Two imaging technologies are used: analog and digital. An analog system re-flects light through a series of mirrors and lenses directly to a drum, creating a latent image. The drum is applied to the paper, leaving a pattern created by static electricity. Black powder called *toner* then adheres to the statically charged places, creating a copy.

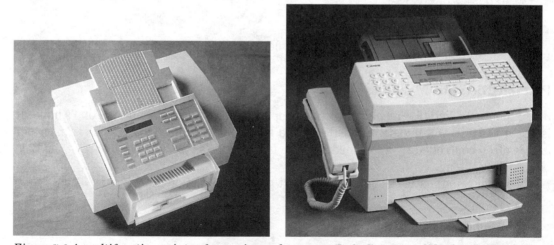

Figure 7-3 A multifunction printer, fax, copier, and scanner. (Left: Courtesy of Hewlett-Packard. Right: Courtesy of Canon Computer Systems, Inc.)

Digital copier technology, based upon the same binary logic as computers and CDs, allows for higher-quality prints. It also gives the user the ability to manipulate images, making digital copies superior to analog copies. However, digital technology is more expensive and slower.

Digital copiers can serve as both a printer and a copier, and many can electronically transmit copies by fax. The two main components are the scanner and the printer. Images can be scanned into a computer, where the image is converted into digital signals. Software makes it possible to manipulate and create changes to stretch, condense, reverse, or shade images. Future models will combine into one unit a copier, fax, scanner, phone, printer, and computer.

There are three categories of copier, based on their speed. High-volume units can produce 50,000 to more than 100,000 copies per month at a speed of 50 to 100 copies per minute (CPM). Medium-volume units can produce 20,000 to 50,000 copies per month at a speed of 20 to 50 CPM. Low-volume units come in three types: low-high units that can produce 10,000 to 20,000 copies per month at a speed of 20 to 30 CPM, low-medium units that can produce 3,000 to 10,000 copies per month at a speed of 15 to 20 CPM, and low-low units that can produce up to 3,000 copies per month at a speed of 10 to 15 CPM.

HINT: *Low-volume copiers are called **convenience copiers** and are suitable for small offices or departments where most jobs are only a few pages in length. Most are small enough to fit on a desktop. Others come with their own stand, which can also be used to store paper and supplies. Few special features are available for low-volume copiers.*

Machines that use one or more toner colors are available. They give users a choice of copy color other than the traditional black. More expensive **color copiers** use a photographic process to produce an exact color reproduction of the original. There are also dual-purpose machines that function as either full-color or as black-and-white copiers.

Some copiers can interface directly with a computer. This feature allows color images on the CRT screen to be immediately captured in the copier. This process provides copies of near-photographic quality.

Many features are available on copiers as options. They are often standard features on high-volume machines. They include:

Automatic document feed (ADF): Multiple originals can be placed in the ADF bin without having to feed one original at a time.

Automatic duplexing: Two-sided copying is done automatically.

Electronic editing: Allows users to manipulate the image of the original document in a cut-and-paste approach to produce modified versions.

Multifunction memory: Preset instructions related to specific types of copying jobs can be set into memory for future recall on frequently run jobs.

Reduction/zoom: Reduces or enlarges a version of the original in order to fit the image on a standard sheet or concentrate on a blown-up section of the original document.

Sorters: A bin sorter can collate copy sets by feeding the output into individual racks or slots on a peripheral device attached to the main copier.

Stapler: Automatically staples the comer of each sorted set of papers at the end of a run.

Three-hole punch: Punches each copy as it exits the copier.

Multiple paper trays: Trays are available in several sizes so that when a different size of paper is needed, one tray can be removed and replaced with the desired size. For example, a three-tray system may use one drawer for holding 8½-by-11-inch paper, the second for legal-sized paper, and the third for letterhead, transparencies, or other special stock.

System stand: Offers a total paper capacity of several reams of paper.

Some copiers include built-in electronic information displays to help the user. Some allow for restricted access. Another feature is automatic copy-quality adjustment. Standard serial and parallel interfaces permit the use of copiers with PCs. Other options permit access to local area networks (LANs).

Printers

Printers provide the printed output, or hard copy, from a computer. They vary widely in speed, quality of output, available printing fonts, and cost. When selecting a printer, it is necessary to relate one's office tasks and budget to the available printing hardware. Two categories of printers exist—**impact** and **nonimpact.** Impact printers strike a ribbon, similar to typewriters, whereas nonimpact printers create characters through the use of heat or light or by spraying ink on a page.

DOT MATRIX PRINTERS

Dot matrix printers strike the ribbon with a series of tiny dots to form a character. They are relatively inexpensive and used when the emphasis is on information and not on the visual quality of the output. A top-line dot matrix printer, often called a near-letter-quality (NLQ) printer, has a larger number of pins in its printhead than the average dot matrix printer, typically 24 rather than 9.

HINT: *Impact printers can handle multipart forms and produce up to five or six copies. Dot matrix printers print at a higher speed than letter-quality ones and are good for draft output.*

NONIMPACT PRINTERS

Nonimpact printers are noiseless but cannot make carbons. There are four types of nonimpact printers: ink jet printers, thermal-transfer printers, laser printers (of which there are several varieties), and plotters.

Ink jet printers: spray ink onto the paper in the shape of the character intended. Printer speeds range from two to six pages per minute. They can print in both black and multiple colors.

Thermal-transfer printers: create characters and images by melting a wax-based ink off the printer ribbon and onto the paper. These printers are quiet and produce high-quality output. Their speed is about 4 to 8 pages a minute.

Laser printers: use a laser beam to form images on a light-sensitive drum. These images are then transferred onto the paper a page at a time; thus they are sometimes called page printers. These machines print at a rate of 4 to 8 pages per minute for low-end desktop models and 10 to 17 pages per minute for high-end equipment. Copies are of the highest quality, approaching typeset quality. Laser printers can use a variety of fonts. They can also produce forms, letterheads, and signatures.

PostScript printers: are laser printers that use a page description language, or page-formatting program, called PostScript, which facilitates the printer's communicating with the computer. High-resolution graphics can be printed on PostScript printers. They also have a wide range of available typefaces that can be scaled to various sizes.

Desktop publishing laser printers: are essentially business-quality typesetters. They can handle any amount of graphics and include a range of built-in, high-quality typefaces.

Intelligent printer/copiers: combine the technology of the microprocessor, laser, and photocopier, so they have features of both printers and copiers. They print a page at a time at a rate of 50 to 100 pages per minute. A microprocessor allows them to accept text, graphics, and instructions from computers, word processors, or magnetic media. They produce hard copy directly from the digitized information received.

HINT: *Depending on the number and types of fonts available with your laser printer, you may wish to purchase optional font cartridges. These contain the instructions and memory your printer will need to print the fonts. Soft fonts, on the other hand, are fonts that can be loaded from your computer into your printer's memory; they can be used when your printer has adequate internal memory.*

Plotters: are used for printing computer graphics and are used in computer-aided design (CAD). High-quality output is created by the movement of ink pens over the paper. A variety of color pens are available.

Multifunction Processors

A **multifunction processor** combines the capabilities of a plain paper fax, a laser printer, a copier, a scanner, and a PC fax board. Users can send a fax, print, and make copies simultaneously, as well as scan paper documents directly into a PC for instant storage, manipulation, or duplication.

Offset Printing

Offset printing is of high quality and is used for large-volume production. Usually offset printing is done by a printer or a copy shop, not by someone in the office. Paper, aluminum, or plastic (electrostatic) masters are used for offset printing. Paper masters are good for 25 to 3,000 copies, the plastic for up to 5,000 copies, and the aluminum for up to 50,000 copies.

Phototypesetting

Phototypesetting is a photographic printing process that produces high-quality documents. Characters are formed at high speeds on photosensitive paper or film. This film is then developed and proofread. Material can be input directly through the phototypesetting equipment or on a personal computer and sent to the phototypesetter on a disk. Many varieties of type sizes and fonts are available. Brochures, newspapers, promotional materials, and books are generally prepared with this process.

HINT: *One typeset page is often the equivalent of two typed pages.*

Micrographics

The paper bottleneck in many offices can be efficiently handled with micrographic systems. Micrographics is the process of recording and reducing paper documents or computer-generated information onto film for long-term storage and archival. Records are photographed and reduced so that many small images in color or black and white will appear on a reel or sheet of film. The micrographic media used to store file information are known as **microforms**. A reader is needed to enlarge the microform image and display it for viewing. Microfilm and microfiche are the best-known types of microform.

Micrographics are usually finned and developed by micrographics service bureaus. These companies can also provide for document pickup, inspection and quality control, duplication of microforms, and the sale or lease of micrographics equipment.

MICROGRAPHICS FORMATS

Roll film: the least expensive form of microfilm, is usually found in 16mm, 35mm, or 105mm sizes. The 16mm roll is used for storing 8½-by-11-inch or 8½-by-14-inch records, such as correspondence and legal documents. The 35mm film is used for large records such as engineering drawings, newspaper pages, and blueprints. Roll film can be stored in cartons or cabinets.

Cartridges: use a plastic collar snapped over the film roll, becoming a magazine that self-threads to film readers. Cartridges are used extensively with automated readers, cameras, and automated retrieval systems.

Aperture cards: contain a microfilm image or images mounted on a small card. Information about the microfilm record or records is printed on or punched into the remainder of the card. Aperture cards are used to store large documents such as maps or engineering drawings.

Film jackets: are clear, plastic carriers with one or more sleeves or channels designed to hold 16mm or 35mm filmstrips, or a combination of the two. Jackets are available in a variety of sizes, the most common being 4 inches by 6 inches. Jackets allow the user to update film files easily and quickly by removing outdated strips and inserting newer material.

Microfiche: is suitable for filming reports, periodicals, catalogs, parts lists, and other collections of pages on a permanent, unitized microform. It contains rows of document on a sheet of film about 4 inches by 6 inches. Full-color or black-and-white images can appear on microfiche. A 4-by-6-inch fiche produced with a 24-times reduction ratio can hold up to 98 document images. One produced with a 48-times reduction ratio can hold up to 270 images.

HINT: *About 200 fiche can be filed per inch of space in a file drawer.*

Ultrafiche: is an extension of microfiche; it allows more images per inch than any other type of microform. It is possible to store up to 1,000 pages on a 3-by-5-inch sheet of film.

Film folios: are aperture cards the size of microfiche inserted into jackets.

METHODS TO PRODUCE MICROFORMS

Three methods exist for producing microforms:

1. Photography by micrographics cameras, either rotary or planetary is one method. Rotary photography produces roll microfilm; planetary photography produces fiche.
2. Computer output microfilm (COM) is a method of microfilming in which computer data are printed on film, processed, and duplicated. The use of computer printouts can be minimized or eliminated with this process.
3. Computer-assisted retrieval (CAR) uses a computer to retrieve documents stored on microfilm. CAR systems can utilize bar coding or optical character recognition for indexing. Records can be accessed in various combinations; for example, accounts with an outstanding balance or clients in a specific geographic location could be accessed.

READERS, READER/PRINTERS, AND RETRIEVAL TERMINALS

Microform readers are categorized as follows:

Handheld or *projection readers:* Simple, inexpensive image magnifiers that are held to the eye for viewing or projecting images onto external screens.

Portable readers: Lightweight, briefcase, or smaller-sized full-screen readers powered by a conventional outlet or rechargeable batteries.

Desk or *console reader/printers:* Stationary readers that are also capable of producing full-sized paper copies of microform originals.

Desk or *console retrieval terminals* and *retrieval terminal/printers:* Stationary reading units with automatic image-seeking capabilities. Retrieval terminal/printers produce full-sized paper copies of microform originals. On some reader/printers, the printer is an integral part of the reader; in others it is a modular unit that attaches to the reader.

Computer screens or facsimile: Sophisticated microfilm readers can be tied in with computer systems using a device called a "jukebox." The user calls up a file on the PC, then the computer searches for the document and directs the jukebox to select the proper microfilm cassette for loading into the reader. The image is automatically called up, digitized, and output into the user's PC.

Optical Disk Systems

Optical disk storage systems are state-of-the-art devices based on laser beams and precision optics. An optical disk system is made up of a number of components. Scanners are the major input source for optical disk-based systems. Drives record documents in digital form onto WORM (write once, read many times) disks and retrieve documents from all types of disks. Jukeboxes are automated disk libraries. The control computer manages the system by cross-referencing data, keeping audit trails, and providing necessary reports. Software is used for image enhancement, database management, and operating systems. Monitors give high-resolution images, and laser printers give printed output.

The major differences from micrographics systems are the following:

Packing density: Some optical disk systems can hold up to 400,000 pages of text.

Retrieval: Documents can be retrieved in seconds.

Transmission speed: Optical disks store documents in a digital form, which means they can be transmitted on a local area network (LAN) or telephone line in two or three seconds.

Paperwork flow: Optical disk systems manage the paperwork flow and control the pacing and sequencing of paperwork by automatically prompting individuals to the next step.

Integration with other systems: Optical systems can interface with other electronic systems. Different users can simultaneously access data on the same file or document.

An optical disk system performs the following functions:

- It scans images from either paper or microfilm.
- It stores documents containing letters and numbers as well as graphics.
- It displays documents on a CRT terminal.
- It searches and retrieves documents.

- It prints documents on paper and/or microfilm.
- It copies documents to and from computer hard disks and optical disks.

Optical Character Scanning

An **optical character reader (OCR)** is a computer device combined with software that can copy graphics or read text in a variety of typefaces and styles. The copy is stored in the computer and is reproduced immediately on a CRT for correction and revisions. The accuracy rate for text recognition is about 95 percent, and the technology is constantly improving. Photographs, drawings, and charts can be scanned for use in desktop publishing or electronic filing in black and white or color.

TYPES OF SCANNERS

There are two primary types of scanners. A **handheld scanner** may be held in the hand and manually swept across the document or image. These have a scan width 2 to 5 inches. A **page** or **desktop scanner** can handle a full page at a time.

Page scanners are further divided into three categories:

- *Sheet-feed:* These operate by automatically moving the document to be scanned via rollers in much the same manner as a fax machine.

- *Flatbed:* These have a flat top upon which the document to be scanned is placed face-down, in much the same manner as on a photocopier. Typically, they offer the best scan results and are the most expensive.

- *Overhead* or *copyboard:* These look like overhead projectors. They scan documents and objects from above. Documents are placed face-up on the scanner's flat scanning surface.

SCANNER RESOLUTION

A scanner's **resolution** is the number of dots it can sample for each linear inch of the document. Common resolutions are 75, 100, 150, 200, 300, and 400 dots per inch (dpi). By comparison, most laser printers have a 300 dpi resolution.

INTELLIGENT DOCUMENTS

A new DataGlyph technology enables scanners and papers to carry a library's worth of information on a sheet of paper. The glyphs are small areas on a document marked with tiny dot patterns smaller than a hundredth of an inch wide. Information is compressed in these spaces that would ordinarily cover an entire page and is scanned into a computer to be interpreted.

APPLICATIONS

Scanners have various uses in the office. Among the most important are the following:

- Desktop publishing uses scanners to incorporate images into a computer or onto paper as well as for character recognition of keyed manuscripts.
- Scanners are used with databases to incorporate price lists, tabular data, and other text as well as for image databases such as those used by real estate companies and police departments.
- Scanners are used in information storage to store documents in organizations with intensive paperwork operations, such as banks, hospitals, and government agencies.
- Paper documents can be scanned into a personal computer and transmitted via a facsimile board to a fax machine.

TELECOMMUNICATIONS EQUIPMENT

Telecommunications uses telephone and computer technology to transmit voice, image, data, and textual information from one place to another. The most used telecommunications device today, outside of the telephone, is the facsimile machine, or fax.

Telephones

A variety of telephone equipment is available that can efficiently meet the needs of any organization.

The standard *touch-tone phone* uses a 12-button keypad arrangement. It has ten buttons with the digits 0–9, plus two special buttons, * (star) and # (pound), that activate various automatic electronic features. Many touch-tone phones are also equipped with an automatic telephone dialer that can store from 15 to 31 numbers. It can dial one of these numbers at the touch of a button.

A *call director* is a desktop switchboard allowing a receptionist or executive assistant to pick up calls that come in on 18, 30, or as many as 60 extensions. One receptionist or assistant can be responsible for the phones of a number of people who may not be at their desks. Call directors usually connect to larger switching system devices in the telephone system.

A *speakerphone set* consists of a microphone and loudspeaker and permits the user to carry on a telephone conversation from anywhere in an office without lifting the receiver from its rest. The microphone picks up the user's voice and the loudspeakers broadcast the voice of the party at the other end of the fine. A speakerphone also allows a group of people to talk through one phone.

Cordless *portable telephones* are also available as well as *cellular phones* for use in cars or airplanes.

VOICE MAIL

Voice mail, or *store-and-forward messaging,* combines the technology of a telephone, computer, and recording device. It stores messages for immediate or later delivery. Access to the system is gained by entering a code on a rotary or touch-tone telephone. A recording tells the user to speak the message into the phone and then to dial the voice-mail number of the recipient. The system codes the message into digital data and attempts to deliver it immediately. If the system cannot deliver the message, it is filed in the computer's memory for later delivery. When the recipient dials into the system to get his or her messages, the caller's voice is reconstructed and the message is repeated.

SWITCHING SYSTEMS

Single line telephones are ordinarily used in homes and small offices. They have only a single line available, so it is not possible for two or more people to place calls at the same time.

For larger businesses, however, the routing of calls to and from the public lines of the telephone company to the private fines within an organization is handled through a switching system. These systems include key systems, PBX systems, and Centrex.

Multiline telephones, or *key phones,* allow one person to handle several lines, each with a separate button on the phone. These telephones may be equipped with up to 30 buttons placed above, below, or beside the dial. If a line is in use, a light by the button is lit. To place a call, the caller pushes an unlit line button and dials the number. A flashing light signals an incoming call; to answer it, an individual pushes the flashing line's button and picks up the receiver. If a call comes in on one line while an individual is on another, the second line can be answered after the first caller is put on hold by pressing the hold button. The person on hold cannot hear the other conversation.

PBX systems (private branch exchange) are used by large companies to channel calls through a central switchboard. A PBX requires a full-time operator to connect incoming calls with company extensions. Internal and outgoing calls, however, are made without operator assistance. Outgoing calls can be made directly, usually by dialing "9" to make a connection to an outside line.

A *PABX system* (private automatic branch exchange) has more automated features than a PBX system. It may be attended by an operator or may work unattended. An unattended, cordless switchboard distributes calls automatically to the proper extensions in the order in which the calls are received. Lighted buttons indicate when lines are engaged. These models have replaced older switching systems that required the attendant to manipulate a series of jacks and plugs.

Most PBX and PABX systems feature voice mail. Some systems feature voice recognition, which allows a caller to choose among various options within the voice mail by simply saying a number. For example, a user may speak the personal identification number of the mailbox. The system would then transfer the caller to the correct mailbox and offer a list of options, such as to hear, send, or delete messages. The caller says the number of the option and the system responds with the appropriate function.

Some systems feature *automatic number identification* (ANI), which logs the caller's phone number for the recipient the moment a call is received. This lets a caller record a callback message without having to leave a phone number.

A *Centrex system* allows a call from the outside or a call from one extension to another to be made without an operator. Centrex systems provide direct internal dialing, so that all calls go directly to the number dialed without use of a switchboard. Every telephone extension in the system usually has the same three-digit prefix as the company's main number, and the last four digits are different. If a caller does not know a particular Centrex extension number, he or she can dial the company's principal number and ask the operator to make the connection.

A *Computerized Branch Exchange* (CBX) uses microcomputer technology to add a variety of features to the Centrex system. Program features include automatic callback, call forwarding, call hold, call backup, call waiting signal, three-way conference calls, and call transfer.

Fax Machines

A fax machine, also called a facsimile machine, instantaneously transmits a copy (or facsimile) of a document from one location to another. Pages of the document are fed into the transmitting machine, electronically digitized, and sent via phone lines to the designated receiving fax machine. The receiving machine converts the digital transmission back into characters and prints it out on paper.

TYPES OF FAX MACHINES

There are two types of fax technology available: thermal-paper, which uses specially coated paper, and plain paper, which uses regular 8½-by-11-inch copy paper. Thermal paper comes in continuous rolls that are useful for receiving documents of nonstandard lengths.

Faxes can be:

- Stand-alone, desktop units.
- Personal fax units sized to fit into a briefcase and designed for use at home or when traveling.
- Public fax machines, much like a public phone booth, that are available in such places as hotels, shopping malls, airports, and post offices.
- Units that double as desktop copiers, answering machines, and regular telephones.
- Machines that are compatible with cellular phones.
- Color fax units that transmit and receive color photographs, color slides, video images, color images, color documents, and transparencies.
- Voice-to-fax units that allow users to call a fax machine and leave a voice message that will be converted by the machine into a printed document.

Advantages of fax machines include the following:

Speed: An 8½-by-11-inch page takes an average of 17 seconds to transmit; no rekeying or document preparation is necessary.

Ease of installation: It can be located at any site where power and a telephone outlet are available.

Input flexibility: Sketches, charts, maps, and photographs can be transmitted or received.

Automatic operation: The operator merely needs to insert the copy; the machine handles the rest.

Fax machines range from low-end to middle-range to high-end units. Capabilities and features in each category vary. A low-end unit differs from a middle-range facsimile machine in type of receiving and transmitting paper used; paper roll size; and receiving tray, automatic cutter, and autodial features. High-end fax machines use plain paper. They also include the capability to restrict unsolicited transmissions to and from the units, increased memory capacity for additional automatic features, and faster transmission speeds.

The majority of units installed since 1981 are fully digital and capable of transmitting a page in less than a minute. They are also usually compatible with older, slower machines. Advances in technology now allow the latest machines to send a document in less than five seconds. However, the actual printing can take longer.

FAX FEATURES AND FUNCTIONS

The following are some of the major features and functions of fax machines:

Autodial: Recalls preset numbers from internal memory and automatically dials the destination number of the receiving facsimile unit.

Automatic reduction: The size of the incoming document can be changed to fit the available paper size. This is important because plain paper fax machines must print on standard 8½-by-11-inch paper.

Delayed timer transmission: Documents can be placed into the fax machine, which is then programmed to send the information at a preset time. Newer units have the capability to send to multiple locations at different times.

Fall-back speed: Allows the sending unit automatically to reduce the transmission speed when it senses a problem with the telephone fine quality. Note that reducing the speed helps to ensure a better copy quality on the receiving end.

Interfaces: Allow the fax unit to be connected with other equipment to meet special communications needs. It can receive from TWX/Telex, send and receive from personal computers, and send and receive encrypted messages. (Encryption is the conversion of text into code.)

Sender I.D./time date stamp: Prints the telephone number of the sending fax unit on top of each page received. It also prints the time and date.

Transmission log: Records and prints out a list of all transmissions received. It lists the number of pages of each batch of transmitted documents received, date and time, and sending unit telephone number.

APPLICATIONS

Fax machines are especially useful for these applications:

Business communications: To transmit documents or photos. Faxes are cheaper and faster than overnight mail or private messenger.

Financial accounting: To handle customer credit information requests, process invoices, and forward ledger or statistical data cheaply and accurately.

Sales: To transmit order notices, delivery schedules, spec sheets, drawings, proposals, and price quotes.

Purchasing: To expedite quotations and orders and to speed order confirmations.

Retailing: To speed delivery information, inventory status, and price change notices.

Advertising and public relations: To meet media deadlines and to forward publicity releases, product photographs, and drafts for approval.

Manufacturing and engineering operations: To transmit design and drawing changes or new procedures.

Law enforcement, news services, weather map communications, and medical data transmission are also areas in which fax transmissions are highly useful and highly used.

PC-FAX

The PC-fax is a combination of hardware and software that enables a personal computer to mimic the operations of a fax machine. The hardware is usually comprised of an expansion board or external unit that plugs into the personal computer, a modem, a scanner, and a printer.

A PC-fax has the following features:

Background modes: Users continue to perform other tasks while the system is operating.

Automatic date/time: Documents are printed with date and time.

Autodialing: Allows users to begin transmission by selecting a fax number stored in the system's directory.

Autoanswer: Receives messages without the sender and receiver establishing a voice telephone call.

Unattended or delayed timer: Allows users to preprogram a transmission to occur at a specific time and date.

Automatic polling: Allows users to contact remote units and request transmission of their documents.

Mailbox capabilities: Allows multiple users access to a single local PC-fax system. Users check their individual mailboxes for messages.

Multiple transmissions: Allows users to transmit to various sites in a predefined order.

FAX DIRECTORIES

As the use of the fax as a primary form of communication has grown, fax directories have been published. They offer a comprehensive listing of companies and private individuals using fax machines to send and receive correspondence. The directories include the company name, fax number, and other pertinent information, such as office hours or street address. Such directories also offer on-line databases with similar listings.

HINT: *An on-line data base is useful for PC-fax users, who can use their PCs to review the directory listings.*

PUBLIC FAX SERVICES

Public fax services are available to companies without their own fax machine. Senders must pay a telephone charge, a basic transmittal fee with additional charges for additional pages, and a delivery charge if applicable. The costs and transmission times vary. Recipients may pick up the documents or have them delivered. Delivery in foreign countries is to a business center or designated post office.

HINT: *To locate addresses and telephone or fax numbers of public fax services, use the* Public Fax Directory. *This directory lists public fax service. Directory and fax referral assistance is also available from the toll-free number 800-USA-FAX1.*

Teletypewriters

Another telecommunications device is the teletypewriter; however, it is being replaced by the fax machine. Teletypewriters transmit and receive only alphanumeric information over phone lines; they cannot transmit graphics. Some companies have their own teletypewriter networks. Many companies use one of Western Union's teletypewriter networks, Telex or TWX. "Telex" stands for teleprinter exchange and is generally used for international transmissions. "TWX" stands for teletypewriter exchange. Both systems permit a user to keyboard information and then send it to another Telex or TWX unit over standard telephone lines. The system provides the immediacy of a phone message as well as the documentation of a letter.

Major disadvantages are the following:

- Information must be keyed into the teletypewriter.
- Graphics cannot be sent via Telex.
- The cost is about four times that of a fax.

OTHER ELECTRIC AND ELECTRONIC EQUIPMENT

In addition to the major office equipment outlined in the preceding sections, other equipment includes:

Shredder: Used to shred documents containing sensitive information. Some fit on a desktop while others are large, free-standing units that can handle up to 140,000 sheets of paper an hour.

Electronic copy board: Electronically copies ideas, diagrams, or charts written on the copy board and prints them onto paper for distribution. Used especially for meetings.

Electric copyholder: Allows a line guide to advance down printed copy as a foot pedal or hand switch is operated by a typist. Generally made in four sizes to accommodate letter size, legal size, and two sizes of ledger paper.

Electric letter opener: Opens envelopes automatically.

Electric collator: Collates pages of material automatically.

Electric pencil sharpener: Automatically sharpens lead pencils.

SELECTING OFFICE EQUIPMENT

Rapidly evolving technology, the multitude of vendors in the market, technical jargon, announcements of new products nearly every day, and the threat of companies going out of business make selection of office equipment a difficult task. What is brand new today can be obsolete next year.

The following guidelines will help you evaluate prospective equipment for your office:

1. Analyze your office's needs. A thorough needs analysis helps to determine equipment applications, the number of users, frequency of use, and types of documents produced.

2. Identify available products. Match the available products to the information gathered in the needs analysis. Determine the available products by talking to equipment dealers, reviewing sales literature, and reading office-related trade magazines. Ask the following:

    * What are the benefits that differentiate one brand from another?
    * Will the features meet your departmental needs?
    * Is the equipment easy to use?
    * Is the equipment compatible with other equipment in the office?
    * What software and accessories are available?
    * Is service available after the sale? By whom? Is there an 800 phone number for troubleshooting problems? What are the terms of the warranty?
    * Are the costs of installing the equipment included in the price?
    * Is training free or is there a charge? What type of training is available?

3. Create a comparative chart of available products. Make a list of the information you have gathered by categories in the first column and put the products you have studied across the other columns. In each column, list the comparative information you have gathered on that product. You may wish to assign both a weight and a score, from a low of 1 to a high of 10, for each item. The weight is an estimate of how important each item is. Multiply the weight by the score for each item and then total the weighted scores. In this way you can quantitatively compare the prospective equipment choices.

HINT: *Consider using a spreadsheet program for this purpose. This will allow you to adjust the size of the rows and columns as needed to accommodate available information. The scores assigned to each item can also be automatically totaled for you.*

4. Ask for a demonstration of the equipment and/or a trial use. A thorough demonstration, or preferably trial use, is important before making a final decision. Some dealers will allow prospective customers to use the equipment for one or two weeks at no cost. Both the demonstration and the trial use will provide valuable insights that are not possible through any other form of evaluation.

5. Make a dealer or vendor comparison. A thorough review of the dealer or vendor is needed to avoid problems after the sale. Ask the following questions:

   • How many service technicians are employed?
   • What is the average tenure of technicians and number of placements serviced by the firm?
   • What is the average response time to a service call?
   • Are parts and supplies readily available?
   • Is a list of references available that can be randomly called? Ask the references the same questions you are asking the dealer and compare the answers. Ask if the service was as good six or more months after the sale as it was in the beginning. Also ask the reference to identify any major service problems, along with how they were resolved. Are there any patterns to the answers received from the various references you called?

INVENTORY AND MAINTENANCE OF EQUIPMENT

With more electronic equipment entering the office, the responsibility for maintaining it is increasing. Some recommended procedures will help you do this.

1. Make a card record for each piece of equipment. The record should contain the name, address, and phone number of the vendor or dealer; date of purchase; model number; serial number; and basic information regarding the warranty and/or service contract. These cards should be filed alphabetically and periodically updated

as the equipment is serviced. A yearly inventory of each piece of equipment should also be done and noted on the card.

HINT: *A database software program can facilitate this process. You can use one that is part of a spreadsheet program or use a stand-alone program.*

2. Consider purchasing a service or maintenance contract. These are available for an additional monthly or annual fee. A service or maintenance contract extends the warranty on the equipment for a longer period of time. Most contracts include options for either mail-in or carry-in service. Others will offer a pick-up and delivery service or on-site repair. Some will also provide a temporary replacement.
3. Establish a maintenance schedule. Have the equipment serviced on a regular basis. Prevention through proper servicing can help to avoid unnecessary downtime. The maintenance schedule should be maintained by the equipment operator or, in the case of executives, by their administrative assistants. Service contracts are available that include periodic cleaning and/or testing of equipment components.
4. Use cleaning products on a regular basis. These products include cleaning kits for personal computers, glass-cleaning products for copiers and CRT screens, and dusters for electronic typewriters.

HINT: *Weekly cleaning of personal computers is recommended, focusing on the screen, keyboard, disk drive, printer, and housing to remove dust and dirt.*

TROUBLESHOOTING YOUR PC

Personal computing is more than creating document—it is problem solving. Understanding the task at hand, knowing what the task requires, and determining if there really is a problem comprise the one-two-three scenario of problem solving.

Understanding the Task at Hand

When working with computers, this involves an understanding of:

- The type of processor, that is, 286, 386, 486, Pentium, or Mac.
- The amount and type of memory, including RAM and hard disk.
- The number and type of disks, that is, 3½- or 5¼-inch floppy disks, CD-ROMs, or read/write optical disks.
- The options and adapters, for example, modems, serial ports, and math coprocessor.
- DOS and its commands.
- How to read the CONFIG.SYS and SYSTEM.INI files.
- How to remove and insert the components and operate any switches or change jumpers.

It is critical to both become familiar with your system's documentation and keep the technical support telephone numbers for both your hardware and software easily available. When you call a technical support line for help, be prepared to answer questions about the items listed above and take your time in describing what you perceive to be the problem.

Knowing What the Task Requires

Identify whether it is a hardware or a software problem. If it is hardware-related, first check for loose plugs on the back of the CPU and make sure the power is on for all components. Do not take the CPU apart or remove any of the inner workings. If it is a software problem, don't begin to delete or reinstall the software. You could lose valuable data files. Write down exactly what happened and also any unusual error commands that appeared on the screen. This way you will be better prepared to answer your technical support rep's questions.

Determining if There Really Is a Problem

Shutting down the system and rebooting the computer can often clear up a hardware or a software problem. When it does not, follow these steps:

1. Look for visual clues, such as fan speed, flickering or nonoperational display, broken cables, spilled coffee or other liquids, etc. Dirt around the fan inlet or around the fan, a weak power supply to the system, or a short from the spilled liquid are possible culprits.
2. Listen for audible clues, including noises from disk drives, error codes from the speaker, or snapping/popping sounds from inside the power display. Noticeable groaning when the system starts may indicate a weak or insufficient power supply.
3. Wiggle the connectors on the back of the CPU or unplug them and inspect the pins. They may be loose or bent. If this doesn't help, begin disconnecting cables, one at a time, and replacing each with one from another computer.
4. If you can't reboot your computer, the problem may be related to your CONFIG.SYS or SYSTEM.INI files. In this case, use your emergency disk. If you don't have one, create one as soon as possible. Also, invest in quality utility software— it's good insurance!
5. If your computer is still not working, call your information systems department or the customer support number provided with your equipment.

PURCHASING ENVIRONMENTALLY EFFICIENT HARDWARE

Consider the "green factor" for your PC and peripheral purchases. The "green factor" refers to energy-efficient computers, monitors, and printers that carry the federal Environmental Protection Agency's (EPA) Energy Star logo. Hardware with the Energy Star logo is great for the planet and it contributes to your employer's bottom line. The EPA now publishes listings of Energy Star–compliant computers, monitors, and printers on the Internet (http://www.epa.gov; look under EPA Gopher, Consumer Information). To qualify for this list, products must meet the EPA requirements of using 30 watts or less for PCs, monitors, and printers that print up to 14 pages per minute (ppm) and 15 watts or less for printers that print 7 pages or fewer per minute.

Here are some things to look for when purchasing new hardware:

Packaging

- Packaging made out of recycled materials.
- Containers that use no ozone-depleting materials in their construction.
- Packaging that can be burned without releasing toxic gases.

Computers

- Computers that have power-down capability when not in use and use 30 watts or less in a power-saving mode.
- Computers that use a maximum of 40 watts when in a running mode.
- Computer that use power-down software.
- Computer that have sleep modes for processor and hard drives.
- Eventually, computers that have eliminated cooling fans.

Video Display

- Built-in power manager features that reduce electricity consumption from 0 to no more than 10 watts in sleep mode.
- Low-emission monitors that meet the Swedish low radiation standards.
- Thin, flat panel liquid crystal display (LCD) screens instead of cathode ray tubes (CRTs).
- Recyclable CRT tubes and monitor casings.

Printers

- Power savers that reduce consumption to 10 watts or less in sleep mode.
- Toner cartridge recycling programs with free United Parcel Service (UPS) pick-up.
- Printers that do not deplete the ozone layer.

Computer software consists of programmed instructions that direct and control a computer's operations. Mainframes, minicomputers, and personal computers all use software. Software programs can be purchased from equipment manufacturers, vendors whose specialty is designing software, or retail software stores.

Software falls into two categories: systems software and applications software. Systems software governs the operation of the computer. Applications software includes programs that perform specific applications, such as word processing.

SYSTEMS SOFTWARE

Systems software includes operating systems, programming languages, and utilities. An **operating system** is a group of programs that act as an interpreter and manager for the computer, display monitor, and any peripherals, such as a printer. The operating system also directs and interprets information moving to and from disk drives. Some operating systems are multitasking systems, that is, they can process more than one task at a time.

Microsoft Corporation's operating systems MS-DOS, Windows 3.x, Windows 95, and Windows NT are the most popular. Windows 95 and Windows NT (used for computer networks) are next-generation operating systems that are intended to unlock the 32-bit processing power of 486 and Pentium computers. The 3.x Windows system is intended for 16-bit processors. Faster access speeds and better multitasking capability are the major advantages of switching to the new 32-bit system. In addition, the new windows graphical interface is supposedly easier to use.

Benefits include a friendly interface; support for long file names (up to 255 characters); plug and play technology that automatically installs compatible disk drives, sound cards, printers, scanners, and fax modems; 32-bit multitasking that enables end-users to run several programs simultaneously; faster printing; improved video performance; and an electronic in-box that supports faxes, e-mail, and on-line services. Internet connectivity is another benefit of the new Windows operating system. Microsoft provides TCP/IP and Winsock, the software need to connect to the Internet. Here are some guidelines when installing Windows 95:

CHAPTER 8

OFFICE

COMPUTER

SOFTWARE

1. Protect your investment in your current Windows 3.x setup. Begin by backing up all of your data files. It's not necessary to back up your applications. Also, back up the following Windows directory files: *initialization* (.INI) files, *registry* (.DAT) files, *password* (.PWL) files, and *Program Manager group* (.GRP) files.

2. Back up all critical *real-mode drivers* specified in *CONFIG.SYS* and *AUTOEXEC.BAT,* as well as your CONFIG.SYS and AUTOEXEC.BAT files located in the root directory of your startup drive.

3. Proprietary network configuration files and logon scripts plus any file crucial to the operation of any part of your system all need to be backed up.

4. Maximize disk space by compressing (Zip) seldom-used directories or files. You can also eliminate backup, temp, and duplicate files.

5. Use a utility program, such as Win 95 Advisor, to prepare your system for the transition. This program will enable you to check the compatibility of your hardware devices and software with Windows 95. It will also determine if your system has enough disk space or which part of your hardware configuration needs to be upgraded, as well as providing recommendations and options to help you plan ahead and avoid problems.

6. Upgrade any utility protection program you may have installed, such as Norton Utilities (NU). NU's *trade-up edition,* for example, includes a pre-installation tune-up to ease your migration to Windows 95. The utility and virus protection system you used with Windows 3.x won't work under Windows 95. Also, make sure that your system does not have the antivirus check enabled in the system's BIOS. Consult your system's hardware manual for assistance if needed.

7. Run SCANDISK.EXE with surface scan for problems with the files and condition of the media. Windows 95 automatically runs this file to check for problems on your hard disk; however, setup cannot continue until they are fixed, delaying the installation. Check your MS-DOS documentation for assistance,

8. Remove any Terminate and Stay Resident (TSR) programs, such as Norton Desktop for Windows or PC Tools, since they will interfere with the installation.

9. Remove all third-party disk cache programs and replace them with SMART-DRV.EXE provided with MS-DOS or Windows 3.x during the install. Be sure to remove all references to it from your CONFIG.SYS and AUTOEXEC.BAT files.

10. Remove all third-party Windows Desktops or shells, such as Side Bar by Quarterdeck.

11. During setup you will have to determine under which directory you want to install Windows 95, select the type of setup, and create a startup or rescue disk.

Keep a telephone help-line handy. Don't spend endless hours trying to solve an installation problem. Call Microsoft for help! In the United States, call 206-635-7000; in Canada, call 905-568-4494. Text telephone services are available for the deaf or hard-of-hearing using a TT/TDD modem and dialing 206-635-4948 in the United States and 905-568-9641 in Canada.

Other popular operating systems include OS/2 by IBM, a multitasking system that works for single users as well as within networks; UNIX by AT&T, a multiuser, multitasking operating system as well as several variants such as Ultrix and Xenix; and Macintosh by Apple Corporation, an operating system with a graphical user interface.

Programming languages are special languages that allow users to communicate with computers. The most frequently used are C, a general-purpose programming language; FORTRAN, which was developed by IBM for scientific, engineering, and mathematical operations; COBOL, which was developed especially for business applications and in which English-like statements are used; Pascal, a flexible language useful for scientific programming; RPG (Report Program Generator), which is used on many small computers to generate reports; and BASIC, an interactive language that allows communication directly with the computer. Microprocessors as well as many small, business-oriented computers use BASIC.

Utilities are special programs that perform such tasks as copying files or transferring files from one storage medium to another. Examples of typical utilities include:

System protection utilities: These programs operate in the background constantly, monitoring vital system resources and data integrity and automatically taking corrective action when needed. Generally, tools for system protection and data recovery are provided. For example, Norton Utilities by Symantec optimizes and defragments your disks to improve access times and enhance the chance of full recovery in the event of a crash. Automated 32-bit file optimization supports most common compression formats.

Document transfer utilities: Exchanging data files across different operating system platforms—that is, between MS-DOS, Windows, Macintosh, and UNIX—is complex. In the past, documents were saved in an unformatted ASCII text format or translators were used to convert files. Document transfer software provides portability to documents so you can use them across platforms, networks, and operating systems.

Data compression utilities: Electronic file transfer via a modem can benefit from file compression software. Examples of typical compression applications include e-mail file attachments, Internet file uploads and downloads, files containing voice or video clips, and transfer of slide presentations to duplicating services. To compress a file is to reduce the size of that file without losing any of the information inside it. Compression provides the obvious benefit of reducing the amount of time required to transfer files from one computer to another, saving online phone charges. A popular and reliable compression program is PKZIP from PKWare, Inc. PKZIP for Windows is a 16-bit program and is also compatible with Windows 95. In addition to compressing files from 50% to 70%, and in some cases over 90%, you can also create, open, and extract from ZIP archived files. Even files that have been stored over multiple disks can be extracted. The capability to store Windows 95 long file names and to protect a ZIP file by encrypting it with a password are other benefits of this software. PKZIP for Windows is compatible with ZIP files created on other PKZIP platforms, including DOS and OS/2. You can download a shareware version from PKWare's Internet home page.

APPLICATIONS SOFTWARE

Applications software consists of programs that enable the computer to perform specific office applications. Applications include word processing, spreadsheets, graphics, desktop publishing, accounting, database management, personal information management, desktop management, project management, and records management. Other software used in offices includes integrated software, groupware, shareware, communications, local area network (LAN), and linking software.

Word Processing

Word processing is the single most commonly used PC application. A word processing program allows the user to enter, edit and print text documents, such as letters and reports. The functions available in a word processing program will vary, depending on the brand and cost of the software as well as the size of the machine's memory.

Selection of a word processing software program should be based on the functions needed to create typical office documents. For many users, the new 32-bit application packages are worth the upgrade cost and will certainly improve productivity. For example, if you are a Microsoft Office user you will find better multitasking versions included in the suite consisting of Word, Excel, PowerPoint, Access (professional), and Schedule+ (a new component to the suite that manages calendars, tasks, and contacts for one or more people in a group). Other features include a unique Office Binder to store all of the letters, reports, spreadsheets, and other files for a project; an Answer Wizard, which allows you to ask for help in your own words; support for long filenames; right-mouse-button functions; and a replacement for the floating toolbar of launch buttons called the Shortcut Bar. With this new bar you can get at documents and other icons without minimizing the window you are working on, as well as open the appointment, task, and contact dialog boxes in Schedule+.

Basic features of word processing programs include:

- Bookmarks.
- Compact install option.
- Cross-platform compatibility with Word 6.0 for Windows.
- Drag and drop editing.
- Envelope printing (including irregular sizes).
- File conversion.
- File management.
- Format painter.
- Grammar and spelling checkers.
- Headers/footers.
- Help (context-sensitive).
- Hyphenation (automatic).
- Index generation.

- Integration with spreadsheets, graphics, databases.
- Macro capabilities.
- Mail Merge.
- Modular installation.
- Most recently used file list.
- OLE visual editing.
- Outlining.
- Paragraph and character styles.
- Shrink-to-fit previews and printing support.
- Special characters and symbols.
- Style gallery.
- Style sheets.
- Tabbed dialog boxes with preview windows.
- Table of authorities and figures generation.
- Table of contents generation.
- Text wrapping (automatic).
- Thesaurus.
- Tip of the day.
- Wizard assistants.
- Word, character, and line count.
- Zoomable editing views.

Spreadsheet Software

A spreadsheet program is an electronic replacement for an accountant's columnar ledger, pencil, and calculator. Spreadsheets can be used to calculate budgets, track sales and budgets, prepare financial statements, and analyze financial problems. They may be used as journals or ledgers and to generate data for management information reports.

Spreadsheets permit data to be moved, changed, inserted, deleted, and formatted without rekeying. Spreadsheets automate calculations so that the user enters only a set of numbers and appropriate formulas in order to find totals, averages, percentages, or the like.

There are four basic spreadsheet designs: traditional, linked, three-dimensional, and relational.

Traditional: The simplest form of spreadsheet is the traditional spreadsheet. It is a grid of cells identified by a column letter and a row number. Each cell may contain a number, a label, a formula, or a function. A label is a piece of text that usually functions as a title or the heading for a column or row. A formula is an equation used to calculate an answer given the numbers in the spreadsheet. A function is a common computation that can be invoked with a brief command; for example, many spreadsheets have a function to sum the numbers in a column or row and another function to calculate the average of the numbers in a column or row.

Linked: Linked spreadsheet designs use data from separate spreadsheets without having to copy values or build giant models. Linked spreadsheets have the ability to coordinate information in different spreadsheets. Any changes made in one spreadsheet will be automatically changed in the corresponding cells of each of the connected spreadsheets.

Three-dimensional: A three-dimensional (or 3-D) spreadsheet design adds depth by providing a third axis. Each cell has three coordinates that identify it: row, column, and page.

Relational: A relational spreadsheet design separates data files from the spreadsheets themselves. Data identification is by name, supports more than three dimensions, and provides automatic consolidation.

Determining which spreadsheet design is best in a particular office requires taking a look at the nature of the information to be processed. Adaptability, flexibility, and ease of operation are also important factors to consider.

Basic features of any spreadsheet program include the following:

▲ Automatic calculation assistance.

▲ Format option: Indicates how the numbers should be printed, including currency, percent, fixed, and scientific notations.

▲ Variable column widths.

▲ Move or copy cells and ranges.

▲ Insert or delete columns or rows.

▲ Functions: Shortcut formulas to make calculations, e.g., SUM (@SUM) to add a series of numbers, AVG (@AVG) to find the average of a series, MAX (@MAX) to find the largest number in a series.

▲ Extract and consolidate data.

▲ Edit a cell.

▲ Store, print, and edit.

▲ What-if table creation: Allows the user to evaluate the alternatives in calculations by changing figures.

▲ Solver function: Allows users to choose a desired result and suggests the best way for them to get it.

▲ Templates: Invoices, expense reports and tracking, and more.

▲ Outlining: Allows the user to view only the most important parts of a worksheet.

▲ Supports add-ins, which are software programs that work with spreadsheets to increase capabilities such as word processing, desktop publishing, better two- or three-dimensional graphics, or more cells per screen.

▲ Windows: Splits the screen into two or more sections horizontally or vertically to enable the user to see two sections of a long or wide spreadsheet on one screen.

▲ Graphics: Modules that turn numeric data into line, bar, or pie charts.

Accounting Software

Accounting software is used to manage financial data. It serves as a vehicle for inputting information about business transactions and organizing that information into meaningful management reports.

Accounting software packages can be broken into modules, or they can be fully integrated to include any or all of the following: accounts payable, accounts-receivable, general ledger, order entry, sales analysis, invoicing, inventory control, job costing, purchasing, payroll, fixed assets, and report writing.

Features of accounting software include the following:

▲ Production of reports.

▲ File export: can exchange data with spreadsheets and databases.

▲ Audit trail.

▲ Multi-user operation.

▲ Network support.

▲ Security.

▲ Customization of system for the business.

Graphics Software

Graphics software permits the display of graphs, charts, and other line art work whether on screen or on paper. It adds visual interest to reports and presentations.

Presentation graphics are images generated by computer that can be printed on overhead transparency film or photographed for 35mm slides. Graphic images can also be printed on paper, with varying degrees of quality, using computer printers or plotters. Some software packages allow the user to project the images electronically through a liquid crystal display (LCD) panel or show them directly on a PC screen. (Additional information on graphics software can be found in Chapter 19, Office Publishing.)

Common graphics programs include the following:

Computer graphics metafile (CGM): CGM, or drawing, programs produce objects that can be manipulated at any time. Such programs, also known as vector graphics or object-oriented programs, are composed of rectangles, ovals, lines, and text that can be arranged and edited. Such programs are suitable for business graphics because corrections and revisions are easy to do and printouts generally look better than those done with paint programs.

Graphics interchange format (GIF): A graphics file format that handles 8-bit color (250 colors) and achieves compression ratios of approximately 1.5:1 to 2:1. GIF files include a color table, which includes the most representative 256 colors used in the image. GIF file sizes are based on the actual number of colors used. Thus images with fewer colors take up less space in the computer.

Joint photographic experts group (JPEG): A standard for compressing images with a high compression capability. Ratios of 10:1 to 20:1 may be achieved with little noticeable loss. JPEG++ is an extension of JPEG that allows picture areas to be selected in different ratios, e.g., the background image could be compressed higher than the foreground.

Musical Instrument Digital Interface (MIDI): A standard protocol for the interchange of musical information among musical instruments, synthesizers, and computers; it is used for storing music on digital media. A MIDI interface on a multimedia computer can record a musical session.

Moving Picture Experts Group (MPEG). A standard for compressing video used in CD-ROMs and video CDs. Some MPEG boards can magnify the image to fill a full screen. MPEG-2 is a full-screen video standard.

Paint programs: A series of dots are "painted" on the screen from a palette of available colors. Paint programs are the easiest graphics programs to use. However, they do not allow the degree of editing that other graphics programs offer.

PICT (Macintosh draw format): Such programs work like CGM programs to generate objects.

Sound files: These come in either WAV or VOC formats: The VOC format is an unofficial standard for DOS programs; it is limited in the duration and range of sounds it can represent. The WAV format is used with Windows; it provides a much wider range of sounds than VOC. Sounds are often used to alert the user that a program is booting or that a nonfunctioning key has been struck.

Spreadsheet graphics files: These are graphics modules within spreadsheet programs that turn numeric data into bar, fine, pie, or X-Y charts. There are also a number of separate charting programs that permit charts to be generated from worksheet data.

Tagged image file format (TIFF): Through the process of scanning, photographs, artwork, and letters are captured and saved as a tagged image file that can be manipulated by any program that works with TIFF files.

Before investing in graphics software the following factors should be taken into consideration:

1. Most graphics software will run better on newer, more advanced computers with faster processors.
2. Most packages are more productive on a hard disk machine.

3. A super video graphics array (SVGA) card is the most helpful in running graphics programs (See the Display Monitors section of Chapter 7.)

4. Most software programs require a windowing environment, such as that on a Macintosh computer or on a PC using Microsoft Windows.

5. A pointing device such as a mouse or light pen is needed if the software runs under a windowing environment or if the user intends to make illustrations that resemble free-hand drawings.

6. Access to an ink jet or thermal transfer printer will increase one's options in producing color visuals with graphics software.

7. The ability to import or export files from or to other programs is an important feature.

Major features of graphics software include the following:

▲ Graph, text chart, and drawing tools.

▲ Ability to crop, rotate, re-size drawings.

▲ Templates.

▲ Macros.

▲ Ability to import and export various files to and from other programs.

▲ Standard symbols.

▲ Multimedia: text, data, voice, video, graphics.

▲ Drag and drop.

Desktop Publishing Software

Desktop publishing is defined as the writing, assembling, and designing of publications, such as business reports, newsletters, brochures, and trade journals, with the use of a personal computer. Through the use of desktop publishing software (DTP), pictures or graphics are combined electronically with words on the same page. DTP software includes draw or paint programs, clip-art programs, and page layout programs. (See Chapter 19, Office Publishing, for more details on desktop publishing software.)

Features of desktop publishing software include the following:

▲ Clip art images.

▲ Text creation and editing.

▲ Graphics creation and editing.

▲ Different fonts and character sizes.

▲ Interactive page layout (usually utilizing a mouse) and a graphic display of the page.

▲ Output devices support.

▲ Batch composition: All pages are automatically composed according to preset page and typographic specifications.

▲ Ability to import text and graphics from other programs.

▲ Control over hyphenation, justification, leading (fine spacing), kerning (intercharacter spacing), etc.

▲ Tools for document distribution on the Internet, e.g., HyperText Markup Language (HTML).

▲ Automatic page numbering.

▲ Automatic repagination once a document has been edited.

▲ Wizard assistance guides.

▲ Design templates.

Database Management Software

A database is a collection of information. Database management software is the set of instructions used with a computer to organize, store, and retrieve data.

Data are placed into "files" relating to a particular subject, such as customer lists, accounts receivable, and inventory or personnel records. Within the files are individual records pertaining to individuals or groups. Information in each record is broken down into different blocks, such as name and address, which are called fields.

Database programs are used by businesses to maintain inventories and process customer orders. Banks use databases to handle checking and savings accounts. The use and purpose of databases is limited only by your imagination.

Database management software can be placed into four categories: flat-file, relational, programmable, and library.

Flat-file databases: are menu-driven programs that work with only one data file at a time. They are designed for people who need to organize facts in a very simple manner. These are the easiest databases to use.

Relational databases: use multiple forms and multiple disk files to store information. Information that appears on different forms is entered only once into the computer.

Programmable databases: are designed for computer programmers who need to construct large and complex systems.

Library databases: employ routines that allow a user to manipulate data files and maintain records and keys in stored order. These are intended for sophisticated users.

Features of database management software include the following:

▲ Input forms and queries.
▲ Report generation.

▲ Onscreen creation of forms

▲ Rearrangement of files without destroying existing data.

▲ Security mechanisms.

▲ Math capability.

▲ Menu-driven operations.

▲ Documentation.

▲ Onscreen interactive tutorials.

▲ Onscreen help.

▲ Networking capability.

▲ Record locking: Allows only one user at a time to make changes to a record in a database file.

▲ Multiuser capability.

▲ Application templates, e.g., contact manager, inventory control, etc.

▲ Wizard assistance guides.

Personal Information Management and Desktop Management

Personal Information Management (PIM) software and Desktop Management Software programs help organize and manage the details of daily office life. Both categories of software generally provide notepads for composing letters or lists, a text editor, electronic calendars, calculators, alarms, onscreen lists of things to do, and pop-up directories for names, addresses, and telephone numbers. PIM software also aids in decision making by recognizing patterns, pointing out relationships, assigning priorities, and providing for cross-referencing the data between categories. For example, a customer contact can be cross-referenced with a particular salesperson, a territory, or a product category. ACT and Sales Suite are examples of popular PIM software programs.

On the other hand, typical Desktop Management software programs, such as Lotus Organizer and Sidekick, are patterned after paper-based organizers or desktop planners. Capability is generally provided for storing phone numbers and messages, creating multiple lists, keeping track of appointments, and recording notes. When keeping track of each department member's appointments, they can also be useful for scheduling meetings. This category of software is usually less complicated and generally easier to learn than PIM software.

Project Management Software

Projects are not the typical ongoing administrative activities, such as opening the mail, preparing information for the payroll, or processing invoices. A project generally consists of a set of nonroutine tasks performed in a specific sequence leading to a goal. It usually has distinct start and finish dates and a limited set of resources. Planning to move 50 people to a new floor by a specified date or developing a new advertising campaign are examples. Keeping track of the many concurrent activities and preparing periodic status reports can be difficult, time-consuming, and prone to error. Project management software can track one or more projects concurrently. The object of project management software is to keep track of project schedules and costs. Typical tasks include keeping track of needed resources, coordinating and allocating resources, and monitoring deadlines and budgets. Features of project management software include:

Capability to share data with other programs and also to incorporate features such as drag-and-drop editing and long file names.

Unique planning wizards and templates to monitor actions as well as offer suggestions, e.g., a Gantt Chart Wizard for creating a graphic visualization of the key project milestones.

Planning features to organize the details of a project into a manageable structure and identify the high-risk tasks that could severely impact the project if missed, such as a "baseline chart" for comparing the current schedule with the original plan. Also, a "resource tools" feature to help one inform management of bottlenecks and shortages in advance.

PERT chart and resource graph view screens that can be combined to see the information and understand the relationships among tasks. Tracking capability for up to 9,999 tasks per project and 9,999 resources per project.

Capability to move data easily among spreadsheets, slides, and reports as well as other documents, other programs, and other databases compliant with the Open DataBase Connectivity (ODBC) standard.

Enhancement of teamwork through capability to route projects to team members via e-mail and to collect task status information via e-mail.

Preformatted reports showing current activities, costs, assignments, and workloads that are available, or the creation of custom reports.

Records Management Software

Records management involves managing and controlling office information. Typical applications include maintaining a records center, tracking active and inactive records, making note of vital records, creating archives or historical records, and developing a record retention schedule.

No one system is right for all users. Criteria for judging all records management software, however, are: support, vendor stability, quality of documentation, ease of use, error handling ability, and value (how well a package addresses user needs).

Features of records management software include the following:

▲ Keyword search: searches for and selects a word for retrieval.

▲ File management.

▲ Retention maintenance: a system for purging inactive files according to a schedule.

▲ Destruction notification: supplies a form notifying the user of erasure of a document.

▲ Request processing.

▲ Records retrieval and inventory.

▲ File tracking.

▲ Generation of reports.

▲ Space allocation: the assignment of a given amount of characters.

▲ Bar coding.

▲ Mixed media: allows more than one type of device for storage of records, e.g., microfilm, microfiche, or floppy disk.

▲ Computer-assisted retrieval (CAR): used with micrographics.

Integrated Software Suites

Integrated software suites are related groups of software programs that can do more than one function. Functions work together so that information can be transferred from one application to another. Integrated software can consist of word processing, database management, spreadsheet, graphics, and desktop management.

Multiuser integrated software operates in a network environment. Such software includes inter-workstation electronic mail, shared file storage, and many business applications.

The following are the two types of integrated software:

All-in-one: These allow users to move between applications without leaving the program.

Modular: These provide a "family" or suite of programs produced by the same software house and sharing similar commands. They permit the sharing of information among individual stand-alone programs. When selecting integrated software, it is important to know how the product integrates applications. A file-conversion utility is less desirable than a cut-and-paste approach, because with the former, the application usually must be abandoned when the utility is activated.

Features of integrated software suites include the following:

• Seamless integration with word processing, spreadsheet, graphic presentation, desktop management, and database management programs.

• Online interactive help (wizards, coaches, etc.) and templates to assist in creating documents, databases, and presentations.

• Capability to share work over a network with team support tools.

• Capability to copy files, worksheets, tables and charts by "dragging and dropping" them into other applications, documents, or mail messages.

• Automatic error and spell check correction.

Groupware

Groupware is a term describing software to support people working in groups connected via computer and communications technologies. This software is designed to enable computer users to work together within facilities over local area networks, as well as beyond the walls of a building through telecommunication systems. Typical groupware applications include conferencing, workflow, calendar, e-mail, and distributing data among groups. Another term used to describe this activity is computer-supported cooperative work (CSCW).

Some of the main features of groupware include:

Ready-to-run application templates: for common groupware applications, such as team issues, customer service, meeting tracking, status reporting, reservation scheduling, and more.

Document database: for users to access, track, store, and organize any number of objects and data types, including text, numerical data, structured data, images, graphics, and sound and video images.

Electronic messaging: so users can send and receive e-mail across a variety of mail systems, including the software program cc:Mail.

Replication technology: that provides everyone working on a document with the same up-to-date information. Groupware also performs replication between servers and desktop clients, allowing employees in the field to dial in at regular intervals and have their records updated.

Administrative tools: for network administrators, both local and remote, to maintain servers, support users, load software, set up replication schedules, manage disk space, and create new accounts.

Modular construction: to allow network administrators to start with core capabilities and build strategic business process applications for their organizations as needs require.

Shareware

Shareware programs are software programs that can be distributed and copied at little or no cost without breaking copyright laws. Shareware is distributed through electronic bulletin boards, on-line information services, user groups, and shareware catalogs from a mail-order company that specializes in shareware programs.

A user who decides to keep a shareware program is expected to register with and pay a fee to the software company that created the program. After registering and paying the fee, the shareware user will receive support and manuals for the shareware.

HINT: *The Public Software Library in Houston maintains one of the largest collections of public domain software and shareware for IBM PC and Macintosh computers. For a free copy of the library's PC newsletter, call 800-242-4775.*

Communications, Network, and Linking Software

Communications, network, and linking software programs enable a computer to transmit and receive information from another computer over telephone lines. They can also link a PC to a mainframe, minicomputer, or other PCs, and transfer files from one application program to another.

In order to transmit and receive information, a *modem* (Modulator-DeModulator) is needed. A modem is a device that is used to convert digital signals into analog (voice-like) signals for transmission over a telephone line. At the other end of the line, another modem converts the analog signals back into digital form. A modem is also known as a data set.

Local area networks (LANs) are used to distribute information throughout an office via different terminals (called nodes) connected to a central information repository (called a server). The server allows people to share peripherals and data files. The server functions like a traffic cop, managing the flow of information between the computers hooked together on the LAN. Thus, a LAN allows people in a department to share information with each other electronically as well as to share common resources like printers and large hard disks. A LAN electronically ties functions together for better communications among individuals, departments within the office and/or satellite offices or locations, and it reduces equipment costs, since different PC users can share expensive peripherals, such as laser printers.

SELECTING SOFTWARE

The following general guidelines will help you evaluate prospective software:

1. Perform a needs analysis, either through a survey, questionnaire, or interviews of other users. A thorough needs analysis helps to determine the software applications needed, who the users are, frequency of use, types of documents produced, the operating system currently in use (if applicable), the computer hardware available, and the printer requirements. It can also indicate what your future needs are likely to be.

2. Identify available packages. Determine the available packages by talking to software manufacturers, software dealers, reviewing sales literature, and reading office related trade magazines. Ask the following questions:

   ▲ What are the benefits that differentiate one brand from another?

   ▲ What tasks need to be done?

   ▲ Will the features meet the needs of the end-user?

   ▲ How easy are the package's features to learn in relationship to performing the task?

▲ What is the availability and compatibility to other equipment and software already being used? Will the software interface with existing hardware and software?

▲ Is support available after the sale? By whom? Is an 800 phone number available for troubleshooting problems? Is there a user group that you can join? Are there others within the organization who have knowledge of the software to assist when problems occur? What kind of maintenance or upgrading is available for software? Are there add-on packages for the software available?

▲ Is training free or is there a charge? What type of training is available?

HINT: *Software decisions drive hardware decisions. Match available packages to the information gathered in the needs analysis.*

3. Establish a comparative grid, or matrix, of available packages. Make a list of the information gathered by categories in the first column and put the packages studied across the tops of the other columns. Fill in the comparative information at the appropriate cell intersections. You may wish to assign both a weight for each category and a score for each package, from a low of 1 to a high of 10. Multiply the weight by the score in each cell and then total the scores in each column. In this way you can quantitatively compare the prospective software package choices.

✓ Ask questions.

✓ Start the search process at least 90 days before software is needed.

✓ Perform a methodical software selection process.

✓ Remember good software recognizes the importance of people in processing while poor software only tolerates people.

✓ Comparison shop.

✓ Consult current users of the software for references.

✓ Know your needs.

✓ Determine if after-purchase support is available.

✓ Purchase on facts.

✓ Keep asking "Does the software fit my needs?"

Figure 8-1 Guidelines for buying software.

4. Request a demonstration of the software and/or a trial use. A thorough demonstration, preferably with trial use, is necessary before making a final decision. Both the demonstration and the trial usage will provide valuable insights that are not possible through any other form of evaluation, helping you to determine if the software is easy to use.

HINT: *Small organizations with limited budgets should consider integrated software, which can combine a few categories of tasks. The larger the organization, the more specialized the software usually needs to be.*

ASSORTED SOFTWARE ISSUES

Establishing a Software Inventory

Managing software is an important function of the administrative assistant. With the addition of more and more personal computers into the office and home, maintaining an inventory of software has become important. Such an inventory not only shows what software is available but also provides a degree of consistency and standardization in the software used.

A software inventory can be done manually or electronically through a database management system. An inventory sheet (or file, if maintained on the computer) for each software package should be completed. An inventory sheet contains important information concerning the software: name of the software, version number, number of copies, serial number, users' names, and vendor information.

By maintaining an inventory sheet, upgrades in the software by the manufacturer can be easily made. Notification of these changes can be quickly incorporated into the appropriate departments. Security and copyright issues can be better managed, protected, and documented.

Backing Up Software

With larger hard drives, the most effective way to back up is to use a tape backup system. These systems are easy to install and generally include a tape drive, backup software, and one preformatted tape. Even if software is not included or you don't like the software, you can purchase Norton Backup from Symantec. It is easy to use and very fast.

Here are some tips on using a tape drive system:

• Tape backup systems are designed to back up from 40 MB into the gigabyte range. When purchasing a tape system, you need to relate the capacity of your hard drive to the capacity of the system you are planning to purchase. Most software backup systems provide for compression, which means you can squeeze 400 MB on a tape designed to store only 200 MB.

- Use the software program's maximum compression command to fit more information on a tape. You can experiment with the compression ratio for optimum results. Text-only files compress better than graphics files or files ending with .EXE.

- Although you can use only one tape, it is recommended that you alternate among three or four tapes. This provides a safety net in case a tape goes bad and also promotes greater tape longevity.

- Keep your tapes stored at room temperature and in a safe place, such as a locked file drawer. Data security is paramount when you have a lot of data stored on something so small that it can fit into one's pocket.

- Save hours of time by buying preformatted tapes. The additional cost is minimal.

- Keep your tape heads clean by periodically cleaning them with a cotton swab and rubbing alcohol. Or you can buy a tape backup drive cleaning kit.

- Always match the type of backup tape to your backup drive requirements. Some drives use DC (data cartridge) tapes and others use QIC (quarter-inch cartridge) tapes.

- When your drive fails, assuming the drive is not damaged, you need to restore it initially by using your "emergency" DOS disk. Next, install the tape backup software, replace the backup tape, and select Restore. Be sure to select the option to overwrite all files that were installed with your "emergency" DOS disk.

Computer Viruses

Computer viruses are self-replicating blocks of computer code that enter a computer through a modem or network, or locally through a contaminated diskette. By replicating themselves thousands or millions of times, viruses may tie up the computer's processor and block other functions. Virus "infections" spread just as biological viruses do—by contact. As healthy diskettes and programs come in contact with an infected system, the virus merges into healthy programs or disks, causing an infection. The insertion process takes only a fraction of a second.

A virus may destroy data, reformat a disk, wear out its drive, or flash a harmless message on the screen. A virus not only affects PCs, but it can also attack mainframes and minicomputers.

A number of things can indicate that a virus has infected or attempted to infect a system. Unexplained system "crashes," programs that suddenly don't work right, data files or programs that are mysteriously erased, and disks that become unreadable are all possible signs of a virus.

Products are available to help a system recover from a virus attack. There are three categories of antiviral programs:

- Infection prevention products, which stop the virus from repeating and infecting the system.

- Infection detection products, which detect an infection soon after the infection occurs. These products identify the area of the system that has been infected. Such products check the program when it is run for any changes. If a change from the original is detected, the user is notified of the affected area.
- Infection identification products, which identify specific virus strains in systems that are already infected and usually remove the virus and restore the system to its correct state, prior to the infection.

To help prevent the risk of viral contamination, companies should have a data backup procedure scheduled, at least once a week for moderate users and one or more times a day for heavy users. Access to backups should be controlled so their availability and integrity are guaranteed. The backups should be carefully dated and kept for several months, at least. Access to programs and data should be restricted to an "as needed" basis.

Some additional steps to follow to help keep a good system from becoming infected include the following:

1. Floppy-disk–based systems should be started only with a specific, clearly labeled boot, or startup, diskette. Only one boot diskette should be assigned to each PC. It should be clearly marked as the boot diskette.
2. Never boot a hard disk system from a diskette. If an infected floppy is used to boot the system, it can infect the hard disk system.
3. Never put shareware programs into a hard disk's root directory. This protects the root directory, which serves as the base for other subdirectories within the system. Most viruses can affect only the directory from which they are executed. In a LAN, avoid placing shareware in a common file-server directory that makes it accessible to any PC in the network. Viruses can also be downloaded into the system through bulletin boards or via disks from traveling executives who use other computer systems. Disks that have been used elsewhere should be checked prior to use (through the use of an antiviral program).
4. In a shared resource system, where data is transported between PCs or printers, the output data should be put on a floppy disk. No other files including system files should be on the floppy disk.
5. Software should be tested before it is used on the system. Backing up an infected disk will create a second infected disk.
6. There should be strict policies regulating the downloading of software from other systems, since a virus can be transferred from the originating computer.

Software Copyright Issues

Copyright infringement is on the rise, primarily because employees do not know the scope of the laws against it. According to the law, an author or creator of a work owns all the rights to any form of it, including the right to copy and distribute it. Title 17 of the U.S.

Code states that "it is illegal to make or distribute copies of the copyrighted material without authorization." The only exception is the user's right to make a backup copy for archival purposes.

An employee who makes duplicates of a copyrighted story, book, or report and distributes them to fellow employees is violating the law. Unauthorized duplication of software is a federal crime. Penalties include fines of as much as $100,000 and jail terms of up to five years. In addition, the material in question can be impounded or destroyed.

Major PC-software companies as well as many smaller ones are bringing suits in court that will hash out just what constitutes legal copying of a computer program. Eventually, laws may change as computer networks become more widely used. Companies may end

1. (Company/Agency) licenses the use of computer software from a variety of outside companies. (Company/Agency) does not own this software or its related documentation, and unless authorized by the software developer, does not have the right to reproduce it.

2. With regard to use on local area networks or on multiple machines, (Company/Agency) employees shall use the software only in accordance with the license agreement.

3. (Company/Agency) employees learning of any misuse of software or related documentation within the company shall notify the department manager or (Company's/Agency's) legal counsel.

4. According to the U.S. Copyright law, persons involved in the illegal reproduction of software can be subject to civil damages of as much as $50,000, and criminal penalties, including fines and imprisonment. (Company/Agency) does not condone the illegal duplication of software. (Company/Agency) employees who make, acquire, or use unauthorized copies of computer software shall be disciplined as appropriate under the circumstances. Such discipline may include termination.

I am fully aware of the software use policies of (Company/Agency) and agree to uphold these policies.

_____
Employee Signature and Date

Figure 8-2 Sample corporate employee agreement: company/agency policy regarding the use of personal computer software.

up charging for organizing, adapting, and updating the products instead of charging by the copy.

Management should work with the company's legal department to develop policies related to copyright issues. These policies should be discussed with employees to educate and remind them of the consequences. (See Figure 8-2.) The simplest and best policy is to have one authorized copy of a software product for every computer upon which it is run.

The Software Publishers Association produces a self-Audit Kit that describes procedures appropriate for ensuring that a business or organization is "software-legal." SPA is located at 1101 Connecticut Avenue NW, Suite 901, Washington, DC 20036; 202-452-1600.

Software Training and Certification

Many software vendors, e.g., Novell and Microsoft, provide certification training for their software products. This training includes certification based on a series of examinations that test one's mastery of critical competencies. By becoming certified, one is recognized as an expert in the designing, developing, and implementing of software support solutions. Typical certification designations include Certified System Engineer, Certified Solution Developer, Certified Product Specialist, Certified Trainer, and Certified LAN Specialist.

CHAPTER 9

OFFICE

SUPPLIES

Office supplies such as pens and pencils, file folders, and paper are consumable, disposable, and easily replaced. Changes in technology and an increased variety of equipment found in offices, however, have resulted in an increase in the number and type of supplies. Knowledge of inventory control, vendors, and the different types of products available helps in organizing supplies for efficient office use, in identifying the best sources, and in purchasing with the qualities and features needed in a particular office.

PURCHASING OFFICE SUPPLIES

Office supplies can be purchased through a variety of sources, including office supply stores, salespeople representing dealers and stationers, mail-order firms, warehouse stores, and discount merchants. Some manufacturers also sell directly to large customers.

Sources of Office Supplies

The following are important sources of office supplies:

Wholesalers: Wholesalers buy finished products from manufacturers and store, market, and deliver the products to dealers; they rarely sell directly to the consumer.

Retail stores: These are office supply stores with walk-in and phone customers; their inventories are generally limited. Because their customers buy in smaller volumes, product cost is relatively high. However, they are convenient for most customers and a good source for rush orders in emergencies.

Contract stationers: These firms have sales representatives who call on customers; some have retail stores; some limit their selling to medium or large accounts in metropolitan areas. They carry large inventories and thus can offer better prices. They offer discounts based on the size of the account and negotiations with the customer.

Mail-order firms: These firms sell through catalogs; customers order by phone, mail, fax, or computer. They range from firms with small, specialized inventories to ones with a large variety of products. They are the best source of supplies for small and medium-sized businesses and home offices. Most emphasize express shipping.

Specialty stores: Such firms specialize in one type of product, such as computer or copy supplies; they offer hard-to-find supplies.

Office products superstore chains: These are warehouse stores with floor-to-ceiling shelves; they buy products directly from manufacturers and offer good discounts. They are good for the small- and medium-sized business used to buying supplies at retail price through dealers. Some charge a membership fee; many have catalogs for customers to look at before coming to the store; and some may deliver orders for a fee.

Warehouse stores: These stores carry office supplies in addition to general merchandise; they are very competitive in price. They are usually cash-and-carry and their offerings may be limited. They buy from the best price sources, so they use various sources and buy from manufacturer's close-out sales.

Additional methods of purchasing supplies are outsourcing and group purchasing. Outsourcing is the process of arranging with a firm specializing in placing orders for others. Group purchasing involves different businesses joining together to purchase supplies. Both methods allow opportunities for discounts not available to a smaller business and provide just-in-time ordering to avoid storage problems. Another way to avoid storage problems is contracting directly with a supplier. A central storage area is then no longer needed since supplies are delivered directly to the department when they are needed.

Choosing the Best Source

It is best to choose one source for most supplies instead of buying from a variety of dealers. Your main supply source might not carry every item needed, but a specialty supplier or mail-order firm can fill those orders if necessary. Every company should have a local emergency source that has a delivery service available for rush orders.

Retail prices shown in catalogs (except mail-order ones) are a starting point for choosing a supplier. Businesses can negotiate discounts of up to 20 percent from some dealers. Some catalogs have multiple-column price charts for quantity discounts; but even if there is no quantity discount chart, you should always ask for a discount quote. Another way to save money on large-volume purchases is by asking several companies to bid on merchandise. Although this takes time and paperwork, it may be worth the effort to get a low price.

A large part of the cost of buying office supplies is the cost of placing and receiving orders. Businesses that shop with discount and wholesale stores need to determine whether the time and expense involved in this process is worthwhile, whether it is more cost-effective to order from a catalog, or whether it is best to order from a sales representative who might make recommendations that improve efficiency and productivity.

The following factors should be considered when choosing a source for office supplies:

Price

- Is the price full retail or discounted?
- Are prices guaranteed?
- Are prices published or is it necessary to call each time an order is placed?

HINT: *Good values and competitive prices should be available on most of the items needed.*

HINT: *Occasionally compare dealer net prices to make certain you are getting the best price.*

HINT: *Choose a supplier based on overall price levels rather than by price shopping on one item.*

Placing an order

- Is it convenient, whether by phone, by mail, by fax, by computer, or in person?
- Does the sales representative suggest alternative products to save money or suggest quantity discounts?
- Is the catalog index easy to locate and use?
- Are prices clearly marked?

HINT: *When calling in an order, ask if the items you are ordering are on sale.*

Receiving an order

- How quickly are orders shipped?
- Are rush deliveries available?
- Do the freight charges increase if the order is partially shipped?
- Is the order consistently accurate?
- Are you notified of substitutions ahead of time?

HINT: *Most orders should be shipped within 48 hours.*

HINT: *Do not accept unordered quantities or extra merchandise.*

Billing

- How long does it take to receive the bill?

HINT: *A bill should be sent within a week of delivery.*

HINT: *Become familiar with credit policies in order to maintain a good credit standing and to take advantage of discounts.*

Returns

- How many days do you have to return merchandise without penalty?
- Is there a simple return policy?
- Are warranties honored?
- Is there a guarantee of 100 percent satisfaction?

HINT: *A good supplier may allow up to 90 days to return merchandise with no penalty.*

Buying in Bulk

Offices may buy large quantities of products and receive volume discounts. This works well if there is enough storage area. The shelf life of the product may determine the quantity to order.

HINT: *Buy only what you can use in a reasonable amount of time.*

Generic Supplies

Buying generic supplies can mean a 15 to 50 percent savings. Some good generic products are available, but some generic products that appear to be the same as name brands do not have the same quality.

The cost savings realized by purchasing a generic product often may be offset by the lack of a guarantee or a major manufacturer backing the product. The only way to tell whether or not to use a generic product is by trial and error and having a willingness to take a risk.

Freight Charges

Unless supplies are purchased locally, the customer pays freight charges. Dealers may give free delivery, free delivery on selected items, or only customer-paid delivery. For lightweight items, freight is 2 to 5 percent of the cost; for heavy items, it can be as much as 20 percent. Listed below are freight terms that office supply dealers use:

▲ F.O.B. (free on board): Customer pays freight from the location mentioned after the letters.

▲ F.O.B. Dealer: Customer pays freight from dealer to customer.

▲ F.O.B. Factory: Customer pays freight from the factory where the product is made to customer.

▲ F.O.B. Point of Origin: Customer pays freight from where the item is loaded onto the truck to the customer.

▲ F.O.B. Destination or F.O.B. Delivered: Freight is paid by the dealer.

▲ Prepaid: Freight is paid by the shipper.

▲ Prepaid and Add: Freight is paid by the shipper but the price is added to the customer's bill.

▲ Freight Collect: Customer pays freight to the trucker when the shipment arrives.

HINT: *Weigh additional costs such as small-order charges, insurance, and handling fees.*

CONTROLLING OFFICE SUPPLIES

Every organization needs a method for controlling office supplies. If individuals or individual departments order their own supplies, the company may miss out on preferred pricing or extra services it would otherwise receive. Inventory and usage tracking are essential to manage supplies.

The following are some steps to take in establishing a system for controlling office supplies:

1. Designate a specific area for storage of all office supplies and lock the area. Note, however, that one person besides yourself should have a key in case of an emergency. Frequently used, inexpensive items such as paper clips or staples, however, can be located in an unlocked closet or drawer that is readily accessible by all office workers.
2. Appoint a supplies supervisor to set procedures to prevent waste. Typically this is the office manager.
3. Determine typical usage of supplies. Estimate monthly, bimonthly, and annual usage so that you know how often to order each item.
4. Establish a budget. Break the budget down into product categories to determine whether too much money is being allocated to certain items. The budget will help in future planning.

HINT: *Breaking down the budget into items is also a way to compare costs. Toner cartridges, for example, can be itemized and yields determined for different printers.*

HINT: *If you know how much is spent on individual items each year, you can negotiate prices with dealers.*

Store office supplies with in-house labeling of categories. Here are some suggested categories: *Paper products*—writing paper, forms, file folders, envelopes, labels, computer and copy paper. *Writing instruments*—wood pencils, mechanical pencils, all types of pens, and markers/highlighters. *Computer/copy supplies*—disks, toner cartridges, and tapes. *Ribbons*—ribbons for all office machines. *Miscellaneous supplies*—rubber bands, staples, paper clips, and other small items.

HINT: *Label products in stock according to the machines they fit.*

Keep the supply storage area in order. Arrange supplies so the most often used ones are easily accessible—and do not pile supplies so high that stacks of items have to be moved to obtain what is needed. Small items should be stored in labeled boxes.

Keep a minimum number of supply items on the shelves to avoid stockpiling. But be sure you know when to reorder. Put a rubber band and a reorder slip around the "last batch" of stock to indicate that it is time to reorder. Note that reordering time must reflect the time necessary to process the order, obtain the supplies, unpack them, and place them on the shelves.

Be sure that supplies are labeled with expiration dates when applicable.

Store materials by location numbers giving the drawer, shelf, bin, and/or slot. Label each location with the cabinet number (if more than one), location number, and brief description of the supply. For example, the label "II-3 Env. 10" could be used for Cabinet II, shelf 3, No. 10 envelopes.

HINT: *A supply area can look messy if items do not have designated storage locations.*

Distribute a master inventory list of available supplies with location designations to everyone who has access to the supply area.

Develop an inventory sheet describing supply types and quantities. Post the sheet in the supply area. The person in charge notes reductions in or additions to supplies.

Develop a supply requisition form. Preprint commonly used items on the sheet. Circulate periodically (perhaps as often as once a week) and purchase only what appears on the sheet.

HINT: *The form should help remind users to request any items they will be using for special projects in their departments.*

HINT: *Check the supply area at least once a week.*

When a supply is low, prepare either a stock requisition, if the supply is carried in-house, or a purchase requisition, if it must be ordered elsewhere. If you are authorized to do so, call or fax the order and prepare the necessary paperwork for the accounting department.

Before placing an order, look for items on sale. Low-cost and quickly used products are the most likely to be on sale. Order a one- or two-month supply.

Establish a schedule for ordering, which may be weekly or monthly. Random buying wastes time and money. Know delivery schedules. For low-value or low-volume items, order as much as a year's supply (as long as it will not deteriorate on the shelf).

HINT: *If you have a schedule for ordering, you will avoid handling charges for small orders and you may save on freight charges.*

Have current office supply catalogs available for employees.

Check each incoming order to be certain the items received are the ones that were ordered. Place the new supplies behind or beneath the other supplies. Inform the purchasing department that the supplies have been received.

Buy case lots or cartons to save money and avoid partial shipments.

Order by phone, Telex, or fax for faster service. Ask for "rush" service and plan an emergency shipping method.

HINT: *Preplanning avoids costly rush orders.*

SPECIAL STORAGE REQUIREMENTS AND SHELF LIFE

Paper, ribbons, and copier and laser printer cartridges all have special storage requirements.

Paper

Paper is very susceptible to atmospheric conditions. Paper has a shelf life of over a year. Forms and printed products have shelf lives of six months to a year. These storage suggestions for paper will help increase its shelf life:

- Immediately replace the lid after removing reams from a packing box.
- Keep paper sealed in its original, moisture-resistant wrapper.
- Never store more than one partially unwrapped ream on an open shelf, since fading can occur. Color stock fades more easily than white.
- Avoid cold, damp, rooms, areas of high heat or humidity, and exposure to direct sunlight.
- If the paper storage area is not climate-controlled, keep a relatively low inventory for infrequently used sizes and colors. Extreme changes in the environment can cause paper to warp.
- Keep stocks of paper on pallets, off the floor. Stack no more than six cartons high, with each carton upright. Improper stacking of cartons or dropping a carton on its corner can damage paper.
- Move paper from storage to user areas at least 48 hours before it is needed to allow the paper to adjust to the temperature in the operating environment. The greater the temperature difference, the longer this adjustment period will be. Some paper manufacturers recommend stabilizing unopened cartons one hour for every degree of difference between the storage and user areas.
- Use older paper first.
- Do not place other objects on top of paper, whether it is packaged or unpackaged.

Ribbons

Ribbons should be stored at normal room temperature, away from heat, light, and humidity. Most ribbons have an estimated average shelf life of up to two years, although some dry out in six months.

Laser Printer and Copier Toner Cartridges

Laser printer and copier toner cartridges should be stored in the aluminum bag in which they were originally packaged. Keep them in a dark cabinet away from direct sunlight and rest them in a horizontal position, not vertically. Room temperature should be between 32 and 95 degrees Fahrenheit, and they should be protected from high humidity.

PAPER

Paper accounts for a major part of most company supply budgets. There are many types of papers for different purposes, including paper for copiers, fax machines, computers, and special printers, and letterhead for correspondence. Purchasing paper that can be used on more than one kind of equipment, such as paper that can be used for copy machines and laser printers, simplifies ordering, handling, and stocking of paper. It can also save your company a significant amount of money. Below are some considerations to bear in mind when selecting paper.

Grades

Paper can be purchased in economy, standard, or premium grades. Better grades provide increased brightness and greater contrast between copy and paper, an important paper characteristic for laser printers because the text appears more legible. Table 9-1 describes paper grades, their brightness, and their uses.

HINT: *Coordinate the brightness levels of all paper for consistent good appearance.*

HINT: *A lower level of brightness makes the paper appear yellowish.*

Content

The content of paper is the amount of wood pulp, which affects durability and appearance. Office paper is either cotton fiber bond or sulphite bond.

Cotton fiber bond (or "rag") is made of cotton pulp combined with chemically treated wood pulp. It is available in grades indicating the amount of cotton pulp combined with the wood pulp: 25 percent, 50 percent, 75 percent, 100 percent, and extra 100 percent. Cotton bonds have a watermark, which is an impression, pattern, or symbol on the paper that signifies its quality. The higher the cotton content, the more durable the paper. Table 9-2 describes the uses of different types of cotton fiber bond.

Note that cotton bond may not perform well on laser printers and copiers, although some manufacturers make a 25% cotton paper specifically designed for laser printers.

Table 9-1
PAPER GRADES

GRADE	BRIGHTNESS	USES
Economy	81	Suitable for everyday use and internal correspondence; used when appearance is less important than economy.
Standard	84	Gives a professional but not a formal look; suitable for interoffice communications.
Premium	86½	Company letterheads; good for laser printers or copiers.

Table 9-2
USES OF COTTON FIBER BOND

CONTENT	USES
100% cotton	Legal documents, certificates, prestige stationery, and vital records.
75% cotton	Permanent records, prestige letterhead, and executive correspondence.
50% cotton	Semipermanent records and letterhead.
25% cotton	Most popular letterhead bond; also used for price lists, report forms, circulars, and bulletins.

Table 9-3
GRADES OF SULPHITE BOND

GRADE	CHARACTERISTICS
#1	Has a watermark; looks so good it is difficult to distinguish from a more expensive cotton bond; cost-effective for letterheads, especially if the letterheads are used in a copier or a laser printer, where permanence is not essential.
#4	Most popular for copying and laser printing; only available in a smooth finish; least expensive since it is made from lower quality pulp and has a very white appearance.

Sulphite bond is made from chemically treated wood pulp. This paper is also known as xerographic paper, because it is typically used for copiers and laser printers. It is smoother and less expensive than cotton-content bond, so it has less of a tendency to curl up and jam in a copy machine or laser printer.

Although sulphite bond comes in five grades, numbered 1 through 5, only #1 and #4 are recommended for general office use. Table 9-3 gives the characteristics of these two commonly used paper types.

Finish

Paper comes in a variety of finishes, which determine the paper's look and feel. Smoother finishes are less expensive and work better with most office machines. Generally a smooth, regular finish communicates an impression of higher quality than a rough surface. However, the choice of finish is often based on personal preference. Table 9-4 describes three commonly used finishes.

Paper with a textured surface typically does not work well in laser printers or copiers because of its greater potential for misfeeding and paper jams. Smoother paper avoids these problems and also ensures sharper resolution of details. Laser printer paper specifically designed for certificates and documents is available that has the look and feel of parchment.

Table 9-4
PAPER FINISHES

FINISH	DESCRIPTION	USES
Smooth	Few irregularities.	Works well with copiers and laser printers; most popular for letterhead.
Linen laid	Embossed with a linen design, with a fairly rough feel and appearance.	Creates superior impression. High-quality letterhead.
Ripple	Wavy, glossy finish, with the indentations darker than the higher spots.	Document papers, certificates.

Weight

Paper weight is the weight of one ream (500 sheets) of paper, which is called the basis weight. The weight is a measure of the thickness and density of paper. In English units, the basis weight is the weight of 500 sheets of 17-by-22-inch paper. Measured in metric units it is the weight in grams of one square meter of paper. Office paper weights range from 9 to 28 pounds. In general, paper specifications should follow the recommendations of the equipment or paper manufacturer. Table 9-5 gives paper weights for common office uses.

Color

Many companies now prefer neutral colors such as ivory, off-white, gray, and blue for important correspondence. Firms that use colored paper or letterhead with color want their message to stand out from others. Research has shown that direct mail on colored paper increases readership, retention of detail, and response from readers.

Colored paper can make the following materials more effective:

- Annual reports.
- Brochures.
- Color-coded documents.
- Direct-mail pieces.
- Dividers for reports.
- Letterhead.
- Memos.
- Product information.
- Sales materials.

Colored paper can also improve interoffice communication by using it to:

- Distinguish department correspondence (e.g., green for accounting, yellow for personnel, etc.).

Table 9-5
PAPER WEIGHTS FOR COMMON OFFICE USES

USE	WEIGHT (LB.)	DESCRIPTION
Adding machine rolls	12–16	Standard size is 2¼ by 3⅛ inches but is usually expressed as 2¼ inches by 165 feet. Rolls specific inner (ID) and outer (OD) diameters of the core. This measurement is crucial to fitting the roll on the machine.
Cash register rolls	12–16	Same as for Adding machines.
Dot matrix printers and daisywheel printers		Recommended: Xerographic (#4 sulphite); 84 brightness, smooth. The higher the groundwood, the lower the price. Available in continuous fanfold sheets as well as cut sheets. Sizes: 9½ by 11 inches (8½ by 11 inches when perforated edges are removed); 14⅞ by 11 inches. Green bars: Used for statistical work where easy reading of data is important. Blue bars: Used when printouts are to be copied, since the blue bars do not show. Higher grades of paper, such as 25 percent cotton bond, are available for letterhead paper.
	10–12	Short-term use.
	15	Average use; lighter handling and less permanence.
	18–20	For reports to be stored for several years, where appearance is important, or for high-speed printers.
Copier paper	20	Recommended: Xerographic (#4 sulphite). Refer to the heading in this chapter on *Copier Problems Caused by Paper.*
Envelopes	24	Opaque; heavier weight than letterhead paper; check user's manual for compatibility with postage meters, mailing machines, and laser printers. Refer to the section in this chapter on Envelopes for additional details.
Laser printer	16–28	Refer to user's manual for weight specifications. Most laser printers cannot accept extremely heavy paper stocks and work best with a very smooth sheet of paper such as xerographic or specially formulated laser printer paper. Colors and cotton bond are available.
Letterhead		Recommended: 25 percent cotton bond; 86½ brightness. Note: Not all letterhead works well with laser printers.
	20	Most popular weight.
	24	More body, generally used for special purposes.

- Avoid wasting time; this can be done by color-coding documents that look similar (e.g., color-code legal documents that look alike but have different contents).
- Call attention to information. Use a bright, visible color for information that must be read immediately, such as companywide information posted on bulletin boards. Reserve tan or gray for confidential information; such a document will stand out if it is in the hands of the wrong person.
- Add a festive mood to holiday announcements or party flyers.

Bear these points in mind when using colored paper:

Equipment compatibility: Check the user's manual for specifications to be sure the paper is compatible with the equipment.

Laser printers: Not all colored paper can withstand the heat of laser printers. Avoid paper with a colored coating that has been added after the paper is produced. The paper should be of the same quality as white paper used in the laser printer.

Letterhead: Use light-colored paper for letterhead because it has the best contrast and readability.

Photocopying: Try photocopying any document on colored paper before ordering large quantities to see if the result is a shadowed copy.

Multipart Forms

Carbonless paper produces copies without the use of carbon paper. Chemical coatings in the paper form an image when pressed with a pen, typewriter, or printer. It is used especially for forms needed by several departments.

Multipart continuous carbonless paper is available for computers. Chemical carbonless paper will produce up to five legible copies if handwritten and seven if computer generated. Mated mechanical carbonless paper should produce 9 handwritten copies or 12 to 20 if machine imaged.

Fax Paper

Most fax machines use rolls of thermal paper or plain paper. (See the section Fax Machines in Chapter 7 for more information.) For thermal machines, consult the user's manual and purchase the recommended type of thermal paper because different machines use different degrees of heat.

Copier Problems Caused by Paper

Copy paper should be properly placed in paper trays. Most paper manufacturers provide loading instructions on their packages (usually an arrow indicating which surface is to be printed on). Some copiers discharge the sheet the same way it is placed in the tray, while others turn it over.

HINT: *To test how a copier works, mark one side of a sheet and run it through to determine the imaging side.*

HINT: *When purchasing a copier, it is important to have a demonstration on the various thicknesses of paper to determine the minimum and maximum possible.*

Table 9-6 provides a quick reference for solutions to copier problems.

Recycled Paper

More people are aware of the limited supply of natural resources and recycle office paper. To facilitate recycling, offices have recycling containers for used white and sometimes colored paper next to wastepaper baskets and near copiers. Building maintenance staff collect the paper for recycling.

On the other side, recycled paper is available for copiers and computers, as well as for writing and memo pads. File folders and mailers may also be made from recycled fibers. Recycled paper may be white or colored, and it may have some cotton content.

Buy a small quantity at first, then check the results. From an environmental point of view, the best recycled paper is 100 percent recycled with a high post-consumer content (paper that was recycled after use at home or in the office) and is either not de-inked at all (i.e., the ink was not removed from the printer's waste) or is bleached without chlorine.

Listed below are some points to consider when buying recycled products:

Table 9-6
SOLUTIONS TO COPIER PROBLEMS

PROBLEM	CAUSE	SOLUTION
Feed difficulties	Heavy-stock paper, such as letterhead, may cause static buildup.	Use lighter-weight paper.
Misfeeding	Uneven edges or excessive curl; mixing different paper weights in the same tray or cassette.	Turn the paper over or use another ream.
Jamming in the finish bins or sheets sticking together	Excessive curl.	Turn the paper over.
	Moisture.	Check storage conditions.
	Low humidity.	Ask vendor to check static eliminator.
Wrinkling	High moisture content resulting when the paper is incorrectly wrapped or stored in a damp location; paper has been left too long in the copy machine.	Check storage conditions; use another ream.

- Test the product with your equipment and see if it meets your needs.
- Compare bids from vendors of virgin products to see if the switch is worth it. Some recycled paper products (such as legal pads and copy paper) may be comparable in price to virgin products, but the costs of some recycled and virgin products can vary greatly.
- Explore the possibility of purchasing recycled products with money the company earns from selling recyclable waste materials.
- Promote the program. Make sure company employees, customers, and vendors know your company is recycling and buying recycled products. Include statements like "Printed on recycled paper" on all publications. Develop news releases, advertising, and public service announcements.

ENVELOPES

Envelopes come in hundreds of styles and sizes to accommodate all mailing purposes. Although other sizes are available, Table 9-7 shows the most common types and sizes of envelopes. Listed below are the characteristics and typical uses of business envelopes.

Commercial and official envelopes (also called business or regular)

- Usually 24 lb. bond for first-class, airmail, or bulk-rate mail handling.
- No. 9 envelope fits into a No. 10 envelope.
- Available with an inside blue tint for confidentiality.
- Cotton fiber bond envelopes should always match letterhead stationery.
- May have a window to use for invoices, statements, addressed documents, or payroll checks. A window eliminates retyping, reducing errors and saving time.

Table 9-7
COMMON ENVELOPES

TYPE	SIZE	DESCRIPTION
No. 6¾	3⅝ by 6½ inches	Commercial
No. 9	3⅞ by 8⅞ inches	Official
No. 10*	4⅛ by 9⅛ inches	Official
No. 11	4 1/2 by 9½ inches	Document/policy
No. 12	5 by 11½ inches	Document/policy
No. 14	9 by 12 inches	First-class mailer
	10 by 13 inches	
	10 by 15 inches	
	12 by 15½ inches	

*The envelope used most often for correspondence.

Kraft envelopes

- Durable, thick, heavyweight stock (up to 50 lb.).
- Bleached or unbleached paper (a dark tan color).
- Available in a full range of sizes.
- Closures may be string and button, clasp, gummed, or self-stick. String and button and clasp envelopes can be reused. Clasp envelopes have gummed flaps for extra strength and security.
- Have wide usage, from storing small coins to mailing large catalogs.

Tyvek™ envelopes

- Available in No. 14 size.
- Made of polyolefin fibers bonded together by heat and pressure, making the envelopes rip-proof, puncture-proof, and water resistant.
- Because they weigh about half as much as paper, they can save postage.
- May incorporate a seal in the closure to reveal tampering, and a window on the flap changes to the word "opened" if the flap is lifted.

Interdepartment delivery envelopes

- May have either a string and button tie or resealable adhesive.
- Some have drilled holes to make contents visible.
- Available in Tyvek™.
- Available in colors such as red, yellow, blue, or orange.
- Transmittal information can be printed on one or both sides.

Laser printer envelopes

- Check the user's manual for envelope use.
- Must be of good construction, with a well-creased fold and no more than two thicknesses of paper.
- Should not have a paper weight greater than 24 lbs.
- Adhesives must not scorch, melt, offset, or release hazardous emissions when going through the laser printer.
- Most laser printers cannot accept window, string and button, or clasp envelopes.
- Usually, larger envelopes are more difficult to feed into the printer.
- Poorly constructed envelopes may result in a jammed printer or a wrinkled envelope.

See the following section on Labels for an alternative to envelope use with laser printers.

LABELS

Labels are available in many sizes and widths, ranging from one to four labels across a page. Labels have been developed specifically for laser printers and copiers. White labels are common; however, clear labels are available to blend into white, patterned, or colored envelopes to look neater and more personalized. Two commonly used sizes are 2⅝ by 1 inches and 1⅓ by 4 inches. Generally, the labels are self-adhered to paper 11 inches in length.

TRANSPARENCIES

A wide variety of overhead transparency film is specially developed to work on various types of office machines. Check the transparency box for compatibility with your printers and copiers since transparencies require a surface coating.

FILING AND RECORDS MANAGEMENT SUPPLIES

Most manual filing systems use file folders, labels, and guides. These products are available in a variety of sizes, shapes, colors, and styles. Filing supply choices depend on individual preferences and needs.

File Folders

There are two basic types of file folders. (1) Manila file folders are made of heavyweight stock that resists tearing, folding, and bursting. They are typically a light creamy color but are also available in a variety of colors. (2) Kraft file folders are made of unbleached sulfite stock in a dark tan color and are preferable when strength and rigidity are required. They look clean longer than manila folders, but they are more expensive.

Letter-size file folders are 9½ by 11¾ inches. The 9½-inch height includes the tab.

Both manila and kraft folders are described by the thickness of the folder, measured in points. One point is equivalent to 0.001 inch . As the point size increases, so does the durability and price of the folder. Typical weights for manila folders are 9½- and 11-point stock.

Table 9-8
FILE FOLDER SIZES

WEIGHT	POINT	USE
Medium	9½	Two or three times a week (semiactive) or less (inactive).
Heavy	11	Several times a day (active).
Extraheavy	17	Numerous times a day (very active); a common weight for guides.
Superior rigidity	25	Guides; available in pressboard (a hard, dense stock).

Typical kraft folders weights are 11- and 17-point. Table 9-8 lists the various sizes and uses of file folders.

In order to be cost-effective, the minimum weight of folders for a task should be used. When transferring files for storage information should be transferred to lighter-weight, less expensive folders. The heavier folders should be reused for active files.

TAB CUTS

A basic file folder has a tab made out of the same material as the folder. Most styles of folders are made with front flaps undercut to create the tab heading area. Special-purpose folders may have tabs that double the thickness of the folder from the top of the tab to the top of the undercut (called "double tab" or "two-ply" file folders). These tabs are good for active files. Other tabs are made of stronger material such as plastic.

The tab cut determines the number of tabs across the top edge of the file folder. Table 9-9 describes the different cuts. Folders usually are packaged with an equal number of tabs so the labeled tabs in the file drawer are staggered evenly.

OTHER FOLDER TYPES

There are several other important types of file folders:

Plastic file folders: Made of durable and flexible polyethylene or polypropylene, these are good for heavily-used folders because they resist spills and stains and are rarely damaged by handling. Many have a nonslip surface to prevent sliding when stacked. They come in a variety of colors and are good for a color-coded system.

Table 9-9
TAB CUTS

CUT	DESCRIPTION	USE
Straight	Tab length is the full width of folder.	Multiple labels; extra long headings.
Half	Tab length is one-half the width of folder; tabs are staggered in sets of two.	Long headings.
Third	Tab length is one-third the width of folder; tabs are staggered in sets of three.	Most common; most folder labels are designed for this folder and do not fit other cuts.
Fifth	Tab length is one-fifth the width of folder; tabs are staggered in sets of five.	Less room for writing; most popular for numerical filing systems.
Two-fifths	Tab length is two-fifths the width of folder; tabs are either right of center or far right.	Long headings.
Shelf or end cut	Tab is on the end of the folder instead of the top; scored expansion bottoms accommodate more material.	Open shelf filing systems where records are stored in horizontal rows rather than in file drawers.

Hanging file folders: Most file drawers are equipped for a hanging file system or can be converted by using a metal frame. Files hang at a uniform level from rodlike projections or hooks at the top, allowing tabs to remain visible and preventing folders from sliding down into the drawer. Many have removable plastic tabs into which paper labeling tabs can be inserted—and removed and changed, and tabs can be used in a variety of positions. They are available in a range of colors and thus can be used in a color-coded system.

Interior manila folders: Shorter than regular manila folders, these are specifically designed to be used inside hanging file folders to make it easy to remove material from the hanging folder without taking the folder out of the drawer. The height and tabs are designed so as not to block or interfere with hanging folder tabs.

Bellows (expansion) folders: These are available with pockets and may be labeled alphabetically or numerically.

Box bottom hanging folders: These folders have flat, reinforced bottoms for filing heavy, bulky material; closed sides keep smaller items from slipping out.

File folders with fasteners: Folders are available with fasteners attached in various positions to secure papers inside them; self-adhesive varieties are available as well as the standard version with plastic or metal prong fasteners that thread through the folder.

LABELS FOR FILE FOLDERS

File folder labels are available in self-adhesive, dry back, and removable types. They come in either sheets or rolls. They may be white or white with a color border. A wide range of border colors is available, including coral, lavender, and black as well as the traditional colors of yellow, blue, and red. File folder labels can also be one color, ranging from lightly tinted pastel shades to neon colors. Self-adhesive label protectors, which are clear Mylar laminate, can be used to protect top or end tabs on folders.

Self-adhesive labels for hanging file folders can be applied to plastic folder tabs or to their paper inserts. If the labels are put on the outside of the plastic tab, the tab inserts are unnecessary. These labels will not snag or peel off and are available in a variety of colored borders.

Preprinted inserts are also available for tabs; they eliminate typing of labels. The inserts are usually alphabetical, numerical, daily, monthly, or by states. Legal exhibit labels are also available preprinted.

GUIDES

File guides are used for dividing file drawers into categorized sections, thus preventing misfiling and wasting time. File guides can be 18-point manila, for inactive to semiactive files, or 25-point pressboard for semiactive to active files. Manila guides cost less than pressboard but are less durable. Guides are available with plain tabs, and monthly, daily, or alphabetic preprinted tabs. File guides are available for hanging file folders. Tabs are either made of the same paper as the guide or made of plastic or steel.

Out guides indicate that an entire folder has been removed from the files. Out guides range from 11- to 17-point paper with either end or tab cuts. Usually they are a bright color such as red or orange, The guide may include a printed form on which to write the date and by whom the file was removed or it may have a small pocket for a charge-out card.

COLORS

Color folders allow the classifying and coding of files by color. Color coding can be done with colored labels, file folders, hanging file folders, or labels. Color coding has several advantages, including the following:

- It guides the eye to correct files and reduces filing and retrieval time.
- It increases filing accuracy because misfiled items stand out.
- It provides additional subdivisions of filed material beyond label headings.

Storage Boxes

Corrugated cardboard filing boxes can be used for long-term storage of checks, documents, cards, forms, printouts, and tapes. The boxes usually need to be assembled. They have built-in handles and can be ordered with a color-coded system, which can save as much as 50 percent in filing and retrieval time. Some boxes are constructed to stand up under more than half a ton of stacking pressure, which maximizes storage floor space.

WRITING INSTRUMENTS AND CORRECTION SUPPLIES

New colors, improvements in style, a variety of types, and a wide range of prices provide many options. Because each writing instrument has advantages for its recommended use, it is likely that you use several different kinds. Many formerly low-end products have been developed with high-tech, aesthetically pleasing designs. Despite increased use of computers and electronic typewriters, office professionals still write some things in pen, marker, and pencil.

Pens

Pens are available in the following types:

Ballpoint: Most popular office pen, ballpoints may either be disposable or have a changeable refill. The ink dries quickly and does not smear, it writes through carbon copies, and it may be erasable. Store ballpoints point down for longest life.

Fountain: Enjoying a resurgence in popularity, fountain pens have a prestigious look. They can use a variety of brightly colored inks. Some are disposable, while others are refillable or have disposable ink cartridges.

Rollerball: These are becoming very popular for office use. They are available in several colors. The tips have a metal ball encased in a plastic or metal stem. Because they write darker and smoother than ballpoint pens, they are good for drawing, ruling, and detail work as well as writing. They can write through carbon copies; they are usually nonrefillable. Some rollerball pens are available with permanent waterproof ink, which is popular in banks and financial and legal offices as well as in humid climates.

Porous point or *felt tip:* These flow easily and have the crisp, precise lines of a ballpoint; however, their points are made of plastic, which may soften with age. The ink is often brighter in color than that of a ballpoint, and they are usually disposable. Although they will not write through carbon, they are good for detail work, ruling, sketching, and labeling floppy disks.

Markers

Markers are available for highlighting information, writing on surfaces, and writing on white boards and transparencies. Below are descriptions of various markers:

Highlighters: These are often used to call attention to information in reading material with bright see-through colors such as yellow, pink, and orange. They can make very fine or very bold lines, depending on the tip. Some can highlight on thin paper without bleeding through; some are nonsmearing and thus can be used to highlight over ink; some will not show up on copies.

Permanent markers: These are good for writing on nonporous surfaces such as cellophane, glass, metal, and transparent tape. They are suitable for mailing labels since the ink does not run when wet. They are not recommended for ordinary writing because the ink bleeds through paper. The ink dries quickly and will not smear. They are available in a wide variety of colors, but some have a distinctive irritating odor. Chisel (or wedge) tips can make fine, medium, or bold strokes; bullet tip (pointed) makes a heavier mark.

Easel pad markers: Designed to write on easel pads, these are available in a variety of colors. Look for chisel tip and waterbased ink that will not bleed through paper.

Dry erase markers: These are designed for use on whiteboards only; they cannot be used on paper because they dry out quickly. They are available in many colors and have little odor, and they erase with a dry cloth or eraser. Some may also be used on glass, unpainted metal, and glazed ceramics. Whiteboards and dry erase markers are popular because they eliminate chalk dust around computers.

Visual aid markers: Available in both permanent and erasable (if waterbased) forms, these are used for writing on acetates, such as transparencies. Available in a wide range of colors, they are designed to remain brilliant and clear under heat and light.

Pencils

Traditional woodcase lead pencils are still found in many offices, although mechanical pencils have become very popular because they have different lead thicknesses and low prices.

The older turn-type mechanical pencils held only one lead at a time and needed frequent reloading. The newest and best mechanical pencils advance the lead automatically and insert new leads as old ones are used up. Lead is available in widths of 0.5, 0.7, and 0.9 millimeters. The 0.5-mm lead is the most popular and is used for general writing and detail work, heavier lines can be drawn with 0.7- and 0.9-mm lead. Mechanical pencils are good for drafting, accounting, and general office work.

COMPUTER, FAX MACHINE, AND COPIER SUPPLIES

Changes in technology have resulted in a greater variety of equipment in the office, and so there is a wide range of supplies for equipment such as computers, fax machines, and copiers.

Computer Disks

Computer disks come in various sizes, depending on the computer used. The most popular size is the 3½-inch disk. The 3½-inch disk is small and easy to carry.

Disks can be ordered preformatted for PCs. They are available in colors that allow for color-coding data. Some disk manufacturers offer a service to restore lost data at no charge, and other disks are certified to be 100 percent error-free and have lifetime guarantees of free replacement. Although many disks look similar, there are differences in the way data is stored, depending on the computer system used. The following are typical abbreviations for disks:

▲ SS   =   single side (data stored on one side)

▲ DS   =   double side (data stored on two sides)

▲ SD   =   single density

▲ DD   =   double density

▲ QUAD =   quad density (also called high density)

The density indicates how closely the computer spaces the magnetic spots when it records a file. Most disks are double density (DD) and may also be used on single-density machines.

Disk Storage

There are boxes with roll tops or hinged lids in oak, polystyrene, transparent acrylic, or plastic to store 3½-inch disks. Some boxes have locks for security, movable dividers, built-in handles, the ability to pop up for an easel display, or can be attached to the side of the monitor.

Plastic three-hole punched disk holders fit in 8½-by-11-inch notebooks. There are also three-ring holders designed to keep documentation together with disks. For convenient storage in file folders or binders, there are self-adhesive pockets with pressure-sensitive backs that stick to most surfaces.

Traveling diskette holders come in a range of sizes, including a 20-disk carrying case with X-ray protection and a wallet-sized nylon holder for antistatic protection.

Disk Mailers

Disk mailers are designed with a sturdy construction to offer protection from bending, static, and moisture. The mailers provide a preprinted address area with first-class postal identification and a warning such as: "Caution: Do not bend or fold. Avoid exposure to all magnetic fields."

Surge Protectors

Computers are sensitive to problems with the power supply. Such problems include surges, spikes, drops, noise, brownouts, and blackouts. Surges generally last longer than spikes, but both usually occur so fast that they are not noticed. Noise interference can be transmitted to the power line by things such as nearby radio and TV stations, loose electrical connections, and fluorescent lights. (See Table 9-10 for power problems and causes and Table 9-11 for protective devices.)

A loss of power or a sudden surge of power can cause serious damage to the circuitry of a computer, disk drive, printer, and communications equipment as well as erase valuable data. A surge protector is a cost-effective method of insuring that computers, printers, and fax machines are protected from unpredictable weather or current changes. Surge protectors divert any excess electricity out the ground line and away from electrical equipment. Surge protectors prevent hardware damage and data transmission errors.

Table 9-10
POWER PROBLEMS AND CAUSES

PROBLEM	EFFECT	POSSIBLE CAUSES
Surge	Increase in voltage	Switching of other equipment on or off.
Spike	Sudden increase in voltage	Lightning, utility company load-switching, power coming on after outage.
Outage	No voltage	Weather, power-line breaks, power system failures.
Sags/brownout	Decrease in voltage	Power company reduction during high demand periods, overloads.
Noise	Interference	High-frequency voltages from local electrical devices, including fluorescent lights.

Table 9-11
POWER PROTECTION DEVICES AVAILABLE

DEVICE	SURGE	SPIKE	SAG	OUTAGE	NOISE
Surge protector	Yes	Yes	No	No	Some
UPS (uninterruptible power systems)	Yes	Yes	Yes	Yes	Some
SPS (standby power systems)	No	No	No	Yes	No
Power conditioner	Yes	Yes	Yes	No	Yes

Some surge protectors have desktop remote controls and alarms to warn when the voltage drops below safe levels. Other surge protectors protect against spikes coming over the phone lines and are ideal for fax machines, modems, and answering machines.

Fax/Phone Line Sharing

Instead of adding another phone fine, equipment is available to add a fax machine to an existing telephone line without interfering with the phone or answering machine already there. There are models designed for single-line, two-line, and multiple-line phone systems. They are compatible with tone and rotary (pulse) dialing, which allows continued phone operation during power failures.

Laser Printer and Copy Machine Toner Cartridges

Toner cartridges are used by laser printers and some copy machines. Toner is a dry, powdered substance that is attracted to electrically charged areas on the machine's photosensitive revolving drum. Toner cartridges can be ordered in color for some copy machines.

Toner should not be exposed to direct sunlight or room light for more than a few minutes because it uses a developing process similar to that of film in a camera. Light can cause the developing roller inside the cartridge to be damaged.

Some service bureaus can recharge toners, either locally or through the mail. If the recharging is done by mail, the empty toner cartridge is shipped in its original box, where it is recharged and returned. Note, however, that some laser printer manufacturers recommend against refilling cartridges because it may cause damage to the printer.

RIBBONS

Ribbons for the same machine may look alike or took totally different due to packaging, colors, and design features. Different part numbers in the user's manual represent differences in design, ink color, length of ribbon, and material, so it is possible for one type of ribbon to have more than one part number. If a ribbon was manufactured by the original equipment manufacturer and made in strict compliance with the device, it carries the abbreviation "OEM."

One way to avoid duplicating orders of ribbons is to establish an in-house list of machines and their ribbons. The list would include statements such as "Margaret's typewriter in Personnel takes X ribbons."

Ribbons for printing calculators and cash registers are nylon and are available in black, purple, or a combination of black and red.

Typewriters use correctable ribbons with lift-off tape or tabs, and nylon or poly ribbons, depending on the model type and manufacturer's recommendations.

Printers use nylon ribbons. The width, length, caliper, and thread count vary with each specific ribbon. For the highest performance of printer ribbons, check the owner's manual for complete instructions on installation. Most ribbons have safety clips installed on the ribbon for protection during shipping and storage. It is important to remove all clips before installation or the ribbon might not advance, causing light printing, jamming, or breakage of the ribbon.

CHAPTER 10

THE

OFFICE

WORKSTATION

A basic element of every office is the workstation. The workstation is a place where the worker can think and perform an assigned set of tasks. For the administrative assistant, the workstation is the action center for organizing and processing information, telephone calls, electronic messages, and files; for greeting visitors, maintaining reference materials, and performing other executive-support activities.

TYPES OF OFFICE WORKSTATIONS

The development of open-space planning has changed the look of offices significantly. Open offices use panels to create a maze of workstations consisting of systems furniture. Systems furniture includes partitions, desks or work surfaces, storage units, and accessories. Although offices with fixed walls and conventional furniture are still prevalent, the open office concept provides the greatest amount of flexibility for meeting changing business and financial trends.

A workstation is designed according to the needs of each individual office professional. There are workstations for receptionists, secretaries, administrative managers, supervisors, middle managers, and executives. Each workstation is designed to provide the necessary privacy, work surface, and storage for the task(s) being performed.

The workstation must physically support a variety of daily tasks. One's physical and psychological well-being are upset by bad design or poorly-adjusted office components, such as the desk, chair, and computer. "Syntonic" is a term that means receptive to and in harmony with the environment. Syntonic design integrates or "harmonizes" all aspects of planning to create an office support system that maximizes productivity while meeting human needs. The integration of people, tools, and the workplace is necessary for efficient offices.

COMPONENTS OF A WORKSTATION

The workstation is composed of office seating, work surfaces, storage containers or files, and privacy panels.

Seating

The most important component is the office chair. (See Figures 10-1 and 10-2a.) It has to support office profes-

CHAIR EVALUATION CHECKLIST

	YES	NO
A. HEIGHT		
1. Is the range of height adjustment adequate?	___	___
2. Can the chair height be easily adjusted?	___	___
3. Can the adjustment be made from the seated position?	___	___
4. Are adequate footrests available?	___	___
B. BACKREST		
5. Does the chair have a high backrest?	___	___
6. Does the backrest interfere with arm movements?	___	___
7. Is the lumbar support adequate?	___	___
8. Is the tension of the backrest adjustable?	___	___
9. Does the backrest tilt back?	___	___
10. Does the backrest lock in position?	___	___
11. Can the backrest be adjusted up and down?	___	___
12. Can the backrest be adjusted forward?	___	___
C. ARMRESTS		
13. Does the chair have armrests?	___	___
14. Are the armrests appropriate for the job?	___	___
15. Are armrests optional?	___	___
16. Do armrests interfere with movement?	___	___
D. SEATPAN		
17. Does the seatpan have a rounded front edge?	___	___
18. Does the seatpan tilt?	___	___
19. Is seatpan tension adjustable?	___	___
20. Does seatpan lock in position?	___	___
E. SAFETY		
21. Is the chair stable?	___	___
22. Does the chair have a 5-leg base?	___	___
23. Are casters matched to the floor?	___	___
24. Can casters be changed?	___	___
25. Are all adjustments safe against self or unintentional release?	___	___
26. Does chair meet all applicable fire codes?	___	___
F. COMFORT		
27. Is the chair adequately padded?	___	___
28. Are materials appropriate?	___	___
29. Is the chair comfortable?	___	___
G. OTHER		
30. Can the chair be easily maintained?	___	___
31. Can maintenance be performed in the field?	___	___

Figure 10-1 Chair evaluation checklist.

Figure 10-2 a: An ergonomic chair with adjustable height, gel-filled, flipper armrests for proper support during mousing activities. A pneumatic lifting mechanism is also available to easily adjust the height of the chair along with a back-height adjustment of up to 4 inches. (Courtesy of Haworth, Inc.) b: This workstation cluster of two administrative/secretarial support workstations are divided by panels with overhead storage units. The power and communications cables are hidden and managed through a wire raceway incorporated into the panel system. A reception-height counter is used for managers to drop-off or review work. (Courtesy of Haworth, Inc.)

sionals in the performance of most office tasks. Lower back pain, the number-one office health problem, is often caused by improper seating. Some researchers believe that there is no one correct seating position. The user, therefore, should be able to adjust the chair to his or her specific anatomical or physical characteristics and favorite seating positions.

Desirable features to consider when selecting an office chair include the following:

Height adjustment: Most office chairs can be raised or lowered to make sure one's feet touch the floor properly. Height adjustment is also important to ensure that one's arms maintain a correct angle for keyboard use. Very short people can use a slanted footrest to support their feet.

Lumbar support: A slight concavity in the lower back of the chair is important to minimize lower back pain. It helps to support the normal alignment and the natural curve of the lower spine, in a manner similar to the standing position.

HINT: *A thin pillow will provide support if the back of the chair is flat.*

Side arms: A chair with side arms helps to take pressure off the wrist when keyboarding and also can support leaning positions.

Waterfall seat: Prolonged sitting cuts off blood circulation to the legs. A sloping, rounded front edge on the seat takes strain off the thighs. Such a seat, called a waterfall seat, improves circulation.

Forward tilt: This feature locks the seat in a forward tilting position. This is very helpful when keyboarding for long periods of time.

GUIDELINES FOR WORK SURFACES

	YES	NO	N/A
1. Is there adequate space to perform all tasks?			
2. Is there adequate space for all equipment?			
3. Can any workspace be shared?			
4. Can the workspace be adapted for either right or left hand use?			
5. Are all items of equipment and job aids which must frequently be used within the normal arm reach of the worker?			
6. Does the arrangement of the work area allow access to all equipment and job aids without excessive twisting?			
7. Are equipment, documents, writing surfaces, telephones, etc., arranged in the most efficient way?			
8. Is adequate space provided for storage of copies, handbooks, documents, and personal belongings?			
9. Are different heights necessary for different tasks?			
10. Are the heights of all working surfaces correct?			
11. Are working surfaces adjustable in height?			
12. Are surfaces user-adjustable?			
13. Can working surfaces be tilted?			
14. Is the surface thin enough to allow adequate leg space and a correct working height?			
15. Is there adequate legroom so the worker can adopt different postures?			
16. Is the area under the work surface free of obstructions that might interfere with movements between different tasks?			

Figure 10-3 Guidelines for work surfaces.

Back tilt: This feature helps one recline, which is at times comfortable and necessary. Several manufacturers' chairs allow the user to lock two or three angles.

Base and casters: A five-star base prevents tipping. Dual-wheel or single-wheel casters allow easy movement over both hard and soft surfaces.

Work Surfaces

Much office work is done on the most important work surface, the desktop. (See Figure 10-3.) Other work surfaces may hold equipment, paper-flow sorting trays, telephones, and writing and reference materials.

Because there are various sizes and shapes of paper and office equipment, the surfaces must have adequate depth. A surface must be a minimum of 24 inches deep, for example, to hold binders with printouts, and 30 inches deep to accommodate a personal computer. Sometimes it is possible to adjust the height of the work surface to better accommodate an individual's needs.

Storage

Adequate storage space improves the organization of an office's workspace. Recorded information is stored on many media, such as paper, magnetic floppy disks, microfilm, microfiche, CD-ROM, and optical disks. Each medium requires its own unique type of storage container. Fixed or mobile pedestals, binder bins, overhead flipper door cabinets, and lateral or vertical file cabinets help in organizing and storing information media, reference manuals, and supplies. (See the sections on Managing Paper-Based Records and Computer Software in Chapter 12 for more information.)

Privacy Panels

Privacy panels are movable walls that can be as short as 40 inches high or as tall as the ceiling. Open-plan offices use movable panels that are lower than ceiling height to provide privacy. Since all desks, partitions, and other equipment can be moved easily, the workstations can be rearranged in a matter of hours, instead of days. (See Figure 10-2b)

WORKSTATION ADJUSTMENT

Ergonomics is the study of the relationship between the worker and the work environment. (The term comes from the Greek words *ergon* meaning "work" and *nomos* meaning "law.") It takes into account the individual characteristics of the worker. Ideally, every office workstation should meet the physical, psychological, and work requirements of the individual.

Ergonomic principles are partly based on the study of anthropometrics. This involves the measurement of size and proportions of the human body. The height of a table and the width of a seat pan, for example, should fit the bodily dimensions of workers.

Ergonomic principles are also based on biomechanics, the study of the human body's structure and functions. Activities such as sitting for long periods, bending, lilting, and reaching can strain various body parts. Working positions should try to minimize fatigue and wear and tear on the body caused by such activities.

To conform to these principles, five focal points of adjustment are essential in any workstation: seating, work surface, video display terminal, lighting, and storage.

Seating

Because office professionals spend most of their time in a chair, it is a crucial factor in comfort and efficiency. The proper chair must fit the individual and the job. A starting point for determining correct chair height is to equal the distance from the floor to the crease behind the knee. The height of the chair should be set to distribute body weight as evenly as possible, 14 to 17.5 inches for women and 15.5 to 19.2 inches for men.

Other important features include the following:

- Swivel-tilt, which allows freedom of movement so users can respond easily to changes in task requirements
- Easy-to-reach, adjustable controls, including a height adjustment handle on chairs with a pneumatic lift and a tension-control knob
- Adjustable armrests to minimize strain on the forearms and wrists
- Adjustable back support for the upper back

Work Surfaces

Most work surfaces are 26 to 29 inches high. Since people vary in height, this is not always satisfactory. Most office professionals prefer a work surface located slightly above elbow height. This allows the arms to rest on the surface without leaning forward too far.

Video Display Terminals

Office workers often spend many hours a day looking at video display terminals (VDTs). Prolonged work at the terminal can lead to repetitive stress injuries (RSIs). Pain in the lower back, carpel tunnel syndrome, forearm pain, and upper shoulder strain are examples of RSIs. Other keyboarding-related complaints include headaches, eye strain, and worry about electromagnetic frequency (EMF) from the VDT screen.

Here are guidelines for working at a VDT:

- The VDT should rest on the work surface and preferably not on top of the CPU (i.e., the disk drive). Most workers prefer the centerline of the screen to be slightly below eye level.

- Provide for keyboard height adjustability so that the wrists can be kept in a neutral position with the feet flat on the floor.
- Ensure that the lower arm and extended hand form a straight line parallel to the keytops. For maximum safety and comfort, specify a keyboard tray that slopes downward in a negative slope away from the operator to offset the positive slope of most computer keyboards. Research finds the tilt-down keyboard tray to be the best in providing for optimum comfort and low RSI risk.
- Specify a palm rest, not a wrist rest. Consider products that are integrated into the keyboard tray. This allows for micro breaks and support of the forearm.
- In order to minimize neck strain and related headaches, suggest the use of a copy holder to provide for the proper alignment of copy with the CRT.
- Use a mouse platform that allows the mouse to be positioned within the elbow zone to eliminate shoulder abduction.

HINT: *Adjustable VDT tables with two surfaces ensure good posture by allowing the keyboard and screen to be adjusted independently to the appropriate levels.*

HINT: *CRTs generate light, certain inaudible sound waves, radio-frequency radiation, X-rays, electromagnetic fields, and static electricity. Few of these emissions are reported to be harmful in the levels emitted. The general guideline is to sit at least 36 inches away from the backs and sides of the VDT monitor and up to 30 inches or an arm's length, away from the front of the monitor. Also, purchase a low-radiation VDT screen.*

HINT: *Hundreds of products identified by the manufacturer as ergonomic are now on the market. Be selective by identifying the problem you wish to solve and by asking for research to support the manufacturer's ergonomic claims.*

Lighting

Glare and brightness in a work environment, especially where VDTs are used, can cause eye fatigue and hamper employee productivity. (See Figure 10-4.) Appropriate lighting can reduce if not eliminate most problems. Workers need to have as much control as possible over their individual workstation (lighting) to assure visual and physical comfort. Ways to adjust the lighting within a workstation include (1) the ability to dim overhead lighting and (2) the addition of a desk lamp for lighting for specific tasks.

Indirect, ceiling-mounted or ambient light in combination with adjustable, task-specific lighting works best to help eliminate computer lighting problems. Light levels should serve for all tasks within the office.

HINT: *The National Lighting Bureau is a good source of information on lighting issues and working with lighting consultants. This bureau has published a number of guides related to VDTs and lighting systems. The NLB is located at 2101 L Street NW, Suite 300, Washington, DC 20037.*

CHECKLIST FOR OFFICE LIGHTING

	YES	NO	N/A
1. Is the level of illumination proper for hard copy tasks?	___	___	___
2. Is the level of illumination proper for VDT use?	___	___	___
3. Are task lights provided as necessary?	___	___	___
4. Are lights flicker-free?	___	___	___
5. Are lights clean and well maintained?	___	___	___
6. Is the worker's field of view free of sources of glare?	___	___	___
7. Is the worker's field of view free of reflections from display screens, keyboards, desk, papers, etc.?	___	___	___
8. Are windows covered with blinds, drapes, or other means of controlling light?	___	___	___
9. Are lights covered with glare shields?	___	___	___
10. Are panels used to block glare and reflections?	___	___	___
11. Are workstations positioned to avoid glare and reflections?	___	___	___
12. Are VDTs fitted with filters to reduce reflections	___	___	___
13. Are VDTs equipped with brightness and contrast controls?	___	___	___
14. Can VDTs or tables be tilted to reduce reflections?	___	___	___
15. Are contrasts within the visual field within recommended limits?	___	___	___
16. Are reflectances of walls, floors, and ceilings within recommended limits?	___	___	___

Figure 10-4 Checklist for office lighting.

ORGANIZING THE WORKSTATION ENVIRONMENT

An office space plan shows the organization and placement of workstation components, including work surfaces, filing and storage cabinets, and chairs. Office space plans should meet the psychological and physiological needs of workers. As the users of workstations, office professionals should have some say in such planning.

One's state of mind can directly influence efficiency. For example, when a worker perceives his or her office space to be unsatisfactory, poor morale is the result. Personal preferences regarding placement of the telephone, personal computer, and other office tools are also essential.

HINT: *Most people do not like to sit with their backs to the hallway nor to have more than one entrance into a workstation.*

Environmental disturbances from lighting, noise, and climate (including heat levels and air quality) can cause physiological stress. (See Figure 10-5 for a workstation comfort checklist.)

Planning Office Space

Space planning for administrative staff workstations in large companies is usually done by interior designers or facility managers. However, administrative staffs should have

---

A "yes" response to any of the following questions indicates the need to make an adjustment in your workstation environment and may require an accessory:

1. Do you use a visual display terminal (VDT) more than 4 hours per day?

2. Are you required to maintain stressful body positions for extended periods of time? (examples might include using a mouse or a digitizing tablet)

3. Are the height, location, and orientation of the workstation furniture, computer, and other features fixed and not able to be adjusted to accommodate your body size and posture preferences?

4. Do you constantly lean forward rather than sitting back in your chair when keying at the computer?

5. Do you have itching or dry eyes?

6. Does the room lighting cause glare or make the VDT screen hard to read?

7. Is the room temperature uncomfortable—too hot, too cold, too stuffy? Do you experience fatigue, especially by two or three o'clock in the afternoon?

8. Does the office environment seem excessively loud and noisy from equipment sounds or workers talking?

9. Are you continually getting out of your chair to get reference manuals or other source materials when working at the VDT?

10. Do you experience extreme bending and reaching for files, manuals, and other information in your workstation while working at the VDT?

Figure 10-5 Workstation comfort checklist.

some input into the design of their workstations, to help arrange the work space properly to match the tasks. In small offices, administrative assistants may set up their own workstations,

To organize a workstation for maximum task support, begin with a task analysis. This is a process that profiles what people do and maps this onto a physical setting to see how people do it. Demands associated with different activities will fall into common categories. This information aids the planner in determining proper lighting, acoustics, and workspace requirements.

The next step in the design of a workstation space plan is to divide the workstation into work focus zones. These are the locations in the workstation where a specific type of work is done. Office tasks can be put in six basic categories: data entry; information acquisition; information transaction; analysis and problem solving; creative and imaginative thinking; and meeting and conferring. An office space plan should allow space for each type of work that will be done there.

The third step is to plan the arrangement of work resources, equipment, and materials within each zone. Resources should be positioned for case of equipment operation, with materials easily reached and visual displays comfortably placed for ease of viewing.

Managing Cables

As advances in information technology continue, the changes in today's office equipment continue at a pace faster than most offices can handle. This sometimes requires the rearrangement of office interiors, including reorganization of wiring. Managing the cables is usually left up to the electricians and facilities design managers.

LAN Management

Vital to a successful office is the ability to tie all company information together. In order to achieve that goal, a local area network (LAN) usually needs to be established. A LAN allows people in a department to share information with each other electronically as well as to share common resources such as printers and large hard disks.

LANs are comprised of cables—twisted-pair, coaxial, and fiber optics—connected to controller cards installed at each computer. More recently, wireless LANs have been developed that use radio frequencies or infrared light instead of cables.

WORKSTATION ACCESSORIES

There are many accessories that add to the efficiency of a workstation and that can personalize it. These range from paper management accessories to computer support accessories.

Paper Management Accessories

By aiding the storage and retrieval of paperwork, paper management accessories help to control paper usage within the workstation. Paper management accessories include desk racks with paper holders, as well as vertical and horizontal paper trays and organizers that mount onto wall panels or inside a cabinet. Forms, computer printouts, and reference material can easily be stored in these accessories. Some accessories can be transported to the next workstation. Other accessories include paper holders for computer printer paper and paper catchers for continuous form paper as it moves through the printer.

Computer Accessories

Computer accessories are intended to help users save space, protect data, and increase comfort. Accessories include antiglare filters or screens, monitor arms and swivel bases for adjusting monitors to user comfort, articulating drawers for keyboards, and workstation furniture designed specifically for computers.

HINT: *Glare can be reduced and contrast improved with a light background and dark text or graphics.*

Additional accessories include copy holders, disk files, switching systems, static mats, computer tool kits, footrests, surge protectors, and security and antitheft devices.

Personal Accessories

The way a workstation is decorated and maintained reflects its user's efficiency, professionalism, taste, and status. Policy on personal accessories varies from company to company and department to department.

Here are guidelines to follow when personalizing the workstation:

- Minimize clutter. A work surface that is bare except for the project being worked on and a few stylish accessories conveys an image of control and taste.
- Only those items being used should be on the primary work surface. Calculators, business card files, paper clip containers, extra pens and pencils should be put away when not in use.
- The "in" box should be well managed. An overflowing "in" box represents its owner's lack of efficiency besides taking up valuable work space. A wall-mounted "in" box is more efficient but it, too, needs to be properly managed.
- Keep projects organized. Projects should be neatly labeled and filed out of the way, not kept in a heap on the corner of a work surface.
- When selecting art for the workstation, restraint and respect for the corporate culture are paramount.

Arthritis: inflammation of a joint or joints.

Carpal tunnel syndrome: a compression of the median nerve as it passes through the carpal tunnel in the heel of the hand.

Chronic low back pain: general soreness and fatigue of the low back; pain is usually constant, and it accompanies most activities.

Constriction: binding, squeezing, or shrinking blood vessels so that circulation is reduced.

Cubital tunnel syndrome: compression of the ulnar nerve as it passes through the notch of the elbow.

Cumulative trauma disorder: damage to body tissue by outside forces that has built up over time.

Degenerative disc disease: a breakdown of the discs that separate the vertebrae of the spine.

DeQuervain's disease: an inflammation of the tendon and/or its sheath at the base of the thumb.

Digital neuritis: compression of the nerves along the sides of the fingers or thumbs.

Epicondylitis: an inflammation of the tendons at the elbow. Also called tennis elbow (lateral or outside part of the elbow) or golfer's elbow (medial or inside part of the elbow).

Ganglionic cyst: swelling of the tendon and sheath due to the buildup of synovial fluid inside the sheath. The cyst usually causes a bump under the skin.

Nonspecific backache: general soreness and fatigue of the lower back.

Raynaud's disease: a constriction of the blood vessels in the hands and fingers. Also called "white finger."

Rotator cuff tendinitis: inflammation of one or more tendons at the shoulder. Also called "pitcher's shoulder."

Sprain: overstretching of overexertion of a ligament that results in a tear or rupture of the ligament.

Strain: overstretching or overexertion of a muscle or tendon.

Tendinitis: inflammation of the tendon inside the sheath.

Tenosynovitis: inflammation of the sheath around the tendon.

Thoracic outlet syndrome: compression of the nerves and blood vessels between the neck and shoulder often associated with prolonged overhead work.

Trigger finger: a common term for tendinitis or tenosynovitis that causes painful locking of the finger(s) while flexing.

Ulnar nerve entrapment: compression of the ulnar nerve as it passes through the wrist, often associated with prolonged flexion and extension of the wrist and pressure on the palm.

(*Source:* CTD News Online, from the Center for Workplace Health Information, "Fit-ting the job to the worker: An ergonomics program guideline (4 of 5), Appendix A.)

Figure 10-6 Medical terms for musculoskeletal disorders.

- Fabric panel walls should be kept clear. Mounting things to the fabric panels will keep it from absorbing sound.
- Use fabric art on solid walls to improve acoustics.
- Accessories that are permanently on the work surface should be chosen for utility and style. An accessory should pass the following test: Does it give its owner pleasure to use it and look at it? Is it in good taste?

HINT: *Diplomas and certificates on the wall usually advertise insecurity and lack of taste, except for doctors and lawyers.*

PART III

SPECIALIZED

OFFICE

PROCEDURES

Successful companies keep their employees informed and involve them in decisions that affect employee welfare. Publications, such as policy and procedures manuals, job description manuals, and company newsletters, can have a positive impact on the employer-employee communication process. Since office professionals have good organizational and formatting skills, they often assume major responsibilities for preparing these documents.

POLICY MANUALS

A **policy manual** incorporates general guidelines governing how a company will operate to accomplish its purposes. Policies may be covered in one manual, and procedures that describe how to do certain activities or tasks may be covered in a separate manual; or they may be combined in one manual. If they are combined, policy statements and procedures must be clearly separated and identified.

Although the board of directors makes the final decisions regarding company policies, top-level managers are responsible for seeing that the policies are written and carried out. They may write the policy statements themselves, hire technical writers, or assign the writing to someone else within the company.

Even a small company will find a policy manual helpful to communicate employee responsibilities and outline the firm's mission and goals. To lessen the possibility of an employee initiating an unfair treatment action against the company, and to be sure the policies comply with state and federal laws, an attorney should always review policy statements and prepare any disclaimer notices the company includes in the manual. Middle-management, supervisory, union, and employee input is always necessary and is especially important in the initial and evaluative stages of the process.

Purpose

To function effectively, employees need a good overall understanding of what the organization hopes to accomplish. Policy manuals are given to employees to provide that information and to explain the guidelines under which they must function.

Since policy manuals are written documents, all em-

CHAPTER 11

OFFICE

MANUALS

AND

PUBLICATIONS

ployees will receive the same information. If managers apply the policies uniformly, employees should receive fair and equal consideration. In turn, a policy manual gives companies some protection from legal suits that may result from employee dissatisfaction.

Content

The amount of information in a policy manual varies with the type and size of the company and with the level of its employees. Exceptions to policies will sometimes occur, so do not try to incorporate every case into one general statement. The following are policy manual topics, divided into two categories, company information and general personnel policies:

COMPANY INFORMATION

- Historical summary
- Company goals/mission statement
- Philosophy and basic beliefs

HINT: *Include how the company got started and what it stands for today.*

- Board of director's policies—authority, organization, meeting notification, and conduct
- Conflict of interest—board members, management, employees
- Stockholders—voting rights, responsibilities
- Organization chart
- Departmental responsibilities
- Company organization/subsidiaries/branch offices—location, function
- Commitment to customer service
- Commitment to employees
- Public relations—handling confidential information, information clearance
- Product lines and services
- Building usage/building names—authorization for outside use by groups, selection of building names
- Budget and finance—responsibility, financial reports, distribution of reports
- Company closings/takeovers/mergers
- Political activity
- Ethics/theft
- Commitment to a safe workplace
- Commitment to environmental concerns
- Involvement with local community
- Disaster recovery

GENERAL PERSONNEL POLICIES

- Affirmative action and equal opportunity position
- Recruitment standards/applications/reference checks
- Personnel files—content, maintenance, access

HINT: *Under the Americans with Disabilities Act (ADA) and the Family and Medical Leave Act, employers must place medical information in a separate file. Prepare explicit guidelines for accessing medical or personnel files.*

- Benefits, such as insurance, pension, and savings
- Retirement/vesting/401k plans/Keoghs
- Vacation schedules/accrued vacation
- Company services, such as company store, merchandise reductions, education, childcare, and elder care
- Performance appraisals/promotions/incentives/transfers
- Grievance procedures/probation/termination
- Leaves, such as emergency, illness, personal, jury duty, bereavement, maternity, family, military, and educational
- Hours of operation/overtime provisions/outside employment limitations
- Attendance and punctuality—expectations, disciplinary action
- Dress codes
- Holidays
- Payroll provisions, such as pay periods, and exempt or non-exempt status
- Part-time work/student employment/temporary help/outside business centers
- Work-related injuries/insurance/compensation limits
- Drugs/alcohol—prohibited use, testing, disciplinary actions
- Illness in the workplace/life-threatening diseases/confidentiality of medical records/AIDS/HIV issues
- Sexual harassment—definition, disciplinary actions
- Safety/building security
- Office furniture and decor
- Copyright protection
- E-mail issues—ownership, privacy
- Patents/inventions/trademark usage
- Purchasing—equipment requests, vendor selection, contracts
- Travel—approval, restrictions, ownership of frequent-flier miles
- Mail services/telecommunications/printing—availability, restrictions
- Records retention/destruction guidelines
- Working at home/mobile offices

- Use of off-site equipment—restrictions, authorization, purchase
- Conference attendance/speaking engagements/honorariums
- Civic responsibilities/jury duty/membership in local professional organizations
- Charity/office contributions/office celebrations

If a policy is new or controversial, such as testing for drugs or e-mail ownership, a short factual statement justifying the policy is helpful. (An example appears in Figure 11-1.) In such cases, send a cover memorandum along with the policy to all employees explaining the rationale for the new or changed policy.

All policy changes must have appropriate approval. Check all changes for content with a lawyer. Also check to determine whether a disclaimer notice protecting the company is necessary. Do not write or distribute a memorandum concerning a change in policy to employees before that policy change has been cleared by all the necessary parties. Always include an effective date on new or revised policy statements.

XYZ COMPANY

3000 SERIESPERSONNEL AND AFFIRMATIVE ACTION

A.   Personnel

3920   Drug-Free Workplace

Congress signed the Drug-Free Workplace Act of 1988 into law on November 18, 1988. XYZ Company receives federal money and is, therefore, subject to the provisions of the Act. In an effort to comply with the Act and to continue to provide employees with a safe, drug-free environment at XYZ Company, the Board of Directors has adopted Board Policy 3920, Drug-Free Workplace.

Employees are prohibited from engaging in the unlawful manufacture, distribution, possession, or use of a controlled substance in any building or on any property under the control and use of XYZ Company. (See Health and Safety Code 11007 for a definition of the term "controlled substance.")

Any violation of this policy by an employee of XYZ Company may result in (1) requiring the employee to participate satisfactorily in an approved drug abuse assistance or drug rehabilitation program; or, (2) carrying out disciplinary action up to and including termination.

Reference: Health and Safety Code 11007
               Drug-Free Workplace Act of 1988

Adopted: July 31, 19—

Figure 11-1 Policy in report form.

The tone of a policy reflects management's attitudes toward employees. Avoid using phrases that sound autocratic or condescending. Use a positive approach when writing policies.

HINT: *Use: All full-time employees are entitled to ten days of sick leave per year. Do not use: No more than ten days apply toward sick leave per year.*

All policy changes are made in writing, and employees must receive adequate notice. It must be clear that any changes made supersede the previous policy.

Format

The first policy manual produced by a company takes considerable time to develop and compile. Once begun, new policies may be added without rekeying the entire manual. (For a comprehensive discussion on formatting and designing manuals, see Chapter 18.) Specific guidelines for organizing the final copy of the policy manual follow:

- Check policy manuals from other companies for format possibilities.
- Store policy manuals in three-ring binder notebooks. New or revised policies may be inserted or old ones removed as needed.
- Use notebooks with attractive cover designs that can be used for more than one year.
- Begin each policy statement on a separate sheet of paper. A new policy statement should always begin on a right-hand page. Continuation pages may be printed on both sides or on one side only. Since pages in a policy manual may change because of insertions of new policies or increases or decreases in the number of pages in a revised policy, do not number policy manual pages consecutively. Instead, indicate the number of pages devoted to each policy:

3005   Equal Employment (page 2 of 2)

- Highlight disclaimers by placing them on a separate sheet of paper or in a boxed format at the beginning of a document. Use bold or larger typeface to separate the disclaimers from the rest of the text.
- State the name of each policy in a title line. If using a memorandum to inform employees of a new or revised policy, show the exact title of the policy and its number in the subject line of the memo.

3680   Memberships in Local Civic Organizations

SUBJECT: Board Policy 3680 Memberships in Local Civic Organizations

- Create a template for policy formats. Your company may use such headings as purpose, policy, definitions, provisions, and references.
- Organize the manual so policies that include similar topics are near each other. Cross-reference those items that pertain to more than one policy:

> **Leaves: Sickness**
>
> **Leaves: Emergency**
>
> **Leaves: Personal**
>
> **Leaves: Jury (See also Civic Responsibilities)**

- Use dividers to set apart major categories of policies within the same manual, such as Board of Directors, Management, and Personnel.
- Develop a numbering system that uses numbers and letters and allows for expansion.

> **1000 Series**   BOARD OF DIRECTORS
> **A. Organization of the Board**
>   **1000 Authority**
>   **1005 Officers**
>   **1010 Meeting dates**
>   **1015 Agendas**
>   **1020 Meetings**
> **B. Conflict of Interest**
> **C. Compensation**
> **2000 Series**   MANAGEMENT
> **3000 Series**   EMPLOYEES

- Indicate whether the policy statement is new or whether it is a replacement for a previous policy. Indicate the date the policy becomes effective at the bottom of each page.

> **Replacement for Policy <u>3020,</u> dated <u>8/27/92</u>**
> **or**
> **New Policy** _____
> **Effective Date** _____<u>1/2/97</u>_____

- Include codes, references, or regulation numbers that apply to the policy at the bottom of the last page of the statement. Omit lengthy references to the law within a policy statement.

> **Reference: Section 703, Title VII of the Civil Rights Act.**

HINT: *Keep a master list of major policies. Include the names and numbers of the proce-*
       dures that pertain to each policy. When the policy is changed, check the master list
       and make the appropriate changes in the procedures.

- Prepare a detailed index of the policy manual. Keep the index current as new policies or changes are made. Distribute the updated index material with each new policy or policy change.

Evaluation

A company may involve personnel other than top management in the process of evaluating policy statements. Office professionals may be asked to review the policies on an individual basis, or they may be asked to review them as members of a committee. The
following questions will assist the office professional in providing input into the evaluation
process:

- Were suggestions and ideas solicited from employees? The more involved the employees are in the process, the more support they will provide when the time comes
  to implement the policies.

HINT: *To simplify this process, provide employees with suggestion forms that include*
       spaces for the policy number and title and for the suggested change(s). Names and
       departments are optional. Recommend a separate suggestion form for each policy.
       Provide a convenient central location or e-mail address to return the suggestions.

- Is the manual attractive? The way material is packaged makes a statement about
  the importance of the policies as perceived by top management.
- Are the policies clearly stated? Is the language direct and simple?
- Is the reason for a new or controversial policy explained?
- Is it easy to locate the policy by topic? Is the organization of the manual logical?
- Are there any omissions in the policy statements? Are there statements that could
  be misinterpreted?
- Is the manual concise? Excessive reading material can be intimidating, and em-
  ployees may therefore ignore it.
- Has the manual been checked for proper grammar, punctuation, word usage, capi-
  talization, and word division?
- Are the policies up to date? Is there a plan for a periodic revision and review of the
  policies?

HINT: *When employees make suggestions about policy statements, file them in an ap-*
       propriate subject folder and use them for the next revision or review. Maintain a
       file for each subject covered in the policy manual.

- Is a policy manual distribution list maintained?

HINT: *If your department is in charge of distributing manuals or policy statements, assign that responsibility to one person or do it yourself Prepare a list of employees to whom the manuals must be distributed and have these employees sign their names as they receive their copies. Signing the form acknowledges receipt and acceptance of the manual's content or policy changes.*

Policy Manual Software and Technology

Software based on expert system technology is available to assist policy writers in identifying policies as well as in writing them. (See Chapter 3 for expert system information.) The user selects the policy topics and then responds to preprogrammed questions about these policy selections. Based on the answers given and the software's stored information, a policy for a specific company can be written. The user can edit, accept, or change this policy by using the word processing feature of the program or by exporting the material to another word processing program.

Online in-depth background material that includes explanations, pros and cons, and legal requirements for most of the policies eliminates much of the basic research that is usually necessary in writing policy manuals. The software creates a table of contents and formats the policies. It provides periodic updates to comply with state and federal laws. The software may be written for a certain state, so caution is necessary when working with legal information.

When manuals are created online, stored electronically, and then sent via a network, the costs of printing, distributing, and storing manuals decreases. With this technology, office personnel retrieve and print sections of the manual as needed. Companies with offices in different states may want to adapt their policies to comply with the laws of that state. A policy written online can handle such situations. Groupware programs allow managers and employees to exchange ideas about policy issues and give policy writers the opportunity to collaborate and share opinions.

Receiving an employee's signature indicating that the policy or policy change has been read and accepted is still necessary. These forms become a part of an employee's personnel file and may be important in a legal situation.

PROCEDURES MANUALS

Written procedures are necessary for policies to be carried out effectively. A **procedures manual** provides employees with instructions for implementing policies and for performing specific activities or tasks. An **employee handbook** is another term to describe this type of manual. Supervisors or the people usually doing the tasks write the procedures.

Purpose

Well-written procedures manuals are simple and easy to understand. Even employees who have never performed the tasks or activities before should be able to follow the detailed instructions without difficulty. Since all employees receive the procedures manual, everyone has the same instructions, and therefore tasks should be performed similarly in all departments.

Specific written procedures save time since new employees need not ask coworkers or supervisors for assistance if they can refer to their procedures manual. Experienced employees use procedures manuals to remind them how to do tasks or activities that they perform infrequently or as a reference when training others.

Content

The content depends on the policies established by the board and the type of procedures manual being written. One type of procedures manual may deal only with a specialized topic area, such as a company correspondence manual. Another may involve procedures for one department area, such as the accounting department or the mailroom. Yet another may include general information and procedures that apply to everyone in the organization. Some sample topics for the latter type of manual include the following:

INTRODUCTORY INFORMATION

- Organization chart
- Responsibilities of departments/divisions
- Floor plans/office numbering systems/maps
- Names and telephone numbers or extensions of top management and department heads
- Telephone numbers of division secretaries
- Hours of operation
- Glossary of frequently used words, trademarks, and accepted abbreviations

PERSONNEL INFORMATION

- Time cards/paychecks/payroll tax information/payroll data changes
- Vacation requests/holidays
- Leaves—procedures, forms, notification
- Jury duty
- Resignations—timelines, forms, notification
- Tardiness/absenteeism—notification
- Insurance—coverage, forms, claims

- Company library use/recreational facilities
- Education—tuition reimbursement, on-site training
- Physical examinations/substance abuse testing
- Childcare/elder care—applications, costs
- Performance evaluations—probation, procedures, timeliness, forms
- Grievances—appeals, procedures, timeliness, forms
- Retirement—benefits, pension fund disbursements, forms
- Breaks/lunch—cafeteria privileges, hours, infractions
- Parking/keys/security/passwords/company visitors
- Injuries—reporting procedures, forms
- Relocation—benefits, family provisions
- Work away from office—responsibility, evaluation

TASK-RELATED INFORMATION

- Supplies purchase and control—authorization, forms
- Equipment—selection, purchase, repair, operation
- Fax/electronic mail—restrictions, user directions
- Software—backup, selection, copyrights
- Document creation
- Computer assistance—on and off premises
- Reprographics—forms, services, approval, copyrighted materials
- Travel—approval, reports, reimbursement, forms
- Records disposal/transfer
- Mail services
- Telephone/voice mail—coverage, services, protocol
- Meetings—notice, room reservations, catering requests, forms
- Files—access, security, control, coding
- Company vehicles—responsibility, reservations, forms
- Recordkeeping—banking, billing, receipts, payments

Writing Procedures

When the procedures apply to the entire organization, managers and supervisors write the procedures for their particular areas of responsibility. When the procedures are task related, office managers, supervisors, or their designees write the procedures. When the procedures concern office tasks, the designees are often office professionals. They perform the tasks and have the most knowledge about the steps involved.

Writing clear procedures requires logical thinking and attention to detail. The following suggestions will assist in writing procedures.

- Clarify the reasons a procedure is necessary by answering these questions before beginning to write:

▲ Who will perform the task? For example, procedures for new employees require more detail than those written for the experienced workers.

▲ What is the purpose of this procedure? Why is it done *this* way?

▲ What equipment and supplies are required?

▲ With what work area or areas is this task associated? Who is involved in the activity?

▲ What is the first step? The next?

- Examine the current company procedures manual. Prepare a list of changes or recommendations made since the last revision. If preparing a manual for the first time, review other company manuals to determine how these organizations write or format procedures.

- Request assistance from coworkers. For example, if you are writing a procedure for handling petty cash, ask the person who performs the task to list the steps in consecutive order.

HINT: *Before describing how to do a task, watch it being done. Use a tape recorder to record notes while the person is working.*

- Include only the information needed to complete the tasks. Excessive explanatory material slows a worker's progress in completing a task. Note, however, that although a subtask may seem obvious to someone who does it regularly, a new worker will not necessarily know that each step is necessary.

- Select a title for the procedure carefully. The most effective titles are brief but clear. For example, "Educational Benefits Process" is not a clear title; a more definitive title is "Educational Tuition Reimbursement—Applications."

- Divide the task into its logical parts. For example, a procedure might be necessary to clarify changes in reprographic services. In this case, a logical breakdown is to write instructions for using the convenience copier, the centralized printing center, or off-premise commercial services. Use subheadings and list the procedures by service area.

- Select a numbering system and use it consistently throughout the procedures manual. One example of a numbering system for a section of a procedures manual follows:

    36. Travel
       F. ...
       G. **Company Automobiles**
          1. **Approvals and authorizations for use**
          2. **Timelines**
          3. **Reservation procedures**
          4. **Accident reporting**

> 5. **Automobile care and maintenance**
> 6. **Forms (attached)**
> H. ...

This example identifies "Travel" as a section heading. Within that section, one sub-heading is "Company Automobiles." Under that subheading are suggested paragraph headings involving procedures for requesting the use of a company automobile.

- Identify who is to do the task. Divide the procedure into two parts: *Who performs the activity?* and *What action is required?* Another format identifies who is to perform the task and then lists responsibilities below.

- Use short, imperative sentences rather than lengthy narrative ones.

HINT: *Use: Obtain Form No. 942, Educational Benefits Approval, from the secretary to the assistant personnel director in the Human Resources office. Do not use: Educational leave is available to employees and may be applied for by obtaining Form No. 942, Educational Benefits Approval, from the secretary to the assistant personnel director in the Human Resources office.*

- Use a job title, as in the above example, rather than the name of the individual, since an individual may change his or her position. Be consistent when using titles. For example, do not refer to the division secretary in one step and to the same person as an assistant to the division manager in a later step.

- Indicate the meaning of an abbreviation the first time it is used, such as Purchase Requisition (PR). Place the abbreviation in parentheses. The abbreviated form is then acceptable in the remaining steps of the procedure. Define all the technical terms used in a procedure.

- Present only one step at a time. Number each step in chronological order as it should occur.

- Do not begin an instruction on one page and continue it on the next page. Complete the entire instruction on one page.

- Use graphs, flow charts, and equipment diagrams when applicable. Use caution with photographs. In the reproduction process, photographs may become fuzzy, causing a loss of detail that may make the photographs less useful.

- Provide samples of the forms required to do a task. Use code letters or numbers to designate the information that is placed on each line. Here is an example of a portion of a reprographic work order that illustrates the use of code letters to refer to instructions.

No. of Copies: _____ G _____
Account to be Charged: _____ H _____

The letters G and H refer to codes listed on a separate sheet. For example: (G) Indicate a number 1–20. (The maximum number of copies allowed is 20.) (H) Use the three-digit account number assigned to the project. (Your supervisor has the number.)

- Identify *very* clearly any warnings for dangerous jobs or precautions about possible problems. Write the warnings in all necessary languages. Place the warnings at the beginning of the instructions and repeat them if they are part of one of the procedural steps. In order to draw attention to the warning, highlight it, place it in bold type, or capitalize it.

HINT: *If language appears to be a barrier to understanding any activity, write the entire procedure in the languages needed.*

- Have an employee who is unfamiliar with the task try to do it by reading the procedure. Rewrite and clarify if necessary.
- Summarize the steps at the end of each procedure. Since experienced workers may forget how to do a step, a summary can be helpful so as to avoid starting at the beginning and reading each step to locate the problem.
- Indicate the status of the procedure—new or revised. (See information on format under Policy Manuals section.)
- Refer the user to additional manuals, such as special forms manuals or correspondence manuals, to complete a task. Include cross references when needed to clarify the procedures.
- Identify the policy or government regulation that pertains to the procedure. When the policy or law changes, procedures are likely to change also. More than one procedure may be affected. The policy or regulation identification on *all* the affected procedures makes it less likely that a procedure will be missed in the revision process. Here is an example of a reference line with a regulation code number and also a company policy number:

Reference: California Education Code 72292, Governing Board Policy 3110

- Proofread procedures for punctuation, capitalization, grammatical accuracy, and spelling. Edit content and avoid wordiness. Conciseness saves disk space and production costs.
- Avoid sexist language. Use "his or her" or the plural form "their."

Format

The memo and the report are the two most common formats used to announce a revision in a procedure or a new procedure. A memo is more appropriate for short proce-

TO: Telephone Users
FROM: Sandra Orlando
SUBJECT: Telephone-Long-Distance Access
DATE: May 21, 19—

The following procedures are necessary to access your Extended Class of Service (ECOS) for long-distance telephone calls. Using this procedure will make long-distance access more expedient for you and will provide prompt service to our customers.

1. Obtain your Extended Class of Service (ECOS) account code from your immediate supervisor. Retain the code in a location that will not be readily available to other employees.

2. Pick up the telephone headset and dial the desired outside number.
   a. If the number dialed is within your Basic Class of Service (BCOS), your call will go through.
   b. If the number dialed is outside your BCOS, you will hear a feature set tone (the tone you hear when you use the #7 call forward).

The effective date for these procedures is October 19—. Please add this to your procedures file.

jmm
Attachment

Figure 11-2 Procedure in memo format.

dures. The memo should include a statement explaining the purpose of the procedure and why it must be followed; then the instructions follow. (A sample appears in Figure 11-2.) Employees should also be asked to add the document to their procedures manuals.

A report is usually divided into two sections—the heading (which includes background information) and the instructions. The report form is used when the procedure is lengthy. A sample of a portion of a procedure written in report form appears in Figure 11-3. An accompanying memo usually reminds employees to remove the old procedure and add the new one in its place or to insert the new procedure.

The following suggestions apply to both formats unless noted otherwise. (For a comprehensive discussion on formatting and designing reports, see Chapter 18.)

- Use a looseleaf binder for procedures. Use 8½-by-11-inch paper. Looseleaf binders offer the greatest flexibility since new pages can be inserted easily. These binders are easy to use, since they open flat and are easy to store upright on a desk.

XYZ COMPANY

Reference: Board Policy 3920
                        Drug-Free Workplace
Effective Date: April 20, 19—
Previous Revision: NA
Procedure: Drug Abuse Violations
Distribution: Department Managers

DRUG ABUSE VIOLATIONS (page 1 of 2 pages)

PURPOSE

XYZ Company is committed to providing a drug-free workplace for its employees. To ensure this commitment, department managers need to be aware of employees exhibiting behaviors that may be drug-related and follow these procedures.

DEPARTMENT MANAGERS

1. Contact the Director of Human Resources immediately if an employee is suspected of drug dependency. Document your concerns and outline a plan of action.

2. Confront the employee displaying behaviors of being under the influence of drugs. (See Attachment A for a list of behavioral clues.) Determine whether the employee is at risk to self or other employees.

3. Release an employee who is at risk or who is unable to complete the remainder of his or her assigned activities for the remainder of the day or shift. Arrange for transportation to the employee's home.
   a. Ask the employee to contact a friend or family member to drive.
   b. Drive the Employee home yourself.
   c. Request taxi service to take the employee home. Complete a taxi voucher form and submit it to Accounting.

Figure 11-3 Procedure in report format.

- Place procedures online so employees can access them via their computers.
- Consider laminating the materials or placing them in plastic sheet holders if the procedures are used regularly in areas where dust and dirt accumulate.
- Use a type font that is large enough to be read easily; for example, 10 point or larger. In some areas where machines are used, the procedures may be posted at a distance and therefore require large type. (See Chapter 19 for more information.)
- Position the visual aids so they are close to the related text. Label the visual aids consistently throughout the document; for example, "Figure 7: Completed Expense

Report." A visual aid is effective only if it adds to the written material and if each part is clearly labeled. If the part is not referred to in the text, do not label it in the diagram. If a diagram is reduced in the duplication process, be sure it remains readable.

- Use a list format. Indent the steps from any narrative that precedes them. The visual effect emphasizes organization and helps the reader follow instructions easily.
- Identify the summary steps by indenting the abbreviated steps or by placing a box around the summary.
- Prepare a detailed table of contents and an index for your notebook or computer file when organizing the procedures.
- Identify pages as follows: "Page 2 of 4 pages."
- Display any forms as originals or in reduced formats and place the instructions for completing the forms on separate pages. Place the forms on the left and the instructions on the right to facilitate their use.

JOB DESCRIPTION MANUALS

A **job description manual** is a compilation of specific jobs within a company that describes the jobs and lists duties and requirements. In large companies, the Human Resources Department is usually responsible for preparing and maintaining the manual. In all companies, input is necessary from those who perform the jobs and from their supervisors. Job descriptions must be in compliance with state and federal laws.

Purpose

Job descriptions provide management with information that is helpful in hiring, placing, and promoting personnel or useful in restructuring or eliminating positions. Supervisors use job descriptions when they evaluate employees' work. Ideally, they should compare actual work performance to the specifications listed in the job description. In large companies, Human Resource personnel do the initial screening and rely heavily on job descriptions. Screening applicants is easier if the job descriptions are clear and identify specific requirements for specific areas. Companies are very aware of discrimination charges and other legal consequences that can result from hiring or termination decisions. Well-written job descriptions communicated to employees can assist in the defense of these decisions.

Content

Job descriptions from other companies may be good models for determining format and content for your manual. Other information sources include interviews with workers and supervisors, observations by Human Resource personnel, formal job analyses by outside consultants, or job description software. The best information sources are the people who do the jobs.

Two ways to facilitate the collection of information from employees are (1) questionnaires and (2) task diaries completed during a specified period of time. The advantage of the questionnaire is the inclusion of the same questions for all employees, which makes data categorization and interpretation easier. As office professionals perform new tasks or assume responsibilities for additional activities, they should record this information and bring it to the attention of their supervisors. This information is useful for performance appraisals as well as for writing or revising job descriptions.

Job descriptions should include the following information:

- General information, such as name, department, job title, classification, work area location, and supervisor's title. Job titles are important since they lend prestige to positions and are used to compare jobs with similar titles. Assign a title that is definitive; for example, "payroll benefits analyst" rather than "accounting clerk."

HINT: *The Dictionary of Occupational Titles is one source of job titles. The publication and periodic supplements are available at most libraries or from the U.S. Department of Labor, Employment and Training Administration, 200 Constitution Avenue NW, Washington, DC 20001.*

- Salary structure information, such as salary range, regular and overtime hours, full- or part-time status, and exemption status. An *exempt* status means that some positions are not subject to certain provisions of the Fair Labor Standards Act (FLSA); for example, overtime and minimum wage. Managerial and professional positions often fall into this category.
- Job overview. The overview is a brief summary of the job. Using one description for "similar" jobs can be misleading; therefore, some companies prepare a job description for each position in the company. For example, an overview of an entry level sales division assistant position might be "provides data entry support for the Software Sales Division. Communicates with customers and sales personnel."

HINT: *One side of the job description sheet includes the general information, summary, and duties; the reverse side outlines the job qualifications and specifications. Follow a similar format for all job descriptions. (A sample job description appears in Figure 11-4.)*

- Duties. Duties are those which the job now entails. Do not list duties that have been changed or eliminated. Identify duties by the frequency with which they are done—daily or monthly—and in order of their importance. An unrealistic list of responsibilities or qualifications can hinder finding good employees. Such a list may also be a violation of the ADA.

HINT: *When describing duties, use action verbs, such as those listed in the section Work Experience in Chapter 2. Describe duties rather than specific tasks; for example,*

Position title:	Administrative Secretary
Division:	Sales and Marketing
Department:	Marketing Research
Reports to:	Department Manager
Salary status:	Exempt

JOB SUMMARY:

The executive secretary, under the general supervision of the department manager, performs routine secretarial duties as well as a variety of tasks that require planning and organization to meet deadlines and quality standards. The position requires interpersonal skills necessary to coordinate the work flow among the six to eight office support staff members in the department.

DUTIES AND RESPONSIBILITIES:

- Composes routine correspondence
- Opens, routes, sorts, and prioritizes the department manager's mail
- Maintains the department manager's calendar
- Responds to mail, other messaging input, and telephone inquiries or to surveys from other agencies
- Gathers information and prepares sales reports
- Maintains confidential files
- Prioritizes departmental work
- Delegates tasks to clerical staff
- Supervises department office support staff, temporaries, and student interns
- Edits product releases and brochures to maintain consistency in format and content
- Schedules conference and exhibit assignments on the computer calendar for department staff members
- Makes all travel arrangements for staff
- Organizes weekly materials for department meetings and maintains file for agenda items
- Prepares press releases
- Recommends staff procedure changes
- Collects, compiles, and delivers office payroll time sheets to Personnel

—Continued—

Figure 11-4 Job description.

"organizes monthly conference meetings" rather than "prepares monthly agendas" or "sends out notices of meetings."

- Supervisory responsibilities, such as number of employees supervised and the type of supervision provided.

Job Description
Administrative secretary
Page 2 of 2 pages

QUALIFICATIONS:
- A.A. degree
- Five years' support staff experience
- Advanced English usage, proofreading, and editing skills
- Decision-making and management skills
- Computer literate
- Proficiency on _____ software
- Operate skills on basic office equipment
- Written and oral communication skills
- Interpersonal and problem-solving skills
- Report-writing skills
- Knowledge of advanced public relations procedures
- Keyboarding skill of 70 words a minute
- Ability to organize, schedule, and follow instructions
- Ability to maintain confidential or sensitive information

PHYSICAL DEMANDS AND WORKING CONDITIONS:
Positions are primarily sedentary.
Worker may be required to attend off-premises meetings or conferences.

LICENSE REQUIRED:
Possession of a valid and appropriate driver's license

CAREER LADDER:
Executive assistant
Confidential administrative assistant

Approved: Richard Bennett
Date of Approval: January 26, 1997
D.O.T. Reference: NA

Figure 11-4 (continued.)

- Intercompany contacts; for example, daily contact with a specific department or with customers.
- Working environment; for example, size of office; single workstation or multiple workstations; job safety; travel requirements; physical requirements; type or level of pressure, such as the requirements of high production quotas.
- Education required for the position; for example, high school, four-year degree, special licenses, and certification, such as the CPS rating.
- Experience and skills required for the position. Job standards require careful analysis and identification and must comply with the ADA and the Equal Opportunity Act. Do not include standards that are unrelated to job duties.
- Date of job description's last revision.

HINT: *Job descriptions require reviews. Rather than updating a job description when it is needed for a job announcement, establish a timeline for periodic evaluations of all job descriptions, such as once every six months. Using electronic document storing procedures expedites the process.*

HINT: *Documentation of tasks performed and of time spent on these tasks is helpful information at performance review time. By writing your own job descriptions, you should be able to negotiate for a title change, increased pay, or a promotion.*

Job Description Software

Job description software provides a good starting point for writing job descriptions. It decreases the research, writing, and input time. The sizes of the databases vary from the *Dictionary of Occupational Titles* to specialized libraries for specific occupations. Most software allows you to search by key word as well as by job title; some even allow job description searches by aptitude.

Other software creates job descriptions similar to the way policy manuals are written. (See section Policy Manual Software and Technology in this chapter.) The software includes job descriptions with prewritten summaries and essential duties, which may be revised or accepted by the user. The user then responds to questions concerning such areas as physical requirements, supervisory responsibilities, language and math skills, and qualifications. The type and number of questions may vary with the software. Based on the answers to the questions, the software provides standard wording for each subsection. The user may also accept or change these statements or add comments.

Other software features include headline and section customization and ADA adaptations. The software is helpful in writing first drafts. It provides a consistent writing pattern and covers topics that may otherwise have been omitted.

Companies using job description software must edit the prewritten descriptions carefully. Someone who understands the job and requirements is the best person to do this task.

WORKSTATION MANUALS

A **workstation manual** or **desk manual** provides a source of information unique to a specific position. The employee at the workstation prepares the information. The manual does not circulate throughout the company and is not an official company publication.

Purpose

The workstation manual serves as a guide for a temporary worker substituting for an absent employee or as an introduction for a new employee. Referring to the manual when questions arise will save time and create less tension in the office. In addition, the manual provides the supervisor with an overview of the many tasks that are performed at a particular workstation.

Content

Some information in a workstation manual may also be included in a procedures or special-topics manual. It is, however, necessary to make a precise cross reference to the original source. The following items are recommended when compiling a workstation manual:

- Overview of the position.
- Organization chart.
- Products/subsidiaries.
- Location of personnel /telephone numbers:

    ▲ Immediate supervisor/duties

    ▲ Supervisor's superior

    ▲ Supervisors for whom work is performed

    ▲ VIPs within the department or organization

    ▲ VIPs outside the organization, such as customers, clients, suppliers, and lawyers

    ▲ Key personnel responsible for specific areas

    ▲ Office personnel to contact for assistance

    ▲ Frequently called numbers

    ▲ Distribution lists including names of people who receive copies of the typical documents produced in your office

- Tasks to be completed daily with recommended timelines.

HINT: *To identify typical daily tasks, refer to your time management logs. (See Chapter 3.)*
       Indicate whether the tasks are typically completed in the morning or in the afternoon.

Tasks completed periodically; for example, the monthly replenishment of petty cash.

- Current committees/projects in progress.

  ▲ Chairpersons
  ▲ Meeting dates
  ▲ Responsibilities/special procedures
  ▲ Timelines

- Telephone etiquette.

  ▲ Standard office greeting/number of rings allowed before answering
  ▲ Long-distance call procedures and charges
  ▲ VIP calls—those which the supervisor always takes
  ▲ Transfer procedures
  ▲ Outside call procedures
  ▲ Message taking and distribution procedures
  ▲ Screening preferences
  ▲ Paging and forwarding procedures
  ▲ Personal use of office telephone
  ▲ Responses to frequently asked questions

HINT: *A quick reference outline is helpful in explaining how the telephone system works;*
       for example, how to transfer or forward a call. Keep it simple so information can
       be quickly obtained.

- Mail handling.

  ▲ Times of delivery and collection
  ▲ Incoming mail/mail register
  ▲ Distribution responsibilities/items to route
  ▲ Outgoing mail
  ▲ Overnight/courier services
  ▲ Network protocol/fax and electronic mail procedures

- Filing.

  ▲ System explanation

  ▲ Coding procedures

  ▲ File label preparation

  ▲ Charge-out procedures

  ▲ Tickler file maintenance

  ▲ Shredding or disposal procedures

  ▲ Confidential information

  ▲ Directory arrangement/contents of directories/template directories

HINT: *If files are in a locked drawer or cabinet, identify the people who have access to specific files. Keep the list of people up to date.*

- Correspondence.

  ▲ Formats

  ▲ Special terminology, trademarks, and abbreviations

  ▲ Signatures required

  ▲ Stationery and envelopes

  ▲ Copies—number and distribution

  ▲ Form letters

HINT: *Sample formats of letters, memos, reports, and envelopes are helpful. Identify formatting requirements and the use of special notations, such as attention, subject, distribution, and attachment lines.*

- Forms.

  ▲ Purpose

  ▲ Samples

  ▲ Location

  ▲ Required copies/distribution

  ▲ Approval/required signatures

HINT: *A completed form is more helpful than a blank form. Identify the source of information for completing each form. If calculations are necessary, give instructions to show how to obtain the figures.*

- Supplies.

  - ▲ Location
  - ▲ Requisition procedures

- Travel.

  - ▲ Travel requests
  - ▲ Travel preferences of supervisor
  - ▲ Frequent flyer numbers
  - ▲ Travel agents/electronic ticketing
  - ▲ Itineraries
  - ▲ Ticket pickup/delivery
  - ▲ Mileage reimbursement
  - ▲ Expense reports

- Equipment repair.

  - ▲ Reporting procedures/forms
  - ▲ Telephone numbers

- Computers.

  - ▲ Operating procedures
  - ▲ Assistance/hotline numbers
  - ▲ Security
  - ▲ Log-on instructions/backup procedures
  - ▲ Instruction manual location

- Software.

  - ▲ Types
  - ▲ Access codes
  - ▲ File naming procedures
  - ▲ File location
  - ▲ Precautions/security
  - ▲ Instruction manual location
  - ▲ In-house staff who have different software expertise

- Reprographics.

  ▲ In-company services/location
  ▲ Copy limitations/chargebacks
  ▲ Request forms/rush requests
  ▲ Repair service
  ▲ Overhead transparencies/special requests
  ▲ Publication and copyright guidelines

- Visitors.

  ▲ Frequent visitors—names and positions
  ▲ VIP visitors (those whom the supervisor will always see)
  ▲ Security procedures
  ▲ On-site accidents—reports, steps to take

- Meetings.

  ▲ Minutes/agendas
  ▲ Scheduling procedures
  ▲ Room/food requests

- Recordkeeping.

  ▲ Bank deposits/reconciliations
  ▲ Timecards
  ▲ Petty cash

- General.

  ▲ Technical terms, abbreviations
  ▲ Special reference materials
  ▲ Breaks/lunch
  ▲ Parking/office keys/security
  ▲ Dress/office appearance
  ▲ Precautions
  ▲ Efficiency hints

- Employer information.

  ▲ Professional memberships—meeting dates and dues

  ▲ Anniversaries/birthdays

  ▲ Family—names and telephone numbers

  ▲ Social security, passport, and credit card numbers

Writing Procedures

A workstation manual requires attention to detail and constant review. The following procedures will assist in organizing the manual.

- Make a list of all the tasks performed and responsibilities involved with the position before beginning to write. Include information on material locations as well as hints or precautions. Individual index cards work well. Sort the cards and place them in categories; for example, place all telephone-related tasks together. When you do a new task, include instructions in the manual. If procedures change, be sure to bring the desk manual up to date. Date each sheet and check periodically to see if information is still accurate.
- Obtain input from your supervisor. Prepare a copy of the manual for his or her desk.
- Use cross-references. For example, a specific task may require the shredding of all draft copies. Rather than describing the shredding procedure each time it is needed, direct the user to the one section where it is described in detail.
- Compile the materials into a three-ring looseleaf notebook. Arrange the material by subjects. Use dividers to separate the sections. Number pages consecutively.
- Store the instructions on a separate disk or create a training directory on the hard disk. A new employee will then have access to up-to-date instructions.

HINT: *A temporary agency may help its employees by preparing disks of workstation instructions for those companies who are its major clients. Temporary workers could then become familiar with procedures before beginning a job.*

- Prepare a detailed table of contents. The person relying on the manual wants the information quickly.
- Obtain input from the people who use the manual. Include a "comments" sheet at the front of the manual for this purpose. Consider these comments when making revisions.

- Review the tasks periodically, and note any changes in the margins of the manual. This eliminates preparing new sheets each time a change occurs, yet it keeps the manual up to date. Prepare new inserts as needed.

INSTRUCTION MANUALS

A new piece of equipment or a software package usually comes with an **instruction manual** or an **owner's guide.** A **quick reference guide,** which is a shorter version of the instruction manual, may also be available.

Department supervisors should keep at least one copy of all instruction manuals in a centralized location. Each user should have access to the instruction manuals.

Purpose

Instruction manuals explain how to use specific products. They can also answer repair questions. Checking the manual before calling the repair center can save time and expense. When you call a hotline number for assistance, the person who responds to your question may refer you to a section in the instruction manual for future reference. Instruction manuals are also useful in training sessions and often serve as the textbooks.

Content

Instruction manuals vary in format, size, and style, but they all include similar topics, such as the following:

- Disclaimer notices
- Warranty and liability statements
- Copyright protection
- Table of contents
- Unpacking/setup procedures
- Installation procedures
- Equipment diagram and list of parts
- Care and handling of equipment
- Getting started
- Standard operating procedures
- Precautions
- Advanced operations
- Glossary
- Appendices
- Troubleshooting pointers

- Warranty registration
- Site-license agreement

Evaluation

Well-written instruction manuals can be helpful in learning how to operate new equipment or software, whereas poorly written manuals cause frustration and wasted time. The following questions can help to determine the potential effectiveness of an instruction manual:

- Is the language simple and clear?

HINT: *Before a salesperson leaves the demonstration, ask to see a copy of the manual. Work through the steps of the first several procedures. Omissions or difficulties in following the first few procedures usually are signs of a faulty manual.*

- Are terms explained?
- Is the material written logically? Is it arranged from the simplest to the most complex tasks? Is it direct or is there excess information that causes confusion?
- Is it readable? Are the steps in a procedure numbered? If not, are there lead-in statements such as "To make a copy of a volume, choose option B"? Are there sufficient headings and subheadings to divide topics? Are the paragraphs short?
- Do diagrams accompany instructions? Showing what happens after an instruction has been followed is helpful.
- Is there an index and is it easy to use?

HINT: *To test the thoroughness of an index, select several items and see if the pages provide the necessary information.*

- Is there a hotline number that can be called for information?
- Does it permit a beginner to get started with the main task and learn others as needed?
- Is a quick reference guide available? Is each procedure summarized for easy reference or review?
- Is the manual well bound so that it will not fall apart with use? Is it a convenient size? Does it stay open and lay flat?
- Does it have a section listing error codes? Are cautions clearly identified?
- Are care and handling instructions clear?
- Are peripheral devices and limitations identified?
- Are there appendices for extra information that is not found in the instructions?

CORPORATE STYLE GUIDES

Style guides are useful to companies for maintaining quality and consistency in their documents. If a company wants a style guide, it must commit the time and resources to develop its own since each guide is unique.

Purpose

A company style guide sets standards and answers those questions that always seem to cause problems. Well-designed style guides eliminate guesswork and provide a consistent and time-saving writing tool. They do not replace such writing aids as dictionaries or grammar and spell checkers.

Style guides are also helpful for project work. If a corporate guide is not available, develop a style sheet for the project. You can also make one for use at your own desk and include all those troublesome spellings or word-usage questions that frequently occur.

Content

The style guide originates in-house with input from many potential users. The content and size of the guide vary. Although the *process* involves the differing opinions of how "things should be done," one person should coordinate the final version of the style guide. Some items to consider include the following:

- Purpose of the style guide
- Copyright material
- Guidelines for preparing tables, graphs, and diagrams
- Labeling graphics in text
- Creating graphics for presentations
- Use of logos
- Nonsexist writing
- Ethnic designations
- Document report formats
- Use of boxes, bullets, numbers
- File and directory naming conventions
- Accepted abbreviations and formats
- Use of acronyms
- Proofreading symbols
- Scientific math formula formats
- Spelling of frequently misused words
- One-word, two-word/hyphenated words
- Word usage
- Number writing

- Active/passive voice
- Reading levels

HINT: *Organizing and writing a corporate style guide could be a challenging project for CPS members in a firm. They have access to samples of documents and are aware of successful styles and procedures. A style guide needs to be used and followed in order to be effective in saving time and in producing quality documents. Actively seek out evaluations and comments. Hold seminars explaining the usage of the guide. Be certain management supports the style guide.*

REFERENCE MANUALS

A **reference manual** is a source for checking specific information. Examples of reference manuals include dictionaries, atlases, office manuals, directories, and thesauruses. Since office professionals refer to these reference manuals frequently, they should be kept within easy reach. Computerized versions of such reference sources as dictionaries and thesauruses may also be accessible as separate software packages, on CD-ROMs, or as integral parts of many software programs. Databases with directory information are also available. See the section on Reference Sources for Home-Based Businesses in this chapter.

Dictionaries

Standard unabridged and abridged dictionaries are indispensable for spelling, definitions, word division, and pronunciation. In addition, some dictionaries include foreign words and phrases, grammar rules, abbreviations, forms of address, directories of colleges and universities, weights and measures, metrics, signs and symbols, and common English names. Unabridged dictionaries can include twice as many words as the standard abridged dictionary. Specialized dictionaries are available for such areas as law, medicine, accounting, insurance, electronics, and education.

Thesauruses

A thesaurus can be helpful in writing or editing documents. It provides alternatives for words that are used frequently. Instead of repeating the same word in a sentence, a synonym can be selected from the thesaurus.

HINT: *Dictionaries and thesauruses should be up to date. Check for new editions in Books in Print, which is available at most libraries. Recommend new editions when these references become five to seven years old.*

Atlases

An atlas provides geographical information in the form of maps (often in color), with names of large cities and capitals. It also presents information on climate, air routes, the solar system, and the economy, in addition to census data and other statistical and demographic information. An atlas is useful in making travel arrangements, setting up geographic files, checking world locations, verifying spellings, and determining mileage.

Directories

Directories contain names, addresses, and special data about people or businesses. Types of directories include telephone directories, toll-free number directories, ZIP Code directories, and city directories, as well as various types of professional membership directories.

Telephone directories of large cities are on file in libraries or central telephone offices. Companies can also rent telephone directories that include addresses from telephone companies. Another resource is Pacific Bell Smart Resource Center (800-848-8000), from which you can purchase state and specialty telephone directories; some of which are national in scope.

The National Five Digit ZIP Code and Post Office Directory is a valuable reference source for checking the accuracy of ZIP Codes on outgoing mail. The directory is arranged by geographic location. A copy may be purchased at the counter in your main post office, or you may contact the U.S. Postal Service or your local library.

City directories list names, addresses, and occupations of the residents in a city or area. They may also contain a list of businesses and their officials or owners. Private companies collect the information and publish the directories.

Polk's Directory lists entries by specific city. Entries may be accessed by the entrant's name, address, telephone number, and place of work. You may obtain copies by writing to Polk's, 7168 Envoy Court, Dallas, TX 75241. Haines and Company publishes *Haines Criss-Cross Directory*, which covers an area rather than a specific city. Copies can be ordered from Haines at 8050 Freedom Avenue NW, North Canton, OH 44720. Check with your local public library for additional information.

HINT: *To locate a particular directory, check the local library for the Guide to American Directories, which describes the many trade and professional directories published in the United States, or the Directory of Directories, which identifies business directories by country, state, and region, as well as by the type of business or the products available.*

Computerized reference services are valuable sources of information. Your public library is an excellent place for locating such sources. The Directory of All On-Line Databases from Cuadra Associates in Los Angeles or Computer Readable Databases from Gale Research in Detroit give the names of thousands of accessible databases available on-line throughout the world.

Office Reference Manuals

An **office reference manual** is an indispensable source of information for office workers. This type of manual offers suggestions and information on a variety of office topics. The use of one office reference manual throughout the organization is more efficient than having separate manuals for each department. In a Professional Secretaries International® research study on reference materials, 52 percent of those surveyed indicated they made the recommendations about which office reference manual to purchase.

An appropriate selection of a reference manual requires research and input from the prospective users. Once input has been obtained, recommend that a committee of office professionals use this information to make the final selection.

If all office professionals use the same office reference manual, they should have the opportunity to attend training sessions regarding the contents and the effective use of these manuals. Recommend that a group of office professionals be responsible for presenting information on the reference manuals at all orientation sessions for new employees.

Other Reference Materials

Other useful references include books of quotations, etiquette guides, and parliamentary procedure manuals. For matters of editing and printing style, consult *The Chicago Manual of Style* (University of Chicago Press) and the U.S. Government Printing Office's *Style Manual.*

SPECIALIZED LIBRARIES

Some companies establish their own specialized libraries. These libraries are usually private and available to company employees. Although some specialized libraries may be limited to a few major subject areas, their specific holdings are comprehensive and current. Even small companies can create mini-libraries by using a centralized location to keep such items as specialty magazines, brochures, newsletters, workshop notices, and employee manuals. Someone needs to keep the area up to date. The materials may be in different formats; e.g., annual reports or job openings may be on video or minutes may be on audiotapes. Access to a specialized library that does not contain classified or confidential information may be possible for people who are not company employees or members of an association. An explanation that outlines the need for the specialized information (preferably in writing) should be prepared before requesting access to any special collection.

Several reference indexes are available to assist in locating special library information. *The Directory of Special Libraries and Information Centers* provides addresses, telephone numbers, and the titles of those in charge of special libraries, archives, research libraries, and information centers. Another directory, *New Special Libraries,* provides regular updates to this directory. Large document collections are also available in electronic form with search and retrieval features.

REFERENCE SOURCES FOR HOME-BASED BUSINESSES

Online services, local libraries, and printed materials provide home-based business owners with many sources of business-related information. The costs vary. Some sources may be more reliable than others.

Commercial Online Services

Online services, such as CompuServe, America Online, and Prodigy, offer huge public databases at your desk and allow you to interact with users from around the globe. Subscribers pay a monthly fee and any other charges for extra services. The majority of commercial online services offer several free hours to try out their programs. Most commercial services offer gateway access to the Internet, so e-mail can be sent and received. To decrease expenses, you compose your messages offline and then send them. In your search for information, you can print the data online, which is slow and expensive, or download the material to a disk and print it later.

Bulletin Board Systems (BBS)

Government agencies, private businesses, and individuals with special interests are the organizers of bulletin board system information. Most services are free or rely on voluntary contributions. Shareware, discussion forums, and electronic mail are popular services. The Small Business Administration (SBA) has an online bulletin board service.

Shareware

Shareware offers you a chance to try out the software to see if it suits your needs before you buy it. If it does, you send in the money that the writer of the shareware suggests. Shareware usually does not include detailed documentation but often includes a "Read.me" file with basic instructions. Members of computer clubs often have shareware for exchange. Local freenets offer bulletin board services and provide access to local businesses, events, and area information. Check the local telephone directory or the public library for a contact.

CD-ROMS

These compact disks with read-only memory store huge amounts of data at relatively low costs. You cannot change the data or write to the disk, If you have CD-ROM capabilities on your computer, you can subscribe to such information services as dictionaries, telephone directories, encyclopedias, reference manuals, clip art, and shareware. Disks are updated at regular intervals. Any program can be loaded in memory while you are working on an application so you can mark data and transfer it to your current task.

Printed Materials

The Government Printing Office has many publications on a variety of business subjects. Order them from the Superintendent of Documents, U.S. Government Printing Office, Washington, DC 20402. For a copy of AT&T's toll-free directory, *Business Edition,* contact the National Association for Information Services, 1150 Connecticut Avenue, NW, Suite 1050, Washington, DC 20036.

U.S. Small Business Administration (SBA)

The SBA provides information and service to small businesses at minimal or no cost. Small Business Development Centers, which are sponsored by the SBA, offer the expertise of universities, local businesspeople, and the government through counseling and workshops. Access to the services is by computer and modem through online programs, through SBA's bulletin board, or by contacting a local SBA office. Your local SBA office also has information on the Service Corps of Retired Executives (SCORE), a group of business retirees who assist small business owners.

Professional Associations

In addition to contact with other professionals, professional association membership includes such items as publications, seminars and conferences, insurance, and equipment and software information. The *Encyclopedia of Associations* at local libraries gives contacts for and descriptions of the organizations.

Local Libraries

Books as well as current magazine articles in specific interest fields are available through public, community college, or university libraries. University libraries often have separate business libraries. Nonstudents may have to pay a minimal fee. Public libraries keep clipping files of local businesses. If materials are not available locally, libraries may order materials from other libraries through interlibrary loans.

Internet

Local service providers or commercial online services provide access to the Internet, or you can establish your own site. Check your local telephone directory for Internet providers and compare costs and services. See Chapter 22 for more information on the Internet and the World Wide Web.

Service Bureaus

Information services and bureaus will do the research or survey that a company needs. These bureaus are helpful when time is short or specific area expertise is limited. Information on market demographics, shopping patterns, government regulations, and international markets are a few areas in which information bureaus specialize.

Radio/Television

Radio and TV broadcasts are available for home-based business owners and cover such topics as government regulations, equipment, financial advice, marketing, business opportunities, and telecommunications. Check local listings for time and topics.

COMPANY NEWSLETTERS

Company newsletters provide businesses with opportunities to communicate with employees (referred to as internal newsletters), or with vendors and current or potential customers (referred to as external newsletters). Management determines the purposes of the newsletters and approves their final publication. The emphasis in this chapter is on internal newsletters.

Because of their organizational skills and their knowledge of word processing or desktop publishing, office professionals assume a major role in producing internal newsletters. They may have responsibility for collecting the information, editing the material, writing articles, or printing and distributing the final copy. Desktop publishing software allows companies to produce newsletters of high quality at a low cost. Simple layouts with attention paid to design details give a professional appearance to company-produced newsletters and other materials published in-house. Local bulletin board or online services as well as shareware and freeware offer clip art, fonts, and software for newsletter preparation. See Chapter 19 for newsletter design suggestions.

Another type of newsletter is one designed specifically for office professionals. These newsletters include such items as practical suggestions and timesavers, product information, course suggestions, grammar tips, and sources for information. This type of newsletter also provides an excellent means of promoting membership in professional organizations.

A firm may wish to create a home page on the Web for staff only. Up-to-date announcements, job listings, directory updates, employee news, and computer techniques are some uses for such a page, which, in turn, would decrease e-mail clutter. After one month or some other designated time, there should be an automatic deletion of the material.

This section deals primarily with the content and writing of the newsletter. For a discussion of its physical design, see the section on designing a newsletter in Chapter 19.

Content

Determining newsletter content requires a clear understanding of management's goals in publishing the newsletter and the number of issues to be published. For example, is the immediate goal to introduce new ideas? to boost morale? to communicate management's activities? to make announcements? to provide information? to feature individuals in personal or work activities? Is one general issue published monthly or is this a weekly bulletin? Knowledge of these goals not only clarifies the content but also determines the order of the articles in the newsletter.

HINT: *Keep a folder of newsletters from other companies to see what is appealing. Check the local library for books on writing interesting newsletters.*

Examples of content ideas and possible headlines for newsletter articles include:

▲ Messages from management.

Example: "A Message from the President" or "Straight from the Top."

▲ Forecast reports.

Example: "A New Year: What Does It Hold for XYZ Company?"

▲ New products/services.

Example: "XYZ Company Receives Recognition by Chamber of Commerce."

▲ Policy changes and explanations.

▲ Current legislation or news items that impact the company.

Example: "Water Conservation—Our Responsibility."

▲ General company information.

Example: "Your Financial Future/New Savings Plan for XYZ Employees."

▲ New technology.

▲ Personnel moves.

Example: "Roberts Named Sales Operations Manager" or "Donaldson Promoted."

HINT: *Rather than simply featuring an employee who has moved along a career ladder, go a step beyond and include advice from the individual. For example, "Roberts, XYZ's New Sales Manager, Gives 12 Tips for Getting Customers."*

▲ Education/training.

Example: "Check Out These New Courses." ___✓___ Internet Basics, ___✓___ Presentation Graphics

▲ Employees' work-related achievements/team accomplishments.

Example: "We Do It Best as a Team" or "The Suggestion That Worked."

▲ Presentations made by employees.

Example: "Peters Addresses Professional Secretaries International®."

▲ Health and safety reminders.

Example: "Take Time to Check for Safety."

▲ Cost-saving reminders.

▲ Ethics issues.

▲ Feature articles on employees/new employees

Example: "Inside XYZ Company" or "Profile/A Closer Look."

HINT: *It is often difficult to become acquainted with coworkers. Distribute a form for employees to complete (voluntary) and include one or more "features" in each issue.*

▲ Calendar of events/activities within the company.

▲ Surveys/suggestions.

Example: "What Employees Need at XYZ Company."

HINT: *Once a survey has been taken, always report the results. Follow-up articles are also interesting; for example, the above survey can be followed with an article on how XYZ Company is meeting these needs.*

▲ Employees' personal achievements/awards.

Example: "On Our Own Time."

▲ Attendance/longevity records.

▲ Tours, community events, volunteers.

▲ Announcements—births/deaths/retirements.

▲ Recreational activities/scores.

▲ Request for newsletter items.

HINT: *Get ideas from as many employees at all levels as possible. Include a form each time the newsletter is published that makes it easy for employees to respond.*

Editing/Writing Newsletters

The editing task is less demanding if writers are carefully selected or if one person does the writing. Rewriting poor copy is often more difficult than writing the original copy. Rewriting can also cause friction with the author and may change the original intent of the article. Several suggestions for writing and/or editing articles follow.

- Answer the basic reporting questions—who, where, when, what, why, and how—in the first paragraph. Articles must be informative and creative and yet practical for the readers.
- Write a headline that highlights the action in the first paragraph; for example, "Dayton Corporation Sponsors $3000 Scholarship." Use secondary headlines in smaller type.

Rank information in a story. After the lead sentence, which is the attention getter, continue to write the material as you have ranked it. If space runs out, you still have the most important parts of the story included.

Establish a timeline and monitor it regularly. Include articles that are timely. Past events should not be written about as if they are still occurring. The calendar of events must be up to date and should not include dates of events that have already passed.

HINT: *New programs may create interest and appear timely but do not include them unless their progress can be described. An announcement of a program in the planning stages can be premature and can confuse readers.*

- Eliminate statements that are not relevant to the major point of the article. Information in the articles should not be repeated.
- Use the language of the audience for whom the newsletter is written.
- Write short paragraphs—four to six lines—to maintain interest. Use one new idea in each paragraph. Subheadings and captions are effective. Keep the sentences short. Vary line and paragraph length.
- Distinguish opinions from facts. If it is an opinion, state this in the article. Avoid superlatives or judgmental statements.
- Avoid using customer or vendor names unless you have authorization to do so. Some companies may interpret the use of their names as product endorsements.
- Place regularly occurring material in the same location each time the newsletter is printed. Use the same heading for the column. For example, the "Calendar of Events" may be boxed on the lower left corner of the last page of each issue.
- Indicate the approximate number of words an article should have when you ask others to write. Request that the articles be double-spaced, have headlines, subheadings, and captions, and include photographs or illustrations if applicable.
- Request vertical black and white glossy photographs. They are easier to use in columns where space is limited. Try to obtain action photos rather than still photos. If using two photographs on the same page, vary the sizes.

HINT: *A company may obtain permission to use photographs of its employees at the time employees are hired. Check with the Human Resources Department or with your supervisor to be sure proper procedures for photo releases are followed.*

- Consult with the author of an article before making extensive editorial changes. If writing the article, check the accuracy of all facts. Get written permission before writing about a person and a sign-off acceptance signature after it is written or after it has been changed extensively.
- Proofread carefully. Be careful with substitutions like "in" for "it" or "your" for "you." Use your software spellcheckers as well as a reference manual and dictionary. If interviewing for a news story, check spelling and details before leaving the interview. It is especially important to check the spellings of names and products. Use a style guide for consistency.
- Put the date, volume, and number on the front of each issue in the same location.
- Include the name, address, and telephone and fax numbers of the company as well as the name of the editor. Include the dates of publication. Box the information on the first or last page. Note the example that follows.

> Published biweekly for present and retired XYZ Company
> employees. For additional information, contact the editor, (Name).
>
> AMC
> 1220 Becker Road
> Eau Galle, FL 32611
> Telephone (407) 296-5433
> Fax (407) 756-6586

CHAPTER 12

RECORDS

MANAGEMENT

Predictions were made in the early 1980s that increased use of computers would mean less paper in offices. What has actually occurred, however, is the exact opposite: paper use has grown. Each day American businesses produce an estimated 1 billion pieces of paper. Office professionals are constantly dealing with mounting piles of paper and a diminishing amount of storage space.

Records management includes management of paper records, micrographics, magnetically stored documents, and optical information systems. Records management starts with the creation or receipt of information and ends with the destruction or storage of the information. Office professionals must be aware of available systems and options in order to manage records with the most efficient and productive methods.

REDUCING PAPER WASTE

Below are suggestions for reducing paper waste:

- Review and change documents on the computer screen before printing to reduce the number of hard copies and paper drafts. Create only the number of copies actually needed.

HINT: *Use the Print Preview feature of your word processing program.*

- Use e-mail whenever possible; avoid printing unimportant e-mail messages. Adopt policies concerning the desired length of reports, memorandums, and other documents.
- Reuse paper printed on only one side to print drafts or staple the sheets together to make no-cost scratch pads.
- Use double-sided photocopying whenever possible.
- Route general information–type documents instead of making copies for each person or post notices on a bulletin board.
- Purchase white legal pads rather than the traditional yellow ones. Colored paper requires bleaching, which raises the cost of producing recycled products.

- Check number of copies selected or press reset before copying to avoid getting multiple copies when you need 1.
- Buy small stick-on notes to use in place of full-page fax cover sheets.
- Donate computer printouts and other paper to nursery or elementary schools. Students can use the clean side for painting and drawing.
- Adopt a recycling program and adhere to it.
- Use form-filling computer software.

TYPES OF RECORDS

Records can be either active or inactive. Active office files should contain only useful, current information. Records consulted frequently, several times a month or more, are considered active. They must be immediately accessible and should be in the main file area. Semiactive records are ones referred to approximately once a month. They may be stored in less-accessible drawers or cabinets either in active storage or elsewhere on the same floor. Records used infrequently, less than once a month, are considered inactive. Inactive files need not be in the immediate work area. Inactive records can be moved to a basement, a storage unit or warehouse off-site, or natural underground caves specifically used for long-term storage. Off-site storage may use low-cost equipment, maximizes space, and costs less per square foot than office floor space. Because the records are inactive, a delay in retrieving them is acceptable.

RETAINING RECORDS

You should develop a records retention schedule to avoid keeping information longer than needed. A retention schedule tells how long to keep records in the office, when to destroy them, and when to transfer them to inactive storage facilities. In determining how long to retain records, consider the following:

- How useful and how active the record is. Move inactive records to another storage area.
- Legal retention requirements for federal, state, and local government agencies. Research these requirements carefully and consult with an attorney.
- Long-term value to the organization for research or to the community for scholarly purposes.

HINT: *Charitable and religious organizations usually retain a recorded history of their development.*

Table 12-1 lists suggested retention schedules for some business records.

Table 12-1
SUGGESTED RETENTION SCHEDULE FOR BUSINESS RECORDS

ACCOUNTING	YEARS
Accounts payable ledger	6
Accounts receivable ledger	25
Audit reports, external	P
Audit reports, internal	10
Bank reconcilement papers	2
Bonds, registered	P
Budget worksheets	6
Capital stock records	P
Cash disbursement ledgers	6
Cash receipt registers	15
Check register	6
Checks, cancelled	6
Contracts	P
Correspondence, accounting	6
Cost accounting records	6
Dividend register	P
Donations	10
Expense reports	6
Financial statements	P
General journal	10
General ledger	P
Inventory records	P
Invoices	6
Licenses: federal, state, local	P
Payroll register, year end	P
Payroll register, weekly/monthly	15
Profit and loss statement	P
Stock certificates, cancelled	15
Stock ledger, reports and records	P
Trial balance sheets	P

EXECUTIVE/LEGAL	YEARS
Annual reports	P
Affidavits	10
Copyrights	P
Correspondence	10
Mortgages	5
Patents and Trademarks	P
Research reports	20
Speeches, publications	10

INSURANCE	YEARS
Accident reports	10
Claims, workers' compensation	10
Expired policy	10

MANUFACTURING	YEARS
Bills of material	20
Blueprints	30
Correspondence, general	6
Customer specifications	20
Drafting records	8
Inspection records	10
Operating reports	10
Production reports	5
Quality control reports	5
Test data	20
Work orders	2

PERSONNEL	YEARS
Accident reports	8
Attendance records	3
Daily time reports	3
Employee file (after separation)	5
Medical folders, employee	25
Pension plan	P
Time cards	3

PLANT AND PROPERTY	YEARS
Appraisals	P
Deeds, titles	P
Leases	6
Maintenance & repair to buildings	10

PURCHASING	YEARS
Contracts	5
Correspondence	6
Quotations	3
Receiving reports	6
Vendor contracts	P

P = Permanent records which need to be available for manual review.

VITAL RECORDS

Approximately 1 to 3 percent of business records are vital. Vital documents are those necessary for continuous operation of the business in the wake of fire, flood, earthquake, or other disaster. These records can be used to reconstruct a company's legal or financial status and to preserve the rights of the organization, its employees, customers, and stockholders.

Vital records include:

- Insurance policies.
- Documents of incorporation or partnership, certifications, licenses, leases, deeds, and titles.
- Tax returns and supporting materials.
- Warranties for office equipment, computers, and machinery.
- Copyrights.
- Personnel records.
- Financial records such as accounts receivable balances.
- Banking and payroll records.
- Pension and profit-sharing documents.
- Word- and data-processing backup tapes or disks.
- Company policy manuals and departmental procedures manuals.

Not all vital records are stored forever; only the most recent update of some information, such as accounts receivable, is considered vital.

Copies of vital records should be made for protection. Vital records can be protected using one of the following methods:

Dispersal: Copies may be stored at different locations during routine distribution of materials. This method is often used when companies have several locations. Dispersal may also be to banks, insurance companies, government agencies, or accounting firms.

Duplication: Copies of vital records can be made as part of regularly scheduled duplication; they may be in any medium, whether disk, microfilm, or paper.

On-site storage: Vital records can be stored in fireproof cabinets, vaults, or rooms; this is normally acceptable only for temporary storage. There must be proper environmental controls and sufficient security.

Off-site storage: Off-site storage facilities could be company-owned, commercial, or shared with others. They must have environmental controls for temperature, humidity, air circulation, and control of insects and rodents. Access should be restricted to ensure security.

TYPES OF FILING SYSTEMS

Most offices use several different filing systems. There are five major ways to store records, whether those records are on paper or on micrographics or magnetic media. Some offices may use a combination of one or more of the following systems:

Alphabetic: Files are kept under the names of individuals, businesses, and government organizations and filed by the sequence of letters in the alphabet. This is the system used in most offices. It is better for small companies and for individual files. Use standard filing rules for consistency in filing and retrieval. (See Figure 12-1.)

Numeric: In this system, a code number is assigned to individuals, businesses, or subjects. Once the code number is assigned, no decisions have to be made as to how to file records. They are simply filed in numeric order. However, this method requires an index to find material. A numeric filing system works well for records that can be filed by policy numbers, product numbers, patient billing numbers, or customer account numbers. It is also easily learned by those not familiar with English. Numeric filing increases the confidentiality of records.

Subject: Records are filed alphabetically by topic or category rather than by individual name or business name. This method is best for companies that store records by inventory or merchandise names. It is often combined with an alphabetic system. Such a system can be one of the most difficult to design and maintain. Major filing categories often

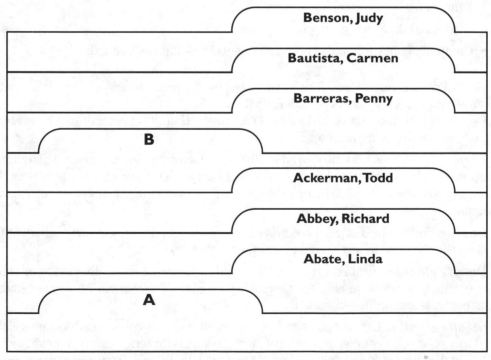

Figure 12-1 Alphabetic style.

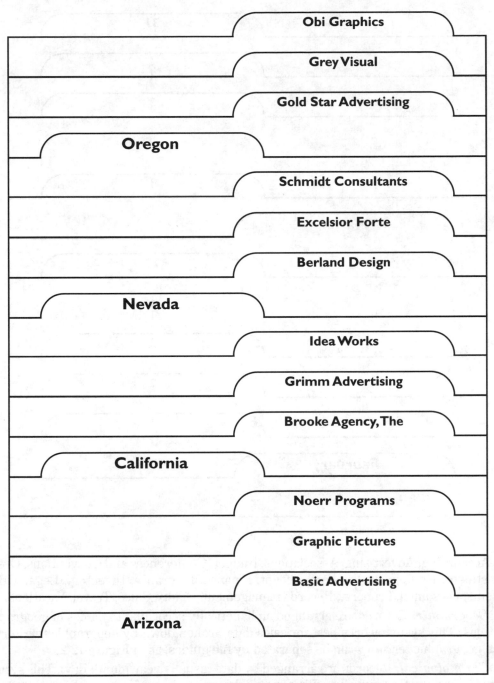

Figure 12-2 Geographic style.

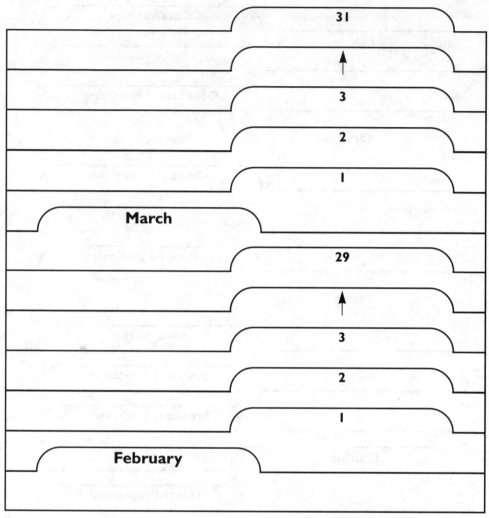

Figure 12-3 Chronological style.

are: Accounting, Advertising, Associations, Budget, Conferences and Conventions, Credit department, Equipment, Expense account, Finance, Insurance, Inventory, Legal, Office systems, Personnel, Property, Records management, Safety, Sales, Travel, Vacations.

Geographic: Records are arranged alphabetically according to names of geographic locations. This system works best for sales data broken down by geographic territories. Each geographic territory can be separated by file guides, as in Figure 12-2.

Chronological: Records are arranged by date (usually year/month/day). This system is used especially for temporary filing and tickler or reminder files. (See Figure 12-3.)

If material may be filed under one or more names or subjects, a cross reference should be made. File the material under one name or subject and file a cross reference to that name or subject under the other. Insert a permanent guide in the proper alphabetical position among the regular file folders for cross reference information.

For example, Dan Imler has a painting service called Dan & Son Painting. All materials are filed in the folder labeled Imler Dan. A cross reference is placed in the files under Dan & Son Painting. The cross reference reads as follows: Dan & Son Painting, see Imler Dan

FILING RULES AND STANDARDS

ARMA, the Association of Records Managers and Administrators, is a professional organization for the records management field that develops and promotes standards for records management.

ARMA Simplified Filing Standard Rules*

1. Alphabetize by arranging files in unit-by-unit order and letter-by-letter within each unit.

	AS FILED		
AS WRITTEN	UNIT 1	UNIT 2	UNIT 3
Professional Artists Inc	Professional	Artists	Inc.
Professional Secretaries International	Professional	Secretaries	International
Rapid Messenger Service	Rapid	Messenger	Service

2. Each filing unit in a filing segment is to be considered. This includes prepositions, conjunctions, and articles. The only exception is when the word "the" is the first filing unit in a filing segment. In this case, "the" is the last filing unit. Spell out all symbols; e.g., as &, $, #, and file alphabetically.

	AS FILED			
AS WRITTEN	UNIT 1	UNIT 2	UNIT 3	UNIT 4
Brinker & Pisenti	Brinker	and	Pisenti	
The Buffy Antiques	Buffy	Antiques	The	
Campbell & Associates	Campbell	and	Associates	
Creative Journeys of Napa	Creative	Journeys	of	Napa
$ and Cents	Dollars	and	Cents	
Flights of Fancy	Flights	of	Fancy	

3. File "nothing before something." File single unit filing segments before multiple unit filing segments.

*Based on ARMA International "Alphabetical Filing Rules." Copyright © 1972, 1985, 1986. All rights reserved. Published with permission of and by arrangement with the Association of Records Managers and Administrators, Inc.

AS WRITTEN	AS FILED			
	UNIT 1	UNIT 2	UNIT 3	UNIT 4
A Grand Innovation	A	Grand	Innovation	
A to Z Bookkeeping	A	to	Z	Bookkeeping
Able Auto Painting	Able	Auto	Painting	
C & W Ford	C	and	W	Ford
C G Products	C	G	Products	
Cooperfield Books	Cooperfield	Books		

4. Ignore punctuation when alphabetizing. This includes periods, commas, dashes, and apostrophes, etc. Hyphenated words are considered one unit.

AS WRITTEN	AS FILED		
	UNIT 1	UNIT 2	UNIT 3
Brides 'n Maids	Brides	n	Maids
Cody's Books	Codys	Books	
Cluckler All-Steel Building	Cluckler	AllSteel	Building
Parker-West Advertising	ParkerWest	Advertising	
Sonoma Package Co.	Sonoma	Package	Co

5. Arabic and Roman numbers are filed sequentially before alphabetic characters. All Arabic numerals precede all Roman numerals.

AS WRITTEN	AS FILED			
	UNIT 1	UNIT 2	UNIT 3	UNIT 4
1 Hour Photo	1	Hour	Photo	
4 Star Foods	4	Star	Foods	
49er Pet Warehouse	49er	Pet	Warehouse	
355 Park Hotel	355	Park	Hotel	
V Star Foods	V	Star	Foods	
A-1 Equipment Rental	A1	Equipment	Rental	
Four Star Foods	Four	Star	Foods	
One Hour Photo	One	Hour	Photo	

6. Acronyms, abbreviations, and radio and television station call letters are filed as one unit.

AS WRITTEN	AS FILED			
	UNIT 1	UNIT 2	UNIT 3	UNIT 4
Am. Patent Services	Am	Patent	Services	
GE Consumer Service	GE	Consumer	Service	
KOLB TV	KOLB	TV		
WSRO 1350 AM	WSRO	1350	AM	

7. File under the most commonly-used name or title. Cross-reference under other names or titles which might be used in an information request.

	AS FILED			
AS WRITTEN	UNIT 1	UNIT 2	UNIT 3	UNIT 4
Dan & Son Painting	Dan (See Imler Dan)	and	Son	Painting
Cellular Car Service	Cellular (See Sonoma Communications Inc.)	Car	Service	
The Violin Shop	Violin (See Loveland Mike)	Shop	The	

Examples for Applying the Simplified Filing Rules

PERSONAL NAMES

1. *Simple personal names:* Use the last (surname) as the first filing unit. The first name or initial is the second filing unit. Subsequent names or initials are filed as successive units.

	AS FILED			
AS WRITTEN	UNIT 1	UNIT 2	UNIT 3	UNIT 4
A. Miriam Harms	Harms	A	Miriam	
Deanna Pebbles	Pebbles	Deanna		
Paul B. White	White	Paul	B	

2. *Personal names with prefixes:* Surnames which include a prefix are filed as one unit whether the prefix is followed by a space or not. Examples of prefixes are: D', Da, De, Del, De la, Della, Den, Des, Di, Du, El, Fitz, L', La, Las, Le, Les, Lo, Los, M', Mac, Mc, O', Saint, St., Ste., Te, Ten, Ter, Van, Van de, Van der, Von, Von der.

	AS FILED			
AS WRITTEN	UNIT 1	UNIT 2	UNIT 3	UNIT 4
Gary D'Alois	DAlois	Gary		
Jesse Del Moral	DelMoral	Jesse		
Andrea C. LaDow	LaDow	Andrea	C	
Peter J. McCabe	McCabe	Peter	J	
Terry V. O'Connor	OConnor	Terry	V	
Linda St. Andrew	StAndrew	Linda		
Jane C. Van Der Slice	VanDerSlice	Jane	C	
Albert Vander Werf	VanderWerf	Albert		

3. *Personal names with personal and professional titles and suffixes:* Suffixes are not used as filing units except when needed to distinguish between two or more identical names. When needed, a suffix is the last filing unit and is filed as written, ignoring punctuation.

AS WRITTEN	AS FILED UNIT 1	UNIT 2	UNIT 3	UNIT 4
John P. Lynch, C.P.A.	Lynch	John	P	CPA
John P. Lynch, Jr.	Lynch	John	P	Jr
John P. Lynch, M.D.	Lynch	John	P	MD
Mr. John P. Lynch	Lynch	John	P	Mr
John P. Lynch, Ph.D.	Lynch	John	P	PhD
Senator John P. Lynch	Lynch	John	P	Senator

4. *Personal names which are hyphenated:* Ignore the hyphen and file the two words as one unit.

AS WRITTEN	AS FILED UNIT 1	UNIT 2	UNIT 3	UNIT 4
Peggy Davis-Farrell	DavisFarrell	Peggy		
Danielle Griffin-Amcor	GriffinAmcor	Danielle		
Carol Lytle	Lytle	Carol		

5. *Pseudonymous and royal and religious titles:* Pseudonyms are filed as written. Personal names which start with a royal or religious title and are followed by only a given name(s) are filed as written.

AS WRITTEN	AS FILED UNIT 1	UNIT 2	UNIT 3	UNIT 4
Dr. Seuss	Dr	Seuss		
Prince Charles	Prince	Charles		
Sister Mary	Sister	Mary		

6. *Foreign personal names:* If the surname is identifiable, file the name as any other personal name is filed. If there is a question about the surname, use the last name as the first filing unit and make a cross-reference from the first name.

AS WRITTEN	AS FILED UNIT 1	UNIT 2	UNIT 3	UNIT 4
Liang Li	Li	Liang		
	Liang	Li		
	(See Li Liang)			
Yang Mo	Mo	Yang		
	Yang	Mo		
	(See Mo Yang)			
Yew Cong Wong	Wong	Yew	Cong	
	Yew Cong Wong (See Wong			
	Yew Cong)			

7. *Nicknames:* When a person commonly uses a nickname as a first name, file using the nickname. Cross-reference from the given name only if necessary.

	AS FILED			
AS WRITTEN	UNIT 1	UNIT 2	UNIT 3	UNIT 4
Susie Sziber	Sziber	Susie		
Bob Tagnoli	Tagnoli	Bob		
Buck Wood	Wood	Buck		
	(See Wood John C)			

BUSINESS AND ORGANIZATION NAMES

1. Business and organization names are filed as written according to the Simplified Standard Rules and using the business letterhead or trademark as a guide. Names with prefixes follow the example for personal names with prefixes above.

	AS FILED			
AS WRITTEN	UNIT 1	UNIT 2	UNIT 3	UNIT 4
A & T Automotive	A	and	T	Automotive
Aardvark Transmissions	Aardvark	Transmissions		
Dee-Jay's Sash & Glass	Deejays	Sash	and	Glass
Kelly Kline Photo Studios	Kelly	Kline	Photo	Studios
U-Save Auto Rental	USave	Auto	Rental	
Van Koonse Glass Co.	VanKoonse	Glass	Co	

2. Subsidiaries of businesses will be filed under their own name with a cross-reference to the parent company if needed.

	AS FILED			
AS WRITTEN	UNIT 1	UNIT 2	UNIT 3	UNIT 4
Comstock Michigan Fruit	Comstock (See also Curtice Burns Foods Inc.)	Michigan	Fruit	
Curtice Burns Foods, Inc.	Curtice (for Divisions see: Comstock Michigan Fruit Iowa Fresh Foods Nebraska Produce, Inc.)	Burns	Foods	Inc

3. Place names in business names will follow the Simplified Filing Standard Rule that each word/filing unit is treated as a separate filing unit.

AS WRITTEN	AS FILED			
	UNIT 1	UNIT 2	UNIT 3	UNIT 4
California Parenting Institute	Californi	Parenting	Institute	
Oakland Coliseum	Oakland	Coliseum		
Sonoma County Transportation	Sonoma	County	Transportation	

4. Compass terms in business names. Each word/unit in a filing segment containing compass terms is considered a separate filing unit. If the term includes more than pass point, treat it as it is written. Establish cross references as needed.

AS WRITTEN	AS FILED			
	UNIT 1	UNIT 2	UNIT 3	UNIT 4
North Bay Regional Center	North	Bay	Regional	Center
North Coast Drywall	North	Coast	Drywall	
North West Design	North	West	Design	
Northwest Community Center	Northwest	Community	Center	

GOVERNMENT/POLITICAL DESIGNATIONS

When filing governmental/political material, the name of the major entity is filed first, followed by the distinctive name of the department, bureau, etc.

This rule covers all governmental and political divisions, agencies, departments, and federal to the county/parish, city, district, and ward level.

1. *Federal:* Prefix with the name of the government and eliminate the department; i.e., of the Interior, Department of the Treasury, etc. File titles of the office, or bureau, etc., by their distinctive names.

   ▲ United States Government; Army

   ▲ United States Government; Federal Bureau of Investigation

   ▲ United States Government; Interior

   ▲ United States Government; Treasury

   ▲ United States Government; Veterans Administration

2. *State and local:* State, county, parish, city, town, township and village governments/political divisions are filed by their distinctive names. The words "county of," "city of," "department of," etc., if needed and as appropriate, are added for clarity and are considered filing units. Note: If "of" is not part of the official name as written, it is not added.

AS WRITTEN	AS FILED UNIT 1	UNIT 2	UNIT 3	UNIT 4
Iowa Highway Patrol	Iowa	Highway	Patrol	
Marin County Library	Marin	County	Library	
City of Healdsburg	Healdsburg	City	of	

3. *Foreign governments:* The distinctive English name is the first filing unit. If needed, the balance of the formal name of the government forms the next filing unit(s). Divisions, departments, and branches follow in sequential order, reversing the written order necessary to give the distinctive name precedence in the filing arrangement.

States, colonies, provinces, cities, and other divisions of foreign governments are filed by their distinctive or official names as spelled in English. Cross-reference written name to official native name where necessary.

AS WRITTEN	AS FILED UNIT 1	UNIT 2	UNIT 3	UNIT 4
Brazil	Brazil			
Paris, France	Paris	France		

MANAGING PAPER-BASED RECORDS

Paper accounts for 95 percent of the filing in the United States. It is estimated that on average a company doubles its total number of records every ten years.

The advantages of paper records are that they are affordable for an office of any size; they are an acceptable form of record for legal purposes; and people are comfortable working with paper. On the other hand, paper records can take up a great deal of space; they are vulnerable to water and fire damage and to loss; file security can be a problem; and only one person at a time can use a paper document.

Paper filing systems should meet the following guidelines:

- Records necessary for daily operations are easily retrieved. Active files are the ones closest to the user.
- Records accessed infrequently are stored in a separate, less-accessible location.
- Access to confidential information is restricted.
- A retention schedule is developed; records are destroyed when they are no longer of value to the company. (See the sections on Retaining Records and on Transfer and Disposal in this chapter.)

Because paper files are so expensive and cumbersome, consider the answer to the following questions before filing paper:

- Must the record be retained in paper form?
- Is it possible to convert the paper record to electronic or micrographic form?
- Is it necessary to transcribe tape-recorded information or will storage of the tape be adequate?
- What is the cost of maintaining the paper-based system? For paper records, consider floor space and labor for handling, filing, and retrieving records. For electronic and micrographic systems, consider time and labor to convert paper records to another format and the cost of any special equipment.

Reorganizing an Existing Paper-based Filing System

If information cannot be accessed quickly and stored easily, it can be organized following these steps:

1. Prepare a written list of existing files.
2. Categorize files as active or inactive. Remove inactive files from the list.
3. Decide whether any materials (speeches, public relations material, client files) need to be separated from the main filing system.

HINT: *A special file should contain enough material to fill up half a file drawer.*

4. Organize the inventory list by broad categories. Usually one heading and two subheadings per category are sufficient. Get suggestions from others who are using the files.

HINT: *Use a word processing outline feature, which makes updating easy and can generate a printed list.*

5. Make any cross references needed. (See the section on Types of Filing Systems earlier in this chapter.)
6. Prepare a summary list, which is a map of the contents of the drawers with broad categories of material contained in each.
7. Prepare labels to put on the actual files. (See the section Preparation of File Folders below for additional information.)
8. Train those who will use the filing system. Distribute the summary list.

Equipment

With the ever-increasing amount of paper in the office, storage has become a major problem for many companies. Filing equipment is available in a wide range of designs and sizes. No more space should be allocated for records than is necessary.

The following are some of the major types of filing equipment and their uses.

Desk-size filing units and two-drawer file cabinets: These are used for files that are accessed daily; they do not, however, utilize space efficiently.

Four- or five-drawer vertical file cabinet: These are the most popular format for active files; the five-drawer version has 25 percent more storage space than the four-drawer version. The letter-size version is the most popular style. A disadvantage is that it can be used by only one person at a time and may not be accessible to those with disabilities.

Lateral cabinets: These are lengthwise units whose drawers or shelves are opened broadside; they are available with two to six drawers or shelves. When open, all records are visible. They may be used as barriers between working areas, and they require 40 percent less floor space than a four-drawer vertical file cabinet.

Open-shelf file units: These lateral units have open shelves like a bookshelf. They are good for high-volume filing and have the advantage of being accessible to more than one person at the same time. All records are visible. Filing and retrieval can be done approximately 20 to 40 percent more quickly than with file cabinets, and they require 50 percent less floor space than a four-drawer vertical file cabinet. Security, however, is a problem.

High-density mobile filing units: These vertical units make a large number of active documents readily accessible. Floor space is saved by not having aisles between the file units; since the units are on tracks or rails, and they are mobile, only one aisle is ever created at a time. Units can be moved either manually (the user pushes the units back and forth) or mechanically. They can increase file space by as much as 200 percent.

Rotary files: Rotation brings records close to the user with little user movement; some versions are automated. Records may be filed vertically or flat. Only one request can be processed at a time, however.

Heavy cardboard boxes: These boxes (12 by 10 by 15 inches) are used for inactive files; they are scaled and labeled and usually stored away from the main work area. Two letter-size file drawers are equivalent to three boxes. The same size is capable of storing both legal- and letter-size documents, as well as odd-size documents and cards. They are structurally secure over a long period of time and provide some degree of waterproofing.

Selection of Equipment

The selection of filing equipment for paper-based records depends upon determining the following information:

1. The amount of floor space available. Vertical file cabinets take up the most space, followed by lateral and open-shelf cabinets. High-density mobile filing units take the least amount of space. Make sure there is adequate aisle space between cabinets. In addition, determine whether moving inactive files to storage will increase the floor space.
2. Number of people accessing the files at one time. Note that vertical cabinets may be used by only one person at a time. As density increases (seven or eight shelves high), accessibility decreases.

3. The method of filing. Determine the most appropriate method: alphabetical, numeric, subject, or geographic. Decide whether to use top or side tabs or bar codes.
4. Number of files pulled each day.
5. Number of refiles each day.
6. Type and size of records.
7. Security concerns. Open shelving is appropriate in a filing area that is accessible only to authorized personnel. In other areas, use cabinets with doors that lock to restrict access.
8. Weight capacity of existing floor. Consult with a structural engineer for load capacity before purchasing new equipment.
9. Corporate growth plans. Are there plans to merge or consolidate operations? Are there plans to move? If at all possible, purchase standard-sized equipment that is usable in other offices or departments in case of reorganization.
10. Corporate budget for filing and storage.
11. Environmental requirements.
12. Accessibility by persons who have disabilities as required by the Americans with Disabilities Act (ADA).

To determine the cost of a system, follow these steps:

1. Compute the current filing inches of space. 175 pieces of paper = 1 file inch; Vertical file cabinet = 25 filing inches per drawer; Lateral file cabinet = 50 filing inches per shelf.
2. Convert filing inches to square feet needed for equipment.

EQUIPMENT	AISLE SPACE (INCHES)	TOTAL SQUARE FEET OF OFFICE SPACE NEEDED
Letter-size vertical file	28	7.5
Legal-size vertical file	28	9.0
30-inch lateral cabinet	6	6.5
36-inch lateral cabinet	6	7.0
42-inch lateral cabinet	6	7.5

3. Multiply square feet times the cost of office space per square foot.

For example, Company A requires 2,000 inches of filing space. If approximately 20 four-drawer vertical file cabinets are used, 150 square feet of floor space is needed. If floor space averages $30 a square foot, the total annual floor space costs are $4,500.

But if high-density mobile files are used, 2,000 inches of filing space would fit in 42 square feet of floor space. If floor space averages $30 a square foot, total annual floor space costs are $1,260.

Standardized Equipment

ARMA has initiated a campaign called ELF, or Eliminate Legal Files. This campaign urges organizations to stop using legal-sized files and legal-sized paper. A legal-size file cabinet is approximately 3 inches wider than a standard one, and the legal paper is costly to handle and file compared to 8½-by-11-inch paper.

Filing Supplies

The type of folders you should select depends on the following:

- Size of records
- Length of time the file is active
- Need for special features such as fasteners, pockets, or closed sides
- Anticipated volume

Here are descriptions of typical types of file folders:

Top-tab: The identifying tab is at the top. Made of either manila or pressboard material, these are used in vertical cabinets or lateral cabinets with drawers.

End-tab: The identifying tab is at the end of the folder. Made of either manila or pressboard material, these are used with flat shelving, lateral cabinets with flat shelves and flipper doors, and lateral units with buckets that slide on rails.

Hanging folders: These are designed to replace the manila or pressboard folder. The label holder can be placed in any position across the top of the folder. They are popular because they make records easily accessible and hold more information than regular file folders. However, they occupy 33 percent more drawer space, thus increasing equipment cost and floor space needs by 33 percent.

Folders with fasteners: These have metal fasteners at the top of the folder. They are used for very active records if records are transferred to several workers or if the internal order of documents is important.

Pocket folders: These are partially enclosed folders that expand from ¾ inch to 3½ inches or more. They are used for odd-sized and loose materials.

Preparation of File Folders

Follow these steps in preparing file folders:

1. Select folder type (see the previous section Filing Supplies).
2. Choose third, fifth, two-fifths, shelf, half, or straight cut folder tabs. (See the section on Filing and Records Management Supplies in Chapter 9 for tab descriptions.)

3. Decide on folder weight. (See the section on Filing and Records Management Supplies in Chapter 9 for more information on folder weights and uses.)

4. Determine the organization of the tabs. There are three main types of organizations (see Figure 12-4):

- **Type one:** Use a set tab position for each category of information to allow for quick retrieval. For example, for an alphabetical list of customers, reserve the first tab position for customers in Arizona, the second position for those in California, and the third position for everyone else.

- **Type two:** Use the first position tab, then the second position tab, and then the third position tab. This is good for a file system that does not change. If it does change, new file folders are added and items are no longer in order. Finding folders then becomes more time-consuming.

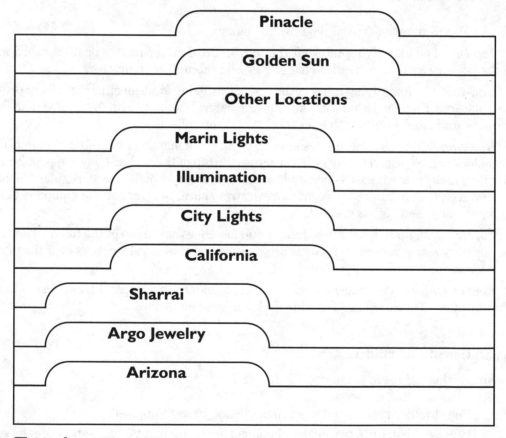

Type 1

Figure 12-4 Three types of tab organiztion.

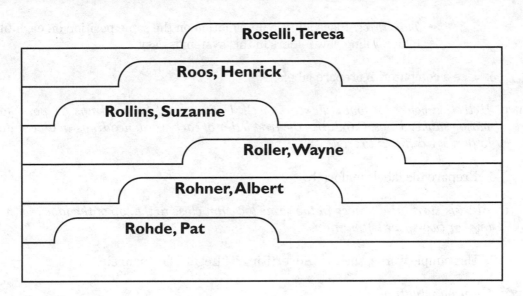

Type 2

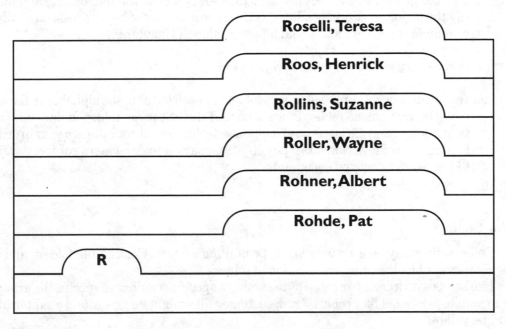

Type 3

Figure 12-4 (continued.)

      • *Type three:* Place all title information on the same position on each file folder. Filing new folders in this system is easy.

   5. Use a computer to prepare labels.

HINT: *Helvetica bold type font style works well. Use 24-point for headings, 18-point for major subheadings. Capitalize the first letter of each word; headings in all capital letters are difficult to read.*

   6. Prepare file labels uniformly.

HINT: *Always start label names in the same location close to the top of the label, with a one- or two-space left margin.*

   7. Use simple words, such as "Advertising," "Legal," "Personnel."

HINT: *Omit punctuation.*

   8. Use file guides. File guides serve as dividers, precede the file folders, and identify the major or subject headings. Guides are made out of heavy pressboard, fiber, or manila stock. (For additional information, see Chapter 9.)

HINT: *Precede every five to ten folders with a guide.*

   9. Include a general or miscellaneous folder for each letter of the alphabet to file any material that has no folder. Place it behind the last name folder under that particular letter, and file material in it alphabetically. Review four times a year in order to purge or refile documents if possible. Start a new folder when a subject has five to ten pages of related documents.

  10. Label file drawers.

Color Coding

Color coding may be used with any type of filing system. Colored file folders and labels allow quick identification and location of folders.

Use labels with a color bar at top by assigning a specific color bar to specific file groups. For example, personnel files could be red, customer files might be green, and creditor files could be yellow.

Use letters or numbers preprinted on a colored and/or patterned background to identify a partial name or subject. For example, the first three letters of a customer's name could be color coded. All customers with names beginning with these first three letters are easily identified as a group. This color-coding system adds an extra step in file preparation.

Solid color labels are recommended only when confidentiality is needed; use pastel colors for easy reading. For example, all personnel files could have yellow labels.

The following should be kept in mind when using color:

- Keep the system as simple as possible; e.g., make all the A's one color, all the B's one color, etc.
- In a numeric filing system use ten colors, since the most common system is based on ten digits.
- Use color folders to indicate certain types of files; e.g., blue could be for correspondence.
- Use different color labels for folders with the same name; e.g., "Steven White, Jr." could have a yellow label; "Steven White, Sr.," a green label.

Filing Documents

Not everything must be filed. Information that will not be used in the future should be thrown away or recycled. Company newsletters, bulletins, newspapers, and vendor catalogs are best placed in a notebook on a bookshelf.

The following tips are helpful when filing:

- Underline or write file headings on documents. Then if an item is removed from the files, it will be refiled in the same folder.
- File documents daily to avoid accumulated filing.
- Remove rubber bands and paper clips; discard envelopes, routing slips, cover memos, and duplicates; staple multipage records together; mend tears with tape.

HINT: *Keep one copy of each draft until the final document is inactive, then discard all previous drafts.*

- Rough-sort documents into major categories; for example, a rough-sort for alphabetic documents is A–L and M–Z.

HINT: *Both alphabetic and numeric sorting organizers are available from office supply sources.*

- File the most recent papers in the front of the folder; place the document facing up, with the top of the page at the left edge of the folder.
- Crease the score marks at the bottom of manila folders when papers are a quarter of an inch thick (about 25 sheets of paper). Manila folders hold approximately 100 pieces of paper. If the folders are not scored for every quarter inch of paper, the file label cannot be seen and the folder will slide into the file drawer or shelf and damage the contents.

- Replace worn folders with new ones.
- Allow 3 to 4 inches of working space in vertical files.

Retrieval and Charge-out

A file can be quickly located if employees charge out files before using them. The following charge-out methods can be used:

Charge-out request: Write down the name of the file (either on a 3-by-5-inch slip of paper or a printed charge-out request); place the charge-out request in an out guide, which is a folder with a pocket for filing documents when the file is missing; remove the charge-out paper when the folder is returned. If the folder is to be used at the filing cabinet, a charge-out request is not necessary.

Out guide: Write on the out guide the name of the folder, when it was removed, and who removed it; place the out guide where the file was located; remove the out guide when the folder is returned. Out guides would be used in the following circumstances in small offices: (1) the file is loaned to someone outside the office; (2) the file is taken outside the office by an employee; or (3) an employee expects to use the file for a week or more. The advantages to using charge-out procedures are as follows:

- Identifies employees using the files.

HINT: *If employees are in a hurry and do not feel they can take the time to complete the charge-out information, assign a special color out guide to be placed in the files in case of emergencies.*

- Allows monitoring of the time a file was taken.

HINT: *Use a color charge-out guide for each week of the month to help identify files missing for longer than necessary. For example, week 1 could be yellow; week 2, red; week 3, green, etc.*

- Determines activity levels for use of the files.

Safety

The following safety precautions should be observed:

- Close all drawers or reference shelves after using them.
- Open only one drawer of a vertical cabinet at a time to keep the cabinet from tipping over.

HINT: *Newer cabinets are equipped with counterbalances to avoid this problem.*

- Weigh down the bottom shelf of lateral equipment before loading the top shelf. Once the cabinet is loaded past the middle shelf, it will not tip over.

HINT: *Store paper or folders on the bottom shelf while loading the cabinet for the first time.*

COMPUTER SOFTWARE

Commercial Software

Electronic computer systems are helping decrease the amount of paper in offices. Word processing, spreadsheet, and database programs are discussed in Chapter 8. All these software packages are available at a reasonable price and can be tailored to meet specific filing needs.

It is essential that electronic files be managed properly. Some of the important steps in managing these files are the following:

- Use consistent standards for logging and naming documents when storing them. Most standards use letters, numbers, or a combination of both.
- Periodically clean up electronic files—either eliminate them or store them on disk. A crowded hard disk slows the access speed of finding information because the hard disk head must move farther across the disk in order to find files.
- Back up important documents. The backup method you should use is determined by the amount of data that you need to store. (See section on Backing Up Software in Chapter 8 for additional information.)
- Store disks and tapes properly, using diskette trays or lateral filing. (See the section on Disk Storage in Chapter 9 for additional information.)

Automated Records Management Systems

Computer software programs known as automated records management systems are used when a paper-based filing system becomes overwhelming to maintain because of the volume of records. These systems can track and analyze the status of documents. The cost of an automated records management system can vary widely.

Automated records management software usually can be operated on existing computer hardware. Information about records, but not their contents, can be viewed on the computer screen. This system typically uses a bar-code system so tracking is done by scanning labels.

Imaging and full-text systems usually require additional hardware, such as optical character recognition (OCR) scanners, and a high-capacity storage system, such as optical disks (optical disks are discussed later in this chapter). Networking capabilities make the system accessible to a wide range of employees. The user can see the contents of records.

The advantages of using an automated records management system include the following:

- It provides a method to track files that are not in the filing cabinet.
- It reduces the possibility of misplaced or lost files.
- It generates reports showing who has taken out files and when they are due.
- It helps in making decisions about which records are to be moved to long-term storage.
- Files requires less storage space.
- Files can be retrieved quickly.
- Data are easily transportable.

The disadvantages include security problems that stem from unauthorized access, the fact that they are easier to destroy than paper records, the ease of alteration, and the initial cost of the hardware and software.

MICROGRAPHIC TECHNOLOGY

Microforms are photographic reductions of larger documents.

Microforms have several advantages. They are an excellent method for storing both active and inactive records, since they take up only a third of the space needed for paper documents. Once recorded, information cannot later be misfiled, since a microform is either a roll or a sheet of film. In addition, microforms are more durable than paper as well as being easily and economically duplicated and economically mailed.

Microforms also have their disadvantages. The initial cost of equipment is high. Readers are necessary (note that readers for microfilm and microfiche are different). Also, microforms must be stored in a controlled environment, and they cannot be updated without refilming.

A microfilm is a roll of film with miniature pictures of pages. A microfiche is a sheet of film with miniature pictures of pages. Both microfilm and microfiche are referred to as microforms.

Microfiche is better for smaller databases; one sheet can store hundreds of images. It is read by placing the fiche on a platen and scanning for the proper index.

Microfilm, although more expensive than microfiche, is one of the most cost-effective methods of storing documents. It is usually used to store large databases of information (typically several thousand images can be stored on one roll of film).

Another way of creating microforms is a method called computer output microfilm/microfiche (COM). Information from the computer is transferred directly to the microfilm/microfiche—it is not printed on paper first. The major advantage of using COM is its speed and the amount of work that can be handled. A COM recorder can film at the rate of 585,000 lines per minute.

Computer-assisted retrieval (CAR) systems can help operators find specific microform images accurately and quickly using a computer. CAR systems consist of (1) a microfilm reader, (2) microfilm cartridges storing the images, and (3) a computer storing the image database. The computer operator enters the document ID number, the database tells the operator which microfilm cartridge to load, and the computer searches for the image.

OPTICAL DISK TECHNOLOGY

Optical disks are similar to CDs in the way they look and operate. Optical disk technology is used with computer systems that communicate with and display images from the optical disk. The disks also work with database software, which organizes and searches the optical disk for the requested images. Optical disks are primarily used by companies with large storage demands, a need to distribute large amounts of information, and high-security requirements.

Optical disks have several advantages. They are not affected by magnetic fields or other problems that might affect a hard disk. They take up less space than paper storage. Information cannot be misfiled because the computer does the filing and searching. Data can be accessed by a number of authorized operators at the same time.

As with other electronic systems, one disadvantage is the initial cost of equipment. In addition, optical disks may not be acceptable in courts of law in some states as a storage medium. And they are not acceptable to tax authorities as a storage medium.

Optical disks can either be CD-ROM, WORM, or erasable. Each technology is designed for a different purpose.

CD-ROM: This is the oldest optical disk technology; CD-ROM stands for "compact disk, read-only memory." Although about the size of a floppy disk, they can store approximately 250,000 pages of text or 40,000 pages of images; these images can be retrieved instantly to a screen or by a laser printer. Once made, however, they cannot be updated.

WORM: These are used for advanced data storage. WORM stands for "write once, read many." This is a more flexible medium than CD-ROM, because data can be added to the WORM disk; however, once added, data cannot be changed (although it also cannot accidentally be destroyed). WORM disks can store handwritten memos, signatures, and drawings and can also be used as backup storage for personal computers.

Erasable storage disks: This disk allows writing, erasing, and reading of data, just as with a computer hard drive. Storage capacity ranges from 500MB to 1GB (gigabyte). The erasable disk is in a cartridge that can be removed from the computer. It can be used for backing up a fixed hard drive and network servers for local area networks.

TRANSFER AND DISPOSAL

When records are transferred from the active filing area to less expensive inactive filing areas, two transfer methods are most commonly used.

The *perpetual* method is used for records that are no longer active because the files have been closed by an event or a date (e.g., legal cases). This method is not suitable for files of a continuous nature. The periodic method is used for records that are regularly transferred after a given time period (e.g., semiannually or annually). Ultimately, vital records are transferred to permanent storage and all other records are destroyed.

A signed authorization is needed to destroy records that have legal retention requirements. This authorization itself becomes a vital record and is proof that destruction was part of normal business operations. If destroyed records are subsequently subpoenaed by a court, the authorization is proof that the records are no longer available.

Three methods of disposal are available. Nonconfidential records can be discarded as waste paper or recycled. Confidential records can first be shredded, then discarded or recycled. If the volume of records to be disposed of is large, a records management service firm can be hired to eliminate them.

FORMS MANAGEMENT

Forms are either on preprinted paper or on a computer screen. They contain permanent information with blank spaces for variable information. From 85 to 90 percent of the costs of filling out forms are for the personnel who complete, process, and use them. The goal of forms management is to minimize the cost of forms and at the same time increase work efficiency and effectiveness. These goals can be accomplished by following these steps:

- Consolidate or eliminate unnecessary forms. Determine if the form is needed. Analyze other forms to find relationships or duplications. Decide whether the forms or items on the form can be combined, eliminated, or simplified.

- Automate forms applications and systems. Maintain a computer listing of all approved forms. Investigate forms design software packages. Become familiar with designing forms using the features of a word processing package. Allow employees to fill in business forms using a computer instead of a typewriter.

- Maintain a forms file that includes specification sheets, design copies, order histories, and copies of all forms.

- Centralize purchasing and printing for cost savings.

- Review all forms annually or when equipment or procedures change.

DESIGNING FORMS

The following are components of effective business form design:

- Use spacing appropriate for equipment it will be used with. For example, check the vertical spacing on the form using the computer printer, an optical scanner, or a wand.

- Include requests for all important information (e.g., area code, ZIP Code). Make certain the instructions are adequate. Avoid unnecessary information and illegal questions.

- Group items so the user can concentrate on one small area at a time. It is best to put the most frequently used items at the top of the form.

- Use checklists and boxes for information. Place instructions above the lines or the boxes.

- Avoid having too many words and lines on a page, and use a combination of dark and light lines to guide the reader's eyes through the form. Use light single lines as guides; use heavy lines for major breaks; use double lines to break up the form into distinct sections or for totals

- Use several type sizes and states, including bold and italic, to draw attention to important items.

- Avoid wide margins unless needed for binding, because wide margins waste paper.

- Make sure lines and boxes are of adequate size to enter data.

- Include a form number and revision date in a standard location, such as a lower corner; identify forms with the organization's name and address. Include the company logo if the form is used outside the organization.

- Use color only if it serves a purpose.

- Use standard form designs and paper size if possible. Avoid sizes that are difficult to file or microfilm. Make certain the form fits in a business envelope. Use paper of appropriate weight and quality.

- Include an adequate number of parts so that as many carbon copies as needed are made when the form is filled out. Multipart forms are often the least costly way to duplicate information.

- Number all pages of multipage forms.

Identify each copy on its face if appropriate; for example, Copy 1—Office; Copy 2—Customer; Copy 3—Accounting

SECURITY OF RECORDS AND DISASTER PROTECTION

Maintaining the security of records is an important part of protecting the assets of an organization. The following tips help secure written, oral, and computerized data:

1. Lock files when they are not in use; secure the office and file keys.
2. Audit who uses the files and for what reasons.
3. Shred confidential documents and printouts that are no longer needed.

4. Avoid leaving confidential information on desks accessible to the public, on the computer screens, in the fax output tray, or in the copy machine.

5. Protect computer passwords and system dial-in phone numbers; change passwords often; do not post passwords in the work area.

6. Log off the computer system when leaving the terminal.

7. Use tamper-proof interoffice envelopes.

Loss from natural disasters such as earthquakes, floods, hurricanes, and tornadoes can be minimized by storing the original vital documents at a remote site and keeping only copies on-site. Consider locations with temperature and humidity control and file protection that sprays the inert gas, Halon, instead of water.

Business records provide management with information to make sound decisions. They also provide a measurement of an organization's stability and its potential for growth.

Office professionals often have the responsibility to collect and present the data required for accurate records. In smaller companies, these responsibilities may include handling cash, checking accounts, bank reconciliations, payroll, and billing as well as journal entries and posting transactions and preparing financial statements. In larger companies these financial responsibilities are more time-consuming and complex; they require a greater level of specialization. Many office professionals use specialized software programs ranging in complexity from simple checking account management to fully integrated systems.

Regardless of the size of the company or the amount of technology used, office professionals must understand basic bookkeeping principles. Owners of home-based businesses need a working knowledge of bookkeeping procedures to communicate with their accountants or to handle the bookkeeping work on their own. Realizing *why* a process is done a specific way will help a worker avoid or locate errors that may occur and make the work more meaningful, challenging, and profitable.

CHAPTER 13

FINANCIAL

RECORDKEEPING

UNDERSTANDING TERMS

The accounting/bookkeeping field uses a language of its own. To do simple bookkeeping tasks or select accounting software, you should know the vocabulary.

General Terms

Financial and managerial accounting are the two major accounting classifications. The goal of **financial accounting** is to prepare financial statements and present them to interested individuals outside the company. **Bookkeeping** involves procedures for recording financial data and is part of the financial accounting process.

Managerial accounting requires much of the same information accumulated in the financial accounting process, but management uses the information to plan, schedule, and control the company's internal activities. Cost ac-

283

counting, financial forecasting (budgeting), auditing, and income tax accounting involve additional specialized accounting functions. Our emphasis is on financial accounting procedures.

Companies operate on either an accrual basis or a cash basis. Operating on an **accrual basis** means that all revenue and expenses are recorded at the time they are incurred regardless of when cash is actually received or expended. Companies operating on a **cash basis** record revenue only when cash is received, and they record expenses only when cash is disbursed.

In the **double-entry** system of accounting, both a debit entry and a credit entry are required in the **journal** and the **ledger** for any transaction that involves an exchange of money or property or that adjusts or corrects existing information. A debit is entered on the *left side* of a ledger account; a credit is entered on the *right side*. When recording transactions, the total debits must equal the total credits.

Most businesses use the double-entry system of accounting, whether they record their entries manually or electronically with a computer. However, some small businesses use the simpler **single-entry** system, in which each transaction is entered only once as a sum due to or owed by the company.

To be consistent and provide an orderly recording of financial information, a company must identify the accounts it expects to use and give a number to each account. This **chart of accounts** is used to identify the accounts that must be charged when making entries in journals and ledgers. (See Figure 13-1.)

HINT: *Most software programs provide numerous choices for a chart of accounts. Select one or customize one that fits your specific business.*

A **journal** is a diary in which daily business transactions are recorded from source documents such as checks, invoices, and cash register tapes. Journal formats vary. Some companies use a **general journal** and record *all* transactions in it. (See Figure 13-2.) Others use a combined journal form. (See Figure 13-3.)

Each account in the chart of accounts has a space in the **general ledger**. (See Figure 13-4.) In addition to a general ledger, companies may use **accounts receivable ledgers** (records of customers who owe money) (see Figure 13-5) and **accounts payable ledgers** (records of creditors to whom money is owed).

Account Classifications

There are several standard classifications of accounts. **Assets** are items that are owned by a company. **Current assets** include cash, inventory, and other assets that have a high probability of being turned into cash readily, usually within a year. **Plant assets** are long-term assets, such as equipment and land, with benefits that carry over into future accounting periods. Asset accounts increase on the debit side and decrease on the credit side of a ledger.

Liabilities are amounts owed or services yet to be rendered by a company. They also are broken down into current and long-term accounts. Accounts payable and salaries

CORNER BOOKKEEPING SERVICE
Chart of Accounts

100–199 ASSETS

110	Cash
111	Petty Cash
120	Accounts Receivable
130	Prepaid Insurance
140	Prepaid Rent
150	Office Supplies
160	Office Equipment
161	Accumulated Depreciation on Office Equipment
170	Office Furniture
171	Accumulated Depreciation on Office Furniture

200–299 LIABILITIES

210	Accounts Payable

300–399 OWNER'S EQUITY

310	D. R. Johnson, Capital
320	D. R. Johnson, Drawing
399	Income Summary

400–499 REVENUE

410	Service Fees

500–599 EXPENSES

510	Salaries Expense
520	Supplies Expense
530	Insurance Expense
540	Rent Expense
550	Utilities Expense
551	Telephone Expense
560	Depreciation Expense/Office Equipment
561	Depreciation Expense/Office Furniture

Figure 13-1 Chart of accounts for a service company.

GENERAL JOURNAL   Page_____

Date		Entry Description	Ref.	Debit		Credit	
19—							
Sept.	4	Equipment		1995	00		
		Accounts Payable/ Donnelly Corp.				1995	00

Figure 13-2 General journal/double-entry system.

Combination Journal for Month of _____ **19** _____   **Page** _____

Cash		Ck #	Date	Explanation of Entry	Ref.	General		Accounts Receivable		Accounts Payable		Service Income	Salaries Expense	Utilities Expense
Dr	Cr					Dr	Cr	Dr	Cr	Dr	Cr	Cr	Dr	Dr
	$1,800	4	June 3	Rent Expense		$1,800								
$980			June 4	Sales				$2,000				$2,980		

Figure 13-3 Combined journal.

payable are examples of **current liabilities.** A mortgage is an example of a **long-term liability.** Liability accounts decrease on the debit side and increase on the credit side of a ledger.

    Owner's equity, which is also called *capital,* or *net worth,* represents the owner's claim against the firm's assets after subtracting the liabilities. In corporations, owner's equity is called *stockholders' equity* or *shareholders' investment.* Owner's equity accounts decrease on the debit side and increase on the credit side of a ledger.

    Revenue results from the sale of goods, the rendering of services, or the use of money or property. Revenue accounts decrease on the debit side and increase on the credit side of a ledger account. **Expenses** are the costs involved in an effort to produce revenue. Expense accounts increase on the debit side and decrease on the credit side of a ledger account. Categories of expenses may include general, selling, and administrative.

ACCOUNTS PAYABLE						ACCOUNT NO. 210
Date	Explanation	Ref	Debit	Credit	Debit Balance	Credit Balance
19—						
Sept. 4	Inv. 9920A	G201		1995 00		1995 00

Figure 13-4 Accounts payable account in the general ledger.

Wm. Weiler Associates				Credit Referrals:		
2092 North Oak Street						
Des Moines, IA 50301						
Telephone: 515-633-9201				Checking Account Reference:		
Fax: 515-633-9222						
e-mail: msmith@wmweil.com						
Comments:						

Date	Entry Description	Ref	Debit	Credit	Balance
Oct. 1	Balance	✔			83,000 89
18	Sales Invoice AJ965	SJ90	396 40		83,397 29
29	CK9065	CR550		83,000 89	396 40

Figure 13-5 Customer's record in accounts receivable ledger.

Financial Statements

Financial statements are reports on the operations or financial position of a business during a given fiscal (or financial) period or on a given date. An **income statement** shows whether a firm operated at a profit or at a loss during a fiscal period, which may be a year, a quarter, or a month. If revenue is greater than expenses, there is a net income; if expenses are greater than revenue, there is a net loss. The **cost of goods sold** section of the income statement represents what you paid for the items you have actually sold. A **balance sheet**

SPORTING GOODS, INC.
Income Statement
For the Month Ended October 31, 19—

Operating Revenue

Sales		$327,000.00	
Less Sales Returns and Allowances	$800.00		
Sales Discounts	500.00	1,300.00	
Net Sales			$325,700.00

Cost of Goods Sold

Merchandise Inventory, October 1, 19—		$80,000.00	
Merchandise Purchases	$150,000		
Less Purchases Returns and Allowances	$3,000.00		
Purchases Discount	6,900.00	9,900.00	
Net Purchases		140,100.00	
Merchandise Available for Sale		220,100.00	
Less Merchandise Inventory, October 31, 19—		85,00.00	
Cost of Goods Sold			135,100.00
Gross Profit on Sales			$190,600.00

Operating Expenses

Selling Expenses			
Sales Salaries Expense	$85,000.00		
Supplies Expense	6,000.00		
Delivery Expense	1,500.00		
Advertising Expense	12,000.00		
Total Selling Expense		$104,500.00	
Administrative Expenses			
Office Salaries Expense	$22,000.00		
Rent Expense	15,000.00		
Utilities Expense	3,000.00		
Insurance Expense	3,000.00		
Office Operations Expense	550.00		
Telephone Expense	1,200.00		
Depreciation Expense/Equipment	500.00		
Total Administrative Expenses		45,250.00	
Total Operating Expenses			149,750.00
Net Income			$40,850.00

Figure 13-6 Income statement.

SPINNETI LAWN AND GARDEN SUPPLIES
Balance Sheet
December 31, 1996

ASSETS

Current Assets

Cash		$25,000.00
Petty Cash Fund		100.00
Notes Receivable		3,000.00
Accounts Receivable	$30,000.00	
Less Allowance for Uncollectible Accounts	600.00	29,400.00
Merchandise Inventory		83,000.00
Supplies		200.00
Prepaid Insurance		2,500.00
Total Current Assets		$143,200.00

Plant and Equipment

Equipment	$15,000.00	
Less Accumulated Depreciation/Equip't.	4,000.00	11,000.00
Total Assets		$154,200.00

LIABILITIES

Notes Payable	$18,000.00	
Accounts Payable	39,000.00	
Salaries Payable	9,500.00	
Sales Tax Payable	5,900.00	
Total Liabilities		$72,400.00

OWNER'S EQUITY

Tony Spinneti, Capital	$81,800.00
TOTAL LIABILITIES AND OWNER'S EQUITY	$154,200.00

Figure 13-7 Balance sheet.

shows the financial picture of a business on a specific date rather than during a fiscal period. It includes three major classifications of accounts—assets, liabilities, and owner's shareholders' equity.

A **statement of owner's equity** shows any changes in the owner's claim as a result of additional investments, net income, or net loss; it also shows any draws against the company by the owner. A **statement of retained earnings** shows the changes in income that have occurred but that have not been paid out as dividends to stockholders. The **statement**

of cash flow shows there is enough cash to cover liabilities. It identifies the changes in cash balances caused by doing business.

Headings are very important on financial statements. Each heading must include the company name, the name of the statement, and the date or time period of the statement. Dollar signs should be next to the first figure in a column and next to all totals. Double rules indicate that a process is complete.

HINT: *Some accounts may be of more interest than others to your supervisor. Highlight these accounts on any financial statements or reports directed to your department.*

Business Structure

The way a business is organized determines its tax and legal liabilities. A **sole proprietorship** is owned and operated by one individual. It is the simplest structure, since all profits or losses as well as all tax and legal liabilities are the owner's. A sole proprietor must meet all local or state licensing and permit requirements and pay quarterly estimated income taxes. If there are employees, the owner must collect payroll taxes like any other employer.

A **general partnership** is a joint venture with the partners sharing skills, profits, responsibilities, and liabilities equally or on a percentage basis. Each partner is liable for the actions of the other partners, and this applies whether the partner is directly involved in the action or not. Partners report profits or losses on their personal tax returns, but the partnership must have an IRS identification number. In a **limited partnership,** a partner invests a specific amount and limits losses to that amount. Profits are distributed according to the partnership agreement. A limited partner has no control in the business; general partners operate it. A legal contract is a wise investment when establishing any type of partnership.

A **corporation** is a separate taxable and legal entity, so personal assets are usually protected. Corporations pay income taxes that are separate from those of the investors. Corporations are also able to obtain capital through the issuance of stock offerings. Two types of corporations primarily used by small family businesses or home-based businesses are the **close corporation** and the **Subchapter S Corporation.** All corporation structures require completion of an Articles of Incorporation form. The Secretary of State's office provides the forms and outlines the requirements to establish a corporation. Legal assistance may be helpful when establishing a corporation if there are other investors involved.

SELECTING SOFTWARE FOR FINANCIAL RECORDKEEPING

Computerized accounting programs range from programs that produce checks and reconcile bank statements to multiuser, fully integrated systems on a network, to expert systems. Computer application modules include programs for check writing, bank reconciliations, point of sale, accounts receivable, accounts payable, inventory control, payroll, job costing, billing, order entry, and general ledger. Software packages are also available for specific industries and job tasks.

The software may be a single application or several integrated applications. Integrated programs allow additional functions to be added as these functions become necessary. Multiuser software depends on a network that allows many users to be online at one time. Spreadsheets are used for analyzing financial data.

Software Considerations

Numerous accounting packages are available, so it is important to investigate them thoroughly before purchasing one. Analyze what works well and what weaknesses exist in the present system. Do not buy more features than you will need.

Here are some questions to ask when you help select accounting software:

- What are the hardware or system requirements? Is there enough storage capacity to run the program *and* handle the number of transactions the business requires?
- Do modules operate individually or do they rely on a general ledger package? Are the modules interactive?
- Is the chart of accounts flexible? Can you mask account format? *Masking* allows a user to specify general ledger account numbers of varying lengths, which permits departmental or other types of subaccounts.
- Are forms predefined or can you create your own formats? Do the financial reports provide information for comparative balances, such as budget to actual or current year to previous year? Do they provide year-to-date balances and indicate percentages of increase or decrease in the various accounts? Does the software provide reports on both cash and accrual operations?
- Are transactions automatically posted to the general ledger immediately after they have been entered? Are recurring and reversing entries made automatically? For example, by coding entries that should be reversed, the software makes and posts the reversing entry on the first day of the next month. Does it allow for batch or real-time posting?
- Is there an effective audit trail procedure? Does the software allow restricted access to users or provide passwords for security to such areas as payroll?
- Does the program allow data to be exported from or imported to other software programs? If so, which ones? Can the data be displayed in colorful, graphic formats?
- Does the software offer contact management features to allow tracking information about customers and suppliers? Is the program capable of printing mailing labels? Will it allow printing on standard business forms?
- How long has the software company been in business? How frequently has the software company updated its software? Do the updates add new features or do they just fix the inconsistencies?

HINT: *Other companies may already use the software you are investigating. Ask for their input before you make a final decision. Check online services that offer accounting software information as well as discussion forums.*

• How difficult is the program to learn? Some programs require an extensive accounting background; others make it easier for nonaccountants to establish a system. Are there onscreen helps and tutorials? Is the documentation easy to understand and indexed for quick reference? Does the software manufacturer have an toll-free number to call for assistance?

HINT: *A software program exists that analyzes a company's needs, compares accounting software programs, and lists several packages that meet the company's specifications. For information about this software, Software Compare, call PTC, 800-323-8724.*

• Is the software designed specifically for handling global transactions? Is it capable of dealing quickly with multiple currency conversions For example, a company doing business under the North American Free Trade Agreement (NAFTA) will want software that handles multicurrencies in French, English, and Spanish. Is there foreign language support onscreen and in the documentation? Can the program print checks and other business forms in the language and currencies of different countries? Can it convert English measurements to metric and vice versa? Does the program collect tax information by country and cover international tax regulations?

HINT: *Increasing numbers of businesses are expanding into global markets. However, all firms do not need international accounting software. If it is needed, select a package that is compatible with the rest of the company's software.*

(Additional help for choosing software can be found in Chapter 8.)

Spreadsheets

Managers need well-designed spreadsheets to analyze such areas as budgets, sales performances, and inventory levels. Spreadsheets show how different variables or figures affect the end results without reentering data for each process.

Some guidelines for preparing spreadsheets include:

• Find out what your spreadsheet can and cannot do. Check its graphic capabilities if your supervisor uses the information for presentations.

HINT: *Spreadsheet software produces many types of graphs. Check for a feature that tells you which type of graph works best for the data displayed.*

HINT: *Specialized add-in software reads a spreadsheet file and displays the data in unique ways. For example, a map add-in can display sales volume ($1–$2 million, less than $1 million, etc.) in color by regions or by states.*

- Check the accuracy of the figures. If a total does not seem accurate, check the formula again or bring it to the attention of your supervisor.
- Maintain notes detailing how you arrived at spreadsheet data and its sources. This is especially helpful when you do the spreadsheet infrequently and forget the procedures.
- Find out if the totals are to be placed at the bottom or on the right of the page. Ask your supervisor if percentages or ratios are necessary or if there is a preference for circle graphs, bar graphs, or another type of display.
- Ask questions if you do not understand the basic spreadsheet concepts or the purpose of the spreadsheet. Elaborate graphics cannot camouflage unclear thinking.
- Design the spreadsheet for its end use. Know the group who will view the spreadsheet. Determine font types, page breaks, spreadsheet name, and type size. To save setup time, try to use similar formats for other work your supervisor requires in spreadsheet form.
- Purge spreadsheets that have formula errors so they are not imported into other documents. Keep a list showing what files are linked to which spreadsheets.

HANDLING CASH RECEIPTS/ACCOUNTS RECEIVABLE

When a business uses a cash register to record its sales, a tape inside the register shows each sale and the total sales for the day. When a business issues receipts for the cash it receives, the receipts should be prenumbered for security purposes. Cash register tapes and copies of the receipts are the source documents for recording sales and cash receipts. Cash and checks should be deposited daily.

If you obtain funds for others, place the money in a sealed envelope and separate it from other cash. Handle checks made payable to cash with extreme care. Indicate the amount on the outside of the envelope and on a sheet of paper that goes inside the envelope with the money. Insist that the money be re-counted by the person accepting it.

Checks

The party who signs the check is known as the **maker** or **drawer.** The financial institution upon which the check is drawn is the **drawee,** and the party who will receive payment is the **payee.**

When checks are received in payment for goods and services, check for signatures, correct dates, and correct amounts. The figure on the check must match the written amount. If it does not, return the check to the maker or obtain written verification of the correct amount.

If the payee's name is written incorrectly on the face of the check, the payee should endorse it as written and then endorse it again correctly before depositing. If a check is received and funds are not available to cover it, call the maker of the check immediately to determine how payment is to be covered. If there is no check after three days, ask for 24-hour payment in cash, money order, or certified check. Retain the dishonored check in your files.

HINT: *A company may call the bank to verify that sufficient funds are available to cover the check at that specific time. The caller will not be told how much money is in the account.*

Endorsement

All checks require immediate endorsement, that is, a signature. An **endorsement** transfers ownership of a check or other negotiable instrument. All checks, as well as traveler's checks, money orders, and bank drafts, require a blank, full, or restrictive endorsement. The place for an endorsement is at the left end of the back of a check.

A **blank endorsement** means only the signature of the payee appears. (See Figure 13-8.) A check with such an endorsement should never be sent through the mail and is not recommended for general business use.

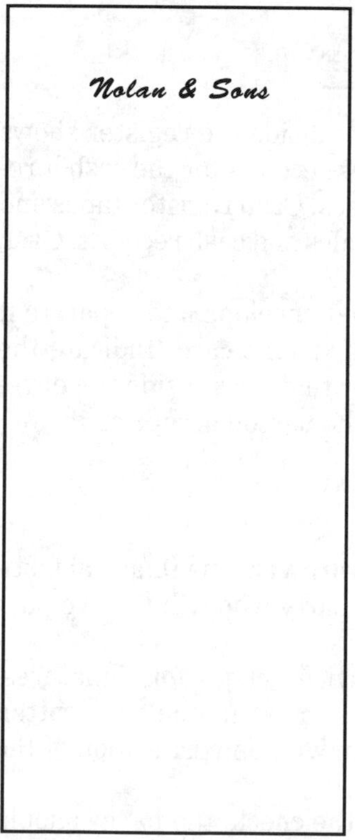

Nolan & Sons	*Pay to the order of* *Aschenbrenner* *Parts, Inc.* *Nolan & Sons* *8643-08*	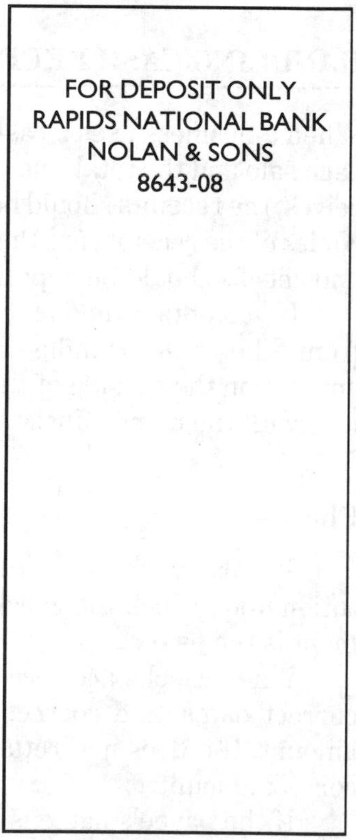 FOR DEPOSIT ONLY RAPIDS NATIONAL BANK NOLAN & SONS 8643-08

Figure 13-8 Blank endorsement. 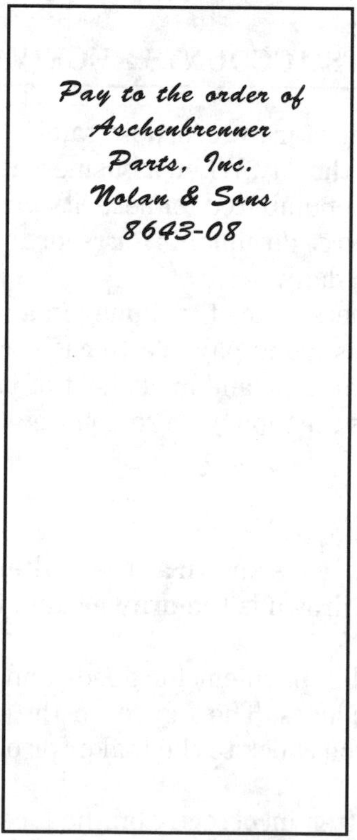   *Figure 13-9 Full endorsement*   *Figure 13-10 Restrictive*
                                   (also, qualified endorsement).   *endorsement.*

Occasionally, a business will use a **full endorsement.** A full endorsement transfers ownership of a check to someone other than the payee. The payee endorses the check and in addition writes "Pay to the order of" and the name of the party to whom the check is being transferred. (See Figure 13-9.)

A **restrictive endorsement** is the most common type of endorsement used by businesses, since it limits the way a check can be used. A typical restrictive endorsement includes "For Deposit Only," the bank's name, depositor's name, and account number. This type of endorsement provides the safest method of transferring a check. (See Figure 13-10.) Most companies use a stamp or machine to endorse checks quickly and safely. For security purposes, keep the stamp for endorsing checks in a locked drawer.

Procedures for Making Bank Deposits

A **deposit ticket** preprinted with the identification number of the bank and the account number of the customer provides a record of the deposit for the bank and for the depositor. A signed **signature card** on file at the bank gives an employee the authorization to make deposits as well as to sign checks. It is necessary to have a signature card on file at the bank for each employee who has this authorization.

The following procedures for handling bank deposits should help you to speed up banking transactions.

- Use coin wrappers, provided by banks, for large quantities of coins. Write the amount, name, and number of the account on the outside of the wrapper before filling it with coins. Inexpensive counters are available that automatically sort coins.

- Place bills of the same denomination face up in the bill wrappers supplied by the bank. If the bills are not all the same denomination, arrange them so the largest denominations are on top and the smaller denominations are on the bottom. Secure these bills with a rubber band. Record the amount of money included in each wrapper.

- Prepare deposit slips in duplicate. Keep one copy until the bank reconciliation process is complete and all deposits are acknowledged.

- List the coins, currency, and amounts for each check on the deposit slip. If checks are drawn on the same bank, list them together. To identify checks, use the name of the bank on which the check is drawn or use the numbers on the top half of the American Bankers Association (ABA) number. ABA numbers indicate the state or city of the bank and the bank number. The numbers in the bottom half of the ABA number indicate a Federal Reserve number and are not necessary on the deposit slip. Arrange the checks so they are in the same order as they are listed on the deposit slip.

- Total the currency, coin, and check amounts and place the total in the appropriate location on the deposit slip and also in the checkbook or check register. A check register not only has check forms but also space to record detailed information about a check.

- Deposit the money by taking it directly to the bank, using the night depository. Never mail coins or currency, only checks. Banks provide special bags to customers for making night deposits. Do not use the bank's drive-up facility if transactions are complicated. Most banks have commercial windows for their customers.

Procedures for Handling Customer Billing/Collections

A company's favorable cash flow depends on prompt payments by its customers. The longer accounts are outstanding, the longer it takes to collect them; some will remain un-collectible.

The billing task is one of the final steps in a sequence that begins with selling merchandise to a credit customer. The **sales invoice** includes all the details of the sale. It is the source document necessary for making journal and ledger entries.

The following are useful procedural guidelines for handling the various stages of billing and collecting:

- Review each item of merchandise on the customer's purchase order to be certain descriptions match stock numbers and prices. Update telephone and address changes.
- Check the pricing options and the credit terms for approval.
- Verify the extensions and recalculate the totals on the customer's purchase order. Indicate that this has been completed by placing checkmarks next to the verified figures.
- Initial the purchase order after completing a task. A purchase order that has a verification stamp with each task listed in sequence is helpful in tracking the sequence of responsibility.
- Prepare multiple copies of the sales invoice and distribute the copies as follows: sales representative/sales, inventory control, shipping and transportation, accounts receivable/accounting, and two copies for the reminder file. To eliminate errors in filing and distribution, use different colors for each copy.
- Post the information on the sales invoice to the accounts receivable subsidiary ledger, which is a record of a customer's new sales as well as payments on previously-purchased merchandise.
- Maintain a chronological file to have control of the dates when payments are due.
- Send invoices promptly. Include penalty clauses for late payments in bold print on the invoices. Some companies prefer cycle billing and send bills to certain preestablished groups throughout the month. Arranging groups by sections of the alphabet, by account numbers, or by geographic locations works equally well for cycle billing. Some companies believe that sending invoices to arrive by the first of the month

improves on-time payments. Others invoice the same day they ship the goods or perform the service.

- Send one of the reminder invoices to notify a customer that payment was due five days after the due date. Include a short note, such as: "This is the amount you owed us on (date). We are sending a copy of the original sales invoice so you can review the details of the purchase you made with us."

- Call the customer two weeks after an invoice due date to inquire if the merchandise was satisfactory and if the invoice and reminder were received and approved for payment. If clients are known to be slow in paying, make this call the *day after* the due date. Have the necessary information available, such as the invoices that have not been paid, amounts of discounts, and returned merchandise credits, so you can answer all questions and do not have to make another call.

HINT: *In order to remember reasons or conversations, use the computer to take notes or write them on the invoice or aged report. Report any changes in a customer's payment pattern to your supervisor.*

- Send the second of the reminder invoices (if payment is still ignored) three weeks after the first reminder. You may also call to ask for a specific amount by a certain day. Do not sound desperate or apologize for asking for payment. Do not question a customer's reasons for not paying. Do not harass the customer; the company may still want their business.

- If necessary, follow this notification with a series of reminder letters. Each letter becomes more insistent, and the time between letters becomes shorter. Do not bother sending notices by special mail services; delinquent payers can simply refuse delivery.

- Send a collection letter that is both courteous and specific; avoid threats. Gimmick letters, such as the "string attached" theme, may work once, but only if a specific course of action is outlined and a direct request for payment is made. Never overwhelm the message with the gimmick. Write clearly. The reader should be able to read and grasp the meaning of the letter in 10 seconds.

- Get to know the people in charge of handling your invoices. Give the process a personal touch. Keep a list of each company's employees who are authorized to charge for merchandise or service.

- Prepare reports to assist management in identifying credit problems and slow-paying customers. An aged accounts receivable report shows those accounts that are overdue by 30, 60, 90, or more than 90 days. (See Figure 13-11.) An aged accounts receivable report arranged by salesperson flags problems unique in specific areas or with specific personnel. A report that arranges outstanding balances from the highest to the lowest identifies those to be collected first. Decisions concerning continued sales to slow-paying customers need to be made by management.

HICKSON DISTRIBUTORS
Aged Accounts Receivable
August 31, 19—

| Customer Name | Inv | Inv Date | Terms | Days | | | |
				0–30	31–60	61–90	90+
Arnold, C.L.	89651	June 15	n/30		359.00		
Bixby Metal	90311	July 15	n/30	865.20			

Figure 13-11 Aged accounts receivable report.

- Select a reputable credit collection agency with a proven collection record as a last step. In normal economic times, anything 90 days and beyond is material for special collectors or an agency. Agencies work on a contingency basis, sometimes keeping a substantial portion of the collections as their fee.

Accounts Receivable/Billing Software

Companies use accounts-receivable software to encourage prompt collections and therefore increase their cash flow. With the increase in the number of service-oriented businesses, time-on-task billing is becoming critical for their success. In these instances, time spent on each process needs to be monitored to see how much it costs to produce the revenue being generated. Although the monitoring may be documented manually, it is more effectively controlled by using a computer program.

Accounts receivable and billing functions may be two separate software modules or they may be combined. The following questions will assist office professionals as they research this software:

- Is there a limit to the number of receivable accounts the software can handle? Is the numbering system flexible?
- Does the software automatically update such records as inventory, job costing, and the general ledger? Is invoicing done within the accounts receivable module or is a separate module for billing necessary?
- Does the software provide the option of handling customer accounts using either the balance-forward method or the open-item method (each invoice is a separate record)? Does it allow the user to identify codes for terms and credit lines so that select customers may receive payment terms different from other customers? Can it figure freight charges on pretax amounts? Does it automatically calculate finance charges and discounts? Does it compare discounts offered to discounts actually taken?

- Does the software print product as well as service invoices? When are invoices printed—at the time they are entered, at the end of the fiscal period, or periodically according to the billing cycle? Is it possible to enter transactions in onscreen forms?
- Are aged reports printed? If so, for how many periods (30 to 60 days, 61 to 90 days, etc.)? Are there other reports showing collections, amounts outstanding, payment due dates, sales by item, individual customer ledgers, and a general ledger control listing? Is there a graphics option for reports?
- Does the software issue a warning when a customer is a slow payer or has an overdue balance? Does it generate appropriate notices and collection letters?
- Is it possible to keep track of the number and amount of sales made by each salesperson? Can data be sorted by such items as ZIP code, customer type, or volume of sales? Can data be reported showing the most popular products and the customers who provided the most revenue?
- Does the software automatically handle repetitive billings? Does it automatically apply finance charges and sales taxes? Can it handle multiple states' sales taxes and prepare the quarterly sales tax returns?
- Is data entry fast? An operator should have to enter only a customer number, an item code, a shipping code, and quantity. Names, addresses, dates, and calculations should be filled in automatically.
- Can the software handle keeping track of time spent on multiple clients' work? Can it produce invoices from this timekeeping?

HANDLING CASH PAYMENTS/ACCOUNTS PAYABLE

Companies pay for most purchases by check. Check forms and stubs vary. Some companies prefer to use their own printed check forms; others use the checks supplied by their banks. A separate **check register** may be used to record information about checks that are issued. Always complete the stubs and entries in a check register before writing the check. If several invoices are paid with one check, list each invoice number and amount on the stub.

Check stubs or check register entries are the major source documents for making journal entries for cash payments. Information for any of these forms must include the amount of the check, the date, the payee's name, the reason for the check (invoice number, reference notation, brief explanation), the balance before the check was written, and the new balance after the check is written.

If it is necessary to stop payment on a check, call the bank immediately to inform the customer service representative of the date and number of the check, the payee's name, the drawer's name, the amount, and the reason for the stop payment. Keep a supply of stop-payment forms in the office; these forms satisfy the bank's request for written verification within two weeks of the transaction. Banks usually charge for stop-payment service. Once the payment is stopped, don't forget to add the amount to the checkbook balance and make the correcting journal entries.

HINT: *Check with the bank to determine how long the stop payment lasts; you may have to renew it in six months.*

Procedures for Preparing Checks

Many checks are computer generated or are produced with check-protector equipment. A **check protector** prohibits someone from making changes in check amounts. The device imprints the amount in figures and words (often in color) on the check. There may still be a need, however, to prepare some checks with a typewriter or a pen. Never use a pencil to write any part of a check. Use a check protector with a counting feature so you can monitor the number of checks imprinted.

The following suggestions are helpful in writing checks:

- Use the current date on checks; do not postdate or predate them.
- Enter the payee's full name as far to the left as possible. Draw a line or type dashes to fill in any remaining blank space to prevent the insertion of other names on the check. Titles such as *Ms.*, *Mr.*, or *Dr.* are not necessary. Verify the spelling of a payee's name.
- If a check is made payable to an individual who is acting in an official capacity for an organization, such as a county treasurer, write the name of the payee followed by a specific title on the check. This makes it clear that the money is going to the organization and not the payee's own account.
- Place the check amount in figures as close as possible to the dollar sign to prevent the insertion of any additional numbers.
- Express the amount of the check in words beginning at the far left of the space provided on the check. Only the first letter of the first word needs to be capitalized. The figures 21 (twenty-one) through 99 (ninety-nine) are the only ones that require hyphens. The word *and* is used only between the dollars and cents amount. If the check is for an even dollar amount, fill in zeros for the cents:

Five hundred twenty-nine and 00/100 ——————— **DOLLARS**

- Express amounts using as few words as possible. For example, the amount $1645.29 takes up less space if written "Sixteen hundred forty-five and 29/100" rather than "One thousand six hundred forty-five and 29/100."
- Circle any amount following a dollar sign that is less than $1. In addition, write "only" before the amount written in words and place a line through the word "Dollars."

$ (.75)

Only seventy-five cents ——————— ~~**DOLLARS**~~

- Do not erase, cross out, or make changes on a check. Write "VOID" on any check that has an error. Make a notation on the stub or in the check register when a check has been voided. File the voided checks.

Check Fraud

Employers are responsible for preventing check fraud and may be held liable if they do not initiate controls or review bank statements on a timely basis. Some reminders for handling checks and initiating controls include:

- Always follow the company's or department's internal control procedures. If there are none, suggest that some be placed in writing. *Never* assume *sole* responsibility for receiving cash, making deposits, writing checks, entering transactions, or reconciling checking accounts.
- Keep blank checks, endorsement stamps, debit cards, authentication signature stamps, and check registers in locked drawers. Notify the company's bank immediately if these items are lost. A laser check-writing system that prints check forms, signature payments, and the magnetic ink character recognition (MICR) image offers considerable security, but keep the MICR security cartridge in a locked drawer when not in use.
- Select password identifications that are difficult to crack. Do not keep your password in a visible location.
- Update the signature cards on file at the company's financial institutions. Promotions, terminations, or resignations mean changes in signature authorizations.
- Be sure the merchandise has been received and the payment reviewed and approved before issuing a check.
- Reconcile the bank statement monthly. Match the list of payables against the bank statement. Report discrepancies in reconciling or in balancing the books to your supervisor immediately.
- Be aware of suspicious-looking checks or checks that appear altered. Some checks are printed on paper treated with chemicals so that if checks are altered, the paper changes color. Other checks will have the word "void" appear when the check is photocopied. KPMG Peat Marwick offers a *Fraud Awareness Guide.* Call 212-872-5850 to receive a free copy.
- Report any excessive complaints from suppliers who are not being paid. Check for inconsistent cash-flow deficiencies. Watch payment requests for goods you never received. If a bank can download the checks received *each day* from your company, you can then identify those that do not appear on a list of checks previously issued. Dishonest employees can prepare extra checks or set up dummy vendors to siphon company funds.
- Purchase check stock from reputable suppliers. Consider shrink-wrapping the check stock; order in small multiples to reduce tampering. Keep the check stock locked in cabinets.
- Shred leftover check stock on closed accounts.

Procedures for Handling Petty Cash

Sometimes a payment is too small to justify writing a check; a petty cash fund is a practical way to handle these small expenditures. Over a year, these expenditures add up to a considerable amount. Usually management designates one person to be in charge of petty cash. The procedures for handling petty cash are as follows:

- Have management establish procedures and amounts for the petty cash fund. Once established, the designated amount in the petty cash fund does not vary unless management decides to increase or decrease it.
- Always keep the petty cash and the blank voucher forms in a locked box or drawer.
- Complete a voucher form for every request for petty cash. (See Figure 13-12.) The person who makes the request must sign the voucher. Obtain a receipt for the money spent and attach it to the voucher.
- Do not allow general access to the petty cash fund.
- Maintain control by prenumbering the voucher forms. If a mistake is made, write "VOID" on the voucher and in the petty cash record.
- Record every disbursement in a petty cash record. (See Figure 13-13.) Check the chart of accounts to identify the appropriate general ledger accounts to charge. All petty cash disbursements increase or decrease the amounts in the general ledger.
- Verify that the cash remaining in the petty cash fund and the total of the vouchers equal the amount for which the fund was established. Complete this verification once a week.

PETTY CASH VOUCHER   No. _____ *86* _____

Date _____   Amount _____

Paid to _____

_____

Purpose _____

_____

Account(s) charged_____

Issued by _____

Amount of purchase _____   Received payment

Cash returned _____

Cash owed _____   _____

Signature

Figure 13-12 Petty cash voucher.

Petty Cash Record for Month						1997			Page_____	
			Petty Cash		Payment Distribution					
Date	Explanation of entry	Vou. #	Received	Paid	Supplies	Advertising Expense	Delivery Expense	Other Accounts		
								Acc't. name	Amount	
19—										
May 1	Established	—	200 00							
	Fund with ck #8196									
1	Labels/ PWP Project	1		8 00	8 00					
2	Floral rental/ OpenHouse	2		30 00				Misc. Exp.	30 00	

Figure 13-13 Petty cash record.

- Replenish the petty cash fund at the end of a specified time period by preparing a check request (or the check) for the amount that will bring the fund to its original amount. If authorized to prepare the check, make it payable to Petty Cash. Cash the check in the accounting department or business office; add the amount to the petty cash box and record the receipt on the petty cash record. Use the cash short and over account when the cash on hand in the fund and the voucher totals are not equal. The cash short and over account accommodates overages or shortages that result from errors made in paying or receiving cash.

- Prepare a summary petty cash report for management. The petty cash report lists the amounts charged to *each* general ledger account and the total petty cash expended for the time period. Stamp the vouchers "Paid" and attach them along with receipts to the report.

- Prepare a journal entry debiting the accounts charged for the disbursements and crediting cash.

HINT: *Replenishing the petty cash fund does not change the original size of the fund. Do not debit or credit the petty cash account at the time you replenish the fund.*

Special Payment Forms

When an ordinary company check is not appropriate or acceptable, one of the following forms of payment may be appropriate:

Certified check: A bank employee stamps "Certified" on the face of an ordinary company-prepared check. This stamp indicates that the amount is available for payment and the bank has earmarked the funds. There is a fee for the service, and a depositor cannot issue a stop-payment order on a certified check. Certified checks need to be included when reconciling the bank statement.

Cashier's check: A bank employee prepares a cashier's check written on the bank's own account rather than on the depositor's account. The depositor reimburses the bank with a payment equal to the cashier's check plus a fee paid to the bank for issuing the check. The depositor may be the payee on a cashier's check and in turn may endorse it to the appropriate creditor, or the cashier's check may be made payable directly to the creditor to whom the payment is due.

Bank draft: A bank draft is helpful when large amounts of money are being transferred from one location to another, when a payment is due in another location, or when payment is due in foreign currency. A bank employee issues a bank draft on funds in another bank rather than on its own funds. The depositor reimburses the bank that issued the draft for the amount and pays the bank a fee.

Money order: Money orders are negotiable instruments and are used most frequently by people who do not have checking accounts. Banks place restrictions on the amount for which individual money orders may be written; however, more than one money order may be purchased for a fee and made payable to a creditor. Money orders are also available for a fee at post offices and at various retail stores.

Traveler's checks: Traveler's checks are useful when it is inconvenient to carry large amounts of cash. At the time of purchase, the user signs the check in the presence of a representative of a financial institution. Each time a traveler's check is cashed, the user signs the check again in view of the person who accepts it as payment. The checks come in various denominations and are also available in many foreign currencies. The numbers on a set of traveler's checks provide a record in case the checks are lost or stolen.

Direct deposit service: Direct deposit service may be used for payroll and many government payments. The company is authorized by the employee to deposit the employee's net pay to a designated financial institution. This eliminates the need for a payroll check. The employee receives only a record of the payment listing such items as regular and overtime hours, gross and net wages, individual tax deductions, and voluntary deductions. Signed authorizations are necessary for employees who wish to participate in direct deposit of their payroll checks.

Automatic withdrawal: A company may authorize the bank to deduct certain designated payments from its checking account and transfer them to the parties to whom the payments are due.

Electronic Bill Payment

Paying bills electronically is another way for businesses to make payments. A description of several of these electronic methods follows:

ONLINE BANKING SERVICE

Online banking services require a touch-tone telephone and personal finance software or special software obtained through financial institutions. Companies or individuals have the benefits of transferring funds between accounts, sending wire transfers, obtaining account balances and statements, and paying bills electronically.

DEBIT CARDS

An online transaction requires the buyer to swipe the card through an electronic reader and enter a personal identification number (PIN) on a keypad. This action signals immediate transfer of funds from the customer's account to the seller's account. If the customer does not have enough money in the account, the transaction becomes void immediately.

A debit card is convenient but also carries some risks. A stolen debit card presents a greater liability to an owner than a stolen credit card. The initial liability for lost cards is similar but *after* two days, the liability increases considerably for debit cards. Debit cards involve annual fees or transaction fees, so they can be expensive for the owners and the sellers. If the merchandise or service is unsatisfactory, a debit cardholder may find it more difficult to negotiate a refund than will a credit card holder.

INTERNET TRANSACTIONS

Because of its global possibilities and low access cost, companies are viewing the Internet as a payment mechanism. However, many other legal and bank regulatory issues need clarification before Internet electronic payments become the norm. See Chapter 22 for additional Internet information.

ELECTRONIC CASH (E-CASH)

Electronic cash is digital money that can move quickly through multiple networks other than the present banking system. Consumers could load up a plastic credit card, which has an embedded microchip, with e-cash. As purchases are made, the amount of digital money decreases. The concept is in its developing stages but may change the way we handle business and personal monetary transactions.

Procedures for Reconciling the Bank Statement

Each month a depositor receives a statement from a bank showing the beginning and ending account balances and any additions or subtractions from the account. Included with the statement are the **canceled checks** (those checks presented and cleared for payment), deposit slips, and credit and debit memos. Credit memos are reminders to add amounts to the ledger accounts and checkbook; debit memos require subtractions.

Some banks retain the canceled checks and simply list the check numbers and amounts on the statements. The depositor has a checkbook in which either carbons or entries are made each time a check is written so a record of the check is available. If a copy of the original check is needed, the depositor may obtain one for a fee from the bank.

Reconciling the bank statement is the process of identifying the differences between the checkbook balance and the bank balance and bringing these two balances into agreement. Companies often use software programs to reconcile their statements. Reconciliation takes place monthly, as soon as possible after the statement arrives.

HINT: *The bank reconciliation process is not a task to treat lightly or to postpone until time permits. The paperwork, or lack of it, provides auditors with important clues about a firm's financial arrangements. Do not delegate this responsibility to a new or inexperienced employee without training the person and supervising the work.*

Banks provide reconciliation forms on the back of the statements mailed to their depositors. Some companies prefer to use their own reconciliation formats. (See Figure 13-14.)

The following steps are helpful in reconciling bank statements.

GRAEBER NURSERY
912463-09
Reconciliation of Bank Statement
June 15, 19—

Bank Statement Balance		$29,642.00
Add Deposits		
June 14		8,320.00
		37,962.00
Less Checks Outstanding, June 15		
No. 2078	$5,815.00	
No. 2082	1,655.00	
No. 2083	62.00	7,532.00
Adjusted Bank Balance		$30,430.00
Checkbook Balance		$31,581.00
Less: Bank Service Charge Expense	81.00	
NSF	1,220.00	1,301.00
		30,280.00
Add: Interest Received		150.00
Adjusted Checkbook Balance		$30,430.00

Figure 13-14 Bank reconciliation company format.

1. Use an appropriate heading that gives the date, account number, and account name, whether you use the bank's form or the company's.

2. Enter the balance found on the bank statement.

3. Verify that all deposits in transit from last month's reconciliation as well as all deposits made since the last reconciliation are listed on the statement. **Deposits in transit** are deposits that are already recorded in the depositor's books but that did not reach the bank in time to be included in the statement. List any deposits still in transit and add the total to the bank statement balance.

4. Compare the canceled check amounts with the bank statement amounts. If they agree, place a checkmark next to the statement amount. Examine the signatures on returned checks to make sure they are legitimate.

5. Place the canceled checks in numerical order. Compare the canceled checks with the check stub or check register entries. Also, compare the canceled checks with any outstanding checks listed on last month's reconciliation form. Use a checkmark, preferably in color, on the stub or register to indicate the check has cleared the bank for payment. Checks without checkmarks are **outstanding checks** and have not been deducted by the bank at the time the statement was prepared.

6. List the amount of each outstanding check along with its number. Obtain a total amount and subtract it from the bank statement balance. This figure represents the **adjusted bank balance.**

7. Enter the current balance from the checkbook. Be sure the balances in the checkbook and in the cash account in the general ledger agree before doing the reconciliation.

8. Look for any credit memos listed on the bank statement. Credit memos include such items as collections made for the depositor by the bank or deposit slip errors in the depositor's favor. Compare the list with the entries on the stubs or in the check register. Add those items not yet recorded to the checkbook balance. Give a brief explanation of each credit memo.

9. Add any interest that has been earned on the checking account to the checkbook balance.

10. Look for any debit memos listed on the statement. Debit memos include such items as payments the depositor has authorized the bank to deduct automatically, such as mortgage or insurance payments, deposit slip errors that decrease the depositor's cash, or nonsufficient funds notifications. These latter notices let the depositor know that a check that was accepted in good faith was not payable by the drawer's bank due to lack of funds. Subtract those items not yet recorded from the checkbook balance. Include a brief explanation for each debit memo.

11. Subtract fees for overdrafts and for credit card discount fees. The latter are charges made by the bank for handling bank charge card slips.

12. Once these additions and subtractions are completed, the result indicates the **adjusted checkbook balance.** Compare the adjusted bank balance and adjusted

checkbook balance. If the balances do not agree at this point, try these procedures to find the errors.

- Compute the amount of the difference between the adjusted bank balance and the adjusted checkbook balance. The amount may be an outstanding check that was omitted from the list or a deposit that was not added.

- An amount may have been added to a balance when it should have been subtracted or vice versa. Divide the difference by two and the answer may provide a clue. Look for any checks, credits, or debits that equal the answer.

- A decimal slide may occur, such as writing $15 for $150. Divide the difference between the two balances by nine. If the answer is a whole number with no remainders, decimal slide may have occurred. For example, suppose the adjusted checkbook balance is $925 and the adjusted bank balance is $790. The difference of $135 divided by nine is $15, a whole number. This figure may be the one causing the discrepancy.

- If these methods are not successful, begin at the point of the last reconciliation and add and subtract all entries in the checkbook again.

- Finally, if all else fails, contact the bank.

13. Place the notation "reconciled," the date of the reconciliation, and any corrections, including reasons, on the next available stub in the checkbook or on the next available line in the check register. Write "Correction made (date) from ($x) to ($y)" on the check stub on which the error was made.

14. Journalize and post any adjustments pertaining to the checkbook side of the reconciliation. All debit memos result in a decrease to cash.

15. File the bank statements in chronological order by date with the most recent form on top.

16. File the checks in numerical order in a separate file designed for check retention. Legal requirements for retaining financial records are not the same in all states due to different statutes of limitations.

HINT: *As canceled checks are filed each month, color code them to identify the retention periods. For example, code all checks that must be kept permanently with a red sticker. A column indicating the retention period for records is also helpful in a check register.*

HINT: *Review each month's outstanding checks to investigate checks that have not cleared. Write or telephone the payee to find out if the check was received. If a deposit is not listed on the bank statement and is not in transit, contact the bank as soon as possible to locate the deposit.*

Personal Finance/Accounts Payable Software

Single proprietorships often find that personal finance software for single-entry or double-entry accounting is adequate for monitoring cash flow and reconciling bank statements. For other companies, stand-alone or fully integrated accounts-payable software works best. Answers to the following questions will be helpful in assessing accounts payable or personal finance software.

- Is the program designed for single-entry or double-entry bookkeeping? How much accounting theory is required to operate the program?
- Is there automated check writing? Once the amount in figures is entered, does the amount in words automatically appear? Are onscreen check forms used? Are the amounts entered automatically in a check register? Is the general ledger automatically updated? Is there an option to indicate reminder dates for cutting the checks? Are discounts automatic or is there an option for an operator override?

HINT: *Every bill should be paid within 30 days to avoid late charges. Company policy determines early payments to take advantage of discounts. Analyze every invoice when it arrives to verify the billing information.*

- Are checks printed in order of voucher number or due date? If multiple invoices are paid with one check, are all invoice numbers listed?
- If a check is sent out monthly (for example, the rent payment), is there a shortcut so the entire check does not have to be reentered? Is it possible to set up levels and dates for payments? For example, the first level might include the payroll and other fixed expenses.
- Are transactions categorized into deductible and nondeductible tax items?
- Does the software produce cash forecasts, general ledger, accounts payable ledger, and cash flow reports? Do the statements provide year-to-date analyses as well as current fiscal period information?
- Does the software record and print purchase orders? Can the purchase orders be organized by type; for example, order items, services, professional, pending, or no purchase order needed? When purchases are received, is the inventory automatically updated?
- Do vendors' accounts indicate such items as name, address, phone number, terms offered, and payment deadlines? Is there online vendor account inquiry so you can determine how much was paid to date? Is it possible to print a report of all vendors as well as selected vendors? Can the vendors' lists be prioritized?

HINT: *An interactive voice-response system allows vendors to ask questions about when they will be paid or when a check was mailed. The vendor punches the purchase order number to receive current account information that the accounts payable department downloads each night.*

- Are reports available for late shipments or returns and allowances? Is there a report for discounts lost (discounts not taken because of employee neglect or management's lack of interest)?
- Does the software perform the bank reconciliation or is separate home-banking software needed? Does it flag unusual transactions? Can the reconciliation changes be posted to general ledger accounts?

HINT: *Overdrafts, bounced checks, and debit/credit memos cause unnecessary service charges and decreased cash flow. Analyze the bank statements and update the checkbook and general ledger promptly.*

- Can the software still be used if the business expands? Can the software support multiple checking accounts?

HANDLING PAYROLL

Every company needs a record of the time its employees work, the amount of wages or salaries paid, and information necessary for completing budgets and tax reports. Office professionals assume various levels of responsibility for payroll tasks, ranging from completing their own timecards to completing federal tax documents. Many companies use computers to do payroll or have contracts with commercial payroll service organizations. Others use their bank's or accountant's payroll services or the software these organizations provide to them. Many small companies still do their payroll manually. Those who understand the concepts of payroll accounting have a level of expertise that is helpful when interacting with CPAs, accountants, and managers and when supervising other employees.

Payroll Records

Most companies find that several types of records will provide them with the information they need to meet the requirements of federal and state regulations affecting payroll. Whether the payroll is done manually or on the computer, the same information is needed.

A **master employee list** of all employee names, numbers, addresses, Social Security numbers, phone numbers, departments, hourly rates, overtime rates when applicable, and the number of exemptions provides the basic source of information for the payroll and personnel departments.

A **timecard** or **report** shows the hours worked by each employee. This manual procedure requires careful review and a supervisor's signature. Formats for time reporting vary widely for employees paid hourly wages, for those paid weekly or monthly salaries, and for those hired on a commission, piece-rate, or job-costing basis.

Some companies issue employees plastic timecards with magnetic strips. Employees insert their cards in a card terminal; the machine recognizes the code, records the appropriate in and out times, and links the information to the payroll processing software. Managers can request a printout of everyone who is working at any hour. Workers have the advantage of confidentiality and accurate recording.

The **payroll register** or journal summarizes information for a specific payroll period and includes time and earnings information on every employee on the payroll. If space permits, a separate column in the payroll register for each deduction is best. Otherwise, a supplementary record is necessary for each deduction. The totals on the payroll register provide the data needed for journal entries. (A sample register appears in Figure 13-15.) Office supply stores stock similar forms.

An **employee earnings record** is maintained by most companies. (See Figure 13-16.) This record provides a place to accumulate payroll data from one period to the next so that at the end of a fiscal year Wage and Tax Statements, or W-2 forms, may be sent to each employee. When recording the payroll manually, the earnings record helps to determine the point when an employee reaches the maximum deduction for such taxes as FICA, state unemployment, or federal unemployment. Once these amounts are reached, taxes no longer have to be deducted from the employee's earnings, and employer contributions and tax expenses are no longer required.

Payroll Taxes and Other Deductions

Payroll deductions, such as income taxes and FICA taxes, are mandatory. Other deductions may be optional, such as union dues, charitable contributions, insurance premiums, and savings plan contributions.

PAYROLL REGISTER

WEEK ENDING JANUARY 14, 1997   DEPARTMENT: **SALES**

Emp. no.	Employee name	Marital Status	W.H. Allowance	Earnings			Taxable Earnings				Deductions							Net Paid	Ck. No.	Accounts Charged	
				Reg.	O.T.	Total	FICA	Medi-care	FUTA	SUTA	FIT	FICA	Medi-care	SIT	Union dues	Other	Total			Sales Salaries	Office & Adm. Sal.
Totals																					

Figure 13-15 Payroll register.

Employee Earnings Record

Employee: _____   Employee #: _____

Address: _____   Date Employed: _____

_____   Withholding Allow:. _____

_____   Marital status: _____

Telephone: _____   Regular Rate $: _____

Department: _____   Overtime Rate $: _____

Social Security Number:_____   Date Terminated: _____

Hours		Earnings			Accumulated Earnings	Deductions							Net Pay	Ck. No.
Reg.	O.T.	Reg.	O.T.	Tot.		FIT	FICA	Medi-care	SIT	Union dues	Other	Tot.		

Figure 13-16 Employee's earnings record.

FEDERAL INCOME TAX (FIT)

The employee's number of exemptions (earnings not subject to income taxes), marital status, payroll time period, and gross wages determine the amount of that employee's FIT deduction. Form W-4, completed by the employee, provides the authorization for deducting an appropriate amount of federal income tax from an employee's gross wages. The federal government furnishes tax-withholding tables in the booklet *Circular E: The Employer's Tax Guide.* Income taxes withheld by the employer are recorded as liabilities of the company.

STATE, COUNTY, OR CITY INCOME TAX (SIT)

The same procedures for determining federal income tax deductions also apply for calculating state, county, or city income taxes. The forms to fill out vary in each state and locality. Special tax-withholding tables are available from the appropriate government agencies.

FICA TAX

The FICA tax (Federal Insurance Contribution Act) covers Social Security, old-age, disability, and survivor benefits as well as Medicare for persons over 65 years of age. The federal government sets the percentage of gross wages to be taxed and the maximum base on which the tax must be paid. FICA and Medicare have different bases. The base and/or the percentage usually increase from year to year.

The employer is responsible for paying FICA taxes to the government equal to the total amount contributed by all employees in each payroll period. To determine the amount, multiply the total in the FICA taxable earnings column of the payroll register by the current FICA percentage rate. The contributions withheld for employees are liabilities of the business, and the employer's matching contribution is a payroll tax expense.

HINT: *The employer must deposit federal income taxes withheld and the FICA taxes (employees' and employer's contributions) in a timely manner with a bank authorized to accept such payments. If the deposit is not made according to the rules, the employer faces a fine. In case an emergency keeps you out of the office, be sure someone else is aware of the need for the prompt deposit of these taxes.*

UNEMPLOYMENT TAXES (SUTA/FUTA)

State unemployment taxes (SUTA) temporarily assist employees who become unemployed as a result of changes they cannot control, such as mergers, layoffs, and cutbacks. SUTA rates and tax bases vary from state to state.

Federal unemployment taxes (FUTA) help defray the costs incurred by the states in administering unemployment programs. Employers receive a credit (the maximum percentage is designated by law) against their federal unemployment tax for monies they pay to the state.

To determine the SUTA and FUTA amounts, multiply the totals in the FUTA and SUTA taxable earnings columns of the payroll register by the appropriate tax rates. For information on bases and rates, contact the state unemployment commission. Unemployment taxes are expenses of the business.

OTHER PAYROLL DEDUCTIONS

Deductions other than those mandated by law include such items as contributions to retirement accounts or plans, insurance premiums, and union dues. Retirement plan vesting rights and payroll termination dates must be carefully documented so payouts are accurate. The employer records pension payments as an expense of the business and records employees' contributions as a liability.

In the case of insurance premiums, the employer records any amounts withheld from the employees as a liability. Employees often pay their union dues through payroll deductions. The employer records this deduction as a liability and at the appropriate time transfers the dues to the union treasurer.

PAYROLL FORMS AND REPORTS

The employer records and transfers to the appropriate agencies the amounts deducted from employees' earnings or contributed by the company. The following forms and reports are necessary to document employees' authorizations for deductions and the prompt transfer of contributions.

Form SS-4: If an employer does not have an employer identification number, which is used on all payroll forms and reports, Form SS-4 must be completed. It is available at any IRS or Social Security office.

Form SS-5: If an employee does not have a Social Security number, he or she must complete Form SS-5. The Social Security Administration provides the forms.

Form OOAN-7003: Employees must complete this form if they change their names.

Form W-4: All new employees must complete a Form W-4 (Employee's Withholding Allowance Certificate), on which they indicate the number of withholding allowances they wish to claim. The employer files these forms and uses the number of allowances the employee indicates to compute federal and state income tax deductions. Each exemption represents an amount of income that is not taxable. Employees are responsible for requesting any changes in the number of withholding allowances.

Form W-2: Each year on or before January 31, the company must provide its employees with W-2 forms (Wage and Tax Statements) for the preceding year. Employees need these multipart forms to prepare their personal federal and state income tax returns. The employer distributes copies to the Social Security Administration; state, city, or local tax agencies; and employees, who receive several copies to file with tax returns and to retain in their files. The employer retains a copy in the office files. If an employee loses a W-2 form, the company reissues another form with the word "reissued" on the new statement. A reissued Form W-2 should not be sent to the Social Security Administration.

Form W-3: An employer must send a Form W-3, the Transmittal of Income and Tax Statements, along with copies of all the W-2 forms to the Social Security Administration. The due date for the W-2 forms and the W-3 transmittal form is the last day of February. Optical scanners are used for reading the W-3 forms, so the information must be typed, and none of these forms may be stapled or folded. Dollar signs may not be used, but a decimal point should be included with the monetary amounts on the forms.

Form 8109: Each time employers deposit income tax and FICA deductions and contributions, they complete Form 8109 (Federal Tax Deposit Form). Once a company obtains an employer identification number, federal tax deposit coupon books are mailed to the company automatically. Form 8109 must include the amount deposited, the tax period, and the type of tax being deposited.

Form 941: Every three months, employers report the amount of income taxes and FICA taxes deducted or contributed on a Form 941 (Employer's Quarterly Federal Tax Return). Form 941 is due at the regional IRS office one month after the quarter ends. For example, the first quarter ends March 31, and the report is due April 30. Any undeposited tax amounts for the quarter are also due at this time.

Form 940: The employer reports FUTA taxes already submitted during the year on Form 940 (Employer's Annual Federal Unemployment Tax Return). The form is due on January 31 of the next year. Any undeposited tax amounts are also due at that time.

Payroll Software

Payroll is often one of the first areas that companies computerize or outsource. The payroll module can operate as a separate system or be integrated with the general ledger system. Personal finance software is not adequate to handle payroll. The following questions will be helpful in selecting the best software:

- Is there a limit on the number of employees the program can handle? Is there a limit on the number of deductions that can be handled? Are reports generated for each type of deduction per pay period?

- Can different compensation modes be accommodated, such as salary, commission, hourly wage, tips, piece rate, pay advances, vacation pay, bonus, per diem, and contract?

- Are sufficient tax tables available? Which taxes are included? Does the software company offer tax updates each year? What is the cost? Are both manual and automatic calculation modes available? Can the user set any of the tax rates?

- Does the software print checks? Is there flexibility in the type of check used? Using a laser printer and special toner, companies can now print the magnetic ink character recognition (MICR) coding at the bottom of a check.

- Does the software allocate costs of payroll materials and supplies to the appropriate project and update the figures? Are employees able to record their hours spent on projects in real time from their desktop computers so instant project costs are available?

- Does the software accept employees' electronic time clock entries to update payroll records? Does it support multi-frequency payroll periods?

- Can payroll expenses be distributed by department? For example, an employee may be assigned to more than one department with different pay rates. Can departmental time card reports be generated? Is the software capable of handling multiple state requirements?

- Does the software maintain quarterly, monthly, weekly, and year-to-date earnings and deduction accumulations? Are W-2 forms automatically prepared at the end of the year? Can they be prepared automatically at other times as well? Does the software automatically update each employee's earnings and deductions? Does it support electronic filing of tax payments and reports?

- Is a check register prepared specifically for payroll each period? Is the general ledger automatically updated? Are there reports categorized by job classification, department, and employee?

- Does the software track sick time and vacation time so that when a person leaves the company the amounts he or she is owed are available?

- Can payroll data be exported to spreadsheets?

- If using a payroll service provider, is the system compatible with yours?

OUTSOURCING

Outsourcing began as a strategy used by large companies to cut costs. Today, businesses of all sizes use it as an ongoing movement to shift work previously done in-house to suppliers or outside service-provider firms who manage the entire operation. Home-based business owners may decide others can provide the services they need. Such areas as payroll, travel planning, printing, and mail distribution are office services that are commonly outsourced. Employee leasing is also a form of outsourcing.

Advantages

If keeping pace with competitors requires huge investments of time, money, and personnel, companies may find an expert outsource provider who will do the work or portions of it more economically. Here are some additional advantages of outsourcing:

- Administrative, recruitment, training, and supervision costs as well as behavior and attitude problems are the responsibilities of the outsource provider.
- Outsource providers supply the resources and assume the liabilities.
- Funds designated for high-cost updated equipment are now available for research or product and service improvement.
- Managers or small business owners can concentrate on their product by limiting their need for in-depth knowledge of technical operational details or constantly changing regulations.
- Companies can gain access to expert specialists and high-level technology they may not have in-house.
- A contract determines the length of a commitment to an outsource provider.
- Employees may receive better health insurance coverage with fewer hassles for the employer.
- Since hiring and terminating become more stable, the work force has a consistent core and is not oversized at off-peak times.

Disadvantages

Outsourcing is not the same as downsizing, although they often occur at the same time. Some disadvantages of outsourcing include:

- Employees are unsure about job security. They are not pleased with "outsiders" coming in to do some of their tasks or with losing their work to the outsource firm. Some of these "outsiders" may have been hired by an outsource firm and are now working at their old jobs.
- Companies find it difficult to develop a team spirit or expect company loyalty or pride from the outsource workers or from the in-house employees.

- Managers and small business owners relinquish some controls they once had over their operations.

- Because managers fail to analyze costs of doing the job in-house, comparisons with costs of outsource providers are inaccurate or nonexistent.

- Managers view outsourcing as temporary measures and do not plan for long-term outsourcing commitments. They are often in a rush and do not research their providers.

- Employees feel a loss of self-esteem when managers single out their department's function as less important to a firm's central core of operations.

- The quality and ethics of the outsource workers may not meet a company's standards.

- Employees are not a part of the decision-making process and thus view outsourcing as a management strategy. On the other hand, management views unions as stumbling blocks in the outsourcing process.

- Security of the company's information may be at risk at off-company premises.

Outsourcing Considerations

To save costs and trouble later, a Statement of Work should accompany an outsourcing contract. To prepare the statement, managers need answers to numerous questions.

- Which operations are best provided by an outside provider and which should be retained by the business?

HINT: *Office professionals need to be in the loop that makes these decisions. Recommend areas for outsourcing that free you for more management responsibilities. Do some research on outsource providers in your community to get answers to the questions in this section.*

- What are the tasks and responsibilities of each party? Who is responsible for the reports management requires? Are rates competitive with those of other firms?

- How quickly are jobs needed? Can the provider meet the deadlines, handle rush jobs, and make last-minute changes?

- Is the provider financially stable? Does it have competent staff? Who does its backup work? Can it provide the training for new procedures and equipment? Is it fully bonded and insured?

- What is the quality of similar work done by the outsource company? (Be sure to ask for samples to review.) Does the outsource company have sufficient experience with the jobs or processes that you want outsourced? Are companies that are using or have used the outsource company satisfied or not?

- If the work is done off-site, how will the data be accessed and downloaded by the business and the provider? Is the equipment compatible? How will the processes interface with each other?
- Who is responsible for monitoring the performance standards?

HINT: *Office professionals are logical evaluators of many outsourced jobs. Design the procedures for monitoring completed jobs and discuss them with your supervisor.*

- How will information be safeguarded? Who owns the materials produced by the outsourcer? Is the outsourcer paid by the hour or by the project?

HINT: *Your company's code of ethics and performance standards need to be communicated. Take the time to develop a congenial working relationship with the workers and the agency or the person to whom the work has been contracted. Volunteer to be one of the company's liaisons with the outsource provider, and use the opportunity to communicate successes and criticisms.*

Employee Leasing

In a leasing arrangement, an employment-management company hires a company's employees and then leases them back to the company. The leasing company assumes responsibility for benefits and payroll. Good leasing companies carry comprehensive insurance on their employees. Before using an employment-management company to lease employees, check with former clients to determine if they really saved money and if employees reacted favorably. Be certain the company is sound financially.

HINT: *Several states require licensing of employee-leasing companies. Call the National Association of Professional Employer Organizations, 703-524-3636, for state regulations. Check with an attorney to determine if a proposed company is in compliance with the regulations.*

KEEPING FINANCIAL RECORDS FOR HOME-BASED BUSINESSES

In addition to financial records, several related topics such as taxes, permits, insurance, and loans require the attention of home-based business owners. Pricing decisions and ways to cut costs are also concerns. See the checklist for starting a new business (Figure 13-17).

Permits/Licenses

Most incorporated areas have zoning regulations, zoning laws, and ordinances governing a business operating from a home in a residential neighborhood. These regulations, if ignored, can result in substantial fines for the owner. Since the regulations vary, check

CHECKLIST FOR STARTING A NEW BUSINESS

1. Check zoning regulations. _____
2. Select the type of business structure. _____
3. Name the business. _____
4. Develop a business plan. _____
5. Obtain sufficient capital. _____
6. Open a business checking account. _____
7. Register the name with appropriate authorities. _____
8. Select an accountant or tax adviser. _____
9. Determine fiscal year. _____
10. Obtain permits and licenses. _____
11. Obtain an Employee ID Number if applicable to business. _____
12. Select your office space. _____
13. Obtain quotes for equipment and supplies. _____
14. Check lighting and electrical requirements. _____
15. Design the office layout. _____
16. Select equipment and supplies. _____
17. Purchase appropriate insurance. _____
18. Order business cards. _____
19. Install a telephone line for the business. _____
20. Establish a pricing policy. _____
21. Set up a bookkeeping system. _____
22. Advertise your product. _____
23. Release an announcement to local media. _____
24. Establish answering machine or voice-mail conditions. _____
25. Hire personnel if necessary or use an outsource provider. _____

Figure 13-17 Checklist for starting a new business.

with a county and/or city zoning authority to be sure you are not breaking any laws. You may need a professional license to operate in your state, but before paying your fee, be sure that you can obtain one for a business with a residential address.

The Chamber of Commerce may have a set of materials that includes all the necessary forms for new business owners. If it does not, obtain a fictitious name statement or d/b/a (doing business as) form and file it with the county clerk's office. The form, required by law, identifies the sole proprietor responsible for the company. Display one in your place of business and give one to your bank when you open a business checking account.

HINT: *Always open a business account. Do not mingle personal and business funds.*

The government requires an identification of your business by Social Security number or an **employee identification number (EIN).** Sole proprietors usually use their Social Security numbers, but if you have employees, use independent contractors, or pay sales tax, you need an EIN. A local IRS office or accountant's office has IRS Form SS-4, which you need to get the EIN.

You may need other business permits. Your state and city offices have that information. These permit requirements vary for different cities and states.

Loans

Most small business owners fail because they underestimate expenses or it takes longer to make a profit than they expected. Plan to have reserve money to cover your fixed expenses for at least 18 months and to cover living expenses of 6 to 8 months. If you need additional money, apply for a loan from a bank or the Small Business Administration's Microloan Demonstration Program (202-205-6490). Try to locate a bank that offers business loans for small borrowers but does not treat the loans as consumer loans with the attendant higher interest rates. Less appealing sources of capital are loans from relatives or friends or from credit cards.

HINT: *Interest rates mount quickly on loans. Never place your credit rating or the family home at risk because of out-of-control borrowing.*

Business Plan

Banks require a business plan from loan applicants. Write your business plan or use a business planning software program that leads you through the following sections:

- Cover sheet. Identify the business name, address, telephone number, and your background.
- Business description. Describe how the business will be structured, the startup date, the experience you have, and the reasons it will be successful. Describe your product or service in detail. Include a capital equipment and supplies list.

- Marketing strategy. Identify your prospective clients and the reasons they will buy your services or products. Compare your plan with your competitors' offerings and then describe your promotional and pricing plans.
- Financial goal. Include fixed and indirect expenses and monthly net profit-and-loss projections for the first year in addition to your sources of startup capital. Include a personal income statement, balance sheet, and latest tax return.

Taxes

The government does not deduct federal taxes from the self-employed, so you must pay estimated quarterly income taxes and a self-employment tax. The self-employment tax includes your contribution to Social Security and Medicare taxes and the matching amount an employer would have paid. If you hire an independent contractor, you do not have to withhold income taxes or Social Security and Medicare amounts from the employee's wages. The IRS has specific rules for identifying independent contractors versus employees, so be sure to review its guidelines.

Home-based business owners are entitled to certain tax deductions. Some of the major deductions include:

- Equipment and supplies. The IRS sets a limit of first dollar amounts every year, so keep all purchase records.
- Health insurance. The deduction is a percentage of your premium and is an adjustment to your income.
- Home office expenses. The IRS allows the deduction of expenses such as utilities, insurance, mortgage interest, property taxes, and maintenance. To be able to deduct these expenses, you must use the office for business only and it must be your principal place of business. To determine the percentage to use to figure your deduction, calculate the square footage of your office and then the percentage of the office space as compared to the square footage of your entire home.

HINT: *A tax accountant can offer good advice about home office deductions and any changes that occur in this sensitive area. For a free copy of* Tax Strategies, *a self-employment survival letter, write to Barbara Brabec Productions, P.O. Box 2137, Naperville, IL 60567.*

- Business expenses. You can deduct travel and entertainment expenses, but keep detailed records such as an appointment list and a gas and mileage log.
- Business loss. If you have a loss on your books for the year, you may write it off against income claimed that year or you can carry it back or forward several years.
- Self-employment tax. One-half of the taxes paid are deductible.

- Tax-deferred retirement plans. Home-based business owners are eligible for a Simplified Employee Pension (SEP) plan or a Keogh plan. Both plans allow a contribution of a certain percentage of your net earnings.
- Sales taxes. State regulations vary in taxing service businesses. Some states may require a sales tax, so check with the state office to determine whether you have to file a sales tax report.

Pricing

Pricing a product or service is a challenge. If you charge too much, your clients will get their work done by someone else. If you don't charge enough, your expenses may exceed your income or prospective clients will question the quality of your service or products. Ask these questions as you determine your pricing strategy.

- Who are my potential clients? What authority do they have? What economic class, education level, age group, gender, and occupation do they represent?
- What will it cost me to produce, advertise, sell, and deliver my product or service? What are my overhead costs? How much do I need for living expenses? How much do I want beyond living expenses?

HINT: *You can always offer a special rate once you have established your price. Do not set the price too low and then raise it immediately. Customers do not appreciate this tactic.*

- What are my competitors charging? Does higher price mean better work in my field? Do prospective clients have other choices in my area? How does my product differ from that of my competitors?

HINT: *Perhaps you can offer additional services such as free pickup and delivery or guaranteed on-time satisfaction. Find a marketing tactic that will work for you, but make it somewhat different from your competitors'.*

- What prices are outside provider companies charging for similar services? Does my professional organization publish suggested rates? For example, the National Association of Secretarial Services (NASS) is the association for people who have their own secretarial businesses.

HINT: *For consulting, accounting, or secretarial rates, check with former employers to find out how much they paid temporary agencies or outside contractors for similar services.*

- What type of rate is best for my work—daily, project, or hourly?

HINT: *Many companies use a daily rate when they budget for outside providers. Don't forget to include planning time in your rates. To be precise in hourly billing time, use a software program designed for time and billing purposes.*

Insurance

Home-based businesses require several types of insurance coverage, such as property, liability, and loss of income. Here are some suggestions for securing adequate business insurance.

PROPERTY INSURANCE

You can obtain an endorsement to your homeowner's policy, which would extend personal property coverage to business property, or you can obtain a full commercial business policy. More insurance companies are beginning to offer specific home office policies that include property coverage, accounts receivable, lost valuable papers, and business income. Cost and extent of coverage will determine your choices.

HINT: *The best "insurance" for data loss and payment records is backing up your completed work or making copies of records and storing them away from your home office.*

LIABILITY INSURANCE

Coverage requirements depend on the type of business. If you have clients coming to your home, you will need insurance for personal liability. Your homeowner's umbrella policy or renter's insurance may not cover business liabilities. If your business is part-time or of a nature whereby clients are not on your premises, an endorsement to your homeowner's policy may suffice.

A **general liability** policy covers personal injury, advertising injury, and product liability. Consider the policy that covers damage to clients' property while in your hands. Some home-based business owners require separate **professional liability** policies to protect them from professional mistakes, such as accounting errors, misplaced commas, or bad advice. Contact your professional association for policies that cover risks unique to your profession.

MEDICAL INSURANCE

Federal law (COBRA) allows you to continue a company's medical insurance coverage for 18 months after you leave. The company you leave must have at least 20 employees. You pay the premiums to your former employer. Check your spouse's or partner's policies to see if you can qualify for coverage. Contact the Chamber of Commerce or your professional organization; they may have access to group plans.

Workers' Compensation

If you have employees, you need workers' compensation insurance, which pays employees for costs that involve job-related injuries. The cost depends on occupation and salary. Check with a workers' compensation office in your state.

Cost Considerations

Home-based business owners need practical suggestions for cutting costs and preserving capital. Some ideas follow:

- Build up a reserve to cover yourself during slow periods.
- Use the free Small Business Administration resources, including their online services.
- Save mailing costs by sending invoices with products or advertisements.
- Order checks from mail-order companies. Be sure they look professional.
- Time telephone calls and faxes to take advantage of lower rates.
- Use a business center when you need access to equipment or services you can't afford or use only occasionally, such as a conference room or mail and fax services.
- Download shareware or freeware software from one of the online services.
- Use a lockbox to speed up cash flow. All payments go to a post office box that you rent. The bank picks up checks several times during the day and processes them immediately. The bank photocopies the checks and forwards them to you for recording. Another way to improve cash flow is to ask for partial payment when the contract is signed or the job begins, or you might consider dealing primarily with cash customers.
- Use volunteers from job centers to do labeling or stuffing tasks. Rely on family members to assist in busy periods.
- Buy only equipment, supplies, and inventory that you need. Consider leasing your equipment, which allows you to use capital for other purposes and provides some protection against obsolete equipment. Know how much lease interest you are paying and check the buyout clause carefully.

Company representatives who travel must have economical, informative, and accurate travel plans. Office professionals have an active role in travel planning; they make the travel arrangements, obtain and organize the information, and handle the follow-up tasks after the traveler returns.

OBTAINING TRAVEL INFORMATION

Sources to use in making travel arrangements include a commercial travel agency, an in-house travel manager, a transportation department acting as a travel service, or on-line electronic travel services. Some companies use out-sourcing to handle travel arrangements. In addition, you can make reservations or obtain schedule and information by calling the airlines, hotels or motels, and car rental agencies directly. Numerous travel-oriented magazines and other publications also provide excellent reference sources.

Commercial Travel Agencies

Commercial travel agencies can efficiently arrange business or personal trips. A company usually selects a travel agency and then establishes an open credit account with that agency. Especially if you work for a small company, you may play a major role in selecting a travel agency and agent. To make a wise selection, you should answer the following questions:

- What agency or agencies are other local firms using? Are they satisfied with the services they receive?
- Have any complaints about poor service been filed against the company? The local Better Business Bureau can supply this information.
- Is the agency a member of a travel trade association such as the American Society of Travel Agents (ASTA) or the Association of Retail Travel Agents (ARTA)? Membership in ASTA, for example, indicates that criteria governing an agent or agency's financial status and ethical practices have been met and the agency has been in business with the same owner for at least three years.

HINT: *If a problem occurs with a travel agent or agency, immediately send copies of all correspondence, dates of*

CHAPTER 14

TRAVEL

PLANNING

telephone calls, names of people contacted, agencies involved, and any documentation involving the action to the ASTA Consumer Affairs Department, ASTA World Headquarters, 1101 King Street, Alexandria, VA 22314. Ask for their free booklet, "Avoiding Travel Problems."

- Is the agency currently approved by the International Air Transport Association (IATA)? Is it a member of the Airline Reporting Corporation (ARC)? These organizations regulate travel agencies' operations and collect their money.

- Are the agents certified? The Institute of Certified Travel Agents offers two types of proficiency designations: the Certified Travel Counselor (CTC) and the Destination Specialist (DS). To obtain a CTC rating, agents must complete an advanced program in travel management and have at least five years' experience in the travel industry. To receive the DS rating, agents must have expertise in one or more specific destination areas of the world and have a year of travel experience.

HINT: *To obtain a list of CTCs in a local area, send a stamped, self-addressed envelope to the Institute of Certified Travel Agents, 148 Linden Street, P.O. Box 82-56, Wellesley, MA 02181.*

- Have the travel agents traveled extensively themselves? Do they appear willing to investigate alternative arrangements, give you the best schedules and prices, and take the time to answer questions? How many years of experience do they have? How can you reach them if there is an emergency?

- Is the agency independent, part of a national franchise, or a member of a consortium? A **consortium** is a number of smaller agencies who have formed a group to obtain benefits that the larger agencies receive.

- Is there a charge for any part of the service or for extra service? Since the major domestic airlines capped commissions paid to travel agents, some travel agencies charge a fee for services.

- Does the agency specialize in business travel? Does it book hotel accommodations for large groups? Can it compare costs of meeting rooms and make conference arrangements?

- What type of computer reservation system (CRS) does the agency use? Does the CRS keep looking for lower fares or better seating arrangements and inform you before the date of travel? Is it possible for the agency to send tickets to companies electronically? Are the boarding passes attached or enclosed with the tickets?

- Is the appearance of the travel agency professional? Is the layout of the office inviting? Are the brochures current and attractively arranged?

- Are the billing procedures acceptable? How are refunds handled if flights are canceled? Are summary statements prepared that list each trip, date, and cost of trip by employee? Is it possible for the agency to track mileage to be applied to frequent-flyer benefits? Is it possible to provide expense account analysis?

- Does the agency sell tickets on discount carriers? Does it sell discounted or consolidator tickets? Check the restrictions and prices on consolidator fares.

In-House Travel Departments/Travel Management Firms

Because travel costs are a significant budget item, companies require detailed records of money spent. On-site travel managers can provide immediate attention to travel needs and expenses. Some companies outsource all their travel work to firms specializing in travel. In addition to contracting with travel suppliers for low-priced reservations, these firms provide a variety of reports to management that can help track a company's preferences and costs. Either arrangement allows companies to contract for lower costs and maintain the caliber of services they need.

Online Databases/Software Systems

By using a microcomputer and modem, you can access an online commercial system, such as CompuServe, for travel information. Examples of topics on which travel information is available through an online service include:

- Up-to-date flight information; flight restrictions.
- Lowest airfares; on-time statistics; train travel.
- Credit card arrangements.
- Airline meal selections; seating preferences and availability.
- Flight changes; layover times; baggage allowance.
- Hotel and restaurant information for the United States and overseas; banquet and meeting room facilities; local events; city guides.
- Weather information and Department of State travel advisories.
- Car rental information.
- Overseas travel information; weather, holidays.
- Tourism offices.
- Travel discussions.
- Suggestions and tips on travel.

If you do not have access to an online service, call the Official Airline Guide (800-323-4000). After you enter the reservation, you will receive a faxed copy designating available seats and costs.

With a travel software program, you have access not only to airline computer reservation systems but also to your company's travel policies and a list of specific contracted suppliers. The system provides an itinerary after you indicate time and location and allows you to book flights, hotel rooms, and car rentals. It also gives you access to the company's or an individual's travel history and preferences.

CD-ROMs are another source of travel information. In addition to the items mentioned above, CD-ROMs provide specialized information on such topics as attractions, scenic routes, road atlases, maps, and area guides. Many tourist bureaus are organizing their promotional materials for CD-ROM distribution.

Published Travel References

State travel and tourism departments provide information on outstanding features of their states. The Chamber of Commerce is a good source for local information. Public libraries and bookstores often have copies of consumer travel publications as well as tourist guides. Auto clubs supply information on lodging, restaurants, and places of interest to its members.

HINT: *The Phone Booklet lists hundreds of toll-free numbers for airlines, lodgings, car rentals, trains, and buses. The annual publication also lists state, city, and international travel and tourism offices. To receive a copy, write to Scott American Corporation, Department EM, Box 88, West Redding, CT 06896.*

Travel reference guides provide detailed information about domestic and foreign air and rail transportation and accommodations. To use these references effectively, it is necessary to keep them up to date. Their use can save online computer time or telephone contact time with a travel agent; however, the references are expensive, and the price may be too high for a small firm. Following are several published travel references:

Official Airline Guide® (OAG®): This guide provides subscribers with detailed airline schedules. Cities are arranged alphabetically and listed by destination and origin with the airlines that service them. Information for each flight is arranged chronologically by the time of departure. Times are stated in local times. Additional information includes flight numbers, days the flights operate, number of stops and in which cities, food service, types of aircraft, baggage allowances, and the airline's toll-free number for reservations. Ground information includes distances to the city from the airport, types of airport transportation available, car rental agencies and their toll-free numbers, and helicopter services. An electronic edition is also available.

HINT: *The guide is large and cumbersome. It is easiest to photocopy the relevant pages and work with them.*

OAG® Pocket Flight Guide *and* Executive Flight Planner: These pocket guides are quick references for checking scheduled direct flights and are especially helpful when there are delays or flight cancellations. They also include airline reservation telephone numbers of all carriers in each listed city, departure and arrival times, names of airlines and flight numbers, class of service, type of aircraft, and stops en route. The guides are updated monthly.

Official Frequent Flyer Guidebook: This book lists airline, hotel, and car rental frequent flyer programs. Updated yearly, it gives information on joining and how to claim awards, as well as frequent-flyer tips. Information about cost and shipping can be obtained by calling 800-487-8893.

OAG® Travel Planner Hotel and Motel Redbook: Published four times a year, this reference contains detailed hotel listings (some with ratings), airline and ground information, car rental and rail directories, airport diagrams, country and city maps, and currency conversion rates. A section for each country features a calendar of events, banking and business hours, consulate office information, and travel document requirements. A North American edition, *OAG® Business Travel Planner,* is also available. The *OAG® Worldwide Hotel Directory,* an electronic source, is especially helpful for non-U.S. locations.

Official Hotel and Resort Guide: Several volumes contain descriptive information about hotels, motels, and city attractions. Maps, room rates and ratings, number of rooms, fax and Telex information, e-mail addresses, and telephone numbers are useful when trying to determine the best accommodations. The guides come in a looseleaf format with updated pages mailed regularly to subscribers.

Hotel and Travel Index: The listings in this reference are alphabetically arranged by country, state, and city. Publication of this large, comprehensive index is on a quarterly basis. It is available in single issues or by subscription and includes telephone numbers, e-mail addresses, Telex and fax information, addresses, number of units, and credit cards accepted.

Official Railway Guide: Rail timetables and fares for Amtrak as well as for trains in Canada and Mexico are available in this guide, which is published eight times a year. Information on large-city commuter rail transit services is useful to business travelers.

Thomas Cook Timetables: Schedules for Europe are available in the *Thomas Cook Continental Timetable.* The *Thomas Cook Overseas Timetable* lists schedules for all other worldwide railway systems. Both guides show maps of the area traveled, visa requirements, and time zones.

The Official National Motorcoach Guide/The Official Canadian Guide: These guides include fares and schedules for bus lines in the United States, Canada, and Mexico. Copies are available monthly. Single issues may be purchased.

UNDERSTANDING TRAVEL TERMS

Regardless of your source for professional travel assistance, you should understand the terms and acronyms you will encounter. Most important are terms used in airline travel, accommodations, and car rental.

Airline Travel Terms

Business travelers have three classes of airline service from which to choose:

First class: offers wider seats and more space than other classes of service. It also offers quality food service, free drinks, and attentive, personalized service. First class is the most expensive seating.

Business class: less expensive than first class, but the passenger also receives special benefits, such as a quiet working atmosphere. Special streamlined check-in procedures are usually available for both first-class and business-class passengers.

Coach-class: seats are not as wide, and there is limited leg room. With more passengers moving around the cabin, coach class is less quiet and less appealing as a working area. It is the least expensive class of service.

With a **direct** flight, the plane makes stops in one or more cities, but passengers do not change planes. A **nonstop** flight has no stops between the departure and arrival cities. A **connecting** flight requires a plane change.

Fare structures are determined by destination and also by such factors as the amount of advance purchase time required, class of seating, the refundable status of the ticket, and the day of the week and time of travel.

HINT: *Nonrefundable tickets have penalties attached if plans change and the trip is not made. The entire cost of the ticket or a percentage of the cost may be lost. If the cancelation is due to a family medical emergency, a physician's letter will void the penalty. When making reservations, be sure to request information about the penalties for canceled trips.*

For a traveler on **standby status,** there is a possibility that a seat will become available at the time of the flight. If one is available, the person travels as a regular customer. A traveler on a **waitlist** is one who wants to fly at a time when the flight is already filled. The traveler's name is placed on a numbered list. If a seat becomes available as the result of a cancellation (within 24 hours of flight time), travelers are accepted from the waitlist in the order of the assigned number and type of booking.

A **stopover** involves spending more than 12 hours in a location that is an interruption in the trip. An **open-jaw** trip is one in which the passenger returns to a city other than the one in which the trip originated. An **open ticket** is valid between two cities but indicates no specific reservation. For example, it may be used if a return trip cannot be finalized at the time the reservations were made.

Most airlines offer **frequent flyer** incentives to encourage customers to use their services. Members may take free upgrades in class of service, or save the miles and take a discounted fare trip or a free trip later, or use the credits toward other gift awards.

Airline club services are available for an annual fee. Members may use these airport facilities for making telephone calls (local calls may be free), photocopying, storing luggage, using the fax machine, or working or relaxing in a quiet area. Meeting rooms may also be booked, and refreshments are available. For a fee, some clubs allow travelers to get day passes. Mini-offices (freestanding *Ziosks)* are becoming available for rent by the hour in some airports. Quarters are cramped, but they are equipped with a desk, fax, phone, television, and chair or couch. Reserve the Ziosks in advance.

Accommodation Terms

Hotel rates and service depend on the type of plan offered. **Budget hotels** have low prices and cater to the traveler on a limited budget. **Executive** rooms are deluxe accommodations and expensive. **Business-class/corporate-class** rooms often have in-room workstations with up-to-date equipment. The cost is higher than the usual corporate rate. Some businesspeople prefer **all-suite** hotels, with living room, bedroom, bath, and often kitchen facilities. This type of arrangement is useful when meetings are to be held in hotel rooms, for extended stays in one location, or for foreign business visitors. Rooms are often advertised with ratings; a four-star rating is very high. A **concierge** is a hotel employee who assists guests with such tasks as obtaining electronic equipment, making theater reservations, or suggesting restaurants. A concierge may be assigned to a specific floor or floors in a hotel. A **business center** provides guests with access to centralized office equipment and assistance.

The **American plan (AP)** is a rate that includes, in addition to the room, all meals daily. The **modified plan (MP)** offers breakfast and dinner. The **breakfast plan (BP)** includes full breakfasts each day. The **continental plan (CP)** includes a continental breakfast (often muffins or sweet rolls, juice, and beverage) each day. The **European plan (EP)** offers no meals. A **rack rate** is the official posted rate of a hotel room. **Corporate rates,** which must be requested, are available to business travelers and are less than the quoted normal daily hotel or motel rates. The **frequent-stay benefit** allows regular customers to receive discounted rates or extra services such as upgrades in rooms, late check-outs, car rental discounts, and special attention to reservations. Some frequent-stay programs have incentive ties to frequent-flyer membership programs. **Adjoining** rooms are next to each other but may not have a door between the rooms. **Connecting** rooms have a door between rooms.

Car Rental Terms

Car rental agencies use different classifications when describing their cars. Most agencies use the term **deluxe** to describe their largest, most expensive model. A **standard** model is a full-size car. A **compact** is regular size, and a **subcompact** is a small car.

A **drop-off charge** is the amount a car rental agency charges when a car is rented at one location but returned to another. Most contracts include **unlimited mileage,** and the driver pays a set amount for a designated time period; with a **limited mileage** plan, the payment is based on the number of miles traveled.

A **collision damage waiver** increases the cost of a rental car. Most travelers will not need these waivers since they are covered by their own personal automobile insurance policies, by their companies' policies, or by their credit card plans.

MAKING RESERVATIONS

When making reservations of any type—airline, hotel, or car—company policy as well as the preferences of the person traveling are important considerations. If other company employees are traveling also, you may be required to work with others to coordinate travel arrangements. To insure a trip free from annoying distractions, reservations must be accurate and complete. You should handle these tasks prior to making reservations:

- Research the travel policies of the company. Well-written policies specify such items as whose signatures are required for travel approval, per diem allowances, travel restrictions, procedures for using company credit cards, and the documentation necessary for expense reports.
- Identify travel agencies, airlines, car rental agencies, and hotels and motels that the company prefers to use. Your travel agency or a travel outsource firm should have this information in its database. Keep a file to update these preferences along with telephone numbers and contacts.
- Maintain a permanent file of the traveler's preferences that includes these items:

   ▲ Preferred days of the week for travel.

   ▲ Departure times (early morning, mid-day).

   ▲ Type of airline and seating arrangements.

   ▲ Frequent-flyer/frequent-guest numbers and information.

   ▲ Restrictions on costs.

   ▲ Location of hotel; type of accommodations; services needed at hotels or motels; types of room and location of room; rooms allowing or prohibiting smoking.

   ▲ Type and size of car; ground transportation.

HINT: *Membership in associations such as the American Management Association or the American Automobile Association allows special hotel and car rental rates. Some companies also have accounts or contracts with specific hotels and car rental agencies that allow them special rates for their employees. Always give the name of the organization and member number for which a special rate is available when making the reservation.*

- Verify the trip details, such as destination, dates, and meeting times and places with the traveler.
- Prepare a planning preference guide to use when making reservations or when using a travel software program. (See Figure 14-1a, b.) Before making the final reservations, be certain the traveler approves the arrangements. Include two alternate

flight reservation plans unless the traveler specifies one specific time period only. Most software programs give you numerous choices.

HINT: *Box in or highlight the information that must be given to the travel agent or reservation assistant so you do not forget information when making reservations. Record every detail about the reservation made.*

HINT: *To make the planning guide easily recognizable, use colored paper. Keep a copy of the guide in the files. It is an excellent source for preparing the itinerary.*

- Begin a trip folder for each person who is traveling. Collect all materials that pertain to the trip and file them in the folder. Place all written confirmations, appointments, addresses, and telephone numbers in a large envelope that fits in the folder. Include hotel brochures, restaurant suggestions, maps of the city, and transportation options that will be helpful when the traveler arrives at a destination. This trip folder will be the basis for organizing the materials that will accompany the traveler on the trip.
- Weather information (current and three-day forecasts) is available for U.S. and foreign cities by dialing 1-900-WEATHER. There is a per-minute charge. You can get telephone access codes for every country on wallet-sized cards by calling 800-331-1140. The magazine *Business America*'s year-end issue includes U.S. and foreign business holidays for the next year.
- Remind the traveler to write or call the people with whom meetings are being scheduled. Document travel arrangements and dates of visits as well as addresses and telephone numbers that might be used while at this location. Request directions to the meeting locations as well as directions within the building, such as floor and room numbers. Confirm all meeting dates and times two days before the traveler leaves.
- Keep profiles on each traveler for whom you make arrangements. Include telephone numbers, people to contact in emergencies, physicians, passport numbers or copies, and credit card data.

Airline Reservations

The airline reservation is the first reservation made after the trip has been approved and tentative appointments have been scheduled. The following information is needed before booking the flights:

- Departure city, date, and time.

HINT: *When booking a flight, request information on flights scheduled before and after the one that is actually being booked. Include this information as a note on the itin-*

TRAVEL PLANNING GUIDE (A)

Name: _____ Department:_____

Credit card: Type:_____ Card #: _____ Exp. date: _____

Frequent flyer info. Airline: _____ Number: _____

Preferences of traveler: Place a check mark in the column labeled "Information Given" each time a reservation is made through a travel center. Many travel agencies also keep this information on file for their clients

Information Given	
	Airline preferences
_____	Carrier:_____
_____	Seating: _____
_____	Days of week:_____
_____	Departure times: _____
_____	Special needs: _____
_____	Other:_____
_____	**Accommodation preferences**
_____	Hotel/motel/other:_____
_____	Hotel/motel location:_____
_____	Floor/room location: _____
_____	Type of accommodations: _____
_____	Services needed: _____
_____	**Car rental preferences**
_____	Model, type, size: _____
_____	Services needed: _____

Name:_____ Department: _____

Telephone: Work _____ Home:_____Fax: _____

Airline: _____ # of people traveling: _____

Destination: _____ Travel dates: _____

ROUTING

Departure

Date	Departure		Arrival		Airline/Flight #.	Airport
	City	Time	City	Time		

Restrictions_____
_____

Return Trip

Date	Departure		Arrival		Airline/Flight #.	Airport
	City	Time	City	Time		

Restrictions_____
_____

Figure 14-1a Travel Planning Guide. (Option A)

TRAVEL PLANNING GUIDE (B)

Departure

Date	Departure		Arrival		Airline/Flight #.	Airport
	City	Time	City	Time		

Restrictions_____

Return Trip

Date	Departure		Arrival		Airline/Flight #.	Airport
	City	Time	City	Time		

Restrictions_____

Class of service: _____ Seat:_____ Type of plane: _____

Special meals: _____ Verified:_____

Booking date: _____ Option: _____ Name of agent: _____

Confirmation date:_____ Name of agent: _____

Airline telephone: _____

Cos:t_____ Method of payment:_____ Ticket pickup: _____

Flights preceding option selected: _____

Flights following option selected: _____

Transport to destination:_____ Distance to destination: _____

Comments:_____ Travelers approval:_____

Hotel/Motel Accommodations

Hotel/motel name: _____

Address: _____ Telephone: _____

Booking date: _____ Confirmation #: _____

Date of arrival:_____ Date of departure: _____

Type of room: _____ Number of people: _____

Check-in time: _____ Check-out time: _____

Meeting facilities/size: _____ Banquet facilities/size:_____

Directions to/from hotel:_____

Courtesy transportation: _____

Cost: _____ Guaranteed arrival: _____ Method of payment: _____

Special services: _____ Cancel by: _____

Reservations agent:_____ Traveler's approval:_____

Car rental

Company name: _____

Name of driver(s): _____

Car model, type, size: _____ Special services: _____

Dates car needed: _____ Incoming airline/flight number:_____

Pickup location: _____ Drop-off location:_____

Cost: _____ Method of payment:_____ Date of reservation:_____

Agent: _____ Traveler's approval: _____

Figure 14-1b Travel Planning Guide (Option B).

erary so alternative arrangements can be made in case a flight is delayed or there is a seat on an earlier flight.

HINT: *To save time and to obtain the best selection of fares, indicate general departure times, such as early morning, rather than exact hours. Most airports are busiest from 9 a.m. to 11 a.m. and from 4 p.m. to 7 p.m.*

- Arrival date, time, and destination.

HINT: *Distances from cities to airports vary. Allow sufficient time between scheduled meetings and airline departure and arrival times. Be especially careful with scheduling during rush-hour traffic periods.*

HINT: *Nonstop flights to the destination city are most desirable, but check the costs. If a flight requires a connection in cities where the weather may be bad or where a terminal change is necessary, allow sufficient time between flights.*

- Restrictions on costs; special rates for conference groups.

HINT: *Companies may request that employees stay over a Saturday night to save on airline fares. Be sure to consider the extra hotel charges when comparing rates. These fares are usually nonrefundable. Always request the airline's regulations for restricted or discounted fares.*

- Number of people traveling.
- Names, addresses, and telephone numbers of passengers.
- Frequent-flyer mileage information.

HINT: *When using frequent-flyer credits for free trips, make reservations directly with the airline. Maintain a list of frequent-flyer mileage numbers so that they are available when reserving the flights. Make sure the agent has the frequent-flyer numbers so that credit can be given for each trip.*

- Class of service; type of flight; seating preference; smoking or nonsmoking; handicap accommodations if applicable; baggage limits and carry-on restrictions for international flights.

HINT: *Smoking is not banned on all international flights. Check the smoking policies when making reservations.*

- Special meals, such as vegetarian, all fruit, low fat, low sodium, kosher, Hindu, and Muslim.

HINT: *Verification of special-request meals should be made approximately 48 hours before flight time to assure availability of the meals. Order the special meals at the
time the reservation is made.*

• Electronic equipment availability.

HINT: *Airlines have various electronic services available. On some flights travelers can
make and also receive telephone calls. For a personal aircall number for receiving
calls, call 800-890-3939. Some airlines have fax services. Check with the airlines to
determine their restrictions for operating electronic equipment, including computers, while on the ground or in the air.*

• Airline and flight numbers.
• Name of destination airport or airports.
• Type of ground transportation and where to get it; cost; and mileage to city center.

HINT: *Find out about insurance on rental cars from the company insurance agent. What
coverage does the company provide for collision and liability? Are there places
where the coverage is not valid? In case of an accident, who should be contacted?
Are any types of cars not covered by the company's policy? Does the policy cover
all drivers?*

• Shuttle service.

HINT: *Shuttle reservations are not necessary. Passengers purchase tickets through a machine or en route. Check for luggage restrictions since some shuttle flights allow only
carry-on bags.*

• Arrangements to pick up tickets; method of ticket payment.

HINT: *When making reservations with an airline that offers ticketless travel, be sure to
record the confirmation number and ask for an itinerary. If a reservation is lost
or there is a billing mistake, such information is crucial since you have no printed
ticket to back you up. Check with the airline to see if seat selection is available before arrival at the airport.*

• Airline telephone service.
• Airline club availability.
• Airline service centers.

HINT: *Airline service centers offer services similar to those of airline clubs; however, travelers do not have to be members. Travelers pay only for the services they use. Since
charges vary from center to center, check costs carefully.*

- Name of agent making the reservation.
- Date of booking.
- Date of confirmation.

HINT: *Some airlines require that you confirm a return flight 24 to 48 hours before departure. This is always a standard procedure on international flights.*

- On-schedule information.

HINT: *FlightCall, a service offered through the Official Airline Guide® (OAG®), provides information indicating whether a flight is on time. Using FlightCall is often quicker, though more expensive, than calling the airline. The number is 900-786-8686. A travel agent or your online travel service can provide ratings on airlines' on-schedule performances. The higher the number on a scale of 1 to 10, the better the airline's on-schedule performance.*

- Safety information.

HINT: *Aisle seats are best if a quick departure is necessary. More leg room is available with bulkhead or exit (emergency) row seats. Travelers in emergency row seats must be willing to open emergency doors if a need arises.*

Hotel or Motel Reservations

Travel agents or travel management firms can reserve hotel or motel accommodations. You can also call the hotel or motel directly or use toll-free reservation numbers provided by the larger hotel and motel chains. Online services provide you with accommodation locations, price ranges, ratings, and number of rooms. The following information will be helpful in making hotel or motel reservations:

- Name of person and company.
- Arrival date and time; departure date and time; whether you want a guaranteed late arrival.

HINT: *If the reservation is guaranteed late arrival, the hotel charges the customer whether the room is used that evening or not. If changes in accommodations are made while en route, the person traveling must inform the hotel or motel to avoid charges. Some hotels require one to three days' notice if reservations are canceled. When making the reservation, find out the cancellation policy of the hotel or motel.*

HINT: *Hotel Reservations Network (800-964-6835) is useful for booking accommodations in major cities at discounted prices. Their service is especially useful when hotel space is difficult to locate. When dealing with hotel clearinghouses, be sure to clar-*

ify who is to be paid and how cancellations are handled—through the clearinghouse or the hotel.

- Cost restrictions.

HINT: *Promotional rates may be available. Ask for them when making the reservation. Call the hotel directly rather than the 800 central reservations number to check on special rates. Don't accept rack rates. Hotel or motel room taxes as well as costs for extra amenities such as parking or equipment rentals can be expensive. Always request this information when comparing lodging accommodations.*

- Number of persons per room; bed size; smoking or nonsmoking room or floor; separate secure floor for women; room location (e.g., away from vending machines); top, first, or concierge service floor.
- Method of payment (credit card number).

HINT: *Since credit cards are used so frequently, keep a list of personal and corporate credit card numbers in a special file. Mark it "confidential" and keep it in a locked drawer.*

- Frequent-guest information.
- Specific location of hotel or motel.

HINT: *Careful booking is required since there may be several hotels in the area that are part of the same chain. Request specific location information—city, address, telephone numbers, and proximity to meeting location. Online services provide directions and maps.*

- Type of plan, such as European, continental, or modified.
- Courtesy airport pickup and return; hours of operation; pickup location; procedures to obtain the service.

HINT: *Some hotels provide complimentary transportation to certain nearby business locations. A rental car may not be necessary.*

- Check-in and check-out times; express registration availability.
- Laundry/cleaning services; hairdressers (appointments necessary?); evening drinks/refreshments; room-service hours; telephone service/extra charges; pool; exercise facilities; continental breakfast.

HINT: *If travelers arrive late and have to leave early the next morning, they may not use the extra services. Select hotels or motels that match a traveler's needs.*

- Secretarial services; private office suite availability; equipment availability; modem capabilities.

HINT: *Specific information may not be available by calling a toll-free number when making reservations. To be certain of equipment facilities, call the concierge at the hotel.*

HINT: *Some hotels reserve a floor for business travelers. There is usually an executive lounge where guests can relax, obtain concierge assistance, and mingle with other businesspeople. Others have business centers with up-to-date equipment and software, telephone and fax services, and secretarial assistance.*

HINT: *The Association for Computer Training and Support publishes* Traveling with a Laptop Computer. *A free copy is available by sending a stamped, self-addressed envelope to ACTS, 27 Sagamore Road, Raquette Lake, NY 13436.*

- Health club facilities.
- Business advisors for briefings on protocol in foreign countries; access to online news services.
- Suites or conference rooms; banquet and meeting facilities.

HINT: *Hotels are very helpful in arranging group meetings or conferences. Contact the hotel sales manager or convention sales coordinator for information.*

- Confirmation number.

HINT: *Hotels may overbook or lose a reservation. Always request written confirmation of a hotel reservation. Obtain the name of the reservation clerk and the confirmation number. Request information about the type of equipment available and its compatibility with the items the traveler will be bringing.*

Car Rental Reservations

Car rental agencies have rental locations at airports or short distances from airports, at some hotels, and at downtown or suburban locations. When making car rental reservations, the following items of information will be helpful:

- Dates for which the car is needed; pickup and drop-off times; pickup and drop-off locations.

HINT: *Agencies typically do not charge for cancellations; however, some do for popular models such as vans or convertibles. Pickup and drop-off locations off the airport premises may be less expensive than those at the airport. Be sure to obtain addresses and directions for nonairport locations.*

- Name of person renting and names of drivers; age limitations of drivers.

HINT: *Drivers need to be 25 years old. A few agencies rent to drivers under 25, but the cost is higher. Check for additional drivers' charges if several people are traveling together. All drivers must be present at the car rental desk to be designated as first or second drivers.*

- Flight number of arriving flights if applicable.
- Cost restrictions; discounted rates; out-of-state or out-of-country restrictions.
- Limited or unlimited mileage; gas charges.
- Model, type, and size of car; smoke-free or not.

HINT: *When renting a car for use abroad, you may encounter unknown models. Ask the agent to identify a U.S. car that would be similar to the foreign model. Obtain the agency's fleet sheet, which indicates such items as the type and size of cars available, size of trunks, and fuel capacities.*

- Drop-off charge; late drop-off charge.

HINT: *Rental firms charge a fee for late returns. When reserving the car, ask about such penalties. Make a note on the itinerary to indicate the time a car must be returned.*

HINT: *Pickup and return procedures often take time, especially when the airports are busiest. When reserving a car, include express check-in on the list of your comparison features.*

- Frequent flyer coupon restrictions and information; frequent renter information.
- Cellular telephone availability and cost.
- Computerized maps.

HINT: *Car rentals with computerized directional systems are helpful in unfamiliar territory. A user identifies the location and destination and a map shows directions (including multilanguage directions) on a screen on the dashboard. There is an extra charge for this feature. Another feature, the police alert device, is useful in an emergency. Pushing a button enables police to identify the location of the car.*

- Insurance coverage.

HINT: *If a car is rented outside the United States or Canada, additional insurance may be needed. Document and date all contacts you make with insurance carriers or credit card companies regarding insurance coverage.*

Company Cars, Planes, Charter Flights, and Trains

A company may provide a car for an employee to use for business travel. Someone in the company is responsible for reserving the cars and keeping maintenance records on them. Since other employees also use company cars, it is important to reserve the car as early as possible in the trip-planning process so one is available when needed.

Automobile manufacturers are experimenting with installing electronic equipment and work areas into cars and minivans so they can be converted into mobile offices.

State or city tourist bureaus issue road maps and city maps as well as general information about the area. It takes time to obtain these materials, so such information needs to be requested early in the planning process. Online access provides information that you can download and use.

HINT: *If a person travels to certain locales frequently, maintain a file of maps, lists of good restaurants, limousine services, and other information for those areas. Arrange the materials by city or state and keep the files up to date.*

HINT: *To make expense reporting and record keeping easier, prepare a mileage chart showing the number of miles between cities to which the person often travels.*

If a company has its own planes, consult the person who keeps the records for reserving a seat. This person is usually responsible for contacting the pilots, verifying departure dates and times, and following the guidelines for determining which employees (and family members, if applicable) are eligible to use the service.

When a number of people travel to the same meeting or when they go to cities not served by commercial airlines, chartering a small plane may be economical and time-efficient. To identify companies that operate charter flights, check the Yellow Pages of the local telephone directory under "Aircraft Charters and Rentals." To obtain information about the cost of a charter flight, you must indicate the length of the trip. the number of stops, size of plane, overnight stays for crew members, in-flight catering, jet or nonjet, and the number of passengers.

Other information you should request includes insurance coverage, safety and experience records of the pilots, amenities available on the plane, and arrangements for ground transportation.

For those who wish to avoid airport traffic and lines and who have short distances to travel, rail service is an alternative. Stations are usually in the center of the city, making arrival at business appointments more convenient. Train travel in many foreign countries is fast and comfortable, and significantly less costly than travel by air.

ARRANGING INTERNATIONAL TRAVEL

With international business activity expanding, more company employees are traveling to destinations outside the U.S. As you organize the details involved in international travel, you will need information about travel documents requirements, customs, security, medical assistance, and currency payment options.

Sources for Obtaining Travel Documents

The documents necessary for travel vary from country to country. Sources of information about a country's entry requirements or travel restrictions include the following:

- Airline offices serving the countries being visited.
- Travel agents; travel management firms.
- Foreign government tourist bureaus with offices in the United States.
- *Foreign Entry Requirements* (U.S. Government Publication M-164), which includes such information as required travel documents, immunizations, embassy or consulate addresses and telephone numbers, time required for processing travel documents, and currency regulations.
- *U.S. Consuls Help Americans Abroad* (A U.S. Government Publication).

HINT: *For free copies of both booklets, write to the U.S. Department of State, Bureau of Consular Affairs, Room 5807, Washington, DC 20520. Another more general publication,* Your Trip Abroad, *is available from the Superintendent of Documents, U.S. Government Printing Office, Washington, DC 20402-9371.*

- Embassies or consulates in specific countries.

HINT: *Embassies are located in capital cities. Consulate generals are branches of embassies, and consulates are offices with limited responsibilities; the officers are consuls or vice-consuls. For locations of these embassies or consulates, check* The Congressional Directory; *a copy is available at most public libraries. Consulates and embassies are helpful in emergencies or when trying to contact a person traveling in a foreign country.*

- Citizens Emergency Center for Travel Advisory Information, Department of State, Washington, DC 20520, which issues warnings about areas of political unrest, terrorism, currency restrictions, and hotel shortages in specific regions or countries.
- Online travel forum services.

PASSPORT

A **passport,** issued by the U.S. Department of State, is required for every U.S. citizen who plans to travel in a foreign country. It is valid for ten years and gives a citizen the right to leave the U.S., receive protection, if necessary, within the country being visited, and reenter the U.S. after traveling. A passport is not necessary for a citizen traveling to Mexico, Canada, the West Indies, the Caribbean, and some South and Central American countries. It is wise to apply for a passport well in advance since it may take three to six weeks to obtain.

First-time passport applicants need to appear in person at a State Department passport office, at an appropriately designated courthouse (federal, state, or county), or at a U.S. post office. Everyone in a family needs an individual passport. The applicant needs to complete a form (DSP-11) and bring the following:

- Proof of identity—driver's license or government identification card.
- Proof of citizenship—birth certificate, certificate of naturalization, certificate of citizenship, or report of birth abroad of a citizen of the United States. If these are not available, secondary proof, such as a baptismal certificate, voter registration verification, elementary school records, or insurance papers, is also acceptable.
- Photographs—two identical 2-by-2-inch color or black-and-white photographs taken during the past six months. The Yellow Pages in the local telephone directory will indicate those photography studios where passport pictures are taken and processed. The date of the photograph and the owner's signature should be written on the backs of the two photographs. Make several extra copies of the photographs. In case a passport is lost in a foreign country, extra photographs can expedite getting a replacement passport from the U.S consulate.
- Fee.

If a person had a passport in the past and now wishes to renew it, a shorter form (DSP-82) mailed to the nearest passport agency is acceptable. The necessary documents include the application form, the old passport, two photographs, and the fee. If a passport has expired and an immediate foreign trip is necessary, applying in person at a U.S. Passport Office (located only in major cities) with proof of departure will be sufficient to get a passport issued on the spot. It is time-consuming to stand in line at the passport office and may not be geographically feasible.

HINT: *If you are not near a passport office, call 800-272-7776 (Washington Passport and Visa Service). They will process applications in 24 hours to ten business days. Fees vary and shipping charges are extra.*

HINT: *Passport numbers and dates for renewal should be recorded in the "travel preference" folders maintained for all managers in order to remind the users of dates when passports must be renewed.*

HINT: *Order a 48-page passport with space for numerous visa stamps if the person travels a great deal to foreign countries.*

VISA

A **visa** is a permit to enter a certain country for a specific purpose on a specified date. If a visa is required in a country, the consulate of that country issues one by stamping the passport. A travel agent can obtain a visa for a traveler by sending the passport, an application, and any necessary fees to the appropriate consulate office. Many countries in Asia, the Middle East, Africa, and Eastern Europe require visas. In a very limited number of cases, a visa may be issued upon arrival in a country. Passport offices do not issue visas. Some countries require letters of reference or proof from travelers that they have transportation in and out of the country; some restrict the length of stay. Apply for a visa early; it takes time for the document to be processed.

TOURIST CARD

The tourist card grants entry to a country without a passport or visa. Tourist cards for a country such as Mexico are available from the country's embassy or consulate office, official tourist offices in the United States, some travel agencies, airlines serving that country, or at the port of entry. To get the card, travelers need proof of citizenship, such as a passport or birth certificate.

INTERNATIONAL DRIVING PERMIT

The permit verifies that the data on a regular driver's license is valid; the information is written in the language of the country in which it is needed. Many countries now allow driving with just a U.S. or Canadian license. To obtain a permit, a fee, a completed application, and two passport photographs are required. Permits remain in effect for one year from the date of issue and are available from the American/Canadian Automobile Associations (AAA/CAA). AAA/CAA can advise you of the countries where permits are necessary. Even with the permit, you will need a valid U.S. or Canadian driver's license. Association membership is not necessary to get a permit.

INTERNATIONAL CERTIFICATE OF VACCINATION

The United States does not require vaccinations before returning; however, some countries do request documentation of certain vaccinations for such diseases as cholera or yellow fever before entering. **International certificate of vaccination** forms are available through local or state public health offices or passport agencies. The form requires a physician's signature and the health department's stamp.

HINT: *For up-to-date international health information, order a copy of* Health Information for International Travel, *U.S. Government Printing Office, Washington, DC 20402.*

*It lists required and recommended vaccinations by country and recommends ways
to maintain health while traveling. Always use a current copy, since regulations concerning proof of vaccination change. There is a fee for the booklet. The Centers for Disease Control (CDC) International Travelers Hotline, 404-332-4559, is another source
for region-by-region information concerning required vaccinations. The Public
Health Office may also have this information, but always ask the date of their sources.*

HINT: *If vaccinations are needed, remind the traveler to allow time for the vaccinations
to become effective, such as five days for cholera. If multiple vaccinations are required, time may be needed between inoculations.*

CERTIFICATE OF REGISTRATION

The **certificate of registration** allows a traveler to register any personal foreign-produced
item, such as a watch or camera so it does not become subject to duty. Documents, such as
a bill of sale, jeweler's appraisal, or receipt, are proof of prior possession. When proof is
not available, travelers should take the item to a customs office, port of entry, or international airport to obtain a certificate.

CUSTOMS DECLARATION

Articles purchased in certain foreign countries and brought back to the United States are subject to **customs declaration**; there are, however, exemptions. The Department of the Treasury, U.S. Customs Service, publishes *Know Before You Go* and *Customs Hints for Returning
U.S. Residents,* which are designed to assist travelers who have made purchases in foreign
countries. For additional customs information, call a U.S. customs office in a major city.

HINT: *Checkpoints between the countries that make up the European Community no
longer exist, simplifying passport checks and customs clearances. Remind travelers to keep their merchandise receipts in case they are needed for U.S. customs.*

Foreign Currencies

Once travel plans are completed, there may be a need to obtain foreign currency. Traveler's checks in dollars or a foreign currency are two ways for business travelers to handle
money. Worldwide travel companies, such as American Express, banks with foreign exchange
facilities, and some travel agents, through airline-sponsored reservation systems, sell traveler's checks in foreign currencies. The customer may receive foreign traveler's checks by registered mail or, for an additional fee, by overnight delivery, or they may be picked up in person.

Credit cards are accepted in most foreign countries. Charges are based on the day's
exchange rate which may be more favorable than the conversion rate involved with traveler's checks.

Large banks and American Express or Thomas Cook offices usually have certain currencies available for those travelers who want cash before they arrive in a country. For currencies of less frequently visited countries, call Ruesch International (800-424-2923) for speedy delivery. Current exchange rates are published in some local newspapers and in *The Wall Street Journal,* or they may be obtained by calling the bank or the reference librarian at the public library.

Medical Emergency Procedures

As firms expand trade with less-developed countries, they will need to provide their employees with information not only on the country's culture but also on its potential health and safety hazards. Business travelers also need information about the medical assistance that is available in the countries in which they will be traveling. Office professionals can help with this research and share the information with others in the firm.

Travelers with health conditions need to carry sufficient medication on their person—*not* in their checked baggage. They also need such items as their doctor's telephone number and a medical summary of problems, treatments, prescriptions (pharmacist/physician proof may be necessary), and allergies. Medic Alert tags, which are available by calling 800-344-3226, identify a traveler's medical problem and provide an identification number and an emergency toll-free number.

All raw food, salads, and fruit with their skins can cause illness. Contaminated water should not be drunk (no ice cubes) or used for brushing teeth.

The State Department's Citizens Emergency Center (202-647-5225) provides material on health conditions throughout the world. The Center for Disease Control (CDC) hotline (404-639-1610) provides information on possible health hazards in specific countries. Also, the CDC publishes *Health Information for International Travel,* which is available from the Superintendent of Documents, U.S. Government Printing Office, Washington, DC 20402.

U.S. consulate officers maintain lists of certified local English-speaking physicians and specialists and will contact family members when there are emergencies. Credit card companies and travel assistance companies have emergency hotlines and offer similar services. Some additional services include making evacuation arrangements, monitoring hospital care, translating medical information, and locating blood that has been properly screened.

HINT: *There is space in the passport for identifying people to call in case of an emergency. Keep a copy of this page from all travelers' passports in the office. It is especially helpful to assistance groups when they have to contact family members.*

HINT: *The International Association for Medical Assistance to Travelers (IMAT) is a nonprofit organization that publishes a list of English-speaking doctors worldwide and gives free information about food and water risks, as well as diseases for many countries. This information should be less than a year old, so do not rely on an old copy in your files.*

Foreign medical offices may want payment at the time of service. Therefore, travelers should carry information on their policy type, group or individual policy number, and type of coverage.

Cultural Awareness

Company employees who represent their firms in foreign countries will find it helpful to acquire general information about the countries as well as knowledge of the customs and values of the people with whom they will be working. Office professionals can assist in collecting and organizing this information so it can be used by anyone who travels internationally or associates with foreign visitors.

GENERAL INFORMATION

Find out as much as possible about topics such as economic climate, history, the political party in power, education, recreational facilities and events, business ethics, and negotiation strategies. A current atlas will provide general information about a country. People who have visited the country, businesspeople who have done business there, or college professors who teach language or area studies courses are also excellent resources for general information about specific countries.

LANGUAGE

Everyone appreciates a visitor's attempts to communicate in the native language of the host country. Small electronic language translators are available, often with correct pronunciations. Practice the pronunciations for such appropriate courtesy phrases as "Thank you" and "It was a pleasure meeting you." If business is to be conducted in English, the English used must be understandable. Superlatives such as "fantastic" or "absolute disaster" are confusing. Two-word verbs, such as "break up" or "win back" should be avoided. Acronyms, slang, and jargon, such as "ballpark figures," are difficult for foreigners to interpret.

HINT: *International hotels may have business centers that provide interpreters and translators. Check with the U.S. hotels that have international branches.*

GREETINGS/ADDRESS

Greetings range from handshakes to bows to friendly slaps on the back. For example, handshakes are a common form of greeting and saying goodbye in the western European countries. Japanese businesspeople often bow and then shake hands.

Addressing someone with his or her title and last name is appropriate in most countries. Determine who will be visited, and write down the pronunciation of each name. Place this information in the appropriate meeting folder.

CONVERSATION

Politics and religion are inappropriate topics. Don't discuss illegal aliens in Mexico or China in Taiwan. It may be rude to discuss business during a social occasion. Express an interest in the traditions and culture of the country.

EYE CONTACT

To Americans, eye contact signifies honesty; but in some countries, such as India, avoiding eye contact signifies respect.

BUSINESS CARDS

Business cards are very appropriate in international situations. It is courteous to print one side of the card in English and the other side in the language of the country visited. When a business card is presented, accept it graciously and place it on the desk in a prominent location.

TIME

In some countries, meetings and appointments often begin late; however, this does not devalue the importance of the business to be conducted or provide a reason for others to be late. In other countries, however, promptness is imperative. Afternoon breaks of two hours or more are common in many European countries. In such cases, appointments are best made for the morning hours.

Central European businesses may close during July or August for vacation. Long weekends are also customary. Banks and some businesses in the Middle East are open on Saturday and Sunday but closed on Friday.

Time differences between various parts of the world affect travel preferences as well as optimum meeting times. (For a map of U.S. time zones, see Figure 14-2; for worldwide time differences, see Table 14-1.) Jet lag may make it necessary to allow some time for readjustment. Avoid scheduling meetings too close to arrival time at the destination city.

Holidays vary from country to country. Some are regional or local only. To avoid scheduling appointments on holidays, check with the country's consulate or embassy in the United States.

MEALS AND TIPPING PRACTICES

In some countries, such as Greece or Spain, the time for the evening meal is relatively late. In other European countries, the main meal may be mid-day. Huge banquets are often given in China. Travelers to Asian countries may wish to learn to use chopsticks. Pork is not eaten in the Middle East. Toasting is very common in European countries.

Tipping practices vary. Prepare a list of tipping suggestions for each country the traveler plans to visit and include it with the materials to be taken on the trip. Current tourist

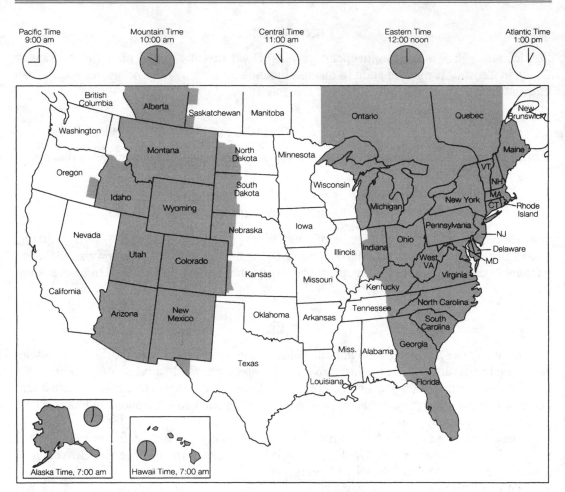

Figure 14-2 U.S. time zones.

manuals found in bookstores or public libraries are useful sources of information for tipping practices. In many countries, a percentage tip is included on the bill, so additional tipping is not necessary.

BODY LANGUAGE

Head shakes may have different meanings or even opposite meanings in various countries. A nod may simply mean that the message has been heard; it does not necessarily indicate agreement. Requesting feedback is appropriate and wise at various stages of a discussion.

In Japan, it is polite to use both hands when receiving or giving items, such as business cards. In India, it is inappropriate to use the left hand for such purposes.

Table 14-1
TIME DIFFERENCES AROUND THE WORLD

COUNTRY	TIME ZONE			
	EST	CST	MST	PST
American Samoa	-6	-5	-4	-3
Argentina	+2	+3	+4	+5
Australia (Sydney)	+15	+16	+17	+18
Austria	+6	+7	+8	+9
Belgium	+6	+7	+8	+9
Bolivia	+1	+2	+3	+4
Brazil	+2	+3	+4	+5
Chile	+1	+2	+3	+4
Colombia	+0	+1	+2	+3
Costa Rica	-1	+0	+1	+2
Cyprus	+7	+8	+9	+10
Denmark	+6	+7	+8	+9
Equador	+0	+1	+2	+3
El Salvador	-1	+0	+1	+2
Fiji	+17	+18	+19	+20
Finland	+7	+8	+9	+10
France	+6	+7	+8	+9
Germany	+6	+7	+8	+9
Greece	+7	+8	+9	+10
Guam	+15	+16	+17	+18
Guatemala	-1	+0	+1	+2
Guyana	+2	+3	+4	+5
Haiti	+0	+1	+2	+3
Honduras	-1	+0	+1	+2
Hong Kong	+13	+14	+15	+16
Indonesia	+12	+13	+14	+15
Iran	$+8\frac{1}{2}$	$+9\frac{1}{2}$	$+10\frac{1}{2}$	$+11\frac{1}{2}$
Iraq	+8	+9	+10	+11
Ireland	+5	+6	+7	+8
Israel	+7	+8	+9	+10
Italy	+6	+7	+8	+9
Ivory Coast	+5	+6	+7	+8
Japan	+14	+15	+16	+17
Kenya	+8	+9	+10	+11
Korea	+14	+15	+16	+17
Kuwait	+8	+9	+10	+11
Liberia	+5	+6	+7	+8

EST: Eastern Standard Time; MST: Mountain Standard Time; CST: Central Standard Time;
PST: Pacific Standard Time.

Table 14-1 (*continued*)

COUNTRY	EST	CST	MST	PST
Libya	+7	+8	+9	+10
Luxembourg	+6	+7	+8	+9
Malaysia	+13	+14	+15	+16
Monaco	+6	+7	+8	+9
Netherlands	+6	+7	+8	+9
New Zealand	+17	+18	+19	+20
Nicaragua	-1	+0	+1	+2
Nigeria	+6	+7	+8	+9
Norway	+6	+7	+8	+9
Panama	+0	+1	+2	+3
Paraguay	+1	+2	+3	+4
Peru	+0	+1	+2	+3
Philippines	+13	+14	+15	+16
Portugal	+5	+6	+7	+8
Romania	+7	+8	+9	+10
Saudi Arabia	+8	+9	+10	+11
Senegal	+5	+6	+7	+8
Singapore	+13	+14	+15	+16
South Africa	+7	+8	+9	+10
Spain	+6	+7	+8	+9
Sri Lanka	+10½	+11½	+12½	+13½
Sweden	+6	+7	+8	+9
Switzerland	+6	+7	+8	+9
Tahiti	-5	-4	-3	-2
Taiwan	+13	+14	+15	+16
Thailand	+12	+13	+14	+15
Tunisia	+6	+7	+8	+9
Turkey	+8	+9	+10	+11
Russia (Moscow)	+8	+9	+10	+11
United Arab Emirates	+9	+10	+11	+10
United Kingdom	+5	+6	+7	+8
Vatican City	+6	+7	+8	+9
Venezuela	+1	+2	+3	+4

GIFT GIVING

Appropriate gifts include products from the United States or an illustrated book. The quality of the gift is important. In some western European countries, a gift is not given at the first meeting. Giving a banquet for Chinese businesspeople is an appropriate gift, but receiving a clock as a gift is considered bad luck in China. No gifts of liquor should be given in the Middle Eastern countries, since alcohol is forbidden by the Muslim religion. Return dinner invitations or theater invitations are customary forms of gifts in most countries. In cultures where group work is respected, give a gift that all members of the group will enjoy.

Colors are significant and should be considered when choosing gifts; for example, white and black are associated with mourning in Japan. The same is true of purple in Latin American countries. Red and gold are good colors in China.

AGE AND SEX

Age is highly honored in some countries. A younger person, therefore, may be less successful in business negotiations. In other countries women may find it difficult to conduct business transactions.

CORRESPONDENCE

Generally, business letters from foreign countries are formal and courteous; use correct titles. Review letters from your foreign correspondents and use similar phrasing when writing to them. Do not send a form letter; write an individual response.

The tone of your own business correspondence should not be overly familiar. The use of clear, precise English is helpful to a foreign reader. Short sentences limited to one idea and paragraphs of seven to eight lines will clarify major points. If several points are made, precede them with "first," "second," etc. To avoid confusion in dates, write them out; for example, use "October 8, 1997," rather than "10/8/97," which may be interpreted as August 10.

If measurements or money are mentioned in correspondence, use metric units and current monetary conversion rates. To avoid misunderstandings, indicate both the dollar amount and the amount in the appropriate foreign currency. (For metric equivalents and conversions, see Table 14-2.)

DECISION MAKING

A company's trustworthiness is an important factor in conducting foreign business. To establish a favorable perception of trustworthiness, such items as the history of the company, its founders and personal information about the people attending the meeting are helpful and may be sent to the foreign company before the visit.

In some countries the most important matters are left until the end of a meeting; in others, omitting details suggests evasiveness. Knowing such differences before a meeting and organizing the materials accordingly can aid in negotiations.

In some Asian countries decisions are often made by a group, not left to one person. The time needed to make decisions, therefore, may be lengthy, which can be a factor in scheduling meetings or business trips.

References for Foreign Travel

Numerous guides exist on customs, etiquette, and general information about foreign countries. Some provide terms and pronunciations for specific industries. Other resources include airline magazines, tourist books, and a foreign country's tourist office.

Table 14.2
APPROXIMATE CONVERSIONS TO METRIC MEASURES

WHEN YOU KNOW	MULTIPLY BY	TO FIND
Length		
Inches (in)	2.5	Centimeters (cm)
Feet (ft)	30.0	Centimeters (cm)
Yards (yd)	0.9	Meters (m)
Miles (mi)	1.6	Kilometers (km)
Area		
Square inches (in2)	6.5	Square centimeters (cm2)
Square feet (ft2)	0.09	Square meters (m2)
Square yards (yd2)	0.8	Square meters (m2)
Square miles (mi2)	2.6	Square kilometers (km2)
Acres	0.4	Hectares (ha)
Volume		
Teaspoons (tsp)	5.0	Milliliters (ml)
Tablespoons (tbsp)	15.0	Milliliters (ml)
Fluid ounces (fl oz)	30.0	Milliliters (ml)
Cups (c)	0.24	Liters (l)
Pints (pt)	0.47	Liters (l)
Quarts (qt)	0.95	Liters (l)
Gallons (gal)	3.8	Liters (l)
Cubic feet (ft3)	0.03	Cubic meters (m3)
Cubic yards (yd3)	0.76	Cubic meters (m3)
Mass (weight)		
Ounces (oz)	28.0	Grams (g)
Pounds (lb)	0.45	Kilograms (kg)
Short tons (2,000 lb)	0.9	Tonnes (t)

Source: U.S. Department of Commerce, National Bureau of Standards, Washington, DC.

Two excellent sources of information are the Business Council for International Understanding, The American University, Washington, DC 20016, and the David M. Kennedy Center for International Studies, *Culturegrams*, Brigham Young University, Provo, UT 84604, 800-528-6279. *The Business Travel Survival Guide* by Jack Cummings is a good source for tipping practices and gift-giving suggestions. *Do's and Taboos Around the World, Do's and Taboos of International Trade*, and *Do's and Taboos of Hosting International Visitors* are helpful guides for acceptable etiquette in foreign countries.

ARRANGING TRAVEL FUNDS

Company guidelines for obtaining travel funds are usually very specific and require strict adherence to established schedules and procedures. Company credit cards, cash advances, and personal payments to be reimbursed later are ways to fund travel.

Corporate Credit Cards

A company often issues corporate credit cards to individual employees. These cards remain the property of the company. A list of all employees who are issued individual credit cards for travel purposes must be kept up to date so that when an employee leaves the company the expenses charged to that credit card are cleared before another employee receives the card privileges. Corporate credit cards that allow access to cash via ATMs decrease the need for cash advances.

Cash Advances

A cash advance allows a traveler to receive funds before leaving on a business trip. Since all costs are not known in advance, it is necessary to estimate such expenses as food and business entertainment. A typical cash advance form requires the following information before the accounting office issues cash or a check:

- Date of request.
- Purpose of trip.
- Travel location.
- Dates of trip.
- Amount requested—may or may not require a breakdown of individual expenses.
- Signature of person traveling.
- Approval of supervisor.

To be sure the amount received matches the amount requested, count the money received from the accounting office, and do not sign a receipt form until this has been verified. Place the cash or check in an envelope for the manager, include a copy of the signed request form, and obtain a signature from the person who accepts the money. File that signed copy in the preliminary trip folder; it will be helpful in preparing the expense claim. Someone has to document to whom a cash advance was given, how much was actually spent, and when unspent funds were returned. Expenses on corporate credit cards are simpler to track.

Personal Payments

When payments for travel expenses are handled personally by the traveler, receipts for all expenditures are necessary for reimbursement. Since some of the payments may have been on the traveler's personal credit card, it is advisable to make copies of all receipts. The traveler's copy accompanies the expense claim.

HINT: *For IRS and expense claim purposes, request cash register receipts for food and miscellaneous expenses rather than a fill-in-the-blank tab.*

HINT: *For information about foreign exchange rates, call a local bank. Know the currency of the traveler's destination, including smaller denominations. It is helpful to ob-*

tain a small amount of the local currency before the trip for tips, cabs, or meals upon arrival.

HINT: *Exchange rates are usually better overseas than at home. Once abroad, banks rather than airport agencies or hotels often offer the best rates. Advise travelers to exchange money as needed; some countries will not reexchange leftover currency when a traveler leaves.*

Letters of Credit

Handling travel funds with a letter of credit allows a traveler to obtain funds up to a designated amount from banks. Such a letter states that the person is a customer in good standing at the bank issuing the letter. The letter acts as an introduction in financial institutions and allows the bearer to make withdrawals up to the amount of the specified credit line.

Automatic Teller Machines (ATMs)

Users punch in their personal identification numbers (PIN) and receive the amount in the local currency. Banks deduct the amount withdrawn (U.S. dollar conversion) and a service charge from users' home bank accounts.

HINT: *ATMs are popular in Europe, but they may not always accept another country's cards. Check with the company issuing the ATM card for a list of its usable ATM locations and its charges.*

Traveler's Checks

Some banks or corporate travel companies sell traveler's checks without a commission. American Express accepts telephone orders for traveler's checks and mails them first-class. If traveler's checks are lost or stolen, they can be replaced. Unused checks may be used on other trips. Travelers may purchase traveler's checks in foreign currency and thus eliminate the need for currency exchange. Since some countries impose surcharges for cashing traveler's checks, purchase the checks in larger denominations to limit the number of transactions.

Smart Cards

The card resembles a credit card in size. A traveler buys an amount of money from a bank, and this amount is digitized on a microchip on the card. When the card is used, the amount of the purchase decreases the card's balance. In foreign countries, where the cards are popular, a traveler purchases a smart card for a specific purpose, such as long-distance telephone calls within the country. Using the card eliminates the need for having the correct coins when making phone calls from public phone booths.

Reducing Travel Costs

Because of restructuring and downsizing, companies are evaluating travel and entertainment expenses to determine how to cut costs. Office professionals need an awareness of these travel management strategies:

- Travel policy. Developing a comprehensive travel policy is the first step in establishing a travel management program. The following are suggested areas to include in a travel policy:

  ▲ Who may travel/booking procedures.

  ▲ Who approves travel/credit card authorization.

  ▲ Designated travel company.

  ▲ Class of travel/designated airline, hotel, and car rental agency.

  ▲ Expense ranges/per diem rates.

  ▲ Reimbursement procedures.

  ▲ Insurance coverage.

  ▲ Meals and entertainment.

  ▲ Frequent-flyer benefits/ownership.

  ▲ Miscellaneous expenses.

The policy needs to be communicated to employees in such a way that they accept it, and it needs to be enforced in such a way that all are treated fairly.

- Travel consolidation. Consolidating travel arrangements with one agency or with one hotel, airline, or car rental agency generates savings and upgraded services because of the volume of travel purchases. If the travel agency provides detailed reports on travel spending habits and suggestions for saving money, companies can analyze their travel needs and make adjustments.
- In-house travel manager/designated employee. Centralizing travel responsibilities with a designated employee or manager eliminates the time consumed by individuals planning their own trips. An in-house manager can obtain better prices and prepare contracts with travel firms in line with the company's travel policy. The company can also prevent travel policy abuses.
- Corporate charge cards. Companies issue these cards to travelers to control expenses and make it easier and faster to track and report major expenditures. The card reduces the need for large cash advances. Companies can select and code restrictions to prevent misuse. One check or transfer covers the costs each month. Discount dining cards for participating restaurants also produce savings when employees travel to the same locations regularly.

- Frequent flyer, lodger, renter programs. Taking advantage of these programs offers such perks as service upgrades or free trips or rooms. The programs are interrelated; for example, frequent flyers may receive hotel savings and car rental coupons.
- Conference calls/teleconferencing/videoconferencing. Once initial meetings are over, companies often find that they can conduct the rest of their business with a conference call. A videoconference may also be acceptable. Both alternatives require clear objectives and a block of uninterrupted time. Sending several employees to an off-site conference is costly; a teleconference may be more cost-effective.

Specific cost-saving suggestions regarding travel arrangements include:

- Reserve flights as early as possible. The biggest discounts are for 14 to 30 days in advance. Reserve the least expensive flight even if it is not with the individual's frequent flyer airline.
- Investigate Saturday night stay-over requirements. They may not result in savings if lodging and food costs are expensive.
- Reserve a flight that lands at a smaller or less congested airport. Try to schedule meetings at hotels/motels near the airport to eliminate the costs of car rentals or other ground travel. Taxes on car rentals are especially high in foreign countries; taxis and limousines may be cheaper.
- Start a database of the best hotels in each city to which company employees travel most frequently.
- Ask for upgrades on every reservation. Established customers often receive extra amenities.
- Downgrade the size of the rental car unless the car's safety record is worse than average.

PREPARING THE ITINERARY

The **itinerary** is a chronological outline of travel plans prepared for each person who is traveling. Even though the airline prepares a flight itinerary, it is helpful for the traveler to have more detailed information presented on a day-by-day basis.

The planning guide provides an excellent source of information for the itinerary. Itinerary formats may vary, but the information is similar on all. (See Figure 14-3.) This information includes:

- Dates and times of departure and arrival.

HINT: *Include the day of the week as well as date. If the international date line is crossed, be sure the dates are accurate. If the flight crosses time zones, use the local arrival time. Indicate the number of hours of flying time between destinations.*

ITINERARY
SANDRA MCNEELEY
May 6–8, 19—
National Pharmaceutical Sales Conference

WEDNESDAY, MAY 6

1:30 p.m.	Leave Chicago/O'Hare Field
	American Airlines Flight No. 836
	Nonstop; lunch
5:10 p.m.	Arrive Boston/Logan Int.
	Hotel Transportation Provided
	Phone: 617-267-9314
	Hotel: Revere Square Hotel, 9135 Revere Square
	Dates: May 6 and 7
	Confirmation No. 156J92CD (by Joan)
	Guaranteed Arrival

NOTE: *Upon arrival, contact Tom Kennedy regarding conference presentation.*

THURSDAY, MAY 7

7:30 a.m.	Breakfast meeting with Donald Hallahan and Courtney Watson, Revere Square Coffee Shop
	Advertising Review Promotion Campaign

NOTE: *Contact conference headquarters for conference handouts.*

10:00 a.m.	Presentation to National Pharmaceutical Sales Conference, Decker Hall, Revere Square Hotel
11:45 a.m.	Luncheon with Jon Blake, new account, Pullman Room, Regency House
4:00 p.m.	Meeting with all regional sales managers, Hall B, Revere Square Hotel
7:30 p.m.	Conference Banquet, Boston Room, Revere Square Hotel

FRIDAY, MAY 8

7:30 a.m.	Breakfast meeting with Tom Kennedy, Hotel Coffee Shop
10:00 a.m.	Exhibits Review with Sandra Milo, Grand Ballroom, Revere Square Hotel
12:00 noon	Conference Luncheon, Boston Room, Revere Square Hotel
3:10 p.m.	Leave Boston/Logan Int. American Airlines Flight No. 462 Nonstop; snack
5:30 p.m.	Arrive Chicago/O'Hare Airport

Figure 14-3 Sample itinerary.

- Departure and arrival cities.

HINT: *A city may have more than one airport. For example, New York has both La-Guardia and Kennedy. Choose the airport closest to the meeting location. Clearly identify the destination airport on the itinerary.*

- Airline; flight numbers; seat assignment; meals provided.
- Airport transportation; cost; times of operation; telephone numbers of limousine services.
- Car rental agency; type of car; charge card used.
- Lodging accommodations; confirmation numbers; written confirmations; telephone, fax, or Telex numbers; e-mail address; guaranteed arrival time; date reservation was made; name of person who made the reservation; credit card used; services available, such as exercise facilities or secretarial.
- Daily appointments; address; room and building; time of meeting; names of people involved; reason for meeting; contact persons and their office and home telephone numbers.

HINT: *If social engagements are scheduled, indicate the type of dress required.*

- Reminders for each appointment, such as where to find materials needed for each meeting or personal information about the people at the meeting.

HINT: *If an appointment is some distance away from the airport, indicate its distance so the meeting can end on time. Highlight times when a connection time is short or extra materials are needed. Leave a reminder if a task must be completed, such as making a reservation if a return time or date was left open.*

When the itinerary is up to date, prepare two copies for the traveler (one to carry and one for the luggage), one copy for the office files, and one copy for the manager in charge. The traveler may also wish additional copies for family and/or friends.

ORGANIZING TRAVEL DETAILS

Even though materials may be collected as soon as the initial plans for a business trip are in place, it is not always possible to complete everything before the trip begins. Some last-minute tasks include the following:

- Check the tickets against the information in the trip planning folder. Check the itinerary to be sure times, dates, and locations match the tickets.
- Organize materials and supplies that will be needed for the trip. A checklist for each traveler is helpful. The following are examples of items to include on the list:

▲ Copy of itinerary.

▲ Tickets.

▲ Motel or hotel information.

▲ Money, letters of credit, or traveler's checks.

HINT: *If traveler's checks are used, give the traveler a list of the check numbers, to be kept separate from the checks. Keep a second list in the office. Each time a traveler's check is spent, it should be recorded. In case of loss, the check numbers will be available for a refund. (See the section Special Payment Forms in Chapter 13 for a discussion of traveler's checks.)*

▲ List of airline, hotel, and car rental toll-free numbers. In cases of delays or missed connections, the traveler can call the airline directly rather than wait in line to be rebooked by an agent.

▲ Speeches and reports.

HINT: *In case the original copy of a speech gets misplaced, e-mail or fax a copy to a specified individual at the location of the meeting. Send handouts ahead of time so they will not have to be carried on the plane. Allow sufficient time for the items to reach their designated locations and verify that they were received. If the materials are sent to a hotel, indicate the name, date of arrival, and specific meeting for which they will be used. If they are sent to a business, address the package to a specific person in that organization.*

▲ Business cards; company letterhead and envelopes, preaddressed mailing envelopes; company forms, Post-it™ notes, manila envelopes, legal pads, folders; paper clips, stamps, notepads, tape, rubber bands, calendar.

▲ Notes on the area, on special customs, and on etiquette (for foreign countries).

▲ Items that must be delivered; wrapped gifts.

▲ Airline timetables; maps.

▲ Expense account forms; office checks.

HINT: *The traveler may need a reminder to keep track of expenditures, so include a blank expense claim form and an envelope for receipts. If the expense claim is filled out while traveling, the details are more easily remembered than if the traveler waits until returning to the office. Travelers often use business diaries to record expenses.*

▲ Passport; visa.

▲ Vaccination certificates; international driver's license or permit.

▲ Medical prescriptions/medications.

▲ Names and telephone numbers of doctors and emergency contacts.

HINT: *Since medical and eyeglass prescriptions are important and difficult to replace, be sure they are in the materials to be carried by hand. Include a personal health information card with blood type and allergies.*

▲ Credit cards; lost card telephone numbers.

HINT: *A list of card numbers and toll-free numbers of the credit card companies is helpful in case the cards are lost. Prepare a list for the office and one for the traveler.*

▲ Frequent-flyer numbers.

▲ Telephone credit card; emergency telephone numbers.

▲ Portable slide projector or overhead projector.

▲ Slides or transparencies.

HINT: *Audiovisual presentations are less frustrating if the materials are sequenced and numbered before the trip begins.*

▲ Laptop computer; batteries; charger; extra disks, software; summary of keystrokes to activate the modem, fax, printer, and programs.

▲ Portable fax; dictation equipment; calculator; portable printer with paper; spare ink cartridges; portable photocopier; cables.

▲ Adapters for three-prong plugs (some locations may have only two-prong outlets); car battery adapters for electronic equipment, adapters for use in foreign countries.

▲ Surge suppressor; battery packs.

HINT: *Make copies of this list for use in organizing travel materials. Ask the traveler to check the items that need to be packed. Include one completed copy in his or her files and keep one in the office.*

• Contact the airline, travel agency, hotel or motel, or car rental agency if any changes in travel plans are made. Confirm the airline reservation a day before departure.

• Place materials for each appointment in a separate folder and place them in envelopes with clasps. Prepare a label with the company name and date of appointment for each folder as well as for the envelope. Number each envelope in consecutive order according to the information on the itinerary. In case the envelopes are mixed up, the numbers will make it easy to rearrange. Include helpful information such as recent correspondence, an annual report of financial information, names of people contacted previously, officers' names, and product or service updates for each company.

- Place airline tickets and confirmations in a special envelope labeled "Tickets." Do not pack the tickets, passports, visas, or traveler's checks in the luggage that is to be checked. If a ticket is lost or stolen, the traveler must buy a new one. The airline will reimburse the traveler for the cost of this purchase, but it may take as long as four months to receive the refund.

- Contact the airline to determine the number, weight, and size restrictions for luggage that may be carried on the plane. Sort materials in two groups—one for hand-carried luggage and one for checked luggage.

- Make photocopies of airline tickets, passport identification page, driver's license, and credit cards. Keep one set at the office and give the other set to the traveler.

- Obtain a list of people who should be given the traveler's out-of-town number. Make arrangements for contacts with you at regularly scheduled times.

TRAVEL EMERGENCIES AND SAFETY

Travelers can minimize travel safety problems if they are prepared to handle emergency situations. Office professionals can assist travelers by identifying potential hazards and suggesting precautions. Some suggestions are:

- Recommend that an international traveler register with a nearby U.S. embassy or consulate. A family may leave messages with the Citizens Emergency Center, 202-647-5225. The consulate contacts the traveler and follows up with the family. Suggest that the traveler write names of contact people on the pages provided in the passport.

- Establish a procedure for financial emergencies in case of loss or theft of a wallet, handbag, or airline tickets. In foreign countries, consulate offices will assist a traveler in contacting employer or family. Travelers' aid desks at airports can provide some help if money and all identification have been lost or stolen. Funds may be wired through a bank or through Western Union.

- Clarify company legal assistance. In foreign countries a consul can provide names of attorneys but cannot obtain jail releases. If there are complications, call the Citizens Emergency Office at the State Department (202-647-5225) or the International Legal Defense Council (215-977-9982).

- Make copies of the front pages of the passport and include them along with two passport photographs in the traveler's packed materials. Having these extra items as well as a driver's license or birth certificate may speed up the replacement of a lost passport at a consul's office. Also keep a copy in the office files.

HINT: *If a passport is stolen or lost, it should be reported to the police and to the passport division of the nearest U.S. consulate. The consul will need the police report and positive proof of citizenship.*

- Record airline ticket numbers and date and place of issue on the itinerary. This information is also helpful if the airline ticket is lost or stolen and a replacement is necessary—the traveler reports the loss to the airline's refund department, completes a form, and sends it to the credit card company for reimbursement.

- Record numbers of traveler's checks and keep the list at the office. Request the telephone numbers and the procedures for reporting and replacing lost or stolen traveler's checks from the company selling them. All companies do not have the same procedures. Report the loss to police and the company that sold the checks.

- Report credit card losses to the police and to the company issuing the card. Keep a list of these corporate credit card telephone numbers available. Send a copy with the traveler so card losses can be reported promptly.

- Reserve a window seat or one near the rear of the plane when traveling through high-risk countries. Passengers in first-class and aisle seats are often targeted by hijackers.

- Make reservations at hotels and motels with good security. Travel agents can check safety factors for you. Concierge floors or business centers often have restricted access or special security features. Other security features include plastic access cards (instead of keys), 24-hour front desk service, and inside entry to motel rooms.

- Remind travelers to take these precautions while staying at hotels:

  ▲ Do not open a hotel/motel door to a stranger. Verify with the front desk if a potential visitor announces "Room Service" and you haven't ordered any.

  ▲ Use the door locks and chains. Never leave the door to the room ajar.

  ▲ Check the locks on deck or patio doors and windows to be sure they work and have locks.

  ▲ Locate a fire escape. Check the number of doors to the escape (in case of poor visibility because of smoke).

▲ Check with the concierge or front desk about the safety of areas around the hotel before walking or jogging alone.

▲ Use the hotel safe for important papers and valuables.

▲ Request that check-in personnel write the room number on paper rather than announce it.

▲ Do not use the "Make Up Room" sign. Call housekeeping to tell them when to make up the room. (This sign is an obvious disclosure that no one is in the room.)

▲ Do not use cabs that are not legitimate. Ask someone at the hotel to suggest a reputable taxi company.

▲ Carry the name of the hotel with you. It helps with pronunciation or if you forget the hotel's name and address.

▲ Use luggage labels with last name and initials only and the company address.

• Remind travelers who are driving to take these precautions:

▲ Keep car doors locked when driving and when leaving the car.

▲ Avoid rest areas that are unattended or that have few people in them. Choose well-lit gas stations and pay phones.

▲ Rent a vehicle that does not advertise "rental car" by license or company identification.

▲ Request an in-car telephone when reserving a rental car.

▲ Contact the police in case of a breakdown. Do not leave the car if someone stops to help. Know how the rental car works *before* you leave the car rental agency.

▲ Understand metric speed and mileage used in other countries. See Tables 14-2 and 14-3.

▲ Inform the office of any route or destination changes.

• Include identification and an itinerary inside checked luggage as well as in carry-on items. Do not leave baggage out of sight. Travelers should contact the airline when bags are missing and complete a written report. It is necessary to have the claim checks and to describe the luggage. Airlines reimburse passengers if baggage is lost or damaged, although some items are exempt from reimbursement (such as electronic and photographic equipment). For some employees, trip cancellation insurance may be an appropriate safeguard.

- Recommend that expensive jewelry and watches be left at home when traveling. Dress should be conservative. Outward displays of wealth attract thieves and muggers.
- Do not discuss travel plans with callers or people coming in to the office. Take their messages and relay the information to appropriate individuals. This practice protects both the traveler and the family.
- Book flights that do not make connections in airports with unacceptable security. Open areas and areas around lockers and telephone booths are not the safest places in airports.
- Contact the American consulate if serious disturbances break out while you are in a foreign country.

COMPLETING FOLLOW-UP TASKS

Well-planned business travel includes monitoring the office tasks that must be completed after a manager's absence. While the manager is away, the office professional assumes responsibility for the daily office tasks necessary to operate efficiently. When the manager returns, the office professional often prepares the expense report and follows up on the tasks resulting from the trip.

Handling Tasks During a Manager's Absence

You should decide which tasks the manager must handle upon returning to the office and which you can handle without immediate supervision. The following suggestions will assist you in organizing work so time is used efficiently.

- Maintain a day-by-day activities list. Highlight the priority action items to alert the manager who calls the office regularly. Compile questions that need to be asked when he or she calls. Identify the best time to contact the manager. Obtain fax numbers and e-mail addresses for the places where the manager has scheduled meetings. Clarify how paychecks or money transfers should be handled *before* the trip begins.
- Understand the parameters of authority while the manager is away from the office. Discuss emergency procedures and delegation of tasks *before* he or she leaves. Know who has been authorized to handle emergencies and to make major company decisions. When another manager has been designated to be in charge, be sure all pertinent items and telephone calls are directed to that person. Know who has the authority to sign paperwork.
- Maintain folders for mail received and actions taken. Label the folders as follows:

  ▲ Immediate attention
  ▲ Actions completed

HINT: *Maintain a log of each task or action taken. For easy reference, attach this log to the inside of the "Actions completed" folder. Include a copy of the paperwork connected with each action.*

> ▲ General reading.
>
> ▲ General correspondence.
>
> ▲ Signature/approval required.
>
> ▲ Phone calls; visitors; appointments made; activities in the office.

- Compose routine correspondence as needed. Sign the letters as follows:
    Sincerely yours,
    Barbara Williams
    Executive Assistant to J. T. Todd
- Forward mail, use e-mail, or fax items to predesignated locations. Maintain a record of these items along with dates they were forwarded. Keep copies in a folder labeled "Items sent to (name)." If mailing items, number each item and inform the manager of the number of items enclosed. Indicate the number and type of items being forwarded and keep a list for the office files.
- Maintain a list of all telephone calls and all appointments made each day. Prioritize the calls and keep a list that will be helpful to a manager. Always update the appointment calendars. Place in parentheses to identify they were made in the manager's absence. As directed, cancel and reschedule appointments and committee meetings during the manager's absence.

Completing Expense Reports

Completing expense reports is another task that requires attention after a trip is over. Some businesses require receipts for all company money spent; others have per diem allowances, which require only receipts for expenses above the limits. Follow explicitly the company guidelines for categorizing travel expenses. If you have questions about travel expenses, discuss them with the person submitting the expenses. Study company policy and ask for clarification when needed.

When filling out expense reports, you should:

- Complete the expense claim paperwork as quickly as possible. If a receipt is missing or a gap in activities is evident, it will be easier for the manager to remember the event now rather than later.
- Use spreadsheet software or software designed to set up expense reports.
- Review the receipts and notes made by the manager while traveling. If any part of the trip was canceled, check the monthly credit card statements carefully for excess charges.

- Categorize the receipts by transportation, registration, food, lodging, business entertainment, and miscellaneous (tips, tolls, parking, telephone and fax charges, secretarial services, postage charges).

HINT: *Expense report software allows travelers to dial a toll-free number, which is always available, to report expenses. The program then checks the figures, matches them to the limits set by the company, and recommends payment. The program offers several options for expense report formats.*

- Attach all required receipts to the expense claim forms. The IRS requires receipts for expenses of $25 and over. Make copies of each receipt for the files. Keep these receipts for five years. Legitimate business expenses include the following:

  ▲ Transportation (airline, shuttle, railroad, bus, taxi, limousine, or rapid transit); car rentals; automobile costs at the current IRS rates or established company rates per mile; parking fees; flight insurance

  ▲ Lodging

  ▲ Laundry and cleaning costs; telephone, fax, mail, and shipping charges; business supplies

  ▲ Exhibit charges; conference registration fees

  ▲ Conference room charges

  ▲ Business entertainment expenses

  ▲ Meals, tips

- Indicate the type of entertainment, names of clients (titles and companies represented), dates, location (city, state, and street location), duration, and the purpose of the meeting when itemizing the business entertainment expenses on the claim form. The IRS reviews these amounts very carefully and specifies that they must relate to the business being conducted. The expenses may be incurred directly before or after a business activity takes place as well as during the activity. File the detailed written documentation with a copy of the expense report.

HINT: *Travel, Entertainment, and Gift Expenses, a booklet published by the IRS, lists rules for handling deductible travel expenses. You can obtain a copy from the IRS or, in many cities, from the public library. For up-to-date rulings on spousal travel deductions and requirements, refer the traveler to a tax adviser.*

- Compare the total expense incurred with the cash advance made. If money is owed to the company, get a check for the difference from the traveler and attach it to the expense report.
- Review the completed expense claim carefully. Check all calculations at least twice. Obtain the necessary signatures and submit the claim for payment. It is important

to have the necessary documentation and to be sure the claim is accurate the first time it is submitted so reimbursements will not be delayed.

Handling Post-Travel Tasks

When the traveler returns to the office, numerous tasks will need completion. Some suggestions for handling these follow-up activities include:

- Avoid scheduling lengthy, important meetings the first day or two after the trip.
- Explain what activities have taken place during the traveler's absence. Schedule time on your appointment calendar to discuss the items in the "Immediate attention" and "Actions completed" folders.
- Compose thank-you letters for courtesies that were extended to the traveler during the trip. Write the appropriate follow-up letters. Send gifts when appropriate.
- Replace all materials that were removed from the files for use during the business trip. The checklists of materials that were packed for the trip provide a reminder of those items that were taken out of the office. If necessary, prepare computer files or folders for new contacts or subjects that were the result of the trip.
- Record comments about travel and hotel preferences in the travel preference folder.
- Contact the airline's consumer affairs office to file a complaint or report on good service. Complaints may also be made to the U.S. Department of Transportation, Consumer Affairs Division, Room 10405, 400 Seventh Street SW, Washington, DC 20590 (202-366-2220). To report safety matters, call the Federal Aviation Administration (800-255-1111).
- Contact the home office of the car rental agency or call the American Car Rental Association (202-223-2118) to file a complaint about a car rental.

CHAPTER 15

MEETING

PLANNING

AND

MANAGEMENT

Successful meetings are the result of careful planning and management. There are two types of meetings. A **formal meeting** is a structured, planned meeting with a prepared agenda, such as an annual sales meeting, yearly conference, or convention. An **informal meeting** is generally held on company premises and can be held regularly or called at the last minute.

PLANNING A MEETING

Whether the meeting is formal or informal, the process of planning for a meeting is the same. Certain questions must be answered by the person calling the meeting so that the meeting planner can act:

- What is the purpose of the meeting?
- How long will the meeting run?
- Who should attend?
- What equipment and aids will be needed?
- Where should the meeting be held?
- When is the best time to hold the meeting?

To determine the time and place of the meeting, you need to notify participants of the meeting and determine their availability. Reserve at least three convenient dates and times. Ask them to hold these times open until they are called back later in the day to confirm the meeting's date and time. After contacting all participants, review the schedule to see what date and time are acceptable to all. You may have to undertake this process several times to arrive at an acceptable date and time.

Depending on the complexity of the meeting, scheduling, budget, and other forms may be necessary. Such meeting forms may be available through the company or, if not, an office supply store may carry standard forms. The American Management Association produces a manual, *Conference and Workshop Planner's Manual*, that contains sample planning schedule, budget, equipment and supply checklist, registration form, and speaker-appraisal forms.

Meeting Functions

The functions involved in planning and running a meeting depend on how the organization operates, the type of meeting, and whether the planning and execution of the meeting rests with one person or with committees. All or some of the following functions must be addressed in planning a meeting:

- Budget.
- Agenda.
- Attendees.
- Meeting notices and agendas.
- Guests, speakers, or program participants.
- Site and facilities.
- Equipment and audiovisuals.
- Exhibits and demonstrations.
- Refreshments and meals.
- Minutes and proceedings.

Notification of Meeting Participants

Notification of participants can be made by telephone, mail, or computer through e-mail or network communication system, if available. The meeting planner should make a list of those to be notified, make sure all have been informed, and check responses so that a final list of attendees can be prepared. Participants should be informed of the day, time, and place of the meeting, the topic to be discussed, and the identity of other participants. An agenda and supplementary material should also be distributed; for example, directions to the meeting location are often provided.

In addition, supplementary material should be gathered for the meeting. The meeting room should have enough chairs, pads, pencils, and paper. All charts and graphic material should be displayed, and any audiovisual equipment and/or computer technology should be checked and set up for use.

Agenda

An agenda is a list of all matters to be brought up at the meeting. Agendas vary with the type of meeting. Informal meeting agendas simply list the items to be discussed during the meeting. Formal meeting agendas detail times, events, speakers, and locations of events.

HINT: *All papers and documents pertaining to matters that will be discussed at the next meeting should be kept in a meeting folder. The folder should contain copies of the meeting notice, a list of those to whom notices were sent, drafts of resolutions to be taken up at the meeting, and an outline of the minutes of the last meeting. An agenda can be prepared from material accumulated in the current meeting folder.*

In formal meetings, the bylaws of an organization usually state the order of business of the meeting, and an agenda can be prepared from this model. A typical agenda for a director's meeting might include:

(a)   **MEETING OF THE HIGHER EDUCATION**
               ADVISORY COMMITTEE
                        May 17, 19—

                        AGENDA
1. Discuss latest product proposal.
2. Review new product literature.
3. Update list of potential clients.
4. Report on previous sales calls to top six universities.

(b)   **SALES MEETING CONFERENCE**

                     Monday, March 16, 19—

8–9 a.m.	Breakfast	Tiffany Room
9–10:30 a.m.	Opening Session	Ballroom A
	James Hughes, Senior VP	
10:30–11 a.m.	Break	
11 a.m.–Noon	Selling to Higher Education	Ballroom A
	Peter Mann, Consultant	
Noon–1 p.m.	Lunch	Terrace Room

                     Tuesday, March 17, 19—

8–9 a.m.	Breakfast	Terrace Room
9–10 a.m.	Marketing Communications	Ballroom A
	Tina Sanford, Mgr.	
10–Noon	Individual seminars	
	(Consult packet for seminar	
	information and locations)	
Noon–1 p.m.	Lunch	Evergreen Room

Figure 15-1 Sample agendas for (a) informal meeting, (b) formal meeting.

- Reading of the minutes of the last directors' meeting.
- Presentation of reports of officers and committees.
- Adoption of a resolution approving the minutes of executive committee meetings.
- Current business.

The agenda should list each item to be acted upon. A copy of the agenda with copies of all minutes, reports, and resolutions attached should be furnished to each participant. (See Figure 15-1.)

Meeting Coordination Software

The personal computer can be a valuable tool when planning meetings. Spreadsheets, project management software, personal information management or desktop management software, and scheduling software can be used to coordinate and keep track of the many details. (Refer to Chapter 8 for detailed information on these software programs.) A scheduling program specifically designed for meeting planners is recommended for anyone who spends considerable time with this type of activity. This type of software integrates e-mail, calendaring, and scheduling functions. Generally, you can have access to meeting participants' schedules, confirm room space, arrange for equipment, and send meeting notices via e-mail. Some schedule software programs include a "meeting wizard" function to guide you through the steps of the meeting planning process.

Meeting Room Facilities and Supplies

As soon as a date for the meeting has been determined, a meeting room must be selected. Most companies have conference rooms available for small meetings of company personnel. For large meetings, an off-site area may be selected. This may entail reserving a ballroom in a hotel or teleconference rooms in a number of cities. In selecting a meeting site several factors must be considered:

- Size of group and purpose of meeting.
- Budget.
- Ambience, acoustics, privacy.
- Ventilation.
- Support services (e.g., catering, audiovisual equipment).
- Dependability of service.

Once a meeting room has been selected, you must determine how the room is to be set up. There are numerous arrangements to select from, depending on the number of people participating and the size of the room itself. Common room setups include:

Theater style: Suitable for large audiences; designed for lecture presentation and/or audiovisuals; speaker is visible, on raised platform.

Classroom style: Suitable for taking notes; works well with long, narrow room; attention directed to speaker.

Boardroom style: Good for small groups; communication facilitated; formal setting.

U-shape style: Allows speaker access to each participant; good for medium-size group; promotes interaction.

T-shape style: Good for panel discussion; accommodates small groups.

Roundtable style: Informal; prompts discussion; good for small group work.

Meeting-room facilities should be checked for lighting, heating, and ventilation. Microphones, slide projectors, computers, overhead projectors, multimedia equipment, video machines, screens, and the like need to be properly set up and working. During the meeting, be sure to provide enough memo pads, pencils, water and glasses, and ashtrays (if smoking is permitted). If coffee or tea is to be served, check your supplies and equipment (if the meeting is held at the company's facilities) or arrange for them to be served by someone else.

HINT: *Several publications are available as references for meeting facilities. They include* Successful Meetings, *published by Bill Communications, Inc., 633 Third Avenue, New York, NY 10017, and* Official Meeting Facilities Guide, *published by Reed Travel Group, 500 Plaza Drive, Secaucus, NJ 07096. Professional organizations for meeting planners can also provide information and insight into meeting planning and facility selection.*

APPLICATIONS OF ELECTRONIC COMMUNICATIONS

Communication systems can be used to hold informal or formal meetings, ranging from 2 people to 25,000. In each case, technology can play a vital part in relaying information.

One form of meeting is teleconferencing. With the rising costs of travel, the increased demands on executives' time, and the global emphasis in business, teleconferencing allows people at different locations to hear and see one another without leaving their offices. Teleconferences can be broken into three general categories: audiographic, audio, and video. Although these methods differ in the technologies used, they have several things in common, they:

- Use a telecommunications channel and station equipment.
- Link people at multiple locations.
- Are interactive, providing two-way communications.
- Are dynamic, allowing the active participation of users.

Audiographic Teleconferences

Audiographic teleconferences transmit words, numbers, or graphics. Such teleconferences include the following:

Desktop computer conferences: Individuals use computer terminals and telephone lines to access a host computer to communicate with one another. Participants do not have to be gathered at telephones or in conference rooms at the same time. They input their comments on the computer at their convenience, as long as the comments are given prior to the deadline established by the conference manager. The advantage of a computer conference is that all participants can review and comment on any material filed in the host computer on their own schedules, in their offices.

Slow-scan video: A camera scans an image from top to bottom for transmission over a phone line to a receiving monitor. It is best used for transmission of documents such as blueprints and schematics.

Freeze-frame video: Freeze-frame or slow-scan television adds visuals to an audio teleconference. Graphics are placed in front of a standard closed-circuit TV camera. The camera is connected to a scan converter that changes the picture into a still image that is then sent over a telephone line or other link.

Faxes: Faxing involves the transmission of an exact copy of something over communications lines.

Electronic blackboard: Similar to a classroom blackboard, this device sends graphics over an ordinary telephone line. Meeting participants write on the board, and the writing appears on a monitor (screen) in the other locations.

Electronic mail (e-mail): This is a message system for sending information from one person to others. E-mail systems are usually programs on computer networks.

Teleconferences

Telecommunications technologies are playing a vital role in linking business executives worldwide. Electronic meetings are now able to take place in the office or in the conference room and are referred to as **teleconferencing.** Computer, audio, and video teleconferencing involves specialized equipment that links two or more locations and provides for interactive participation among the users. Office assistants often have the dual roles of meeting facilitator and technology expert. Questions such as the following need to be asked:

- What software are the participants using?
- Are the video boards compatible?
- What is the baud rate of the modems?
- Is a conferencing bridge service available (when more than two sites are involved)?
- Is a public video conferencing room available?

Computer-based conferences allow participants to work together on a variety of documents from any distance via the personal computer and a computer modem using *groupware software.* (See Chapter 8 for details on this type of software.) This type of meeting lacks the advantage of face-to-face communications. To counter this disadvantage, graphical images called *avatars* (also referred to as agents, characters, or bots) are used to represent each person on the computer screen. *Virtual chat rooms* can be created, using the *avatars* to represent participants in an electronic meeting working on group projects. Digital photographs or any graphic can be used for an *avatar.*

Audio teleconferences involve the transmission of sound only. Generally, the office assistant's role is connecting a number of people from various locations at a given time. This is usually done through the company's telephone carrier or a telecommunication company's bridge service. Typical equipment requirements include an ordinary telephone for an individual or a speaker-phone when two or more persons are present in a room. Larger audioconferences use a special microphone, such as the Polycom SoundStation™, to effectively facilitate a group audioconference. This type of system provides full 360-degree coverage within a room.

Video teleconferencing allows one or more people to interact via a television camera from the *desktop* or a *conference room*. **Desktop videoconferencing** has the advantage of allowing participants to see one another and concurrently interact on documents, such as spreadsheets or reports. Participants use a PC equipped with a videoconferencing software package, a video camera built into the video display screen or attached to it, and a headset for voice communications. **Video conference rooms** have more sophisticated cameras and audio equipment, and they provide for larger numbers of participants. Two pieces of specialized hardware are often used in conference rooms: (1) a *video visualizer,* which is used to input documents, photographs, slides, and 3-D objects directly into the video production equipment, and (2) a *smart whiteboard,* which uses lasers to scan the surface and report any digital input to an attached computer. Most whiteboard software incorporate special tools for annotating images and connect one site to another via a pair of modems. Using a special modem and software, voice and data can be combined into one simultaneous connection, allowing participants to send a file or a remote presentation and talk at the same time.

Using Electronic Equipment in the Meeting Room

The workplace is shifting from one-person, one-task operations to group interactions and meetings. As a result, technology is being used more and more to bring people together. Meetings now include sophisticated electronic equipment. Video conferencing is becoming the affordable alternative to project reports, planning sessions, sales training, product development meetings, and financial reviews.

There are a number of organizations that specialize in teleconferencing, providing services ranging from consultanting to installing a complete system. The use of outside sources depends on the degree of involvement expected of office professionals as well as their knowledge of the equipment. Users of such equipment should expect to be trained by professionals. Training includes control panel operations (the "buttons" used to operate the equipment), graphics capabilities, seating arrangements, room scheduling, and troubleshooting.

As an office professional, you may be expected to prepare the visuals to be used during the meeting. Try to keep them simple, bold, colorful, accurate, and informative. Always make them easy to read by mixing upper- and lowercase letters and justifying the left margin. The following guidelines will help to make your visuals more readable:

- Minimize the complexity and use one idea per visual.
- Do not be wordy.
- Keep the length of the text short, about six or seven lines per visual.
- Do not crowd the visual with more than one illustration.

- Use words with few syllables, two or three at most.
- Keep the letters large and bold so they can be read from the back of the room.
- Keep the number of type sizes per page limited to a maximum of three.
- Use of a maximum of four colors per visual is recommended.

Several table shapes have been developed for teleconferencing. They include the following:

- Canoe-shaped—an oval table with participants seated side by side along one side.
- Keystone—a solid "V" shaped table, with users sitting along both outside edges facing one another.
- Curved—a table bent in a crescent shape, with users seated on the long edge of the curve.

The canoe and curved formats have the advantage of placing every person the same distance from both cameras and video monitors.

General guidelines for watching a video on a monitor are as follows:

- People should be seated about 10 feet from a 19-inch image and about 9 feet from a 27-inch screen.
- Minimum viewing distance from a standard monitor is two to four times the width of the image. For color monitors, however, viewers must be at least six feet from the image.
- Maximum viewing distance from a monitor is estimated to be between 12 and 14 times the image width.
- Seat placement within 45 degrees of the center of the screen is acceptable.
- A screen should be angled 5 degrees below a viewer's straight vertical line of sight for the best results.
- Seats should directly face a monitor.

Taking Minutes

Minutes are an accurate recording in outline form of the actions that occurred in a meeting. For informal meetings, the minutes should be brief and simple. Formal meetings require more complex minutes.

You may be asked to take minutes during the meeting. Skillful minute-taking is an art that takes practice to develop. Here are some guidelines to follow:

- Get a copy of the agenda beforehand if you were not the person who prepared it. If technical or unfamiliar jargon is used, find a way to familiarize yourself with common terms. Minutes of past meetings, handouts for the meetings, and glossaries of relevant subjects are appropriate sources.

- Take thorough notes.

HINT: *Consider using a small tape recorder. You will have to get permission to do so from every participant. If even one objects, do not use it.*

- Record verbatim all resolutions, amendments, decisions, and conclusions.

HINT: *A resolution is a formal statement of the group, approved by a vote of the group. After a resolution is drafted and approved, it must be signed, distributed, and incorporated into the minutes. Resolutions may be for achievements, sympathy, promotion of special events, etc. Each paragraph in a resolution begins with the words WHEREAS or RESOLVED, either in capital letters or underlined.*

- Record all important statements verbatim.
- Use eye-catching symbols to mark any item that may need action.
- Write a rough but complete draft as soon as possible and submit it for review to the supervisor in charge of the meeting.
- Transcribe the minutes as soon as possible after the meeting. Do not add your own opinions. Be sure you have the chairperson approve and sign the minutes before they are distributed.
- Send handouts to anyone who was absent from the meeting.
- Include any follow-up meeting information at the bottom of the minutes, such as the date, time, and location.
- Correct the minutes at the next meeting, if necessary. For formal meetings, corrections are made on the official copy with red ink (if possible) and initialed in the margin. Minutes should never be erased or rewritten. If corrections are extensive, they should be written on a separate page and attached to the original minutes. A marginal note should be included at the side of the item in the original minutes indicating a correction is attached.

When putting formal minutes into their final form, use the following outline:

1. Name of group, place, date, and time of meeting.
2. Listing of those present, identifying officers and other officials.
3. Call to order; approval of minutes of previous meeting as is or with corrections and/or amendments.
4. Reports of officers and committees.
5. Unfinished business; discussion, motions.
6. New business and action taken.
7. Motions, including names of those involved in total motion, if amended, and names of seconders.

MEETING OF PLANNING COMMITTEE
September 7, 19—

ATTENDANCE
The monthly meeting of the planning committee was held in the conference room of Manville Hospital at 10 a.m. on September 7, 19—. Dale Stetzer, Vice President of Marketing, presided. Present were Mary Farr, George Rowen, Sue Gates, Ted Smith, and Larry Taylor.

REPORTS/MOTIONS/NEW BUSINESS
1. Sue Gates presented a report on the proposed east wing renovation. Further information is to be given at the October 9 meeting.
2. George Rowen reported on the progress of the sewer project. Completion is expected by early spring, 19—.
3. A new service contract was approved for the computer equipment.

MEETING DETAILS
The next meeting of the planning committee will be held on October 9 at 10 a.m., Conference Room A, Manville Hospital.

ADJOURNMENT
The meeting was adjourned at 12 noon.

_____
Peter Ren, Recorder

Figure 15-2 Sample minutes.

8. Date and location of next meeting.
9. Adjournment and time of adjournment.
10. Signature of secretary and, if required, the chairperson.

Corporate minutes should be typed on plain white paper (watermarked for official corporate stockholders' and directors' meetings). If the minutes are brief, double-space the body and triple-space between paragraphs. If the minutes are long, they should be single-spaced for the text and double-spaced between headings. When side subheadings are used, it is not necessary to indent the paragraphs. Allow a one-and-one-half-inch left margin and a one-inch right margin. The title should be capitalized and centered. (See Figure 15-2.)

When filing the minutes, be sure to include all handouts and the agenda for future reference. By law, corporations are required to keep minutes of stockholders' and directors'

1. Three months prior to meeting:

_____ a. Book a meeting location.

_____ b. Identify and contract with support services

_____ c. Notify attendees regarding details of meeting

_____ d. Prepare travel arrangements for attendees,

_____ e. Identify local events and get information.

_____ f. Plan a program of formal and recreational events

_____ g. Plan a topical program and identify speakers.

_____ h. Invite speakers and VIP's.

2. Three weeks before meeting:

_____ a. Confirm menus, room setups, and supplies with the hotel, in writing

_____ b. Reconfirm speakers, formal and recreational events.

_____ c. Mail agendas and other pertinent information.

_____ d. Reconfirm attendees.

3. One week before your meeting:

_____ a. Ship material to hotel for delivery at least 24 hours ahead of your arrival.

_____ b. Confirm arrival of materials prior to your departure to the meeting.

_____ c. Make arrangements to collect from the hotel, pack and ship back to your office any unused materials.

_____ d. Bring a master set of handout materials with you and make arrangements for duplicating additional materials if necessary.

_____ e. Confirm food and beverage requirements at least 48 hours prior to the meeting.

_____ f. Bring your own supplies of tape, shipping labels, paper clips, pens, pencils, note pads, badges, scissors, masking tape, magic markers, etc.

4. Upon arrival at the meeting location:

_____ a. Meet with the convention coordinator and confirm all details and walk through the meeting site.

_____ b. Confirm with the audiovisual coordinator that needed equipment will be available.

_____ c .Meet with the bell captain and the maitre d'.

_____ d. Confirm the attendees list with the front desk and the room assignments if possible.

_____ e. Arrange for any gifts that are to be delivered to the attendees' rooms, e.g., fruit basket.

_____ f. Double check that meeting room locations are posted in the hotel lobby.

Figure 15-3 Meeting planner's checklist.

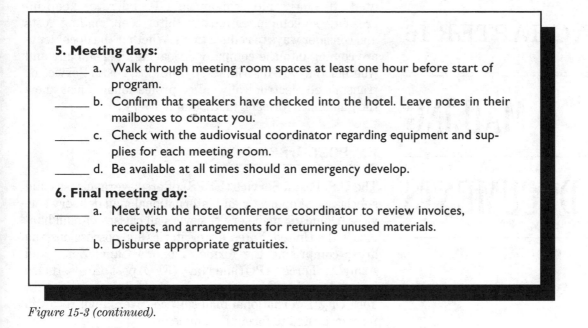

5. Meeting days:

_____ a. Walk through meeting room spaces at least one hour before start of program.

_____ b. Confirm that speakers have checked into the hotel. Leave notes in their mailboxes to contact you.

_____ c. Check with the audiovisual coordinator regarding equipment and supplies for each meeting room.

_____ d. Be available at all times should an emergency develop.

6. Final meeting day:

_____ a. Meet with the hotel conference coordinator to review invoices, receipts, and arrangements for returning unused materials.

_____ b. Disburse appropriate gratuities.

Figure 15-3 (continued).

meetings. Such minutes are considered legal records and should be guarded against tampering.

Follow-Up Activities

After the meeting, you must follow up on a number of details, including distribution of the minutes to proper individuals, collection of any extra materials, review of charges and receipts, and writing of "thank you" letters to speakers, participants, and hotel staff (if appropriate). It is also important to maintain an accurate meeting folder for reference.

The checklist in Figure 15-3 is a helpful reminder to keep in front of you throughout the process of planning for a meeting.

CHAPTER 16

MAILING

DOCUMENTS

Once documents have been created, they must be distributed efficiently and economically. Postal rates keep increasing, so companies must monitor their mailing costs and consider ways to reduce them. Whether the documents are coming into the company or leaving the company and whether they are distributed by the U.S. Postal Service or transmitted electronically, office professionals must know the guidelines for each method of delivery.

U.S. POSTAL SERVICE

The U.S. Postal Service (USPS) offers several classes and subclasses of domestic and international mail delivery services. Domestic mail service covers all classes of mail handled in the United States, its territories and possessions, the areas comprising the former Panama Canal Zone, and Army/Air Force (APO) and Navy (FPO) post offices. It also includes mail for delivery to the United Nations in New York City. International mail service covers mail received from or posted to foreign countries.

The U.S. Postal Service Classification Reform of 1996 provides changes in the rates, the classes of mail, and the procedures for preparing mailings. For detailed information about the USPS changes, check the Domestic Mail Manual (Issue 50), which is available from the Superintendent of Documents, P.O. Box 371954, Pittsburgh, PA 15250-7954 (202-783-3238) on a subscription basis or from local post offices. Max It also outlines classification reform and is available from USPS, 475 L'Enfant Plaza SW, Washington, DC 20260-2405.

Local post offices have copies of *Time-Saving Information for Your Business*. To be placed on a mailing list to receive a free USPS newsletter, write to Memo to Mailers, National Customer Support Center, U.S. Postal Service, 6060 Primacy Pkwy, #101, Memphis, TN 38188-0001. Both items include updates on mailing services and helpful tips for handling mail.

Each company must carefully analyze its mailing operations. To assist with the classification reforms and future special service changes, check with the Postal Business Centers in metropolitan areas nationwide. Your local post office can give you the telephone numbers of the centers. Local postal service personnel offer informational meetings designed to help mailers understand how they can cut costs under the Classification Reform.

First-Class Mail

First-class mail consists of such items as letters; postal cards (sold by the post office); postcards (sold commercially); bills; typewritten, handwritten, or photocopied messages; price lists; statements of account; checks; printed forms; and computer-generated matter with the characteristics of business or personal messages.

Sealed first-class mail items are not subject to postal inspections. First-class mail may be sent special delivery, certified, COD, or registered. The sender may also obtain a certificate of mailing. (See Special Services for Domestic and International Mail.)

To qualify as first-class, items must weigh 11 ounces or less and be at least 0.007 inch thick. Items that are ¼ inch thick or less must be at least 3½ inches high, at least 5 inches long, and rectangular in shape. First-class postal rates are based on weight, with the charge for the first ounce higher than the charges for the second and succeeding ounces. Rates for postcards and postal cards are less than for regular first-class items.

Airmail is no longer a domestic classification, but international mail still uses the airmail classification. The USPS forwards all first-class mail without charge for one year if it is informed of the new address.

HINT: *Less confusion results when companies inform their clients of address changes and complete change-of-address forms furnished by the USPS before they move. Remind employees within the department to complete change-of-address forms if they leave the company and want their mail forwarded.*

First-Class Subclasses and Categories

The two current subclasses of first-class mail are (1) cards and postcards and (2) letters and sealed packages. Each subclass has an automation rate and a nonautomation rate category. Options within these catagories allow mailers to receive reduced rates on bulk first-class mailings. (Bulk mailings are mailings of many pieces.) To qualify for the reduced rates, mailers must do some of the work usually done by the USPS. They must also follow specific USPS procedures and meet certain eligibility requirements. Local post office personnel can assist mailers in selecting the appropriate option and provide information to prepare the mailings accurately. Several of the general requirements are:

- A minimum of 500 items must be in a single mailing.
- The mailer pays an annual fee, which allows the mailer to obtain rate discounts. This fee is not the same as the one-time fee for a permit imprint. The permit imprint allows users to mail items without placing postage on them if payment is made from a previously established deposit account at the post office. The permit imprint may be stamped, copied, or printed on the envelope but not handwritten or typewritten.
- Each piece must include a complete delivery address with correct ZIP code, ZIP + 4 code, or the numbers in the barcode.
- Each piece must be appropriately marked; for example, "Presorted first class."

Table 16-1
WHICH POSTAGE STATEMENT TO USE

IF YOU ARE MAILING THIS TYPE	USE THIS STATEMENT
First-Class (all rates except Priority Mail)	
Permit imprint	3600-R
Postage affixed	3600-P
Priority Mail	
Permit imprint	3605-R
Postage affixed	3605-P
Periodicals	
Regular and science-of-agriculture	3541-R
Nonprofit and classroom	3541-N
Standard Mail (A) (Regular and Enhanced Carrier Route)	
Permit imprint	3602-R
Postage affixed	3602-PR
Standard Mail (A) (Nonprofit)	
Permit imprint	3602-N
Postage affixed	3602-PN
Standard Mail (B) (Parcel Post and Bound Printed Matter)	
Permit imprint	3605-R
Postage affixed	3605-P
Standard Mail (B) (Library Mail and Special Standard Mail)	
Permit imprint	3608-R
Postage affixed	3608-P

Source: The Mailroom Companion, March 1996.

- Mailers must complete forms that indicate the total number of items in the mailing. (See Table 16-1.)

- Letters in the address should be a uniform size, and the line spacing must be consistent. Black ink on a white background is preferred. Check with the Postal Service for use of colored envelopes.

- To obtain the automation rate, mail must be 100 percent delivery-point barcoded. The bar code must be on the addressed side of the envelope or package within the bar code read area. All the Postnet bars have the same width and spacing. Software programs can apply the bar codes to your labels and envelopes. If you use return envelopes or business reply cards, do not forget to include bar codes on them as well. (See Figure 16-1.)

- Letters and postcards must be prepared in 1- or 2-foot trays. The USPS provides bundling materials such as trays, sacks, labels, separator cards, and rubber bands (if needed) without charge.

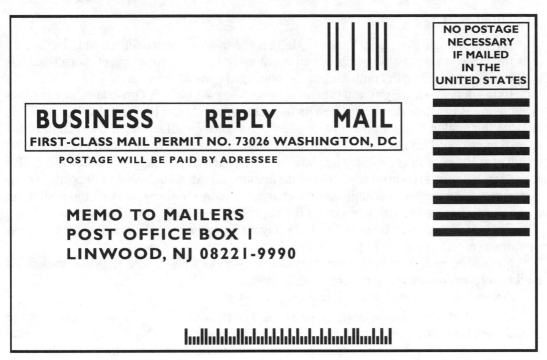

Figure 16-1 Business Reply Mail.

- All customer addresses on automation and presort mail require updating within 6 months of the mailing by using a USPS-approved address update device. To obtain the presorted rates, mailers must use a certified process at least once a year to make sure five-digit ZIP codes are accurate. If you use a software supplier's services, be sure the services or products meet USPS accuracy standards. Call the National Customer Support Center (800-238-3150) for a list of certified software suppliers.

Priority Mail

Priority mail is first-class mail that weighs no more than 70 pounds. Delivery time is listed as one to three days.

Rates depend on the weight of the item and the zone to which it is being mailed. Priority mail offers a flat rate for all material that can fit into a special priority mail envelope. The envelopes are available at local post offices.

Customers may request pickup service and pay one fee per call, not per item. Priority mail packages may be insured or sent COD. Mailers can obtain certificates of mailing. For extra fees, return receipts, restricted delivery, special delivery, certified, and registered services are also possible.

Expedited Mail

Expedited mail (formerly Express Mail), is the fastest service for mailing documents that the USPS provides. Expedited mail is not acceptable for mailings of more than 108 inches in length and girth combined, or for packages over 70 pounds.

Rates depend on weight and type of service. The cost includes insurance against loss or damage. If the item does not reach its destination within the time established, refunds are due the mailer. Expedited mail also offers a flat rate for all material that can fit into a special envelope. This flat-rate service saves time, since the envelope does not have to be weighed at the post office but may be placed with the company's outgoing mail or in a USPS collection box. An expedited mail corporate account allows a company to deposit an estimated amount of expedited mail postage charges. When sending an expedited mail item, write the corporate account number on the appropriate expedited mail label.

Expedited mail may be sent COD. By paying an extra fee, mailers may also request a return receipt, which offers proof of delivery.

Expedited mail is available for international service. The USPS provides expedited mail envelopes, boxes, and tubes at no extra cost.

Several options for expedited mail are available:

Expedited mail custom designed service: The customer signs an agreement with the Postal Service that outlines such specifics as pickup times and days, delivery dates and times, and service levels. The customer receives a guarantee for timely and consistent service according to the individual agreement specifications.

Expedited mail next day service: Two types of service are available: post office to post office (Label A) and post office to addressee (Label B). (See Figure 16-2.) Mail deposited by a cutoff time designated by the local postmaster (often 5 p.m.) is delivered to the addressee the following day, or it may be picked up at the post office if the post office is open for regular service. Expedited mail next day service is not available in every city. Check with the local post office before preparing an item for expedited mail. Every post office has a copy of the Expedited Mail Next Day Service Network Directory. In this directory mailers can locate those post offices with expedited mail next day service.

Periodicals Mail

Publishers and news agents use this service to mail newspapers and periodicals in bulk. To mail single issues of newspapers or magazines, use standard mail (A) or (B).

Periodicals mailers will have to meet higher standards pertaining to circulation and advertising. The item must be published at least four times a year. Publications should have informational printed sheets that are not designed primarily as advertising or as promotional pieces. Circulation records must be available for periodic examination by Postal Service personnel. Subscription orders and receipts are the only enclosures allowed in periodicals mail; other types of enclosures require additional postage. To obtain automation rates, pieces must be barcoded using certified equipment addresses must be matched using approved software.

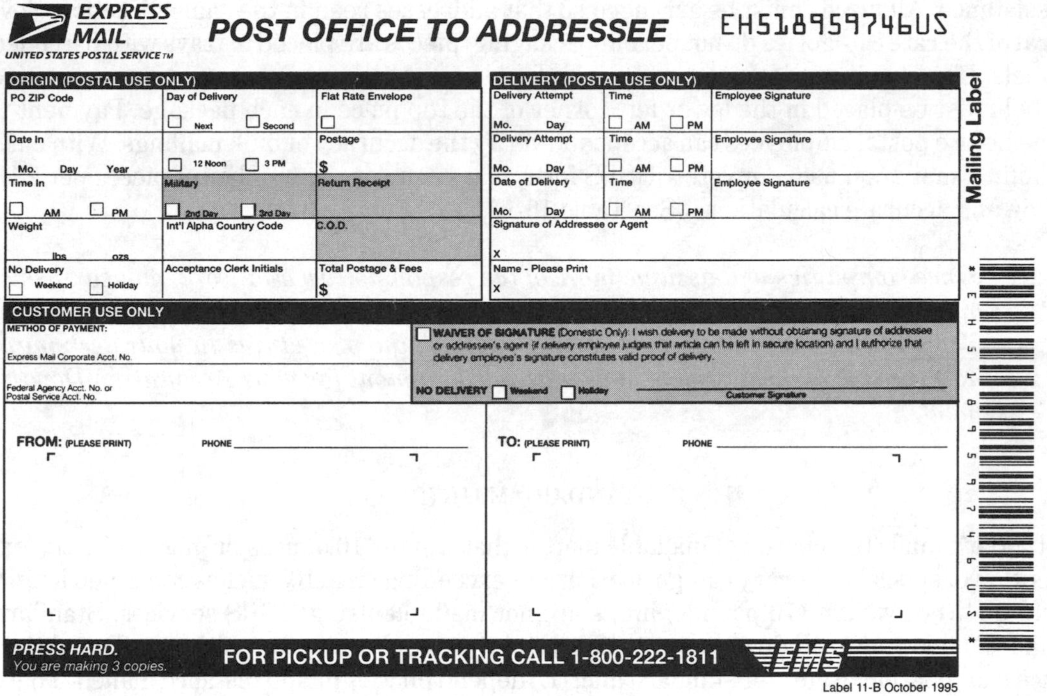

Figure 16-2 USPS Expedited Mail Form (formerly Express Mail).

Standard Mail

Under Classification Reform, standard mail consists of mail previously known as third-class and fourth-class mail. Former third-class mail is reclassified as standard mail (A) and fourth-class mail as standard mail (B). Both standard mail (A) and standard mail (B) have specific eligibility and preparation requirements.

STANDARD MAIL (A)

Circulars, catalogs, booklets, printed matter, and photographs may be sent as standard mail (A). Standard mail (A) rates are available to businesses and qualified nonprofit organizations. The rates for the nonprofit groups are lower than the rates for business mailers. To qualify for standard mail (A) rates, items must weigh less than 16 ounces. Postal Service personnel may inspect standard mail (A), whether it is sealed or unsealed.

Standard mail (A) rates may be used for material with the same general message sent to different addresses. At least 200 pieces or 50 pounds will qualify for bulk-mail rates. The greater the degree of automation assumed by the mailer, the lower the rate for bulk mailings. Special services, such as certified or registered, do not apply for bulk mailings.

Standard Mail (A) must be properly sorted, bundled, labeled, and put in trays or sacks. Mailers have numerous sorting options, so it is wise to check with the local post office for assistance. All pieces must be arranged so that addresses read in the same direction. Several of the rate categories do not permit packaging; pieces are placed in trays with barcoded labels. If packaging is required, material is banded and an appropriate pressure-sensitive label must be placed in the lower left corner of the top piece in each package. Payment is due before postal employees can accept and verify the accuracy of bulk mailings. With each mailing, mailers must complete a USPS form that requires the number of pieces per ZIP code and accurate calculations. (See Table 16-1.)

HINT: *Since companies will assume more of the responsibility and work, you can assist by organizing a set of notes that outline the new procedures under Classification Reform. Fill out a USPS form and file it with the procedures in your desk manual. Always make a copy of your mailing statement for your Accounting Department.*

STANDARD MAIL (B)

Standard mail (B) consists of mailable matter that weighs 16 ounces or more, with the exception of special or library categories. Parcels exceeding size (108 inches combined length and girth) or weight (70 pounds) limits are not mailable using USPS services. Standard mail (B) does not include a guaranteed arrival time, and it may be subject to Postal Service examination. Rates for standard mail (B) depend on weight and distance mailed. There are eight postal zones in the United States; zone charts are available from local post offices.

Standard mail (B) bulk mailings must be separated by zones, and the correct USPS form must accompany each mailing (See Table 16-1). Parcels must weigh the same amount but may be different in size and content for bulk mailings.

Under the standard mail (B) parcel post category, instructions, packing slips, or invoices may go inside a parcel at no extra cost. Attach a letter to the outside of a parcel and pay the first-class rate for the letter and the standard mail (B) rate for the package. Another way to include a letter is to place it inside the package, mark "Letter Enclosed" on the outside of the parcel, and pay the appropriate postal rates for the parcel and letter.

Another standard mail (B) category, bound printed matter, includes promotional, advertising, and educational items. Material must be permanently fastened with at least 90 percent of the sheets imprinted with letters, figures, or characters. For details concerning special rate and library rate categories, check with the local post office. The USPS is planning additional reform proposals for parcels in 1997.

International Mail

The USPS offers land (surface) mail and airmail services to most foreign locations. Information on postal rates and fees is available in the Postal Service publication International Postal Rates and Fees. Companies with extensive international communications should have a copy of the International Mail Manual, which is available from the Superintendent of Documents by subscription.

International mail is classified into several categories. LC mail and AO mail fall under the *postal union* classification of international mail.

LC mail (lettres et cartes): Items include letters and letter packages, postcards, and aerogrammes. The weight limit for LC mail is 4 pounds.

AO mail (autres objets): Items consist of *printed matter* and *small packets*. Printed matter includes identical copies of material reproduced by computers or a process other than handwriting or typewriting. Small packets consist of small merchandise items, samples, or nonpersonal documents.

Parcel post (colis postaux): This classification is similar to domestic standard mail (B). It includes items that do not require LC rates, and it is possible to insure the items. Customs regulations are under the jurisdiction of destination cities.

Express mail international service (EMS): This is the fastest service available through the USPS to foreign countries. Weight limits and the allowed contents vary depending on individual country restrictions. Most deliveries are made within three days.

International surface air lift (ISA): This system for sending all types of printed matter is faster than surface mail. Mailers take their bulk items to designated airports (a list of these airports is available at local post offices) to be flown to the designated foreign countries. Once the items arrive, they are sent by surface mail delivery to the addressees. Costs are lower than airmail shipments. Rates vary from country to country.

Global priority mail: This new service is for correspondence and packages that are important but not urgent; the maximum weight is 4 pounds. It is processed with expedited mail and receives priority handling. The envelopes are flat rate, and a customs label must be placed on packages weighing 1 pound or more. Although the USPS strives for delivery within four to five days, this time is not guaranteed. The USPS does not provide tracing or tracking of global priority mail.

SPECIAL SERVICES FOR DOMESTIC AND INTERNATIONAL MAIL

As an office professional, you should understand the special services provided by the USPS. Since these services often involve fees, purchase only those that are necessary.

The forms for domestic and international special services are not the same.

Business Reply Mail/Courtesy Reply Mail

Business reply mail consists of postage-paid envelopes or postal cards that are enclosed with other mailings to encourage recipients to respond. Mailers pay postage only on replies that are returned. Mailers pay the regular first-class postage plus a handling charge. Courtesy reply mail is a preprinted envelope or card that is provided to the sender, but the addressee pays the postage. Such envelopes are often enclosed with invoices.

Business reply mail users require a permit, which is available for an annual fee. The words "First-Class Mail Permit No. xxx" and the name of the post office issuing the permit (city and state) must appear on the address side. (See Figure 16-1.) In a few countries, an international business reply service is available.

Certificate of Mailing

The certificate shows that the Postal Service accepted the item and provides proof that an item was mailed. (See Figure 16-3.) It does not indicate that the item arrived at its destination and does not include insurance. The certificate is available for all classes of mail, and it applies to domestic and international mail. The person sending the item completes the certificate of mailing and pays the fee.

Certified Mail

Certified mail is a domestic mail service that provides proof of mailing and delivery for items sent by first-class or priority mail. The destination post office keeps a record of delivery for two years; the post office where the item was mailed does not keep a record.

For an additional fee, a return receipt or a restricted delivery receipt is available to the mailer as evidence that the delivery occurred. Mailers of certified mail may request special delivery service for an extra fee.

HINT: *The Postal Service provides blank certified mail receipts. Enter the addressee's name and address. Check the boxes indicating the appropriate receipts needed.*

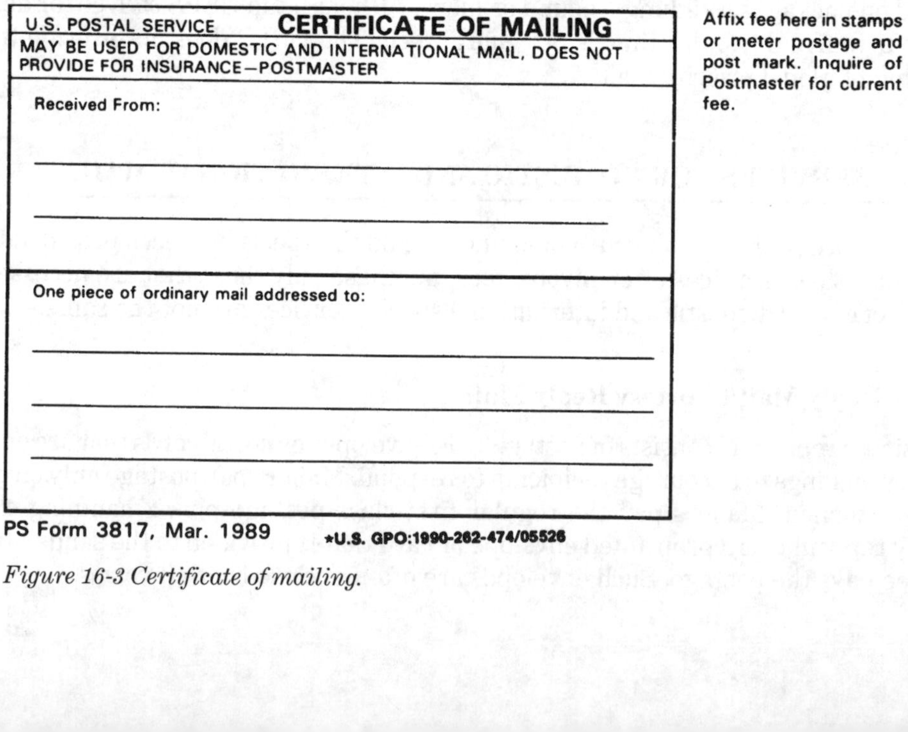

U.S. POSTAL SERVICE **CERTIFICATE OF MAILING**	Affix fee here in stamps or meter postage and post mark. Inquire of Postmaster for current fee.
MAY BE USED FOR DOMESTIC AND INTERNATIONAL MAIL, DOES NOT PROVIDE FOR INSURANCE—POSTMASTER	
Received From:	
One piece of ordinary mail addressed to:	

PS Form 3817, Mar. 1989   ★U.S. GPO:1990-262-474/05526

Figure 16-3 Certificate of mailing.

P 281 764 159

US Postal Service
Receipt for Certified Mail
No Insurance Coverage Provided.
Do not use for International Mail *(See reverse)*

Sent to	
Street & Number	
Post Office, State, & ZIP Code	
Postage	$
Certified Fee	
Special Delivery Fee	
Restricted Delivery Fee	
Return Receipt Showing to Whom & Date Delivered	
Return Receipt Showing to Whom, Date, & Addressee's Address	
TOTAL Postage & Fees	$
Postmark or Date	

PS Form **3800**, April 1995

Fold at line over top of envelope to
the right of the return address

CERTIFIED

P 281 764 159

MAIL

Figure 16-4 Certified mail.

Enter the certified number on the return receipt card, self-address it, and attach it to the item being certified. Mark the date, attach the correct postage, and mail at any post office or deposit in any USPS mailbox. (See Figure 16-4.)

Return Receipt/Restricted Delivery

A return receipt signifies to the mailer that delivery of an item took place. The return receipt may indicate to whom and the date delivered or it may indicate to whom, date delivered, and delivery address. A restricted delivery allows a mailer to designate who can receive the item being mailed. Both receipt forms are available for certified, registered, COD, and expedited mail and for mail insured for designated amounts. They apply to domestic and most international mailings. Fees for return receipts do not cover damages or losses to the items sent. (See Figures 16-5 and 16-6.)

Return Receipts for Merchandise

Return receipts for merchandise are available only for priority mail and standard mail (A) and (B). They allow the mailer to obtain a mailing receipt, a return receipt, and a record

SENDER:
- Complete items 1 and/or 2 for additional services.
- Complete items 3, 4a, and 4b.
- Print your name and address on the reverse of this form so that we can return this card to you.
- Attach this form to the front of the mailpiece, or on the back if space does not permit.
- Write *"Return Receipt Requested"* on the mailpiece below the article number.
- The Return Receipt will show to whom the article was delivered and the date delivered.

Is your RETURN ADDRESS completed on the reverse side?

I also wish to receive the following services (for an extra fee):

1. ☐ Addressee's Address
2. ☐ Restricted Delivery

Consult postmaster for fee.

Thank you for using Return Receipt Service.

3. Article Addressed to:

4a. Article Number

4b. Service Type
- ☐ Registered   ☐ Certified
- ☐ Express Mail   ☐ Insured
- ☐ Return Receipt for Merchandise ☐ COD

7. Date of Delivery

5. Received By: *(Print Name)*

8. Addressee's Address *(Only if requested and fee is paid)*

6. Signature: *(Addressee or Agent)*
X

PS Form **3811**, December 1994   Domestic Return Receipt

Figure 16-5 Domestic return receipt.

Return Receipt for International Mail

UNITED STATES POSTAL SERVICE ™

Administration des Postes des Etats-Unis d'Amérique

(Registered, Insured, Recorded Delivery, Express Mail)

Avis de réception

Par Avion

Postmark of the office returning the receipt *Timbre du bureau renvoyant l'avis* **C5**

Return by the quickest route *(air or surface mail)*, a découvert and postage free.

A renvoyer par la voie la plus rapide (aérienne ou de surface), à découvert et en franchise de port.

The sender completes and indicates the address for the return of this receipt.
(A remplir par l'expéditeur, qui indiquera son adresse pour le renvoi du présent avis.)

Name or Firm *(Nom ou raison sociale)*

Street and Number *(Rue et no.)*

City, State, and ZIP + 4 *(Localitié et code postal)*

UNITED STATES OF AMERICA   Etats-Unis d'Amérique

PS Form **2865**, October 1992

Figure 16-6 International return receipt.

of delivery. They are not available for international mailings. Special delivery service can be obtained for a fee. Articles with return receipts for merchandise must be mailed at a post office; they cannot be deposited in collection boxes.

Registered Mail

Registered mail is the most secure means of delivering valuable and important mail. The post office gives the mailer a receipt, and a USPS employee records the arrival of registered mail at each point along its way. When delivery is made, the mailer receives notification. (See Figure 16-7.) The post office compensates the mailer if a registered item does not reach its destination.

First-class mail, priority mail, and COD parcels may be registered. Additional insurance and restricted delivery receipts are available for additional fees. Mail to most foreign countries may be registered.

HINT: *Valuable items such as stock certificates, merchandise, or jewelry should be registered. Send any item that cannot be replaced, valuable or not, by registered mail.*

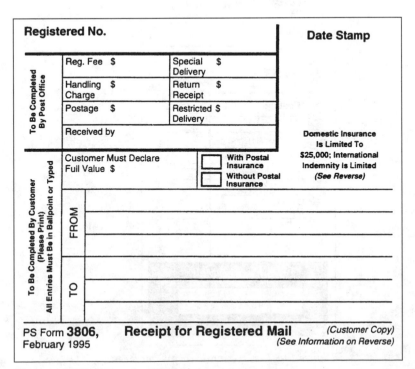

Figure 16-7 Registered mail receipt.

Insured Mail

Insurance is available to guard against loss or damage to items mailed at standard mail (A) and (B) rates or to standard mail (A) and (B) matter mailed at first-class rates for real value of the items. Do not overstate the value. Return receipt and restricted delivery services are available for extra fees. Insured mail must be taken to the post office; it cannot be deposited in a collection box. An appropriate endorsement for insured mail is stamped on the parcel.

The post office at which the item is mailed does not keep a record of insured mail. The person receiving the mail signs a receipt that is filed at the destination post office. (See Figure 16-8.)

The receipt is necessary if a claim for loss or damage is ever made. Write the name and address of the addressee on the receipt and file it until you know that the parcel arrived safely.

Insurance is not available for LC mail, small packets, or printed materials. Maximum coverage varies according to the country.

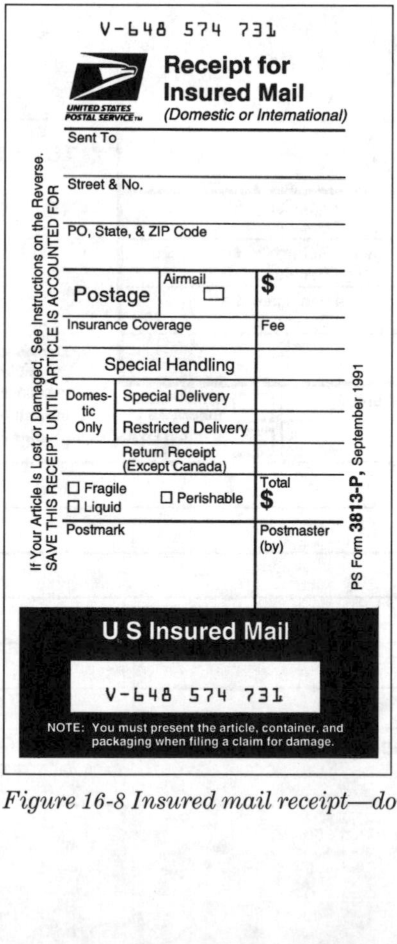
V-648 574 731
UNITED STATES POSTAL SERVICE
Receipt for Insured Mail
(Domestic or International)
Sent To
Street & No.
PO, State, & ZIP Code
Postage | Airmail | $
Insurance Coverage | Fee
Special Handling
Domestic Only | Special Delivery
Restricted Delivery
Return Receipt (Except Canada)
☐ Fragile ☐ Liquid ☐ Perishable | Total $
Postmark | Postmaster (by)
If Your Article is Lost or Damaged, See Instructions on the Reverse.
SAVE THIS RECEIPT UNTIL ARTICLE IS ACCOUNTED FOR
PS Form 3813-P, September 1991
U S Insured Mail
V-648 574 731
NOTE: You must present the article, container, and packaging when filing a claim for damage.

Figure 16-8 Insured mail receipt—domestic.

Special Delivery

Postal Service messengers try to deliver special delivery mail the day it arrives at the post office, including Sundays and holidays. However, to make special delivery feasible, send the items so they will arrive during normal business hours rather than over a weekend. Do not use a post office box as the address. Some post offices hold special delivery mail addressed to a post office box at a general delivery window. If the post office is not open, the item may not reach the addressee any faster using special delivery than it would by regular mail.

The fee for special delivery service, which must be paid in addition to regular postage, does not cover insurance against theft or loss. Fees depend on weight and the class of mail. Special delivery is available in most countries, but each country has its own delivery regulations. Check with the local post office before using the service.

Special Handling

Mail marked "Special handling" receives preferential handling in dispatching and transporting. Special handling applies to standard mail (A) and (B) and is available for COD and insured items. It does not include special delivery service or "special" care in handling fragile or breakable items. The weight determines the fee. The special handling fee is in addition to standard mail (A) and (B) postage. The service is available for international mail for parcel post, printed matter, and small packets only.

Collect on Delivery (COD)

COD service allows mailers to send merchandise for which they have not been paid; payment for the merchandise and cost of mailing are collected when the package is delivered.

First class, standard (A) and (B) and expedited mail may be sent using COD service. Special handling, special delivery, registered mail return receipt, or restricted delivery services are all available. COD service is not available for international mail. The COD fee includes insurance against loss or damage and an amount to cover the potential failure of the addressee to pay for the merchandise. (See Figure 16-9.)

Payment may be in cash or by a check payable to the sender. When cash is involved, the sender receives a money order from the Postal Service for the amount collected.

ALTERNATE DELIVERY SERVICES

Other delivery services are available besides the USPS. The costs, delivery times, and types of services offered vary. The advertising pages of a local telephone directory include companies that offer freight, delivery, and shipping services under such headings as air cargo, package express service, and delivery service. Individual companies can provide information on rates, service charts, and limitations on items transported.

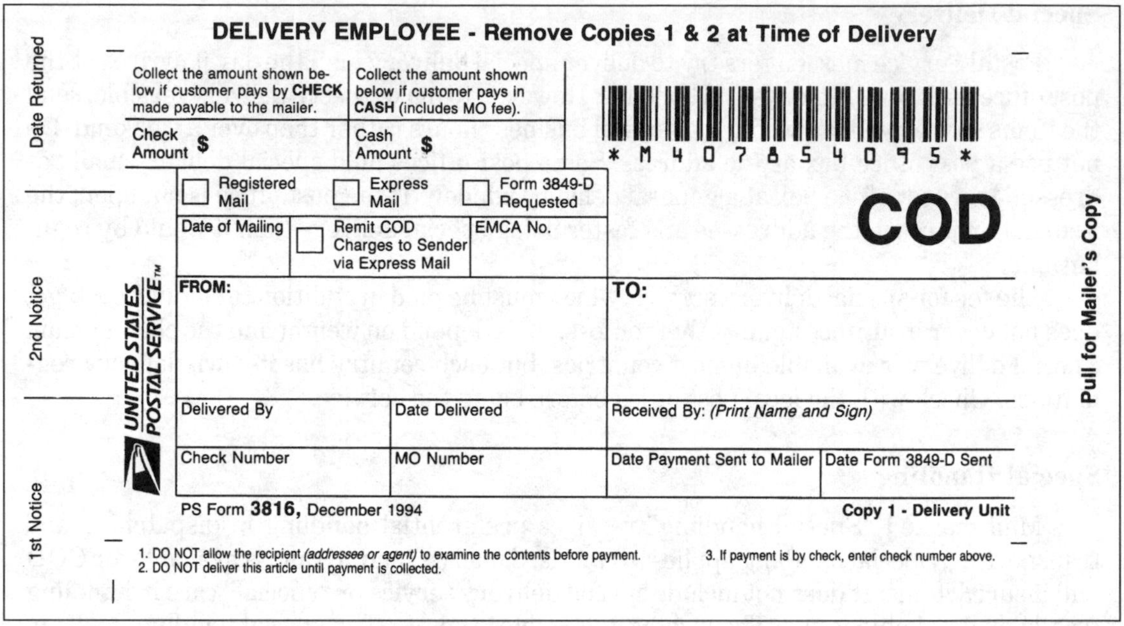

Date Returned | 2nd Notice | 1st Notice

DELIVERY EMPLOYEE - Remove Copies 1 & 2 at Time of Delivery

Collect the amount shown below if customer pays by **CHECK** made payable to the mailer.	Collect the amount shown below if customer pays in **CASH** (includes MO fee).
Check Amount $	Cash Amount $

* M 4 0 7 8 5 4 0 9 5 *

COD

☐ Registered Mail ☐ Express Mail ☐ Form 3849-D Requested

Date of Mailing	☐ Remit COD Charges to Sender via Express Mail	EMCA No.

UNITED STATES POSTAL SERVICE™

FROM:		TO:	
Delivered By	Date Delivered	Received By: *(Print Name and Sign)*	
Check Number	MO Number	Date Payment Sent to Mailer	Date Form 3849-D Sent

PS Form **3816**, December 1994 **Copy 1 - Delivery Unit**

1. DO NOT allow the recipient *(addressee or agent)* to examine the contents before payment.
2. DO NOT deliver this article until payment is collected.
3. If payment is by check, enter check number above.

Pull for Mailer's Copy

Figure 16-9 COD delivery.

United Parcel Service (UPS)

The United Parcel Service (UPS) delivers packages to individuals and businesses. In addition to ground service, air service—next day or second day—is available to destinations within the United States and many other countries. Sonic Air, which is a wholly owned subsidiary of UPS, specializes in same day service that includes pickup within an hour of the request and an average delivery time of four to six hours anywhere in the United States. Other customized services are also available.

Mailers can request door-to-door service or they may drop off the item at a UPS facility or collection box. Fees differ depending on the service.

The sender must fill out a form that requests the sender's name and address, the recipient's name and address, and the contents of the parcel. The package must weigh 70 pounds or less. The size limitation for a package is 108 inches, length and girth combined. In addition to the protection against theft or damage already included in the basic UPS rate, the mailer may purchase additional insurance coverage. UPS is linked with commercial online services and offers package-tracking software. Its customer automation system electronically manages package and billing information and can produce the financial reports that management needs.

Air Express

Numerous private companies, such as Federal Express, provide air express or courier express service for domestic and international deliveries. These companies will pick up a firm's or individual's letters, parcels, or heavy freight items and provide same day, next day, or second day delivery. Same day services are the most expensive. In addition to speed, charges depend on the size and weight of the parcel. Volume discounts are often available.

HINT: *FedEx has free software (also available on the Internet) that allows you to connect to FedEx, complete shipping and billing information, call for pickup, and print labels and bar codes. Requirements are a computer, modem, and laser printer; register with FedEx to get started.*

Most courier companies are expanding their international markets. Some operate their own planes; others rely on commercial flights. To increase convenience, firms are developing branch office services on a 24-hour basis with other companies; for example, Kinko's offers FedEx service. Other firms are competing by adding more hubs, offering faster service, or expanding to more cities. All major firms can track a lost item. Guaranteeing the arrival of the shipment or returning the fee for a lost item is part of the service offered by most companies. Call the local customer service number or the 800 number for refunds.

Since costs and arrival times vary, go over these details when calling for service:

- Value of the parcel(s).
- Delivery date.
- Number of packages.
- Service; for example, same day, overnight, international, or second day delivery.
- Pickup service, latest time to call, charges.
- Weight of each parcel.
- Destination.
- Type of merchandise.
- Day of the week for pickup as well as delivery.
- Money back guarantee.

HINT: *If your company does not have one person monitoring costs, it becomes everyone's responsibility to cut costs and improve service. Organize your work so it is not necessary to use expensive delivery services at the last minute. Use these services only for documents that must get delivered the same day or overnight.*

Some air express advisers will help companies analyze their needs at no charge. To assist them, keep records of where deliveries go, when and how often they are sent, and how much it costs.

Several carriers offer logistics services (warehousing) so that a company can store products at the carrier's location. When a product is needed, the carrier pulls the product from the inventory and ships it according to company instructions.

Local Transport Services

Companies located in small cities may have to depend on local bus service for some deliveries. The cost is reasonable, and insurance is included in the basic charge. Depending on local schedules, same day service as well as Sunday and holiday service may be possible. In addition to rate information, the local bus company offices can indicate any limitations concerning the size and weight of a parcel.

Small businesses or individuals contract for local delivery services. Local messenger services make intracity deliveries the same day. Some promise delivery within the hour.

ELECTRONIC MAIL

Electronic mail (e-mail) is a cross between a telephone call and a letter. It is a software application that lets you compose, send to anyone with an e-mail address, and receive messages online at your convenience but with some sense of urgency. Standard features of an e-mail system allow a sender to use the computer keyboard to input a message. Once the address or mailbox of the recipient is located, the message is transmitted to the addressee's computer by activating a transmit key. At the receiving workstation, the recipient checks the mail received, selects a message to view, displays it on the monitor, and then downloads it for printing, or routes it to someone else. Some advantages and special concerns of e-mail are discussed below.

Advantages

Advantages of e-mail include:

- *Speed.* A message arrives quickly, and the recipient has the option of responding immediately or prioritizing messages for later action.
- *Convenience.* Messages do not have to be written or received during normal business hours; the system is operable 24 hours a day. E-mail is good for reaching people who are difficult to contact or who are in other time zones. It minimizes telephone tag. Messages do not have to meet interoffice mail or USPS pickup deadlines. Telecommuters can stay in touch with their coworkers and supervisors.
- *Idea exchange.* Ideas flow more spontaneously than with formal meetings with planned agendas. Appearance, age, shyness, and speaking ability seem less important.
- *Scanning capability.* Subject lines give a recipient an opportunity to review the messages and select those requiring immediate action.
- *Cost.* Messages are inexpensive when compared to alternative forms of communication.

- *Sender identification.* Most e-mail software automatically places the sender's name in the FROM line, which authenticates the origination of the message.
- *Destination reliability.* If the addresses are accurate, there will be minimal transmission errors. Messages do not have to go through another individual.
- *Simplicity.* Using e-mail requires some basic instructions, but it does not require in-depth computer expertise.
- *Information access.* Office professionals have access to information that they can share and respond to simultaneously. One message may go to numerous recipients, which eliminates routing information or sending memos.
- *Document linkage.* "Threading," or attaching key words to messages, allows their integration with other documents or computer files for accurate retrieval. Threading informs people about the relationship of various projects.

Special Concerns

Special concerns of e-mail include:

- *Privacy.* Even the use of a personal password is no guarantee that a message will not be read by management. Messages may be altered and/or forwarded to others beyond the person you contacted without your knowledge.
- *Destination reliability.* If it's important, request the receiver to indicate receipt. If the receiver has several e-mail addresses, send the message to all addresses. Be certain the e-mail address is accurate.
- *Delayed response.* Although a sender may expect an immediate response, the receiver may not prioritize the message in the same manner.
- *Message impact.* E-mail cannot provide cues such as body language, tone of voice, and use of humor or sarcasm. Situations involving personnel problems are handled more effectively with face-to-face contacts. A letterhead carries more weight and prestige for important correspondence.
- *Inappropriate messages.* Because of e-mail's simplicity, people send messages that are not clear or are written in anger. Poor communicators will not become good communicators because of e-mail. Electronic mailboxes become clogged with general information or lengthy documents that seem more appropriate for a company bulletin board or paper form for later reading.
- *Volume.* Information overload may cause the recipient to filter messages identified by key words and send the others to a "folder" for later attention—or just ignore them. Message senders tend to become wordy with a blank screen in front of them. It becomes easy to send messages to people who really don't need them.
- *Overwork.* People tend to be "on call" 24 hours a day at home, in the office, on vacation, and while traveling. There is a "need" to check e-mail for messages, which may then generate other tasks.

- *Employee misuse.* Employees waste time using the system for messages unrelated to work.
- *Carelessness.* Because of e-mail's informal style, those sending messages may be careless in proofreading or using correct grammar and style.

Message Composition

Office professionals often must compose e-mail messages for their supervisors or send their own e-mail. The following guidelines provide assistance:

- *Keep the message short; limit it to one screen.* Readers can handle viewing a screen of information but dislike paging up or down to check facts or connect ideas. State the facts the reader needs and be specific about the action, if any, to be taken. Divide lengthy messages into several communications and send them with individual subject lines. If you include several topics in one message, the reader may find it too cumbersome to respond quickly or will omit several of your concerns in the response. It's also difficult to file messages with several topics.
- *Write in a businesslike manner.* Avoid slang expressions or abbreviations, especially with international e-mail. Avoid clever first liners or overused openers such as "First the good news, then the bad news."
- *Use a descriptive subject line.* Recipients who receive many e-mail messages use the subject line to prioritize their responses. Do not deceive the reader with an enticing but inappropriate subject. Be specific in identifying subjects. For example, "Insurance Benefits" is too general; instead, use "Dental Insurance—Increased Benefits."
- *Do not use all caps for the entire message.* A few words in all caps is acceptable for emphasis, but an entire message in all caps is considered "screaming" or "shouting." Messages in all caps are difficult to read.
- *Omit sarcasm or too much humor.* Limit emotive language, such as smiling faces. Do not send an angry message. Criticizing or ridiculing an idea or individual is called "flaming." If you would not write it in a letter or memo or do not want it used in court, do not say it in e-mail.
- *When replying to a message,* especially if time has elapsed, remind the recipient what action had been requested. Use a line or two from the original message. For example, include the original question with your answer.
- *Write clearly.* If you have to send a second message to explain your first one, you have not saved time. Outline your thoughts before you send your message. Identify facts and acknowledge your own opinions.
- *Proofread.* Correct grammar, spelling, and punctuation affect others' opinions of you. (See Chapter 20.)

- *Highlight key ideas* by numbering them or using bullets and indenting them from each margin. Use white space generously. Avoid long blocks of solid text.

E-Mail Procedures/Etiquette

Companies need to implement procedures and etiquette guidelines for creating, distributing, and storing e-mail documents. Office professionals should take the initiative and recommend training sessions in which message content, format, style, and etiquette are covered. Some suggestions for e-mail procedures and etiquette protocol include:

- Do not leave e-mail messages onscreen when you are away from your desk.
- Do not copy or send software or information that is copyright-protected.
- Avoid attaching lengthy files to e-mail messages. Unless the file is essential, it often takes the recipient more time to download than it's worth.
- Use interoffice memo headings, but then use the recipient's name in the first paragraph when you want a more personal greeting; for example, "Mary, here are the up-to-date job cost figures that you requested this morning."
- Know the audience to whom your e-mail is addressed. Use appropriate language and formality. Use acronyms only for informal internal messages. Some commonly used e-mail acronyms include:

FAQ	Frequently asked questions
FYI	For your information
PLS	Please
RFC	Request for comments
YR	Your
IMO	In my opinion
MSGS	Messages
NLT	No later than

- Maintain an electronic index of all incoming and outgoing communications.
- Indicate the time when e-mail messages will be checked. Check and respond to messages at least once a day, if only to indicate receipt.
- Use a screening technique or "filtering" process that automatically routes a document according to its content, priority, file size, or date. Senders should prioritize these messages with a 1-, 2- or 3-priority, with 1 being the highest.

HINT: *Office professionals can screen messages that are received for their supervisors and place them in files identified "Urgent," "Action," and "Information."*

- Do not use e-mail for personal or sensitive messages; it is not private. Supervisors or colleagues may see messages by accident or on purpose. Avoid gossip, sexual innuendos, or critical remarks about another person or group. Do not use e-mail to discuss proprietary information.
- Inform a sender when a message reaches you by mistake rather than ignoring or deleting it. Forward it with a note that you received the message by mistake.
- Establish e-mail storage procedures similar to those for filing paper documents. For example, a procedure might be to purge documents within 30 to 60 days and archive important messages on disk, tape, or paper.
- Maintain distribution lists by adding or removing names promptly upon request. Include only those people who have a need to receive the information from your office. Request that your own or your supervisor's name be removed from other senders' lists when information is not needed.
- Do not attach an unauthorized message to another person's message. Do not print and distribute another person's message without approval.
- Include e-mail addresses on letterhead and business cards. A suggestion to use the company e-mail address may be left on the voice-mail answering message.

Legal Issues

Legal conflicts occur over e-mail ownership and privacy rights when specific guidelines are not published and communicated. Establishing an e-mail policy and having employees sign a form indicating they have read it can prevent many of these problems. Here are some suggestions to include when writing a policy on e-mail:

- Employer property. The e-mail system is company property—not that of its employees. Management reserves the right to monitor, review, and disclose information that must be accessed in the absence of an employee or when policies regarding business use and harassment or misuse must be investigated.

HINT: *Supervisors need to monitor with caution. Contact an attorney for consultation.*

- Business use. The e-mail system is for business use only. Using it for harassment, flaming, or making illegal or other inappropriate comments is prohibited. Companies may be liable for their employees' e-mail messages and conduct.
- Proprietary information. Use of the system to transmit trade secrets, share confidential information with competitors or other employees, or solicit personal business is prohibited.
- Privacy. Time periods need to be established for changing passwords. Personal passwords do not guarantee privacy. If e-mail is allowed for personal use, be specific about acceptable and unacceptable use. No laws protect the privacy of employees' e-mail to date.

- File retention. Establish erasure policies and regular file-retention periods for e-mail. In dealing with sensitive information, include hard-drive reformatting and backup devices as part of retention procedures.
- Discipline. Violations of the e-mail policy result in discipline, including discharge.

E-Mail on the Internet

E-mail is a popular feature of the Internet. Subscribers to major online services, private company networks, shareware, and freeware can exchange messages via the Internet. Commercial online services are not directly on the Internet but provide a gateway to receive and send mail. Sometimes these gateways become clogged, and transmission delays then occur. The same procedures and message composition techniques apply for Internet e-mail as for company network e-mail.

INCOMING MAIL

Incoming mail includes USPS mail, special courier deliveries, intercompany correspondence, and electronic messages. Although incoming mail may arrive throughout the day, most USPS mail arrives at specified times. Office professionals facilitate the handling of these documents by prioritizing, opening, and distributing them as soon as possible after they are received.

Sorting Incoming Mail

In companies with centralized mail departments, USPS mail is delivered by mailroom messengers or robotic mobile delivery carts programmed to stop at designated locations. In other companies, postal carriers deliver the mail to each person's desk or to one person who then distributes it.

Once the mail is delivered, arrange it according to importance. Check the address of each item to be sure it has been delivered to the correct location. Return all mail that does not belong to the department to the mailroom or to the post office.

The following are useful categories for sorting mail by priority:

First priority: expedited mail; certified, registered, insured, or special delivery mail; special courier deliveries; telegrams; urgent e-mail.

Second priority: personal or confidential mail. If a supervisor gives you permission to open personal, confidential, or private mail, attach a note to indicate that the envelope was marked as such.

Third priority: first-class mail, e-mail messages, interoffice mail, priority mail, airmail.

Fourth priority: packages.

Fifth priority: periodicals mail—newspapers and magazines.

HINT: *Magazines and newspapers may be important to a supervisor. Do not put periodicals mail aside for later handling, but include it in each mail distribution.*

Sixth priority: Standard mail (A)—catalogs, advertising materials, pamphlets, and booklets.

Supplies for Opening the Mail

Several supplies are helpful in opening the mail.

- Letter openers. Small mail opener machines, either manual or electric, can save considerable time. Some models automatically feed the envelopes, even ones of various sizes. In addition, such equipment can open the envelopes on one end (or on one side and one end), stack the envelopes, and count them.

HINT: *When using a manual letter opener, place the envelope on a hard surface with the flap up. To cut the envelope, insert the letter opener halfway under the flap and quickly move it forward and outward. Avoid jagged edges or tearing the envelope by using a sharp opener and by holding it properly.*

- Date and time stamp.
- Mail record, special services record, mail-expected record, or a combination of these records. (See the section on Recording Incoming Mail below.)
- Stapler, paper clips, adhesive message pad, pencils, and transparent tape.
- Mail stop directory. If mail needs to be routed to another location, include the mail stop location (if applicable) as well as the name.
- Routing slips.

Procedures for Opening the Mail

The following procedures are recommended for opening mail and removing the contents:

- Arrange the envelopes so the flaps face the same direction before opening them by hand or machine. Open all envelopes first; then remove and unfold the contents. To prevent discarding an enclosure, hold each envelope to the light to make sure the envelope is empty. Clip each envelope's contents together. Do not discard the envelopes until you have verified the addresses.
- Use a date stamp to record the receipt date of each item. Once the contents have been removed, stamp the document in the same location; for example, in the upper right on correspondence or on the back of catalogs. Include the time a document is received if it is important. The date and/or time may be handwritten, hand-stamped, or machine-stamped.

- Tap the lower edges of the envelope to allow the contents to fall to the bottom and avoid cutting them. If an item is cut, use transparent tape to repair the damage.
- If an envelope was opened when it should not have been, write "Opened by Mistake" on the envelope and initial it.
- Review each document for the sender's name and address, enclosures, and date. If the address on the envelope and document differ, clip the return address from the envelope and staple it to the letter. Make a note to verify the correct address with the sender. Once verified, change all mailing list notations and circle the correct address on the correspondence just received.
- Record an omission of a date or a major discrepancy between the date on the letter and the date of the postmark on a piece of adhesive notepaper. Attach the note to the correspondence for your supervisor's attention. Staple the envelope to the document. Any discrepancies may have consequences in legal matters.
- Verify the receipt of all enclosures. If an enclosure is missing, circle the enclosure line and indicate that the item is missing. If the amount in the message is different from the amount on an enclosed check, indicate the discrepancy next to the enclosure notation. Record the missing item(s) on the mail record and make a note to contact the sender as soon as possible.

HINT: *Unless your supervisor wishes to see each check, prepare a list of incoming checks and other reimbursements and submit the list to your supervisor daily. Include the date of the check, the maker, and the amount. A copy of the list is also helpful when the payments are submitted to the accounting department. If your supervisor is the payee, distribute those checks directly to her or him. Attach the check to the accompanying correspondence and place it in a folder. Make a photocopy of the check.*

- Attach an enclosure to a document with a staple or a paper clip. Attach small enclosures to the front of documents and attach enclosures that are the same size or larger to the back of documents.

HINT: *A staple may damage an attachment, such as a photograph. Fold a small sheer of paper in half and place the attachment between the fold and document. Use a paper clip to attach them together.*

- Check suspicious-looking packages—no return or fake return addresses; bulky, sloppy, or lopsided packaging; specific addressee with misspellings; too much postage—for possible bombs. Call the Postal Inspection Office and the police. Store the item in a remote area until it is checked by a technician.
- Draw a line through the last name that appears on an interoffice envelope and save for reuse. Check that all contents have been removed. Forward e-mail messages that should be handled by another department.

- Check parcels for first-class mail, such as an invoice or letter, that may be attached to the front of the package or enclosed inside.

- Verify that the contents of the package match the packing slip or invoice as well as the original requisition. Indicate the acceptance of the materials listed on the invoice with a signature or other designated approval before sending the invoice to accounting for payment. Note on the mail record that the ordered materials were received.

- Indicate that enclosures have been distributed to another location by writing a note on the original copy of the letter and on the mail record.

Recording Incoming Mail

In addition to recording the date and time that materials arrive, keep a record of the mail. The mail record is a daily list of mail received with follow-up actions and dates. The list is easily maintained on the computer. A review of the record indicates how a document is being handled and to whom a document was routed. It helps in locating and tracing correspondence. Record those items that appear to need additional handling as well as certified, registered, expedited, priority, and first-class mail; interoffice mail; airmail; e-mail; and personal mail.

A special services record lists only those documents requiring the sender to pay additional fees, such as certified, registered, and expedited mail. The mail expected record lists mail that is still expected, such as materials that have been ordered or items that are being sent under separate cover. If the mail expected is very limited, a note on your "to do" list is sufficient. File these mail records in an 8½-by-11-inch notebook at your desk. Establish separate records for each special one-time event, such as a special publication or a conference that requires registration fees.

Annotating Mail

In addition to reviewing and recording mail, reminders or comments may be placed in the margins of the correspondence, with underlining or highlighting of key facts. Refer only to the items that require your supervisor's attention; excessive annotation is ineffective. Before making notations on the correspondence, obtain your supervisor's consent. If the documents are distributed to other departments, the marginal notations or underscores may not be appropriate.

Nonreproducing pencils are useful when annotating correspondence since the notations do not reproduce when photocopied. Adhesive notepaper also works since it is easily removed before copies are made for distribution. Use a highlighter only with your supervisor's approval.

Many incoming documents require only brief acknowledgments or transmittal of material. Draft responses to such correspondence for your supervisor's signature or under your own name. Discuss your ability to handle certain types of correspondence with your supervisor. Prepare a list of the actions you take ("Items I Handled") and place it with the incoming mail distribution for your supervisor to review.

Distributing Incoming Mail

Once the mail is sorted by importance, it can then be divided into such categories as:

- Immediate action required.
- For reply/routine mail.
- For reply/other employees.
- For reply/office assistant.
- No reply needed—information only (e.g., thank-you notes, acknowledgment letters).
- Magazines, newspapers, publications.
- For reading (e.g., announcements, reports not included in the first two categories, advertisements).

The earlier the mail reaches the right desk, the more time there is to respond to those items that require immediate action. Try to set aside the same times each day for handling the mail. Use these procedures for quick, effective distribution:

- Sort the first-class mail into such categories as invoices, client concerns, orders, or correspondence from suppliers.
- Use a consistent system for presenting the mail. Place it in folders or arrange it according to priority, with the most important documents on top.

HINT: *To identify priorities, use different colored folders. For example, place the documents for immediate action in a bright red folder. Code e-mail messages into "Urgent," "Action," and "Reading" categories.*

- Place incoming mail in the same location on the supervisor's desk each time it is delivered. If folders are not appropriate, place a bulky item such as a book on top of the mail. Place the top sheet face-down so the materials are not visible to others.
- Assist your supervisor in handling the magazines and trade publications that he or she receives. Request a prioritized list of topics and publications. Prepare a list of articles in each magazine that correspond with these subjects. The supervisor can then select the magazines and articles to read. A second method involves preparing file cards for the articles that fall in an interest area. File these cards in the subject folders for each interest topic. A third method is to photocopy the table of contents of a magazine and highlight those articles in which the supervisor may be interested. Place this list in a folder marked "For Reading." Always keep reading files and subject lists up to date.
- Route materials to other departments or other employees by using routing slips or e-mail. Routing slips may include names of employees who should review the ma-

terial or take action. After the first person is finished with the material, he or she initials and dates the routing slip and passes the material on to the second person on the list. "Date received" and "date sent" may be included on the slip.

HINT: *The last person on a routing list should know what to do with the document once everyone has read it. Include on the routing slip the name of the person to whom the material should be returned or indicate if it can be discarded.*

- If there are a number of people who must see the document, photocopying or sending it by e-mail may be more expedient than routing the document. The size of the document and the time needed to copy or download will determine the best procedure. Keep the original copy in the originating office.
- If actions are necessary, prepare a duplicate and attach it to the original kept in the office. This prevents the same document from being routed again. Making a note in the mail-expected record to indicate to whom the item was routed or the action expected is also helpful.
- Share materials from the files with other employees who are asked to take action on an assigned task. Attach these files when routing the materials. Make a notation in the mail record to indicate that the file materials are being routed.
- Ask for assistance in determining which advertisements and catalogs to save, if any. Store them in a separate location away from general files. Discard the older editions as soon as new ones are received.
- If an employee has left the company, forward personal correspondence to the employee's home. Cross out the company address on the envelope and write the forwarding address and the words "Please forward." If the document appears to be business related, forward it to that person's replacement, or to the immediate supervisor if a replacement has not been named.

OUTGOING MAIL

Efficient handling of outgoing mail speeds the communication process. Processing the mail so it is not delayed and following the USPS guidelines for addressing mail are responsibilities of office professionals. Under the 1996 Classification Reform, the Postal Service offers considerable discounts for mail that is properly screened, addressed, and bundled.

Processing Outgoing Mail

Before sending the mail to the mailroom or depositing it for delivery, several steps are needed to process it:

- Check that all letters have a signature. Be sure all attachments and enclosures are included.

- Combine mailings. If there are two letters to one company, place them both in the same envelope. Use both sides of the paper for lengthy reports; this practice saves paper and also postage costs.
- Check that all correspondence has been dated and that the address on the envelope matches the inside address. Verify the accuracy of the addresses by checking the current address list and making appropriate changes. When inserting the material in the envelopes, be sure the correct letter goes in the proper envelope.
- Verify the ZIP Code with the address on the original correspondence or locate it in the ZIP Code directory. Check that each piece of mail meets USPS dimensions and weight limits.
- Deposit all metered mail on the date stamped. Do not place metered stamps on the envelopes one day and wait until another day to do the mailing. If the mail does not make the last pickup, take it to another collection box or to the post office.
- Change the date on the postage meter each morning before other tasks are started. Electronic metering systems automatically advance the date, give accurate readings for whatever item is on the scale, and allow you to compare postal rates with FedEx and UPS. Metered mail is processed faster than stamped mail, since it does not have to be canceled at the post office. Newer postage software uses computers and laser printers for mail metering and printing, so a postage meter may not be necessary.
- Avoid waiting until the end of the day to deposit mail. Take mail to the mailroom several times during the day. Mail deposited by 2 p.m. has a chance of being processed by 5 p.m. for next day delivery.
- Order postage for the postage meter when the remaining postage is enough for three days of mail. Reorder by telephone or take the meter in to the post office to be reset.
- Use the USPS order forms to order stamps or envelopes. USPS also has a service for ordering stamps by telephone. There is a charge for the service.
- Sort the mail into local and out-of-town bundles.
- Use window envelopes only if the address has four or fewer lines. More than four lines will not be fully visible in the window section.
- Inform mailroom personnel when a large mailing is planned.
- Weigh all mail. Do not guess. Use a scale that measures to a fraction of an ounce. Check the scales periodically with the USPS scales to be certain they are accurate.
- Use postal cards to make routine announcements to clients and to send short messages to customers. Use business reply cards or envelopes for return responses. They are less expensive than stamped, self-addressed envelopes. Make sure that any return documents fit the return envelope.
- Place tape over a metal clasp on an envelope. This avoids damage to the envelope if it gets jammed in the sorting machine. Write "Please hand stamp" on the outside of the envelope if it contains bulky items. Use pressure-sensitive seals rather than staples when mailing announcements or newsletters.

HINT: *If materials must be clipped together or stapled, fold so that the paper clips or staples are in the inner fold of the document. Paper clips can get bent and cause a jam in a sorting machine.*

- Mark envelopes with the notation "Do Not Bend" when you send photographs, certificates, or transparencies. Use cardboard for extra protection.
- Obtain full value for the amount of postage used. If paying for one ounce, weigh the letter to determine if another announcement or promotion piece can be included. This eliminates two separate mailings.
- Use the smallest and strongest containers possible for wrapping packages. Do not use string and wrapping paper, since packages may also be processed by machines; use a filament tape. Do not use newspaper for protecting the contents; use lightweight stuffing.
- Include a letter with any disk that is being transmitted through the mail. Do not rely solely on a file named "Read.me" on the disk. Identify the contents of the disk and the sender in the transmittal letter and on the disk label. This procedure causes less confusion should the disk and letter be separated. Also, identify the software program and the hardware used.
- Prepare disks for mailing by placing them in cardboard or heavy plastic wrap before putting them in a box or padded envelope. On the outside of the box or envelope, indicate a disk is enclosed.
- Consider using a service bureau to handle bulk mailings or considerable amounts of international mail. Foreign postal services have established centers in the United States to deliver mail abroad.

Folding and Inserting Mail

Machines are available to fold, seal, and stamp mail. Correct folding and insertion give letters a professional look and make them easy for the reader to open and unfold. The steps involved in folding and inserting materials for the No. 10, No. 6¾, and window envelopes follow. Always use a flat surface for neater folds.

No. 10 Envelope
- With the document face-up on the desk, fold up the bottom third of the page first.
- Fold the top third of the letter down over the bottom third so the top edge is ¼ inch from the first fold.
- Insert the item so the open side of the document is at the back (side to be sealed) and to the top of the envelope.

No. 6¾ Envelope
- With the document face-up on the desk, fold the bottom half of the paper to ¼ inch from the top. Leaving the ¼ inch makes it easier for the reader to separate the pages.

- Fold the document in thirds. Start with the first one-third fold from the right side. Continue with the second one-third fold from the left side so the edge is ¼ inch from the right side.
- Insert so the last fold is toward the bottom of the envelope and the open edge faces the back of the envelope (the side to be sealed). Insert the document so the open edges are on the stamp side of the envelope.

HINT: *If the folds are not parallel with the top and sides, the letter will look sloppy when unfolded. Fold the sections so they are exactly the same width. Avoid uneven edges and folds that are at angles.*

Window Envelope

- With the document face-up on the desk, fold up the bottom third of the page first.
- Fold the top third of the document in the opposite direction so the edge touches the first fold.
- Insert the document so the last fold is at the bottom of the envelope and the address shows through the window.
- Postal guidelines call for a space of ¼ inch between the side and bottom edges of the window and an address.

HINT: *Fold enclosures with the document or insert them so they are in the fold of the document.*

Addressing Envelopes

The USPS has provided guidelines for addressing envelopes so its mechanical and electronic equipment can read the addresses and speed the delivery of mail. (See Figure 16-10.)

State abbreviations: Use the standard two-letter abbreviations as given in Table 16-2.

ZIP Codes: Use nine-digit ZIP Codes, if known, or the five-digit ZIP Code. Letter-sorting machines sort envelopes by ZIP Codes. Optical character readers read the last two lines of an address. Bar code readers can process mail with imprinted bar codes at extraordinary speeds. Most countries have postal code systems. Canadian and British postal codes consist of numbers and letters arranged in two groups of three characters each; for example, F3N 4B2.

Address placement: Mail can be processed more quickly if the address is placed in a designated location on the envelope and arranged in a specific sequence. The USPS recommends the following for address placement:

- Locate the address lines within the OCR read area.
- Align the address so each line is straight.
- Allow an area 4½ inches wide and ⅝ inch from the bottom of an envelope for printing the bar code. Do not mark anything within the bar code boundaries.

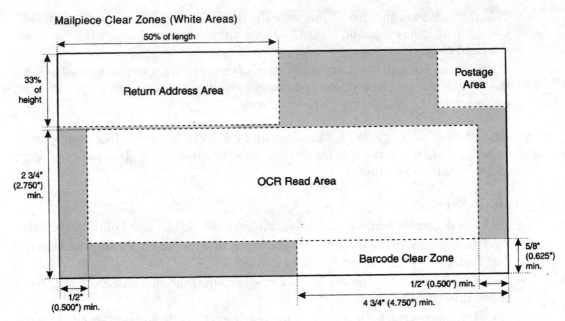

Mailpiece Clear Zones (White Areas)

Figure 16-10 Format for addressing an envelope.

- Use black ink on white envelopes. Bright colors and reverse printing are not recommended.
- Use USPS abbreviations. (See Table 16-3.)
- The return address should appear on the front of the envelope, not on the back. Block the return address two lines from the top and three spaces from the left side of the envelope,

Address format: The USPS recommends the following guidelines for formatting the address:

- Align each line of an address at the left.
- Put the address in all caps.

HINT: *Titles of respect should be used when appropriate. Do not combine titles and degrees; for example, "Dr. Mary Smith, M.D." is redundant.*

- Omit punctuation marks but include the hyphen in the ZIP + 4 code; for example, 94702-6401.
- Limit the address to four to six lines.
- Always type addresses in the same place. On No. 10 envelopes, begin 14 lines from the top and 5 spaces to the left of the center. On No. 6¾ envelopes, begin on line 12 and at the center.

Table 16-2
STANDARD ADDRESS ABBREVIATIONS

UNITED STATES AND POSSESSIONS

Alabama	AL	Montana	MT
Alaska	AK	Nebraska	NE
Arizona	AZ	Nevada	NV
Arkansas	AR	New Hampshire	NH
American Samoa	AS	New Jersey	NJ
California	CA	New Mexico	NM
Colorado	CO	New York	NY
Connecticut	CT	North Carolina	NC
Delaware	DE	North Dakota	ND
District of Columbia	DC	Northern Mariana Islands	MP
Federated States of Micronesia	FM	Ohio	OH
Florida	FL	Oklahoma	OK
Georgia	GA	Oregon	OR
Guam	GU	Palau	PW
Hawaii	HI	Pennsylvania	PA
Idaho	ID	Puerto Rico	PR
Illinois	IL	Rhode Island	RI
Indiana	IN	South Carolina	SC
Iowa	IA	South Dakota	SD
Kansas	KS	Tennessee	TN
Kentucky	KY	Texas	TX
Louisiana	LA	Utah	UT
Maine	ME	Vermont	VT
Marshall Islands	MH	Virginia	VA
Maryland	MD	Virgin Islands	VI
Massachusetts	MA	Washington	WA
Michigan	MI	West Virginia	WV
Minnesota	MN	Wisconsin	WI
Mississippi	MS	Wyoming	WY
Missouri	MO		

CANADA / DIRECTIONAL ABBREVIATIONS

CANADA		DIRECTIONAL ABBREVIATIONS	
Alberta	AB	North	N
British Columbia	BC	East	E
Manitoba	MB	South	S
New Brunswick	NB	West	W
Newfoundland	NF	Northeast	NE
Northwest Territories	NT	Southeast	SE
Nova Scotia	NS	Southwest	SW
Ontario	ON	Northwest	NW
Prince Edward Island	PE		
Quebec	PQ		
Saskatchewan	SK		
Yukon Territory	YT		

Table 16-3
FREQUENTLY USED POSTAL ABBREVIATIONS

ABBREVIATIONS FOR STREET DESIGNATORS (STREET SUFFIXES)

Alley	ALY	Fork	FRK	Pines	PNES
Annex	ANX	Forks	FRKS	Place	PL
Arcade	ARC	Fort	FT	Plain	PLN
Avenue	AVE	Freeway	FWY	Plains	PLNS
Bayou	BYU	Gardens	GDNS	Plaza	PLZ
Beach	BCH	Gateway	GTWY	Point	PT
Bend	BND	Glen	GLN	Port	PRT
Bluff	BLF	Green	GRN	Prairie	PR
Bottom	BTM	Grove	GRV	Radial	RADL
Boulevard	BLVD	Harbor	HBR	Ranch	RNCH
Branch	BR	Haven	HVN	Rapids	RPDS
Bridge	BRG	Heights	HITS	Rest	RST
Brook	BRK	Highway	HWY	Ridge	RDG
Burg	BG	Hill	HL	River	RIV
Bypass	BYP	Hills	HLS	Road	RD
Camp	CP	Hollow	HOLW	Row	ROW
Canyon	CYN	Inlet	INLT	Run	RUN
Cape	CPE	Island	IS	Shoal	SHL
Causeway	CSWY	Islands	ISS	Shoals	SHLS
Center	CTR	Isle	ISLE	Shore	SHR
Circle	CIR	Junction	JCT	Shores	SHRS
Cliffs	CLFS	Key	KY	Spring	SPG
Club	CLB	Knolls	KNLS	Springs	SPGS
Corner	COR	Lake	LK	Spur	SPUR
Corners	CORS	Lakes	LKS	Square	SQ
Course	CRSE	Landing	LNDG	Station	STA
Court	CT	Lane	LN	Stravenue	STRA
Courts	CTS	Light	LGT	Stream	STRM
Cove	CV	Loaf	LF	Street	ST
Creek	CRK	Locks	LCKS	Summit	SMT
Crescent	CRES	Lodge	LDG	Terrace	TER
Crossing	XING	Loop	LOOP	Trace	TRCE
Dale	DL	Mall	MALL	Track	TRAK
Dam	DM	Manor	MNR	Trail	TRL
Divide	DV	Meadows	MDWS	Trailer	TRLR
Drive	DR	Mill	ML	Tunnel	TUNL
Estates	EST	Mills	MLS	Turnpike	TPKE
Expressway	EXPY	Mission	MSN	Union	UN
Extension	EXT	Mount	MT	Valley	VLY
Fall	FALL	Mountain	MTN	Viaduct	VIA
Falls	FLS	Neck	NCK	View	VW
Ferry	FRY	Orchard	ORCH	Village	VLG
Field	FLD	Oval	OVAL	Ville	VL
Fields	FLDS	Park	PARK	Vista	VIS
Flats	FLT	Parkway	PKY	Walk	WALK
Ford	FRD	Pass	PASS	Way	WAY
Forest	FRST	Path	PATH	Wells	WLS
Forge	FRG	Pike	PIKE		

- Single space the address.
- Avoid nonstandard print fonts, such as script, and styles, such as italic or condensed.
- Use the last line of the address for the city, state, and ZIP + 4 code. Leave one space or two between the state and ZIP Code.
- Use the line above the last line for the street address or post office box number. It is not necessary to use both. Use the correct ZIP Code for either the delivery address or the post office box number.

HINT: *If a return address includes both a street address and a post office box, address your correspondence to the PO box. Mail may be picked up from the box earlier in the day and on weekends. If the business moves to another location, the PO box usually stays the same.*

- Put suite numbers or apartment numbers on the same line as the street address. If the address is too long, put the suite or apartment number on the line above the street address.
- Identify the addressee on the top line of the address. The department name, if applicable, should appear on the second line and the company name on the third line.
- Use an "attention" line on the second line of an address if necessary.
- Put special service notations such as special delivery, certified, or registered two lines below the stamp in all capital letters. Underscores are not necessary. The information must be above the OCR read area.
- Put handling instructions such as Confidential and Personal three lines below the return address and above the OCR read area. Capitalize the first letter of each word and underscore.
- When addressing mail to foreign countries put the name of the country on the last line in all capital letters.

HINT: *Address formats differ in foreign countries. In European countries, the street name often appears first with the number following it. Write the address exactly as it appears on the letterhead.*

INTEROFFICE MAIL

Interoffice mail may be delivered by mailroom personnel or intercompany transport or by e-mail via the computer. Most companies have distinctive envelopes for interoffice mail. Light brown envelopes with space for names and departments/locations of the recipients are the most common. They are 9½ inches × 13 inches or 4 inches × 9½ inches. The smaller size is appropriate for small notes. Avoid using the smaller envelopes for documents that must be folded to fit inside.

Interoffice envelopes are reusable. The sender crosses out the previous name, inserts the material, and fastens, but does not seal, the envelope, usually with an attached string. Interoffice mail accumulates and is collected at scheduled intervals during the day.

HINT: *If the material is confidential, use an ordinary envelope and seal it. Label it "IN-TEROFFICE MEMO" in the upper right corner so it will not get mixed in with the other classes of mail. Some companies have special envelopes for confidential interoffice mail that are labeled as such.*

DIRECT MAIL

Before investing time and money in a direct-mail campaign, you need to set objectives and select target markets. Once the market is targeted, obtain mailing lists that are accurate and current. Effective mailing lists are easy to reuse and manipulate.

You can prepare your own in-house lists, or rent, buy, or lease them. The lists may be rented for one-time use or more than once if stated in the original agreement. Those who compile and own the lists can identify illegal use of their lists. Use the list only as specified in the rental agreement.

HINT: *When ordering a mailing list, allow at least six weeks to order and receive the list, sort the names, and prepare the mailing. Time the mailing so it reaches potential clients at the beginning of the week or at seasonal slack times. During the holiday season and around tax deadlines or accounting closing periods, direct-mail literature receives less attention.*

Mailing lists can be compiled from such sources as the following:

- Company sales invoices.
- Company payroll records.
- Replies to advertisements.
- Business license applications.
- Professional organizations; for example, Kiwanis, Chamber of Commerce.
- Utility companies.
- Voting lists.
- Auto registration lists.
- Magazine subscribers.
- Tax lists.
- Warranty registrations.
- City directories.
- Telephone directories.
- Responder lists (people who have bought by mail from someone else).

HINT: The Directory of Directories, *an annual publication from Gale Research Company, has listings for organization and business directories.*

In-house preparation of mailing lists requires time and planning. Begin by identifying the appropriate fields to include in setting up a database. Then revise the fields as necessary once the database is established.

Several suggestions for specific fields include:

- Name/address/telephone number/e-mail/fax.
- Social Security number (if known or applicable).
- Income level/sales volume.
- Job title of the person making the inquiry or purchase.
- Number of years the organization has been in the business.
- Age category of individuals (when applicable).
- Geographic area.
- Product areas.
- Amount of order.
- Date of first purchase; date of last purchase.
- Frequency of orders.
- Peak buying times.
- Code for products in which an interest is shown.
- Category of the company; for example, manufacturing, real estate, finance.
- Level of inquiry; for example, branch office, department, project group.

Companies use mailing lists for activities other than direct mail. Up-to-date lists are also needed for such activities as sending out newsletters or informational bulletins, maintaining vendor addresses, and customer billings. In deciding whether to use first-class or standard mail (A) bulk mailing for the direct-mail campaign, consider that first class is faster but standard mail (A) is much cheaper. First class cannot be opened by USPS personnel and is forwarded or returned if undeliverable.

Mailing lists may be maintained on address labels, address plates, file cards, computer printouts, or as a database.

HINT: *Printing directly on an envelope is more personal; a recipient will be more likely to open it rather than toss it away.*

HINT: *If numerous lists exist in different departments, bring address changes to the attention of other departments to avoid wasted postage costs and returned mail.*

List processing or mail management software allows users to prepare and sort lists more efficiently. Select software that verifies your mailing lists against the USPS National Database (USPS CASS-approved ZIP + 4). The software adds, corrects, and prints ZIP + 4 and carrier and delivery route bar codes. Some software has a change of address system utility, a database that has all address changes filed during the last three years. It eliminates duplicate records and gives you departmental charges and marketing reports for accounting.

You may find that direct mail campaigns and maintaining mailing lists are not productive tasks. Outsource providers handle these jobs as well as other bulk mailings.

To remove your name or your company's name from commercial and/or nonprofit mailing lists, contact the Mail Preference Service of the Direct Marketing Association, 6 East 43rd Street, New York, NY 10017. Another way to decrease the influx of direct mail is to request companies with whom business is transacted to stop renting the company name to other organizations.

PART IV

OFFICE

COMMUNICATIONS

Well-written correspondence is one of the most important factors in communicating a strong, positive corporate image. The office professional is expected to know how to correctly and attractively format correspondence for maximum impact using the most productive means available. In addition, many office professionals are expected to compose written communications for others.

For years the formats of memos and letters did not change. Computers, however, now allow the design of personalized form letters, printing of envelopes from prepared address lists, and discovery of errors by spelling, grammar, and style checkers. All of these advances in technology have brought about streamlined, uncluttered correspondence designed to improve operator productivity.

CHAPTER 17

WRITTEN

CORRESPONDENCE

TIPS ON COMPOSING CORRESPONDENCE

Before going into the specifics of various types of correspondence, it's best to begin with a handful of general guidelines regarding all types of correspondence that the office professional should keep in mind.

- Write only when circumstances are appropriate. In some instances, it may be better to place a phone call, handle in person, or send an e-mail message or fax.

  Be aware that anything put in writing may be shown to others, even if it is not intended for them. Therefore, do not put anything in writing that you would not say publicly or you would not want published with your name. Never send correspondence in anger.

HINT: *Wait 24 hours before sending a negative reply or something written in anger. You may decide not to send it after cooling off. This hint especially applies to e-mail messages.*

HINT: *Understand the needs of your receiver. Some people respond more quickly to e-mail than written correspondence; others prefer telephone communications.*

- Know your audience. Determine what relationship exists or what relationship you wish to achieve. Demonstrate sensitivity to the needs and interests of the reader. Personalize correspondence if possible.

   You may need to know the following items for audience analysis: occupation or position, gender, age range, education, income, and experience.
- Have a specific objective. For example, ask for information or attempt to make a sale. Every piece of correspondence should have the subtle objective of building goodwill for your organization.

HINT: *Always know the purpose before writing. It helps to answer this question: What do I want my reader to do (or know) when they finish reading what I've written?*

- Use the active voice. Voice shows whether the subject acts or is acted upon. In the active voice, the subject performs an action: Our accountants completed the audit; We shipped your order on Friday, December 3. In the passive voice, the subject is acted upon: The audit was completed by our accountants; The order was shipped on Friday, December 3. The active voice is more direct, even though both sentences state the same information.

   The passive voice is often used to soften the impact of negative news: Your order will be shipped when the enclosed order blank is returned. This is less negative than the active voice: We will ship your order when you return the enclosed order blank.

HINT: *Many computer grammar and style checkers can analyze sentences for active or passive construction.*

- Be concise. Use specific, concrete words. Eliminate unnecessary words. Avoid clichés and jargon.

HINT: *The average sentence length should have fewer than 20 words.*

HINT: *Keep paragraphs to three or four sentences.*

HINT: *Computer thesaurus programs can suggest synonyms and help you avoid repeating the same words. Computer grammar and style checkers can point out unnecessary words or statements.*

HINT: *Use lists. All items must be parallel.*

WORDS AND PHRASES TO AVOID:	USE:
accompanied by	with
according to our records	(avoid)
acknowledge receipt of	(avoid)

as of this day	today
at the present time	now, presently
at your earliest convenience	(be specific)
attached please find	enclosed
be cognizant of	know that
consensus of opinion	consensus
deliberate upon	think about
disbursements	payments
due to the fact	because
enclosed please find	enclosed
forward	send
free of charge	free
herewith	(leave out)
increment	increase
in compliance with your request	as requested
in reference to	about
in the amount of	for
in the event of	if, in case
kindly	please
to our previous...	when we last
per your request	as requested
re	regarding
scrutinize	read, examine
subsequent to	after, since
take the liberty of	(avoid)
thanking you in advance	thank you
this is to acknowledge	(avoid)
up to this writing	until now
utilize	use
vitally essential	vital or essential

- Be polite and courteous. Be positive by stressing what you can do instead of what you cannot do. Use the "you" attitude to convey warmth and friendliness. The "you" attitude is writing from the reader's point of view by emphasizing "you" and minimizing "we" and "I."

HINT: *Some companies prefer the use of "we" rather than "I" in order to show that the writer is speaking for the company. Use "we" or "us" to show others share the message.*

- Get straight to the point unless the news is bad. Make the purpose of the correspondence obvious. Arrange material from general to specific. Start with a general statement and add facts that explain the statement.

HINT: *The last paragraph is remembered the longest, so important information should be stated or restated there.*

- Reply promptly. If you cannot respond to a letter in a week, acknowledge it immediately and say when the requested information will be available: Thank you for your letter. The information you requested will take several days to research. As soon as we have the information,...

HINT: *When saying "no" to a request or job applicant, delay the reply for a week so it does not appear that little thought was given to the response.*

- Use proper grammar, spelling, and punctuation. A computer grammar and style checker helps point out potential problems with sentence structure, punctuation, and writing style. A computer spelling checker locates misspellings and typographical errors.
- Check for accuracy of dates and figures.

E-Mail Writing Tips

More and more, e-mail is substituting for paper mail, especially for internal communications, because of its speed. E-mail creates a paper trail that increases the lifespan of the message and may leave either a positive or negative impression with the reader. Many people with e-mail access have not been trained to use it, have poor writing skills, or think they can ignore the formalities of writing. Many major universities maintain online writing labs through the World Wide Web. Also see Chapter 16, Mailing Documents, for additional e-mail writing suggestions.

The following tips help in writing e-mail messages:

- Practice the same rules of writing as you would if you were sending the correspondence through traditional channels; but at the same time, keep the message short.
- Keep the line length to approximately 60 characters. Know whether your system has word wrap or not.
- Avoid sarcasm, pomposity, and anger.
- Proofread carefully onscreen since many e-mail systems do not have spell check.
- Avoid all caps, which has the effect of "screaming" to the receiver.

Be aware that many organizations feel e-mail composed and sent at work is the property of the company. Some companies regularly check e-mail messages with the justification that the company can be liable for your e-mail. It is also possible for your e-mail to be altered without your knowledge. In addition, if someone else has access to your password, they can send e-mail in your name. With most e-mail systems, it is easy to send copies to others without your knowledge.

International Communication Suggestions

The global nature of communications demands an understanding of how people in other cultures communicate. Americans are typically more informal than the rest of the world, deemphasizing rank, status, and position.

When communicating with individuals in cultures where formality is expected—such as Latin America, Europe, and Japan—follow these suggestions:

- Use last names, titles, and other indications of rank and status. Never use first names unless invited to do so. In many Latin American countries, the title is more important than the name. The French prefer flowery and effusive language, and Dear is perceived as too familiar.

- Write individual letters to people of higher status. Avoid mass mailings and form letters. Know who should receive copies of correspondence.

- Avoid trying to "cut through the red tape" to get the job done. Red tape is honored in some cultures.

- Demonstrate some knowledge of other languages, even though individuals in other cultures may be communicating in English.

- Avoid using words that have more than one meaning, industry-specific jargon, or abbreviations. Humor typically does not translate well. Be aware of using sports-related terms, such as "give me a ballpark figure," or terms that might not be understood in other cultures, such as "keep your nose to the grindstone."

American messages are sometimes too direct for individuals in cultures where it is important to get to know a person before doing business. To overcome this difficulty, use faxes, e-mail, and letters to share information in order to build a relationship. The professional or personal information shared depends upon the culture of the other country.

COMPONENTS OF LETTERS

Letters may include some or all of the following:

- Date.
- Inside address.
- Attention line.
- Salutation.
- Subject line.
- Complimentary closing.
- Writer information.
- Initials of typist.
- Notations.

The inclusion of a component depends on the purpose of the correspondence and the letter style used.

Date

All letters should include a date. Write the date as, for example, January 15, 19—. Spell out the month. Or use the military style of 15 January 19— to avoid punctuation and save keying time. Place the date two or more lines beneath the letterhead; the shorter the letter, the more space is needed beneath the letterhead. Place the date either at the left margin or the center of the page, depending upon the letter style used (see the section on Letter Styles later in this chapter).

HINT: *Use the date feature of your word processing program to insert the date.*

Inside Address

The inside address contains everything necessary for delivery of correspondence: the name, job title, company name, street address or post office box number, and the city, state, and ZIP/Postal Code.

NAME

- Check on the correct spelling of the recipient's name.
- Use a courtesy title if it is known. Courtesy titles include Dr., Mr., Mrs., and Ms. (See the section on Salutation below for determining whether to use Ms., Mrs., or Miss.)

HINT: *If you do not know whether you are addressing a man or a woman with first names like Lynn or Pat, omit the title of Mr. or Ms.*

- Omitting earned titles such as Dr., M.D., or the Reverend may offend the reader, especially if that person has written your company using his or her title. Courtesy titles are not used if the earned title is included, and only one earned title is used: e.g., Louise F. Granger, M.D. (not Dr. Louise F. Granger, M.D.).
- Esquire (abbreviated as Esq.) can be used after the name of a lawyer, but no courtesy title should then be included: e.g., Shannon A. Duff, Esq. (not Ms. Shannon A. Duff, Esq.).
- Use a job title if the name of the person is not known.
- Use a period after most courtesy and earned titles (except Miss).
- Spell out Professor and Reverend.

JOB TITLE

- Omit the job title if the exact title is not known.
- Place it either on the same line with the name, separated by a comma, or on the next line.

COMPANY NAME

- Check on the exact spelling and punctuation of the company name.
- Type the name exactly as it appears in the company's official letterhead, including The, Inc., or Co. If the name is long and requires another line, indent the second line 2 or 3 spaces.

STREET ADDRESS OR POST OFFICE BOX

- Spell out numerical names of streets and avenues if they are numbers less than 10: e.g., Seventh Street, Third Avenue, 15th Street.
- Use figures for all house numbers except One: e.g., One Commerce Boulevard, 2 Park Avenue, 102 Sunnyslope.
- Spell out Avenue, Street, Boulevard, etc.
- Place a PO Box number after the street address:

      3489 Westwood Road
      PO Box 4388

HINT: *Use the street address for overnight delivery.*

- Omit periods after abbreviations: e.g., PO Box 34, Elm Street, NW

  The trend toward dropping periods in the inside address is a result of USPS requests to eliminate punctuation on envelopes. Also, addresses on computer databases generally do not include punctuation.

CITY, STATE, AND ZIP

- Include the full name of the city with no abbreviations. For example, San Francisco instead of SF.
- Use the two-letter state or province abbreviation recommended by the USPS. (See Table 16-1 in Chapter 16.)
- Place the ZIP or postal code one space after the state or province abbreviation.
- Use the ZIP + 4 code if known.
- A comma is not necessary between the city and the state, but one may be used.

The inside address should be single-spaced and placed at the left-hand margin. Locate it not less than two lines nor more than twelve lines below the date; placement depends on letter length. For longer letters, place closer to the date; for shorter letters, avoid extending the inside address beyond the middle of the page. Avoid going beyond the center of the page with the inside address. If necessary, carry over information to the next line, which should be indented five spaces. Avoid having more than six lines in an address; it may be necessary to combine lines.

Here are some examples of inside addresses:

Ms. Sarah Raintree
Sales Manager
Interim Personnel, Suite 203
4378 Southwest Boulevard
Chicago, IL 60637

Dr. Gail Radtkey
Vice President
Lawrence Galleries
3892 Independence Avenue
Phoenix, AZ 85773

Cameron Jacobson, M.D.
968 Lakeville Highway
Napa, CA 94943

Mr. Roger Weiss, President
Creative Leisure
5948 Industrial Road
Trenton, NJ 38943

Alexandra T. L. Freeman, Personnel Coordinator
4783 Redwood Highway
PO Box 5012
San Rafael, CA 94530

INTERNATIONAL ADDRESSES

When keying an international address, spell out the full name of the country on a separate line in all capital letters.

Ms Gertrud Baumann
AR Research
Doblinger Hauptstrasse 38
1190 Wien
AUSTRIA

When writing to Canada, the territory or province may be spelled out or abbreviated. The Canada Post prefers addresses to be spelled out.

> **MR. HENRY SMITH**
> **14 MERRIWETHER LANE**
> **OTTAWA ON CANADA**
> **K1A 0B1**

Attention Line

An attention line is used when correspondence is addressed to a company but sent to the attention of an individual. If the recipient's name is known, put the name in the inside address, use a proper salutation (see the section Salutation below), and eliminate the attention line. The USPS recommends placing the attention line first in an address. To be consistent, the attention line should be placed in the same position in the letter. Place the attention line at the left margin as the first line of the inside address. A colon is optional after the word Attention.

> **Attention Sharon Flanagan**
> **Campbell Press**
> **3902 Oakridge Drive**
> **San Jose CA 49857**
>
> **Dear Ms. Flanagan:**

or

> **Attention: Sharon Flanagan**
> **Campbell Press**
> **3902 Oakridge Drive**
> **San Jose CA 49857**
>
> **Dear Ms. Flanagan:**

Salutation

A letter should always be addressed to an individual if the name is known. Below are suggested salutations.

ADDRESSED TO AN INDIVIDUAL

The most common salutation is Dear. Whether the first name or last name with title is used depends on the relationship between the writer and the recipient. Most people find it annoying to be addressed by their first name if they do not know the writer.

Use Ms. when addressing a woman, unless previous correspondence indicates she prefers the title Mrs. or Miss. Many women prefer the neutral term of Ms. over a term that denotes marital status.

If a person has an earned title such as M.D., Ph.D., or Ed.D., use Dr. in the salutation. Spell out the title Professor.

Avoid substituting a designation of business rank or position for a name; use "Dear Mr. Jones," not "Dear Personnel Director Jones." Similarly, write "Dear Ms. Reynolds," not "Dear Editor Reynolds."

The Honorable is used for individuals with high offices at the federal, state, or city levels. This title is still held after retirement. Table 17-1 provides sample salutations used for clergy, elected officials, military officers, and education officials.

WHEN RECIPIENT'S NAME OR GENDER IS NOT KNOWN

Traditional salutations of Dear Sir or Madam are inappropriate if the recipient's name is not known. Dear Ladies and Gentlemen is another option. You may also address the recipient by title: e.g., Dear Screening Committee, Dear Board Members, Dear Credit Manager. If the gender is not known, you may use the first and last name, as in "Dear Lynn Crichton."

A salutation can use either open or closed punctuation. Either is correct, but the style must be consistent in a letter. Open punctuation means there is no punctuation after the salutation or closing. Closed punctuation uses a comma after the salutation when the first name is used; a colon after the salutation when a title and last name are used; and a comma after the closing.

Abbreviate the titles Mr., Mrs., Ms., Messrs., and Dr. Spell out all other titles. Key the salutation two lines below the inside address. If you will use a standard window envelope, start two inches from the top of the page.

Subject

The subject line describes the purpose for writing a letter. The subject line is not necessary in business letters but is used when drawing the reader's attention to the contents of the letter. It is particularly helpful if recipients, such as government agencies, receive a volume of correspondence. No punctuation is needed.

HINT: *Avoid re, an outdated Latin expression meaning the same as "subject."*

Complimentary Closing

The most popular and appropriate closing is Sincerely. Sincerely yours and Cordially are also well-accepted closings. Respectfully yours is used when writing to a high official, including the President of the United States or a high church official. If a closing has more than one word (such as Sincerely yours), capitalize only the first word.

Place the closing two lines below the last line of the letter. Use a comma after the clos-

Table 17-1
SAMPLE SALUTATIONS

PERSON	INSIDE ADDRESS	SALUTATION
Elected Officials		
Chief Justice	The Chief Justice Supreme Court	Dear Mr. Chief Justice
Governor	The Honorable Richard Swan	Dear Governor Swan or Dear Governor
Judge	The Honorable Rosa Bezzari	Dear Judge Bezzari
Mayor	The Honorable Carolina Jung	Dear Mayor Jung
President	The President	Dear Mr. President Dear Madam President
Speaker of the House	The Honorable José Perez The Honorable Julia Payne	Dear Mr. Speaker Dear Madam Speaker
State Senator	The Honorable Lisa O'Leary	Dear Senator O'Leary
State Representative	The Honorable Mary Carter	Dear Representative Carter
U.S. Representative	The Honorable Betty Hamilton	Dear Representative Hamilton or Dear Ms. Hamilton
U.S. Senator	The Honorable Sam Nelson	Dear Senator Nelson or Dear Mr. Nelson
Vice President	The Vice President	Dear Mr. Vice President Dear Madam Vice President
Education Officials		
	Dr. J. Barbara Hall	Dear Dr. Hall
	Professor Quinlan Jones	Dear Professor Jones
Clergy		
Protestant clergy	The Reverend Sarah Gilligam	Dear Dr. Gilligam (with a doctoral degree) Dear Ms. Gilligam (without a doctoral degree)
Bishop of the Episcopal Church	The Right Reverend Randolph Jones	Dear Bishop Jones
Methodist Bishop	The Reverend George Rojas	Dear Reverend Rojas
Mormon Bishop	Mr. Gerald Hornaby	Dear Mr. Hornaby
The Pope	His Holiness, The Pope	Your Holiness
Cardinal	His Eminence, Paul Cardinal Bernardi	Your Eminence or Dear Cardinal Bernardi
Priest	The Reverend Father Peter Smoll	Dear Father Smoll
Nun	Sister Mary Margoilis or Mary Margoilis, R.S.C.J.	Dear Sister
Rabbi	Rabbi Benjamin Stein	Dear Rabbi Stein

(Continued)

Table 17-1 *(continued)*

Military		
First Lieutenant	First Lieutenant, Craig Garcia	Dear Lieutenant Garcia
Lieutenant Colonel	Lieutenant Colonel, Samuel Jacobson	Dear Colonel Jacobson
Noncommissioned officers in Army, Air Force, and Marine Corps	Master Sergeant Roger Webb	Dear Sergeant Webb
Enlisted person in Navy	SN Charles Brown	Dear Seaman Brown

ing if using closed punctuation; use no punctuation if using open punctuation. (See the section Salutation earlier in this chapter for a definition of open and closed punctuation.)

Writer's Name and Signature

All letters should include the name and title of the writer. Enough space should be left between the complimentary closing and the typed name of the writer for a signature.

NAME

- Place the writer's name four lines under the closing to allow space for the signature.

HNT: *Reasonably priced software is available to replicate actual handwriting. This software can be used to place signatures on documents.*

- Use the first name with or without the middle initial as preferred by the writer; place a period after a middle initial if used.
- Place earned titles after the name; place periods after earned titles if appropriate: e.g., Karen Fisher, CPS; Martin Pena, M.D.

JOB TITLE

- Place the writer's job title on a line below the typed name:

Sincerely,

Ronald Rubik
Sales Manager

Sincerely,

Debbie Paulsen
Administrative Assistant
to Ronald Rubik

- If the letter is signed by someone other than the writer, sign the writer's name and use your initials.

Sincerely,
Sylvia J. Crinski
gk
Sylvia J. Crinski
Vice President

- Professional, military, or academic titles appear after the writer's name:

Sincerely,

John Toten, M.D.

Sincerely,

Leslie Duggins, CPS

Reference Initials

The typist's initials are often included but may be omitted. Use lowercase initials at the left margin and place them two lines below the writer's title. If desired, the author's initials can be put in all caps preceding the typist's initials.

SJ/ms
ms

Enclosure Notation

Enclosure notations include information such as the number and nature of enclosures.

- Place notations at the left margin two lines below the last notation.
- Enclosure may be written out or abbreviated Enc. More than one enclosure can be noted as follows:

> **Enclosures 2**
> **Enclosure—Software**
> **Enclosures**
>   **Software**
>   **Documentation Manual**
> **File Name Notation**

File Name Notation

The use of computers has made it necessary to include file name notations on correspondence. The file name needs to be as meaningful as possible, with the length depending upon the operating system software used. Place it on the line below the reference initials.

HINT: *Reduce the font size to make it less noticeable.*

Delivery Notation

If the correspondence will be delivered in a way other than first-class mail, include that information below the file name notation. Place it on the line below the file notation. Notations may appear as By Federal Express, By certified mail, By fax, By messenger, By registered mail.

> **ser**
> **drrison.doc**
> **By Federal Express**

If a letter has been faxed first and then mailed, include a "'confirmation" notation on the letter so the recipient realizes it is the original of the fax. Place this information on the second line below the date line.

> **June 5, 199—**
>
> **Confirmation of fax sent on June 5, 199—**

Copy Notation

- "cc" means carbon copy. Since carbons are obsolete in many offices, the notation "c" for copy followed by a colon is commonly used. The notation "bcc" or "bc" is used for "blind" copies, that is, for copies that the recipient of the document will not necessarily know about. Tab once after keying the notation; otherwise the names may not align when fonts are changed.

c: Adele Richards
Marvin O'Leary

Postscript

A postscript is used to strongly express an idea deliberately omitted from the body of the letter. The postscript is keyed two lines below the last notation. Key "PS:" or "P.S." and space two times.

ser
drrison.doc

PS: Send your registration materials back today for preferred reservations!

LETTER STYLES

Most companies have designated letterhead and developed a letter style to identify, communicate, and project a corporate image. Letter styles are typically based on their perceived impact on others. Today many office support personnel who use word processing and desktop publishing programs create their own letterheads.

The most common letter styles are the block, simplified block, and modified block letter. Because of word processing software, the block letter style is the most frequently used. The less centering and indenting in a letter, the easier it is to keyboard and revise, which increases productivity. Productivity can also be increased by having one standard letter format instead of having different styles for different writers.

The following general formatting rules apply to letters, no matter what style is used:

- Use a standard line length, which is typically 6 inches (left and right margins of 1.25 inches). Line length can be decreased for shorter letters. A line length longer than 6 inches is difficult to read. Start a new page if the letter runs long rather than increase the margins to more than 6 inches.
- Press Enter four times after the date. The space may be increased or decreased depending on the length of the letter.

- Single-space the body; leave a blank line between paragraphs.
- Use short sentences averaging no more than 20 words.
- Include at least two sentences in a paragraph. Unless for effect.
- Keep paragraphs approximately the same length. Avoid more than 10 lines of type in a paragraph; divide a longer paragraph into two shorter ones.
- Use left justification only. Research shows that full justification is more difficult to read.
- Use tabulated lists to make a letter look more interesting. Discreet use of italics or bold print also adds interest.
- Begin lists at the left margin with a number followed by a period. Use the automatic numbering word processing software feature for proper placing and indenting of succeeding lines.

Block Letter

In a block letter, all lines are flush with the left margin. (See Figure 17-1.)

FORMATTING SUGGESTIONS

- Press Enter two times after the inside address, salutation, the subject (if any), and before the closing.
- Press Enter four times after the closing for the writer's information.
- Press Enter two times after the writer's information for the initials of the typist and notations.

Simplified Block Letter

This letter style reflects a trend toward eliminating the salutation and complimentary close. All lines are flush with the left margin. A subject line is used in place of the salutation. The simplified letter is the most efficient letter style to type. (See Figure 17-2.)

- Key the inside address with initial caps or in all capital letters.
- Press Enter three times after the inside address.
- Omit the salutation and use a subject line. The subject line may be initial capped or in all caps.
- Press Enter three times after the subject line and begin the body.
- Omit the closing.
- Press Enter four times after the body for the writer's information. The writer's name and title may be initial capped or in all caps.

June 5, 19—

Mr. Greg Lichau
Lark Creek Inn
Box 6329
Tahoe City, CA 95730

Dear Greg:

Thanks to you and your staff for the superior job you did in handling our group again this year. We like to come to Lark Creek Inn because we know the meeting rooms are comfortable and pleasant and the food is excellent.

Next year we are planning our conference for August 12–16. If by any chance our original dates become available, please notify us. We would also like to reserve our dates several years in advance for the last week in July.

Thank you again for all you did to help make our conference a success! We look forward to working with you again next year.

Sincerely,

Michelle Bryant
Conference Coordinator

ik
Lichau.doc
c: Richard Fong

Figure 17-1 Block letter.

June 5, 19—

Mr. Michael Troy
Human Development Associates
203 S. Willits
Visalia, CA 93291

YOU DID AN OUTSTANDING JOB!

"Thanks" hardly seems like an adequate word to express my appreciation
for all the time, effort, and planning that went into our conference, Mike.
You were so responsive to our needs and so willing to make changes.

You did an excellent job again this year and really gave the balance we
were looking for. I had a million little things to worry about, and it was a
relief not to worry about you or your presentation.
I knew you would do a great job!

The enclosed evaluations are our best ever and reflect your ability to
deliver the training we wanted. Thanks again, Mike, for everything you did
to make our conference a success

Michelle Bryant
Conference Coordinator

ik
troy.doc
c: Caroline Hing
Enc.

Figure 17-2 Simplified block letter

September 11, 19—

Ms. Michelle Bryant
Conference Coordinator
The Learning and Guidance Center
6543 Lincoln Way
San Francisco CA 94367

Dear Michelle:

Thank you so much for letting me observe your conference at Lark Creek Inn on June 1. Your leaders did a marvelous job of relating to the participants as well as educating them in leadership, presentation styles, and problem-solving skills.

My experience will be relayed to the educators I work with. We have a lot to strive for with your conference as a model. Congratulations on a wonderful conference!

Sincerely,

Sandra Mandici
Project Consultant

lp
bryant.doc
c: Ben Louis
Enc.
P.S. I am using Mick's delegation suggestions.

Figure 17-3 Modified block letter.

Modified Block Letter

The modified block letter is somewhat more traditional. The date, closing, and writer's information start at the center. All other lines are flush with the left margin. This format looks balanced on the page. (See Figure 17-3.)

FORMATTING SUGGESTIONS

- Press Enter two times after the inside address, salutation, and the subject (if any) and before the closing.
- Press Enter four times after the closing for the writer's name and title.
- Press Enter two times after the writer's name and title for the initials of the typist, if any.
- Press Enter two times after the typist's initials for any notations.

Multipage

The first page of a multipage letter should be keyed on letterhead. The rest of the pages should be keyed on plain paper of the same size and quality as the letterhead. At least three lines of the letter should go on the last page with the closing (if used) and the writer's signature.

A heading should be placed at the top of the page that includes the name of the addressee, page number, and date in either of the following formats:

Dr. Christine Davis   Page 2   April 19, 19—

Dr. Christine Davis
Page 2
April 19, 19—

FORMATTING SUGGESTIONS

- Leave a 1-inch top margin unless word processing software is used and the heading is in a header, in which case the heading would be ½ inch from the top of the page.
- Start the body three lines below the heading.
- Use the same side and bottom margins as on the first page.

FORM LETTERS

A form letter is a letter sent to many people, usually about a repetitive or routine situation. Form letters save time in letter writing and keyboarding. A form letter is useful when people repeatedly ask for the same information. Form letters about products or the company can be prepared in response to customers who write with questions, requests, or complaints. They are also useful when the same information needs to be sent to more than one person, company, or group; for example, a letter sent to a list of customers.

Form letters should appear as if they were written for the recipient. This is easily done with the mail-merge function of many word processors. (See Chapter 8, Office Computer Software.) The following are suggestions for personalizing form letters:

- Use company letterhead and matching envelope.
- Include the recipient's name, title, and address in the inside address.
- Use a personalized salutation; for example, "Dear Ms. Garza."
- Customize by adding specific information if known; for example, "I enjoyed talking with you this morning."
- Personally sign each letter.

MEMO STYLES

A memorandum, or memo, is a short, informal message used in-house. The tone depends upon the relationship between the reader and writer. Because memos are to people in the same organization, jargon and technical terms may be used and the tone may be more informal than correspondence leaving the company.

A heading such as Memorandum, Memo, or Interoffice Correspondence is printed or keyed at the top of the page. Most memos contain the headings To, From, Date, and Subject instead of an inside address, salutation, closing, and signature line. (See Figure 17-4.)

HINT: *Word processing software programs have a memo template that can be used or modified.*

TO: This line includes the name and job title of the individual(s) who will receive the memo.

When a memorandum is sent to a group, a distribution list identifying the individuals who are part of the group can be keyed after the reference initials. If copies of the memo are to be sent to other individuals, the notation "c:" is keyed below the distribution list and followed by the name(s) to whom the copies will be sent.

bj

Distribution:

Cynthia Cramer
Jerry Eastman
Deborah Lesniak

c: Elizabeth Rea-Medina

Memorandum

To   Steve Posgate, Allan Brody, Tracy Brennan, Brett
              Rouzer, Antonio Ruiz, Janet Sandberg

From   Michelle Bryant, Conference Coordinator

Date   May 23, 19—

Subject   Conference Details

The registrations are arriving and plans are under way for the
fifth Leadership Conference to be held June 1–4 at Lark Creek
Inn, Lake Tahoe.

Enclosed is the form confirming your attendance. Please fill this
out and return it to me by May 28 so I can proceed with the
room reservation list and make other necessary arrangements at
Lark Creek Inn.

mj
Enclosure

Figure 17-4 Memo.

FROM: This line includes the writer's name and title (if necessary). Writers sign their name or initials to show they have read and approved the contents.

DATE: The month is written out with a comma separating the day from the year: e.g., January 20, 19—. Military style of 20 January 19— is acceptable to avoid punctuation and save keying time.

HINT: *Create a template using your word processing program and set up the date as a coded field so you do not have to key the dates.*

SUBJECT: Use a concise phrase with action verbs if possible on this line.

The following general formatting rules apply to memos, no matter what style is used:

- Use a 6-inch line.
- Begin the first line 1 inch from the top of the page unless letterhead paper is used. If letterhead is used, begin at least two lines below the letterhead.

- Key TO, FROM, DATE, and SUBJECT in all capitals or initial caps. A colon after each heading is optional. Leave one blank line between lines of the heading.
- Leave two blank lines after the last line in the heading before the body.
- Single-space the body; leave a blank line between paragraphs.
- Align paragraphs at the left margin unless using a memo template.
- Place the typist's initials two lines below the last line of the body.
- Place the enclosure notation two lines below the typist's initials.

ADDRESSING ENVELOPES

Mail addressed according to the USPS guidelines helps insure accurate delivery. (See Chapter 16, Mailing Documents.)

- Use paper with a minimum basis weight of 20 pounds.
- Include a return address in the upper left-hand corner if preprinted envelopes are not used.
- Line up addresses flush left.
- Allow at least 1-inch left and right margins.
- Place address horizontally.

HINT: *Use word processing software to address envelopes. The bar-code feature is also available. The software package will automatically place the address on the envelope at the location suggested by the USPS.*

- Put address in all capital letters with no punctuation or initial caps with punctuation.

HINT: *For many years, the USPS preferred addresses to be in all upper-case letters with no punctuation. Now lowercase letters with punctuation are acceptable.*

- Typewrite or computer print. Use easy-to-read type styles, not italics or script. Securely fasten stickers and labels to prevent damage when going through automated equipment.

Mailing Labels

Word processing packages provide predefined label options for laser printers. Mailing labels can also be created using the mail merge feature.

HINT: *Do not use labels that are separating from the backing sheet or that are wrinkled or damaged in any way. The printer may be damaged.*

HINT: *Do not feed a sheet of labels through a laser printer more than once. The label adhesive is designed for only one pass through the printer. Damage to the printer may occur.*

SAMPLE CORRESPONDENCE

Announcement Letter

An announcement letter is similar to a press release. It is a way to improve visibility and provide a reminder of a firm or products. An announcement may be made for the following reasons:

- Opening of a company or division.
- New product or service.
- Change of address.
- New staff.
- Promotion.
- Anniversary.
- Acquisition.
- Merger.

SUGGESTED FEATURES

- Communicates pride; some are very formal with only a few sentences.
- Gives appropriate information such as names, dates, and addresses; has a clear purpose.
- Addressed to the public or a company; envelopes addressed to individuals.
- Uses company letterhead or a specially printed white or cream card with black ink.

SAMPLE ANNOUNCEMENT OF NEW SERVICE

Milan, Inc., is pleased to offer 24-hour customer service for your convenience. Call toll-free 1-800-489-5984.

SAMPLE ANNOUNCEMENT OF NEW EMPLOYEE

Hirschfield and Nadler Law Office is pleased to announce that Patricia Issel has joined our staff as an associate in our probate department.

SAMPLE ANNOUNCEMENT OF A PROMOTION

The President and Board of Directors of AMS Industries, Inc., are pleased to announce the promotion of Charles Leoni to Vice President. Mr. Leoni has been the Sales Manager for AMS in San Francisco for the past ten years and will join our corporate staff in Houston.

Letter of Apology

Mistakes will occur, and it is important to apologize for them in a prompt letter of apology.

SUGGESTED FEATURES

- Blames the company, not a specific person or department.
- States what is being done (or was done) to correct the error.
- Explains how the error was made.
- Apologizes for the error.
- Reassures the customer that steps are being taken to reduce the chances of error in the future.
- Closes positively.

SAMPLE LETTER OF APOLOGY

Your book order was shipped air express on November 2. You should have the books by now.

In investigating the problem, we discovered your order code was entered incorrectly in the computer. Consequently, your order was shipped to another school. Since we pride ourselves on our data-entry procedure, mistakes like this are very infrequent. However, our computer programmer is adding an extra safeguard to our order program so we can avoid errors like this in the future.

I appreciate receiving notification of the problem in enough time to send the books before classes started. We believe you will be pleased with the revised edition of Administrative Procedures.

Best wishes for a successful school year.

Confirmation of Appointment

A confirmation of an appointment need not be sent for every appointment, but it can be used to verify a verbal conversation.

SUGGESTED FEATURES

- Is brief and limited to appointment information, including date, time, place, and names.
- Is sent out immediately after the appointment is made.

SAMPLE LETTER OF CONFIRMATION

This is to confirm our appointment on Monday, September 2, at 9:00 a.m. in Room 4026, 4th Floor, of the Economic Development Building, 722 Capitol Mall. A public parking garage is located directly across the street at 7th and Capitol.

I look forward to continuing our discussion on your proposal.

Letter of Congratulations

Letters of congratulation build goodwill. They may be sent for the following occasions:

- Promotions and appointments to new positions.
- Achievements.
- Awards and honors.
- Introduction of a new product.
- Marriages, births, and anniversaries.
- Retirements.

SUGGESTED FEATURES

- Expresses interest sincerely and enthusiastically.
- Avoids negatives.
- Begins with the expression of congratulations.
- Mentions the reason for the congratulations.
- Ends with an expression of goodwill.

SAMPLE LETTER OF CONGRATULATIONS FOR RECEIVING AN AWARD

Congratulations for receiving the Distinguished Achievement Award from the National Media Association! I was so proud when they announced your name and the audience gave you a standing ovation.

No one is more deserving of this award than you. Congratulations on your consistent accomplishments. We are all celebrating for you.

SAMPLE LETTER OF CONGRATULATIONS FOR RECEIVING AN APPOINTMENT

Congratulations on your appointment as Vice President of The Travel Center. You have worked hard, and I am thrilled your efforts have been rewarded. You will bring dynamic leadership to your position.

Our company offers any help you need as you move into your new position. We're behind you all the way!

Employment Rejection

Examples of sample cover letters to use in a job search are in Chapter 2. Unsolicited letters of application should be answered briefly and immediately.

SUGGESTED FEATURES

- Conveys thanks for the interest in the firm.
- Indicates positions are not available.
- Expresses luck in job search.

SAMPLE LETTER OF REJECTION

Thank you for your interest in North Bay News. Presently we do not have any positions available that match your background.

We will keep your resume on file and contact you if your experience meets our needs. We wish you success in your job search.

Meeting Notification

Meeting notifications should be in writing. If the meeting will always be on the same day, same time, and same place, notification is sent when the meeting time and place are set, along with a listing of all the dates. If any dates are altered from the original schedule, notification should be in writing.

SUGGESTED FEATURES

- Is brief and limited to meeting information, including date, time, place, and names.
- Is sent out immediately after the meeting date is set.
- Includes any special items to be brought to the meeting; for example, budget figures, reports, or personnel manual.
- Includes a tentative agenda and asks for input.

SAMPLE NOTIFICATION LETTER

Our regular staff meeting would fall on March 23 this month. Since many of us will be in-volved in planning for our national convention, the date has been changed to March 15 at 1:00 p.m. in the Board Room.

Attached is a tentative agenda. If you have any item you would like to add, please let me know by March 10. We will be discussing sick-leave policy, so bring a copy of the regula-tions distributed on January 20.

Letter of Resignation

The letter of resignation is used to notify your supervisor that you are resigning from a position. Generally the letter should be positive, since these letters typically stay in a personnel file. If you resign because of a lack of promotional opportunities or be-cause you did not receive a promotion, you may prefer to express those disappointments in the letter of resignation. Derogatory comments about the staff or company should be avoided.

SUGGESTED FEATURE

- Includes the effective date, which is typically two weeks in advance of leaving.

SAMPLE FRIENDLY LETTER OF RESIGNATION

I am resigning effective June 1, 19__, after five years of stimulating and productive work at Ferraris, Inc. As you know, I will be moving to Seattle to take a position as administra-tive assistant to the president of Environmental Controls.

Moving back to Seattle fulfills a dream of being able to work environmental field in my hometown. I will miss all the good friends I've made at Ferraris, and I will particularly miss working with you. Thank you for making me part of the team.

SAMPLE LETTER OF RESIGNATION FOR LACK OF PROMOTIONAL OPPORTUNITIES

I am resigning as your administrative assistant effective June 1, 19__. Although I have learned a great deal working with you, I had hoped to have an opportunity to expand my responsi-bilities. I feel I need to find a position that will give me the chance to use more of my talents.

Thank you for all your help and support during these last three years.

Request Letter

A request letter should be clear and precise. Be brief and specific; cover only the infor-mation requested. If information is needed from two separate departments, write two letters.

SUGGESTED FEATURES

- Include all information necessary, such as item number, quality, price, color, and where to ship.
- Use list form, which is easier to read than a letter.

SAMPLE SIMPLE REQUEST LETTER

Please send me 15 copies of your free brochure, "Telephone Techniques." We plan to use this brochure in training our support staff.

Thank you.

SAMPLE REQUEST LETTER

The Harrison House is recommended as a good meeting facility near the Kansas City Airport. Our Board of Directors is meeting October 5–8, 19__, and we need a meeting room and accommodations.

Date	October 5–8
	Arriving October 4. Staying the nights of October 4, 5, 6, 7; departing October 8.
Number	15. Need a room with a large enough table to comfortably seat 15; video projection and overhead projection availability. 15 single-occupancy rooms.
Food Service	One evening banquet; four luncheons. If possible, meals in a room separate from the meeting room.

Please send rates, meeting room sizes, recreational facilities, and catering menus. We will be making a decision on the meeting by March 1. I look forward to hearing from you.

Sympathy Letter

Sympathy letters are written when a colleague (no matter what position in the company) has lost someone to death.

SUGGESTED FEATURES

- Expresses how you feel about the news.
- Recalls something positive about the deceased.
- Makes an offer to be of help or comfort.
- Uses a sympathy card or is handwritten on personal stationery.

SAMPLE SYMPATHY LETTER

I was shocked to hear about Jeff. He was so active and healthy.

Jeff was a wonderful, supportive man. He was always calm, even in times of crises. We all know how close you were and how much you will miss him.

I am thinking of you at this difficult time. Please let me know if there is anything I can do to help.

Reports provide essential information for everyday operations and decision making. Businesses could not function without written reports. A fundamental component of many office professionals' jobs is to correctly format reports for their supervisors. In addition to formatting, some office professionals decide on content and write reports.

Reports range from informal interoffice memos describing seminar attendance to bound formal reports such as feasibility studies. Reports are categorized according to subject, intended audience, and length. Each type of report requires a different format and organizational style, and these vary widely from one organization to another.

CHAPTER 18

REPORTS

SHORT REPORTS

Short reports are also called informal, semiformal, or semitechnical reports. They get right to the point, with objective reporting of facts in one to three pages. The subject of the report determines the number of subdivisions it has, if any. Short reports are typically routine and have a limited audience of coworkers or an immediate supervisor.

A short report will answer the questions who, why, where, when, what, and how. Some companies follow a specific procedure for organization of reports, while others leave the organization up to the author. A short report typically includes the following components:

- Purpose.
- Findings.
- Conclusion or Summary.
- Recommendations.

HINT: *Some employers prefer to find the recommendations at the beginning of the report instead of the end to avoid having to read the entire report.*

Detailed information such as drawings, charts, or cost analyses are usually placed at the end of the report in a section referred to as "Attachments" or "Appendices."

If a report is for in-house use, it is usually in memo format, while those reports going outside the company are typically written in the form of a letter. Memos are the least formal type of report format. Some companies may use standard, printed, letterhead forms. Memos use a heading with the following lines: To, From, Date, Subject. There is no need for an inside address, salutation, complimentary close, or signature line. Be sure to include the name and job title of individual(s) who will receive the memo or a copy of it. (See Figure 18-1.)

FORMATTING SUGGESTIONS

- Use a 6-inch line. Leave a 1-inch top margin unless using letterhead.
- Start the body of the report on the third line after the last line of the heading.
- Use single spacing with block paragraphs.

(For more detailed information on memos, see the section on Memo Styles in Chapter 17.)
     A letter has to appear more formal, especially if the report is directed to someone outside the company. It should be on company letterhead. (See Figure 18-2.)

FORMATTING SUGGESTIONS

- Use a 6-inch line. Lines of more than 6 inches are tiring to the eye.
- Allow a top margin of 2 to 2½ inches, depending upon the depth of the letterhead.
- Allow a bottom margin of 1 inch.
- Use single spacing with block or indented paragraphs and one blank line between paragraphs.
- Begin the body on the second line after the salutation.

(For detailed information on letters, see the section on Letter Styles in Chapter 17.)
     If the report is more than one page, type the continuation page on a blank sheet of paper. Leave a 1-inch top margin. Begin the body on the third line after the heading.

HINT: *A header command on a word processing program can add the required information and the page number.*

FORMATTING SUGGESTIONS

- Leave at least two lines of a paragraph at the bottom of a page. Carry over at least two lines to the next page.
- Do not divide the last word on a page.
- Always include at least two lines of copy after a heading before starting a new page.

TO   Maria Gravelez, Supervisor

FROM   Judith Witmore, CPS, Administrative Assistant

DATE   August 3, 19—

SUBJECT   Evaluation of PSI Convention in Salt Lake City

After attendance at the Professional Secretaries International Convention in Salt Lake City, July 20–25, 19—, I recommend that at least one support staff member have the opportunity to attend each year. The information distributed at the convention is extremely valuable and will be beneficial to all support staff at Western Bank.

The sessions ranged from technical to practical to personal. Even with the variety of the sessions, nearly all workshops focused on the central theme of expanding and enhancing the contribution of secretaries in the workplace.

The sessions I attended were as follows:

1. Selecting Office Products
2. Anatomy of a Merger
3. How to Get Your Article Published in *The Secretary*
4. Secretarial Stress: The Hidden and Controlling Factor

Over 50 companies exhibited the latest in office technology, demonstrating everything from fax machines to filing systems.

The convention was truly outstanding and a highlight of my professional career. I will be sharing what I learned with the other office professionals at Western Bank at our monthly meeting.

Figure 18-1 Short report in memo form.

December 7, 19—

Mr. Gary Thomas
Public Relations Director
Clemmons, Jones, and Grantz
3894 South Geary
San Francisco CA 94132

Dear Mr. Thomas:

This is the third issue of your company newsletter that I have coordinated and edited. I have the following recommendations, which I think
will enhance this communication.

Format
The two-column format does not provide much flexibility in layout and
design. We are restricted in placement of pictures and columnar headings. It is my recommendation that we move to a three-column format.

Pages
The number of pages has ranged from four to ten. The first newsletter
had ten pages, and subsequent issues gradually decreased to four. I recommend that a standard number of pages, preferably four, be set for
the newsletter. If there is any additional information that needs to be
included in an issue, it can be added as an insert.

—Continued—

Figure 18-2 Short report in letter form.

Gary Thomas
Page 2 of 2
December 7, 19—

Printing
We have used Mountain Printers because they gave the best quote.
As you know, we had to reprint the last issue because of the poor
quality of the photos. I have previously worked with Zenith Printers.
The cost is approximately 10 percent higher, but the quality is consis-
tently excellent.

Use of Color
We have used color in every headline. This format seems to make
the newsletter look "busy." I recommend we use color only on the
masthead, dates, and flag sections. It will not only reduce the cost but
also improve the appearance.

It has been a pleasure working with your professional staff. I am eager
to hear your reactions to these recommendations. I will be out of the
office until December 15. Please call me at 415-555-1257 any time
after that date so we can talk.

Sincerely,

Sarah Williams, CPS
Consultant

Figure 18-2 (continued.)

LONG REPORTS

A long or formal report gives detailed information about a subject and usually requires extensive research. The audience may include stockholders or top-level managers. Such reports may influence long-range financial or organizational decisions. Often they are designed and printed out-of-house if they are important enough.

Long reports may include some or all of the following components:

PRELIMINARY PAGES:

Cover, letter of transmittal, title page, table of contents, list of illustrations, abstract or executive summary.

BODY:

Introduction, background, problem, purpose, scope, main discussion (70 percent of the report), conclusions, recommendations.

BACK MATTER:

Glossary, references/bibliography, appendix

Many businesses have a standard format, described in a style guide, to follow in writing a report. A standard format minimizes misunderstandings between the author and the person or persons keying and/or designing the report.

Table 18-1 gives details on a format typically used in business reports. Word processing software programs provide report templates and styles to use or modify. These features allow some flexibility in appearance and spacing (see Chapter 19). For additional formatting suggestions, see the specific topics in this chapter.

Text Flow Suggestions

Standard typography rules are used to control the minimum number of paragraph lines displayed on a page and the lines of text that should be kept on the same page. The following are the standard rules:

1. Leave at least two lines of a paragraph at the bottom of a page. Carry over at least two lines to the next page.

HINT: *Use the widow/orphan feature of your word processing software to eliminate this problem.*

2. Keep headings and sideheads with the first line of the next paragraph.

HINT: *Use the keep with next or block protect feature of your word processing package.*

Table 18-1
BUSINESS REPORT FORMAT

Margins	Bound: 1.5-inch left margin; 1-inch right
	Unbound: 1-inch left margin; 1-inch right
Top of first page	2-inch margin
Succeeding pages	1-inch margin
Bottom	1 -inch margin
Page Numbers	
Preliminary pages	Use sequential lowercase roman numerals beginning with i for the title page. Center at the bottom of the page. The title page has no number.
Body	Use sequential arabic numerals beginning with 1 for the first page. They may be in one of two styles:
	1. At the top of the page at the right margin.
	2. Centered at the bottom of the page. When using word processing software, the default position for page numbers is .5 inches from the top and bottom of the page.
Spacing	
Body	Double-spaced with .5 inch paragraph indentions or use the report template in your word processing software.

   3. Avoid dividing a short paragraph.

HINT: *Use the keep lines together or block protect feature of your word processing package.*

   4. Begin chapter titles at the top of a page.

HINT: *Insert a page break before the chapter title.*

   5. Indent quoted material ½ inch from both margins. Either double- or single-space.
   6. Avoid dividing a quote or list of items unless at least two lines are at the bottom of a page and two lines are on the next page.

COVER

The cover should reflect the style of the rest of the report. An attractive cover helps persuade the reader to open the report and read it. A well-designed. cover makes it easy to understand the subject of the report. For an important enough report, these elements should appear on the cover:

- Title of the report.
- Name(s) of report writer(s).
- Name and address of the company.

FORMATTING SUGGESTIONS:

- Illustrations should be used only if they are relevant and of high quality.

- Simple typography should be used, and it should be stronger than the type size and typeface chosen for the inside.

- The paper should be heavier than the paper used for the report itself.

- Standard covers can be preprinted that include the company name and address and a cut-out window. The title of the report appears on the title page and will show through the window.

- The same elements that appear on the title page can also be printed on the cover page. (See the section on Title Page below.)

- A cover page is not necessary for reports that are somewhat less formal. A title page can be used as the cover for such reports.

- The top margin should be 2 inches and the bottom margin should be 1 inch.

HINT: *Your word processing software may have a cover page template.*

LETTER OF TRANSMITTAL

A letter of transmittal may be used to convey a report from one organization to another, or from one person to another. It may be bound as part of the report or it may be attached to the front. A letter of transmittal summarizes the purpose, scope, and major recommendations of the report. (See Figure 18-3.)

A cover letter may be used instead. A cover letter includes a simple statement such as "Enclosed is a copy of…." If reports are regularly distributed inside a company, a letter of transmittal is not necessary.

TITLE PAGE

A title page is usually the first page of a document after the cover. (See Figure 18-4.) It usually contains the following elements:

- Title. The title should be brief yet informative.
- Name(s) of report writer(s). Include the title(s) of the writers and their contribution to the project or report (e.g., coordinator, editor, analyst).
- Name and address of the company or organization preparing the report.
- Date the report was written.
- Any agency or order numbers.

February 10, 19—

Mr. Louis Johnson
President
Pacific Telecommunications
4783 South Pima
Tucson AZ 85745

Dear Mr. Johnson:

Enclosed is the report, "Improving Computer-User Comfort," that you
asked our company to prepare. The report summarizes current
research on the effects of computers on health and recommends
changes for your computer users.

We interviewed over 500 Pacific Telecommunications employees in the
last six months and consulted with health experts in eye and wrist
fatigue. We also reviewed all the current literature available for computer health hazards.

Our recommendations are as follows:
1. Antiradiation screens should be available for computer monitors.
2. Wrist supports should be used to help maintain proper wrist position
   during computer use and possibly reduce the risk of carpal tunnel
   syndrome.
3. Employees need adjustable chairs with a stronger back support.

You should find our report useful in reorganizing your computer area
for maximum comfort. If you have any questions or would like to discuss
our recommendations, please let us know.

Sincerely,

Janet Wong
Consultant

Figure 18-3 Letter of transmittal.

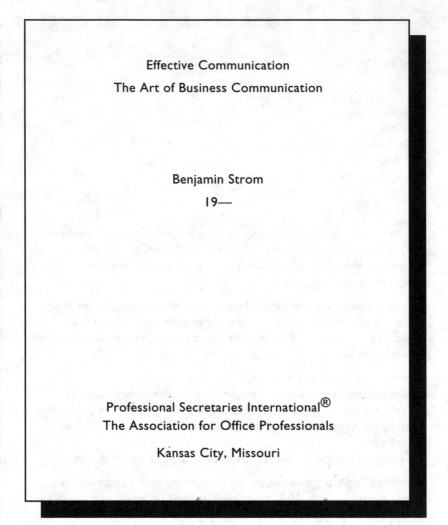

Figure 18-4 Sample title page.

- Name of the firm for which the report was prepared (e.g., *Prepared for Professional Secretaries International).*

FORMATTING SUGGESTIONS

- All title page elements do not have to be included, nor must they be in the order given above.
- The layout should be consistent with the document, however. If the chapters start on the same line on the page, the title should start on that same line.

- A 6-inch line length is typical.
- The reader's eye will usually start a quarter of the way down the page.
- Avoid putting the longest line at the top of the page or below the visual center.
- Allow enough space for the left margin given the binding that will be used.
- The title page is actually counted as small roman numeral i, even though no number is typed on the page.
- A short title may be in bold print and initial caps. A long title in bold print and capital letters is difficult to read and takes up too much space.

HINT: *Your word processing software may have a cover page template that can be used as a title page.*

TABLE OF CONTENTS

The table of contents lists the major sections of the report and the page numbers as well as all appendices. It allows the reader to see how the report is organized, what topics are covered, and where to find specific information. The table of contents may include a list of subdivisions and any subheadings that may be included under each subdivision. Include subheadings only if there are two or more, but do not include *any* subheadings if their inclusion would make the table of contents too long. (See Figure 18-5.)

Include a brief summary of the contents of each chapter if the subdivision titles are not sufficiently descriptive or if the contents need to convince the reader to look at the report.

If space is limited, the title page and table of contents may be combined on the same page.

FORMATTING SUGGESTIONS

- The left and right margins may be different from those of the report. The subdivisions and page numbers should be close enough together so the eye can link the two.
- Rules (lines) can be used to separate subdivisions instead of leader lines (rows of dots).

HINT: *Use the tab leader feature of your word processing program.*

- The top margin should be 2 inches from the top of the page and the bottom margin 1 inch from the bottom of the page.
- This page is counted as small Roman numeral ii, centered on the bottom of the page.

Table of Contents

Introduction
- Why Communication Is Important 1
- Your Goals in Communicating 2
- How Personality Affects Communication 3

Section 1: Communication Model
- The Communication Model 5
- Barriers to Effective Communication 8
- Overcoming Communication Problems 9

Section 2: Nonverbal Communication
- Eye Contact 11
- Gestures 15

Section 3: Interpersonal Communication
- Appearance 17
- Voice 20
- Facial Expressions 25

Section 4: Summary 28

ii

Figure 18-5 Sample table of contents.

HINT: *Use the table of contents feature of your word processing software to generate the table of contents.*

LIST OF ILLUSTRATIONS

This is a list of any illustrations and tables with their page numbers. (See Figure 18-6.) The single entry "Illustrations" and the page number is listed in the table of contents. If there are few illustrations, they can be listed in the table of contents.

Illustrations

iii

Figure 18-6 List of illustrations.

FORMATTING SUGGESTIONS

- It is not necessary to use the same margins as the report, but you should use the same margins as the table of contents.
- If there is a list of illustrations, it is counted as small Roman numeral iii, centered on the bottom of the page.
- The top margin should be 2 inches and the bottom margin 1 inch.

HINT: *Use the table numbering feature in your word processing software to automatically number tables and illustrations. This feature will also generate separate lists of tables and illustrations.*

ABSTRACT OR EXECUTIVE SUMMARY

The abstract or executive summary is a summary of what the report contains, including problems and conclusions. It may contain a listing of key points in sentences or miniparagraphs. Readers can see the contents of the report without having to read it. The abstract or executive summary immediately precedes the text, but it does not always have to appear on a separate page. Sometimes it is included in the cover letter preceding the document. If space is available, it may be on the title page or cover.

FORMATTING SUGGESTIONS

- The abstract may be less than a page; an executive summary is often two or three pages.
- If these elements are used, it is counted as the next small Roman numeral, centered on the bottom of the page.
- The top margin should be 2 inches and the bottom margin 1 inch.

Here is a sample summary:

"Improving Computer User Comfort" summarizes the current research on the effects of computers on health and recommends changes for computer users. Employees were interviewed and health professionals were consulted. Current literature was reviewed.

It is recommended that the following accessories be made available for computer users: antiradiation screens for computer monitors, wrist supports to help maintain proper wrist position during computer use and possibly reduce the risk of carpal tunnel syndrome, and adjustable chairs with a stronger back support.

BODY OF THE REPORT

The body is the main text of the report and should be organized according to the nature of the report. Listed below are the sections included in most reports.

Introduction: An introduction tells the reader why the report was written and helps interpret what follows. It can be in a larger type size than or have different line spacing from the rest of the report.

Main discussion: The main discussion should be organized according to major topics and subtopics. Headings help readers identify major subjects and are included in the table of contents.

Conclusion: The conclusion ties everything together for the reader by presenting the findings of the report. Conclusions should be based on the information and documentation in the report and contain no new information.

Recommendations: Recommendations suggest what should be done based on the findings or point out areas in which further study is needed. Not all reports have recommendations.

TEXT HEADINGS

Headings are important because they allow the reader to see how a report is organized. Headings can be one of the following types:

Centered on a line by itself. Leave two blank lines above and one below the heading, which should be all capitals or initial caps and bold.

Flush left on a line by itself. Leave two blank lines above and one below the heading, which should be all capitals or initial caps and bold.

A *paragraph heading* begins a paragraph and is followed by text on the same line. Leave one blank line above the heading, which can be bold or italic and should be followed by a period. Begin the text two spaces after the period.

Before selecting a subheading style, decide how many levels of subheadings are needed. Headings should be limited to a maximum of three levels.

If one head level is used, it should be flush left.

If two head levels are used, one should be flush left and the other a paragraph heading *or* one should be centered and the other flush left.

If three head levels are used, one should be centered, one flush left, and one a paragraph heading.

FORMATTING SUGGESTIONS

- Use either upper- and lowercase or all capitals. The choice is determined by the length of the majority of headings; long headings are more difficult to read in all caps. When using upper- and lowercase, use lowercase for "the," "a," "to," "of," "with," "for," "by."
- The report title should be bigger and/or bolder than the strongest subheading.

HINT: *Use the style headings available with your word processing package.*

- A heading can be one size larger in the same weight as the text.

HINT: *Use the outlining feature of your word processing program to review your headings.*

HEADERS AND FOOTERS

Multipage documents include headers and/or footers. A header is information that prints at the top of the second and the following pages; a footer is the same information, but printed instead at the bottom of the page. Headers and footers typically are not printed on the first page of a document. They may have more than one line of text.

By using word processing software, different headers or footers can be created for even pages, odd pages, and (if appropriate) the first page. For example, the chapter title can be printed on the even pages and the text of the first head level on the odd pages. Page numbers are appropriate in either the header or footer.

HINT: *If the fonts are changed for the entire document, the fonts of the header and/or footer typically must be changed also.*

HINT: *If a multipage document is printed two-sided, odd and even headers or footers are more professional.*

TABLES

Tables are used to present statistical data to explain written text. All tables present data in vertical columns and horizontal rows. (See Figure 18-7.)

FORMATTING SUGGESTIONS

- Maintain equal space between columns.
- Leave at least half an inch of white space above and below the table.
- The typeface may differ from that of the report. Sans serif figures are often preferred to serif figures (see the section on Type and Printing Styles in Chapter 19 for an explanation of serif/sans serif). Times Roman and Helvetica are usually legible and narrow, which means more information can be placed in the table.
- Try to keep the table vertical so readers will not have to turn the page to read it. Use a double spread over two facing pages for a wide table.

Table I
Annual Salary Ranges by Title
(rounded to the nearest dollar)

Title	Quoted Salary Range	Average Salary Range
Administrative Assistant	$12,000–60,000	$25,555–27,605
Administrative Secretary	42,000–50,000	25,183–29,109
Executive Secretary	14,000–45,000	22,849–28,069
Secretary	8,320–48,000	21,116–24,218
Secretary/Receptionist	10,400–28,000	17,643–19,647

Source: Secretarial Want Ad Survey.

Figure 18-7 A sample table.

- If the table will not fit on the same page as the text referring to the table, put the table on the page immediately following the reference in the text. If necessary, reduce the table by photocopying so it will fit on the same page as the reference to it.
- Use margins equal to or wider than the report's margins.
- Use consistent line spacing for all tables in a report. If you are using a word processing program, experiment with spacing between lines.

Table Numbers

Tables can be numbered Table 1, Table 2, Table 3, etc., in the order they are mentioned in the text and with "Table" capitalized. It is not necessary to number tables if a report has only one table, widely scattered tables, or tables that can be easily described and found.

Tables should be numbered separately from illustrations, such as Table 1, Illustration or Figure 1. However, if the report has many tables, graphs, and charts, they can all be called Exhibit and numbered in sequence.

Tables can also be placed in an appendix. Tables in an appendix are numbered separately from those in the text. For example, Table A-1 would be Table 1 in Appendix A.

FORMATTING SUGGESTIONS

- Use either all capitals or an initial capital, i.e., TABLE 1 or Table 1 and bold.
- The table number can be set flush left on a line by itself with the title directly below it.
- The table number can also be on the same line with the title, followed by a period or a dash, or sometimes both: Table 1. Annual Salary Ranges by Title; Table 1—Annual Salary Ranges by Title; Table 1.—Annual Salary Ranges by Title

HINT: *Use the table numbering feature of your word processing software.*

Table Titles

The title of a table should be short and direct. Omit articles such as "the" and "a" and phrases such as "summary of."

FORMATTING SUGGESTIONS

- Center the title or place it flush left.
- Do not use punctuation after a title unless it is a full sentence.
- Words should be capitalized with letters in both upper- and lowercase, except for articles and short prepositions, which should be in lowercase. Titles in all caps are difficult to read and take up more space.

- If a title runs two lines, the lines should be similar in length, with the first slightly longer than the second. If the title is flush left, the second line may be either flush left or indented. Otherwise both lines must be centered.
- Leave white space before the body of the table.
- Use bold type for an effective table title.

Subtitles

A subtitle gives an explanation of the table. It may list abbreviations or explain how the data were obtained. The subtitle should apply to the entire table and not just to one or two columns. Place specific information about columns in footnotes. (See the section on Footnotes, Endnotes, and Text Notes below for additional information.)

FORMATTING SUGGESTIONS

- The subtitle may be in the same style as the title or in parentheses.
- Place the subtitle on a separate line below the title.
- The type size is usually smaller than that of the title.

Column Headings

Single words or concise phrases are used above all columns in a table. Two lines may be necessary to explain columns.

FORMATTING SUGGESTIONS

- Use enough white space between column headings so the table does not look crowded.
- Use bold type for effective column headings.
- A column heading spanning two or more columns is called a spanner head. The spanner head may be separated from column heads by a space, a rule, or a different typeface.
- Use upper- and lowercase letters.
- Center the column head if it is narrower than the column text; otherwise leave it flush left.
- Avoid abbreviations and symbols that may not be understood by the reader.

Figures

Align columns of numbers at the right:

4504
23
2

Dollar Amounts

Omit decimal points and zeros when the figures are whole amounts. However, if one amount contains a cents figure, every amount requires the cents. Place the dollar sign next to the first amount. Align the dollar sign vertically with the column containing the longest figure. (See the examples below.) Do not use commas in four-digit numbers unless the numbers appear in the same column with larger numbers.

$$\begin{array}{ll}
\$\quad 20 & \$\quad 20 \\
1000 & 1,000 \\
350 & 35,000
\end{array}$$

Decimals

Align the decimal points of every figure in a column. All figures should have the same number of decimal places.

$$\begin{array}{l}
10.000 \\
5.535 \\
7.750
\end{array}$$

Percentages

A percent sign follows the first figure in a column of percentages. However, percent signs are not necessary if you use the word *percent* or *percentage* in the column heading:

MEMBERS RESPONDING	PERCENT OF MEMBERS RESPONDING
50.2%	50.2
30.7	30.7
28.2	28.2

Parentheses

Parentheses around figures signify a negative amount. If some, but not all of the figures include parentheses, the figures should still align on the right:

$$\begin{array}{r}
(340,400) \\
2,500 \\
(50)
\end{array}$$

Dates

Right align a column of dates by the last figure:

January 5, 1998
June 12, 1998
October 2, 1998

Total Amounts

The total is usually shown as the last row in a table of figures. The total should be clearly labeled and easy to find. However, it may be omitted if it is obviously a total. When a percentage adds up to 100, the *total* is optional. If the percentages do not add up to 100, a total should be given with a note such as "Percentages do not add up to 100 percent because of rounding."

	35
	2,365
	796
TOTAL	**3,196**

The word *total* should be indented from the left margin of the table and may be in all caps and bold.

HINT: *If using a word processing package, add shading to the total row.*

Word Tables

Word tables should be simple. Entries should be brief, with or without rules. Runover lines can be flush left as shown or indented several spaces.

FORMATTING SUGGESTIONS

- Set in all caps and indent.
- Use bold type for heading and title.
- Set off with one blank line above or below.
- Do not use periods.

Footnotes

Footnotes include source notes, spelling out of abbreviations in a table, and explanations of specific items in a column. They are placed immediately below the table.

Source notes are required when the table is reprinted from another source or when the table has been created using data from another reference. Source notes should be placed before any other table notes:

Raised symbols in a table refer the reader to notes. Common symbols are *, †, ‡, and §.

FORMATTING SUGGESTIONS

- Set footnote in a smaller type size than the table.
- Set the words *Note* or *Source* in italics.
- Begin footnotes flush left.
- Place a period at the end of each note.

CHARTS AND GRAPHS

A chart or graph shows numbers in picture form. This representation of data can often have a greater impact than a table of figures. Tables are used when readers need precise statistical details; charts and graphs are used when readers are concerned with the overall effects of statistics. But note that too much information in one diagram is confusing; it is better to have two small charts than one large chart.

Charts and graphs are easy to produce using computer software. The following information is entered into the computer:

- Title of the chart.
- Subtitle (if needed).
- Heading for the x-axis (horizontal axis) and y-axis (vertical axis) if creating a bar or line chart.

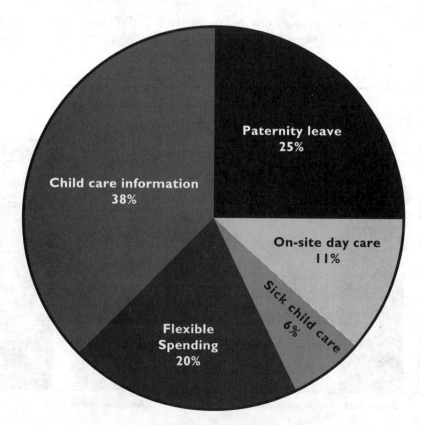

Work/Family Conflicts
% of Companies Reporting Programs

Figure 18-8 Sample pie chart.

- Numbers for each entry in the chart or graph.
- Footnotes, if needed.
- Appropriate type of graph.

The software then creates the graph on screen.

The three most popular ways of presenting statistical information in graphic form are pie charts, bar charts, and line graphs.

Pie Charts

Pie charts are used to show budgets, sales, and costs at a particular time. They are not effective for showing trends over a period of time. And if there is a large gap between the highest and lowest figures, it is difficult to show the smallest numbers accurately. The size of a section or wedge of the pie chart is proportional to the quantity the wedge represents. (See Figure 18-8.)

Do not use more than six sections in a pie chart; it is difficult to read a pie chart with more sections. Avoid listing small slices of the pie separately; combine small slices into a

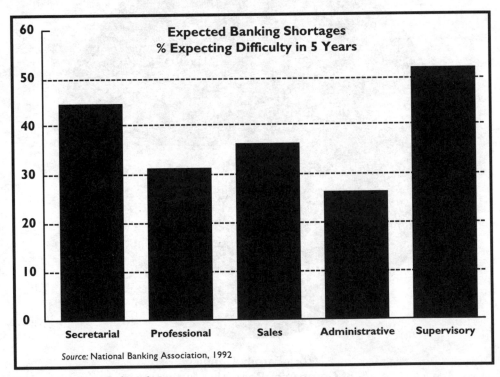

Figure 18-9 Sample bar chart.

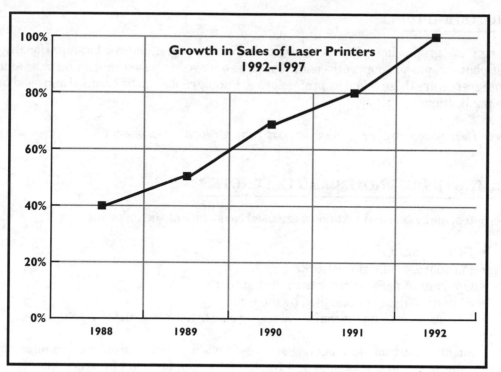

Figure 18-10 Sample line graph.

category called "Other" or "Miscellaneous." Make the slices add up to an exact figure: 1, 100%, $1, or a rounded multiple of one of these.

Bar Charts

Bar charts are used to show information over a period of time or to make comparisons. Bar charts allow for more complex comparison of information by presenting data in multiple bars. The height of a bar is proportional to the quantity it represents. Vertical bars are used to show increases in quantities. Horizontal bars are used to show increases in distance. As on pie charts, if there is a large gap between the highest and lowest figures, it is difficult to show the smallest numbers accurately. (See Figure 18-9.)

Line Graphs

A line graph is effective in illustrating trends or comparisons over a period of time. Limit the number of lines to three if they cross one another, four if they do not intersect. (See Figure 18-10.)

PHOTOGRAPHS

Using photographs in a report is a way to increase interest and readership. Usually the best photographs of people are candid shots, as opposed to posed shots. The most skillful photographs are those taken by professionals. Photographs can be scanned and used in office publications.

HINT: *Hire photographers who work part-time for local newspapers.*

FOOTNOTES, ENDNOTES, AND TEXT NOTES

Footnotes, endnotes, and text notes are used to document the following:

- Direct quotes.
- Paraphrases of written works.
- Opinions of persons other than the author.
- Statistical data not compiled by the writer.
- Visuals such as photographs, tables, or charts not constructed by the author.

Many formats exist for documenting sources used in a report or to provide information outside the main text. Footnotes are positioned at the bottom of a page, endnotes are placed at the end of a report, and text notes are notes in parentheses within the body of the material itself.

Footnotes and endnotes are easy to do using word processing software. The footnote will be automatically positioned on the page in the appropriate place with a superscript (raised number) in the text. If there are many footnotes on a page, the report will look unattractive; the reader's eye must move from the body of the text to the bottom of the page. The endnote feature puts endnotes at the end of the document. Endnotes necessitate flipping back to the end of the report to find the reference.

FORMATTING FOOTNOTES

- Use a type size two sizes smaller than that of the text, if possible.
- Single-space the footnotes; double-space between footnotes.
- Indent the first line of each footnote 1½ inches or place it flush left.

FORMATTING ENDNOTES

- Place endnotes after appendices. If there are no appendices, the endnotes follow the body of the report.
- Center the heading "Notes" 2 inches from the top of the page.
- Begin keying the first endnote two blank lines below the heading.

- Single-space endnotes; double-space between endnotes.
- Indent the first line of each endnote 1½ inches or place it flush left.
- Use the same margins as in the report.
- Number the pages as part of the report.

FORMATTING TEXT NOTES

- Text notes immediately follow the information given in the report.
- If there are only a few references in the report, all bibliographic data can be placed in parentheses. (See Figure 18-11.)
- When there are numerous references in the body of the report, give the name of the author and the page number of the text in parentheses immediately after the information presented in the report. List the sources in full at the end of the report.

REFERENCE NOTES, REFERENCE LIST, AND BIBLIOGRAPHY

Several different styles may be used for citing sources in footnotes, endnotes, or text notes. Footnotes are placed at the bottom of the page on which the citation appears. Endnotes are compiled at the end of the chapter or report, listed in the order in which they appear in the text. Text notes are given in parentheses in the body of the text. The style shown below is for business reference notes. (Academic style differs slightly in that the place of publication precedes the publisher and date, with a colon after the place.)

BOOK WITH ONE AUTHOR:

1. Carolyn J. Mullins, *The Complete Writing Guide to Preparing Reports, Proposals, Memos, Etc.*, Aaron Publishing Co., Englewood Cliffs, NJ, 1996.

Pay Equity
Childcare workers are paid less than plumbers; physiotherapists are paid less than brewery workers; experienced secretaries are paid less than delivery truck drivers (Barbara Carlson, *Working Report*, Universal Publishers, New York, 1992, p. 85). These statistics seem shocking but they are true. They attest to the widespread pay inequities between female- and male-dominated professions.

Figure 18-11 Text notes in a report.

TWO OR MORE BOOKS BY THE SAME AUTHOR:

2. Carolyn J. Mullins, *The Complete Writing Guide to Preparing Reports, Proposals, Memos, Etc.*, Aaron Publishing Co., Englewood Cliffs, NJ, 1996.
3. ———, *Report Writing*, Cooper Press, New York, 1997, p. 54.

BOOK WITH TWO AUTHORS:

4. Mark Louis and Margaret Emke, *Successful Writing*, Cooper Press, New York, 1997.

BOOK WITH THREE OR MORE AUTHORS:

5. Milton Hoover and others, *Report References for the 1990's*, P.J. Thomas Co., Boston, 1992.

BOOK TITLE WITH EDITION NUMBER:

(the edition number is given when the book is not in its first edition):

6. Harry Shadle, *Economics of Business*, 3rd ed., Iowa State University Press, Ames, 1994.

BOOK WITH CORPORATE AUTHOR:

7. Professional Secretaries International®, *How to Get Your Article Published in* The Secretary, Kansas City, MO, 1995.

ARTICLE IN A MAGAZINE OR PROFESSIONAL JOURNAL:

8. William Smith, "Accessories Improve User Comfort," *The Secretary*, 50:8, October 1997.
9. Ron Zemke, "The Ups and Downs of Downsizing," *Training*, 27:11, November 1997, p. 27.

ARTICLE IN A MAGAZINE OR PROFESSIONAL JOURNAL WITH NO AUTHOR CITED:

10. Green Ballots vs. Greenbacks," *Time*, 136:22, November 19, 1996, p. 44.

ARTICLE IN A NEWSPAPER:

11. Sabin Russell, "Dow Advances 36 Points in Strong Session," *San Francisco Chronicle*, December 13, 1996, C1.

TECHNICAL PAPER PRESENTED AT A CONFERENCE:

12. Diane B. Hartman and Lorraine F. Colletti, "Secretarial Stress: The Hidden and Controlling Factor," Professional Secretaries International Convention, Salt Lake City, UT, July 25, 1996.

SPEECH OR CONVERSATION:

13. Bernard F. White, U.S. Department of Labor, Washington, DC, speaking to the 59th annual American Vocational Association Conference, Cincinnati, OH, December 5, 1996.

A bibliography lists all the references relevant to the report, while a reference list gives just the ones cited. In a reference list, an author's first name precedes the last name; in a bibliography, the name of the initial author is reversed, with the last name appearing first. The works are numbered in a reference list but unnumbered in a bibliography. Works appear in a reference list in the same sequence that the information they contain appears in the report, while in a bibliography they are listed alphabetically by author. Reference lists and bibliographies are usually punctuated and capitalized in the same way. And both are positioned at the end of the report before attachments.

FORMATTING SUGGESTIONS:

- Place the title 2 inches from the top of the page.
- Use the same margins as in the report.
- Begin each reference at the left margin.
- Indent the second line five spaces.
- Single-space each reference; double-space between references.
- References without authors are alphabetized by title.

Here is a sample bibliography:

"Green Ballots vs. Greenbacks," *Time*, 136:22, November 19, 1996, p. 44.

Hartman, Diane B. and Lorraine F. Colletti, "Secretarial Stress: The Hidden and Controlling Factor," Professional Secretaries International Convention, Salt Lake City, UT, July 25, 1996.

Hoover, Milton and others, *Report References for the 1990's.* P.J. Thomas Co., Boston, 1992.

Louis, Mark and Margaret Emke, *Successful Writing*, Cooper Press, New York, 1997.

Mullins, Carolyn J., *The Complete Writing Guide to Preparing Reports, Proposals, Memos, Etc.*, Aaron Publishing Co., Englewood Cliffs, NJ, 1997.

————, *Report Writing,* Cooper Press, New York, 1997.

Professional Secretaries International®, *How to Get Your Article Published in The Secretary,* Kansas City, MO, 1995.

Russell, Sabin, "Dow Advances 36 Points in Strong Session," *San Francisco Chronicle,* December 13, 1996, C1.

Shadle, Harry, *Economics of Business,* 3rd ed., Iowa State University Press, Ames, 1994.

Smith, William, "Accessories Improve User Comfort," *The Secretary,* 50:8, October 1997, p. 31.

White, Bernard F., U.S. Department of Labor, Washington, DC, speaking to the 59th American Vocational Association Conference, Cincinnati, OH, December 5, 1996.

Zemke, Ron, "The Ups and Downs of Downsizing," *Training,* 27:11, November 1997, p. 27.

GLOSSARY

A glossary is an alphabetical listing of specialized vocabulary and definitions. A glossary is necessary if the readers will be unfamiliar with the terms used in the report.

FORMATTING SUGGESTIONS

- The heading "Glossary" is centered 2 inches from the top of the page.
- Leave two blank lines after the heading.
- Use one of the following styles: (1) Two columns—put the terms in alphabetical order in the left column and definitions in the right. (2) Hanging indentation—begin each term at the left margin, followed by a colon, then give the definition; indent the second line five spaces from the left margin. (3) Paragraph style—indent each term five spaces from the left margin, followed by a colon, then give the definition; the second line is flush with the left margin.
- Terms may be in bold.
- Use periods at the end of definitions if they are written as sentences.

HINT: *Use the glossary feature of your word processing package to create the glossary.*

APPENDICES

Appendices include the supporting material for the report. Items in an appendix may be questionnaires, statistics, detailed test results, descriptions of data, or cost comparisons. Appendices appear in the order referred to in the report. Each appendix is assigned a letter; e.g., Appendix A, Appendix B, etc.

FORMATTING SUGGESTIONS

- Type the heading "Appendix A" centered 2 inches from the top of the page.
- Leave two blank lines after the heading.

COMPUTER PRESENTATIONS

Graphic presentation software makes it easy to develop highly professional presentations. This method can be used with a group or in a booth at a trade show to attract the attention of participants. The presentation can also be sent on disk to customers or off-site employees.

The following are suggestions when designing a computer presentation:

- Select a background that will project well.

HINT: *Blue backgrounds make words easy to read when projected.*

- Avoid the temptation to create complex visuals, which will distract from the message.
- Include one major idea in each visual. When presenting, paraphrase rather than read the visual.
- Include transitions (an eye-catching way to move from slide to slide) and builds (the highlighting of one subtitle at a time).
- Print copies of the visuals as handouts. Most computer presentation programs will automatically reduce the size of the visuals so that several can be printed on a page.
- Place a black visual at the end of the presentation so you know you have finished.
- Include graphs, charts, graphics, and tables to increase visual interest.

HINT: *Invest in a software clip art collection; such collections will greatly increase the number of graphics available and they are reasonably priced.*

- Use the spell check feature and proofread carefully. The visuals should be perfect.
- Check the location where the presentation will be given to make certain the presentation projects properly.

HINT: *When dealing with equipment in a remote location, plan to arrive at least 45 minutes ahead of time for troubleshooting.*

HINT: *If you are presenting in a place you are not familiar with, always have a hard copy of the visuals made into transparencies in case the equipment does not work properly.*

HINT: *Bring an extension cord with three-way adapter plugs. If you are using an over-head and projection plate, bring an extra transparency bulb.*

A disadvantage of computer presentations is the inability to personalize them. If you wish audience input, bring along a flip chart or make certain a board is available for writing. Also the audience can be distracted by the transition from one slide to another.

Office publications have four functions:

- To capture attention
- To focus interest
- To create a desire
- To motivate to action

Each step of the publishing process, from writing copy to choosing paper, should contribute to one of these functions.

There are two methods of creating newsletters, brochures, and flyers. One method is to decide on content for a publication and use specialists such as graphic artists and typographers to decide layout, suggest graphics and paper, and determine type size. Another method, which is becoming increasingly popular because of advances in technology, is to use computers and software to create and design publications.

TYPESETTING VERSUS DESKTOP PUBLISHING

In conventional publishing, after the design and editing of a document are completed, it is given to a typesetter. The designer specifies the typeface (including italics and bold), type size, line spacing, and line length. Any artwork is usually done by the designer or an artist. Once the layout is completed, the originator must proof the copy and approve it for printing.

Desktop publishing (DTP) involves using the computer to create both text and graphics for a camera-ready publication, that is, one ready to be photographed and printed. Because of the capabilities of the software, changes are easy to make. Output is done on a laser printer.

In-house DTP eliminates the need to hire outside graphic artists and typesetters to produce publications and offers the following advantages:

- It speeds up production because it is no longer necessary to accommodate the schedules of specialists.
- It saves money after the initial equipment purchase because some or all of the work is completed in-house.
- It is easier to make changes and corrections.
- It offers more internal control over the design and production schedule.

CHAPTER 19

OFFICE

PUBLISHING

- It provides greater security for confidential or sensitive documents.
- It allows a business to have more professional-looking everyday documents.

Whether a typesetter is used or not, the printing process remains the same. Small jobs can be printed out and then reproduced on a copy machine, with larger publications completed by a professional printer.

Understanding the intricacies of DTP means learning new software as well as designing layout and comprehending printing terms and vocabulary. Many firms designate employees or departments for these needs.

DESKTOP PUBLISHING HARDWARE AND SOFTWARE

Listed below are suggestions for hardware and software selections:

- A PC or Macintosh computer with high-capacity hard drive and at least 16 MB of RAM (random access memory).
- Laser printer.
- Scanner.
- Optional: CD-ROM drive, which allows for easy access to graphics and fonts.
- Desktop publishing program or word processing software.

HINT: *Most word processing programs can do a good job of DTP.*

- Graphics software, which may include clip art, fonts, and photographs.

Also see Chapter 7 for descriptions of hardware and Chapter 8 for descriptions of software.

TYPE AND PRINTING STYLES

Various typefaces, or shapes of type, and sizes of characters are used in publishing. Different typefaces can greatly affect the appearance and legibility of a document and help deliver the appropriate message. A typesetter will have hundreds of typefaces from which to choose, but the DTP selection is more limited.

Typeface

Different typefaces produce appearances that convey characteristics such as high-tech, plain, conservative, feminine, masculine, or classic. Companies use different typefaces to reflect a style and corporate identity. Table 19-1 lists some specific typefaces that convey certain images.

Table 19-1
TYPEFACE CHARACTERISTICS

IMAGE	TYPEFACE
Classic	Baskerville, Caslon, Garamond, Goudy Old Style
Clean, modern	Century Schoolbook, Bodoni
Ultramodern	Futura
Conservative	Franklin, Rockwell, Clarendon, Italienne, Egyptian, Italia, Memphis, Prestige Elite
Mainstream	Baskerville, Caslon, Times Roman, Souvenir, Cooper

The major distinction between typefaces is the presence or absence of serifs. **Serifs** are the small curves added to the ends of strokes; **sans serif** typefaces lack these small curves. Here are two different typefaces, one with serifs and one sans serif:

Desktop Publishing (serif)
Desktop Publishing (sans serif)

Most of the differences among typefaces are in the lowercase letters. The one letter that most often differs from typeface to typeface is the lowercase g. Listed below is the letter g in a variety of typefaces:

g   Garamond
g   Times Roman
g   Bookman
g   Gothic

Table 19-2 lists some common serif and sans serif typefaces.

Research has shown that sans serif is harder to read than serif type. Sans serif is also difficult to read in boldface or italics. Sans serif type is recommended mainly for headings and headlines.

Table 19-2
COMMON TYPEFACES

SERIF	SANS SERIF
Times Roman*	Helvetica*
Bookman	Optima
Palatino	Avant Garde
New Century (also called Century or Century Schoolbook)	Futura

*Most common typefaces

Table 19-3
TYPEFACES FOR DIFFERENT PUBLICATIONS

PUBLICATION	TYPEFACE
Advertising	Sans serif (e.g., Helvetica)
Books	Serif (e.g., Garamond, Souvenir, Optima)
Technical books	Sans serif
Charts	Sans serif (e.g., HeIvetica, Avant Garde)
Documents (lengthy)	Serif
Magazines	Serif
Newsletters	Serif (e.g., Times Roman, Bookman, Trump, Palatino)
Reports	Sans serif
Signs	Sans serif
Table	Sans serif (e.g., Helvetica, Avant Garde)

Table 19-3 lists the recommended typefaces for various sorts of publications. Here are a few miscellaneous but important facts about typefaces to bear in mind:

- Typefaces with different names can be identical because although a typeface *itself* cannot be copyrighted, the typeface *name* can be.

- Typefaces with geographic names (Venice, New York, Geneva) may cause problems when brought into page layout software. The characters are wide, with wider spacing between letters, and they look less attractive when printed.

- Times Roman and Helvetica are usually standard on DTP systems; others can be purchased on disk and downloaded or copied onto the hard disk.

Type Size

The size of the type determines whether people read a publication. A small type size is doomed to failure. The size of type is measured in picas and points. The pica and point system dates back to the time when all type was produced in metal or wood. A *pica* is one-sixth of an inch. Each pica is divided into 12 **points.** A point is $1/72$ of an inch. The size of type is called the **point size,** and is approximately equal to the distance from the top of an h to the bottom of a q.

$$
\begin{array}{rcl}
1 \text{ inch} & = & 6 \text{ picas} \\
1 \text{ pica} & = & 12 \text{ points} \\
72 \text{ points} & = & 1 \text{ inch}
\end{array}
$$

Twelve-point type, for example, is type that measures 12 points from the top to the bottom of the letters. DTP software programs provide measurements in fractions of points and

Table 19-4
DIFFERENT POINT SIZES OF TWO TYPEFACES

TIMES ROMAN (SERIF)	HELVETICA (SANS SERIF)
This is 7 point.	This is 7 point.
This is 10 point.	This is 10 point.
This is 12 point.	This is 12 point.
This is 18 point.	This is 18 point.
This is 42 point.	This is 42 point.

sometimes in centimeters and millimeters. The range of type sizes available depends on the printer used and the fonts available.

Table 19-4 shows examples of Times Roman and Helvetica in different point sizes. Notice that Helvetica tends to look larger than Times Roman, although they are the same point size. For a document with a lot of text, the characters per line make the number of pages; i.e., the more characters on a line of text, the shorter the document. Listed below are some common uses of common type sizes:

Brochure to fit in No. 10 envelope	14–36 point
Copyright notice or other fine print	6 point
Formal announcements and invitations	10, 12, or 14 point
Newsletter body	10 or 12 point
Text	10 or 12 point
Overhead transparency	18 point or larger

HINT: *For the subtitle, use a larger point size than for the text, and use an even larger size for the main title (14 points or larger). If 12-point type seems too large, use a lighter weight type (see next section).*

Type Style

Each typeface usually has a series of different **weights,** or letter thicknesses. Most computerized typefaces should have at least a bold weight and an italic. Tables 19-5 and 19-6 show different weights of Helvetica and the uses of different styles.

Table 19-5
WEIGHTS OF HELVETICA TYPE

This is an example of Helvetica typeface in light weight.
This is an example of Helvetica typeface in bold weight.
This is an example of Helvetica typeface in italic.

Table 19-6
USES OF DIFFERENT TYPE STYLES

STYLE	USE
Bold	Main titles and subtitles; used to draw attention to the most important thing first. Avoid setting large blocks of text in bold because nothing will stand out.
Italics	Quotations, names of books and magazines, emphasized words. Avoid setting large blocks of text in italics because research shows people read italic type up to 20 words per minute more slowly than regular type.
Capital letters	Only used if a few individual words need emphasis. A long title in capitals may take up too much space or be difficult to read.
Underlining	Avoid (left over from the days of typewriters); use italics or bold for emphasis.

Fonts

A font is a particular style and size of a typeface. It is also called a **type family.** A font includes capitals, lowercase, small caps, punctuation marks, and mathematical symbols. Below is a font of Times Roman:

ABCDEFGHIJKLMNOPQRSTUVWXYZ
abcdefghijklmnopqrstuvwxyz

Leading

Leading is the distance between lines of type; it is often called line spacing. Line spacing does not alter the size of the typeface or lengthen the line; it merely moves the lines farther apart. Short lines (e.g., 45 characters on a line) need less space between them than long lines (e.g., 80 characters on a line). DTP software usually has a 2-point leading default, which is acceptable for most publications.

Extra leading for bold type increases legibility and may be needed to lighten its color or weight. Sans serif type might also need extra leading to help the reader's eye drop to next line of text. Below are two sample pieces of text with different leading:

A type set on its own body size without
additional line feed is said to be
"set solid."

A 12-point type with 3 points of extra space
is called "12 on 15 pt" or $^{12}/_{15}$ pt.
Printers refer to this as 3-point leading.

Suggestions for a Professional Appearance

Here are some suggestions to guide you in making type choices:

1. Use no more than two typefaces (a headline face and a body copy face) in a document. The two typefaces should be different enough to be distinguishable from one another. Often the best mix is a serif typeface with a sans serif one.
2. Choose the most readable typeface. Ornate typefaces are difficult to read, as this example shows:

Holiday Greetings

Type should be determined by the audience. Young or older readers need larger text type so it can be read easily, while busy executives need type that can be scanned quickly. Avoid using a script typeface, which looks like handwriting, for more than a few lines of copy, because it is tiring to the eye.

3. Determine the reading distance before determining the type size. Posters, for example, take a larger type size than a booklet.
4. Lengthen the line or reduce the type size to save space, rather than changing the typefaces.
5. Type may be either right-justified (even along the right margin) or ragged right (uneven at the right margin). Justified text is associated with typeset copy; however, some people feel justified text is harder to read than ragged right. If text is ragged right, paragraphs should have one line of space between them and not be indented. If the text is justified, paragraphs should have one line space between them and be indented.
6. Avoid leaving a blank line between paragraphs.

HINT: *Use your software to leave additional space above and below paragraphs.*

7. Use one rather than two spaces after the period at the end of a sentence.

HINT: *Use the search and replace feature to change two spaces to one space.*

8. Do not use asterisks to begin items in a list; instead, use bullets or other symbols.

Columns

The width of the column depends upon the purpose of the publication. The following table suggests uses for different numbers and widths of columns:

COLUMN WIDTH	USE
One	Newsletters, pamphlets
Two	Newsletters
Three	Newsletters, publications that mix text with graphics and or boxes
Four	Indices, lists, dictionaries
Five or Six	Newspapers

GRAPHICS AND ILLUSTRATIONS

A graphic or illustration in a publication enhances the text and makes it more interesting. Graphics and illustrations can include original drawings, photographs, charts, and graphs. Research shows twice as many people will read a publication if it is supported by photos or artwork.

Original Drawings

Original drawings can be done using paint or draw programs on computer or by hand. They should correlate with items to be emphasized in the text. Cartoons can be added for humor but should not be overused. The drawing should be of the same quality as the publication.

Clip Art

Clip art is art done by professional artists and is copyright-free. It is typically arranged by topic or by themes, such as business or holidays. A wide variety of clip art is available, particularly on CD-ROMs.

When selecting a program, find out which companies supply images in the subject areas desired (e.g., business, travel, health). Then ask for sample drawings to make certain the artwork meets your standards. Some clip art companies will create special artwork or convert logos into clip art files.

It is very important to be aware that most drawings in newspapers, magazines, and other commercial publications are copyrighted; they are *not* clip art. Check with the publisher before reproducing.

Charts and Diagrams

Charts and diagrams not only provide visual interest but also supply information in a smaller amount of space than would be used by a verbal explanation. Diagrams should be kept simple and not used if they require a great deal of explanatory information.

Photographs

Scanners can be used to add photographs to publications. When using photographs, avoid pictures of people holding trophies, shaking hands, or a group just smiling into the camera. Try to use candid shots of people doing their jobs. Readers enjoy human interest. Readers also prefer large photographs. If you know you are taking photographs that will be reproduced, use black-and-white film.

If you must include head shots of people, try to use a similar format. The same amount of head and shoulder should appear in each photo, and the relative sizes should be similar. If you are identifying people in a line, identify as "From left:…"

Use captions to describe or explain the action in the photo. The caption should be below the photo it describes and run a maximum of four lines.

Pull Quotes

Pull quotes are quotations used as a graphic device, especially when no graphic artwork is available. Pull quotes summarize surrounding material and draw attention to it. Pull quotes are set in a larger type with boxes or rules around them.

Design Graphics

Rules are lines for borders or boxes. They are used to separate categories of information (e.g., numbers and words), to draw attention to information, or to decorate. They are best used sparingly. Use vertical rules to separate columns and horizontal rules to separate topics within a column.

Screen tints are shadings or fill patterns that look like light versions of the ink. They are useful in highlighting blocks of type, such as a table of contents, and in helping organize data in calendars.

Reverses consist of printing the background rather than the image (e.g., white words on a black background). They are hard to read and are best used for display type in calendars or nameplates.

Special Concerns About Using Graphics and Illustrations

Before adding any graphics or illustrations to a publication, ask yourself the following questions:

- Are words adequate or are graphics needed to bring attention to the message?
- Will graphics help explain part of a text?
- Is there a place, person, or event frequently referred to in the text whose illustration would aid the audience's understanding?
- Is there a step-by-step process that could be illustrated?
- Is there a mood or style that could be captured by graphics?

The following suggestions should be kept in mind when using graphics and illustrations:

- Use them only if they add to the message.
- Mix them with text instead of isolating them at the beginning or end of a page.
- Avoid complicated graphics—keep them simple.
- Place the graphic or illustration on or near the same page as the text that it depicts.
- Unless they are purely decorative, illustrations should be accompanied by captions. Captions should be in a smaller type size than the text; if they are in the same type size as the text, they should be in bold, italic, or a different typeface (preferably sans serif).
- Include a source line (reference) for an illustration if appropriate.
- Use illustrations that are in different sizes and shapes to add interest. At least one visual on a page should be substantially larger than others to attract reader interest. Readers usually see visuals first and move from print to visuals while reading.

DESIGNING PUBLICATIONS

Publications that best accomplish their goals are ones that have both their content and the audience clearly identified. Whether designing a brochure, advertisement, or newsletter, it is important to ask and answer the following questions:

- What is the goal? To persuade? impress? explain? boost morale? If goals are high, higher-quality publication may be necessary. Quality is determined by the design, paper, and photography.
- Who is the audience? Employees? Association members? Investors?
- What are the budget restraints?
- How will it be distributed? Mailed in an envelope? Sent as a self-mailer? Inserted in other publications? If it will be a self-mailer, leave part of the back page for the return address and a mailing label. Make certain to dummy the back page before printing, so the newsletter does not appear to be upside-down when opened.
- Is art needed? Not all publications need art. If costs are limited, clip art or scanned art can be used.

Whether a brochure, newsletter, or advertisement is being created, the following steps are suggested:

- Make a rough layout using pen and paper before using the computer. Drafting ideas on paper helps visualize and formulate objectives as well as accounting for the design limitations of the publication.
- Select the typeface. (See the section on Typeface earlier in this chapter.)
- Determine type size for the body copy, headings, and other text blocks.
- Decide whether to use right-justified or ragged right text.

HINT: *Most readers find ragged right text easier to read.*

- Determine what graphics will be used.
- Avoid bias based on gender, race, age, ethnic background, physical ability, or sexual preference.
- Use the active, not passive, voice.

HINT: *Use the grammar checker on a word processing package, which will search for the passive voice.*

- Keep the writing simple.

HINT: *The grammar checkers on most word processing packages indicate the grade level of your writing. Write at about the seventh grade level for general understanding.*

HINT: *Reduce the grade level by decreasing the number of complex sentences and eliminating multisyllable words.*

- Keep sentences short.

HINT: *A sentence of 17 words is considered standard. Long sentences make content more difficult to understand.*

- Check for correct spelling, grammar, punctuation, inconsistencies, and inaccuracies.
- Decide on color. Research shows about three times as many people will read a publication if it is in color. A study by *Advertising News Review* found the greatest legibility is given by black type on a yellow background. Green on white ranks second, with blue on white third. The worst combination for legibility is red ink on green paper. Color, however, should be used sparingly. Ordinary text should not be printed in color; rather, color should be used for nonverbal elements, such as boxes or rules.

Most popular DTP and word processing programs have prepared templates designed by professionals. There are templates for newsletters, brochures, flyers, business cards, and numerous other common publications. The templates help you to be consistent within each page and within a publication and help add balance to a page. They have specific margins, columns, fonts, and type sizes already selected; however, these elements are all easy to modify.

Designing a Brochure

Brochures created for customers and–or the public are intended to present a positive image of the company. The rules for designing a brochure are fairly simple:

- Writing should be clear and concise.
- The typeface should be easy to read.
- The title will be more prominent if it is set in a sans serif typeface.
- Since either the front or back will be seen first, benefits should be listed in both places.
- Contemporary colors should be used. Good colors are off-white, light yellow, buff, goldenrod yellow, pink, and very light tan. Avoid green (unless it is bright teal or turquoise)—it is too restful to elicit action.
- Shading is frequently used to draw attention to layout elements.
- Price information and graphics, if appropriate, should be included to allow the reader to see what is being described. If price information changes frequently, include that information as an extra sheet. Always position benefits before the price.
- The company logo should be in a prominent position, usually on the cover, to promote the name. If the logo is purely graphic, the name should be repeated close to the logo.
- Company name, address, and fax and phone numbers should be included.
- Bullet points can be used with hanging indentations.
- Photographs should be contemporary. Use action shots, and crop unnecessary background to eliminate distractions.
- Leave sufficient white space.

When creating a brochure, keep in mind how the document is to be folded. The type of fold chosen should be one that can be handled by the printer's machine. (Figure 19-1 shows two suggestions for folds.) Panels must be unequal to accommodate folds.

Any folded brochure must be designed carefully so that there is no artwork or copy on the folds. A brochure using either of the folds shown in Figure 19-1 can be used as self-mailers or inserted in a No. 10 business envelope. These brochures can also be included with a one-page letter and still be mailed at the one-ounce postal rate. Envelopes may not be available to fit odd-size folds.

HINT: *The tear-off registration portion of a brochure should not include important information on the other side.*

Designing a Flyer

A flyer is used to publicize an event or product. Flyers are usually read quickly and often read at a distance. Because of this, type should be large and spare. Type too large, however, may detract from the message. The usual flyer is printed on 8½-by-11-inch paper.

Laser printers need ¼-inch to ⅜-inch margins. If you are printing small numbers, using a color printer with good-quality paper will make flyers look professional. It is also possible to print one original on the color printer and then have full-color photocopies made on a color copier machine. You can purchase a variety of paper with preprinted, colorful borders to add visual interest.

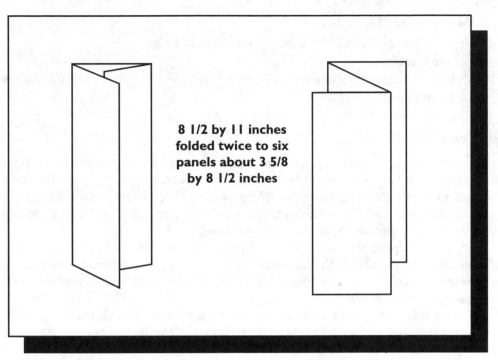

Figure 19-1 Two types of brochure folds.

Designing an Advertisement

Because there are so many ways to lay out information for an advertisement, there are no typical page layouts and few rules. Simple one-page advertisements are usually on 8½-by-11-inch paper.

The design of a poster is different from the design of a magazine advertisement. The poster must use attention-getting visuals with little text. The visuals for a magazine advertisement do not need to be so striking, since the advertisement will be seen up close and will probably contain more text than a poster.

The following are suggestions for designing advertisements:

- The design should immediately get the reader's attention, either with a headline or an image. Visuals should reinforce the message in the copy.
- Avoid unnecessary words. Either get right to the point or lead up to the point in a way that captures the reader's interest.
- Do not use too many images or large-type headlines.
- Avoid a typeface that is hard to read.
- Use the company logo consistently for continuity.
- Use rules, not underlining, for a coupon response advertisement. And make certain there is enough space for the coupon to be filled out legibly.

- Use plenty of white space.
- Use thin-lined borders to make a wide ad appear taller.
- Center headlines.
- Make certain that information is accurate. It is illegal to give false or misleading information in an advertisement.

Designing a Newsletter

Newsletters are designed to provide information to readers on a regular basis. Most are four or eight pages long on $8\frac{1}{2}$-by-11-inch paper. It is important to understand the audience well in order to write and design a successful newsletter. Listed below are some suggestions:

Know the audience. If the publication has reluctant readers, use design techniques such as large type combined with extra white space.

Design a nameplate (the top of the front page). The nameplate is also called the flag. The nameplate should include the name and subtitle of the newsletter and the publication date. The inclusion of the following elements is optional: logo, illustration, photo, issue number, slogan, publisher, editor.

Include a masthead (the area with business information). The masthead should have the same content and stay in the same location (typically the second page) from one issue to the next. The masthead includes the name and address of the sponsoring organization and the editor's name. The inclusion of the following elements is optional: frequency of publication, subscription costs, names of key officers and contributors, copyright notation, and International Standard Serial Number (ISSN) (used by librarians to catalog publications). Newsletters mailed second class must display either an ISSN or post office identification number in the nameplate, masthead, or return address.

Determine the content. A table of contents on the front cover draws attention to articles in the newsletter. Some content suggestions for a company newsletter are as follows:

- Job-related information.
- Personnel policies/practices.
- Effect of external events on job.
- News of departments/divisions.
- Organization stand on current issues.
- Stories about other employees.
- Personal news (births, birthdays, etc.).
- Training/professional development.
- Technical information.

Compose headlines before writing articles to help focus on what the article will say. The headline must:

- Convey the point of the article.
- Be from the reader's point of view.

- Relate to the story.
- Be in the present tense with an action verb and subject.
- Be specific.

Do not capitalize every word in a headline—only the first word and proper nouns.

Determine the writing style. The writing style should be consistent with company or association image. Newsletter articles are usually less formal than magazines, books, and reports. Use natural conversational tone, with concentration on "you, yours."

Choose the number of columns. Also look at newsletters produced by others for ideas and inspiration. And bear the following format hints in mind:

- Most readers look at headlines, photos, and captions first while skimming.
- The inside pages are seen together, so the layout should be tied together with design graphics. Headlines can be set across a whole page, for example.
- Once the basic format is determined for a newsletter, keep it for succeeding issues. Consistency makes content easier to find and lets the designer concentrate on content for each issue.
- More than 90 percent of newsletters in the United States are $8\frac{1}{2}$ by 11 inches. If the publication is four pages, print on an 11-by-17 sheet folded once to become $8\frac{1}{2}$ by 11. An eight-page publication is made with two 11-by-17 sheets or one 17-by-22 sheet folded and trimmed.
- Bottom margins are always slightly larger than top and side margins to make it appear that copy is centered on the page.
- Run main stories over two columns in a three-column newsletter to gain impact.
- The newsletter title, page number, and date are often repeated across the top of every page. Page numbers may also be printed at the bottom of a page.
- Author identification can be placed at the beginning or end of an article. An author's background can be summarized at the end of an article.
- Use headers and footers to repeat the publication title, name of author, and page number. Page numbers are appropriate at either the top or bottom of the page.

Select typeface and size, bearing the following points in mind:

- Stay with just a few typefaces and sizes. Serif type is easier to read for long sections of type. Sans serif type can be used for headlines or captions, as long as it is compatible with the typeface used for the body.
- Make the most important headlines large and place them near the top of the page.
- Choose a thin typeface, such as Times Roman or News Gothic, for narrow columns.

Decide on graphics. Refer to the section on Graphics and Illustrations earlier in this chapter, and follow these suggestions:

- Graphics should contribute to a specific objective.
- Use rules and screen tints to organize information that is not text or in captions.

Do not crowd the page with text and/or graphics—leave plenty of white space (blank space between text and graphics). The average length of sentences should be about 15 words; paragraphs should be three to four sentences and no longer than seven lines long.

HINT: *Avoid white space in the middle of a page. Add emphasis to headlines by surrounding them with white space.*

Decide whether text will be right-justified or ragged right.

Design calendars carefully. The calendar should appear in the same place in each issue and should not have important items that may be clipped out on its reverse side. When properly designed, a calendar serves as an advertising tool. Include the location and date for each listed activity. Categorize by location activity, or date based on the readership. The design should make it easy for readers to find what they want.

Use trivia facts, boxed quotes, or clip art for filler if the text does not end at the bottom of the page.

Divide long articles and place them on more than one page.

Choose color. Most newsletters are printed in black with a second color used sparingly.

Use bullets and dingbats (typographical design elements).

Add oversize initial caps to help mark new sections of copy.

PRINTING METHODS

Printed output can be produced either with a laser printer or with phototypesetting equipment.

Publications produced on a computer can be stored on disk and printed at a typesetting service bureau that has a professional quality printer. Some bureaus are self-service and charge by the hour for computer rental time. Other bureaus charge for each finished page. Before sending a large project to a typesetting service bureau, send small samples to several and see which one is best. Many bureaus accept files by modem. Obtain quotes from printers to get the best price.

Preparing to Print

Before you print through a service bureau, the printer should be consulted about resolution, lines per inch, and whether to print on paper or film. The following steps should be taken before sending work to a bureau:

1. Take carefully proofread hard copy (laser-printed) to the service bureau. (If the publication is sent by modem, send a fax as confirmation.)

2. Find out what file format the bureau prefers (e.g., PostScript).
3. Deliver a list of fonts with the publication. Ask ahead of time how wants the service bureau wants the fonts set up.
4. Ask whether the version of software they are using is compatible with the software you used to create the file.
5. Bring the original graphics file if the document was created with a page layout program.
6. Proofread the copy again once it has been printed.

Methods of Printing

The choice of a printing or copying method depends on the following factors:

- Number of copies
- Budget
- Deadline
- Print quality

The two main ways to print multiple copies of office publications are by photocopying and offset printing. Printing by office copier is quick and convenient. Lines and large areas of black can be copied adequately, but fine details or photographs do not reproduce well. This method is not recommended for more than 100 copies.

Offset printing involves making photographs or film of the camera-ready copy. A plate is made from the photographic film; separate plates are made for each color. Note that once the film is made, it is extremely expensive to make corrections. This method results in much better quality than printing by copier. *Quick printers* are good for short runs needed quickly. *Commercial printers* are used for longer runs and more complicated jobs.

Paper

Paper costs can represent half the cost of the printing and influence the qualify of a publication. Printers usually make suggestions on weight and type of paper because these decisions can be very technical.

Binding

Binding contributes to the overall impression created by a publication. There are binding methods that are mechanical and others that do not require equipment. Table 19-7 describes binding systems that can be used in the office without sending the material to a printer.

Printers and binders offer a wide range of binding options. The type of binding should be decided on before the material is printed so that the margins are appropriate. Word processing and page layout programs can be used to adjust margins appropriately.

Table 19-7
BINDING SYSTEMS

BINDING METHOD	NUMBER OF SHEETS
No equipment:	
Two-pocket portfolios	15
Prong-style report covers	100
Punchless	125
Slide lock	30
Paper punch:	
Two-piece plastic and pressboard report covers	600
Vinyl ring binders:	
½ inch	100
1 inch	200
1½ inches	325
2 inches	500
3 inches	600

HINT: *Custom binders are available for camera-ready artwork. View binders with plastic overlay on the front, back, and/or spine can help you customize binders quickly and economically.*

Stapler needed:	
Stapled report cover	15
Plastic ring punch-and-bind machine:	
Either manual or with an electric motor; binds on side or top.	12–425 (depending on equipment)
Adhesive tape machine:	
Uses adhesive tape to bind punched reports to special report covers designed for the machine.	Short reports
Thermal binding system:	
Uses a heat-sealing process to adhere pages to a one-piece, preglued spine and cover.	40–600

HINT: *Thermal binding systems are used with DTP to improve the appearance of sales presentations, reports, and other important documents.*

HINT: *Since printers usually subcontract binding work, it may be less expensive to contact a binder initially.*

DESKTOP PUBLISHING GLOSSARY

Printers and graphic artists use certain terms that may be unfamiliar. Figure 19-2 lists some definitions.

ALLEY: Space between two columns of type-set material.

BOXED COPY: Text with horizontal and vertical lines (or rules) around it.

CAMERA-READY: Of a quality appropriate for final copy and ready to be printed or photographed.

CLIP ART: Art designed by professional artists that is copyright-free and commercially available. The art may be printed on paper or stored on a data disk for a DPT program.

CROPPING: Cutting an illustration to fit a given area or to remove unwanted background along the edges.

DESKTOP PUBLISHING: The process of designing and producing a publication with a computer.

DTP: An abbreviation for desktop publishing.

FLAG: See NAMEPLATE.

FONT: A typeface in a particular style and size. Some DTP software programs use this term in place of TYPEFACE.

GRID: A skeleton of the finished printed page showing vertical columns, margins, and the space between horizontal lines.

HALFTONE PROCESS: A photograph broken up into fine dots for reproduction.

LASER PRINTER: A computer printer that uses a laser beam to form images on paper, a page at a time.

LAYOUT: The arrangement of text and images on a page.

LEADING: The distance between type lines, measured in points from the baseline of one line of type to the baseline of the next line. Also called *line spacing*.

MASTHEAD: The information in a newsletter that includes the business information, such as name and address of sponsoring organization.

MOUSE: A hand-controlled input device that gives commands to the cursor or icon on the screen.

NAMEPLATE: The top of the front page that includes the name and subtitle of the newsletter and publication date. Also called *flag*.

NETWORK: A system of interconnected computer systems and terminals.

PAGE LAYOUT PROGRAM: DTP program that allows placement of text and pictures on the screen before printing.

POINT: Unit of type measurement. One point is approximately equal to 1/72 of an inch

RAGGED RIGHT: The uneven alignment of text along the right margin.

READABILITY: Relative ease with which a printed page can be read.

RIGHT-JUSTIFIED: The even alignment of text along the right margin.

RULES: Lines of various thickness and pattern used to divide and box text on a page.

SANS SERIF: Characters of a typeface without SERIFS.

SCANNER: Hardware that reduces an image into a grid of dots that can be stored in the computer.

SERIFS: The short lines terminating the main strokes of certain letters in a typeface.

TEMPLATE: A page grid that has been created as a guide and can be used repeatedly for similar documents.

TYPE STYLE: An assortment of styles of a typeface, such as italic and bold.

TYPEFACE: An assortment of characters of one particular kind of type. Some DTP software programs use the word FONT instead.

TYPESETTING: The preparation of characters in a printed typeface created by a traditional metal type or by the photocomposition process.

WHITE SPACE: The blank space between text and graphics on a page.

Figure 19-2 Desktop publishing glossary.

CHAPTER 20

PROOFREADING

AND

EDITING

Printed office documents should be written correctly and formatted attractively. Office professionals with high-level proofreading and editing skills can take pride in meeting professional standards. Reference books, dictionaries, and English grammar and usage manuals are essential sources for answering proofreading and editing questions. Some proofreading and editing jobs may be effectively completed by outside service providers.

Proofreading and editing are separate but integrated skills; both require concentration on the details involved in producing error-free documents. **Proofreading** entails checking copy for errors in spelling, punctuation, capitalization, word division, statistical data, and format. It takes place at two stages—first while editing the material and again after printing the final document.

Editing is a process to ensure that the content of a document is accurate, clear, and complete; that the material is organized logically and free of grammatical errors; and that the writing style is appropriate for the purpose. Editing should be completed before the final copy is printed to avoid the cost of revising or rewriting.

PROOFREADING DOCUMENTS

Whether proofreading copy on a computer screen or on printed copy, it is easy to miss errors on your first review of the material. The efficient proofreader makes separate checks for mechanical accuracy, format, and statistical data.

Format

An attractive-looking document can affect a reader's impressions of a company. Do the following when checking the overall appearance of a document:

- Scan all pages to be sure headings and subheadings as well as the spacing between these headings are consistent. If one heading begins with a verb, use verbs for other headings at the same level. Check the paragraph indentations for consistency.
- Check that page numbers are consecutive and in the same location on each page.

- Check enumerations for omissions or inaccurate numbering or lettering. In deleting or adding material, it is easy to forget to renumber the remaining items.

- Check that the top, bottom, and side margins are in proportion to each other. Bound reports require a wider left margin than unbound reports. (See Chapter 18, Reports.)

- Follow the company style manual if there is one. However, take the initiative to recommend companywide adoption of new formats if a document's appearance can be improved or productivity increased with the recommended changes.

- Scan outlines for number and letter accuracy. Avoid an A without a B or a 1 without a 2.

- Compare figure and table labels to the reference in the text. When you move, add, or delete material, the references may shift or get out of sequence.

- Determine whether consistent typestyles and fonts were used.

Mechanical Accuracy

Producing quality documents requires precise and careful attention to details. The following points should be helpful:

- Learn basic spelling and word division rules in order to avoid repeated checking of reference sources. But be sure to check the dictionary or a reference manual if in doubt.

- Avoid excessive word division at ends of lines, especially several lines in succession.

- Be aware that errors often occur in: (1) items that are enumerated; (2) long words (syllables are often omitted); (3) words at the margins or at the bottom of a page; (4) words with double letters; (5) proper names; (6) headings, subheadings, and titles; (7) word endings, such as -*tion,* -*ed,* or -*s;* (8) sentences with beginning and closing marks of punctuation, such as quotes and parentheses; (9) words or phrases printed in all caps; and (10) words that are similar such as *than* for *that* or *now* for *not.*

- Check carefully for transposed letters, figures, or words.

- Compare the inside address of a letter with the original source, and then check the inside address with the address on the envelope to be sure they agree. Check that all enclosures are included and all copy notations are identified. Be sure that mailing instructions have been noted.

- Examine line endings and beginnings to be sure a word like *to* or *that* has not been printed twice.

- Recheck proper names to be sure they are spelled correctly. Titles must be accurate. If words are not familiar, proofread letter by letter.

Table 20-1
PROOFREADERS' MARKS

EXPLANATION	NOTATION IN MARGIN	EXAMPLE
Add space	#	our tuition plan
Align vertically	‖	‖ A. Software
		‖ B. Hardware
Capitalize	caps	Mary harrington
Center copy	⌐ ⌐	⌐CHAPTER I⌐
Close up space	C	a recent let ter
Delete	⨍	proofreading⨍
Double space	ds	ds to work.
		Thank you for
Insert	∧	two requests merit (have)
Insert apostrophe	⌄	companys payroll
Insert colon	(:)	Include the following items
Insert comma	∧	your prompt helpful response
Insert hyphen	=/	well equipped
Insert parentheses	(/)	to obtain ten(10)
Insert period	⊙	We have her check⊙
Insert quotes	⌄/⌄	She said, I will increase sales.
Insert semicolon	(;)	She spoke we listened.
Let it stand	stet	arrive today at 5 p.m.
Move down	⊔	⊔ Table 12-2
Move left	⊏	⊏ proofreader can use
Move material		Last month's sales
Move right	⊐	⊐ facsimile services
Move up	⊓	⊓ SECTION 2
New paragraph	¶	¶ We will attend
No paragraph	no ¶	no ¶ Next fall
Single space	ss	ss Please return the
		office supplies.
Spell out	sp	sp Jan 19
Transpose	tr	th last payment
Underline	_____	The word their
Use boldface	bF	The task of editing
Use italic typeface	ital	a bona fide transaction
Use lowercase	lc	My recent Request
Verify data	?	The 10 a.m. meeting ?

Statistical Data

Errors in figures suggest carelessness and cause embarrassment for a company. Proofreading numbers takes special care. Here are some suggestions for ways to proofread statistical data.

- Count the items in a series or in a tabulation on the original copy; then compare this count to the number of items on the final copy.
- Verify the accuracy of the arithmetical functions on both the original and the printed copy. Take the extra time to verify extensions and all totals.
- Verify the accuracy of all numbers by checking them twice. Check for transposed numbers. Check the decimal alignment within tabulations. Be sure the number of zeros is correct.
- Check with the writer when you are not sure about spacing or using upper- or lowercase letters in formulas.

Proofreading Marks

Both you and the writer should be able to interpret and use proofreaders' marks. To use the marks, identify the location of the error in the copy itself and note the type of error in the margin closest to the error. Table 20-1 shows the standard marks proofreaders use to indicate changes on printed matter.

EDITING DOCUMENTS

Productivity increases when a minimal number of printed revisions of a document are necessary. If the writer and the office professional work as a team, the editing process should be smooth. If the writer is inexperienced or careless, an office professional who has an excellent grasp of basic grammar, an understanding of the content of the material, and an appreciation for appropriate writing style can be invaluable. Be aware, however, that some writers do not appreciate having their work changed.

Language Usage

Well-written communications reflect a company's competence and reliability. Try to insure that the principles of grammar are consistently followed.

- Review the rules of grammar by taking refresher classes at a local college, by reviewing English grammar books at the public library, or by using an up-to-date handbook for office professionals.
- Use a thesaurus to avoid repetition or overuse of a word, but be sure that the substitution does not change the meaning of the sentence.

HINT: *Sometimes you know the meaning of a word but not the word itself. Check the Random House Word Menu by Stephen Glazier, which organizes material by topics.*

- Check for parallel structure; e.g., that all items in a list begin with a verb.
- Check that all sentences are complete.
- Be aware of language-usage problems in areas such as: (1) noun/verb agreement; (2) homonyms; (3) word usage, such as *less* versus *fewer* or *that* versus *which*; (4) dangling participles and split infinitives; (5) pronouns/antecedents; and (6) active/passive voice.
- Use the services offered by grammar hotlines. Faculty members and graduate students at many universities and colleges answer questions from callers about spelling, punctuation, capitalization, number style, and grammar. These services are usually free.

HINT: *A free copy of the* Grammar Hotline Directory *is available each January from Tidewater Community College Writing Center, 1700 College Crescent, Virginia Beach, VA 23456. To receive a copy of the directory, send the college a stamped, self-addressed No. 10 envelope.*

Content

A well-written communication contains complete information and follows a logical thought pattern. Suggestions to achieve this clarity include the following:

- Be sure the document answers the who, what, when, where, why, and how questions.
- Identify the purpose of the document succinctly and directly.
- Begin new paragraphs when introducing new ideas.
- Make sure all dates are correct by checking them against the office calendar; make sure the days of the week mentioned match the dates given.
- Eliminate vague statements that lack precision or completeness. Be sure the intent of the document is clear.
- Eliminate excess verbiage; keep the facts and ideas new.
- Make the transitions from point to point smooth rather than abrupt.
- Ask a layperson to read the material to see if it makes sense.

Style

An appropriate writing style stimulates a reader's interest in the message. To attain this goal, try to do the following:

- Present information in a logical format, with a smooth flow from sentence to sentence and from paragraph to paragraph.

- Strive for an *average* sentence length of 16 to 20 words. If successive sentences are very short, a communication may seem curt. If sentences are too long, they may be difficult to follow because they bury information.
- Use a writing style that is appropriate for the reader. Evaluate the situation to determine whether the tone of the document should be formal or informal.
- Use words that clarify rather than confuse. Avoid unfamiliar words. Short words are preferable to long ones.
- Eliminate archaic, trendy, or slang expressions.
- Select the correct verbs. If necessary, use a thesaurus to find verbs that are appropriate. Eliminate long runs of adjectives and adverbs.

PROOFREADING BY YOURSELF

Teaming up with a coworker is the best way to proofread lengthy documents or statistical information. One person reads aloud to a second person who checks the copy. However, since a coworker is not always available, the following suggestions are for proofreading alone.

- Place a 3- by 5-inch card below the line you are proofreading on your final copy and your finger below the line on the original copy. This forces you to slow down your proofreading rate as you move from line to line.
- Read the copy character by character and then reread it for content. Finally, scan the entire document for format consistency.

HINT: *If the document is not too lengthy, read the material from right to left rather than the usual direction of left to right. This forces you to read each word.*

- Count lines to compare the number of printed lines with the number of lines on the original copy.
- Listen to machine-dictated material a second time while proofreading the printed copy.
- Do your proofreading during a quiet period so you can concentrate on the copy. When you are proofreading a lengthy document, take frequent breaks to prevent your eyes from getting tired.

PROOFREADING COPY ONSCREEN

Proofreading onscreen immediately after putting the information into a computer is more productive than bringing it back onscreen later. The more editing you can do onscreen, the less time it will take to review the final printed copy. The following suggestions should prove helpful for onscreen proofreading:

- Strive for "first printing, final copy." Revising always takes time.
- Use the spell checker as a routine check for obvious errors. (Update the dictionary in the program to include terms or acronyms unique to your specific company or area.)
- Use a plastic ruler to remain on the correct line when proofreading onscreen, or move the cursor from line to line as you proofread. If possible, ask someone else to proof the screen as you slowly read aloud from the original copy.
- Divide the document into convenient viewing sections for proofreading; for example, paragraph by paragraph or 10 to 12 lines at a time.
- Check a revised document carefully. Words are often omitted or rekeyed, or a new paragraph is inserted without deleting the old. Or a paragraph can be moved without deleting it at its original position. Review the copy that comes immediately before and after the revisions as well.
- Make sure references to other pages are accurate. For example, your text might refer to a list on page 8, but after you revise the copy, it's on page 7.
- Have a coworker read/spell information while you make corrections at the keyboard.
- Always proofread the final printing.

SPECIAL CONCERNS ABOUT PROOFREADING AND EDITING

A current reference manual, dictionary, thesaurus, and word division dictionary are invaluable aids. To insure uniformity in style and English usage, recommend that everyone in your company use the same reference books.

Even though your word processing software includes a hyphenation feature, check line endings for undesirable word breaks. Avoid unnecessary blank space at the end of a line.

If space does not permit an addition or revision on a page, use a separate sheet of paper on which each insertion is identified as A, B, or C, and correlate these letters with the appropriately identified locations for the insertions on the document. Make editing remarks in another color. Use an erasable pen so it's easier to correct your comments.

Never rely solely on your memory; always verify pertinent facts, such as dates, figures, and times. Errors in dates often occur at the beginning of a new year.

If letters sit on a desk for a few days, the dates may be old and the material can be confusing if there is a reference to "next week" or "within a few days." Check the dates before sending the documents.

Prepare a style sheet that outlines the format, shows correct spellings of proper names, and lists words that cause spelling or hyphenation difficulties. Style sheets are also valuable to keep on file for future use with similar documents.

It is often advisable to put the copy aside for a while and come back to it later with a fresh eye to proofread the final copy.

Review all notations made by someone who proofreads your copy. These are suggestions, not "corrections." You do not have to accept all the suggestions.

USING SOFTWARE TO PROOFREAD AND EDIT

Programs that identify misspellings and incorrect grammar and analyze writing style are not substitutes for good proofreading and editing skills, but they can be very useful.

Reference Software/CD-ROMs

An electronic dictionary, like a traditional dictionary, contains word definitions, syllabification, inflected forms, and parts of speech labels. Some may include pronunciations. An electronic thesaurus offers numerous synonyms for words. Once loaded, these software references can be called up while you are working on a document. Specialized versions for such areas as law, medicine, and engineering are helpful. Always check the copyright date of the source material. You will want the versions with the most recent dates.

Another type of dictionary software can help you locate a word you may have forgotten. If you can think of only a vague meaning or concept, key in a descriptor or two; the program provides a list from which you can select. This type of dictionary includes idioms, word origins, spelling, parts of speech, and definitions.

CD-ROMs provide numerous resources for office professionals to use while working on other documents. Because they can hold so much data, most CD-ROMs include a dictionary, thesaurus, world atlas, ZIP code directory, business writing style guide, book of quotations, and world almanac. Other features vary with the packages.

Spelling, Grammar, and Style Checkers

Spell checker, grammar, and style checker software programs are available as stand-alone packages or they may come as one package. The stand-alone packages may or may not work with other software that you use.

Word processing software has its own built-in spell checkers; some also include grammar-check and style-check features as well as thesauruses.

Spell checkers are expandable, so you can add abbreviations, company-specific terms, and acronyms. Legal, medical, and scientific dictionaries can be included. Some spell checkers check for unintentional repetition of a word, capital letters, and singular or plural word endings. Spell checkers will only check for correct spelling; they do not check for correct use of the word.

Grammar and style checkers identify certain types of writing deficiencies by using rule-based expert system techniques. On this basis, the checkers can only offer tips for improvement; specific corrective actions are still the author's/proofreader's responsibility. Different grammar/style checkers often produce different results and recommendations, so it is imperative that the user be competent in the use of the language.

HINT: *Software will not identify all errors and may indicate that some words or sentences are wrong when they are actually correct. Do not accept suggested corrections without question.*

The following checklist illustrates the many decisions facing potential users of software for checking spelling, grammar, and writing style:

- Is the program easy to use? Is the documentation easy to understand? Is the cost reasonable?
- Does the software check spelling as well as grammar and style?
- Does the software allow the options of checking single words, blocks of text, whole documents, words as they are typed, or words in background windows?
- Does the software check the spelling as the document progresses or does it check the spelling in a batch mode when the document is finished?
- Is the software capable of checking foreign language documents?
- Does the critique indicate excessive use of jargon? negative terms? difficult words? clichés? abstractions? Is there a critique of sentence structure? Does the software recognize such differences as *form* for *from?* Is a summary of the criticisms for the entire document available?
- Does the software check the following language usage areas?

  - ▲ Subject/verb agreement
  - ▲ Passive voice
  - ▲ Awkward phrasing
  - ▲ Sentence structure
  - ▲ Plurals and possessives
  - ▲ Double negatives
  - ▲ Long-sequence prepositional phrases
  - ▲ Long-sequence noun modifiers
  - ▲ Article usage
  - ▲ Superlative versus comparative usage, e.g., best versus better
  - ▲ Split infinitives
  - ▲ Number agreement
  - ▲ Pronoun usage
  - ▲ Capitalization

- Does the spell checker automatically correct a misspelled word or does it present a list of words from which to select?
- When grammatical errors are identified, are there comments explaining the rules? For example, "This sentence may be in the passive voice." Are replacement sen-

tences offered? Are you able to change rules? Can you add rules? If a company has its own guidelines regarding style, it will want to obtain software that allows changes or additions to the rules.

- Does the software perform a second evaluation of a sentence after it has been rewritten? (The second attempt may be worse than the first one.)
- Is a readability grade-level analysis available? How many formulas or indices are available for this readability level? (A readability level indicates the number of years of education the reader needs to understand the document.) Index levels vary from program to program.

HINT: *Most people are more comfortable reading at one or two grade levels below their top reading level. Know the audience that will be reading the document.*

- Are the average number of words per sentence and syllables per word as well as the number of sentences per paragraph shown?
- Can the software be customized? Are you able to select the kind of writing you plan to do—for example, proposal, business letter, memo, advertising, or technical?

CHAPTER 21

ORAL

COMMUNICATIONS

The ability to communicate orally is essential in today's office. All office professionals must be able to listen actively to people inside and outside the company and respond with accurate information to questions and requests. Good communication requires a positive attitude that recognizes the needs of others.

RECEPTIONIST TECHNIQUES

Because the receptionist is often the first contact visitors have with a company, it is vital that the receptionist create a positive impression. Larger offices usually have a reception area with a trained receptionist; in smaller offices, a secretary handles these responsibilities.

Waiting Area

Any waiting area for visitors, no matter what the size, must be clean and comfortable. The following suggestions help make waiting more pleasant.

- Include current magazines with subjects that appeal to both men and women, a daily newspaper, an annual report, and/or company brochures.
- Make coffee and tea available or indicate their location.
- Have a place for coats with enough hooks or coat hangers.
- Do not allow visitors to wait in private offices unless permission has been given.
- Have a separate area for children to play in if they are frequent visitors. Even if children visit infrequently, have a few children's books and toys available.

Greeting Visitors

All visitors should be treated as important guests, with courtesy and respect. You should stop what you are doing, smile, and greet the visitor. Below are some tips for making the visitor feel welcome.

- Greet the visitor with "good morning" or "good afternoon." It is not necessary to rise or shake hands, unless the caller extends his or her hand first. If you are on the telephone, acknowledge the visitor with a nod and smile.

- Greet people by name. Use *Mr., Ms.*, or a professional title and the visitor's last name, unless you are on a first-name basis with the visitor. Refer to your supervisor by title and last name.

HINT: *Take a business card if offered and file it. If necessary, write the visitor's name phonetically on the card to avoid mispronunciations. Brief written notes will also help you remember the caller.*

- Offer to take the visitor's coat; indicate seating verbally or with a hard gesture.
- Keep your work area free of food or drinks; these detract from a professional atmosphere.

HINT: *If you must eat at your desk, make certain it is not in view of anyone who might be visiting; avoid foods with strong odors.*

- Treat everyone, including suppliers and vendors, with dignity and respect.
- Avoid initiating conversations; however, respond to visitors who wish to talk. Talk about company business in generalities and avoid controversial subjects. In answering direct business questions, it is always acceptable to say, "I'm sorry, I don't know the answer to that."
- Follow company policy in allowing unscheduled visitors to see your supervisor. Find out the reason for the visit. If the person refuses to state the reason for the visit, it may be necessary to say something like the following: "I'm sorry, but I'm unable to make an appointment without telling Ms. Garcia the purpose of your visit." When in doubt, ask your supervisor.
- Stop unknown people from going beyond the reception area. Know company policy for handling sales representatives and solicitors. Be familiar with what to do in the case of emergencies or dealing with suspicious characters.
- Keep a list of employees who speak other languages in case a visitor does not speak English. If you have difficulty understanding someone's name, ask them to spell it for you.

Workplace Violence

Employees, supervisors, and managers have become victims of physical assaults in the workplace. Reducing the risk of workplace assaults requires strong management commitment. Employers should develop procedures for workplace security and appropriate training for all employees. Emergency action plans should be in place.

Employers who need assistance in addressing workplace security hazards can contact the Division of Occupational Safety and Health (OSHA), which has available pamphlets, samples of model programs, and videos. The following are violence prevention suggestions:

- Observe what is going on outside the workplace and report any suspicious persons or activities to security or the police.
- Post emergency police and fire department numbers and the company's address by the phone.
- Have a code word that informs other employees there is potential trouble.
- Limit accessible cash to a small amount. Use a time access safe for larger bills and deposit them as they are received.
- Do not fight or argue with a violent person and offer no resistance whatsoever.
- Always move slowly and explain each move before you make them.
- Make no attempt to follow a violent person from the workplace. Lock the door when they leave and immediately call the police. Do not unlock the door until police arrive.
- Write down everything you remember about the person while you wait for the police to arrive.

Keeping a Record of Visitors

Some offices keep a register of visitors for security reasons or to help prepare client billing. The register should include the date, time, name and company, purpose of visit, and other information necessary for record keeping. Smaller offices typically use the appointment notations in a calendar for keeping information.

Introducing Visitors

The visitor should be escorted to the office door. If the supervisor's door is closed, knock before entering.

Proper etiquette requires introducing the visitor first. If the visitor is a lower-ranking company employee, introduce the supervisor first; for example, "Mr. Supervisor, I would like you to meet Mr. McLean, who is in the Graphic Arts Department." For frequent visitors say, "Ms. Manager can see you now; please go right in." (For additional information, see Chapter 6, Business Ethics and Etiquette.)

Delayed Appointments

No matter how carefully scheduling is done, appointments may be delayed. If the supervisor is running later than scheduled, explain the delay to the visitor. If possible, try to give the approximate length of the delay so the visitor can decide whether to wait or reschedule the appointment. If possible, call the visitor ahead of time to notify them and explain the delay. If a visitor's meeting is taking longer than scheduled, call and remind the manager about the next appointment or take in a reminder note.

TELEPHONE PROCEDURES

The telephone should be used property by everyone in a firm, including executives, managers, customer representatives, receptionists, and secretaries. What is said over the telephone and how it is said helps or hurts a company's image. Proper use of the telephone establishes a positive impression that the company's employees are friendly, efficient, and helpful.

Telephone Courtesy

Telephone etiquette is vital to creating a courteous and pleasant company image. Below are general suggestions for telephone usage:

- Speak directly into the telephone, holding the mouthpiece about an inch and a half from your lips. Do not eat, drink, chew gum, or key at the computer while on the telephone.
- Keep background sounds, such as a radio, low.
- Avoid talking on the telephone and with a co-worker at the same time. The telephone receiver will transmit sound even though the mouthpiece is covered.
- Use a pleasant, professional tone of voice. Convey through your voice that you are confident, reliable, and capable. Avoid slang, "yeah," and "OK," as well as technical words a caller may not understand.
- Be cheerful and positive.
- Vary your pitch. Keep your pitch just above your best note to open a phone conversation. Use a lower pitch when emphasizing words. Lower your voice and pitch when making telephone calls in an open room.
- Speak loud enough to be heard.
- Enunciate clearly. Use words to identify letters in spelling names and places.

A as in Able	N as in November
B as in Boy	O as in Ocean
C as in Charles	P as in Peter
D as in Dog	Q as in Queen
E as in Edward	R as in Robert
F as in Frank	S as in Sugar
G as in George	T as in Thomas
H as in Henry	U as in Uniform
I as in India	V as in Victor
J as in John	W as in William
K as in King	X as in X-ray
L as in Lincoln	Y as in Young
M as in Mary	Z as in Zero

- Use careful pronunciation.
- Talk slowly enough to be understood. Talk at about the same pace as the caller.
- Address people by their names and titles.
- Use courteous phrases such as "thank you," "please," and "you're welcome."
- Respond verbally with "yes" and "I see" when someone else is talking so they will know you are still there and listening.
- Handle as many calls as possible yourself without asking for a supervisor's assistance.
- End the phone call pleasantly and professionally, preferably using the caller's name; for example, "It's been nice talking with you, Ms. Fortino." Use "good-bye" instead of "bye-bye."
- Let the caller hang up first. Hang up gently and securely.
- Return calls promptly.
- Do not worry about your regional or foreign accent unless others have a difficult time understanding you.
- Follow through with promises.

Answering Incoming Calls

It is important that a secretary and supervisor communicate daily in order to handle incoming calls effectively. According to recent research, seven out of ten customers will refuse to do business with a firm again if they were badly treated on the very first encounter. The following suggestions help a supervisor and secretary keep each other informed. (For additional suggestions about time management, see Chapter 3.)

- Meet the first thing in the morning to go over the schedule and prepare for the day.
- If your supervisor is working under a deadline, find out if anyone else might handle his or her calls or visitors.
- Find out whose calls are expected in order to help screen calls.
- Know ahead of time names of people whose calls should be transferred, no matter what the situation. Be aware that not every call from an important person is urgent.

Phones should be answered according to company policy, if there is one, and in such a way that a caller never has to guess whether it is the right number. Below are some suggested ways to answer phones:

▲ *Answering for the company:*
"Good morning, Professional Secretaries International."
"Professional Secretaries International, Maria speaking."

▲ *Answering for a department:*
"Sales, Maria Carlson speaking."
"Publications, Ms. Goodman. May I help you?"

▲ *Answering another person's phone:*
"Dr. Fenner's office, James speaking.

▲ *Answering your own phone:*
"Purchasing, Glenn Cushner speaking."

Here are some hints regarding proper phone use:

- Smiling when talking on the phone realigns the throat muscles and causes the voice to be softer, the mouth to be more open, and the jaws to be less tense.
- Keep the pitch of the voice in the medium range, which has a calming effect on callers.
- Giving your name enables the caller to address you in the conversation and imparts warmth and friendliness.
- If you are going to be away from your desk, ask someone to answer your phone or forward it to another phone, voice mail, or an answering machine.

The following suggestions help make a positive impression on incoming callers:

- Answer immediately, preferably on the first ring but before the third ring.
- Be prepared. If you are right-handed, place the telephone on your left so the right hand is available to take notes. Reverse the position if you are left-handed. And always have the following available: pen or pencil, message pad, watch or clock for noting the time, company extension numbers, and telephone book.
- Avoid the use of company jargon.
- Determine who is calling if that information is not volunteered by the caller; for example, "May I ask who's calling, please?" or "May I tell Mr. Manager who's calling?"
- Verify the pronunciation and get the spelling of the caller's name.
- Be discreet. Avoid disclosing personal information; for example, "He's not in yet," "She's still at lunch"; "He usually doesn't work on Thursday afternoons—that's his day for golf." Step outside the office if a coworker or host takes an important call while you are there. If they motion you to stay seated, read any materials you may have brought to their office or look out the window. Discretion, however, does not include dishonesty. A secretary should never be expected to lie for colleagues or supervisors; it is unethical.

- Determine which calls are urgent and decide on the appropriate person to handle them. If a call is urgent, it may be necessary to interrupt a meeting or conference discreetly with a note indicating who is waiting on the phone.
- Thank the caller for calling before transferring to the desired destination. (See the section Transferring Calls below for additional information.)
- Develop scripts to cover most common calls.

Dealing with Accents

As the workplace becomes more global, talking with people with accents is common. Below are some tips to improve telephone communications:

- Ask the person to spell his or her name. Spell it back and phonetically write it out, particularly if you are transferring the call.
- Do not pretend to understand. Ask the person to slow down so you can verify the request. Make certain they understand it is your difficulty, not theirs.
- Slow down and listen to the caller's pattern of speech. Repeat key words back to make certain you have interpreted the meaning correctly.
- Keep your voice well modulated. It is not necessary to raise your voice.
- Have a phrase book available. Know the names of those in the company who can speak other languages.

Answering Simultaneous Incoming Calls

In order to answer a phone by the third ring, it may be necessary to interrupt one conversation to answer another line. When several incoming calls occur at once, use the following technique:

1. Put the caller on hold. (See the section Holding Calls below.)
2. Answer the next call.
3. Complete the second call only if it can be handled *quickly*.
4. Return to the original call promptly.

Consider a direct approach to answering a call, such as, "Hello, this is Carol at the XYZ Company. How may I direct your call?"

Holding Calls

Being put on hold irritates many callers. Anyone using a telephone needs to be sensitive to this and do everything possible to be polite and attentive. The following suggestions help promote goodwill, even if a caller is put on hold.

- Ask permission to put the caller on hold. For example, say "May I put you on hold?" or "Is it convenient to hold or would you prefer to call back?"; avoid "I have to put you on hold" or "Can I put you on hold?" Always wait for a response.

- Check back every 30 to 40 seconds while the person is on hold. Thank them for holding and ask if they wish to continue holding. Listening to music helps alleviate the stress of waiting. Avoid keeping callers on hold for more than a minute or two unless that is their preference.

- Inform the caller if the wait is longer than you anticipated; for example: "Thank you for holding, Mr. Customer. Ms. Manager is still on the other line. Do you want to continue holding or would you prefer to have her call you back?"

Transferring Calls

Know how the transfer procedure works on your telephone system to avoid losing a caller during the transfer process. Remember to give the caller enough information to call back in case the transfer process does not work. When transferring calls, the following procedures are helpful:

- Transfer calls only if you are unable to help the caller.

- Ask permission to transfer calls.

- If you do not know where to transfer a call, put the caller on hold and ask coworkers for assistance.

- Give the name and complete telephone number to the caller in case the call is disconnected during the transfer process. For example: "Mr. Customer, I think the Service Department is better able to answer your question than I am. If you don't mind, I'm transferring you to Mr. Howe's office. His number is 483-3002 in case you need to call again."

- Suggest having the call returned instead of transferred if the caller complains about having been transferred several times.

- Give the called party any helpful information. For example, "Carol Sekor of North Bay Construction is holding; she has a question about last month's invoice."

Cutting Short a Call

Sometimes it is necessary to terminate a call. It takes skill to end a call with enough tact that the caller feels good about the conversation. The following suggestions are useful for cutting short a call:

- Give a short, sincere explanation for getting off the telephone; for example, "I'm sorry to cut this short, but I have a visitor waiting to see me" or "Excuse me, but I have a call on the other line."

- Make plans to get back with the caller if necessary; for example, "We have a staff meeting in five minutes; may I call you back?" or "Excuse me, but I'm trying to get a letter ready for overnight delivery; may I call you back?"

Taking Messages

Taking accurate messages is vital when answering the telephone for others. By some estimates, 90 percent of messages contain incorrect information, with errors ranging from names and phone numbers to reasons for calling.

To avoid taking messages or having someone place a call back, try to help the caller yourself; for example: "Ms. Wong is out of the office. I expect her back after 3:00. I'm her administrative assistant and work very closely with her. May I help you?"

If it is necessary to take a message, keep these points in mind.

- Use a form. In fact, fill out a form even if the caller indicates they will call back.
- Include both the time and date.
- Write legibly.
- Verify the caller's name, company name, and phone number by repeating back the information.
- Include as much information as possible to help the caller return the call. Attach to the message slip any material (e.g., files, invoices) that may be helpful in answering the call.
- Deliver the message promptly.

Screening Calls

The purpose of screening calls is to decide whether to transfer a call or take a message. Screening must not offend the caller. The following suggestions are helpful when screening calls.

- Avoid giving the impression that calls are being screened. Avoid asking the caller's name *first* and *then* saying the manager is unavailable. Instead, immediately state that the manager is unavailable and ask if the call can be returned, in the process finding out who is calling. If it happens to be someone the manager wishes to talk with, the call can be transferred or the following statement can be made, "May I put you on hold while I see if I can interrupt her?"
- Use judgment in determining whether the supervisor needs to talk to every important person (including relatives or higher-ranking people) immediately. It may be necessary to say, "Mr. Nunes is in a staff meeting. Do you want me to interrupt him?"
- Transfer a call if it is an emergency.

Placing Outgoing Calls

All businesses make outgoing calls. The manner of handling outgoing calls is just as important as prompt, courteous service for incoming calls. Before placing an outgoing call, you must have a reason for calling and know what you want to accomplish. This takes planning even before picking up the telephone receiver. Use the following guidelines in placing outgoing calls:

- Know the name of the person you want to reach and how to pronounce it. Check the pronunciation and spelling with others if you are unsure.
- Verify the phone number before calling. Keep frequently called numbers in an address book. Calling Information for a number often costs money.
- If you reach a wrong number, do not just hang up; say, "I'm sorry; I must have dialed the wrong number." If the wrong number is long distance, immediately call the operator to receive credit on the phone bill.
- Plan outgoing calls in advance. Have all materials available and make an outline or rough script (but sound natural when talking).
- Group outgoing calls one after another to save time—but leave some time between each call in case someone is trying to reach you.
- Avoid the hours of noon to 2:00 p.m. and any other times you know to be inconvenient. Take different time zones into consideration.
- Identify yourself immediately; for example, "This is Colleen Peppard of Hargrave and Johnson."
- Ask if it is convenient to talk. If it is not convenient, make an appointment to call back; for example: "Can you talk for a minute? I have three items to discuss about the conference next week."
- Avoid calling people at home unless they request that you do so.
- Insist on calling back if the connection is faulty.

Handling Complaints and Angry Callers

Resolving complaints is important to the success of any business. You want to do all you can to retain the customer or client. Angry people may use abusive language, exaggeration, sarcasm, or personal attacks. While you cannot control the angry person, you can control your reaction to the situation.

Here are suggestions for handling complaints and angry callers:

- Listen to the complaint. Listen to both the feelings and the facts. Avoid interrupting until the entire complaint has been stated, getting emotionally involved, reacting to a personal attack, and allowing yourself to get angry.
- Do not interrupt until the caller starts repeating information. This is an important signal.

- To angry callers focusing on their anger or on personal attacks, say, "It would really help if we could focus on the problem."

- If the caller is angry, pause before you respond and respond politely. If the caller is extremely angry, ask if you can call back. If the caller refuses, ask if you may have some time to collect needed information. This additional time may allow the caller to calm down. Putting angry people on hold may upset them more. Instead, put the phone on the desk. Express regret with a statement such as, "I'm sorry for your inconvenience."

- Find a way to agree with their circumstances. Say something like, "I understand what you are going through; I'd be upset too if it had happened to me."

- Ask open-ended questions that allow people to further explain the problem; for example, "You feel the last shipment…? Use a checklist or a script. (Allow the other person to finish the sentence.)

- Suggest three or four alternatives for handling the problem that (1) you are able to do and (2) you have the authority to do. Do *not* say, "Company policy says we can't." A statement like this says you do not make decisions, and the caller may demand to talk to a supervisor. An example of giving alternatives is saying, "I cannot give you your money back, but you can pick out another product of equal value or have credit toward another purchase.

- Transfer the call only if you are certain the individual to whom you are sending the caller can and will take responsibility for solving the problem.

- Follow up in a week to make certain the problem is resolved. Ask if there is anything else that would be of assistance.

Arranging a Conference Call

A conference call is a telephone call involving three or more people. Many computerized phones have a conference call feature that allows the office professional to set up a call from the office telephone.

If the phone system does not have conference call capability, operator assistance is necessary. In the front of most phone directories is information on how to set up a conference call. Charges are added for the number of places connected, distance, and length of conference. If possible, give the operator advance notice of the call.

The steps for setting up the conference call are:

1. Check with the participants on their availability. Do not forget time zone differences.
2. Set the time of the conference call. Either notify the participants by telephone or in writing of the time according to their time zone.

3. Fax or mail an agenda ahead of time. This information helps participants gather materials and be better prepared for the call.

If operator assistance is necessary, dial 0 for the operator and explain that you wish to make a conference call. Give the operator the names and phone numbers of those taking part in the call and the time of the day of the call.

Cellular Phone Etiquette

Cellular telephones are becoming a standard business tool. The following are suggestions for cellular phone etiquette:

- Treat an incoming cellular phone call with the same urgency as a long-distance call.
- When transferring the call, tell the person to whom you are transferring that the call is on a cellular phone.
- Avoid putting cellular phone callers on hold.
- Use discretion when discussing confidential information such as credit card numbers or calling card numbers.
- Select words carefully and use first names only.

HINT: *For those who need added privacy, scrambling devices and enhanced privacy services are available.*

VOICE MAIL SYSTEMS

A voice mail system is a computerized answering machine. Messages are sent, retrieved, and saved on computer. When replayed, the person's voice sounds like it does on an answering machine.

Voice mail has the following features:

- It answers and routes large numbers of incoming calls at once.
- It provides important information, such as office hours or numbers to call for more information.
- It allows direct dialing from different locations to retrieve messages.
- It forwards calls to other locations, such as to home or a hotel.
- It allows callers to leave detailed messages in their own voices.
- It reduces the length of a phone call because communication is one-way.
- It allows people in different time zones to stay in touch 24 hours a day.

- It can send the same message to many people at preprogrammed phone numbers.

The message on the voice mail system should take into consideration the following factors:

- Rotary phones cannot access extensions or use the keypad for codes like touch-tone phones can.
- Some people prefer to talk with people instead of machines: Voice mail should make that option available.
- Avoid catching callers in an "endless loop" of pressing buttons so that they are not able to reach their intended party or get their questions answered.

For example, when you call Professional Secretaries International, you are connected to a recorded voice that says: "Thank you for calling Professional Secretaries International. If you know your party's extension, you may dial it now. If you are calling from a rotary telephone, please hold. If you are calling from a touch-tone telephone, please dial 0 for assistance. Thank you."

Leaving Voice Mail Messages

Voice mail technology has changed the type of messages left. Some people feel they can be as rude as they wish and use any tone of voice they want. Others leave personal, volatile, and potentially devastating messages on voice mail. Researchers think machines make such things easier because they detach people from an event and give permission to do something we would not do otherwise.

When you have a difficult or complex message to deliver and you reach voice mail, it is appropriate to say something like, "I am sorry I did not reach you. Please call me. I have some news."

If the possibility exists that you will have to leave a voice mail message, make an outline of what you have to say and check all facts and figures before placing the call. Avoid sounding like you are reading and include the following information when leaving the message:

- Your name. Spell it if it is not a very common name.
- Your phone number. Say it slowly and leave it at the beginning of the message. Many voice mail systems require listening to the entire message when replaying it.
- Date and time unless you know the voice mail system automatically records this information.
- A complete message. Details can help someone begin work on a project or gather information before returning the call; however, avoid giving too many details so that the receiver does not have to listen and relisten to the recorded message. Smalltalk is not appropriate.
- A good time to return the call when you are in the office.

MEDIA RELATIONS

The most cost effective method of publicizing an event or activity is through the media. News coverage can generate additional registrations, help publication sales, and educate the public about your organization. Larger businesses have public relations professionals but small businesses can still effectively receive media coverage. The following are opportunities to get publicity:

- Anniversaries
- Business news
- Corporate supporters
- Events and activities
- Recognitions
- Seminars
- Technology
- PSI news: elections, growth of chapter, joining with other groups or organizations to accomplish goals, new members, workshops

Establish a contact from your company. This person should consistently send the news releases and make the personal or telephone contacts with the media.

News releases can be sent to radio, television, or newspapers. The following are guidelines for news releases.

- Use professional letterhead and keyboard.
- Give the essential information first; use background and additional information later in the announcement. Keep the length to two double-spaced pages.
- Highlight any celebrity or VIP appearance.
- Proofread names carefully. Make certain it contains no grammatical, spelling, or punctuation errors.
- Avoid industry jargon.
- Be aware of deadlines and make the contact well in advance.
- Always send a personal note or follow up with a phone call when a publication prints your news release or does a feature story.

For newspapers, send a business announcement to the business editor. If you are trying to get a feature story, contact the features editor or reporter. The most professional contact is to send a news release with a letter attached. Ask if there is a staff photographer who could cover an event. If not, enclose high-quality, black and white photographs. Include the name(s) and the person(s) in the picture.

The news assignment editor is the best contact at a television station. Think about what will be interesting to viewers and only contact a television station when you have something special to show.

CHAPTER 22

ELECTRONIC COMMUNICATIONS AND THE INTERNET

Electronic communications and telecommunications allow data to be electronically transferred from one point within an information system to another. In today's office, computers and other equipment can now be linked together to expedite the exchange of information within a business and between organizations. Telecommunications technology is quickly changing the way businesses operate.

Computer networks can be set up to distribute information within a department or an office, through a local area network (LAN), or between different locations through a wide area network (WAN). Databases provide computers with an organized means of storing large amounts of information. Public databases are available that make information available to users for a fee.

The Internet is the world's largest computer network. Millions of people use it to send e-mail, search information databases, and conduct electronic commerce. In addition to being used for communications functions, the Internet is a social system inhabited by computer-literate people and shaped by the infrastructures, standards, protocols, expertise, and values that enable these communications.

COMPUTER NETWORKS

A computer network ties different functions together electronically, allowing for improved communication and greater sharing of information among individuals, departments, other offices or satellite offices, and other locations. Networking can also reduce equipment costs because it allows several PC users to share expensive peripheral equipment, such as laser printers and high-capacity disk drives.

The administration and management of a network is usually handled by a computer professional. Any problems arising in a network usually happen because of technical and programming issues. However, it is helpful for office professionals to understand the function of networking equipment and the terms used to describe it.

Local Area Networks

A **local area network (LAN)** is used to distribute information in an office through different terminals, called **nodes,** that are connected to a central information depository, called a **server.** The server manages the flow of information between computers hooked together on the LAN, somewhat like a traffic cop who manages the flow of traffic. The server also enables users to share peripheral equipment, disk drives, and data files.

The server is connected to each terminal or node in the network by some kind of cable (twisted-pair, coaxial, or fiber-optic). The cable is connected to a **controller card** in each computer terminal. The controller card interprets the messages going to and from the network. Recently, wireless LANs have been developed that use a radio frequency or infrared light to transmit information, eliminating the need for cables.

The configuration, or **topology,** of a LAN is the way each unit fits together and communicates with the network. There are three basic configurations: the star, the bus, and the token ring. (See Figure 22-1.)

Star configuration: Every computer in the network is connected to the server, which is the heart of the star configuration. Each user can communicate with every other user by passing information through the central server. It is the easiest configuration to install.

Bus configuration: Each terminal is connected by cable to the next in the network. Information flows over the wire to all the connected computers. Each terminal acts as a "bus stop" along the wire, but each reads only its own messages.

Token ring configuration: All the network's computers are wired together in a closed circle. An electrical signal, called the **token,** is passed around the ring or network. The signal contains information that is collected and distributed around the network. Users specify where on the ring they want their data or message to go. Although this seems to be the most reliable configuration, the software is complex and has a greater chance of losing or garbling data.

Desktop Management Networking Standards

Several groups are now working on creating desktop management standards to make network environments consistent:

- The Distributed Support Information Standards Consortium (DSIS) promotes the standardization of support and management information across multivendor environments from PCs to mainframes. This group does not make standards; rather, it finds out what requirements from the standpoint of support providers need.

- The Internet Engineering Task Force (IETF) is defining a new information standard for systems called the Host Resources MIB (HRM). This group is working to produce a document that defines MIB (management information base) objects common to all Internet hosts, including UNIX- and DOS-based machines.

- The Desktop Management Task Force (DMTF) was formed to promote a unifying desktop management interface (DMI). If all desktop components were united under one standard, desktop component vendors would need to support only a single in-

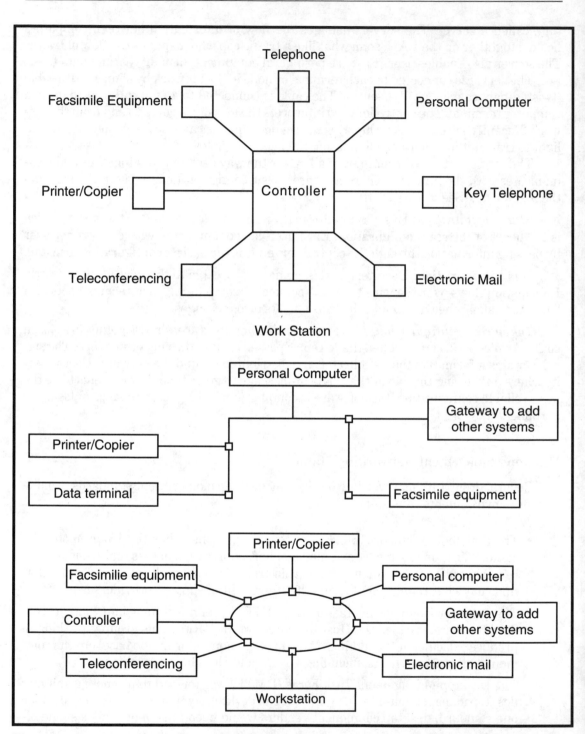

Figure 22-1 Star, bus, and token ring networks. (Courtesy of Frederick R. Feldman of the Feldman Group Inc.)

terface for managing their devices. Likewise, management application vendors would have only one interface for managing components from different vendors.

Electronic Mail

A major application of networks is electronic mail. E-mail is the sending and receiving of messages in electronic form between computers in a network. Messages can be stored, saved, and edited. They can also be forwarded or copied to another user or users. A user can also reply to a message. (See section on Electronic Mail in Chapter 16.)

Voice E-Mail

Voice e-mail is more friendly and personal than regular e-mail. It allows a caller to convey emotions on-line by using your voice instead of the keyboard. Voice e-mail add-on programs enable you to send and receive voice messages exactly like regular e-mail; the only difference is that instead of typing your messages, you digitally record them. The advantages are obvious: input is faster, there are no editing or spelling issues, you can be creative in providing sound effects, and you can include pictures and photographs in your voice e-mail messages.

Modems and Other Interface Devices

Computers operate using *digitally* encoded electronic signals (see section on The Computer in Chapter 7). On the other hand, telephone lines transmit *analog* electronic signals. In order for a computer to transmit and receive information over a telephone line, a **modem** is needed at each end. Modem stands for "modulator-demodulator." A modem translates (or "modulates") digital signals into analog signals for transmission over a phone line. At the other end, another modem converts the analog signals back into digital form for the receiving computer. A modem is sometimes also called a **data set.**

This integration of phone lines and computer systems allows information to be transmitted by voice or as data. Terminals equipped with modems can communicate as easily as humans can by making a phone call. Modems operate at various baud rates or speeds. For example a *28.8 baud modem* operates at a speed of 28.8 kilobits per second. Efficient transmission of voice, graphics, and video images requires even higher-speed modems. A 10-megabyte video clip, for example, takes 46 minutes to transfer from one computer to another with a 28.8 baud modem. This same file could be transferred on a *T1 telephone circuit* (speed rate of 1.5 megabits per second) in 52 seconds and on a *cable modem* (speed rate of 4 megabits per second) in 20 seconds. Cable modems are available from cable TV services and are used to connect a personal computer with a coaxial television cable.

There are various other kinds of interface devices that allow communication between different types of equipment. They include the following:

Port extenders: These devices turn a machine's single communications outlet, or "port," into two or three channels, allowing the machine to interface with more than one device at a time.

Protocol converters: These are also known as "black boxes." They are programmed to convert or translate from the codes and modes, or protocols, of one type of equipment to the protocols of another, and vice versa.

Media converters: These allow files stored on floppy disk by one program, such as a word processor, or on one brand of computer to be converted to a different program, such as another word processing or a composition program, or to a file compatible with a different brand of computer.

The type of phone system used in the office is important when considering modems and other devices. Currently most office phone systems are PBX systems. These are telephone facilities within an office or office building that connect to the public phone network. (PBX stands for Private Branch eXchange.)

However, an international effort to set communications standards has resulted in the **Integrated Services Digital Network (ISDN).** When fully operational, ISDN will let users make complex connections among different telecommunications resources. ISDN will allow the exchange of data, text, voice, graphics, and video over one line. Currently, several different lines must be used. When upgrading a telephone system, a company or office should choose a system that can be upgraded to the ISDN standards in order to meet future requirements.

ELECTRONIC COMMUNICATIONS THROUGH DATABASES

A database provides computers with a means of storing information. It is a large and continuously updated file on a particular subject or subjects.

Databases can be used for various applications. They are limited only by the user's imagination and needs. Small and large companies use databases to maintain inventories or process orders. Banks use databases to maintain checking and savings accounts. The government uses databases to track income taxes owed by citizens. Databases can be private or public.

Private Databases

A private database is one developed specifically for a company or organization that is not available to the general public. An example of a private database would be the customer list for XYZ Company. This database would contain information on customers, their orders, their addresses, etc. It would be used by management and office professionals.

Private databases are generally determined by the computer sophistication of a company. It is important to understand that a well-organized database can quickly help employees analyze, compute, and report what might otherwise take months to do manually.

It could be the responsibility of the office professional to help establish a database or work with the management information system personnel to use and further develop the database.

Public Databases

Information utilities have capitalized on the explosive need for information. An information utility is any organization that will let an individual use its information (or someone else's), usually for a fee. The information utility may use one database or several and offer many services. An individual can search and retrieve information on a variety of topics from airline information, to news and sports, to stock quotes. Different utilities specialize in different types of information.

To reach these information utilities, an individual typically either calls directly or calls through **Telenet, Tymnet, or Uninet** (three services that save long-distance phone charges). When connected with the utility, a person logs on, using a password and account number. Prices for these utilities range from a few dollars to several hundred dollars per hour. Some have sign-up charges, monthly minimums, subscriptions, consulting fees, and other fees associated with their use. A thorough understanding of the fees is necessary to avoid possible billing problems.

Information utilities are an outgrowth of several different technologies. They combine communications technologies (information delivered by phone lines, cable, or television), space technology (satellites), and computer technology (software and computer programming used to assemble large amounts of information or databases and retrieve them).

Information utilities offer various kinds of service, including transaction-based, communication-based, and information-based. **Transaction-based services** include shopping services, computerized classifieds, theater ticket sales, plane reservations, and at-home banking. It is essentially shopping by computer. Within the office, the service that would probably be utilized most is the one for making plane reservations.

Communication-based services include e-mail (see above), computerized bulletin boards, and online conferences. E-mail is a service that is used to send a message to anyone also using the system. A message is sent to a person's electronic mailbox. The next time that person goes to read his or her mad, the message will be there. CompuServe, for example, provides an electronic mailbox service for its subscribers.

Computerized bulletin boards function like real bulletin boards. A message is "posted" in the system and can be read. Usually bulletin boards are devoted to one subject or group of people, such as all users of IBM personal computers or individuals with the same hobby. Most are small and independent, operated by clubs, computer stores, or even by individuals. To use them, a modem, telephone, and computer are needed. Merely dial an access number and log on to the system. To "log on" simply means that an individual has electronically connected into the system—in this case, the bulletin board.

Online conferences or forums are written conversations between two or more people. Such conferences can be a club or professional group "meeting" in different locations by computer.

Information-based services are really electronic libraries. They contain everything from bibliographic research services to stock market quotes to electronic newspapers. This service is particularly useful for doing research reports. Reference information is available in abstract and/or full-text form.

Using online databases requires some special knowledge and involves certain considerations. Professionals are available in many companies to search online databases for the necessary information. However, if the responsibility is the office professional's, several tips are offered here:

- Don't be intimidated. The more you use a database service, the easier it gets.
- Take a course. Many database services offer training sessions.
- Check the bulletin board. Online bulletin boards and communications services can be used for learning more about database searches.
- Be prepared. Know what you are looking for before going online.
- Remember that every database is unique and may require special search techniques.
- When searching through full text, first look at headlines and first paragraphs. Then focus on those that seem most promising.
- If possible, make global searches of all databases that may be of interest.
- Every database is priced differently. Try the less expensive ones first.
- Download the documents you want and read them later to reduce online time. Save them on disk instead of printing.
- If your research needs are varied or infrequent, it may make sense to pay a professional to do the searching.

Information Utilities

Just as there are different services offered, there are also different kinds of information utilities. Each uses different technology. They are (1) **teletext,** (2) **videotext,** and (3) **interactive databases.**

TELETEXT

This is an information utility that sends its information by television. Teletext is a generic term that applies to several different specific systems. One of those systems is used by PBS, NBC, ABC, and CBS in their closed-caption system for the hearing impaired.

Each "page" contains one screen of information and is sent along with the regular television transmission. The system puts the teletext information into the black bars that show up between normal television picture frames.

To use teletext, a special adaptor is required. The pages include a table of contents with the page numbers. When the page number is entered into the adaptor, that page shows up on the television screen.

Teletext has limitations, however. It is strictly one-way communication. It takes about 1 second to transmit 4 pages. If 100 pages are being transmitted, it takes about 25 seconds to broadcast. If information from a particular page is needed quickly, the wait may be irritating.

VIDEOTEXT

This is an information utility that puts information into a computer (text or graphics or both), transmits that information, and displays that information on a modified television set (in the form of pages). Using videotext is much the same as using teletext. An individual sits in front of the television with an adaptor, punches in the numbers of the pages wanted, and the pages show up on the screen. With this system, connection is directly to a computer. The television functions like a computer terminal. The system is asked directly what is wanted, and it will respond.

INTERACTIVE DATABASES

These services are available online (i.e., connected by personal computer terminal to the service's mainframe computer) or offline. The latter type is available through CD-ROM disks. The online type of system uses time-sharing (technology that allows many people to use the same computer at the same time). An interactive process allows a command to be entered to find all information dealing with a specific topic. It is not necessary to look through menus—the system tells what stories or information fit the description. From that listing, a selection can be made of the ones to review. The computer then pulls those articles from the database.

A new technology is the use of CD-ROM (compact optical disks) for providing interactive information. Instead of connecting online using the computer terminal, the subscriber is sent a CD-ROM disk that can be accessed by a special drive attached to the personal computer. Many online databases, such as Educational Resource Information Clearinghouse (ERIC), are now available on CD-ROM. The advantage of CD-ROM is that it saves telephone costs. The disadvantage is that information is not always up to the minute.

THE INTERNET

The **Internet** is a network of 18,000 or more computer networks connected together. On these networks are millions of computers, computer terminals, and users. The Internet has become the world's largest group of computers connecting government bodies, universities, libraries, and businesses. Over the Internet, people can send messages to one another, participate in interest groups, gather research information on any subject imaginable, or

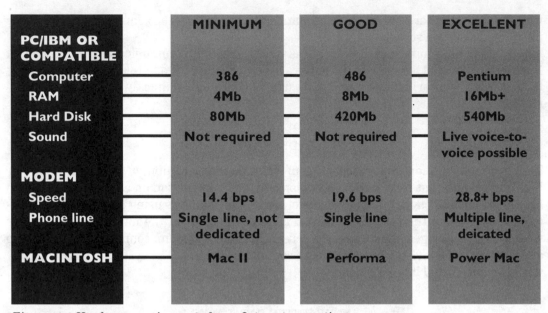

PC/IBM OR COMPATIBLE	MINIMUM	GOOD	EXCELLENT
Computer	386	486	Pentium
RAM	4Mb	8Mb	16Mb+
Hard Disk	80Mb	420Mb	540Mb
Sound	Not required	Not required	Live voice-to-voice possible
MODEM			
Speed	14.4 bps	19.6 bps	28.8+ bps
Phone line	Single line, not dedicated	Single line	Multiple line, deicated
MACINTOSH	Mac II	Performa	Power Mac

Figure 22-2 Hardware requirements for an Internet connection.

even buy and sell. Figure 22-2 lists the basic hardware requirements to get you connected. **Browsers** or **graphical user interfaces** (GUIs), such as Netscape, Mosaic, and Microsoft Internet Explorer, make it very easy to use the Internet. (See Figure 22-3 for a list of major Web Browsers.)

Gopher, developed at the University of Minnesota (named after the school's mascot), is a text-based information-retrieval program on the Internet. A Gopher is a computer server that provides a hierarchy of menus from which you can select text to read, files to download, or other services. Thousands of organizations maintain Gopher servers around the world, all connected via the Internet. Subject search utilities make it easy to work your way through the surf. **Archie** and **Veronica** are companion search tools that use keywords to help you look for information.

A **shell account** provides unlimited access to both Internet and Usenet services and file sites. Most providers will sell you a front end or interface to a *Serial Line Internet Protocol (SLIP) service* or a *Point-to-Point Protocol (PPP) service.* Tools and services provided by shell accounts can be either limited or extensive. They will vary with the provider. Another approach is to connect your computer directly to the Internet via opening your own **SLIP** or **PPP account.** These services provide users with multimedia program access with graphics, video and audio as well as text and links to other pages. Many businesses that require considerable access to the Internet use a direct connection method. In this case, a LAN connection is established through a high-speed NET link. Online services, such as America Online and CompuServe (see Figure 22-4), also provide direct access to their members on the Internet.

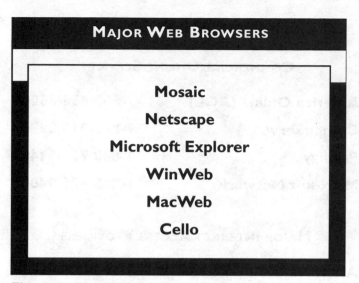

Figure 22-3 Major Web browsers.

Internet E-Mail

A popular benefit of the Internet is the capability to send messages to colleagues around the world without using a postage stamp via Internet e-mail. Your e-mail address is divided into two parts and is determined by the nature of the Internet account that you established—for example, an online service, a shell account, or a direct connection via your LAN through your company's direct, high-speed connection.

The first part of your address is your login name. This is the name of your account or the name you use each time you access the Internet. Usually names are used, such as *jdoe* for *Jane Doe.* However, some people may use a code name. The choice is yours.

A domain name comprises the second part of your Internet address. This name identifies computers and groups of accounts. For example, *gov* is the domain name used by the U.S. government. Subsets or levels of domains are also used. For example, the White House uses *whitehouse.gov* as its address. The higher-level domain is always to the right; the lower-level domain, to the left. Each domain subset is separated by a period, called a "dot." Always check with your service provider or employer, in case of a direct connection, for the correct domain name (see Figure 22-5).

The login name is always to the left of the domain name(s) separated by @, called "at." For example, if you wanted to send a message to the president, you would use this address: *president@whitehouse.gov.* If you are buying access from a service provider for yourself or your company and can pick a domain name, consider your location. For instance, *jdoe@albany.ny.us* refers to Jane Doe of Albany, New York, United States. When sending a message to a group of people, address the message to one person and then cc (carbon copy) and list the addresses of the other e-mail users.

When sending e-mail to someone using an online service such as CompuServe, you

COMMERCIAL ONLINE SERVICES

America Online (AOL)   1-800-454-6500

CompuServe   1-800-848-8990

Prodigy   1-800-776-3449

Microsoft Network   1-800-426-9400

MAJOR INTERNET ACCESS PROVIDERS

AlterNet   1-800-258-9695

Netcom   1-800-353-6600

PSI/Pipeline   1-800-82PSI82

Usenet   1-800-265-2213

Figure 22-4 Major commercial online services and Internet access providers.

SIX MAJOR TOP-LEVEL DOMAIN
TYPES

.gov   FEDERAL GOVERNMENT
.mil   MILITARY
.edu   EDUCATION
.org   ORGANIZATIONS
          (USUALLY NON-PROFIT)
.net   NETWORKS
.com   COMMERCIAL

Figure 22-5 Domain hierarchy.

need to know the identification (ID) or online address of the user. For example, CompuServe IDs consist of five-digit numbers, followed by a comma, followed by two or more numbers. Since you can't use a comma with an Internet address, you have to replace it with a period. A typical CompuServe Internet address will be in this format: *12345.678@compuserve.com.* To send a message while using CompuServe to someone on the Internet, use this format: *INTERNET:president@whitehouse.gov.* Other online services have their own protocol for using the Internet.

Be sure to record and store the Internet and online addresses of your colleagues. Write them down in your Rolodex. Also, when sending e-mail messages avoid hard-to-read ALL CAP messages. Most importantly, if you begin using e-mail, be sure to check your messages daily. Less frequent checking cancels the benefits of this type of communication!

Internet Newsgroups

A **newsgroup** is a discussion group. Anyone with an interest in a topic can participate by posting and replying to messages. Newsgroups do not contain separate file libraries and many are unmoderated. They can be used to discuss business, share information on the best restaurants for entertaining clients, and acquire end-user information on computers or software you may be planning to purchase.

A large number of newsgroups are part of a system called **Usenet**. Independent of Internet, Usenet is also a network of networks. The system's traffic is routed largely over the Internet. Usenet relies on a hierarchical system, going from left to right, for its host addresses. A series of descriptive words is used, separated by periods. For example, the newsgroup *rec.arts.movies* is part of the broader recreational *(rec)* category. Other popular categories include *comp* for computer-related subjects, *news* for information about newsgroups themselves, *sci* for discussions about the hard sciences, *soc* for information about different types of societies and subcultures, and *misc* for all kinds of topics.

Users will encounter a different network culture on Usenet with its own rules and regulations about behavior. Here are guidelines to help you:

- Begin newsgroup surfing by reading the *news.announce.newusers* group for background information.
- Always read messages before you post your own messages to learn what issues have been discussed.
- Read the frequently-asked questions lists posted in individual newsgroups.
- Use lines of 80 characters to format your messages and don't right-justify text. Also, never submit messages in ALL CAPS and do not use special control charters or tabs.
- Use clear and descriptive titles. This helps readers to scan through the messages by subject.
- When replying to a message, summarize the part to which you are responding. Do not repeat the entire message.
- Don't post "me too" messages in response to a query.

Conducting an Internet Search

Finding useful information quickly on the Internet is possible when you use the correct search tools. The number of Web servers and Web pages will continue to grow at a rapid rate, making it necessary to take advantage of the excellent tools that are available for finding information. Subject search utilities make it easy to work your way through the surf. Gopher, Archie, and Veronica are companion search tools that use keywords to help you look for information. Two categories of search tools dominate: subject indexes and search engines—and combinations of the two.

Subject Indexes: These are lists of links organized into subject categories and may provide the best strategy if you are still figuring out what information you need. They are analogous to a table of contents in a book. Subject indexes include **Alta Vista, WWW Virtual Library, The English Server** (from Carnegie Mellon, concentrating on the humanities), **The Whole Internet Catalog,** and **Nerd World.**

Search Engines: Instead of looking through lists and lists of lists (subject indexes), a keyword or key phrase is entered onto a line or into a box and the search engine does the work. All documents containing matching words or phrases in appropriate fields appear on the screen. Keyword searching is a good strategy when you have a specific word or phrase in mind, for example, the name of a technical term or a product. **Lycos,** developed at Carnegie Mellon, is one of the most powerful and frequently used search engines. Other popular search engines include Excite, InfoSeek Net Search (has both a free search and a subscription-based search service), WebCrawler, Open Text Index, New Riders' Office WWW Yellow Pages (one of several "Yellow Page" Web directories offering links to many corporate sites), and The Internet Trailblazer Search (a native American networking group; note, however, that its database is not limited to Native American materials).

Combinations of the above two categories also are available, offering the advantages of both. **Yahoo** is one of the largest and most complete centralized subject indexes with a search engine on the Internet. It has categorized Web sites into 14 main topics and hundreds of subtopics. Others include Planet Earth, with a geographic emphasis, and EINet Galaxy, which is intergalactic in scope.

A multiple access search engine can quicken your keyword search through hundreds of databases. In this group you will find All-In-One Search Page, SavvySearch, Starting Point, CUSI (Configurable Unified Search Interface), and The Internet Sleuth.

When conducting a search, always use more than one index or search engine. Also, when you discover Web pages to which you would like to come back in the future, mark them with your **Bookmarks** menu, which allows you to add pages to your own personal list.

Creating a Web Business Page

Software is now available to assist in getting a business onto the Internet. A Web page is similar to a Yellow Page in the phone book with a major exception. When composing a Web page, the author uses hyperlinked multimedia elements. The standard authoring language is known as **HyperText Markup Language (HTML).** This language allows your documents to include audio, video, text, graphic, and tables. Links can be made to e-mail, Usenet news, and other Web sites.

Large companies of all types are developing home pages to promote their products or provide product-related information. Small businesses, such as florists and CD distributors, are also finding new business opportunities through creating a Web page.

INTRANETS

Because of the increasing availability of encryption and authentication tools, companies can build secure **intranets** (private networks) over the Internet to protect electronic commerce applications. First-generation products, such as firewalls, were insufficient because of their reliance on Internet Protocol (IP) addresses that could be forged. Typically, noncritical, delay-insensitive information, such as e-mail, one-way data transfers and low-bandwidth LAN traffic, is appropriate. Using an intranet to extend a WAN (by linking suppliers, customers, and remote offices) or to communicate internationally is also suitable. Future uses of intranets will include high-bandwidth, two-way communications, including real-time videoconferencing and highly sensitive data.

GLOSSARY OF COMPUTER TERMS

access, to locate (data) for transfer from one part of a computer system to another.

acoustic coupler, a device designed to connect a telephone handset to a modem and a computer.

active-matrix, of or pertaining to a high-resolution liquid-crystal display (LCD) with high contrast, used especially for laptop computers.

adapter, *See* expansion card.

add-in, a component, such as an expansion card or chip, added to a computer to expand its capabilities.

add-on, a product, as an expansion card or computer program, designed to complement another product.

address, a label, as an integer or symbol, that designates the location of information stored in computer memory. Also, to direct (data) to a specified location in an electronic computer.

addressable, (of information stored in a computer) capable of being accessed.

alpha test, an early test of new or updated computer software conducted by the developers of the program prior to beta testing by potential users.

American Standard Code for Information Interchange, *See* ASCII.

analog computer, a computer that represents data by measurable quantities, as voltages, rather than by numbers.

AND, a Boolean operator that returns a positive result when both operands are positive.

applet, a small application program that can be called up for use while working in another application.

application, a specific kind of task, as database management, that can be done using an application program.

application program, a computer program used for a specific kind of task, as word processing architecture, a fundamental underlying design of computer hardware, software, or both.

artificial intelligence, the collective attributes of a computer, robot, or other mechanical device programmed to perform functions analogous to learning and decision making. The field of study involved with the design of such programs and devices.

ASCII, a standardized code in which characters are represented for computer storage and transmission by the numbers 0 through 127. A(merican) S(tandard) C(ode for) I(nformation)

assembler, a language processor that translates symbolic assembly language into equivalent machine language.

assembly language, a computer language most of whose expressions are symbolic equivalents of the machine-language instructions of a particular computer.

author, the writer of a software program, especially a hypertext or multimedia application.

backslash, a short oblique stroke used in some operating systems to mark the division between a directory and a subdirectory, as in typing a path.

backup, a copy or duplicate version, especially of a data file or program, retained for use in the event that the original becomes unusable or unavailable. A procedure for creating a backup. Also, to make a backup of (a data file or program).

batch, a group of jobs, data, programs, or commands treated as a unit for processing.

batch processing, a form of data processing in which a number of input jobs are run as a group.

baud, a unit used to measure the speed of data transfer, usually equal to the number of bits transmitted per second.

bay, an open compartment in the console housing a computer's CPU in which a disk drive, tape drive, etc., may be installed. Also called *drive bay.*

BBS, bulletin board system: a computerized facility, accessible by modem, for collecting and relaying electronic messages and software programs, playing games, etc. Also called *electronic bulletin board.*

beta test, a test of new or updated computer software or hardware conducted at select user sites just prior to release of the product.

binary, of or pertaining to a system of numerical notation to the base 2, in which each place of a number, expressed as 0 or 1, corresponds to a power of 2. Computers use the binary number system to store and process information.

BIOS, computer firmware that directs many basic functions of the operating system, as booting and keyboard control. B(asic) I(nput)/O(utput) S(ystem)

bit, a single, basic unit of computer information, valued at either 0 or 1 to signal binary alternatives.

bit map, a piece of text, a drawing, etc., represented, as on a computer display, by the activation of certain dots in a rectangular matrix of dots.

block, a group of computer data stored and processed as a unit. (in word processing) a portion of text or data marked off for deleting, moving, etc. To mark off (a portion of text or data) for moving, deleting, printing, etc., as in word processing.

board, a piece of fiberglass or other material upon which an array of computer chips is mounted. Also called card.

Boolean operation, any logical operation in which each of the operands and the result take one of two values, as "true" and "false" or "circuit on" and "circuit off."

boot, to start (a computer) by loading the operating system.

BPS, bits per second (refers to the number of data bits sent per second between modems).

buffer, a temporary storage area that holds data until ready to be processed.

bulletinboard, *See* BBS.

bus, a circuit that connects the CPU with other devices in a computer. The data bus transmits data to and from the CPU.

byte, a group of adjacent bits, usually eight, processed by a computer as a unit.

cache, a piece of computer hardware or a section of RAM dedicated to selectively storing and speeding access to frequently used program commands or data.

CAD/CAM, computer-aided design and computer-aided manufacturing.

capture, to enter (data) into a computer for processing or storage. Also, to record (data) in preparation for such entry.

card, *See* board

CD, *See under* compact disc.

CD-ROM, a compact disc on which a large amount of digitized read-only data can be stored. C(ompact) D(isc) R(ead-) O(nly) M(emory).

central processing unit. *See* CPU.

character, any encoded unit of computer-usable data representing a symbol, as a letter, number, or punctuation mark, or a space, carriage return, etc.

character set, the numbers, letters, punctuation marks, and special symbols that can be used by a particular device, as a printer, or in a coding method, as ASCII.

chat, to engage in dialogue by exchanging electronic messages usually in real time.

chip, a tiny slice of semiconducting material on which a transistor or an integrated circuit is formed. Also called *microchip.*

circuit board, a sheet of fiberglass or other material on which electronic components, as printed or integrated circuits, are installed.

CISC, complex instruction set computer: a computer whose central

processing unit recognizes a relatively large number of instructions.

click, to depress and release a mouse button rapidly, as to select an icon.

client, a workstation on a network that gains access to central data files, programs, and peripheral devices through a server.

clock, the circuit in a digital computer that provides a common reference train of electronic pulses for all other circuits. The clock speed, usually measured in megahertz, indicates how fast the computer will carry out commands.

clock speed. *See under* clock.

code, the symbolic arrangement of statements or instructions in a computer program in which letters, digits, etc., are represented as binary numbers; the set of instructions in such a program.

color monitor. *See under* monitor.

command, a signal, as a keystroke, instructing a computer to perform a specific task.

compact disc, a small optical disc on which music, data, or images are digitally recorded for playback. Abbreviated: CD.

compatible, (of software) able to run on a specified computer. (of hardware) able to work with a specified device. (of a computer system) functionally equivalent to another, ususally widely used, system.

compiler, a computer program that translates another program written in a high-level language into a form, usually machine language, that can be executed by a computer.

compression, reduction of the size of computer data by efficient storage.

computer graphics, pictorial computer output produced, through the use of software, on a display screen or printer. Also, the technique or process used to produce such output.

configuration, a computer, the equipment connected to it, plus software, set up to work together. Also, the act of configuring a computer system.

configure, to put (a computer system) together by supplying a specific computer with appropriate peripheral devices, as a monitor and disk drive, and connecting

them. Also, to insert batch files into (a program) to enable it to run with a particular computer.

console, the control unit of a computer, including the keyboard and display screen.

conversion, the process of enabling software for one computer system to run on another. Also, the transformation of data from a form compatible with one computer program to a form compatible with another.

coprocessor, a processing unit that assists the CPU in carrying out certain types of operations. For example, a math coprocessor is a processing unit that performs mathematical calculations using floating-point notation.

copy protection, a method of preventing users of a computer program from making unauthorized copies, usually through hidden instructions contained in the program code.

CPU, central processing unit: the key component of a computer system, containing the circuitry necessary to interpret and execute program instructions.

crash, (of a computer) to suffer a major failure because of a malfunction of hardware or software.

cursor, a movable, sometimes blinking, symbol used to indicate where data (as text, commands, etc.) may be input on a computer screen.

cyber-, a combining form representing "computer," e.g., cybertalk; cyberart.

cyberpunk, science fiction featuring extensive human interaction with supercomputers and a punk ambiance, a computer hacker.

cyberspace, the realm of electronic communication.

daisy wheel, a small spoked wheel with raised numbers, letters, etc., on the tips of the spokes: used as the printing element in some computer printers. Laser and inkjet printers have almost entirely replaced daisy-wheel printers for producing high-resolution text with personal computers.

data base, a collection of organized, related data in electronic form that can be accessed and manipulated by specialized computer software. Also, fund of information on one or more subjects, as a collection of articles accessible by computer.

data bus. *See under* bus.

data highway, *See* information superhighway.

DBMS, database management system: a set of software programs for controlling the storage, retrieval, and modification of organized data in a computerized database.

dedicated, (of a computer) designed for a specific use or an exclusive application: a dedicated word processor.

default, a preset value that a computer system assumes or an action that it takes unless otherwise instructed.

density, a measure of how much data can be stored in a given amount of space on a disk, tape, or other computer storage medium.

desktop computer, a computer made to fit or be used on a desk or table.

desktop publishing, the design and production of publications by means of specialized software enabling a microcomputer to generate typeset-quality text and graphics. Abbreviated: dtp

digital, involving or using numerical digits expressed in a scale of notation to represent discretely all variables occurring in a problem.

digital computer, a computer that processes information in digital form.

directory, a division in a hierarchical structure that organizes the storage of computer files on a disk. Also, a listing of such stored files.

disk, any of several types of media for storing electronic data consisting of thin round plates of plastic or metal.

disk drive, a device in or attached to a computer that enables the user to read data from or store data on a disk.

diskette. *See under* floppy disk.

display, to show (computer data) on a CRT or other screen. The visual representation of the output of an electronic device. Also, the portion of the device, as a screen, that shows this representation.

docking station, a small desktop cabinet, usually containing disk drives and ports for connection to peripherals, into which a laptop may be inserted so as to give it the functionality of a desktop computer.

document, a computer data file.

documentation, instructional materials for computer software or hardware.

dongle, a hardware device attached to a computer without which a given software program will not run: used to prevent unauthorized use.

DOS, an operating system for microcomputers. D(isk) O(perating) S(ystem).

dot-matrix printer, a computer printer that produces characters and graphics by pushing pins into an inked ribbon to form the appropriate pattern, or matrix, of dots.

dot pitch, a measure of the distance between each pixel on a computer screen. A lower number indicates a sharper image.

double-click, to click a mouse button twice in rapid succession, as to call up a program or select a file.

download, to transfer (software or data) from a computer to a smaller computer or a peripheral device.

dpi, dots per inch: a measure of resolution used especially for printed text or images.

drag, to pull (a graphical image or portion of text) from one place to another on a computer screen, especially by using a mouse.

drive bay. *See* bay.

driver, software that controls the interface between a computer and a peripheral device.

dump, to output (computer data), often in binary form, especially to diagnose a failure. Also, a copy of dumped computer data.

edit, to modify (computer data or text).

electronic mail, a system for sending messages via telecommunications links between computers. Abbreviated: e-mail.

e-mail. *See* electronic mail.

emoticon. *See* smiley

end-user, the ultimate user of a computer or a software program.

Energy Star Program, a program of the U.S. Environmental Protection Agency encouraging the manufacture of personal computers that can reduce their energy consumption when left idle.

enhance, to provide with more complex or sophisticated features, as a computer program.

enhanced keyboard, a keyboard having 101 keys, with 12 function keys along the top.

environment, the hardware or software configuration of a computer system.

Ethernet, Trademark. a local-area network protocol featuring a bus topology (all devices are connected to a central cable) and a 10 megabit per second data transfer rate.

execute, to run (a computer program) or process (a command).

expansion card, a circuit board that fits into an expansion slot, used to add sound capability, more memory, etc., e.g., a sound card is an expansion card that permits files containing music, voice, or other sounds to be played on a computer. Also called *expansion board*

expansion slot, a connection to which a new circuit board can be added to expand a computer's capabilities.

export, to save (documents, data, etc.) in a format usable by another application program.

fax modem, a modem that can fax data, as documents or pictures, directly from a computer.

field, a unit of information, as a person's name, that combines with related fields, as an official title, address, or company name, to form one complete record in a computerized database.

file, a collection of related computer data or program records stored by name, as on a disk.

file server, a computer that makes files available to workstations on a network.

firmware, software stored permanently on a ROM chip.

first-generation, being the first model or version available to users.

flame, (especially on a computer network) an act or instance of angry criticism or disparagement. To behave in an offensive manner; rant. Also, to insult or criticize angrily.

flash memory, a type of reprogrammable computer memory that retains information even with the power turned off.

flat-file, of or pertaining to a database system in which each database consists of a single file not linked to any other file.

floating point, a decimal point whose location is not fixed, used especially in computer operations.

floppy disk, a thin, portable, flexible plastic disk coated with magnetic material, for storing computer data and programs. Currently, the 5¼-inch disk (sometimes called a diskette), housed in a square flexible envelope in which the disk rotates while in use, and the 3½-inch disk (sometimes called a microfloppy), housed in a square rigid envelope, are the two common sizes used with personal computers.

flops, a measure of computer speed, equal to the number of floating-point operations the computer can perform per second (used especially in combination with the prefixes mega-, giga-, and tera-) fl(oating-point) op(erations per) s(econd)

font, a set of characters that have a given shape or design.

footprint, the surface space occupied by a microcomputer.

format, the arrangement of data for computer input or output, as the number of fields in a database record or the margins in a report. To set the format of (computer input or output). Also, to prepare (a disk) for writing and reading.

freeware, computer software distributed without charge.

FTP, File Transfer Protocol: a software protocol for exchanging information between computers over a network. Also, any program that implements this protocol.

function key, a key on a computer keyboard used alone or with other keys for operations.

gateway, software or hardware that links two computer networks.

GB. *See* gigabyte

gigabyte, a measure of data storage capacity equal to approximately 1 billion bytes. Abbreviated: GB

gigaflops, a measure of computer speed, equal to one billion floating-point operations per second.

global, (of a computer operation) operating on a group of similar strings, commands, etc., in a single step.

Gopher, a protocol for a menu-based system of accessing documents on the Internet. Also, any program that implements this protocol.

graphic, a computer-generated image.

graphical user interface, a software interface designed to standardize and simplify the use of computer programs, as by using a mouse to manipulate text and images on a display screen featuring icons, windows, and menus. Abbreviated: GUI.

groupware, software enabling a group to work together on common projects, share data, and synchronize schedules, especially through networked computers.

GUI. *See* graphical user interface.

hacker, a computer enthusiast who is especially proficient in programming. Also, a computer user who attempts to gain unauthorized access to proprietary computer systems.

hard copy, computer output printed on paper; printout.

hard disk, a rigid disk coated with magnetic material, for storing computer programs and relatively large amounts of data.

hardware, the mechanical, magnetic, electronic, and electrical devices composing a computer system.

hardware platform, a group of compatible computers that can run the same software.

hardwired, built into a computer's hardware and thus not readily changed. Also, (of a terminal) connected to a computer by a direct circuit rather than through a switching network.

Help, a system for supplying documentation for a software program, accessible on line from within the program.

high-level, (of a programming language) based on a vocabulary of Englishlike statements for writing program code rather than the more abstract instructions typical of assembly language or machine language.

hi-res, high-resolution.

home computer, a microcomputer designed for use in the home, as with game, multimedia, and educational software or electronic online services.

host computer, the main computer in a network, which controls or performs certain functions for other connected computers.

HTML, HyperText Markup Language: a set of standards, a variety of SGML, used to tag the elements of a hypertext document: the standard for documents on the World Wide Web.

hypermedia, a system in which various forms of information, as data, text, graphics, video, and audio, are linked together by a hypertext program.

hypertext, a method of storing data through a computer program that allows a user to create and link fields of information at will and to retrieve the data nonsequentially.

icon, a small graphic image on a computer screen representing a disk drive, a file, or a software command, as a picture of a wastebasket that can be pointed at and clicked on to delete a file.

impact printer, a computer printer, as a dot-matrix printer, that forms characters by causing a printhead to strike at paper through an inked ribbon.

import, to bring (documents, data, etc.) into one application program from another.

information superhighway, a large-scale communications network providing a variety of often interactive services, such as text databases, electronic mail, and audio and video materials, accessed through computers, television sets, etc.

initialize, to set (variables, counters, switches, etc.) to their starting values at the beginning of a computer program or subprogram. To prepare (a computer, printer, etc.) for reuse by clearing previous data from memory. Also, to format (a disk).

inkjet printer, a computer printer that prints text or graphics by spraying jets of ink onto paper to form a high-quality image approaching that of a laser printer.

input, data entered into a computer for processing. The process of introducing data into a computer for processing and/or internal storage. Also, of or pertaining to data or equipment used for input, e.g., a computer's main input device.

input/output, the combination of devices, channels, and techniques controlling the transfer of information between a CPU and its peripherals.

install, to put in place or connect for service or use, e.g., to install software on a computer.

instruction, a computer command.

interactive, (of a computer or program) characterized by or allowing immediate two-way communication between a source of information and a user, who can initiate or respond to queries.

interface, computer hardware or software designed to communicate information between hardware devices, between software programs, between devices and programs, or between a computer and a user.

interlaced, of or pertaining to technology that allows a monitor to display an image with higher resolution than it would otherwise be capable of by refreshing half the lines on the screen during one pass of an electron gun and the other half during a second pass. Interlaced monitors are more subject to flicker than noninterlaced ones.

interleaving, a method for making data retrieval more efficient by rearranging or renumbering the sectors on a hard disk or by splitting a computer's main memory into sections so that the sectors or sections can be read in alternating cycles.

Internet, a large computer network linking smaller computer networks worldwide.

interrupt, a hardware or software signal that temporarily stops program execution in a computer so that another procedure can be carried out.

I/O, input/output.

jaggies, a jagged, stairstep effect on curved or diagonal lines that are reproduced in low resolution, as on a printout or computer display.

job, a unit of work for a computer.

joystick, a lever used to control the movement of a cursor or other graphic element, as in a video game.

KB. *See* kilobyte.

keypad, a small panel of numeric and other special keys on a computer keyboard.

kilobit. *See* kilobyte.

kilobyte, a measure of data storage capacity equal to approximately one thousand bytes (1,024 bytes). Also called *kilobit.* Abbreviated KB.

LAN. *See* local-area network.

language, a set of symbols and syntactic rules for their combination

and use, by means of which a computer can be given directions.

laptop, a portable, usually battery-powered microcomputer small enough to rest on the lap.

laser printer, a high-speed, high-resolution computer printer that uses a laser to form dot-matrix patterns and an electrostatic process to print a page at a time.

letter-quality, designating or producing type equal in sharpness and resolution to that produced by an electric typewriter: e.g., a letter-quality computer printer. Abbreviated: LQ.

light pen, a hand-held light-sensitive input device used for drawing on a computer display screen or for pointing at characters or objects, as when choosing options from a menu.

line printer, an impact printer that produces a full line of computer output at a time.

load, to bring (a program or data) into a computer's RAM, as from a disk, so as to make it available for processing. Also, to place (an input/output medium) into an appropriate device, as by inserting a disk into a disk drive.

local-area network, a computer network confined to a limited area, linking especially personal computers so that programs, data, peripheral devices, and processing tasks can be shared. Abbreviated: LAN.

log in, to gain access to a secured computer system or on-line service by keying in personal identification information.

log off, to terminate a session on a computer.

loop, the reiteration of a set of instructions in a computer routine or program.

lo-res, low-resolution.

LPM, lines per minute: a measure of the speed of an impact printer.

LQ. *See* letter-quality.

machine language, usually a numerical coding system specific to the hardware of a given computer model, into which any high-level or assembly program must be translated before being run.

machine-readable, (of data) in a form suitable for direct acceptance and processing by computer, as an electronic file on a magnetic disk.

macro, a single instruction, for use in a computer program, that represents a sequence of instructions or keystrokes.

mailbox, a file in a computer for the storage of electronic mail.

mainframe, a large computer, often the hub of a system serving many users.

main memory. *See* RAM.

management information system, a computerized information-processing force offering management support to a company. Abbreviated: MIS.

math coprocessor. *See under* coprocessor.

MB. *See* megabyte.

megabit. *See* megabyte.

megabyte, a measure of data storage capacity equal to approximately one million bytes. (1,048,576 bytes). Also called *megabit.* Abbreviated: MB.

megaflops, a measure of computer speed, equal to one million floating-point operations per second.

megahertz, a unit of frequency equal to one million cycles per second, used to measure microprocessor speed. Abbreviated: MHz.

memory, the capacity of a computer to store information, especially internally in RAM while electrical power is on. Also, the components of the computer in which such information is stored.

menu, a list of options or commands from which to choose, displayed on a computer screen. A menu bar is a horizontal list of options near the top of a window. A pop-up menu appears temporarily when the user clicks on a selection. A pull-down menu appears beneath the option selected.

menu bar. *See under* menu.

menu-driven, of or pertaining to computer software that makes extensive use of menus to enable users to choose program options.

MHz. *See* megahertz.

microchip. *See* chip.

microcomputer, a compact computer having less capability than a minicomputer and employing a microprocessor.

microfloppy. *See under* floppy disk.

microprocessor, an integrated computer circuit that performs all the functions of a CPU.

MIDI, Musical Instrument Digital Interface: a standard means of sending digitally encoded information about music between electronic devices, as between synthesizers and computers.

minicomputer, a computer with processing and storage capabilities smaller than those of a mainframe but larger than those of a microcomputer.

minitower, a vertical case, smaller than a tower and larger than a case for a desktop computer, designed to house a computer system standing on a floor or desk.

MIPS, million instructions per second: a measure of computer speed.

MIS. *See* management information system.

modem, an electronic device that makes possible the transmission of data to or from a computer via telephone or other communication lines.

monitor, a component with a display screen for viewing computer data. A monochrome monitor can display two colors, one for the foreground and one for the background. A color monitor can display from 16 to one million different colors.

monochrome monitor. See under monitor.

morphing, the smooth transformation of one image into another by computer, as in a motion picture.

motherboard, a rigid slotted board upon which other boards that contain the basic circuitry of a computer or of a computer component can be mounted.

mouse, a palm-sized device equipped with one or more buttons, used to point at and select items on a computer screen, with the displayed pointer controlled by means of analogous movement of the device on a nearby surface.

MPC, multimedia PC, a system conforming to specifications covering audio, video, and other multimedia components, and able to run multimedia software.

MPR II, a standard developed in Sweden that limits to 250 nanoteslas the electromagnetic radiation emissions from a monitor at a distance of a half meter.

MS-DOS, Trademark. a microcomputer operating system. M(icro) S(oft) D(isk) O(perating) S(ystem).

multimedia, the combined use or integration of several media in computer applications, as text, sound, graphics, animation, and video.

multitasking, the concurrent execution of two or more jobs or programs by a single CPU.

multiuser system, a computer system in which multiple terminals connect to a host computer that handles processing tasks.

netiquette, the etiquette of computer networks.

network, a computer or telecommunications system linked to permit exchange of information.

newsgroup, a discussion group on a specific topic, maintained on a computer network.

noninterlaced, of or pertaining to technology that refreshes all the lines on a monitor's screen at one time while maintaining screen resolution. (Noninterlaced monitors are less subject to flicker than interlaced ones.)

nonvolatile, (of computer memory) having the property of retaining data when electrical power fails or is turned off.

NOR, a Boolean operator that returns a positive result when both operands are negative.

NOT, a Boolean operator that returns a positive result if its operand is negative and a negative result if its operand is positive.

notebook, a small, lightweight laptop computer measuring approximately 8½ x 11 in. (22 x 28 cm).

numeric keypad. *See* keypad.

OCR. *See* optical character recognition.

offline, operating independently of, or disconnected from, an associated computer.

online, operating under the direct control of, or connected to, a main computer.

on-line service, a database service providing information, news, etc., accessed through a modem.

operating system, the software that directs a computer's operations, as by controlling and scheduling the execution of other programs and managing storage and input/output.

optical character recognition, the process or technology of reading printed or typed text by electronic means and converting it to digital data. Abbreviated: OCR.

optical disc, a grooveless disk on which digital data, as text, music, or pictures, are stored as tiny pits in the surface and read or replayed by a laser beam scanning the surface.

optical scanner, *See* scanner.

OR, a Boolean operator that returns a positive result when either or both operands are positive.

output, information made available by computer, as on a printout, display screen, or disk. Also, the process of transferring such information from computer memory to or by means of an output device.

page, a block of computer memory up to 4,096 bytes long. Also, a portion of a program that can be moved to a computer's internal memory from external storage.

page description language, a high-level programming language for determining the output of a page printer designed to work with it, independent of the printer's internal codes. Abbreviated: PDL.

page printer, a high-speed, high-resolution computer printer that uses a light source, as a laser beam or electrically charged ions, to print a full page of text or graphics at a time.

palette, the complete range of colors made available by a computer graphics card, from which a user or program may choose those to be displayed.

palmtop, a battery-powered microcomputer small enough to fit in the palm.

parallel, of or pertaining to operations within a computer that are performed simultaneously: parallel processing. Also, pertaining to or supporting the transfer of electronic data several bits at a time: a parallel printer.

passive-matrix, of or pertaining to a relatively low-resolution liquid-crystal display (LCD) with low contrast, used especially for laptop computers.

password, a string of characters typed into a computer to identify and obtain access for an authorized user.

path, a listing of the route through directories and subdirectories that locates and thereby names a specific file or program on a disk drive (in some computer operating systems). Also, the currently active list of all such routes that tells the operating system where to find programs, enabling a user to run them from other directories.

PC. *See* personal computer.

PCMCIA, Personal Computer Memory Card International Association: (especially for laptop computers) a standard for externally accessible expansion slots that accept compatible cards for enhancing the computer's functions, as by adding memory or supplying a portable modem.

PDA. *See* personal digital assistant.

PDL. *See* page description language.

pen-based, (of a computer) having an electronic stylus rather than a keyboard as the primary input device.

peripheral, an external hardware device, as a keyboard, printer, or tape drive, connected to a computer's CPU.

personal computer, a microcomputer designed for individual use, as for word processing, financial analysis, desktop publishing, or playing computer games. Abbreviated: PC.

personal digital assistant, a hand-held computer, often pen-based, that provides especially organizational software, as an appointment calendar, and communications hardware, as a fax modem. Abbreviated PDA.

PIM, personal information manager.

pixel, the smallest element of an image that can be individually processed in a video display system.

platform, *See under* hardware platform and software platform.

Plug and Play, a standard for the production of compatible computers, peripherals, and software that facilitates device installation and enables automatic configuration of the system.

plug-compatible, designating computers or peripherals that are compatible with another vendor's models and could replace them.

pop-up menu. *See under* menu.

port, a data connection in a computer to which a peripheral device or a transmission line from a remote terminal can be attached. Also, to create a new version of (an application program) to run on a different hardware platform.

portable, (of data, software, etc.) able to be used on different computer systems.

PPM, pages per minute: a measure of the speed of a page printer.

printer, a computer output device that produces a paper copy of data or graphics.

printhead, the printing element on an impact printer.

printout, computer output produced by a printer.

print wheel. *See* daisy wheel.

program, a sequence of instructions enabling a computer to perform a task; piece of software. Also, to provide a program for (a computer).

programming language, a high-level language used to write computer programs, or, sometimes, an assembly language.

prompt, a symbol or message on a computer screen requesting more information or indicating readiness to accept instructions.

protocol, a set of rules governing the format of messages that are exchanged between computers.

pull-down menu. *See under* menu.

queue, a sequence of items waiting in order for electronic action in a computer system.

RAM, volatile computer memory, used for creating, loading, and running programs and for manipulating and temporarily storing data; main memory. R(andom) A(ccess) M(emory).

random-access, designating an electronic storage medium that allows information to be stored and retrieved in arbitrary sequence.

random-access memory. *See* RAM.

raster, a set of horizontal lines composed of individual pixels, used to form an image on a CRT or other screen.

read, to obtain (data or programs) from an external storage medium and place in a computer's memory.

read-only, noting or pertaining to computer files or memory that can be read but cannot normally be changed.

read-only memory. *See* ROM.

read-out, the output of information from a computer in readable form.

real-time, of or pertaining to computer applications or processes that can respond immediately to user input.

recognition, the automated conversion of words or images into a

form that can be processed by a computer.

record, a group of related fields treated as a unit in a database.

red-lining, a marking device, as underlining or boldface, used especially in word processing to highlight suggested additional text in a document.

refresh, to redisplay the information on (a screen) so as to prevent loss or fading. A refresh rate of many times per second is typical for a computer's display screen.

refresh rate. *See under* refresh.

register, a high-speed storage location in a computer's CPU, used to store a related string of bits, as a word or phrase.

relational database, an electronic database comprising multiple files of related information, usually stored in tables of rows (records) and columns (fields), and allowing a link to be established between separate files that have a matching field, as a column of invoice numbers, so that the two files can be queried simultaneously by the user.

resident, encoded and permanently available to a computer user, as a font in a printer's ROM or software on a CD-ROM. Also, (of a computer program) currently active or standing by in computer memory, as a TSR program.

resolution, the degree of sharpness of a computer-generated image as measured by the number of dots per linear inch in a hard-copy printout or the number of pixels across and down on a display screen.

response time, the time that elapses while waiting for a computer to respond to a command.

retrieve, to locate and read (data) from computer storage, as for display on a monitor.

reverse video, a mode on the display screen of a computer in which the colors normally used for characters and background are reversed.

RISC, reduced instruction set computer: a computer whose central processing unit recognizes a relatively small number of instructions, which it can execute very rapidly.

ROM, nonvolatile, nonmodifiable computer memory, used to hold programmed instructions to the system. R(ead) O(nly) M(emory).

routine, a set of instructions directing a computer to perform a specific task.

run, to process (the instructions in a program) by computer.

save, to copy (computer data) onto a hard or floppy disk, a tape, etc.

scalable font, *See under* font.

scan, to read (data) for use by a computer or computerized device, especially using an optical scanner.

scanner, a device that converts text or graphic images into a digital form that the computer can use. Also called *optical scanner.*

screen saver, a computer program that blanks the screen display or puts a moving pattern on it to prevent the permanent etching of a pattern on a screen when the pattern is displayed for a long time. Also, any of a selection of moving patterns available through this program, appearing on a screen if there has been no user input for a specified amount of time.

scroll, to move a cursor smoothly, vertically or sideways, gradually causing new data to replace old on the display screen of a computer.

SCSI, a standard for computer interface ports featuring faster data transmission and greater flexibility than normal ports. S(mall) C(omputer) S(ystem) I(nterface)

search, to command software to find specified characters or codes in (an electronic file). e.g., to search a database for all instances of "U.S." and replace them with "United States." Also, to find specified characters or codes in an electronic file by means of software commands.

serial, pertaining to or supporting the transfer of electronic data in a stream of sequential bits: a serial port. Also, of or pertaining to the transmission or processing of each part of a whole in sequence, as each bit of a byte or each byte of a computer word.

server, a computer that makes services, as access to data files, programs, and peripheral devices, available to workstations on a network.

SGML, Standard Generalized Markup Language: a set of standards enabling a user to create an appropriate scheme for tagging

the elements of an electronic document, as to facilitate the production of multiple versions in various print and electronic formats.

shareware, computer software distributed without initial charge but for which the user is encouraged to pay a nominal fee to cover support for continued use.

shell, a computer program providing a menu-driven or graphical user interface designed to simplify use of the operating system, as in loading application programs.

slipstreaming, the act of updating a software program without adequately informing the public, as by failing to release it as an official new version.

slot, *See* expansion slot.

smiley, a sideways smile face, :) or similar combination of symbols; a winking face, ;-) a sad face, :(used to communicate humor, sarcasm, sadness, etc., in an electronic message. Also called *emoticon.*

software, programs for directing the operation of a computer or processing electronic data.

software platform, a major piece of software, as an operating system, an operating environment, or a database, under which various smaller application programs can be designed to run.

sort, to place (computerized data) in order, numerically or alphabetically.

soundcard. *See under* expansion card.

spell checker, a computer program for checking the spelling of words in an electronic document.

split screen, a mode of operation on a computer that uses windows to enable simultaneous viewing of two or more displays on the same screen.

spool, to operate (an input/output device) by using buffers in main and secondary storage.

spreadsheet, an outsize ledger sheet simulated electronically by specialized computer software, used especially for financial planning.

standalone, (of an electronic device) able to function without connection to a larger system; self-contained.

storage. *See* memory.

store, to put or retain (data) in a computer memory unit, as a hard disk.

subdirectory, a directory hierarchically below another directory in DOS or UNIX.

subnotebook, a laptop computer smaller and lighter than a notebook, typically weighing less than 5 pounds (2.3 kg).

subroutine, a prepared instruction sequence that a programmer can insert into a computer program as needed.

surge protector, a device that provides an alternative pathway for electrical energy when excessive voltage appears on the power line, shunting the energy away from computer circuits.

system, a working combination of computer hardware, software, and data communications devices.

system(s) program, a program, as an operating system, compiler, or utility program, that controls some aspect of the operation of a computer.

systems analysis, the methodical study of the data-processing needs of a business or project.

tag, a symbol or other labeling device indicating the beginning or end of a unit of information in an electronic document.

tape drive, a program-controlled device that reads data from or writes data on a magnetic tape which moves past a read-write head.

telecommuting, the act or practice of working at home using a computer terminal electronically linked to one's place of employment.

telnet, a protocol for connecting to a remote computer on the Internet. Also, any program that implements this protocol.

teraflops, a measure of computer speed, equal to one trillion floating-point operations per second.

terminal, any device for entering information into a computer or receiving information from it, as a keyboard with video display unit.

text editor, a computer program for writing and modifying documents or program code on-screen, usually having little or no formatting ability.

toggle, to shift back and forth between two settings or modes of computer operation by means of a key or programmed keystroke.

touch screen, a computer display that can detect and respond to the presence and location of a finger or instrument on or near its surface.

tower, a vertical case designed to house a computer system standing on the floor.

track, one of a number of concentric rings on the surface of a floppy disk, or other computer storage medium, along which data are recorded.

trackball, a computer input device for controlling the pointer on a display screen by rotating a ball set inside a case.

tree, a computer data structure organized like a tree whose nodes store data elements and whose branches represent pointers to other nodes in the tree.

TSR, a computer program with any of several ancillary functions, usually held resident in RAM for instant activation while one is using another DOS program. T(erminate and) S(tay) R(esident)

UNIX, trademark. A highly portable multiuser, multitasking operating system used on a variety of computers ranging from mainframes through workstations to personal computers.

upload, to transfer (software or data) from a smaller to a larger computer.

user, a person who uses a computer.

user-friendly, easy to operate, understand, etc.

user group, a club for the exchange of information and services among computer users.

utility program, a system program used especially to simplify standard computer operations, as sorting, copying, or deleting files. Also called *utility.*

vaporware, a product, especially computer software, that is announced and promoted while it is still in development and that may never come to market.

VDT. *See* video display terminal.

vector graphics, a method of electronically coding graphic images so that they are represented in lines rather than fixed bit maps, allowing an image, as on a computer display screen, to be rotated or proportionally scaled.

VGA, video graphics array: a high-resolution standard for displaying text, graphics, and colors on monitors.

video display terminal, a computer terminal consisting of a screen on which data or graphics can be displayed. Abbreviated: VDT.

virtual, temporarily simulated or extended by software; virtual memory on a hard disk. Also, of, existing on, or by means of computers.

virtual reality, a realistic simulation of an environment, including three-dimensional graphics, by a computer system using interactive software and hardware.

virus, a segment of self-replicating code planted illegally in a computer program, often to damage or shut down a system or network.

volatile, (of computer storage) not retaining data when electrical power is turned off.

WAN, wide-area network.

wide-area network, a computer network that spans a relatively large geographical area. Abbreviated: *WAN.*

wild card, a character, as an asterisk, set aside by a computer operating system to represent one or more other characters of a file name, as in the DOS command "DEL *.DOC," which would delete all files with names ending in ".DOC."

window, a portion of the screen of a computer terminal on which data can be displayed independently of the rest of the screen. Also, a view of a portion of a document bounded by the borders of a computer's display screen.

Windows, trademark. Any of several microcomputer operating systems or environments featuring a graphical user interface.

wired, connected electronically to one or more computer networks.

word processing, the automated production and storage of documents using computers, electronic printers, and text-editing software.

word processor, a computer program or computer system designed for word processing.

work station, a powerful microcomputer, often with a high-resolution display, used for computer-aided design, electronic publishing, or other graphics-intensive processing. A computer terminal or microcomputer connected to a mainframe, minicomputer, or data-processing network. Also, a work or office area assigned to one person, often one accommodating a computer terminal or other electronic equipment.

World Wide Web, a system of extensively interlinked hypertext documents: a branch of the Internet.

write, to transfer (data, text, etc.) from computer memory to an output medium. Abbreviated: WWW.

WWW. *See* World Wide Web.

WYSIWYG, of, pertaining to, or being a computer screen display that shows text exactly as it will appear when printed.

XOR, a Boolean operator that returns a positive result when either but not both of its operands are positive.

INDEX

ABOUT PROFESSIONAL SECRETARIES INTERNATIONAL—The Association for Office Professionals®

Founded in 1942, Professional Secretaries International®—The Association for Office Professionals (PSI®) is the nation's leading professional secretarial organization with more than 40,000 active members. Representing all office professionals, PSI is dedicated to improving the quality of work life within the office environment by providing oppurtunities for educational, personal, and professional growth.

PSI certifies secretaries with the Certified Professional Secretary® (CPS®) rating and has recently established the Office Proficiency Assessment and Certification™ (OPAC™) program. Discounts on educational products, professional seminars, and conferences are offered. The Secretary®, PSI's official magazine, alerts secretaries to new ideas, office products and services, and new technology applications for implementation on the job.

Professional Secretaries Week®, originated by PSI in 1952, is observed annually the last full week in April.

For more information, write or call:

Professional Secretaries International
10502 NW Ambassador Drive
P.O. Box 20404
Kansas City, MO 64195–0404
(816) 891–6600
Fax (816) 891–9118